THE ROUTLEDGE HANDBOOK TO NINETEENTH-CENTURY BRITISH PERIODICALS AND NEWSPAPERS

Providing a comprehensive, interdisciplinary examination of scholarship on nineteenth-century British periodicals and newspapers, this volume surveys the current state of research and offers an in-depth examination of contemporary methodologies. The impact of digital media and archives on the field informs all discussions of the print archive. Contributors illustrate their arguments with examples and contextualize their topics within broader areas of study, while also reflecting on how the study of periodicals may evolve in the future. The *Handbook* will serve as a valuable resource for scholars and students of nineteenth-century culture who are interested in issues of cultural formation, transformation, and transmission in a developing industrial and globalizing age, as well as those whose research focuses on the bibliographical and the micro case study. In addition to rendering a comprehensive review and critique of current research on nineteenth-century British periodicals, the *Handbook* suggests new avenues for research in the twenty-first century.

Andrew King is Professor of English Literature and Literary Studies at the University of Greenwich, UK.

Alexis Easley is Professor of English at the University of St. Thomas, USA.

John Morton is Senior Lecturer in English Literature at the University of Greenwich, UK.

Ranging from explorations of regional presses to the transformation of periodical scholarship through digitalization, this *Handbook* provides an overview of the history and theory of nineteenth-century British periodicals and newspapers. By offering an expansive view of the state of this rapidly developing field, these 30 essays suggest a variety of routes for that development in both future research and pedagogy. The multiple perspectives demonstrate exciting interventions by periodicals in art, politics, economics, and the everyday life and work of their readers.

Mark Schoenfield, Vanderbilt University, USA,
author of *British Periodicals and Romantic Identity: The 'Literary Lower Empire'*

This *Handbook* succeeds brilliantly in conveying the diversity and depth of the field of nineteenth-century periodical and newspaper studies. At a time when new digital resources have enabled far greater access to this crucial material, this wide-ranging and rich resource—theoretically probing and full of new research and thinking—will quickly establish itself as the first port of call for students and scholars alike. A wonderful and welcome achievement.

Mark W. Turner, King's College London, UK

THE ROUTLEDGE HANDBOOK TO NINETEENTH-CENTURY BRITISH PERIODICALS AND NEWSPAPERS

Edited by
Andrew King, Alexis Easley, and John Morton

Routledge
Taylor & Francis Group
LONDON AND NEW YORK

First published 2016
by Routledge

2 Park Square, Milton Park, Abingdon, Oxfordshire OX14 4RN
52 Vanderbilt Avenue, New York, NY 10017

Routledge is an imprint of the Taylor & Francis Group, an informa business

First issued in paperback 2019

Copyright © 2016 selection and editorial matter, Andrew King, Alexis Easley, and John Morton; individual chapters, the contributors

The right of the editors to be identified as the author of the editorial material, and of the authors for their individual chapters, has been asserted in accordance with sections 77 and 78 of the Copyright, Designs and Patents Act 1988.

All rights reserved. No part of this book may be reprinted or reproduced or utilised in any form or by any electronic, mechanical, or other means, now known or hereafter invented, including photocopying and recording, or in any information storage or retrieval system, without permission in writing from the publishers.

Notice:
Product or corporate names may be trademarks or registered trademarks, and are used only for identification and explanation without intent to infringe.

British Library Cataloguing in Publication Data
A catalogue record for this book is available from the British Library

Library of Congress Cataloging-in-Publication Data
A catalog record for this title has been requested

ISBN: 978-1-4094-6888-2 (hbk)
ISBN: 978-0-367-87986-0 (pbk)

Typeset in Perpetua
by Apex CoVantage, LLC

Printed in the United Kingdom
by Henry Ling Limited

CONTENTS

List of Figures — viii
List of Tables — xi
Notes on Contributors — xii
Acknowledgements — xviii

Introduction — 1
ANDREW KING, ALEXIS EASLEY, AND JOHN MORTON

SECTION I
Production and Reproduction — 15

1 Digitization — 17
   JAMES MUSSELL

2 Technologies of Production — 29
   SHANNON ROSE SMITH

3 Distribution — 42
   GRAHAM LAW

4 Periodical Economics — 60
   ANDREW KING

SECTION II
Contributors and Contributions — 75

5 Writing for Periodicals — 77
   LINDA H. PETERSON

6 Editors and the Nineteenth-Century Press — 89
   MARYSA DEMOOR

7 Illustration — 102
   BRIAN MAIDMENT

v

8	Poetry LINDA K. HUGHES	124
9	Prose BETH PALMER	138

SECTION III
Geographies 151

10	Empire and the Periodical Press MICHELLE TUSAN	153
11	Transatlantic Connections BOB NICHOLSON	163
12	Transnational Connections JANE CHAPMAN	175
13	Periodicals in Scotland DAVID FINKELSTEIN	185
14	Welsh Periodicals and Newspapers LISA PETERS	194
15	Periodicals in Ireland ELIZABETH TILLEY	208
16	Provincial Periodicals ANDREW HOBBS	221

SECTION IV
Taxonomies 235

17	Markets, Genres, Iterations LAUREL BRAKE	237
18	Men and the Periodical Press STEPHANIE OLSEN	249
19	Periodicals for Women KATHRYN LEDBETTER	260
20	Family Magazines JENNIFER PHEGLEY	276
21	Children's Periodicals KRISTINE MORUZI	293

Contents

22	Sporting Periodicals YURI COWAN	307
23	Comic/Satiric Periodicals CRAIG HOWES	318
24	Social Purpose Periodicals DEBORAH MUTCH	328
25	Temperance Periodicals ANNEMARIE MCALLISTER	342
26	Periodicals and Religion MARK KNIGHT	355
27	Theater and the Periodical Press KATHERINE NEWEY	365
28	Art Periodicals JULIE CODELL	377
29	Music Periodicals LAURA VORACHEK	390
	Chronology of the Nineteenth-Century Periodical Press GARY SIMONS	400
	Bibliography	406
	Index	461

FIGURES

1.1	Robert Walker Macbeth, *Our First Tiff*, etching, 22.8 cm × 26.5 cm, 1880.	xx
2.1	"He is scratching, scratching, scratching with a furious-driven nib," *Pall Mall Magazine* 24 (June 1901): 244.	30
2.2	"Applegarth's Patent Printing Machine," *Official Descriptive and Illustrated Catalogue of the Great Exhibition. By the Authority of the Royal Commission*, 3 vols. (London: Spicer Brothers, 1851), 1:275.	35
2.3	"Patent Vertical Printing Machine, in the Great Exhibition Class C, No. 122 / The 'Illustrated London News' (Applegarth) Printing Machine," *Illustrated London News* 18 (May 31, 1851): 502.	37
2.4	Paul Destez, "The 'Graphic' Exhibit at the Paris Exhibition, Awarded a Gold Medal," *Graphic* 62 (September 15, 1900): 375.	41
4.1	Production costs of annuals in the 1820s (adapted from S.C. Hall, "Annuals").	69
4.2	Newspaper production costs in the late 1840s (adapted from J.P., "Daily Press").	70
4.3	Brewing Trade Review Limited, balance sheet for the year ending October, 1887.	73
6.1	"While the Editor Is at Lunch," *Judy: or The London Serio-Comic Journal* 70 (November 1, 1905): 519.	93
6.2	"Some Magazine Editors," *Review of Reviews* 3, no. 17 (May 1891): 508.	100
7.1	H.G. Hine, wood-engraved illustrations for "The Monster City," *Illuminated Magazine* 3 (September 1844): 286.	103
7.2	Wood-engraved headpiece to the index of *Punch* 5 (1843).	104
7.3	Robert Seymour, detail from the wood-engraved masthead for *Figaro in London* 5 no. 239 (July 2, 1836): 105.	105
7.4	Wood-engraved title page for the *Saturday Magazine* 1, no. 20 (October 27, 1832): 153.	109
7.5	Wood engraving showing a "Proposed Metropolitan Subway," *Illustrated London News* 23 (October 29, 1853): 367.	110
7.6	Wood-engraved illustration to "Leaf Insects," *Weekly Visitor* 2, no. 98 (August 19, 1835): 297.	111
7.7	Charles Keene, wood-engraved illustration to George Meredith's *Evan Harrington*, *Once A Week* 2, no. 38 (March 17, 1860): 243.	113

FIGURES

7.8	"The Demon Shows Theresa to Faust," wood-engraved illustration for G.W.M. Reynolds's *Faust*, *London Journal* 2, no. 32 (October 4, 1845): 49.	114
7.9	John Gilbert, "The Ship on Fire," wood-engraved title page illustration for the *British Workman* 107 (November 1863): 425.	117
7.10	Engraved title page to volume 2 of the *Puppet Show* (1849).	119
7.11	C.J. Grant, "The Irish Schoolmaster and His Pupils," *Political Drama, No. 128* (London: Drake, c. 1834).	120
7.12	"A.P.," process-engraved illustration for "Why He Failed," *Strand Magazine* 2 (July 1891): 30.	122
11.1	Full-text search for "Americ*" OR "United States" in twenty-nine British newspapers.	168
14.1	*Baner ac Amserau Cymru* 43, no. 2276 (October 10, 1900): 1.	198
14.2	*Wrexham and Denbigh Weekly Advertiser* 2, no. 70 (July 7, 1855): 1.	199
15.1	Cover of *Dublin University Magazine* 36, no. 212 (August 1850).	214
15.2	Paper issue cover of Charles Lever, *Charles O'Malley, the Irish Dragoon* (Dublin: William Curry, 1841).	216
16.1	Approximate numbers of metropolitan and provincial newspapers and magazines, 1800 and 1900.	223
16.2	Masthead of *Dudley and Midland Counties Express and Mining Gazette* 1, no. 16 (January 2, 1858).	224
16.3	Metropolitan versus provincial annual newspaper sales, 1821 and 1864.	225
18.1	Frontispiece to the *Leisure Hour* (1860), detail.	254
19.1	Copper-plate engraving of the "Princess Royal as She Appear'd at Court on the Queen's Birth-Day," *Lady's Magazine* 12 (February 1781): 62.	262
19.2	Frontispiece engraving featuring fabric swatches from textile manufacturers, *Ackermann's Repository of Arts* 12, no. 72 (December 1814).	263
19.3	Hand-colored fashion plate, *New Monthly Belle Assemblée* 8 (January 1838): 58.	265
19.4	Two-page spread showing arrangement of the "Englishwoman's Conversazione" feature next to hand-colored fashion plates, *Englishwoman's Domestic Magazine* 9 (November 1864): 288.	270
19.5	Frontispiece illustration from the first issue of the *Lady's Newspaper* 1, no. 1 (January 2, 1847): 1.	272
19.6	Embroidery pattern from the *Queen* 55 (January 17, 1874): 64.	273
20.1	Frontispiece of the *Family Friend* 4 (January–June 1851).	277
20.2	"Lady De Vere Makes a Discovery," *London Journal* 43, no. 1103 (March 31, 1866): 193.	281
20.3	"Notices to Correspondents," *London Journal* 43 (March 31, 1866): 208.	283
20.4	Masthead of *Bow Bells* 4 (February 14, 1866): 49.	285
20.5	Cover of the *Argosy* 23, no. 137 (April 1877).	286
20.6	"Laura's Fireside," *Cornhill Magazine* 3 (April 1861): 385.	289
21.1	Reissue cover of *Boys of England* 19, no. 490 (September 4, 1883).	297
21.2	Cover of the *Girl's Own Paper* 19, no. 970 (July 30, 1898).	299

FIGURES

22.1	Page from J. Mason, "The Money We Spend on Sport," *Pearson's Magazine* 1 (May 1896): 534.	309
24.1	"I'll Go Back, I'll Not Pledge the Clock," *British Workman*, no. 98 (February 1863): 1.	330
24.2	"The Harvest Field: Maternal Love," *British Workwoman*, no. 107 (September 1872): 88.	338
25.1	Cover of first issue of *Onward* (July 1865).	346
25.2	Cover of the *Temperance Mirror* 7, no. 81 (September 1887): 193.	349

TABLES

2.1	Selective timeline of technology	33
3.1	Distribution timeline	56
4.1	Debits and credits of annuals in 1829	68
4.2	Debits and credits of a newspaper in the late 1840s	68
4.3	Costs of advertising in the *Brewing Trade Review* 1887, 1891	72

CONTRIBUTORS

Laurel Brake is Professor Emerita of Literature and Print Culture at Birkbeck, University of London. Recent work includes the *Nineteenth-Century Serials Edition*, a digital edition of seven nineteenth-century periodicals (www.ncse.ac.uk) and *The Dictionary of Nineteenth-Century Journalism*, co-edited with Marysa Demoor, in print and online. She also co-edited *W.T. Stead, Newspaper Revolutionary* and a special issue on Stead in *19: An Interdisciplinary Journal*. She is currently co-editing a collection of articles on the *News of the World* for Palgrave and writing *InkWork*, a biography of Walter and Clara Pater. She is editor of volume 5, on Pater's journalism, of the forthcoming *Collected Works* for Oxford University Press.

Jane Chapman is Professor of Communications at Lincoln University, Research Associate at Wolfson College, Cambridge, and Visiting Professor at Macquarie University, Sydney, attached to the Centre for Media History. She is the author of ten books and more than twenty articles and book chapters specializing in comparative media history from the nineteenth century and the world wars, especially imperial/commonwealth journalism history in English and French. She is a long-term grant research team leader for the Arts and Humanities Research Council on World War I and for "Comics and the World Wars—a Cultural Record."

Julie Codell is Professor of Art History at Arizona State University and affiliate faculty in English, Gender Studies, Film and Media Studies, and Asian Studies. She wrote *The Victorian Artist: Artists' Life Writings in Britain, ca. 1870–1910* (2003; paperback rev. ed. 2012). Her edited works include *Transculturation in British Art, 1770–1930* (2012), *Power and Resistance: The Delhi Coronation Durbars* (2012), *The Political Economy of Art* (2008), *Genre, Gender, Race, and World Cinema* (2007), and *Imperial Co-Histories* (2003). With Laurel Brake, she co-edited *Encounters in the Victorian Press* (2004) and with D.S. Macleod, *Orientalism Transposed: The Impact of the Colonies on British Culture* (1998).

Yuri Cowan is Professor in the Department of Language and Literature at the Norwegian University of Science and Technology (NTNU) in Trondheim. In the field of book history, he is interested in textual histories, the material book, periodicals, and constructions of authorship. He has published articles on topics including Victorian sporting writers, ballad anthologies, the Aesthetic Movement, and the reprinting of Victorian fantasy in the 1970s. He is also a founding editor of the peer-reviewed open-access journal *Authorship* and a core member of the Enlightenment News project at NTNU.

CONTRIBUTORS

Marysa Demoor is Professor of English Literature at Ghent University and a life member of Clare Hall, Cambridge. In 2011, she was also the holder of the Van Dyck chair at UCLA. Demoor is the author of *Their Fair Share: Women, Power and Criticism in the Athenaeum, from Millicent Garrett Fawcett to Katherine Mansfield, 1870–1920* (2000) and the editor of *Marketing the Author: Authorial Personae, Narrative Selves and Self-Fashioning, 1880–1930* (2004). With Laurel Brake she edited *The Lure of Illustration in the Nineteenth Century: Picture and Press* (2009) and *The Dictionary of Nineteenth-Century Journalism* (2009). Her current research focuses on the cross-fertilization between Northern Belgium and Britain in the long nineteenth century.

Alexis Easley is Professor of English at the University of St. Thomas in St. Paul, Minnesota. Her first book, *First-Person Anonymous: Women Writers and Victorian Print Media*, was published by Ashgate in 2004, and her second monograph, *Literary Celebrity, Gender, and Victorian Authorship*, was published by Delaware UP in 2011. Her most recent publications appeared in several recent essay collections, including *Women Writers and the Artifacts of Celebrity*, *Women in Journalism at the Fin de Siècle*, *Centenary Essays on W.T. Stead*, *The Cambridge Companion to Victorian Women's Writing, 1830–1900*, and *The News of the World and the British Press, 1843–2011*. She is co-editor, with Beth Rodgers and Clare Gill, of a forthcoming essay collection, *The Edinburgh History of Women's Print Media in Britain, 1830–1900*. She also edits *Victorian Periodicals Review*.

David Finkelstein is Head of the Office of Lifelong Learning and Chair in Continuing Education at the University of Edinburgh. His research interests include media history, print culture, and book history studies. Recent publications include *An Introduction to Book History*, the co-edited *Edinburgh History of the Book in Scotland*, vol. 3, 1880–2000, and the edited essay collection *Print Culture and the Blackwood Tradition*, which was awarded the Robert Colby Scholarly Book Prize for its advancement of the understanding of the nineteenth-century periodical press.

Andrew Hobbs is Senior Lecturer and Research Associate in the School of Journalism, Language, and Communication at the University of Central Lancashire. He is fascinated by print culture and a sense of place. Recent publications include "How Local Newspapers Came to Dominate Victorian Poetry Publishing" (*Victorian Poetry*, 2014, with Clare Januszewski) and "*Lancashire Life* Magazine, 1947–1973: A Middle-Class Sense of Place" (*Twentieth Century British History*, 2013). He formerly worked as a journalist.

Craig Howes is Professor of English and Director of the Center for Biographical Research at the University of Hawai'i at Mānoa and has co-edited the journal *Biography: An Interdisciplinary Quarterly* since 1994. A former president of the Council of Editors of Learned Journals, he is the author and editor of many books, essays, reference articles and reviews on nineteenth-century British periodical literature, English and American literature, life writing, literary theory, American history, and Hawai'i history, literature, and culture.

Linda K. Hughes, Addie Levy Professor of Literature at Texas Christian University in Fort Worth, Texas, specializes in Victorian literature and culture with particular interests in historical media studies (poetry and print culture, periodicals, serial fiction), gender and women's studies, and transnationality. Most recently she published *The Cambridge Introduction* to *Victorian Poetry* (2010); co-edited, with Sharon M. Harris, *A Feminist Reader: Feminist Thought from Sappho to Satrapi* (4 vols., 2013); and co-edited, with Sarah R. Robbins, *Teaching Transatlanticism: Resources for Teaching 19th-Century Anglo-American Print Culture* (2015).

Andrew King is Professor of English at the University of Greenwich. His publications include *The London Journal, 1845–1883: Periodicals, Production and Gender* (2004), three co-edited collections *Victorian Print Media* (2005), *Popular Print Media* (2005), and *Ouida and Victorian Popular Culture* (2013); and several special numbers of journals, including "Gender, the Professions and the Press" for *Nineteenth-Century Gender Studies* in 2008, with Marysa Demoor, and "Angels and Demons" for *Critical Survey* in 2011. He has also published articles and book chapters on popular periodicals and fiction and was an associate editor of *The Dictionary of Nineteenth Century Journalism*. He is currently completing a literary biography of Ouida. He blogs at http://blogs.gre.ac.uk/andrewking/author/ka31/.

Mark Knight is Senior Lecturer in the Department of English and Creative Writing at Lancaster University. His books include *Chesterton and Evil* (2004), *Nineteenth-Century Religion and Literature* (2006, co-written with Emma Mason), and *An Introduction to Religion and Literature* (2009). He has also co-edited two collections of essays (2006 and 2009) and *Literature and the Bible: A Reader* (2013). He has edited several volumes, most recently the *Routledge Companion to Literature and Religion* (forthcoming, 2016) and is currently finishing his new monograph, *Good Words: Evangelicalism and the Victorian Novel*.

Graham Law is Professor in Media History at Waseda University, Tokyo. His books include *Serializing Fiction in the Victorian Press* (2000) and (with Andrew Maunder) *Wilkie Collins: A Literary Life* (2008). He is currently working on a general account of the dominant communications system of the nineteenth century under the title *Periodicalism*.

Kathryn Ledbetter is Professor of English at Texas State University. She is the author of *Victorian Needlework* (2012), *British Victorian Women's Periodicals: Civilization, Beauty, and Poetry* (2009), *Tennyson and Victorian Periodicals: Commodities in Context* (2007), *"Colour'd Shadows": Contexts in Publishing, Printing, and Reading Nineteenth-Century British Women Writers* (with Terence Hoagwood, 2005), and *The Keepsake (1829)*, a facsimile edition, with introduction and notes (with Terence Hoagwood, 1999). She has published articles in various newspapers, magazines, and scholarly journals, including *Studies in the Literary Imagination*, *Victorian Poetry*, *Papers of the Bibliographical Society of America*, the *Journal of Modern Literature*, and *Victorian Newsletter*.

Brian Maidment is Professor of the History of Print at Liverpool John Moores University. He has published widely on a broad range of nineteenth-century topics, including popular visual culture, laboring-class authors, and mass-circulation literature, especially periodicals. His books include *The Poorhouse Fugitives: Self-taught Poets and Poetry in Victorian Britain* (1987), *Reading Popular Prints 1790–1870* (1996), *Dusty Bob: A Cultural History of Dustmen, 1780–1870* (2006), and *Comedy, Caricature and the Social Order, 1820–1850* (2013).

Annemarie McAllister is the author of *John Bull's Italian Snakes and Ladders* (2007), which explores nineteenth-century representations of Italians in periodicals, travel writing, and novels. She is currently working on UK temperance history; her latest book, *Demon Drink?*

Temperance and the Working Class (2014), is a popular history intended to complement the three exhibitions she has curated, including the ongoing virtual site, www.demondrink. co.uk. Her recent article, "*Onward*: How a Regional Temperance Magazine for Children Survived and Flourished in the Victorian Marketplace" (*Victorian Periodicals Review* 48:1) provides a case study that serves as a companion to her chapter in this volume.

John Morton is Senior Lecturer in English Literature at the University of Greenwich. His monograph, *Tennyson Among the Novelists* (2010), considers allusions to Tennyson's poetry in novels written from 1850 to the present day. Other publications include several articles on Neo-Victorian poetry and a book chapter on "T.S. Eliot and Tennyson." He is currently working on a literary biography of the year 1850 and is deputy editor of the *Tennyson Research Bulletin*.

Kristine Moruzi is a Lecturer and Discovery Early Career Researcher in the School of Communication and Creative Arts at Deakin University, Australia. Her monograph, *Constructing Girlhood through the Periodical Press, 1850–1915*, was published in 2012. She is currently completing a project, with Michelle Smith and Clare Bradford, on colonial girlhood in Canadian, Australian, and New Zealand print culture. Her latest project examines links between children and charity in the late nineteenth and early twentieth centuries in British and colonial print culture. With Michelle J. Smith, she edited *Colonial Girlhood in Literature, Culture and History, 1840–1950* (2014) and *Girls' School Stories, 1749–1929* (2014), a six-volume anthology published in Routledge's "History of Feminism" series.

James Mussell is Associate Professor of Victorian Literature at the University of Leeds. He is the author of *Science, Time and Space in the Late Nineteenth-Century Periodical Press* (2007) and *The Nineteenth-Century Press in the Digital Age* (2012). He is one of the editors of the *Nineteenth-Century Serials Edition* (2008) and *W.T. Stead: Newspaper Revolutionary* (2012). Since 2009 he has edited the digital forum in the *Journal of Victorian Culture*.

Deborah Mutch is Senior Lecturer in the Department of English at De Montfort University, Leicester, UK. Her primary research area is the fiction of the British socialist movement. Her numerous publications include a five-volume collection for Pickering & Chatto entitled *British Socialist Fiction, 1884–1914* (2013); an article on the popular fiction of A. Neil Lyons and Charles Allen Clarke, "The Long Recuperation: Late-Nineteenth/Early-Twentieth Century British Socialist Periodical Fiction," for the journal *Key Words* (2014); and a scholarly edition of John Law (Margaret Harkness), *A City Girl* (2015), for Victorian Secrets.

Katherine Newey is Professor of Theatre History at the University of Exeter. She is a literary historian specializing in nineteenth-century British popular theater and women's writing. Her publications include *Women's Theatre Writing in Victorian Britain* (2005), *John Ruskin and the Victorian Theatre* with Jeffrey Richards (2010), and *Lives of Shakespearian Actors: Frances Kemble* (2011). She is currently writing a cultural history of Victorian pantomime.

Bob Nicholson is Senior Lecturer in History at Edge Hill University. He works on the history of Victorian popular culture and is particularly interested in periodicals, jokes, transatlantic relations, and the digital humanities. He was awarded the Gale Dissertation Research Fellowship in 2009 for his study of digital newspaper archives and won the British Library

Labs Competition in 2014 for his proposal to build a digital archive of Victorian jokes. He has written about digital newspaper archives for the *Journal of Victorian Culture*, *Media History*, and *Victorian Periodicals Review*. He blogs at www.DigitalVictorianist.com and tweets @DigiVictorian.

Stephanie Olsen is Research Fellow at the Max Planck Institute for Human Development, Center for the History of Emotions (Berlin). She was previously a postdoctoral fellow at the Minda de Gunzburg Center for European Studies at Harvard University. She is the author of *Juvenile Nation: Youth, Emotions and the Making of the Modern British Citizen*, co-author of *Learning How to Feel: Children's Literature and the History of Emotional Socialization, c. 1870–1970*, and editor of the forthcoming *Childhood, Youth and Emotions in Modern History*. She has published a number of articles on the history of masculinity, childhood, education, and the emotions. Her new research focuses on children's education and the cultivation of hope in the World War I.

Beth Palmer is Lecturer in English at the University of Surrey. Her publications include a monograph, *Women's Authorship and Editorship in Victorian Culture: Sensational Strategies* (2011); a co-edited volume, *A Return to the Common Reader: Print Culture and the Novel, 1850–1900* (2011); and many journal articles on nineteenth-century literature and periodicals.

Lisa Peters is a librarian at the University of Chester. She is the author of *Politics, Publishing and Personalities: Wrexham Newspapers, 1848–1914* (2011) and has contributed to edited books and journals on the subject of Welsh newspapers. Her current research is in the area of newspapers and politics in north and mid-Wales in the late Victorian and Edwardian eras. She is a member of the Print Networks Council.

Linda H. Peterson was the Niel Gray Jr. Professor of English at Yale University, where she taught courses on Victorian poetry, fiction, and nature writing. Her books include *Victorian Autobiography* (1986), *Traditions of Victorian Women's Autobiography* (1999), *Becoming a Woman of Letters: Myths of Authorship and Facts of the Victorian Market* (2009), and *The Cambridge Companion to Victorian Women's Writing* (2015).

Jennifer Phegley is Professor of English at the University of Missouri–Kansas City. She has published numerous articles and books including *Educating the Proper Woman Reader: Victorian Family Literary Magazines and the Cultural Health of the Nation* (2004) and *Courtship and Marriage in Victorian England* (2012). She recently co-edited *Transatlantic Sensations* (2012) and edited a special pedagogy issue of *Victorians Institute Journal* (2011). She is currently working on a project exploring the publishing partnerships of John Maxwell and Mary Elizabeth Braddon and Sam and Isabella Beeton entitled *Victorian Media Moguls: Marital Collaborations, Magazine Marketing, and the Invention of New Reading Audiences in Mid-Century England*.

Gary Simons is an adjunct faculty member in the English Department at the University of South Florida where he completed his PhD in the spring of 2011. A former scientist and businessman, he took early retirement to study Victorian literature. He has published articles on the critical journalism of William Makepeace Thackeray in *Victorian Periodicals Review*, *Victorian Literature and Culture*, and other journals. He serves as editor of the *Curran Index*, http://victorianresearch.org/curranindex.html.

CONTRIBUTORS

Shannon Rose Smith is Assistant Professor of English Literature at the Bader International Study Centre (UK), Queen's University (Canada). From 2013 to 2015, she also served as director of the BISC's Field School in the Digital Humanities. Her current research is concerned with histories of nineteenth- and twentieth-century communication and print production technologies; the Internet and World Wide Web; and the intersection between digital humanities "maker culture" and the participatory art movement. She is currently co-editing special issues of *Victorian Periodicals Review* (2016) and *Digital Humanities Quarterly* (2016). She has also published articles on literary theory, Victorian popular theatre, sport, and urban spaces.

Elizabeth Tilley is College Lecturer in Victorian Literature and book history at the National University of Ireland, Galway. She was an associate editor of *The Dictionary of Nineteenth-Century Journalism* and has published extensively on Irish periodicals and publishing.

Michelle Tusan is Professor of History at the University of Nevada, Las Vegas. She is the author of *Smyrna's Ashes: Humanitarianism, Genocide and the Birth of the Middle East* (2012). Other publications include *Women Making News: Gender and Journalism in Modern Britain* (2005); articles in the *American Historical Review*, *Victorian Studies*, *Journal of Women's History*, and *History Workshop Journal*; and a co-authored textbook for Routledge, *Britain Since 1688* (2015). She is currently writing a book on Britain's response to the Armenian genocide.

Laura Vorachek is Associate Professor of English at the University of Dayton, specializing in Victorian literature and nineteenth-century musical culture. Her work on Victorian music and nineteenth-century periodicals has appeared in *Victorian Periodicals Review*, *Victorian Literature and Culture*, *Victorians: A Journal of Culture and Literature*, *George Eliot-George Henry Lewes Studies*, and *CLIO*, as well as in three edited collections: *Gissing and the City* (2005), *Cultural Crisis and the Making of Books in Late-Victorian England* (2006), and *The Idea of Music in Victorian Fiction* (2004). She is currently working on a study of racial masquerade in late nineteenth-century British literature and culture.

ACKNOWLEDGEMENTS

This project has been, like all large undertakings of this sort, quite a roller coaster—one that was being constructed even as we were riding it. That we have got to the end without falling off or the girders collapsing under us is due to the support and generosity of many. We mean first of all our patient contributors, of course, most of whom are stalwarts of the Research Society for Victorian Periodicals, but also Ann Donahue of Ashgate. She was the one who first suggested we get into the car—and then design the track. Always the very model of a tactful and rigorous editor, she not only pressed the starting button which set us off on this wild ride but enabled the *Handbook* to arrive finally and calmly on terra firma, the reality of publication. Near the exit, Autumn Spalding took over with great charm and tact. We thank them both.

Another Ann, Ann Hale, made sure we were safely strapped into the car at two dangerous moments by bringing order to chaos, operating with vertiginous speed and accuracy to regularize our referencing systems and spellings, and then, with our valued colleague Kathy Malone, compiling the bibliography. Scott Radunzel painstakingly scrubbed the rust off the images with Photoshop and Arianne Peterson smoothed out rough patches with her sharp and assiduous file so language could flow smoothly. Ann, Kathy, Scott, Arianne: we shall always be grateful.

Our consulting editor, Laurel Brake, has many times fearlessly hewn out new tracks into the steep and treacherous terrain of the nineteenth-century press. She advised us from the first on our plan and how we could realize it, encouraging us to take risks and maintain safety, face the new and consolidate the familiar. With enormous pleasure we thank her.

Our anonymous readers were acute and attentive, and we are delighted to acknowledge the way they helped us tighten bolts and redesign bends and chicanes that might well have caused whiplash or worse had they been prematurely opened to public use.

The University of Greenwich helped fuel the project from the beginning, most notably by providing funds for a one-day workshop in 2014 which enabled many contributors to come together to share ideas and expertise. Special thanks to Zoë Pettit, head of Literature, Language and Theatre, and to Sarah Greer (formerly Dean of the School of Law, Humanities and Social Sciences and now PVC Academic at the University of Worcester) for believing in the possibility and value of ambitious constructions like this. We also thank the University of St. Thomas, which provided support throughout the journey.

ACKNOWLEDGEMENTS

Nathan Pendlebury of the Walker Art Gallery in Liverpool helped the editors paint their signboard at the last minute by expediting a request for permission to use *Our First Tiff*, by the Scottish artist Robert Walker Macbeth, on our dust jacket. Richard Morris, the founder of the Registered Charity Heropreneurs, rescued us despite his severe illness by sending Andrew a rare copy of Macbeth's etching of the painting which appears as Figure 1.1.

It is with heartfelt regret that we record here the passing in June 2015 of Professor Linda H. Peterson who, even though she was very ill, was determined to aid our undertaking. Over her illustrious career, she contributed a great deal to Victorian studies not only through her extraordinarily perceptive and exquisitely crafted publications but also through her good humor, wit, grace, and generosity.

Our families, it goes without saying, have watched over us, waved us encouragement, and patiently awaited our return. Special thanks are due to Brett, Laura, and Lesley. While we were still up in the air, another witness happily arrived, Eve Morton. She, like her elder brother Alex, must have wondered what her father was doing—soldering, riveting, and looping the loop at all hours. We thank her for her forbearance and hope that in due course this volume will explain it all to her.

Figure 1.1 Robert Walker Macbeth, *Our First Tiff*, etching, 22.8 cm x 26.5 cm, 1880. From the editors' collection.

INTRODUCTION

Andrew King, Alexis Easley, and John Morton

> Periodical Literature—how sweet is the name! 'Tis a type of many of the most beautiful things and events in nature; or say, rather, that they are *types* of it, both the flowers and stars. . . . The flowers are the periodicals of the earth—the stars are those of heaven. . . . Look, then, at all our paper Periodicals with pleasure, for sake of the flowers and the stars. Suppose them all extinct, and life would be like a flowerless earth, a starless heaven. We should soon forget the seasons themselves—the days of the week—and the weeks of the month—and the months of the year—and the years of the century—and the centuries of all Time—and all Time itself flowing away on into eternity.[1]

This playful passage from an 1829 article in *Blackwood's Edinburgh Magazine* imagines periodical literature as a natural part of everyday life which structures time and imbues it with meaning. It is both ephemeral like the flowers that brighten our lives and permanent like the stars that guide us on life's voyage. Over the course of the nineteenth century, periodicals and newspapers became a ubiquitous feature of daily life, serving as vehicles of entertainment, political discourse, historical retrospection, popular education, and countless other modes of thought. Displacing the centrality and status of oral modes of communication even further than in the previous century, when theories of print and oral cultures were first adumbrated, they prepared the way for the densely mediated society we experience today.[2] Journalism and daily life were increasingly entwined due to improvements in printing technology; advances in methods of information gathering and dissemination; increases in literacy rates; and the elimination of the taxes on knowledge. According to John North, in his introduction to that essential map of the nineteenth-century British press, *The Waterloo Directory of English Newspapers and Periodicals*, there were 125,000 newspaper and periodical titles published in England between 1800 and 1900.[3] Adding in Scotland, Ireland, Wales, and the British Empire (let alone the newspapers and periodicals from elsewhere) raises the number of titles markedly, creating what the

---

1. [Wilson], "Monologue," 948.
2. McDowell, "Towards a Genealogy." Vincent's *Literacy and Popular Culture* remains a key resource for charting this transition.
3. North, introduction.

Saturday Review called a "surging sea of print on which we are all afloat," a profusion of material that was disorienting, threatening, sublime, addictive, and exciting.[4]

Periodicals and newspapers structured readers' days, weeks, and months, providing news, updates on the latest fashions in London, commentary on intellectual and political debates, or the next installment of a gripping serial novel. Eliza Cook wrote in 1849 that a "family would often drink the tea of Lethe, and eat the toast of taciturnity, were they not happily relieved from torpor of thought, and immobility of tongue, by the entrance of a newspaper."[5] At the same time, as illustrated in our cover image and in Figure 1.1, a newspaper (or a periodical) could separate readers from their immediate surroundings, launching them into what Benedict Anderson has called an "imagined community" of national affiliation, the idea of a reading public.[6] Of course, in the nineteenth century, the idea that individuals were no longer confined to the community in their immediate vicinity was not a new concept. Neither was the reality that there were many different communities created and maintained by print. What was new was the diversity of communities, the intensity of the social permeation of print, and the rapidity of its increase (phenomena that many contributors to this volume address). Even while publishers had long recognized that the reading public was divided into particular sectors,[7] some, such as W.M. Thackeray and Wilkie Collins, were still attempting to imagine a unified audience well into the 1850s.[8] The massive and rhizomatic growth of the press increasingly made this vision untenable, especially as prices fell and regulation diminished. Provincial newspapers, women's magazines, children's periodicals, and illustrated fiction weeklies, along with temperance, trade, and myriad other classes of periodicals either sprang into being or proliferated into other formats and titles. By the second half of the nineteenth century, it was generally acknowledged that choice of reading matter marked membership not only in a national framework but also in overlapping sets of niche markets and interest groups. Issues raised in the nineteenth century—for instance, how readers classified and were classified by the media and how media industries were organized and understood by readers and the state—still resonate with us today. Even if our technologies have changed dramatically, we still think through—and experience the effects of—these issues today.

The *Handbook* presents a comprehensive exploration of the rich diversity of newspapers and periodicals that gave birth to today's media saturation. We have designed it to provide readers with a survey of current scholarship and contemporary methodologies, along with indications of areas ripe for further research. It assesses the impact of digital media and archives, which in recent years have provided unprecedented access to rare periodicals and newspapers while presenting a host of methodological quandaries. As James Mussell points out in Chapter 1, "Those familiar with periodicals in print readily notice what has been left out, whether properties related to the shift in materiality (weight, size, the texture of the page, colors of

---

4. "Repose," 110.
5. Cook, "Newspapers," 111.
6. Anderson, *Imagined Communities*, 6.
7. Klancher, *Making of English Reading Audiences*, especially chapter 1.
8. Thackeray, "Half-a-Crown's Worth"; [Collins], "Unknown Public." On this shift in the conceptualization of the market, see King, *London Journal*, 24–25, 36–67.

paper and ink) or the way the resource organizes its content (perhaps making it difficult to browse, for instance)."[9] Yet, he notes, "Just as there are things that it is only possible to learn by consulting the print periodicals in the archive, so there are also things that can only be learned from interrogating data produced from these archival objects."[10] This volume amply illustrates the opportunities and insights that such data can provide.

Previous guides to the field, such as those edited by Vann and VanArsdel, offered maps of the field by directing scholars to paper periodicals and archives. *The Wellesley Index to Victorian Periodicals*, *The Waterloo Directory of English Newspapers and Periodicals*, and *The Dictionary of Nineteenth-Century Journalism* also serve, in differing ways, as finding aids and factual reference guides. The *Handbook* continues the rigorous approach modeled by these forebears, offering guidance to help readers identify and locate material for research and place it in a wider context. However, the *Handbook* differs from earlier volumes by celebrating diversity, promoting broader theoretical discussion of the press, and highlighting new methodological questions and approaches.

The fundamental question we must ask is how we can interpret the wealth of data we find when researching the nineteenth-century press. The *Handbook* collectively answers this question through explicit theoretical discussion but also through proposing answers that differ from one another and are at times contradictory. The striking diversity of the chapters reflects the current heterogeneity of the field. That the *Handbook* embraces heterodoxy stems from our belief that only plural approaches can address the protean nature of our subject.

We hope this volume addresses the needs of scholars who research issues of long-term cultural formation, transformation, and transmission in a developing industrial and globalizing age. Early on, we made the decision to focus on British periodicals and newspapers of the nineteenth century as a whole. While the idea of Romantic and Victorian periodization helps to define academic fields of inquiry and provides manageable boundaries in the vast archive of print, newspaper and periodicals scholarship has rightly become more attentive to the nineteenth century as a whole. This is demonstrated by the coverage of the *Waterloo Directory* (1976–), which spans from 1800 to 1900, and the contents of *Victorian Periodicals Review* (1968–), which often includes research on material from the long nineteenth century, 1780 to 1914. Our decision to incorporate research on periodicals and newspapers from across the century and beyond was also motivated by the fact that many important titles, such as *The Times* (1785–) or the *Strand Magazine* (1891–1950), extend beyond the boundaries of the nineteenth century.

National and geographical limits are just as hard to justify as temporal boundaries.[11] Periodicals and newspapers published within the British Empire were influenced in both form and content by those printed in Germany, France, America, and many other countries. In order to explore intersections between these national contexts, we included chapters focused on empire, transatlanticism, and transnationalism and the press. From the mid-1880s, press directories, inspired by *Sell's Dictionary of the World's Press* (founded in 1884), began to link the individual economies of newspapers and periodicals to a world economy through long articles

---

9. See Mussell, "Digitization," 25 below.
10. Ibid., 28 below.
11. See Ogborn and Withers, "Introduction," 1.

on colonial imports and exports. For example, they classified the press in India according to area, demographics, and kinds of goods imported and exported to different regions. By 1891, *Mitchell's Advertising Press Directory* provided a comprehensive guide to the world's press, including titles produced in Algeria, Pondicherry, Senegal, the French provinces, and many other locales, demonstrating that press advertising was a conduit for exporting British goods during a time of domestic overproduction. By paying for advertisements in foreign papers, British manufacturers were—to varying extents—helping to support the press of many other countries, just as manufacturers from other countries helped finance the British press with advertisements for their products.

In addition to interpreting "British" as a node in an international network rather than as a sealed box, we also wanted to emphasize that "British" was not a synonym for either "English" or "London." As will be clear from chapters 13–16, the majority of newspapers published inside Britain came from outside the metropolis, and there were many in languages other than English. In Britain, newspapers and periodicals were published in Welsh, French, German, Italian, Yiddish, Irish Gaelic, Scottish Gaelic, and other languages. We interpret "Britain" not only as intrinsically diverse within itself but as an extendable conceptual, geographic, and political space that often overlaps with locations of other social groupings not just of nations but of reading communities.

In determining the focus of the *Handbook* we also made the decision to be inclusive of both periodicals and newspapers while wishing to acknowledge the similarities and differences between the two publishing formats. As the *Nineteenth-Century Serials Edition* notes,

> Whereas newspapers are focused around a very delimited notion of the present and are designed to be superseded once that moment has passed, a periodical—despite also being predicated on the notion of the moment—tends to provide apparatus that is oriented to its continuing relevance in the future. Although both newspapers and serials are date-stamped, feature regular departments and foster links between present and past numbers, periodicals offer themselves as having relevance beyond the moment of reading.[12]

Nineteenth-century discussions of the press often differentiated between newspapers and periodicals, as Laurel Brake reminds us in Chapter 17. Perusal of the press directories shows that in 1861 there were 791 newspapers in England, 28 in Wales, 138 in Scotland, 132 in Ireland, with an additional 13 on the Isle of Man and the Channel Islands. Dailies numbered 39 in England, 8 in Scotland, 12 in Ireland, 2 on the islands, and none in Wales. The press directories list 481 magazines (including the quarterly reviews) but do not locate them with such geographical specificity.[13] In Chapter 16, Andrew Hobbs observes that there was a geographical difference between newspapers and periodicals, with the majority of papers produced in the

---

12. "Serials, Periodicals and Newspapers," in "Terminology," *Nineteenth-Century Serials Edition*, http://www.ncse.ac.uk.
13. *Mitchell's Press Directory*, 1861, back of title page, n.p.

provinces and the majority of magazines published in London. Newspapers, in other words, were conceptually defined by place while periodicals were not, even though location affected their production, circulation, and contents.

The 1851 "Report from the Select Committee on Newspaper Stamps," which Graham Law discusses in Chapter 3, highlights the vagueness of the term "newspaper." The same year, Mitchell's *Press Directory* wryly noted how difficult it was to define a newspaper legally, for "'news' are events of recent recurrence, as what is recent is relative: i.e. relates to people's means of information; so that without going so far as to suggest, with some wag, that to ignorant persons Rollin's Ancient History might be news—it is obvious that the idea of what is *recent* is *uncertain*, and the definition of it must be arbitrary."[14] The weekly periodical included time-sensitive content (however recent or old that "news" might be) along with the kind of literary miscellany associated with magazines. The permeability between the newspaper and the periodical was also evident when titles changed their frequency of publication. For example, as Lisa Peters demonstrates in Chapter 14, *Yr Amersau* (1843–59) began as a fortnightly periodical and became a weekly newspaper after 1848. Perhaps most importantly, periodicals and newspapers shared audiences, contributors, editors, and subject matter. Harriet Martineau wrote leaders for the *Daily News* (1846–1912) in the 1850s but simultaneously published her work in periodicals, including the weekly *Leader* (1850–60) and the quarterly *Westminster Review* (1824–1914). Between 1842 and 1848, G.W.M. Reynolds was foreign editor of the *Weekly Dispatch* (1795–1961) while writing for and editing the *London Journal* (1845–1928) and later *Reynolds's Miscellany* (1846–69).[15] Periodicals and newspapers shared an interest in the same subject matter and reprinted material from each other: drama reviews appeared in daily newspapers such as *The Times*; in weeklies such as the *Observer* (1791–), the *Illustrated London News* (1842–1989), and the *Theatrical Journal* (1839–73); and in monthlies such as the *New Monthly Magazine* (1814–84). As the speediest search through a newspaper and periodical database will demonstrate, the weekly *Punch* (1841–2002) was a carcass freely picked over by a wide variety of publications, especially when they needed filler.

There is sometimes a divide between those who study newspapers and those who study periodicals, a division that falls along disciplinary boundaries: nineteenth-century newspapers are studied more in history and media departments, whereas nineteenth-century periodicals are the subject of research in literature departments. To isolate periodicals from newspapers, however, is to create an arbitrary division that obfuscates more than it illuminates. While the distinction between the two publishing media is helpful in some respects—particularly where the economics of publishing are concerned—we need to think of them as a set of binary oppositions that we can easily deconstruct and also as a nineteenth-century British invention—sets in a Venn diagram, with core meanings and huge areas of practice and conceptualization overlapping one another.[16]

---

14. Mitchell, "Law of Newspapers," 40. Rollin's thirteen-volume *Histoire ancienne* had been published in Paris, 1730–38.
15. King, "*Reynolds's Miscellany*," 66–67.
16. Venn diagrams first appeared in a periodical, in the *London, Dublin and Edinburgh Philosophical Magazine and Journal of Science* in 1880 (Venn, "Diagrammatic and Mechanical Representation").

Sectional Debates

The *Handbook*, comprising a sequence of thirty essays, a timeline, and a bibliography, does not require linear reading. Like an issue of a periodical or newspaper, it does not oblige readers to start at page one and read to the last. As with issues of periodicals, non-linearity does not mean neglect of form, for we have juxtaposed chapters we believe overlap in theme, if not approach, so that readers can read them in combination and conversation with each other. What follows is a brief outline of some of the debates and general research topics we hope to highlight through this organization. We have not sought to give summaries of individual chapters but rather to draw attention to overarching research questions raised in the volume as a whole.

The first section, "Production and Reproduction," comprises four chapters designed to help readers think about how we use data to tell different kinds of explanatory stories. It begins with James Mussell's discussion of how recent digitization efforts have dramatically influenced the ways we engage with, understand, and research journalistic texts, focusing first on the technological constraints and enablers of the digitization process and then, by comparing and contrasting the digital data with its paper predecessors, on how these affect our understandings of what has been digitized. The second chapter, by Shannon Rose Smith, goes on to address what stories we can tell about the technological underpinnings of the nineteenth-century press. Rather than simply providing a technological chronology, Smith questions assumptions about the notion of technological progress by focusing on two representations of technological innovation—Applegarth's vertical rotary press and the Linotype—and by probing the ways in which such innovations had to be integrated into narrative frameworks if they were to be accepted. Graham Law's chapter centers on the 1851 "Report to the Select Committee on Newspaper Stamps," offering a panoptical view of how the processes and practices of distribution changed over the course of the nineteenth century. He includes discussion of the fiscal and legal regulations, as well as the technological and economic arrangements, that helped or hindered the press. In the final chapter of this section, Andrew King explores economic considerations that determined the form and content of newspapers and periodicals. Given that the study of print economics has principally been linked with the research of media management, this chapter is keen to show that ideological commitment could be as powerful as capital investment during the nineteenth century. It also provides three different commercial models demonstrating the relative costs of content in newspapers and periodicals.

The next section of the *Handbook* is focused on "Contributors and Contributions." Study of the nineteenth-century press raises the question of what to call those who wrote, drew, engraved, or photographed the material it published. Linda K. Hughes has written persuasively on the problematic decision to omit all poetry from the *Wellesley Index*, an editorial choice which seemed to assume that poets could not be classified as journalists and which belied the important contribution of poetry to the nineteenth-century press.[17] As Andrew Hobbs notes, at least five million poems were published in the provincial press alone.[18] Many writers who

---

17. Hughes, "What the *Wellesley Index* Left Out."
18. Hobbs, "Five Million Poems."

regularly published poetry in periodicals—for example, Algernon Swinburne—contributed a substantial amount of prose to magazines as well. Illustrators, too, contributed to the press in significant ways. In 1863, Baudelaire referred to Constantin Guys, an artist for the *Illustrated London News*, as the "Painter of Modern Life," whose images enabled readers to grasp the details of the Crimean War more clearly than any other source.[19] Baudelaire's repeated use of the term *journalier* ("every-day," "daily") to describe Guy's drawings suggests that for him the news illustrator was the most modern kind of *journaliste*.

Given the diverse roles contributors played in the nineteenth-century press, it is difficult to draw the line between poet, novelist, artist, and journalist. It would be difficult to argue that, for instance, Walter Pater was viewed by his contemporaries as primarily a journalist despite the fact that, as Laurel Brake notes, he "constructed most of his books from his journalism."[20] Many other prominent contributors to nineteenth-century periodicals would potentially have bridled at such a designation, not least Thomas Carlyle, whose own anguished position as a contributor to magazines is discussed by Linda H. Peterson in Chapter 5 below.

This problem of definition arises partly in the different associations we bring today to the terms "journalist" and "journalism." While both words can be traced back hundreds of years, "journalist" only began to be used with any frequency in the wake of the French Revolution, when it was used to refer to someone who wrote for newspapers rather than for periodicals. Although we recognize that in many circles "literary" and "artistic" remain privileged terms, we affirm that journalism is no longer comprised of "subjugated knowledges" locked in a closet, as Brake defined it, echoing Foucault.[21] To prove that, the contributors to this volume demonstrate the importance of recovering the lived economic realities of writers in the nineteenth century, as shown in Linda Peterson's and Marysa Demoor's discussions of the remuneration received by writers and editors.

Of course, genre, just as much as authorship, is a crucial consideration in the history of the press. The fundamental formal categories on the page—illustration, poetry, and prose—functioned in different ways in different contexts. There are several recurring implications of this. One concerns recycling, for the same subject matter was very often either reprinted verbatim, summarized, commented on, or remediated into verbal or visual form. There is much work still to be done on where and when items were first published and on how, when, and why they were reprinted and with what effects (insofar as this is possible to determine). Second, dialogues between readers and textual producers emerge as crucial in determining how we should subdivide umbrella terms such as "news." A focus on reader-producer interactions—rather than on the legal definitions based on content which so preoccupied the 1851 Newspaper Stamp Committee—allows us to see "news" afresh and in a wider perspective so that the role of topical poetry, prose, and illustration can all be taken into account.

Classification proves another preoccupation, for within each formal category that the chapters on poetry, prose, and illustration address, there are also methodological questions of

---

19. Baudelaire, "Peintre," 3.
20. Brake, "Walter Pater," 482. See also Brake, *Walter Pater*, chapters 3–6, and *Subjugated Knowledges*, chapter 1.
21. Brake, *Subjugated Knowledges*, ix.

how they are to be categorized. Brian Maidment shows that the apparently simple term "illustration" is a case in point. Centering on wood engravings, he suggests illustration be analyzed in relation to three subcategories: the representational, the pictorial, and the comic. In the next chapter, Linda K. Hughes points out intersections between verse and various forms of commentary, including memorializations of recent events and demands for change in political consciousness. She reminds us, too, that poetry and illustration often worked in tandem. Beth Palmer, even while marking the most obvious division in prose between fiction and nonfiction, alerts us to the porosity between them and demonstrates how various kinds of prose can be read as symptomatic of power differentials between individuals or social groups. Taken as a whole, all the contributors to this section are concerned with how we can mobilize ways of classifying material to create new ways of understanding both the individual case study and the nineteenth-century press as a whole.

As noted above, geography was important in nineteenth-century press directories. This notion of place had many other resonances in the nineteenth-century press, as is demonstrated in the next section of the *Handbook*, "Geographies." The first three chapters, by Michelle Tusan, Bob Nicholson, and Jane Chapman, stress kinetic geographies of circulation, interrelation, and interactivity rather than maps of fixed points. If empire necessarily suggests dynamics of dominance and subordination—and Tusan considers Scotland, Wales, and Ireland as parts of an English empire—that is not the case with either the transatlantic or the transnational, both of which underline exchange and, to some extent, mutuality as key conceptual underpinnings. By comparing all three chapters, however, another instance of the long-lamented "digital divide" between rich and poor becomes apparent.[22] Digitization has opened up new possibilities for researching first-world publications but these materials are only slowly becoming available to other nations and social groups. The prevalence of paywalls in digital archives provides a further barrier to access, which has consequent effects on both scholarly and public understanding of national histories and identities.[23]

The four authors of the chapters on the Scottish, Welsh, Irish, and provincial press (chapters 13, 14, 15, and 16) raise other questions about how large numbers of periodicals and newspapers can be studied. Finkelstein, acceding to the impossibility of doing justice to the enormous number of periodicals published in nineteenth-century Scotland, focuses on five canonical English-language literary periodicals known for their integration into British literary culture at large. Peters, by contrast, emphasizes the breadth of Welsh print culture by covering a large quantity of both Welsh- and English-language newspapers and periodicals, including material produced for and by the Welsh diaspora in the United States and South America. Tilley elects to exclude Irish Gaelic material and, like Finkelstein, offers case studies of publications that were influential both inside and outside Ireland. Hobbs polemically theorizes the relation of the press to place, raises important questions about the role of quantitative

---

22. Norris, *Digital Divide*.
23. Important initiatives include the *Readex Collection* (which includes African Newspapers, 1800–1922, and Caribbean Newspapers, Series 1, 1718–1876) and the *World Newspaper Archive*.

methods, and demonstrates the usefulness of case studies that demonstrate the "rich profusion of provincial print."[24]

The question of national affiliation presents a challenge. Finkelstein discusses how the title of *Blackwood's Edinburgh Magazine* (1817–1980) seems to denote its Scottishness in an unambiguous way. Yet many readers of *Blackwood's*, particularly in the later nineteenth century, might well have seen it as British, not least because of its generally pro-imperialist outlook, which distinguished it from much of the national press of Scotland, Ireland, and Wales. Likewise, as both Lisa Peters and Elizabeth Tilley demonstrate, a sizeable part of the readership for periodicals from these countries was located in England and beyond the British Isles. The editor of the *Irish Penny Journal*, for example, complained that the unsustainability of his periodical was partly due to the fact that his only regular readers were in England.[25]

The next section of the *Handbook*, "Taxonomies," is designed to contribute to ongoing debates about how newspaper and periodical genres should be defined. The Aristotelian generic classification of texts by form and subject matter is of little help in discussing commodity texts in an industrial age unless notions of form and subject matter are radically reconsidered, and this is, in effect, what most of the chapters in this section seek to do. Implicitly or explicitly, they are focused on identifying the elements, both formal and content-based, associated with particular periodical genres. But they also identify the parameters within which periodicals and newspapers can operate without losing their identities as members of a genre.

In her introductory essay to this section, Laurel Brake argues that frequency, along with price, content, and location, are the primary formal features that determine genre. The long publication cycles of some periodicals may have contributed to their status and value—the quarterlies being more prestigious than the monthlies, and the monthlies being more entertaining than quarterlies but more respectable than weeklies. But this appertained only at a certain time in the century. By the fin de siècle, the quarterlies had lost the greater part of their luster, and the monthly *Blackwood's*, even though it serialized Conrad's *Heart of Darkness* in 1899, had become a tub-thumping mess-hall read for the military with far lower prestige amongst cultural elites than, say, the *Academy* (1869–1916). Similarly, the division between morning and evening dailies is not clear cut when we look at the realities of publication and distribution schedules. As Brake also points out, nineteenth-century advertising guides were not only aware of price, frequency, and place, but also of specific readerships. "Readership" implies not only form but also subject matter, and the taxonomy that follows her chapter is based fundamentally on a classification of readers defined largely by content. That said, throughout this volume we remain keenly alert to the unsettled nature of generic classification. Two particularly significant sources that contribute to this uncertainty are the correspondence columns and advertisements that several chapters mention. Although often considered in passing, they remain ripe for large-scale quantitative study. While huge gaps in newspaper and periodicals databases currently prevent the creation of a truly representative overview, it may be that eventually new taxonomies will emerge by attending to interactivity.

---

24. Hobbs, "Provincial Periodicals," 223 below.
25. Tilley, "Periodicals in Ireland." 210 below.

Gender is one of the most salient characteristics of newspapers, periodicals, and their readerships. We chose to place the chapter on men first to emphasize the need for work in this area, for while there has rightly been a good deal of work on women and the periodical press in recent years, there has been considerably less on men and masculinities. Even if "gender is not a synonym for women" as Terrell Carver reminded us a generation ago, masculinity often remains the silent norm.[26] Starting from the thesis that gendering is always in process and contestation, Olsen considers periodicals and newspapers addressed to men, such as Cobbett's *Political Register* (1802–35), along with sporting or boys' periodicals (both of which are explored in greater depth in later chapters). Acknowledging that most professions were still bastions of middle-class masculinity during the nineteenth century, she also examines professional periodicals such as the *Law Times* (1843–1965) and the *Lancet* (1823–). The title of her chapter is also significant, for she asks us to consider issues of masculinity in material addressed to women and children, and she is alert to how the gender address of a periodical or newspaper can change during its lifetime.

In her examination of women's periodicals, Kathryn Ledbetter is also keen to demonstrate how they pushed the boundaries of gender, not only in terms of content but also in terms of the vocational opportunities they provided. Many periodicals and newspapers had women editors as well as women contributors, and from 1859 the Victoria Press employed women compositors. Over the course of the nineteenth century, women's roles expanded, partly due to the rise of Christian evangelism and its associated press (which justified missionary work and management outside the home). The emergence of a feminist press was crucial in promoting women's work as well. Beginning with the *English Woman's Journal* (1858–63), the feminist press always had a limited circulation, but it was nonetheless influential on print culture as a whole. For example, Mona Caird's explosive 1888 article on "Marriage" in the *Westminster Review* created a furore which led to a subsequent inquiry in the *Telegraph*.[27]

Jennifer Phegley's chapter examines penny and shilling family magazines, emphasizing the genre's hybridity. Such periodicals combined titillation with respectability, entertainment with education, text with image, and solitary reflection with communal reading experiences. Of relevance here is how weekly newspapers such as the *Illustrated London News* (1842–1989) often sought to provide content for the entire family, not just male readers, and this has implications not only for the gendering and genre of a newspaper or periodical but also for its overall identity.

In the next two chapters on children's periodicals and the sporting press, gender intersects with a common set of issues: class, celebrity, interactivity, and interpellation into national and imperial citizenship. What emerges as truly characteristic of each genre is perhaps surprising. Kristine Moruzi notes a significant gendering of the children's periodical market in the 1850s when long-lasting magazines targeting boys and girls as separate identities were established. While gender-inclusive periodicals continued to exist (and of course girls read boys' magazines and vice versa), they were often constructed around celebrity editors or authors. Later in the century, interactivity comes to the fore: competitions, quizzes, puzzles, and correspondence.

---

26. Carver, *Gender Is Not a Synonym for Women*.
27. For detail on Caird's reception following her *Westminster Review* article, see Rosenberg, "Breaking Out."

What had been most characteristic of children's periodicals early in the century—monologic education—came to be fused with entertainment and dialogue.

In his chapter on sporting periodicals, Yuri Cowan not only highlights their concern with issues of gender exclusivity, celebrity, and interactivity but also examines their fascination with numbers and tables and the closely related notions of time and risk management (the fixing of sporting events in the calendar and the prediction of sporting results). The latter can be discerned in the provision of arcane knowledge that might prove advantageous either in practicing the sport itself or in gambling. Such knowledge, when combined with anecdotes and news, can also serve as badges of belonging to groups defined according to criteria more specific than just class, such as supporters of a precise football club, Alpine climbers, polo players, or the sector of the landed gentry marked by an interest in hunting and shooting. Yet, as Cowan points out, the same information, supplied by press agencies, might be relayed and reprinted in various formats across a wide area of the field. This again alerts us to the overlapping nature of our taxonomy: material relevant to any one chapter can appear in almost any other, but here Cowan alerts us to how recycling and overlapping came to be centrally controlled by the changing macro-organization of the press. The rise of press agencies, while known to scholars for a long time, still deserves additional research.

Contributors to the *Handbook* focus less on party politics with its huge social visions, than on practical politics understood as the power arrangements involved in the distribution of resources and, as with temperance, on single-issue politics. They look at how access to the production and consumption of periodicals and newspapers was unevenly spread between social groups and was always open to dispute. Chapters 23–26 are concerned with periodicals and newspapers that attempted to assess present circumstances with the aim of working toward achievable ideals, either in the material world or beyond it.

Contrasting the real and the ideal is one of the key definitions of satire. In his chapter, Craig Howes demonstrates that satirical material was very common across the entire range of elite and popular publications during the nineteenth century. Social-purpose periodicals also strove to address the gap between a troubled world and its ideals, although they usually sought to achieve their aims through less comic means. As Deborah Mutch highlights in her chapter, when defining social ideals, one group's vision of heaven might be another's idea of hell, and this almost always leads to conflict. She links class politics to topics raised in other chapters of the *Handbook*—temperance, religious, and women's activism—in order to illustrate similarities and differences in each group's approach and ideological stance. While there is a long and honorable tradition of studying the radical, feminist, and socialist press, Annemarie McAllister rightly calls attention to a vast but neglected field of discourse—temperance—noting how it empowered not only working-class men but also women and children. Mark Knight, by contrast, asks us to rethink current materialist paradigms not just in our study of the declaredly religious press but of nineteenth-century periodicals and newspapers in general. Knight provocatively questions our fetishization of quantitative methods and Marxian approaches, challenging us to understand religious periodicals on their own terms.

The range of aesthetic interests for both writers and readers was vast, from macramé to grand opera, from walking sticks to the Victoria and Albert Museum, from tending roses in a cottage garden to the dressing of a table for a state dinner. The last part of the "Taxonomies" section focuses on three fields that received a great deal of attention: theater, art, and music. Material relevant to these fields can easily be found in a variety of forms. For example, music for domestic performance appeared every week in the penny fiction weekly *Bow Bells* (1862–97) during the 1860s; art history and reproductions were a feature of the latter years of the *Penny Magazine* (1832–45), which included contributions from Anna Jameson,[28] and the dramatic poses in acting manuals were reproduced in myriad illustrations.[29] Recycling, allusion and reference were the order of the day.

Theater, music, and art each had dedicated titles that separated professionals from amateurs. Study of periodicals and newspapers in each category has suffered from a "grab and run" approach by historians of those fields who, when raiding them for information, have often neglected the medium itself and the conditions under which content was produced. The final chapters in the *Handbook* seek to rectify this. In her chapter, Katherine Newey draws attention to the discursive constraints of theater journalism and its important intersections with the mainstream press. Discussions of the theater, and indeed of all the arts, were concerned that performances should morally improve their audiences, a notion that connects with characteristics of other genres which aimed to narrow the gap between ideal and real. Julie Codell, like Katherine Newey, focuses on the overarching discursive rules that governed what could be said, while at the same time offering a Bourdieu-inflected take on art periodicals. Laura Vorachek highlights the transnational nature of music and in the process alerts us to how much we still do not know about music periodicals and their audiences.

Throughout the *Handbook* we have tried to draw attention to the process of remediation, which demonstrates links between what seem to be disparate titles, genres, and realms of display. For example, the original of the picture reproduced on the *Handbook* dust jacket, *Our First Tiff*, was painted by Robert Walker Macbeth, an artist who had drawn scenes of the Paris Commune for the *Graphic* in 1871 and contributed illustrations to periodicals such as the *English Illustrated Magazine* (1883–1913) and *Once a Week* (1859–80). *Our First Tiff* was not only hung at the Grosvenor Gallery in 1879 but had a resonant afterlife in the press. For *Punch*, the painting was an excuse for a bad but affectionate pun ("a sulky gentleman turning away from a silky lady") while for the *University Magazine* (1878–80), it was an example of bad realism rather than "real" art.[30] Macbeth also made an etching of *Our First Tiff* that was exhibited at galleries; copies were sold for a guinea and were of course advertised in the press. The etched version was subject to a verbal remediation that was different from the painting in that articles and reviews focused on its technical production.[31]

This constant movement of artist and item across, as well as in and out of, the press applies equally well to other kinds of published material. The quotation at the beginning of this introduction, in fact, comes from an article that was probably written as not much more than an

---

28. Holcomb, "Anna Jameson."
29. See, for example, Figure 7.8 below.
30. "Grosvenor Gallery Review"; "Gossip on the Grosvenor."
31. See, for example, "Exhibition of Works in Black and White," 3. We use a reproduction of the etched version as Figure 1.1.

extended filler for the December 1829 number of *Blackwood's* by its editor John Wilson who, around this time, regularly supplied the first and last pieces in individual issues (in this case, the last). Extravagantly extended over several pages, the metaphor of periodicals as stars and flowers in the *Blackwood's* of the *Noctes Ambrosianae* and other witty conversation pieces functions as a rather silly throwaway jeu d'esprit in celebration of the periodical's 148 months of survival—an odd anniversary to mark. Its position and its frothiness suggest that it was a way of ensuring that the issue had a decorous bulk worthy of its retail price. It would amuse regular readers and humorously assure them of the periodical's value in several ways at once. As soon as it appeared, it was freely extracted and circulated, reprinted (with slight variations) in the December 26, 1829 number of the twopenny weekly *Mirror of Literature* and in the *Polar Star of Entertainment and Popular Science* (1829–32), an obscure London quarterly which published compilations of extracts from other periodicals, both British and American.[32] The *Blackwood's* piece very quickly crossed the Atlantic to appear in the *Athenaeum: Spirit of the English Magazines* in January 1830, followed by a slightly different version in the *American Masonick Record and Albany Literary Journal* (March 6, 1830).[33] Almost twenty years later, it was printed yet again in the *Randolph County Journal*, where its source was named as the "Excelsior" and its original context was entirely obscured through excision of any reference to *Blackwood's*.[34] In all its reprints, some with the source redacted, the piece nonetheless still includes almost all the same words. It is still filler in all the periodicals that print it; however, rather than being a fizzy local marker of a particular occasion, it has become a generalized celebration of the periodical press and its social and technological progress. By 1858, it is treated as a serious reflection on the press—as if its ridiculous comparisons of periodicals to stars and flowers had become self-evident poetic truths.

Attention to dissemination, recycling, and repurposing across texts and across nations is easier nowadays than it was before the age of the Internet, as several contributors remark. A focus on the detail, form, and context of our material, while essential, should not blind us to the wider concerns of the press and its multiple and contradictory roles in politics, aesthetics, pleasures, beliefs, the distribution of resources, and the regulation and formation of social groups. Several of the essays included in the *Handbook* challenge us to reconsider how we conceptualize our subject matter at a very basic level—asking, what is a nineteenth-century periodical or newspaper?—as much as they point us in the direction of possible answers. If the approaches, narratives, and topics represented here vary widely, we celebrate this diversity and the energy behind it. This volume is proof of the vitality of our field. Whether we are novices or experienced scholars, it is ultimately our decision and our responsibility to determine where and how we proceed. This *Handbook* aims to illuminate our decisions and responsibilities while lighting the way toward future explorations.

---

32. "Spirit of the Public Journals," *Mirror of Literature*, 440–2; "Soliloquy," *Polar Star of Entertainment*, 336–8.
33. "Periodical Literature," *Athenaeum: Spirt of the English Magazines*, 352–4; "Essayist-Periodical Literature." *American Masonick Record*, 44–5.
34. "Periodicals," *Randolf County Journal*, 4.

Section I

PRODUCTION AND REPRODUCTION

1

DIGITIZATION

James Mussell

It is difficult to overstate the impact of digitization on the study of nineteenth-century periodicals. By transforming periodicals into processable data, digital resources tackle two of the most significant challenges for scholars interested in this material. Firstly, they exert a measure of bibliographical control over what is a complex archive, offering lists of periodicals and indexing their contents. Secondly, they allow anyone with a web browser (and, more often than not, the necessary subscription) to access material from wherever they are, whenever they want. The range of content might vary from resource to resource, but even relying on large (and largely indiscriminate) freely accessible resources over the web, such as *Google Books*, the *Internet Archive*, and the *HathiTrust Digital Library*, provides researchers with a collection that surpasses that of most individual libraries and has much more amenable opening hours. Despite limitations in the quality of the data (page images, transcripts, and metadata), the uneven selection of periodicals digitized, and the often prohibitive barriers to access (mainly in terms of subscription but also the necessary skills to make the most of the resources), it has not been so easy to read nineteenth-century periodicals since the time when they were first published. In fact, given the often-noted difficulties with staying abreast of what was published in the period, one might argue that it is easier today.

Even though only a fraction of what was printed in the nineteenth century has survived, there remains far too much to read in the print archive, and what has survived appears in a perplexing diversity of forms. By transforming periodicals into something else, something digital, we create new ways that they can be interrogated, which, in turn, help us to understand both the surviving printed periodicals and the culture that produced them. It is easy to assume that the more accurate the digital reproduction, the better the resource; however, because of the necessary transformation from one medium to another, complete reproduction of print periodicals in digital form is impossible. Rather than lament this as a shortcoming of digital resources, this chapter takes the way digital resources differ from periodicals in print as a productive starting point. Digital resources are effective because of the ways that the digital medium differs from print. To use digital resources effectively, I argue, it is important that researchers understand how they differ so that the print archive can be approached anew.

The chapter is in two parts. In the first, I account for some of the common features of digital resources by linking them to the way that they are produced. Just as scholars using printed periodicals need to understand something about their mode of production, the same is true when using digital resources. In the second, I consider the relationship between the new digital archive of nineteenth-century periodicals and its predecessor in print. As the power of digital resources results from the way they modify the printed periodicals on which they are based, it is crucial that the two be consulted alongside one another. Such a comparison makes explicit the differences introduced through digitization. However, rather than condemn these as deficiencies—the ways in which the digital resource fails to adequately reproduce aspects of the printed periodical—they are more usefully recognized as opportunities, distinctly digital features that can be manipulated in various ways. Whether in print or digital form, what can be learned about periodicals depends on what can be done with them. Our knowledge of nineteenth-century periodicals to date is the result of the material that survives, often in distinct forms, on the shelves of the archive. But digital resources too have their own lessons to teach about the nineteenth-century press, its modes of production, and the period that it served.

Digitization

Periodical publication has always caused bibliographical problems. Even as nineteenth-century writers praised the press as an icon of modernity, they also lamented the amount of material that was produced and the difficulty of reading it all. There were various attempts in the period to devise ways to stay on top of what was published. Periodicals frequently reviewed each other, allowing their readers to glimpse inside the covers of rival publications. Most periodicals also provided indexes at the end of the volume that allowed readers to search for articles retrospectively. The *Cornhill Magazine*, for instance, indexed the title words for each article it published.[1] As useful as these volume indexes are, readers still had to know which volume was likely to contain the article they wanted. This problem was addressed for newspapers by Samuel Palmer's *Index to the Times Newspaper*, first published in 1868, which indexed the whole paper retrospectively while keeping up with each new issue as it appeared. For periodicals, Sampson Low's short-lived *Index to Current Literature* (1859–60) used title information to derive subject indexes for current periodicals, but it was not until the appearance of William Frederick Poole's *Index to Periodical Literature* (1882) that back numbers were indexed. W.T. Stead, who had instituted the *Pall Mall Gazette*'s shilling biannual indexes in 1884 during his tenure as editor, began his annual *Index to the Periodical Literature of the World* in 1891 after leaving the newspaper and beginning his monthly *Review of Reviews*.[2] Like its predecessors, this was primarily a subject index but, like Low's and unlike Poole's, Stead's indexes were a serial designed to stay abreast of the press year by year.

Digital resources should be situated in this tradition of attempts to exert bibliographic control over the periodical archive. Scott Bennett's "The Bibliographic Control of Victorian Periodicals," published in 1978, described such work as "indexing and inventorying," the two

---

1. See Hetherington, "Indexing of Periodicals," 3–7.
2. See Brake, "Stead Alone" and *Subjugated Knowledges*, 99–100.

primary functions of bibliographic control.[3] For Bennett, recent innovations such as the *Wellesley Index* and *Waterloo Directory* were the latest attempts to open up the historical print archive by listing its contents. However, Bennett looked forward to what he called the "next bibliographic horizon," one that would include "analytical bibliography and textual analysis."[4] Bennett recognized that indexing and inventorying depended upon the fiction that the periodical archive was fixed and consistent, with every run containing the same identical content. However, what survives in the archive are the remains of a complex and competitive publishing process which has subsequently been subjected to a wide range of archival practices. It is an archive characterized by abundance and complexity: indexing and inventorying address the abundance but do so by eliding the complexity.

Digitization necessitates an engagement with both analytical bibliography and textual analysis, although this engagement is not often recognized as such. The choice of which run to scan, for instance, is an editorial decision, as the same publication is likely to exist in different forms. Digitization projects will have their own criteria for selecting one run over another: a large project might simply digitize the holdings of a particular library, not giving much consideration to the status of individual publications; a more focused project, however, might merge different runs in order to provide as complete a set as possible. In either case, a decision must be made to nominate a particular set of materials to represent the publication as a whole, and then a further set of decisions must be made about what content constitutes the periodical proper (and so what might be left out).[5]

The use of specific, individuated copies of a periodical to represent all others means that there is a tension at the heart of all digitization projects. Bennett's critique of "indexing and inventorying" was that these methods did not recognize the bibliographical complexity of the surviving print objects. Indexes such as the *Wellesley* provide information about an idealized version of the periodical that can be applied to the specific material at hand. Something similar happens with digital resources, which offer one particular set of materials, perhaps collated from different runs, as a copy text to stand for all others. This is a common editorial technique, but the use of facsimile page images in a digital resource makes the provenance of the source material persistently present in a way that it is not in a print edition. While most digital resources are a kind of critical edition, attempting to offer a "best" representative text, the page images are also facsimile editions that document particular material witnesses with their own individual histories.

As the periodical must be recreated from scratch in digital form, those doing the digitizing need a good sense of what it is about the source object, the printed periodical, that they want to present. As paper-based printed objects designed (primarily) to be read, simply scanning the pages will produce a sequence of page images that can be distributed over the web,

3. Bennett, "Bibliographical Control," 50. For a further discussion of this chapter, see Mussell, *Nineteenth-Century Press in the Digital Age*, 3–6.
4. Bennett, "Bibliographical Control," 50.
5. For accounts of how two different digital projects went about sourcing their material, see Cayley, "Creating the *Daily Mail*," and "Editorial Commentary."

displayed onscreen, and read more or less as they would in print. The symmetry between the linear sequence of page images and the page sequence in the printed volume can be useful, as it provides a possible structure for the digital periodical that is already understood by its users. However, it endorses the codex form of the bound volume (and the decisions made by various librarians and archivists as to what should be preserved and in what shape) rather than any of the other possible states in which periodicals were issued and read. While this basic resource might be accessed over the web, allowing many people to read it at once, it asserts the page as the periodical's constituent unit and restricts its users to turning them one by one.

To really open up the content on the page, page images need to be accompanied by textual transcripts. The process for creating these is called Optical Character Recognition (OCR), a technology that produces encoded alphanumeric characters from the printed letterforms displayed on the page image which are readable both by humans and machines. It is easy to mistake the OCR-generated transcript as the "content" of the periodical—its processable soul, perhaps—but this reduces content to the words on the page. Natalia Cecire has described OCR as a "strange backwards ekphrasis," where the text becomes an image from which another, corrupted, text is generated.[6] As she remarks, the transcript constitutes a kind of "silent diplomatic edition," offering a version of the periodical's verbal text.[7] Even though it is derived from the page images, the transcript provides a complementary version of what the images represent. Rather than the pure content of the periodical—liberated from the embodied forms of paper and ink, layout and letterform—the transcript serves as a representation of the page that complements the way it is represented in the scan. The transcript provides a processable representation of what is written in the periodical; the image provides a representation of how it looks (which, of course, includes what it says).

OCR is a well-established technology with a wide commercial application. Although fancy typefaces and unusual layout can still cause problems, the performance of OCR likely depends on the quality of the original page impression rather than the text printed on the page. While the letterpress in most periodicals is quite clear, printing errors, degraded type, and closely printed text can obscure the letterforms. This means that some types of periodicals have more accurate transcripts than others: quarterlies and monthlies, especially the more upmarket publications, tend to produce quite accurate transcripts, whereas those produced from cheaper and more frequent publications, especially the more newspaper-like titles, contain significantly more errors.[8] The condition of the volume can also cause problems. If tightly bound, the pages bend when opened, distorting the letterforms; if the leaves are not bound flush to the binding, the resulting images need to be "de-skewed" so that the OCR can run on horizontal lines of text. The quality of the scan, too, makes a difference. The best results from OCR are achieved when the letterpress is starkly defined against the page. This effect can be enhanced by increasing the contrast of the scan; however, because the same image is used as the basis for the one that appears onscreen, such settings misrepresent the appearance of the page. Since they result

---

6. Cecire, "Visible Hand," n.p.
7. Ibid.
8. Tanner, Muñoz, and Ros, "Measuring Mass Text," n.p.; Holley, "How Good Can It Get?," n.p.

in smaller file sizes (compared to grayscale images), bitonal images are considered ideal for OCR. Further, because every pixel is black or white, bitonal images make the back letterpress stand out clearly from the white of the page. However, such scans render engravings, with their subtle use of line, as dense blocks of black and white. Grayscale page images, or in some cases color, are now more common, but these produce larger files that are more costly to store and serve to users. Of course, digital images produced from microfilm can only produce the image that was filmed, and this is likely to be in black and white and under high contrast.

The textual transcripts produced through OCR are seldom entirely accurate, even with further processing (for instance, referencing against a corpus of known words); only a human reader is capable of catching all the errors by checking the OCR against the original source. Although expensive and time-consuming to correct, a corrected transcript makes more of the verbal content of a periodical accessible. It allows the periodical to be subjected to further analysis, for instance through text mining or additional markup (picking out key names, texts, or events), and permits richer modeling of the text's structure. It also enables further functionality such as text-to-speech, which affords blind or visually impaired users better access to the resource's contents.

However, it is difficult to establish the precise accuracy of a transcript. Without a corrected version to check against, accuracy rates cited by vendors remain only estimates. Rather than pay others to correct transcripts, some projects have turned to their potential users. Crowdsourcing correction is cost-effective and, if managed well, can also cohere volunteers into a community of advocates. The success of the Australian Newspapers Digitisation Programme's text correction project (begun in 2008) demonstrated that it was possible to work with volunteers to correct transcripts and mark them up with keywords.[9] *Dickens Journals Online* ran a similar project from January 2011 until May 2012 which provided corrected transcripts for complete runs of *Household Words* and *All the Year Round*, as well as the *Household Words Narrative* and *Almanac*. This textual corpus allowed the project, in collaboration with the Centre for Literary and Linguistic Computing at the University of Newcastle, Australia, to use corpus methods to explore whether Dickens was the author of a previously unattributed article in *All the Year Round*.[10]

There is more to a periodical's contents than what is represented by a series of page images or the linear text of an OCR-generated transcript. The pages of periodicals signal all kinds of other structures. Mastheads (where they appear) indicate that another issue has commenced, other headings do the same at the level of articles, and there are a whole range of textual marks—for example, rules or different typefaces—that give the page texture. In print, the reader processes the signs that mark these structures, allowing the text's materiality to emerge as it is read. In digital form, however, these structural components can also be marked up and encoded so that they become part of the digital object. In a classic examination of the poetics of markup, Jerome McGann and Dino Buzzetti argue that it makes "explicit certain features of that originally paper-based text, it exhibits them by bringing them forth visibly into the

---

9. Holley, "Many Hands Make Light Work."
10. Drew and Craig, "Did Dickens Write 'Temperate Temperance'?"

expression of the text."[11] Markup acknowledges the structural and semiotic functions of formal features and, crucially, makes them operational, enabling a wide range of potential functions. It becomes possible, for instance, to represent structure in various ways, reconfiguring the periodical as required and allowing the different constituent units to be exported and extracted, combined and compared, and subjected to further analysis.

There are different ways to write structure into the digital resource. The end goal is a robust data architecture that delineates the constituent units of the periodical and places them in some sort of order. For less complex periodicals, or those in shorter runs, this might simply be a case of marking up the transcript, perhaps using an established XML schema such as TEI, and associating it with the relevant page image.[12] Some OCR engines even produce transcripts with rudimentary markup that can then be further developed. For more complex periodicals, particularly those with multiple articles on the page, more sophisticated methods are required. Commercial publishers often have their own tools that allow operators to mark up the page directly, delimiting key textual units, such as articles, and adding metadata as appropriate. These marked-up pages are then processed to produce OCR-generated transcripts and image files for the designated textual units as well as the data structure, usually in XML, that organizes them.[13]

Although this seems like a technical process, it is also interpretive, as choices have to be made as to which structures are represented and how. To create a data structure for a periodical, its components need to be classified, named, and related to one another. This is straightforward in many instances; one could use a well-established metadata schema, such as Dublin Core, and there are plenty of precedents when it comes to classifying periodicals. Features such as publication titles, volume numbers, issue numbers, and article titles—metadata recorded on the printed periodicals—are usually easy to identify and mark up. However, periodicals pose their own classificatory problems. Publications often amended their titles over the course of the run, or, for example, they might have published a new series, creating two volumes with the same number. Equally, although the date of publication is usually given on every issue, these dates might not correspond to the actual dates of publication. As dates are also likely to be at different levels of granularity—a day for a weekly, a month for a monthly, or a period of three months for a quarterly—they can be difficult to aggregate, causing problems when searching.[14] All these problems can be solved, but those producing the resource must negotiate between the strictures of a general metadata schema and the idiosyncratic demands of the source material.

Publishers often prefer to devote resources to metadata rather than the OCR-generated transcripts because metadata, once corrected, is likely to compensate sufficiently for any remaining errors when it comes to searching.[15] In such cases, the transcript is still used for searching; however, because the user is given a page image to read, it can be relegated to the

---

11. Buzzetti and McGann, "Electronic Textual Editing," n.p.
12. This method, for instance, was more or less adopted for the index and metadata in the *Internet Library of Early Journals* (1999). See "ILEJ: Final Report."
13. For two accounts of this, see "Editorial Commentary" and Cayley, "Creating the *Daily Mail*."
14. See Mussell and Paylor, "Editions and Archives."
15. See Cayley, "Creating the *Daily Mail*," 6.

index, keeping its errors away from the eyes of users. It is particularly important to correct the titles of articles. As the publishers of the *Cornhill* realized, titles can provide a good sense of an article's content; however, in digital resources, they function more as a set of keywords than as a verbal description. Titles are also useful when it comes to browsing lists of search results. For this reason, publishers of digital resources prioritize corrections to titles. The dominance of Google means that users are familiar with entering a search term and then wading through long lists of results, rarely reaching the end of the list. Metadata plays a vital role here, helping users to decide between articles without having to open them up and read them.

Metadata can also provide the framework for faceted browsing, offering a way for users to visualize a resource's content and take more control over how it is delimited. Faceted browsing requires all content to be associated with various predetermined facets, allowing users to add or take them away to reduce or increase the pool of articles to be read. Brightsolid's *British Newspaper Archive* (2011–), for instance, combines free-text searching, which runs on the underlying OCR-generated transcript, with a faceted browse, displaying metadata categories in a left-hand sidebar that shows the number of hits under each. The state of the transcripts means that such searches will never be exhaustive, but at least readers have a way of managing—and maybe exhausting—their search results.

As Patrick Leary has noted, free-text searching can be very effective, but it raises its own methodological problems. If users want to find an article about something, they need to come up with a search term likely to appear within the article.[16] Given the size of many databases, it is likely that users will find something of use, but the more familiar they are with the material (and the language used within it), the more successful they will be. Metadata can complement free-text searching by opening up the content in different ways, but the extent to which it can be developed and applied depends on the size of the corpus and the resources available. Metadata is particularly important for images since without verbal information they remain outside of the search index. *The Database of Mid-Victorian Illustration* (2007) devised its own schema for describing the content of images, and this was later adapted by the *Nineteenth-Century Serials Edition* (2008) to mark up the images in its periodicals. Gale Cengage's *Illustrated London News Historical Archive, 1842–2003* (2010) relies on the text strings in captions and accompanying articles to make its images searchable but has included metadata so that images can be delimited by type (for example, as a photograph or an engraving). More recently, the team behind the *Database of Mid-Victorian Illustration* have launched *Illustration Archive*, a project that uses a combination of computational means and crowdsourcing to identify images and supply metadata in a large corpus of nineteenth-century books.

Verbal content, too, can be marked up and, as with images, this often necessitates someone reading the content and making a judgment. Gale Cengage uses a standard set of content categories in its various products (for example, "business and finance" or "front page"), which it assigns by hand.[17] This can be very time-consuming, especially if the editors have to make difficult decisions regarding the appropriate categories. To avoid having to read every article in

16. Leary, "Googling the Victorians," 80–2.
17. Cayley, "Creating the *Daily Mail*," 7.

the database, the editors of the *Nineteenth-Century Serials Edition* used text-mining techniques from corpus linguistics to assign metadata categories, including a semantic tagger to identify different types of content.[18] A further solution—one that is increasingly common—is to let users assign their own tags. A number of commercial publishers have implemented this "social" element with varying degrees of success. Three years after its launch, for instance, there is only one instance of the tag "Victoria" in the *British Newspaper Archive*. Even "Titanic," the example provided by the archive, has only been tagged once.

Simply by making nineteenth-century periodicals searchable (and cross-searchable), digitization has transformed both the study of the press and of the period. By providing solutions to many (but by no means all) of the methodological problems associated with working with periodicals, digital resources have placed this material in some sort of order and opened it up. However, these results are achieved through transformation. In such resources, periodicals become databases of articles, searched by an index that reduces their content to sequences of characters derived from page images. Such resources make their contents much more accessible, reinforcing the importance of the periodical press to the period, yet their design necessarily shapes the form periodicals take and what can be done with them. Despite the real and important achievement represented by these resources, they remain predicated on allowing users to read articles one at a time.

Periodicals, Old and New

What is read in a digital resource is not a nineteenth-century periodical but is instead often an image from a page that is accessed and presented in such a way as to simulate the printed object. At present, digital resources take advantage of data to make page images accessible to keyword searching. As the page images are read much as they would be in print, this separates off the "digital" part of the user's experience—for example, browsing, reading about the resource, or entering search terms—and marks it as belonging to the mediating framework of the interface. The page images, which are made accessible by this activity, appear distinct, marked as "content" and offered as a kind of surrogate for the similar (but not identical) reading experience that occurs with print off screen. This distinction between mediating form and mediated content is intended to reduce the difference between digital and print editions, ensuring that users, when they find the content they want, know what to do with it. Most users come to digital resources to gain access to articles and so want to encounter as few barriers as possible. Given the high up-front costs associated with digitization, it is particularly important that their producers (and not just commercial publishers) recognize and anticipate their users' expectations and needs. Yet this model of digitization, which relies on an (undisclosed) index to provide access to images that stand in place of pages, creates a situation where the resource can only ever offer a deficient representation of the printed periodical.

If digital objects are conceived as surrogates of non-digital objects, then they will always be thought of as deficient in some way. This is mitigated by identifying the key features of the

---

18. "Visual Material."

source material—for instance, the way it looks, if it is to be read—and reproducing these at the cost of other, less important features. Those familiar with periodicals in print readily notice what has been left out, whether properties related to the shift in materiality (weight, size, the texture of the page, and the colors of paper and ink) or the way the resource organizes its content (perhaps making it difficult to browse, for instance). In this view, the digital resource, despite its impressive functionality, can only ever fail to capture the richness of the print object. Yet digitization takes place in an economy of loss *and* gain: while it is important to register how a digitized periodical differs from one in print, especially for those who may not be familiar with printed periodicals, conceiving of these differences as deficiencies only tells half the story.

Using data to identify what to read is one possible way of exploiting the digital difference, and it is the one implemented most often. However, data is processable and can be used much more creatively. An uncorrected OCR transcript is already a bountiful source of data, and any further encoding makes it richer. A number of resources use the processable nature of the transcripts to combine different types of materials. Gale Cengage's *Nineteenth-Century Collections Online* (2012–), for instance, brings together a wide range of material from the period to create a cross-searchable database of primary sources. The material was mostly sourced from discrete library and archive collections, but it includes periodical material (although "periodical," unlike "newspaper," is not defined as a content type). Perhaps more useful is their *NewsVault* (2010–), which is designed to search across what Gale Cengage classes as its "newspaper archives," although this includes *19th Century UK Periodicals* (series 1 and 2, 2007 and 2008, respectively), the *Economist Historical Archive, 1843–2007* (2007), the *Illustrated London News Historical Archive* (2010), and *Punch Historical Archive 1841–1992* (2014), as well as their newspaper collections *The Times Digital Archive* (2002), *Sunday Times Digital Archive, 1822–2006* (2012), and *19th Century British Library Newspapers* (2007, incorporated into *British Newspapers, 1600–1900* in 2009).

Gale Cengage can aggregate their resources in this way because of the common digitization strategies adopted by their various databases. However, a number of academic projects have worked to aggregate discrete resources, no matter how they were created. *Connected Histories* (2011–), for instance, brings together a number of different datasets, including those based on periodicals such as *SciPer: Science in the Nineteenth-Century Periodical* (2005–2007), the *Database of Mid-Victorian Illustration*, and the *Proceedings of the Old Bailey Online, 1674–1913* (2003–), as well as related resources such as the *John Johnson Collection of Printed Ephemera* (2008), *Nineteenth-Century British Pamphlets* (2009), and *British Newspapers, 1600–1900*. Each of these resources was produced independently; what *Connected Histories* has done is produce a further set of indexes, derived from data supplied by the contributing projects, which links them together. In some cases, this was semi-structured data from databases and in others, from marked-up XML, but some was produced from uncorrected OCR-generated transcripts. *NINES: Nineteenth-Century Scholarship Online* (2003–) does something similar, using a separate layer of metadata to aggregate the contents of a number of discrete resources. Like *Connected Histories*, *NINES* brings together resources dedicated to digitized periodicals (for instance, the *Nineteenth-Century Serials Edition*), but it also includes databases that incorporate periodicals as part of wider projects, such as the *Yellow Nineties Online* (2010), *Poetess Archive* (2005–), and *Rossetti Archive* (2000–2008), as well as databases that focus on different types of content entirely, such as the *William Blake Archive* (1995–). Both *Connected Histories* and *NINES* allow free-text searching across their constituent resources; however, whereas *Connected Histories* produces its own separate indexes of names, places, and dates in order to redirect users to the specific resource, *NINES* uses metadata prepared by its contributors that enable the entries to function as objects in their own right. This allows users of *NINES* to collect and repurpose this metadata, generating and publishing their own collections based on the objects provided by contributing projects.

These resources partly adopt the same logic as the large databases of nineteenth-century periodicals such as Gale Cengage's *19th Century UK Periodicals* or ProQuest's *British Periodicals* (2006–2007). By aggregating as much content as possible, resources like *Connected Histories* and *NINES* help users locate relevant content by broadening their searchable content. Like the publishers of periodical databases, the creators of aggregated sites argue that the larger the scope of the database, the more chance that users will find the specific information they need. It is undoubtedly true that combining disparate datasets can provide a richer account of the period. Users searching for something in particular will get hits in a wide range of materials, revealing the many traces it has left in the archive (or at least those parts of the archive that are part of the resource). Even canonical figures or events can become defamiliarized as they crop up in unexpected places. Such searches will never be exhaustive, but they do at least juxtapose different types of material, potentially complicating dominant historical narratives.

Periodicals constitute a particularly useful set of materials in this regard, as their inherent miscellaneity can provide specific articles on a wide range of subjects while also offering a range of different views of the same subject. However, while including periodicals amongst other types of content restores them to their central place in nineteenth-century culture, the way in which they are digitized transforms them into a database of articles. These digital resources decontextualize their contents, isolating articles from the pages, sections, issues, and volumes to which they are inextricably connected. While such resources provide access to periodical material of which the user would otherwise be unaware, they encourage a form of research where such material is mined indiscriminately for the content that it contains.

Recently, a number of scholars working with newspapers have begun to take advantage of processable data to explore features of the press that would be beyond the reach of those using more traditional methods. One of the main problems presented by the abundance of periodicals surviving in the archive is how to understand the periodical as a print genre responding to changing cultural conditions over time. Critics since the nineteenth century have offered surveys of the press that describe its main features, but such surveys are necessarily impressionistic, based on whatever periodicals the author has happened to come across. However, the data produced through digitization can be used to detect and make visible patterns within the corpus without having to read its entire contents. Bridget Baird and Cameron Blevins's *ImageGrid* (2012), produced as part of the larger *Mapping Texts* (2010–11) project, uses a bespoke visual interface that functions in a similar way to those used by commercial publishers to segment periodicals and newspapers. Using the tool, they were able to quantify discussions of space within newspapers (in other words, to capture how much content is devoted to a particular location) and track the spaces of the newspaper in which such discussions appeared. Blevins calls this "middle reading," a way of interrogating newspapers that is situated between the close reading associated with traditional literary studies and the distant reading of large datasets.[19] Tim Sherratt's *The front page* (2012) visualizes the newspaper data within *Trove*, the National Library of Australia's digital repository. Taking the data—including the OCR transcripts that were part of the text correction project—Sherratt devised a tool that allows users to explore the constitution of the front page for every issue of every Australian newspaper in the collection.[20] This data can be quickly plotted on a graph, allowing researchers to see the number of words, articles, and article types over time. One further example is *Viral Texts: Mapping Networks of Reprinting in 19th-Century Newspapers and Magazines* (2013–). Drawing on the data from *Chronicling America*, this project visualizes the reprinting of content between publications, allowing users to see relationships between individual titles, as well as the type of content that was reprinted.

Underpinning all these projects is the recognition that there are things to learn about nineteenth-century serials that cannot be discovered from reading them alone. Like newspapers, periodicals were published in a competitive marketplace over time, and so the surviving archive is shaped by a number of formal patterns that are readily discernible through computational methods. However, such methods—and the maps and graphs they tend to produce—seem to take scholars even further away from printed periodicals. If the digital resources based on nineteenth-century periodicals fail to capture the richness of the printed objects or evacuate their "periodicalness," turning them into a database of articles, then these projects transform them further, combining them in ways that solely depend on patterns in the data which are then visualized in some way. Printed periodicals have an important role to play here, reminding scholars what it is that they are attempting to model and making clear the extent to which this content has been transformed through digitization. In fact, as digital resources increasingly provide students and scholars with access to nineteenth-century periodicals, it becomes even more important that these resources be put into dialogue with printed periodicals in the archive.

It is important that this be an actual dialogue, however. If the archival objects are considered the pure, original source for the resulting digital resource, then the digital resource will always seem deficient. Such an approach, which positions digital resources as surrogates for print, misinterprets the relation of printed material to the past. Rather than originals, these archival objects are better considered as what textual scholars call "witnesses," documenting the processes that produced them, the society in which they circulated, and the archival practices that kept them safe. Periodicals in the archive witness these idiosyncratic and composite histories through their material forms: by transforming their materiality, digitization might imperil some of the ways printed periodicals document these histories, but at the same time, it can open up other ways of witnessing the past. For instance, while it is possible to learn about reprinting by looking for repeated material in printed periodicals, digitized transcripts provide

---

19. Blevins, "Coding a Middle Ground." For close and distant reading newspapers, see Liddle, "Reflections on 20,000," and Nicholson, "Counting Culture."
20. Sherratt, "4 Million Articles Later."

a ready way of visualizing repetition and doing so at scale. As it is new material facets that give digital resources their analytical power, the goal of digitization is modification, not simulation.

Rather than use print material to check the accuracy of digital reproductions we should put these media into dialogue so we can learn what each has to offer for historical, literary, and cultural research. Just as there are things that it is only possible to learn by consulting print periodicals in the archive, so there are also things that can only be learned from interrogating data produced from these archival objects. The reason for this is that the print periodicals are themselves a kind of interface. They may look deceptively complete when encountered as a series of bound volumes on the library shelf, but they are actually the surviving fragments of a complex publishing process. Printed periodicals might record a moment from the past, but this moment can only be reconstructed retrospectively by studying the periodical in the form in which it survives. When scholars talk about a particular publication, this is an abstraction based on the individual examples that they have seen; likewise, when discussing a particular issue, this is usually imagined on the basis of material that survives in a particular bound volume. It is these broader, abstract conceptions of periodicals and periodical culture (the "work" in textual scholarship) that digital resources provide an alternative way of studying. The widespread reliance on page images, usually derived from some identifiable source, as reading texts means that the reading experience will always be based on a specific set of printed objects, but digitization, because it is predicated on transformation, allows for richer models than those afforded by simple reproduction. Digital resources might reduce the complexity of printed material, but scholars also do this when they posit the printed periodicals as simple, unitary originals from which digital resources derive. By taking us further away from printed periodicals, digital resources help us understand what it is that the printed periodicals represent.

2

TECHNOLOGIES OF PRODUCTION

Shannon Rose Smith

In the sixth and final entry in the "Common Heroes" series for the *Pall Mall Magazine*, Harold Begbie presents the journalist as one of his unsung heroes (Figure 2.1).[1] Like the other five entries in the series, which ran from January to June 1901, Begbie's account of the journalist included a full-page, wood-engraved illustration and, on the facing page, a twenty-line poem celebrating his day-to-day efforts.[2] Begbie presents the journalist as a late-night figure of industry who works to meet the demand for copy from both the newspaper industry and its customers. Begbie contrasts the indefatigable industry of the journalist with the idleness of the implied reader of the poem. While the former is "scratching, scratching, scratching with a furious-driven nib," the latter is "wrapt in easy slumber in [his] comfortable crib."[3] In celebrating the journalist's capacity for work, the poem also provides a succinct and detailed study of the of the print-culture industry at the close of the nineteenth century and perhaps most importantly, the technologies of production that defined it. The poem shows how the journalist locates material for stories, how stories are turned into copy and thus rendered suitable for printing, and how stories are printed, distributed, and sold to the customer. It also highlights the network of machines integral to the job of producing a newspaper or periodical in 1901: the telegraph, the Linotype, the rotary press, and the railway.

While the image of the journalist caught in a mad flurry of productivity is striking, it is the poem's references to the technologies of production in the print culture industry that twenty-first-century readers are likely to find most absorbing. The poem provides many telling details about the journalist's information-gathering process, including the "clicking of the cables from the ocean's quiet bed," a reference to the transatlantic cable, first laid in 1858, and to the development of news agencies such as Reuters that worked under contract to both newspapers and commercial interests as consolidators and relayers of news from around the globe via telegram.[4] Begbie's anonymous journalist is also represented as preparing material for two formidable machines: the Linotype, with its "loud, harsh, clanging thunder" and "roar" for copy,

---

1. For details of Begbie's biography and literary output, see Maume's introduction to the 2006 edition of Begbie's *The Lady Next Door* (1912).
2. For the other works in the series, see Begbie, "Common Heroes."
3. Begbie, "Journalist," 245.
4. For introductory discussions of the role of the telegraph and news agencies such as Reuters in defining the media space of empire, see Blondheim, *News over the Wires*; Rantanen, "Globalization of Electronic News"; Read, *Power of*

"He is scratching, scratching, scratching with a furious-driven nib."

Figure 2.1 "He is scratching, scratching, scratching with a furious-driven nib," *Pall Mall Magazine* 24 (June 1901): 244.

and the "mighty press," which is represented as stirring like a slowly awakening beast, only to "flap and bang" its "flyers" as the journalist rushes to write his column.[5] Following its distribution through outlets such as the "stall of Mr. Smith" at the railway station, the newspaper containing the journalist's work ends up discarded on the very means of transportation used

---

the *News*; and Winston, *Media, Technology*. For discussion of nineteenth-century conceptualizations of networks, see Otis, *Networking*, and for discussion of nineteenth-century responses to electricity, see Marvin, *Old Technologies*.

5. Begbie, "Journalist," 245.

to move the final product from the printing house to the customer—the train.[6] Begbie's poem illustrates the way in which the journalist occupies the center of a demanding intersection of production technologies, and it reminds readers of the way in which that web of machines was also a part of imperial networks of power. If Begbie's journalist is the point at which the machines and methods of the industry converge, he is also the nexus at which the larger colonial project comes into play. In response to the "flap and bang" of the "mighty press," Begbie's journalist churns out a "Bimetallic column," or, to expand the technological metaphor, a device that will take the temperature of the nation and the empire.[7] While Begbie's celebration of the journalist's work is meant to remind contemporary readers of the mental and physical labor that goes into newspaper production, twenty-first-century readers are more likely to read the poem as a demonstration of the cultural currency of print technology at the end of the Victorian period.

When embarking on a study of different nineteenth-century print culture forms, it is vital to acknowledge that the material conditions for the production of newspapers and periodicals are not the same as those that produced the period's remarkable output of books.[8] As Begbie's poem reminds us, the industrial and technological networks that made up the newspaper industry were different than those associated with other forms of publishing. Having a working knowledge of the different points of intersection in those networks is key to being able to articulate their meaning and influence.

In this chapter, I provide brief case studies of two key pieces of technology that feature in Begbie's poem: the printing press and the Linotype. Through an account of these machines, this chapter will relate changes during this period to two key stages of the printing process: origination and multiplication. While it is necessary to situate each of these components in its respective developmental context, my case studies serve to question the linearity inherent in the notion of technological "progress." As new media scholar Lisa Gitelman notes, when talking about changes in technology such as those which occurred in the nineteenth-century print culture industry, it is assumed that each change inevitably leads to improvement. This tendency to view changes in technology as progress "along an inevitable path, a History, toward a specific and not-so-distant end" is just what I seek to disrupt in this chapter.[9] In the process, I hope to illuminate the cultural constructions that are involved in coming to terms with new media forms and machines, what Alan Liu terms a "new media encounter."[10] I shall not therefore replicate here those general

---

6. Ibid. For discussions of the broader impact of the railway on nineteenth-century life, see Freeman, *Railways*, and Schivelbusch, *Railway Journey*.
7. Lines 12–14 of Begbie's poem include references to key imperial political events, debates, and individuals connected with the Siege of Peking and China's Boxer Rebellion in 1900.
8. As Twyman notes in *Printing*, distinctions should be drawn between the technologies in use for book printing, jobbing, and non-book printing, such as the production of newspapers and periodicals. Twyman argues that whereas book printers worked within a range of industry practices that sometimes remained unchanged for hundreds of years, jobbers and periodical printers had to contend with "new problems to solve, new processes and materials to use, new clients to serve, [and] new kinds of information to translate into print" (2). See also McKitterick, *Cambridge History*, and Price, *How to Do Things*.
9. Gitelman, *Always Already New*, 3.
10. Liu, "Imagining," 1.

histories of nineteenth-century media technologies that are so readily available elsewhere but rather use these case studies to reflect on, and generate further thinking about, those histories.[11]

As new media historians such as Gitelman and Liu, along with media archeologists such as Friedrich Kittler and Jussi Parikka, have noted, the arrival of new media technologies, such as a faster printing press, a cable under the ocean that relays messages, or a machine that does away with the need to cast and set type in two separate processes, is not intrinsically a moment of revolution or progress. It is only understood as such after society is forced to account for the technological change and thus constructs meanings from multiple, conflicting responses. At any given time, a cluster of available narratives can be put to use when responding to a new media form, and as society gradually becomes accustomed to it, the media form gains a kind of invisibility that elides the constructed nature of the meanings attributed to it. As Gitelman explains, that kind of erasure is necessary for a media form to endure.[12]

In offering discussions of the rotary printing press and the Linotype, this chapter aims to address the needs of readers who seek an introduction to the field of nineteenth-century print culture studies by providing a timeline surveying the introduction of different technologies and their attendant effects on print output (see Table 2.1). However, at the same time it disrupts that timeline by offering brief, focused considerations of the shifting socio-cultural narrative terrain around these new media forms, as evidenced in their representation in the very publications they helped to produce. Readers can further contextualize these case studies by locating them in the list of changes in nineteenth-century technology on pages 33 and 34. Each case study will focus in on one iteration of the media form at a key moment: the display of Applegarth's vertical rotary press at the Great Exhibition of 1851 in cooperation with *The Times* and the *Illustrated London News* (Figures 2.2 and 2.3) and the Linotype's exhibition at L'Exposition Universelle de Paris in 1900 as part of a display produced by the *Graphic* and the Linotype Company (Figure 2.4). As part of my strategy to cultivate a critical awareness of the problems inherent in superimposing a timeline of technological progress on changes in nineteenth-century print culture, I will purposefully discuss these items out of their expected order in the linear process of converting "raw material" (news received via telegram) to a final commercial product (a copy of *The Times*).

Case Study: Applegarth's Vertical Rotary Press

In the paragraph introducing Section II, Class 6 of the 1851 Great Exhibition's *Official Descriptive and Illustrated Catalogue*, visitors are promised a vision of all manner of machines demonstrating the application of steam power to manufacture. The language of the introductory paragraph

---

11. For an early account of the complete process of periodical production, see the four-part series "Commercial History of a Penny Magazine" in the 1833 *Penny Magazine*. For a period catalogue of the myriad changes that occurred in print technology in the nineteenth century, see John Southward's *Progress in Printing*. A.E. Musson's "Newspaper Printing" provides a case study of changes implemented at the *Manchester Guardian*, thus shifting the focus to print culture outside of London. Lastly, Michael Twyman's *Printing* provides a detailed account of changes which occurred before, during, and after the nineteenth century.
12. Gitelman, *Always Already New*, 5–6. In her introduction, Gitelman argues that "technology and all of its supporting protocols ... have become self-evident as the result of social processes.... The success of all media depends at some level on inattention or 'blindness' to the media technologies themselves (and all of their supporting protocols) in favour of attention to the phenomena, 'the content,' that they represent for users' edification or enjoyment" (5–6).

Table 2.1 Selective timeline of technology

1794	In France, Firmin Didot names and develops the stereotype, a process derived from the experiments of William Ged of Edinburgh in 1727.
1798	Lithography is invented.
1799	In France, Nicholas Louis Robert is granted a patent for a machine that makes continuous paper (rather than sheets).
1800	First Stanhope press (made of cast iron).
1801	John Gamble, brother-in-law of Nicholas Louis Robert's business partner, takes out a British patent for a continuous paper-making machine.
1803	Continuous paper-making machinery is introduced at Frogmore, Hertfordshire.
1804	The Earl of Stanhope devises stereotyping using plaster.
1806	The first illustration in *The Times*.
1810	Patent and trials of the Koenig steam press on the *New Annual Register*.
1813	The first sea-going steamboat is launched: Richard Wright's *Experiment*.
1814	The Koenig steam press is used to print *The Times*, November 29, 1814.
1822	William Church patents a typesetting machine. Nicéphore Niepce develops the heliograph (the earliest form of photography).
1825	The opening of the Stockton and Darlington railway.
1828	The Applegath & Cowper cylinder press is introduced by *The Times*.
1830	The Liverpool and Manchester railway is opened; it is the first railway to be fully timetabled.
1837	William Fothergill Cooke and Charles Wheatstone patent what will be the first commercial electrical telegraph system.
1839	Invention of the daguerreotype. First screw-propeller steamship, the *SS Archimedes*.
1840	James Young and Adrian Delcambre invent the Pianotyp typesetting machine. Electrotyping is used for first time in UK printing—the April number of the *London Journal of Arts and Sciences*.
1841	Fox Talbot patents the calotype. The Young-Delcambre machine, operated by women, is used to compose the short-lived monthly *London Phalanx*.
1843	Richard March Hoe invents the rotary drum printing press.
1844	First use of the telegraph to report news (the birth of Prince Alfred to Queen Victoria) in *The Times*.
1845	In Saxony, Friedrich Gottlob Keller and paper manufacturer Heinrich Voelter patent a machine for making paper out of wood pulp.
1848	*The Times* employs Applegath's vertical rotary press; it is exhibited at the Great Exhibition in 1851.
1851	London and Paris are connected by telegraph via submarine cable. Reuter begins to send financial information by telegraph between London and the Continent.
1852	Fox Talbot patents "photographic engraving."
1853	Miller & Richard introduce US Bruce typefounding machine (invented in 1838) to Britain.
1856	The Hoe press is deployed by *Lloyd's Newspaper*. India and Europe are connected by telegraph.
1857	Hoe presses and stereotyping are used by *The Times*. Robert Hattersley patents a typesetting machine.
1858	Fox Talbot patents "photoglyphic engraving." The transatlantic telegraph cable is installed. Reuters starts supplying reports for London newspapers.
1863	William Bullock improves Hoe's rotary press.
1866	Hattersley composing machines (based on the Young-Delcambre model) are used by the *Eastern Morning News* (Hull).
1868	Walter rotary presses are used at *The Times* (employing continuous rolls of paper).
1869	The Kastenbein typesetting machine is patented (installed at *The Times* in 1872).
1873	Remington widely markets typewriters.
1875	Robert Barclay patents the rotary offset lithographic printing press.

(*Continued*)

Table 2.1 (Continued)

1876	In the United States, Alexander Graham Bell patents the telephone.
1878	Karel Klíč refines Fox Talbot's photogravure process. The Telephone Company, Ltd. (Bell's patents) set up in London.
1880	In the United States, Joseph Thorne patents a typesetting machine.
1882	In England, Miesenbach patents a halftone process a year after Frederic Ives uses a different halftone method in Philadelphia.
1885	In the United States, Tolbert Lanston invents Monotype.
1886	In the United States, German-born Ottmar Mergenthaler invents Linotype, which is first used by the *New York Tribune*.
1887	The Thorne typesetting machine is used by the *Manchester Guardian*.
1889	Linotype is installed at the *Newcastle Chronicle*.
1891	London and Paris connected by telephone line.
1899	Marconi sends wireless signals across the English Channel and from shore to ship.
1900	Linotype is exhibited at the Paris Exposition Universelle by the *Graphic* and the *New York Times*.

asserts that this extraordinary power can be harnessed to perform extraordinary feats, not only fulfilling "functions which were accomplished formerly only by direct human labour" but also executing these tasks with a "perfection [and] certainty" that exceeds "that attainable in most instances by the highest exercise of human skill."[13] This emphasis on exceeding human capacity is once again present in the *Catalogue*'s discussion of entry 122, a display of a "printing machine, on the vertical principle, as used at the 'Times' office."[14] While the entry is focused on describing how the machine works, it also is careful to note that this new kind of press can ensure "good work" in the "best manner" at a volume previously unseen in the newspaper industry.[15]

The vertical rotary press exhibited at the Crystal Palace in 1851 was the latest incarnation in a series of changes in the printing process implemented by Edward Cowper and Augustus Applegarth, two engineers in the employ of *The Times* tasked with finding ways to print more copies at a higher speed in order to satisfy reader demand.[16] There had already been changes in the technologies of production at the newspaper prior to the introduction of Applegarth's press, a slightly modified version of which could print 12,000 impressions an hour.[17] In 1814, *Times* proprietor John Walter II installed a Koenig cylinder press that used a series of rollers to ink and press the forme—the part of the press bed containing the justified lines of hand-set type. However, like Applegarth's later alternatives to the cylinder press, the machine still had to be fed individual sheets by hand. Applegarth's press, which changed the forme and press bed from a horizontal surface to a vertical, octagonal, rotating bed, was first employed at *The Times*

---

13. *Official Descriptive and Illustrated Catalogue*, 1:257.
14. Ibid., 1:275.
15. Ibid.
16. The *Official Descriptive and Illustrated Catalogue* entry for the vertical rotary press lists Applegarth as the sole patent holder for the press. See the close of entry 122 on page 276.
17. Twyman, *Printing*, 53.

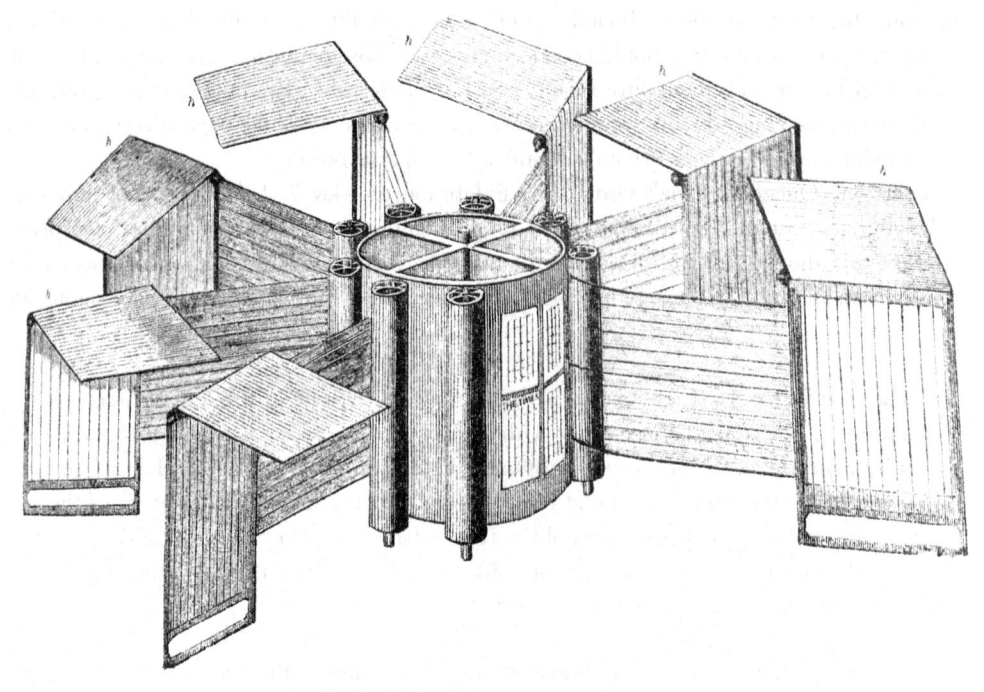

Applegath's Patent Printing Machine.

Figure 2.2 "Applegarth's Patent Printing Machine," *Official Descriptive and Illustrated Catalogue of the Great Exhibition. By the Authority of the Royal Commission*, 3 vols. (London: Spicer Brothers, 1851), 1:275.

in 1848 and shortly thereafter at the *Illustrated London News*.[18] Applegarth's press remained in use until it was replaced by the Hoe horizontal rotary press in 1857, versions of which were employed in both national and provincial papers throughout the 1860s. By the end of the century, reel-fed machines no longer required operators to feed individual sheets by hand. The Walter press, named after *Times* proprietor John Walter III, had been installed in many large-circulation London newspapers, including the *Daily Telegraph*, the *Standard*, and the *Daily News*, as well as in British provincial papers.[19]

Because the Applegarth press was a result of changes driven by *The Times*, rather than by a patent holder seeking to market an independent, commercially successful venture, it had little public exposure prior to its display at the Great Exhibition. The process of negotiation which is intrinsically a part of a new media encounter may exist even if it is absent from the press. There were complex, competing, and conflicting responses to the machine, but this cluster of narratives did not appear in newspapers and periodicals until 1851. In their coverage of the Applegarth press at the Great Exhibition, *The Times* and the *Illustrated London News* focus on exploring and articulating the relationship between man and machine. At the same time that the press is represented as a

18. Ibid.
19. Ibid., 55.

Case Study: The Linotype

In the July 17, 1889 edition of the London *Daily News*, an advertisement was published with a headline proclaiming "Printing Revolutionised." It depicts and describes a machine that it claims is capable of simultaneously executing the operations of setting, spacing, justifying, and distributing that make up the bulk of the compositing process.[25] The advertisement attests to no less than £400,000 invested in its development and a promise of £16,000 savings per year for any newspaper that acquires the machine.[26] The Linotype, a hot-metal casting and compositing machine, was created by a German-American inventor, Ottmar Mergenthaler, and was first used in the offices of the *New York Tribune* in 1886. It offered an alternative way of executing the different operations that made up the origination portion of the printing process.[27] Proving once again that, as Jussi Parikka reminds us, new media always contain traces of old media,[28] the Linotype incorporated some of the principles of operation exhibited by the Pianotyp, a machine that arranged pre-cast type into lines using a keyboard mechanism designed and first manufactured by Young and Delcambre of Lille in 1840. Like the Pianotyp and Tolbert Lanson's Monotype, both of which were primarily used in book production,[29] the Linotype provided a solution to the problem of how to move individual pieces of type faster than the fastest compositor's hand. However, unlike the Pianotyp, the Linotype did not work with pre-cast type; rather, it combined the casting of type with its distribution and justification. This combined process of casting and setting, initiated by an operator sitting at a specially designed keyboard which arranged letters in order of frequency of use, became known as hot-metal casting.[30]

The Linotype was first adopted in Britain in 1889 by the *Newcastle Chronicle* and a year later by the *Leeds Mercury*. It rapidly became ubiquitous, with over 250 in operation in provincial newspapers alone by 1894.[31] In the decade between 1890 and 1900, the machine occupied various places in both the journalistic and popular imagination of British readers and writers, and a cluster of narratives concerning its use, value, potential, and place in the newspaper industry can be traced

---

25. From the fifteenth century to the mid-nineteenth century, the work of compositors remained more or less unchanged. They placed individual pieces of type upside down and from right to left on a small tray called a compositing stick. These lines of type were then placed in frames and justified. See Score, "Pioneers," 274, and Twyman, *Printing*, 22–3.
26. Advertisement for "The 'Linotype' Composing Machine."
27. Twyman, *Printing*, 62.
28. Parikka, *What Is Media Archaeology?*, 3.
29. Like the Linotype, the Monotype was designed to automate the origination portion of the printing process. First sold in Britain in 1897, it comprised two parts. The first was a keyboard which produced a perforated tape in a pattern representative of the line of characters typed by the operator. This tape was fed into a second component, the caster, which produced the individual pieces of type. Twyman, *Printing*, 75. For a period discussion of the operation of the machine, see "Monotype."
30. Because the Linotype had no backspace key, if an operator made an error in transcribing copy, the common convention was to drag a finger down the first two vertical rows of keys, producing the sequence of letters "etaoin shrdlu." After the line was cast, the operator would throw it back into the pot of molten lead, in effect erasing the error. Not all errors were removed in this way, however, and beginning in the 1890s the appearance of the phrase "etaoin shrdlu" in a range of newspapers throughout Britain is evident. See *Linotype: The Film*.
31. Twyman, *Printing*, 62.

through a diverse range of publications. To locate a representative sample of those narratives in the popular press is to observe the process by which this new piece of printing technology was gradually normalized. Alternatively presented as an investment risk, a labor- and cost-saving device, and a threat to hand compositors' livelihoods, the Linotype engendered a mixed set of responses.

A full-page illustrated advertisement in the *Daily News* promised a machine that would increase the "speed or rate of composing . . . at least sixfold" and reported that American compositors were "earning an average of 17 percent more wages."[32] Yet this claim of combined speed and prosperity was challenged by other perspectives.[33] Just as it was viewed as a labor-saving device that would reduce the cost of getting a newspaper out, the Linotype was also represented as a threat to workers.[34] As Melissa Score discusses in relation to the Linotype's cousin, the Pianotyp, attempts to automate the trade were met with resistance in print and in practice.[35]

If the Linotype was imagined as both a blessing and a curse to the printing trade, it was also represented as an unsure opportunity for business investment. In 1895, the *Saturday Review*'s "Money Matters" column scrutinized the Linotype Company's practices of advertising and promotion. Noting that the company had among its founding members two financial adventurers of some renown, John Charles Cottam and Ernest Orger Lambert, the piece was quick to proclaim it "one of the most flagrant promotions of the notorious" pair.[36] It challenged the incongruity between advertisements trumpeting the machine's technological capabilities and projections for its impact on the printing trade. These adverts had appeared in "financial contemporaries" rather than trade journals, an advertising strategy that seemed like a scam that relied on dodgy dealings in shares. The *Saturday Review* was quick to draw parallels between the complexity of the machine's inner workings and the company's financial arrangements. Suspicious of the company's claims of industry impact and its association with figures such as Cottam and Lambert, the *Saturday Review* concludes, "We are sure that it does not appeal to experienced printers to the extent represented by the Company [and] we are not at all sanguine regarding the future of the 'Linotype' machine. . . . We do not see any future before it."[37]

This small selection of representations hints at the range of responses the Linotype provoked in Britain in the 1890s; however, by the time the machine was exhibited in Paris at the Exposition Universelle in 1900, public opinion had, to a certain degree, softened. In its coverage of the exposition, the *Graphic* drew attention to the complexity of operating the Linotype but interpreted

32. Advertisement for the "Linotype" Composing Machine.
33. Ibid.
34. Barry, "Labour Day," 309.
35. Score, "Pioneers," 282–3. Score discusses how the introduction of the Pianotyp into British compositing rooms met with resistance due to the feminine overtones given to the machine through a campaign of representation which by and large depicted it as being operable by young, genteel women in middle-class drawing rooms. As the *Compositor's Chronicle* declares on March 1, 1845, "The art of composing type [is now] so simple and elegant, that ladies may sit down, as to a piano-forte, and set up in type their own sweet effusions, with as much ease as they can commit them in writing." Quoted in Score, "Pioneers," 282.
36. "Money Matters—The 'Linotype,'" 686. An 1889 article in *The Times* titled "Police" reveals a catalogue of Cottam's previous financial misadventures. In an 1898 article titled "$5,000,000 Failure," the *New York Times* reported the spectacular bankruptcy of Cottam's occasional business partner, Ernest Orger Lambert.
37. "Money Matters," 687.

3

DISTRIBUTION

Graham Law

At the beginning of the nineteenth century, most British periodicals were luxury goods affordable only by the wealthy few. From daily journals and newspapers to quarterly reviews, there were hardly more than two hundred distinct titles in print nationwide, the majority local weekly newspapers, and, except for a few subsidized sectarian magazines, even the highest subscriptions fell short of 10,000.[1] A century later, periodicals had been largely transformed into cheap commodities available to the mass of the domestic population, with an expanding market overseas for the monthlies in particular. Divided equally between newspapers and magazines, there were then nearly 5,000 separate titles,[2] with the highest circulations around a million.[3] However, the rate of expansion had been far from uniform, with more than one stutter in growth during the opening quarter of the century and an acceleration much more rapid in the second half. Indeed, at mid-century, with the United Kingdom population already reaching twenty-seven million, there were still only around 560 newspaper titles available,[4] less than a quarter of the total in the United States with its twenty-three million people.[5] With access still difficult for many communities in Wales, Scotland, and Ireland, aggregate sales of daily papers then amounted to little more than 60,000 copies, representing only one for roughly four hundred persons.[6] It was thus fitting that at this juncture there was an extensive inquiry into how British periodicals were distributed. The investigation in question, central to this chapter, was orchestrated by the House of Commons Select Committee on Newspaper Stamps, whose sessions coincided with the Great Exhibition from the spring of 1851.

For the purposes of this chapter, "distribution" should be understood in two ways: in a narrower commercial and a wider socio-political sense. Both represent technical usages deriving from political economy, a field of social inquiry flourishing with the progress of industrialization. The narrower sense designates the means by which the products of industry, whether goods or services, are dispersed among consumers. Here, it covers not only the sale of serial

---

1. Altick, *English Common Reader*, 392.
2. Mitchell, *Newspaper Press Directory*, 1901.
3. Altick, *English Common Reader*, 395–6.
4. Mitchell, *Newspaper Press Directory*, 1851.
5. Coggeshall, *Newspaper Record*, 122.
6. "Report from the Select Committee on Newspaper Stamps," 420.

publications, whether directly through the postal service or indirectly via wholesale and retail agents, but also temporary access in public houses, coffee shops, reference libraries, reading clubs, and the like, as well as the various modes of transportation employed in the process. The second, wider meaning generally refers to how equally or unequally the products of industry, whether commodities, services, or other manifestations of wealth, are shared among the different groups into which society as a whole can be classified. In the context of modern print media, this encompasses the social availability of current intelligence, a term understood broadly to include ideas and opinions as well as factual information. Clearly the distribution patterns regarding periodicals and intelligence changed radically though unevenly over the course of the nineteenth century. As represented schematically in the distribution timeline at the end of this chapter (Table 3.1), the process of development was driven by fiscal and legal reforms reflecting public policy, as well as by technological and/or economic innovations typically initiated in the private sector. Dealing with each of these two aspects in turn, this chapter charts the main currents of change.

Fiscal and Legal Reform

First exacted in 1712, the stamp duty on newspapers was only one of a group of imposts limiting the distribution of information via British periodicals. Imposed by the same act of Parliament intended "to raise large supplies of money" to carry on the War of the Spanish Succession,[7] the other main taxes in question were further stamp duties on printed pamphlets, almanacs, and advertisements, plus an excise duty on paper itself. Considered purely from a fiscal point of view, however, this combination appears counter-productive: penalizing the publication of commercial and political intelligence discourages the use of the very material necessary for growth in returns from the excise on paper, consistently the weightiest in terms of revenue generated. The details of the legislation indeed suggest an ulterior motive that was political rather than financial: back in 1695 the government had abandoned a regime of direct censorship of the press and now wished to explore more discrete and pervasive methods of control.[8] Though the excise duty rose according to the quality of the paper and thus progressively affected all print media,[9] the various stamp duties were set at a flat rate, so that they targeted not merely periodical and occasional publications in general but those cheaper and more ephemeral formats designed to address a broader social readership. Thus, from the beginning the duties also served the purpose of restricting the formation and communication of critical opinion.

Inevitably, the duties in question did not remain static over time. There were frequent changes of detail regarding penalties, exemptions, schedules, and other factors, many having long-term material or ideological effects. For example, after 1743, the selling of unstamped newspapers

---

7. *Statutes at Large*, 327.
8. See Downie, *Robert Harley*, 149–61, and Deazley, *Origin*, 1–29.
9. "For the encouragement of learning," exemptions were granted for "books in the Latin, Greek, Oriental, or Northern Languages." *Statutes at Large*, 355 (§63).

became a criminal offence;[10] in 1765, there was a notorious attempt to impose a similar regime of stamp duties in the American colonies;[11] and from 1794, the paper duty lost its progressive element and was based merely on weight.[12] Already by the last decade of the eighteenth century, each of the taxes had at least doubled, but it was the extended period of Tory rule from the turn of the century that saw not only the imposition of the "Corn Laws," which protected landed interests at the expense of price hikes in staple foods, but also the most punitive changes to the "taxes on knowledge," as they became known among the swelling ranks of their enemies.[13] These opponents increasingly included not only radicals demanding universal education and suffrage without compromise but also liberals committed to free trade, though with paternalistic views of popular improvement and limited visions of parliamentary reform.

In the first place, in the new century the duties on paper, advertisements, and newspapers were raised to vertiginous peaks. For about two decades from 1815, with the newspaper stamp at 4d. and the duty on a single advertisement at 3s. 6d., regardless of size, taxes accounted for about two-thirds of the cover price of established dailies like *The Times*, which in 1828 alone contributed duties totaling nearly £70,000.[14] At the same time, it was impossible to print news at a price affordable by the common people without breaking the law. And, in the second place, there were more laws to be broken. In particular, with the Corresponding Societies still spreading democratic views, a 1798 bill imposed rigid rules concerning the registration and deposit of newspapers,[15] while, following the radical disturbances of 1819, new laws repressing "blasphemous and seditious libels" extended the definition of a newspaper to cover cheap journals of political opinion, at the same time saddling all publishers with a draconian system of bonds and securities.[16] Among the low-priced publications which provoked the latter legislation was William Cobbett's *Political Register* (1802–36), which had been converted into an inexpensive weekly pamphlet with no news but radical views in plenty. By around 1830, the battle against the taxes on knowledge had risen to the top of the radical agenda, with scores of journals now prepared openly to defy the authorities, despite vendors facing imprisonment and publishers facing confiscation of their property. At the vanguard of this "War of the Unstamped" was Henry Hetherington's *Poor Man's Guardian* (1831–35), which franked the words "Knowledge is Power" on its cover in lieu of the revenue stamp required by law. On this occasion, with a mildly reformist government in a Parliament recently reconstituted to reflect the advancing power of capitalism, the conclusion was not crackdown but compromise. By 1836, the duties on pamphlets and almanacs were eliminated, and those on paper, advertisements, and newspapers had been reduced substantially.[17] At the same time, non-fiscal constraints like registration and security requirements remained in place, and the definition of a newspaper had been expanded to

---

10. Deazley, "Commentary."
11. *Statutes at Large*, 179.
12. Dagnall, "Taxes on Knowledge," 354–8.
13. For the fullest first-hand account, see Collet, *History of the Taxes*.
14. Untitled report in *The Times*, 2.
15. House of Commons, "Bill for the More Effectual Suppression."
16. House of Commons, "Bill to Make Certain Publications," 1.
17. For the details, see Law, *Serializing Fiction*, 10.

include sheets devoted to advertisements. Though the reductions impacted the metropolitan more than the provincial press,[18] this new regime of taxes on print media clearly served to significantly reduce the cost and stimulate the growth of both general miscellanies and weekly organs of news. Nevertheless, it still prevented the publication of cheap daily papers and indeed helped to reinforce the quasi-monopoly enjoyed by *The Times*, which, well before the changes, annually accounted for over 10 percent of the newspaper stamps purchased in the entire kingdom. In brief, this was the regime the 1851 Select Committee had to investigate.

Given that the committee's brief also covered the regulations governing postal transmission, its inquiry inevitably gave thorough consideration to both the broader social and the narrower commercial aspects of periodical distribution. Happily, the report submitted on July 18, 1851, was extraordinarily detailed. It contained within its seven hundred pages not only recommendations to the house but also the full proceedings of the committee, including minority proposals by Whig MP Henry Rich;[19] the verbatim minutes of evidence from each of the twenty-three witnesses;[20] and a thick appendix of documents examined, such as lists of prosecutions under the stamp acts.[21] The report provides a fascinating record of the differences of opinion and interpretation which emerged, along with the conflicting interests often underlying them, as well as of the strength of the consensus eventually reached.[22] Given not only the weight of the testimony heard but also the composition of the committee itself—the chairman was the radical MP Thomas Milner Gibson, the president of the Association for the Repeal of the Taxes on Knowledge, who had originally proposed the Commons inquiry—the inevitable conclusion was that news was not a "desirable subject of taxation."[23] In the summary of the supporting evidence listing a lengthy series of problems, the committee drew attention

> to the objections and abuses incident to the present system of newspaper stamps, arising from the difficulty of defining and determining the meaning of the term "news"; to the inequalities which exist in the application of the Newspaper Stamp Act, and the anomalies and evasions that it occasions in postal arrangements; to the unfair competition to which stamped newspapers are exposed with unstamped publications; to the limitation imposed by the Stamp upon the circulation of the best newspapers, and to the impediments which it throws in the way of the diffusion of useful knowledge regarding current and recent events among the poorer classes.[24]

It is instructive to look at each point in more detail.

On questioning, Inland Revenue officers confirmed that the insertion of news under any circumstances, or the inclusion of either advertisements or opinion under certain conditions,

---

18. See House of Commons, "Return of the Titles."
19. "Report from the Select Committee on Newspaper Stamps," xxiv–xxxii.
20. Ibid., 1–480.
21. Ibid., 481–573.
22. For an excellent contemporary critique of the report, see "Report," *British Quarterly Review*.
23. "Report from the Select Committee on Newspaper Stamps," xii.
24. Ibid., xl.

rendered a publication subject to the newspaper stamp. Given such a strict interpretation, the committee judged that "nearly all periodical printed matter, and a large portion of occasional printed matter" would be liable to the duty.[25] Since this was manifestly not the case, they concluded that the officers in fact exercised the arbitrary power of deciding which periodicals to take action against, a state of affairs which in his testimony Collet Dobson Collet, secretary to the Association for the Repeal of the Taxes on Knowledge, condemned as a "disguised censorship of the press."[26] The bureaucrats were shown as a rule to overlook "private" news (typically society gossip) and "class" news (concerning the activities of specific professional and trade groups), while "with respect to comments on news in cheap publications, the law [had] been allowed to some extent to sleep."[27] At the same time, it was not difficult to cite exceptions involving either the suppression of journals or the prosecution of proprietors, especially in the case of publications conducted on a small scale and/or critical of government policy, like the monthly *Norwich and Norfolk Independent, and Police Reporter* (1841) or the *Stroud Free Press* (1848–56). Indeed, a few months after the Select Committee filed its report, the Inland Revenue received another public rebuke. This was in the form of a judgment in the Court of Exchequer in a test case against Dickens's publishers for issuing unstamped a monthly news summary entitled *Household Narrative*, to the effect that accounts of events published at intervals of more than twenty-six days were to be considered as history, not intelligence.[28] In addition, a number of witnesses drew attention to injustices arising from the way the duty was applied. The fact that there were no stamp offices outside London, Manchester, and Edinburgh, meant that publishers elsewhere faced increased costs in the transportation of the pre-stamped sheets. Because there was no alternative to using such sheets, they could not employ rotary presses requiring paper in roll form, and because no refunds were allowed on sheets spoiled in the course of production, they were subject to arbitrary tax increases.

Even greater anomalies existed in the way the duty was treated as a transmission charge, as representatives of the Post Office admitted. One argument made in 1836 for retaining the newspaper stamp was that it guaranteed universal delivery at low cost through the mails. But for unknown reasons, such a privilege, first granted in 1792, was denied both to stamped publications posted in central London and to those directed to British territories overseas. As Henry Cole, organizer of the Great Exhibition, put it, "We give the Americans all the benefit of our intelligence in print, and we cut our colonies off from having it."[29] Publishers in fact made limited use of the postal service; metropolitan papers were increasingly sent to the provinces in bulk by wholesalers, while country journals were delivered mainly by local carriers. At the same time, due to the difficulty of checking whether the 150,000 papers mailed every day were in fact stamped, illicit use of the service was widespread. And, since there was no system of cancellation, it was understood that stamped papers were free to travel by post on multiple

---

25. Ibid., vii.
26. Ibid., 113.
27. Ibid., vi.
28. See "Report," *British Quarterly Review*, 136–8.
29. "Report from the Select Committee on Newspaper Stamps," 405.

occasions. Moreover, since a 1789 statute prohibiting newspaper rental was not enforced,[30] re-transmission facilitated shared access to journals in both rural and urban areas.[31] In the country, this included informal newspaper societies, in which groups of scattered acquaintances could divide the cost of purchase, with those gaining earlier access paying more. In the towns and cities, there was a variety of lending organizations, whether mechanics institutes, cooperative reading rooms, and commercial lending libraries, or taverns, restaurants, and coffee houses, which could all recover some of their costs by selling on used papers via the post. The wholesale newsagent W.H. Smith thus testified that stamped journals were being re-transmitted through the post "to a most enormous extent."[32] More amusingly, the committee learned that the mails were often used for the disposal of waste-paper since there was nothing to stop a bundle of old newspapers "as large as a diving-bell" from being transmitted in perpetuity by the Post Office.[33] Yet the most contentious postal issue was that of partially stamped journals. By a treasury minute of 1838, the publishers of periodicals not classed as newspapers were granted the privilege of registering their titles with the Inland Revenue and printing on stamped paper only those copies to be transmitted via the mail. Since the lengthy list of journals taking advantage of this loophole included middle-class weeklies like *Punch* and the *Athenaeum*,[34] which might strictly have been made to publish entirely on stamped paper, there was considerable resentment from the publishers of weekly newspapers aimed at a popular readership.

The committee's conclusions concerning the impact of the stamp on the "circulation of the best newspapers" referred to established journals like *The Times* or the *Scotsman*. Representatives of both appeared before the committee, expressing strong views in favor of retaining the existing duties. Mowbray Morris, manager of *The Times*, though clear that his own paper would not be damaged by the abolition of the stamp, suggested that, without it, "you would have different kinds of papers published, papers advocating perhaps opinions not quite so advantageous to society."[35] It was a common criticism that papers loud in condemning the Corn Laws as against the freedom of trade were silent concerning the fiscal constraints on the press. Indeed, other witnesses were convinced that *The Times* did have a vested interest in preserving the existing regime. In particular, the editor of the *New York Tribune*, Horace Greeley, the only witness from the United States, where British-style press taxation was precluded by the First Amendment, argued convincingly that the "limited circulation of papers generally is caused by the stamp"[36] and that the quasi-monopoly enjoyed by *The Times* was due to the flat rate of advertising duty. The chairman, however, found it politic to maintain that the "taxes on knowledge" were of benefit to no one, serving to restrict the profitability of the elite organs as well as prevent the publishing of papers for the common people.

30. Aspinall, "Circulation of Newspapers," 42.
31. See Altick, *English Common Reader*, 322–3.
32. "Report from the Select Committee on Newspaper Stamps," 422.
33. Ibid., 263.
34. See House of Commons, "Return of the Titles."
35. "Report from the Select Committee on Newspaper Stamps," 323.
36. Ibid., 439.

At the other extreme, the report categorized "bad publications" into the immoral, low, obscene, and pernicious,[37] covering such genres as scandal sheets, "penny bloods" (melodramatic fiction in weekly numbers), semi-pornographic papers, and revolutionary journals. The expert witnesses in popular literature, notably the Manchester newsagent Abel Heywood, who had suffered imprisonment for distributing the *Poor Man's Guardian*, agreed that things had improved distinctly since the 1830s. He argued that if the stamp duty were removed, allowing news to appear alongside literary matter in the cheap journals, "it would increase the circulation of many of the better class, and decrease the circulation of the worse."[38] Members of bodies actively concerned with social improvement, like the temperance societies and the mechanics institutes, emphasized the "impediments which it [the stamp] throws in the way of the diffusion of useful knowledge regarding current and recent events among the poorer classes,"[39] thus articulating the final and most weighty reason for proposing a change of regime.

Despite the doubts cast on the impartiality of the Inland Revenue, it was not until June 1855 that Parliament finally took action to abolish the penny stamp as an obligatory duty on newspapers, instead making it an optional general charge for the "transmission by post of printed periodical publications."[40] The effect was dramatic and not just on existing journals like the *Manchester Guardian*, which, like other provincial papers, in anticipation of increased sales, immediately reduced its price by far more than the value of the duty and shifted to daily publication, so that the number of newspaper titles published in the United Kingdom doubled within ten years.[41] Due in part to Gibson's persistent opposition to retaining the advertisement duty in reduced form, Parliament had already voted for its abolition by July 1853, while it was not until October 1861, when the House of Lords finally consented to an end to the paper duty, that periodical distribution was free from fiscal constraint. These changes were of course in line with a general shift from indirect to direct modes of taxation—notably, via the introduction of a permanent income tax—that contributed to a long-term reduction of social inequality. This reflected the reasonable view of Adam Smith, the pioneer of political economy, that the "rich should contribute to the public expense, not only in proportion to their revenue, but something more than in that proportion."[42]

A further policy issue raised, though only briefly discussed, by the Select Committee, was that of intellectual property in periodical contents. Because it increased the price of publications, many radicals classed copyright protection among the taxes on knowledge. The primary function of the 1842 Copyright Act was to increase the minimum period of protection to forty-two years. In addition, it had established that, by thus contracting with the publishers, authors could secure rights in material published in collective works such as magazines, though it remained silent on the status of illustrations in the periodical press. And the act had said nothing about the contents of newspapers, thus reinforcing the existing understanding

---

37. Ibid., index, 575–6.
38. Ibid., 381.
39. Ibid., xl.
40. House of Commons, "Bill to Alter and Amend," 1.
41. From 624 in 1854 to 1,250 in 1864 (Mitchell, *Newspaper Press Directory*).
42. Smith, *Inquiry*, 2:446.

that there was no copyright in news itself. This justified the practice, still universal at the mid-century, of editors duplicating material from recently published papers, with or without the courtesy of acknowledgement. In 1851, the Select Committee was persuaded that the stimulus to the creation of cheap newspapers from the abolition of the stamp might damage the existing dailies, which expended large sums on the timely collection of original information. It was thus tentatively suggested that to prevent the "pirating of articles of intelligence from one newspaper to another . . . some short privilege of copyright should therefore be conferred," the term under consideration being a matter of hours rather than years.[43] However, this suggestion was overlooked by Parliament, so that in 1878 the Copyright Commission had to recommend legislation defining "what parts of a newspaper may be considered copyright."[44] In fact, this was only achieved with the 1911 Copyright Act, so that, in this particular if no other, parliamentary inaction encouraged rather than prevented the broadcasting of intelligence.

Technological and Economic Innovations

Fundamental to this section are twin aspects of the long-term process of socio-economic transformation known as the Industrial Revolution. First, technological advances revolutionized not only how goods such as periodicals were made but also how they were circulated, with the power of steam soon driving both press and railway. And second, developments in technical method tended to be rapidly followed, if not accompanied, by shifts in economic mode. Thus, at the end of the eighteenth century, in publishing as in other industries, production and distribution were typically carried out piecemeal by a multitude of small, local firms in private family hands, whereas by the beginning of the twentieth century, both were increasingly dominated by a handful of huge joint-stock, mass-market companies. These radical changes were already under way in the first half of the nineteenth century, though their impact on the periodical industry was restricted until the removal of the fiscal constraints.

Still in the opening decades of the nineteenth century, the motive force of the main transportation systems was either wind-power, as employed in both coastal and ocean-going shipping, or horse-power in the case of carriage by canal or road. Except for the canal barges, used only for unhurried bulk delivery, each contributed to the circulation of print media, whether via public or private agency. In 1811, for example, there were thirteen sailing routes operated by the Post Office itself,[45] regularly conveying newspapers and magazines along with official, commercial, and personal correspondence. Among these services, the longest sailing was to Jamaica, which took six to eight weeks, and the shortest journey was the four hours or so from Port Patrick in southeast Scotland to Donaghadee in northwest Ireland. The Post Office packets represented only a fraction of the lines of distribution by sea, and there were many private carriers to whom mail routes could be contracted. Advertisements in early Australian colonial newspapers reveal not only the nature of shipping contacts with the mother country but also the

---

43. "Report from the Select Committee on Newspaper Stamps," xi.
44. House of Commons, "Copyright Commission," xvii.
45. See *Paterson's Roads*, 1811, 538.

demand for journals from home. As early as 1823, settlers in Van Diemen's Land were informed of the availability of nearly thirty British serial titles which could be transmitted within six months of publication and at a premium of only 25 percent on London prices.[46] Nearer home, the Edinburgh port of Leith served as a conduit not only for the export of highland whiskey but also for the bulk transfer of printed publications between the Scottish and English capitals.

Nevertheless, internal distribution of periodicals in the early nineteenth century relied more heavily on coaches drawn by teams of horses in stages of a dozen miles or so along the metalled road network developed by the turnpike trusts. These had grown from 3,500 to 13,500 miles during the "turnpike mania" of 1750–70, by which time virtually all trunk roads out of London had been improved. The early decades of the nineteenth century saw a slowdown, with the main developments then being in secondary roads, and the overall length peaked at just over 20,000 miles by the beginning of the Victorian era.[47] Between 1750 and 1830, with progress also in vehicle efficiency and safety, average passenger stagecoach speeds increased from 2.6 to 8 miles per hour,[48] while, with changeover times reduced and stopovers eliminated, the typical journey time from London to Edinburgh, say, dropped from twelve days to less than two, and the trip from London to Cambridge, from two days to six hours.[49] Moreover, services allowing the more rapid delivery of newspapers were gradually created, initially by the Post Office and later by private carriers. In 1784, the Post Office began to replace its mounted post boys with rapid night mail coaches, which were exempt from turnpike tolls, allowing London evening papers to be delivered by the next morning within 100 miles or so,[50] and in 1787 a special mail office for handling newspapers was set up, with free mail delivery for stamped papers granted by decree a few years later.[51] From the mid-1820s, express day stagecoach services began to run from the London inns, typically setting off around 7:00 a.m., the Brighton service being one of the first in 1824.[52] These soon permitted the delivery of London morning papers to distant urban centers like Birmingham the same evening. Such expensive distribution arrangements, though, were affordable only for the wealthy few who were anxious for the latest political, legal, and commercial intelligence. Less urgent information in the form of quarterly reviews, monthly miscellanies, and even weekly journals could travel by slower, cheaper channels, whether by fly-wagon and carrier's cart or by coastal and river packet. Finally, the turnpike network at its peak accounted for less than 20 percent of the road system,[53] so that the last leg of transportation to smaller towns and villages remained more subject to the contingencies of weather and was commonly traversed at a slow pace on foot.

If little else, this situation remained largely unchanged as the stagecoach was steadily replaced by the steam train, much to the lament of novelists like Dickens. At its peak in the 1830s, the

---

46. See "Literary Commissions," 2.
47. Bogart, "Turnpike Trusts," 483.
48. Ibid., 484.
49. See Harris, *Coaching Age*, 275–94, and Robinson, *Post Office*, 113.
50. Robinson, *Post Office*, 102–18.
51. Ibid., 95.
52. Wilson, *First with the News*, 43.
53. Bogart, "Turnpike Trusts," 480.

extent of the turnpike system was almost the same as that of the railway network by the end of the century,[54] though over that period transportation by train had made progress in terms of speed, volume, and cost efficiency. By the 1890s, expresses bound for Edinburgh and Cambridge took under eight and two hours, respectively, with hundreds of times the capacity of the old stage-coaches, whether in passengers, mail, or goods. The first public steam railways were transverse lines in the industrial north, but with growth caused by the "railway mania" of the 1840s, the familiar style of arterial development out of London was firmly established. Thus, by mid-century there were already nearly seventy million passengers annually, traveling at top speeds of up to 50 miles per hour on over 6,000 miles of track.[55] The methods of press distribution over this new network in many ways reproduced those under the old turnpike regime. The Liverpool–Manchester railway was first used for postal conveyance in 1830,[56] and the last mail coach seems to have left London for Norwich in 1846.[57] The post was typically carried long-distance in overnight trains, dropping off mail at smaller stations without stopping and arriving in time for morning delivery in the major cities, with dedicated mail trains and special sorting carriages introduced in 1838.[58] Slightly earlier wholesale news vendors in London had begun to use trains for the distribution of periodicals to urban centers in the provinces, offering both early morning express services, arriving well before the mail trains for daily newspapers, and slower bulk services for less urgent journals. And just as coaching inns had offered local customers the chance to browse the latest metropolitan journals, so train stations quickly became hosts to the commercial sale of periodicals and other publications. This was in the form of railway bookstalls catering to the information and entertainment needs of travelers. Termini like London Euston or Bristol Temple Meads, along with junctions like Crewe and Swindon, offered the most comprehensive services, though even branch-line stations would have had at least a paperboy "crying" the news. The station stall had begun as a local affair, with early holders typically being retired railway employees or booksellers from nearby towns, but by mid-century, contracts were awarded for entire lines to companies operating on a grand scale.[59]

Coal-fired steam soon powered the dominant forms of transportation not only on land but also by water. Indeed, the steam engine was put to practical use rather earlier in the latter case. From as early as 1812 the Clyde estuary was plied by steamboat, with combined services (mail, goods, passengers) both to the Scottish Highlands and Islands and to Belfast soon following,[60] and by 1826 most of the Post Office coastal packet services were driven by steam.[61] The first transatlantic service entirely under steam power had to wait until 1838, but with the transition from paddle to screw propulsion, even westbound crossings (against the Gulf Stream) from Bristol or Liverpool to Halifax or New York had been more than halved to under a week by

---

54. See Porter, *Progress of the Nation*, 553.
55. Simmons, *Victorian Railway*, 309–18.
56. Robinson, *Post Office*, 169.
57. Wilson, *First with the News*, 43.
58. Robinson, *Post Office*, 169–70.
59. See Colclough, "Station."
60. See McCrorie, *Clyde Pleasure Steamers*.
61. See *Paterson's Roads*, 1826, 714–15.

the mid-1880s.[62] The opening of the Suez Canal in 1869 provided even more marked improvements in journey times and travel conditions en route to India, the Australasian colonies, and intermediary British ports like Aden and Singapore. Steamship routes both west and east thus became the fastest means of carrying periodicals and other printed information to distant English-speaking communities, stimulating the exchange of news and views in both directions, though with centrifugal forces dominant. In the later Victorian decades, metropolitan newspapers and magazines thus traveled far and wide, with prestigious news organs like the *Illustrated London News* offering editions on lighter paper for transmission overseas, while popular weekly miscellanies like *Chambers's Journal* began to create monthly editions with circulation in the colonies in mind. Local cultural links were also maintained through periodical means: Scottish colonists in eastern Canada, southern New Zealand, or even Patagonia, seemed to have regularly received the Dundee *People's Friend*, a weekly story paper founded in 1869.[63]

In theory at least, Victorian Britain's intellectual property regime held sway throughout the empire. However, this was especially difficult to maintain in the Canadian colonies, with their long open borders with the United States. Since the American government refused any part in the International Union for the Protection of Literary and Artistic Works, which nine nations had signed at Berne in 1886, all but two from Western Europe, there was no copyright agreement between the Old World and the New until the Chace Act of 1891. Thus, virtually throughout the century, material from British periodicals was disseminated much more widely in North America than the periodicals themselves were distributed. From the 1840s, popular American miscellanies like *Littell's Living Age* regularly reprinted the bulk of their literary material directly from British journals, typically with acknowledgement but not permission. More prestigious publishers like Harper's typically made agreements with well-known British authors to pay for advance proofs of new work in serial form to gain a brief advantage over piratical rivals; a number of British publishers tried to expand their reach by arranging for simultaneous American editions of their periodicals, with Dickens's *Household Words* (1850–59) being a well-known example. Many of these processes also operated in the opposite direction, though more rarely. Until the Civil War, British daily papers relied on American journals shipped across the Atlantic for intelligence from the New World, often reprinting stories verbatim. The most common source for *The Times*, for example, was evidently the *New York Courier* (1829–61), a Whig paper that issued a special edition for the British market prior to the departure of each transatlantic steamer.[64]

While the gradual move from steam to electric power had little direct effect on the distribution of periodicals and newspapers, the general process of electrification did have a decisive impact on the dissemination of much of the information they contained. The electric telegraph revolutionized the transmission of urgent intelligence, allowing newspapers to almost instantly report events occurring on the other side of the country, the continent, and finally the globe. For the first time, long-distance communication could along paths independent of physical

---

62. See Bonsor, *North Atlantic Seaway*.
63. Law, *Serializing Fiction*, 119.
64. See "American News for European Readers."

transportation and at far great speed, though land telegraph lines inevitably tended to follow railway tracks and submarine cables to track shipping lanes. The first commercial system was along the initial section of the Great Western Railway from 1839. By 1850, a country-wide network had been pieced together by the Electric Telegraph Company, with nationalization taking place twenty years later. The first operational transatlantic cable went online in 1866, and the circle around the earth was completed early in the twentieth century.[65]

Just as significant as these technical extensions was the formation of the Press Association in 1868 by a group of provincial newspaper owners in need of a common news wire service to compete with the metropolitan press. Including this last example, we have thus far touched on several cases where technical and commercial innovation went hand in hand. To give a more rounded picture of how changing business models specifically affected periodical distribution, it may be best to offer a couple of brief case studies, focusing in turn on the operations of W.H. Smith (newsagent) and Charles Mitchell (advertising agent), the first of whom was among those called before the Select Committee in 1851.

W.H. Smith's started out in the early 1790s as a West End "news walk," a local retailer of stationery and periodicals. The shop provided house delivery for the well-to-do around Grosvenor Square and soon began to supply newspapers and other goods to customers leaving town mansions for country seats at the end of the London season.[66] By the late 1820s, after opening up a periodical reading room on the Strand, the growing firm consolidated its business near Fleet Street. It then adopted the name of W.H. Smith, the younger and more energetic son of the founder, who led the business to become a major wholesale distributor of newspapers to the provinces. Smith regularly used the columns of *The Times* to advertise his enterprise of hiring stagecoaches independently when late sittings of Parliament caused a delay in the press.[67] With the coming of the railway era, he employed a fleet of distinctive red carts to ferry parcels of papers in time for early morning trains, hiring special locomotives if the occasion demanded. Using the correspondence columns of *The Times* to launch an attack on the Post Office,[68] he won an exclusive contract for wholesale provincial distribution of that paper from 1854. The hiring of dedicated newspaper trains with special packing carriages from the 1870s shows that Smith's wholesale business continued thriving in quasi-monopolistic style under the new tax regime.

At mid-century, the bookstall contract for the line from Euston to Manchester was awarded to Smith's, and within little more than a decade the firm had control of retail outlets and station advertising on virtually the whole of the network in England and Wales,[69] with John Menzies soon establishing a similar network throughout Scotland.[70] The stalls offered not only newspapers

---

65. For general background on the development of the telegraph network, see Kieve, *Electric Telegraph*, and Roberts, *Distant Writing*.
66. Wilson, *First with the News*, 9–10.
67. See, for example, advertisements in the form of letters to the editor in *The Times*, March 21, 1829, 3; March 24, 1829, 4; and March 25, 1829, 4.
68. "Post-Office," 7.
69. See Colclough, "Purifying," 27–51.
70. See Gardiner, *Making of John Menzies*.

and magazines but also series of inexpensive books, most notably the latest "yellowback" railway libraries of popular fiction. From 1860, W.H. Smith's also operated a circulating library from their stalls, exercising a conservative influence over literary trends.[71] The firm's countrywide chain of high-street stores, even more prominent today with the takeover of Menzies in 1998, emerged early in the twentieth century after the loss of railway bookstall contracts. Though W.H. Smith did not in fact become a public limited company until 1949, in most other respects the firm's steady development from local London retailer to major provincial wholesaler and then to nationwide retailer, exemplifies the general trend from petty commodity to mass commodity distribution and consumption over the nineteenth century.

The development of Charles Mitchell's business reflects the impact of changes over a similar period in the form and function, as well as the scale and scope, of commercial advertising on the circulation of periodicals. While commercial notices in print publications have a much longer history, it was in the mid-1830s, with a cut in the advertisement duty, that advertising agencies really took off. Among the earliest was Mitchell, "Town and Country Advertisement Agent" at Red Lion Court, off Fleet Street, who seems to have started up on completing his apprenticeship as a newspaper printer in Manchester in 1837. In addition to acting for out-of-town papers, Mitchell made regular use of a press, since within a few years there appeared under his imprint a number of periodical publications, most notably the satirical weekly *Punch* (1841–2002). Soon Mitchell must have decided that the way forward in the advertising business was to issue his own serial on the subject, the *Newspaper Press Directory* (1846–), an annual publication that continues today in the form of *Benn's Media Directory*. Mitchell's pioneering volume appeared in 1846, though it was described in the dedication as the "fruit of anxious labour during a long period of time."[72] In his opening address on the limitations of existing newspaper listings, he specified his aim as "to form a guide to advertisers in their selection of journals as mediums more particularly suitable for their announcements."[73] The detailed characterization of each of the 551 titles, spanning the entire kingdom, thus covered not only factual matters, such as content, price, and format, but also socio-political questions of affiliation and orientation, as well as salient economic features of the area of circulation. There were also articles providing information on relevant legal, fiscal, and commercial issues, including a piece titled "The Philosophy of Advertising." In any event, the "annual" appeared only five times in its first decade, but with the flood of new papers following the change of fiscal regime, it appeared as scheduled after 1856 in editions of increasing size.

Though Mitchell died in 1859, his directory continued to flourish, adding the listing of magazines from 1860, and of Continental, American, and colonial journals from 1878, 1879, and 1885, respectively. At the same time, the firm began to cooperate with overseas partners such as Gordon & Gotch, the Melbourne news and advertising agents covering the entire Australasian market. Thus Mitchell's operation both reflected and stimulated the internationalization of markets for British goods and services, periodical intelligence included. In a similar way, Mitchell's both recorded and contributed to a decisive shift centering on the 1880s—from

---

71. See Colclough, "Greater Outlay."
72. Mitchell, *Newspaper Press Directory*, 1846, iii.
73. Ibid., v.

the small classified notices cherished by *The Times* to the display announcements that helped mass-market manufacturers establish a clear brand identity for their products. Given that the circulation figures provided by official stamp returns had ceased and that audited business accounts providing similar information were not called for before the new century, Mitchell's qualitatively rich surveys of the exponentially expanding periodical industry are today as valuable to media historians as they were in their own day to manufacturers of all kinds. As a rule of thumb, periodicals of the later Victorian decades would typically aim to fill around half of their available space with advertising copy. With the social character of the readership often counting as much as raw circulation,[74] such a balance of content would generate income from advertising exceeding that from subscriptions, thus resulting in a clear profit. This became the standard business model not only for newspaper publishers but also those that produced a range of magazines. As detailed elsewhere,[75] the impact on the new generation of mass-market journals can be seen most clearly in the publishing empire created at the end of the Victorian era by George Newnes. This represents the extreme of commercial journalism, where the periodical "assumes the character of an enterprise which produces advertising space as a commodity that is made marketable by means of an editorial section."[76] Thus, dependence on the advertising-driven business model fostered by agencies like Mitchell's affected periodical function as well as circulation. In the process, the pattern of distribution of intelligence itself, in the broad socio-economic sense, underwent a profound transformation.

The radical socio-economic changes that the later part of this article has tried to cover have been characterized with similar intent, though in rather different terms, by Raymond Williams and Jürgen Habermas, two radical thinkers who responded to the media broadcasting revolution taking place in the decades after World War II. Williams claimed that the "methods and attitudes of capitalist business have established themselves at the centre of public communications," so that with the "widespread dependence on advertising money . . . all the basic purposes of communication—the sharing of human experience—are being steadily subordinated to this drive to sell."[77] Habermas, in turn, argued that due to the increasing intrusion of corporate interests, "rational–critical debate had a tendency to be replaced by consumption, and the web of public communication unravelled into acts of individuated reception."[78] In his view, this inevitably resulted in a weakening of the function of public opinion, defined as the "tasks of criticism and control which a public body of citizens . . . practices *vis-à-vis* the ruling structure organized in the form of a state."[79] Whether we favor the formulations of Williams or Habermas, or indeed neither, it is difficult to escape the conclusion that the technical and business developments transforming the periodical industry over the later Victorian decades resulted in a very different model for the distribution of knowledge from that imagined by the reformists on the Committee on Newspaper Stamps at mid-century.

74. Brown, *Victorian News*, 16.
75. See Law and Sterenberg, "Old vs. New."
76. Karl Bücher, cited in Habermas, *Structural Transformation*, 185.
77. Williams, *Communications*, 32–3.
78. Habermas, *Structural Transformation*, 161.
79. Habermas, "Public Sphere," 49.

Table 3.1 Distribution timeline

	Legal / Fiscal Aspects	Technological / Business Aspects	Periodical Data (High Circulation)	Demographic / Distribution Data
Late 18th c.	1797 Newspaper stamp up to 3½d. per sheet. 1797 Advertisement tax up to 3s. per item. 1798 Bill: newspaper registration required.	1792 W.H. Smith starts up in London. 1796 Invention of lithography. 1799 Religious Tract Society founded.	1795 *The Times* (D, 6d., 4.7k) 1797 *Gentleman's Magazine* (M, 1s. 6d., 4.5k)	1788 GB newspaper stamp returns = 12.8m. 1797 GB revenue from newspaper stamps = £150k. 1797 GB revenue from advertising duty = £75k.
1800s	1802 Fine paper duty up to 3d. per lb. (peak).	1800 Stanhope iron press invented. 1801 Roll paper-making invented. 1803 Stanhope reinvents stereotyping.	1803 *Morning Post* (D, 6d., 4.5k). 1807 *Evangelical Magazine* (M, 6d., 18k).	1801 Pop. of England and Wales: 8.9m. 1803 GB newspaper stamp returns = 16.9m. 1806 UK stamped newspaper titles > 150. 1808 GB newspaper stamp returns = 22.1m.
1810s	1815 Corn Laws introduced. 1815 Advertisement tax up to 3s. 6d. (peak). 1815 Newspaper stamp up to 4d. (peak). 1819 Bill: stamp duty on "seditious" papers.	1814 Koenig steam press invented.	1814 *Edinburgh Review* (Q, 6s., 13k). 1816 *The Times* (D, 7d., 5k). 1817 *Political Register* (W, 2d., 40k).	1811 Pop. of England and Wales: 10.2m. 1813 GB newspaper stamp returns = 26.3m. 1814 UK stamped newspaper titles = 224. 1816 GB revenue from newspaper stamps = £298k. 1816 GB revenue from adv. duty = £132k. 1818 GB newspaper stamp returns = 22.1m.
1820s	1822 Stamp Office transfers back newspapers to BM. 1825 Free postal delivery for all stamped newspapers.	First express daytime stage-coach services. 1825 First steam railway service begins. 1826 SDUK founded.	1823 *Mirror of Literature* (W, 2d., 80k). 1828 *Blackwood's Edinburgh Magazine* (M, 2s. 6d., 6.5k). 1829 *Weekly Dispatch* (W, 8½d., 15k).	1821 Pop. of England and Wales/ UK 12m/20.9m. 1823 GB newspaper stamp returns = 24.7m. 1824 UK stamped newspaper titles = 266. 1826 GB revenue from newspaper stamps = £365k. 1826 GB revenue from adv. duty = £151k. 1828 GB newspaper stamp returns = 28.8m.

	Legal / Fiscal Aspects	Technological / Business Aspects	Periodical Data (High Circulation)	Demographic / Distribution Data
1830s	1830 "The War of the Unstamped" begins. 1832 Reform Act: franchise to 1 in 6 males. 1833 Advertisement tax down to 1s. 6d. 1833 Duties on pamphlets/almanacs abolished. 1836 Newspaper stamp down to 1d. 1836 Fine paper duty down to 1½d. per lb. 1838 Free PO delivery for all stamped periodicals.	1830 Trains first used for postal carriage. 1832 SPCK starts *Saturday Magazine*. 1833 John Menzies starts up in Edinburgh. 1837 P&O (shipping company) win first mail contract UK–Iberian Peninsula. 1837 Invention of chromolithography. 1837 First domestic telegraph line opened. 1838 W.H. Smith first conveys by rail. 1838 *SS Sirius* crosses Atlantic at 10 knots.	More than 400 unstamped newspaper titles issued. 1832 SDUK *Penny Magazine* (W, 1d., 100k). 1832 SPCK *Saturday Magazine* (W, 1d., 80k). 1832 *Chambers's Edinburgh Journal* (W, 1d., 50k). 1833 *Poor Man's Guardian* (W, 1d., 15K). 1837 *The Times* (D, 5d., 11k). 1839 *Northern Star* (W, 3½d., 36k).	1831 Pop. of England and Wales / UK: 13.9m/24m. 1833 GB newspaper stamp returns = 30.7m. 1836 UK stamped newspaper titles = 397. 1838 GB newspaper stamp returns = 49.4m.
1840s	1840 First Railway Regulation Act. 1840 Uniform 1d. post for letters within UK. 1842 Copyright Act clarifies magazine copyright. 1846 Corn Laws repealed.	"Railway Mania" begins. 1843 Hoe rotary press invented. 1844 Wood pulp paper-making invented. 1845 UK railway network = 2.3k miles. 1846 Last London mail coach service. 1848 First W.H. Smith station bookstalls.	1848 *The Times* (D, 5d., 36k). 1849 *News of the World* (W, 3d., 54k).	1841 Pop. of England and Wales / UK: 15.9m/26.7m. 1841 M/F illiteracy rates: 33%/49%. 1843 GB newspaper stamp returns = 59.7m. 1846 UK stamped newspaper titles = 550. 1848 GB newspaper stamp returns = 83.9m.

(Continued)

Table 3.1 (Continued)

	Legal / Fiscal Aspects	Technological / Business Aspects	Periodical Data (High Circulation)	Demographic / Distribution Data
1850s	1851 House of Commons Select Committee on stamp tax. 1851 Window tax replaced by house tax. 1853 Advertisement tax abolished. 1855 Newspaper stamp no longer obligatory.	1850 UK railway network = 6.6k miles. 1854 W.H. Smith gains *Times* wholesale monopoly. 1857 Newspaper stereotyping. 1857 First Menzies station bookstalls.	1854 *Illustrated London News* (W, 6d., 123k). 1855 *London Journal.* (W, 1d., 510k). 1856 *Illustrated Times* (W, 2d., 400k). 1858 *The Times* (D, 4d., 50k).	1851 Pop. of England and Wales / UK: 17.9m/27.4m. 1851 M/F illiteracy rates: 31%/45%. 1854 GB newspaper stamp returns = c.122m. 1856 UK newspaper titles = 801.
1860s	1861 Paper duty abolished. 1867 Reform Act: franchise to 40% males. 1869 Legal deposit rules extended to newspapers. 1869 Telegraph Act grants Post Office monopoly.	1860 UK railway network = 10.4k miles. 1866 Transatlantic telegraph link active. 1868 Formation of the Press Association. 1869 Suez Canal opens.	1860 *Cornhill* (M, 1s., 80k). 1863 *Lloyd's Weekly News* (W, 1d., 350k). 1868 (Dundee) *People's Journal* (W, 1d., 120k).	1861 Pop. of England and Wales / UK: 20.1m/28.9m. 1861 M/F illiteracy rates: 25%/35%. 1866 UK newspaper/magazine titles = 1,257/557 (69:31).
1870s	1870 Education Act sets up elementary system. 1870 Optional newspaper stamp discontinued. 1878 Copyright Commission queries newspaper copyright.	"Newspaper trains" & "packing carriages" become common. 1870 UK railway network = 15.5k miles.	1870 *Echo* (D, ½d., 80k). 1870 *Telegraph* (D, 1d., 190k). 1870 *Glasgow Herald* (D, 1d., 31k). 1870 *Cassell's Magazine* (M, 6d., 200k).	1871 Pop. of England and Wales / UK 22.7m/31.5/m. 1871 M/F illiteracy rates: 19%/27%. 1876 UK newspaper/magazine titles = 1,642/657 (71:29).

	Legal / Fiscal Aspects	Technological / Business Aspects	Periodical Data (High Circulation)	Demographic / Distribution Data
1880s	1880 Elementary education made compulsory. 1884 Reform Act: franchise to 60% males. 1886 Berne Convention: first multilateral copyright treaty, including literary material in periodicals.	Display advertising becomes widespread. 1880 UK railway network = 17.9k miles. 1886 Hot metal type-setting invented (Linotype). 1889 SS *City of Paris* crosses Atlantic at 20 knots. 1889 End of turnpike toll system.	1881 *Weekly Budget* (W, 1d., 500k). 1882 *The Times* (D, 3d., 100k). 1885 *Yorkshire Post* (D, 1d., 47k). 1886 *Glasgow Weekly Mail* (W, 1d., 270k).	1881 Pop. of England and Wales / UK: 26m/34.9m. 1881 M/F illiteracy rates: 14%/18%. 1886 UK newspaper/magazine titles = 2,093/1,368 (60:40).
1890s	1891 Elementary education free of charge. 1891 Chace Act: copyright for alien authors in US. 1897 House of Commons Report opposes opening newspaper postal rates to other periodicals.	1890 UK railway network = 20.1k miles. 1898 Motor vans used for mail delivery.	1893 *Tit-Bits* (W, 1d., 607k). 1896 *Strand* (M, 6d., 332k). 1899 *Daily Mail* (D, ½d., 543k).	1891 Pop. of England and Wales / UK: 29m/37.7m. 1891 M/F illiteracy rates: 6%/7%. 1896 UK newspaper/magazine titles = 2,355/2,097 (53:47).
Early 20th c.	1911 Copyright Act clarifies newspaper copyright.	1900 UK railway network = 21.9k miles. 1901 First trans-Pacific telegraph link. 1903 Offset paper printing invented. 1914 Panama Canal opens.	1911 *Daily Mirror* (D, ½d., 1m).	1901 Pop. of England and Wales / UK: 32.5m/41.5m. 1901 M/F illiteracy rates: 3%/3%. 1906 UK newspaper/magazine titles = 2,440/2,745 (47:53).

Abbreviations: d. = penny; D = Daily; k = thousand; lb. = pound (weight); m = million; M = monthly; M/F = male/female; Pop. = population; s. = shilling; SDUK = Society for the Diffusion of Useful Knowledge; SPCK = Society for the Promotion of Christian Knowledge; W = Weekly.

Souces: Altick, *English Common Reader*; Bogart; Bogart, "Turnpike Trusts"; Bonsor, *North Atlantic Seaway*; Law, *Serializing Fiction*.

4

PERIODICAL ECONOMICS

Andrew King

When we think of "economics" today, the first thing that comes to mind is probably profit and loss: the accountant's columns of bookkeeping so essential to a society founded on the principles of capitalism. Capitalism seems natural to us, and it appears logical that a chapter on periodical economics should explain the debits and credits of periodical production. That I shall do in due course. Yet even though all periodicals, as manufactured and shared artifacts, necessarily involve some kind of economics, commerce does not inhere in all of them. Many operated at a loss commercially while on their own terms they were a success servicing a community or promoting an ideal. Economics contains accountancy; it is not confined to it. A bookkeeper's numbers do not represent material reality; rather, through the lens of economics, as I understand it, reality lies in the relationships that those numbers encode.

This chapter is accordingly split between consideration of what we might mean by "periodical economics" and a guide to the kind and use of materials that might be available to study the relations that made periodicals sustainable. The first section will raise general issues in the consideration of the topic, the second section will point the researcher to some relevant data sources, and the final section will offer a cost breakdown of the production of three different kinds of periodicals. Researchers can use this third part to generate a tick list for making their own calculations and reflections based on whatever data is available. The chapter as a whole is critical of the comforting fantasies of realistic and accurate representation that, according to Mary Poovey, quantitative measurement dangles before us.[1] While stimulated by the arguments of Poovey and others on the representation of finance in the *contents* of print, I am more interested in looking at what enabled those contents to be produced and disseminated in the first place.[2]

Theoretical Issues

In the preface to *Illustrations of Political Economy* (1832–4), Harriet Martineau defines her topic as the "principles which regulate the production and distribution of the necessaries and

---

1. Poovey, "Writing."
2. See, for example, Poovey, "Economics and Finance"; Gallagher, *Body Economic*; Gagnier, *Insatiability of Human Wants*.

comforts of life in society."[3] She goes on to distinguish two kinds of economy, political and domestic. Indeed, the etymological roots of "economics"—a combination of the Greek words οἶκος and νομος—link the household and the law. "Economy" essentially studies the patterns of circulation within or between defined spaces or units, however we may define them—a household, periodical, industry, country, class, sex, "race," individual, political party, or publishing house. When we talk of "periodical economics," therefore, we must be careful to define what units we are investigating as well as what passed between or within them: money, labor, status, knowledge, friendship, and so on. We also need to define how the negotiation takes place and what limits are imposed on what, how, and who are involved in the exchange.

The answers to these questions are not obvious from either a theoretical or an evidential perspective. For example, where do the limits of a "periodical unit" lie? Even when focusing on the economy of a particular title, we may need to regard it as but one part of a wider commercial, political, or social enterprise. As Patrick Leary has shown, *Punch* was but one horse on a team of periodicals owned by what was, *au fond*, a printing business.[4] Notes to the payment sheets for *Macmillan's Magazine*, for example, sometimes show unusually generous payments to friends of the editor, investing money in the consolidation of networks which may exceed the immediate printing context but which may perhaps be useful in the future either to the editor or to the firm.[5] Indeed, house magazines played an important role in publishing firms even if they operated at a loss. *Tinsley's* lost £25 a month, but according to a contemporary, Tinsley believed that the periodical advertised his name and publications and kept his authors together.[6] Its value lay not in its ability to make a profit on its own but in forwarding his entire firm's business strategy. Then again, as surviving letters in the Blackwood archive suggest, periodicals were, and continue to be, regarded as parts of an entire market sector. At one point, for example, William Blackwood III threatened to get a *Times* reviewer sacked by filing a complaint with his "old friend," the editor. Why, he asked, had the requested review not appeared within the week, even though he had sent the reviewer an "explanatory note" with the "early copy"?[7] Blackwood assumed he was operating in a cartel wherein specific firms helped each other and excluded others. *The Times*, for him, was not a free-standing unit of income generation so much as part of an elite and exclusive market sector that sought to minimize risk to capital investment to all who belonged to it. Blackwood's emotional response was derived from his perception that the reviewer had behaved so as to threaten that economic logic.

The value of many social purpose and religious periodicals, by contrast, lay in their perceived ability to promote actions, beliefs, or ideologies more than in balance sheets. The weekly

---

3. Martineau, *Illustrations*, 1:iii.
4. Leary, *Punch Brotherhood*, 160–72.
5. Unbound Pay Sheets for *Macmillan's Magazine* 1889–1907, British Library, Add Ms 55999. See, for example, the March 1891 pay sheet, where a note from the editor, Mowbray Maurice, appended to the name and address of H.L. Havell, reads, "This paper was written at my request. Perhaps you will give the writer a little more than usual—say *ten guineas* instead of *nine pounds*" (emphasis in original).
6. Downey, *Twenty Years Ago*, 247.
7. See William Blackwood III to J.A. McCarthy, June 8, 1886, Blackwood private letter book, National Library of Scotland, NMS 30372, fol. 138.

temperance periodicals of the United Kingdom Alliance were designed primarily to benefit the community by encouraging temperance; despite huge losses, they continued to be published for decades.[8] The Chartist penny weekly *Red Republican* (1850), which serialized Helen MacFarlane's translation of the *Communist Manifesto*, likewise operated at a financial loss. The feminist *Englishwoman's Review* (1866–1910) refused advertisements, and hence income, because to do so would compromise its mission (though unlike the *Red Republican*, it benefited from subvention by a wealthy founding editor, Jessie Boucherett). In all these cases, a kind of sacrificial economics is at work: immediate gain is sacrificed in an attempt to make a better future for others. We can see this logic extending beyond producers in how a reader of the *Red Republican* raised 10s. 6d. from his associates to buy copies of the periodical to place "upon the tables of popular resort."[9] Inspired to create a relay of sacrifice by the *Red Republican*'s politics, he convinced those around him to give up their pennies to persuade others of the periodical's vision. Sometimes, if more rarely, periodicals such as Edward Gordon Craig's *Page* (1898–1901) were created as a kind of therapeutic activity for an individual rather than for a community. Again, this was an undertaking whose commercial possibilities were entirely incidental.[10]

Despite numerous exceptions, most publishers believed that the sale of large numbers of each issue of a periodical was crucial to sustainability. "Sale" is never simple for any commodity and varies according to location and period. At the end of the century, most metropolitan publishers sold defined quantities of their periodicals to wholesalers who then sold them on to a network of retail merchants. These in turn sold them on to customers. For the provincial press, sales were more geographically limited, making wholesalers unnecessary; publishers often sold directly to retailers or to customers from their own premises.

At each relay of a sale, the value of a commodity should ideally increase in what today's marketing experts call the "value chain."[11] Alteration in value at each stage can be quantitatively expressed by a mathematical relation called "mark-up." In its simplest form, mark-up comprises the relation between production cost and retail price, usually expressed as a multiple. It is not the same as "profit" since at every stage of the relay there are also costs: "profit" is (strictly speaking) mark-up minus the costs. Using figures from an 1839 article by S.C. Hall published in the *Art-Union*, we can calculate that the estimated mark-up from production to retail for all the annuals sold in 1829 was 4s. on 12s. volumes and 7s. on guinea volumes. In modern terms, the mark-up would be 50 percent (half of the production cost added to the retail cost), while the profit by the bookseller would be considerably less, comprising the mark-up minus the costs incurred for premises, staff, heating, lighting, bookkeeping, and so on. However, when Hall's article is cited in an 1858 article in the *Bookseller*, the "profit" for the bookseller is stated to be 33 percent, calculated as a third of the sales price.[12] If this mismatch between modern and nineteenth-century terminology is rather confusing, it is nonetheless a comparatively simple

---

8. See Harrison, "World," 154, and see chapter 25 below, 344, 347.
9. "G.J. Mantle" in Harney, "Notices to Correspondents," 125.
10. Claes has discussed the *Page* in some detail in "Towards the Total Work of Art," 179–85.
11. For a discussion of the "value chain," see Porter, *Competitive Advantage*.
12. See "Annuals," 493.

example; one can immediately see how the *Bookseller* extrapolated the "profit" from Hall's figures, even if it used the term differently than we would today. To discuss comparative periodical economics, either over time for one periodical or synchronically across the field, we must therefore be careful to define and sustain our terms, not only contested concepts such as "circulation" but also apparently transparent ones like "profit," "loss," and "mark-up."[13]

If, for distributors, the value chain ended with retail sale, the "value system" did not. Besides enjoying the complex pleasures or social profits that might derive from a product,[14] purchasers might choose to remain within the sphere of commerce by selling the product to the second-hand market or by converting the information gained from the periodical into income (for example, selling dresses made up from patterns printed in magazines, fashion plates, or fiction illustrations[15] or, indeed, selling their own writing back to journals whose rhetoric they had studied carefully). Then again, the periodical might have utility value for a purchaser who, far from being identical to the reader, might give it as a gift unread. The periodical might be used to establish or consolidate friendship or family alliances and so generate unquantifiable but still distinctly economic benefits.[16] More prosaically, users might transform periodical pages into spills to light fires, cut them up to decorate walls, even wrap them around bullets as wadding for guns used in homicides.[17] Old clothes might be recycled into paper that would then be used to print a periodical, which would ultimately be converted into fire, another method of keeping warm—constituting a distinctly economic journey through which value is systematically transformed at every stage. Periodical economics are not then restricted to the account books of their publishers but inhere in every passage of a periodical from one place or state to another.

Finally, the economic unit might extend to the production, distribution, and use of periodicals in an entire region, nation, or beyond. Richard Altick's still-valuable *The English Common Reader* has elements of a national business history, while William St. Clair's magisterial *Reading Nation in the Romantic Period* is a more thoroughgoing example that extends through 1830. The standard story traces a transformation from artisanal family and personal ownership of periodicals at the beginning of the nineteenth century through the growth of public limited companies (especially from the 1880s), to an increasingly rhizomatic ownership structure whose figureheads were press barons such as Alfred Harmsworth and Arthur Pearson. Despite the many useful accounts that trace this narrative,[18] a thorough business history of

---

13. In compensation, one advantage for students of nineteenth-century British periodical economics is that after 1815 inflation was very low, enabling much easier comparison of prices from year to year than those of, say, 1970 and 2010. See Macfarlane and Mortimer-Lee, "Inflation over 300 Years."
14. Chapter 16 of McQuail's *Mass Communication Theory* gives the standard overview of how audiences use texts.
15. On the latter, see, for example, King, *London Journal*, 218, and see Figures 19.2 to 19.4 and 19.6 below.
16. See King, "Killing Time," 162–7.
17. In *Sixty Years of Journalism*, Bussey recounts an undated story of how a double murder was supposedly caused by the *Family Herald* (74–5). An old couple who regularly read the *Herald* were shot by their grandson who used a page of the magazine as wadding in the murder weapon.
18. See, for example, Cox and Mowatt, *Revolutions from Grub Street*; Curran and Seaton, *Power without Responsibility*; Conboy, *Press and Popular Culture*, chapters 4 and 5; K. Williams, *Read All about It*, chapters 3–5; Feather, *History of British Publishing*, chapter 4; Chapman, *Comparative Media History*, chapter 3.

nineteenth-century British periodicals and newspapers based on the detailed examination of primary sources has yet to be undertaken.

Sources

Given the expansive definition of periodical economics outlined above, one could reasonably surmise that the term is akin to Mary Poppins's bottomless carpetbag. For that very reason, we must be clear about the units we are focusing on and the relation between them. In the rest of this chapter, I shall not be concerned with any specific *value system*, but rather with specific *value chains of production and sales*: the debits and credits of commercial periodicals.

Unsurprisingly, there are various ways of reconstructing the value chain depending on what units we choose to analyze and what data are available. First, we need to decide how far back to trace the chain. For instance, taking the publisher Edward Lloyd as the economic unit, we might need to go as far back as the costs of leasing land in Algeria for growing esparto grass from which his mills made paper for his periodicals. Lloyd was unusual in the thorough and very early "vertical integration" of his supply chain, preceding by a decade the same organization of supply better known in other industries (most famously Andrew Carnegie's steel company).[19] Instead of tracing production all the way back to raw materials, though, a more usual practice is to restrict study to the relations between publishers, printers, and authors. In this approach, we consider the publisher's income from wholesale or retail sales as the total budget from which other expenditure is subtracted. While this reflects how publishers liked to present themselves to their authors and to the public, it is a version of a simple, quasi-domestic economics that does not take into account the value of credit bills, banking loans, speculation, public limited liability, or even the late paying of bills.[20] How some of these operated will become apparent when I discuss the *Brewing Trade Review* below.

Periodical publishing costs were on the whole much more complicated than those for book publishing. There was a pretty standard breakdown for book production costs, and consequently, several detailed business histories of book production have been published.[21] Reconstructing the value chain of periodicals is more challenging. Ideally, we could turn to the business records of periodical publishers. As the 1850 *Manual of Book-keeping for Booksellers, Publishers and Stationers* declared, "The books of a tradesman, in whatever department he be

---

19. On Lloyd's paper mills and his farm in Algeria, see Hatton, *Journalistic London*, 195–6. In *The British Paper Industry*, Coleman refers to Longman, who was a partner in Dickinson's large paper-making firm early in the nineteenth century, and to Thomas Routledge, who took out patents on esparto grass paper manufacture in 1856 and 1860 and collaborated closely with Wrigley's paper mill in 1860 and 1861 to produce new and cheaper kinds of paper (247, 342). These examples do not illustrate true vertical integration, however, but synergistic collaborations.
20. Coleman clearly explains the types and advantages of credit available to paper manufacturers from the passing on of bills of exchange. For example, a paper manufacturer could draw a bill on a stationer to whom he had sold paper payable to the rag merchant from whom the stationer had obtained the rag. *British Paper Industry*, 251–4.
21. Recent studies include Bassett, "Living on the Margins" and "Production of Tree-Volume Novels." Weedon, *Victorian Publishing*, and Eliot, *Patterns and Trends* and "Business," remain invaluable overviews, though they treat periodicals and newspapers incidentally.

engaged, should contain every particular which relates to his affairs . . . so full and so well arranged, as to afford ready information on every point on which they may be consulted."[22] Even with the aid of the *Manual*'s systematic explanation, nineteenth-century bookkeeping can often be confusing. This is especially true for family firms, many of which developed idiosyncratic recording practices since, unlike public liability companies (which became increasingly common after an 1857 law regularized them), they had no obligation to make their books available to shareholders or have them verified by external auditors.[23] While the realities of surviving archives are thus often widely different from the procedures the *Manual* recommends, it nonetheless remains useful for its description of what information *should* be available. The following four points comprise a simplified summary:

1. The day book records invoices and daily credit (what the company owes creditors, not what others owe the firm).
2. The cashbook records petty cash going in and out for everything from coal to postage, carriage, or porterage. (Note the careful differentiation between these three forms of distribution.) It also records "pocket money" for staff as well as other receivable and payable accounts.
3. The ledger is the central economic record which might comprise an "inventory": the valuation of goods in hand and the balances of different accounts. A central publication ledger should record costs of paper, printing, advertising, and binding, as well as payments to contributors, though in practice these costs are usually split up in various ways.
4. Stock books record the firm's return on investments.

There are many variants of this schema. For example, the Bentley Papers include a four-volume authors' ledger, a *Temple Bar* ledger, a general magazine and newspaper ledger, and another volume giving *Temple Bar* decennial statistics.[24] Some archives, like Bentley's, Macmillan's, and Longman's, are available in Chadwyck Healey's "British Publishers' Archives" microfilm series, but most publishers' records are available only in paper forms. With luck, the researcher might find marked copies of ledgers with amounts paid and names of contributors, minutes of editorial board meetings, or correspondence to and from the publisher, as in the Blackwood archives at the National Library of Scotland.

While many records can be located online through the National Register of Archives, St. Clair has compiled a convenient list of publishers' archives to circa 1830 in the bibliography of *The Reading Nation*.[25] For the rest of the century, Weedon and Bott's *British Book Trade Archives* is still invaluable. Divided up into lists concerning the various sectors of the book trade, from literary agents and bookbinders to publishers and printers, it helpfully describes the location and contents of archives. Two volumes of *The Dictionary of Literary Biography* give

---

22. *Manual*, iii.
23. On the rise of auditing as a key activity of the accountant in the second half of the nineteenth century, see Brown, *History of Accounting*, 317–22.
24. See Ingram, *Index*.
25. See St. Clair, *Reading Nation*, 724–8.

handy potted histories of publishers and where their archives can be accessed.[26] Less obvious, if equally illuminating, sources for identifying the archives of limited companies are Richmond and Stockford's *Company Archives* and, from 1875 onwards, the *Stock Exchange Year Book*. While much lamented at the time, the records of the "taxes on knowledge" are now extremely helpful. They comprise the gross annual government income from the advertisement and pamphlet duties in London and (separately) Great Britain, along with annual lists of London newspaper publishers, the names of the papers they printed, and the outstanding balances of advertisement duties owed by publishers at the end of each financial year.[27] Overlapping with the stamp duty records by less than a decade, the various press directories, especially those published by Mitchell, May, and Sell, offer basic information about circulation and advertising costs.[28] While the two main mid-nineteenth-century histories of the press, by Alexander Andrews and by James Grant, are not very useful for information about costs, the gossipy monthly *Newspaper Press* (1867–72), edited by Andrews, is well worth exploring.[29] One can also (with less certainty) conduct online searches through various electronic resources, such as the *British Newspaper Archive*, for adverts and reports of relevant court cases which may provide information about the profits and losses sustained by particular periodicals.

For secondary material, assuming the periodical in question falls outside the remit of Sullivan's *British Literary Magazines* or Houghton's *Wellesley Index*, the first ports of call are North's *Waterloo Directory*, the *Cambridge Bibliography of English Literature*, and the biennial bibliographies published in *Victorian Periodicals Review*. William S. Ward's bibliography of secondary material on newspapers and periodicals is likewise a useful resource. Finally, accounts of publishers or general histories of the press might offer information about a specific periodical or analogous periodicals, though older scholarship tends to be reticent or even misleading about financial details.[30]

---

26. See Anderson and Rose, *British Literary Publishing Houses, 1820–1880*; and Rose and Anderson, *British Literary Publishing Houses, 1881–1965*.
27. Figures for the early part of the century are available in Aspinall's two-part article "Statistical Accounts." Aspinall's "Statistical Accounts of the London Newspapers in the Eighteenth Century" is also useful for understanding the stamp returns, as is Wiener, "Circulation and the Stamp Tax." The discursive "Report from the Select Committee on Newspaper Stamps" (1851) is available online without charge; the papers of the Select Committee on Newspaper Stamps for 1837–50 are available through the *House of Commons Parliamentary Papers* database (ProQuest).
28. For more on press directories, see Chapter 17 below.
29. Andrews, *History of Journalism*; Grant, *Newspaper Press*. Andrews's *Newspaper Press* was incorporated into the monthly *Printers' Register* (1863–92) in 1872. The latter, along with the *London, Provincial and Colonial Press News* (1866–1912), is also useful. All three will require considerable beagling.
30. For example, *Family Business* gives an account of W.B. Clowes, the extremely successful printer of the *Penny Magazine* and many other periodicals. The biography unfortunately offers no financial detail, not even on the formation of the Clowes Limited Company in 1880 (Cf. Richmond and Stockford, *Company Archives*, 232–3). By way of contrast, Ayerst's *Guardian* and Wilson's *First with the News* (on the retailer W.H. Smith) pay scrupulous attention to financial matters, as do more recent studies such as Finkelstein's *House of Blackwood* and Fyfe's *Steam-Powered Knowledge*.

Sample Costs

It is now time to turn to specific examples of the ways we can reconstruct periodical economics. My three examples concern very different kinds of periodical, yet they all focus on production costs. Researchers will find abundant instances elsewhere in this volume of the other kinds of economics mentioned earlier, especially in chapters 24, 25 and 26. The first two examples, annuals and newspapers, offer a comparative and critical method based on secondary sources, while the third, a trade monthly, compares the results of a quantitative method based on what used to be called measurement by "column inches" with the audited accounts of the periodical. In all cases my central point recurs: that only in fantasy can economics be reduced to numbers that capture reality; quantitative methods must be combined with qualitative, relational approaches to produce valid research results.

My first example (Table 4.1) is derived from the article by S.C. Hall mentioned earlier in this chapter. It provides an analysis of the estimated sale of 150,000 annuals in 1829, which retailed for £90,000 in total. When the *Bookseller* quoted these figures twenty years later in "Annuals of Former Days,"[31] it offered slightly different figures—a warning to the researcher of how easy it is to miscopy. But in any case, Hall's breakdown was obviously rough and ready: for example, distribution costs (which the *Manual* urged publishers to record) are not mentioned. What is consistent between the two accounts, however, is the list of sources and destinations of financial flow, along with the rough proportions of flow between them. To that extent, the breakdown remains helpful. At the same time, we must acknowledge that it is also only applicable to specific types of expensive periodicals, for few other kinds would require binding in leather and silk. By jettisoning the expensive binding alone, the costs would be reduced by almost a quarter.

My second sample operated according to a very different model. An 1847 article in the *Metropolitan Magazine* by "J.P." offers a detailed breakdown of an imaginary newspaper. Once again, the items and proportional costs in the breakdown are confirmed in general terms by another source, in this case Frederick Knight Hunt's *The Fourth Estate* (1850), though the costs themselves are not identical (for example, J.P. records that an editor is paid £3 8s. less than the figure Hunt provides).[32] Both breakdowns are too detailed to be reproduced here in full, and if scholars choose to conduct in-depth economic analysis of newspapers, they should peruse both articles carefully. Table 4.2 below instead provides a simplified summary of J.P.'s figures. As in Figure 4.1, I have added percentages of production costs (rounded up or down to the nearest whole figure) to enable quick comparison between the tables here and with other cost breakdowns the researcher might find.

Placing Hall's and J.P.'s production costs side by side (Tables 4.1 and 4.2, and Figures 4.1. and 4.2) reveals how the cost of generating content for newspapers was much higher than for annuals (amounting to 62 percent and 18 percent of their total expenses, respectively). Annuals, by contrast, devoted much more of their costs to ensuring their status as aesthetic objects. Less obvious from the tables, since they both record annual figures, is how newspaper finance

---

31. "Annuals of Former Days," 493.
32. Hunt, *Fourth Estate*, 2:196–204.

Table 4.1 Debits and credits of annuals in 1829 (Hall, "Annuals," 172). I have added the percentages.

Debits		
Authors and editors	£6,000	12%
Painters [for pictures and copyrights]	£3,000	6%
Engravers	£12,000	24%
Copper-plate printers	£4,000	8%
Printers	£3,500	7%
Paper makers	£5,500	11%
Binders	£9,000	18%
Silk manufacturers and leather sellers	£4,000	8%
For advertising, &c.	£2,000	4%
Incidental matters	£1,000	2%
[Total production costs]	£50,000	

Credits	
Publishers' profits	£10,000
Retail booksellers' profits	£30,000
[Total income from retail sales]	£90,000

Table 4.2 Debits and credits of a newspaper in the late 1840s (derived from J.P., "Daily Press"). I have added the percentages.

Debits			
Fixed overheads (premises, incl. heating, light, pens, etc.)		£1,000	1.5%
Editorial department		£2,614 10s.	4%
Editor at £15 10s. per week	£819		
Three sub-editors at £10 10s. per week	£1,795 10s.		
Reporters		£9,978	15.4%
Thirty-three reporters at £5 10s. or £2 2s. per week plus expenses	£7,898		
Penny-a-liners at £40 a week	£2,080		
Additional contributors (city article, market intelligence, sporting, etc.)		£1,040	1.6%
Foreign correspondents, overseas mail, etc.		£10,200	15.7%
Counting house (including publisher, advertising clerk, porter, and boy)		£569 8s.	0.9%
Printing (wages of printer, reader, compositor, paper, etc.)		£7,800	12%
Machinery (wages to feeders, takers-off, boys)		£780	1.2%
Petty expenses (e.g., fees to court ushers, cabs, parcels, "Christmas boxes")		£1,040	1.6%
[Total production costs]		£35,021 18s.	
Additional costs			
1d. per sheet cost of paper, 1d. stamp tax, 1d. to newsagent, allowing for sales of 7,500 x 314 days (6 days a week) per year		£29,435 10s.	45.5%
DEBITS TOTAL		£64,657 4s.	

Credits	
Circulation (sales of 7,500 at 5d. x 314)	£47,100
Advertising (£50 per day x 314)	£15,700
CREDITS TOTAL	£64,762

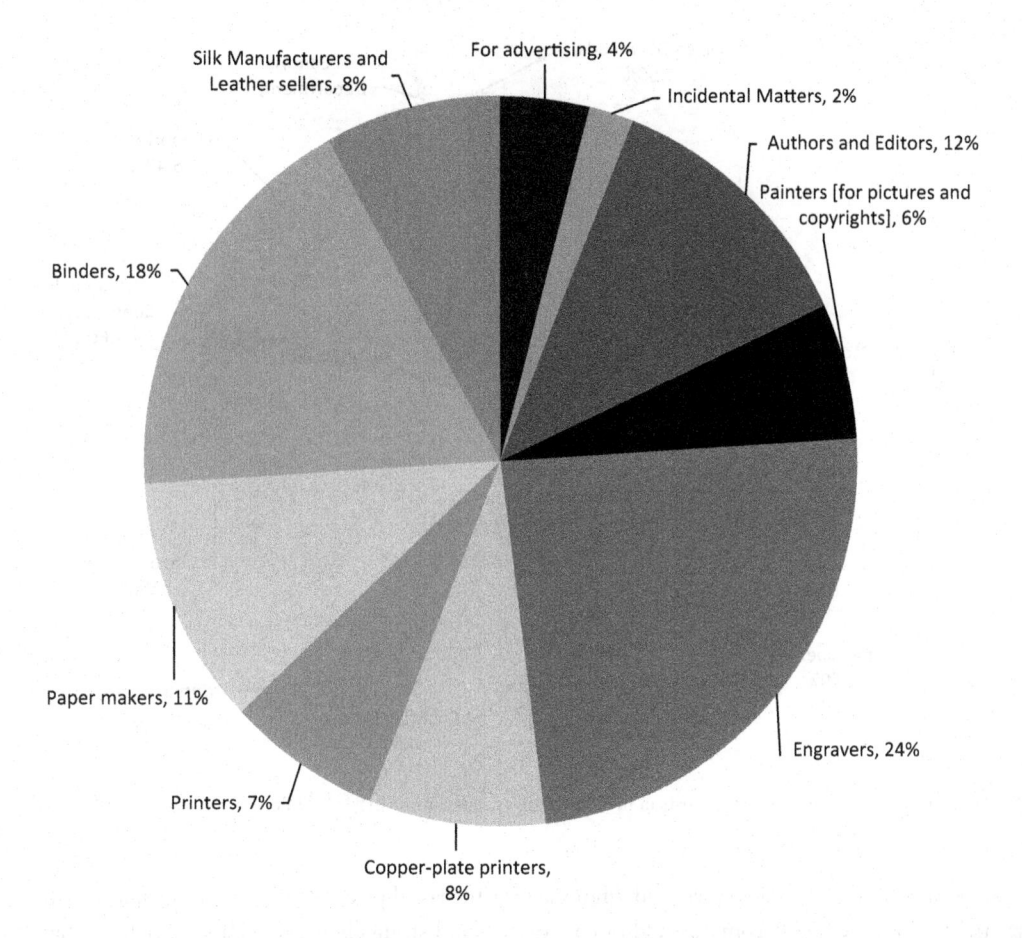

Figure 4.1 Production costs of annuals in the 1820s (derived from S.C. Hall, "Annuals").

Pie chart segments: Silk Manufacturers and Leather sellers, 8%; For advertising, 4%; Incidental Matters, 2%; Authors and Editors, 12%; Painters [for pictures and copyrights], 6%; Engravers, 24%; Copper-plate printers, 8%; Printers, 7%; Paper makers, 11%; Binders, 18%.

was based on cash flow and rapid turnover week by week and month by month, and not, as with annuals, on yearly one-off capital investments. When regarded from the point of view of production costs (let alone their social functions), it is hard to think of these two examples as belonging to the same industry; while today we class annuals as periodicals, in economic terms they were more similar to books.

Even if accounting statements such as the example above might appear to offer the sort of financial transparency advocated by the *Manual of Book-Keeping*, the figures they provide need to be checked both logically and factually. The tables not only conceal differences in the cash-flow models of annuals and newspapers but also provide incorrect data. For example, J.P.'s suggestion that the breakeven point for the newspaper would be achieved by selling 7,200 issues a week is incorrect. Re-calculation of his figures suggests that only a circulation of 7,500 would generate a (very small annual) profit; 7,200 would result in a financial loss. His figures are misleading in other ways, too. For instance, his mark-up of a penny per issue is excessive;

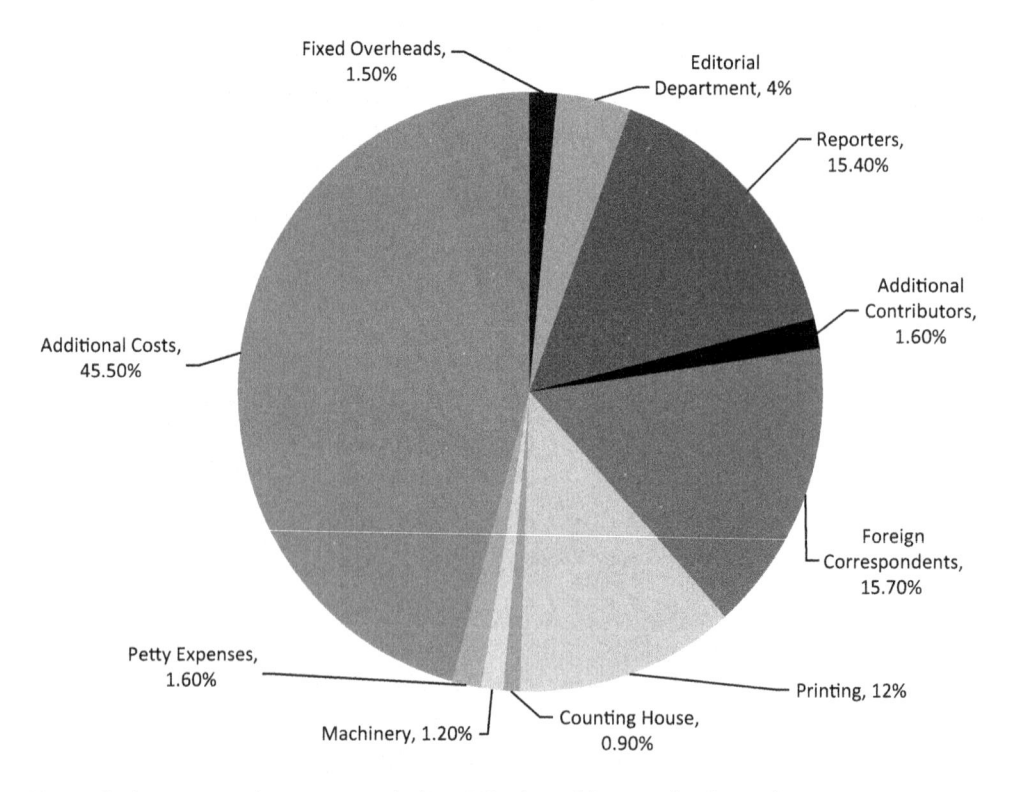

Figure 4.2 Newspaper production costs in the late 1840s (derived from J.P., "Daily Press").

in reality, thirteen copies were sold wholesale for the retail price of eight.[33] This instantly subtracts almost £3,774 from his "additional costs"—and strangely enough allows for his breakeven point of 7,200 issues. Furthermore, J.P.'s figures include two separate charges for paper (under "printing" and "additional costs"), so a further £9,812 might be subtracted from the total debits, bringing the total down to around £50,000 and a breakeven circulation of just over 5,000. Even with this adjustment, J.P.'s overall annual production costs are twice as high as those for the cheapest respectable daily proposed by Hunt three years later. This is not to suggest that his breakdown schema should be dismissed entirely but that we must be cautious in taking figures at face value, for figures always operate in a specific rhetorical context. J.P.'s point was to demonstrate how far price-cutting could go while remaining sustainable, and he manipulated his figures to prove his point. Nonetheless, we can learn from his article that in a competitive newspaper market it was essential to control costs and at the same time to offer a particular "character" or niche, whether political (like the Whig *Morning Chronicle*) or in terms of news values (like *The Times*'s stress on speed, accuracy, and tradition). Where two or more periodicals came to occupy the same niche, a price war could erupt which might end in the

33. King, *London Journal*, 91. Counting thirteen as twelve—the "baker's dozen"—was standard in Victorian accounting procedures.

cessation of one of more of the rivals. To avoid this risk, newspaper prices were standardized in their various segments, often for long periods, until some new force was applied to the market, such as the lowered price of paper and compositing later in the century.

By the mid-1860s, state market control (the "taxes on knowledge") had largely been eliminated, but the costs of news gathering technology had been increasing for some time. (They are significantly omitted as a separate item from Table 4.2, combined no doubt with "foreign correspondents, overseas mails, etc.") The *Morning Advertiser*, for example, was paying about £500 a year in telegraph costs in the 1850s.[34] The costs were so high that by the end of 1858 the main London dailies outsourced much of their overseas news gathering to Reuters for £30 a month.[35] From the 1870s, further cuts could be made to content costs by running serial fiction from Tillotson's Fiction Syndicate, an option many provincial newspapers chose to pursue. In this light, too, it is easy to see why the *Illustrated London News*, with its expensive woodcuts, chose to include fiction beginning with its thirty-fifth number: fiction was simply cheaper content than news.[36]

My final example is very different from the previous two since it compares and contrasts conclusions possible from content analysis of a periodical with the surviving audited accounts (see Table 4.3 and Figure 4.3). The *Brewing Trade Review* (1886–1972) was the monthly organ of the Country Brewers Society: members received a copy as part of their subscription. The *Review* was founded because the periodical hitherto associated with the society had failed to follow the party line at a time of increased taxation and regulation of beer and spirits, which the society was opposed to.[37] The indirect economic and political role of the *Review* must have been considerable since it claimed that members of the society collectively contributed no less than 10 percent of the nation's tax revenue.[38]

Perusal of the periodical itself suggests that its income depended on advertisements and subscriptions (the *Review* listed around 580 subscribers who each paid £1 a year in the late 1880s). Given that spatial quantitative content analysis is useful for periodicals which include content that can be economically differentiated (at its most basic, content versus advertisements), it might give us some idea of income and costs. I have accordingly taken measurements of all the columns from two complete years, 1887 and 1891, so as to generate averages (the actual numbers vary about 5 percent from issue to issue).

Of the sixty-four pages of the *Brewing Trade Review*, thirty comprised adverts, not including the four additional cover pages which also included advertising. The rest of the periodical can be divided into what I shall call "assembled" content (user-generated material or filler culled from

---

34. Grant, *Newspaper Press*, 2:324.
35. See Storey, *Reuters' Century*, 20–31.
36. See Law, *Illustrated London News* for a bibliography of the fiction.
37. The surviving records of the Country Brewers' Society can be found at the Modern Records Centre, University of Warwick. On dealings with the *Country Brewers' Gazette*, see MS 420/CB/1/1/5 (minute book no. 4). There are no folio or page numbers in this ledger, but Finance and General Committee meeting minutes trace the gradual breakdown of this relationship (e.g., September 24, 1884; December 22, 1885; and October 3, 1886). A special sub-committee was set up to deal with the *Gazette* which met December 3, 1885, and July 16, 1886.
38. See, for example, "Country Brewers Society."

Table 4.3 Costs of advertising in the Brewing Trade Review, 1887, 1891

	12 months	6 months	3 months	One insertion
Full page	£36	£20	£11	£4
Half page	£20	£12	£6/10/-	£2/5/-
Quarter page	12	6/15/-	3/10/-	1/5/-
Eighth page	6/15/-	3/10	2	15s.

Small prepaid: Wants, new books, etc., 3/6 under 8 lines per column; over 8 lines 6d. extra
Other display column advertisements, 3/6 per inch

other sources) and "composed" content (original material created for the magazine), representing just over 20 percent and 30 percent of the magazine, respectively. Amongst the fourteen pages of assembled content, we find reports of meetings from constituent brewing associations, standard information about the periodical, biographies and obituaries of prominent members, law reports, relevant market prices, answers to correspondents, and filler. The remaining twenty pages of composed content, focused primarily on legal matters and practical brewing methods, seem to have been written by the manager J. Danvers Power and the editor Dr. E.R. Moritz.

Since the *Brewing Trade Review* regularly published its advertising rates, it is possible to make a rough calculation of its advertising income. As was typical, there were differentiated rates depending on the size and iteration of the given advertisement. Most of the advertising space was taken up by full-page adverts at the twelve-month, full-page rate. Other advertisers ran half-, three-quarter-, and eighth-page adverts for six months, perhaps following the advice of agents of the time, who told their clients that repetition was the best method of persuasion.[39] This was also a happy arrangement for the periodical as it could rely on a certain income for the year. In 1887, an average of twenty full-page ads were repeated throughout the year, amounting to £720 in annual advertising income; by 1891, full-page adverts occupied twenty-three out of thirty-five advertising pages (£828). The remaining fractional adverts generated around £318 in both sample years. The even smaller "prepaid" adverts collectively generated six guineas a month (£75 a year). Combining the income from advertising space and subscription gives a total income of around £1,693 in 1887 and £1,801 in 1891. We can see from this how trade journals such as the *Brewing Trade Review* followed a very different economic model from annuals and newspapers. While they were unlikely to yield enormous returns, they faced low risk on investment once they secured a combined subscription and advertising base.

The audited annual balance sheets, the first of which is given as Figure 4.3, suggest a much more complex picture of the *Review*'s economics. I cannot comment on every aspect here but shall instead point out the most salient aspects. First of all, the *Review* was published by a public limited company, the Brewing Trade Review Limited, which was separate from the Country Brewers Society. The company had been set up with the issue of 1,000 shares that only members of the society could buy. When it was floated on October 29, 1886, there were fifty-two shareholders with between two and fifty shares each. In the mid-1890s there was

---

39. See King, "Killing Time," 158–9.

Figure 4.3 Brewing Trade Review Limited, balance sheet for the year ending October, 1887.

a major concentration of ownership with just five directors buying up almost all the shares between them (though even when the records of share ownership end in 1934 there were still a few individuals with just one share). The changing ownership structure is not only relevant to the intended ideological purpose of the periodical but also to its function as an investment: by 1889 it was regularly giving 10 percent returns per annum.[40]

For the first year, neither the manager (who organized the advertisements) nor the editor was paid, though the company secretary and the bookkeeper were given £25 and £85, respectively.[41] From the second year the manager and editor were paid £150 each, but that soon changed to a system whereby they received half the remaining profit after the dividends plus £50. The Country Brewers Society subvented the *Review* initially with a flat £50 per annum and a room to be used for editorial purposes on the society's premises at 3 Westminster Chambers, London. The subvention was soon raised to £150. In 1889, a different system was instituted whereby the *Review* was paid 7 shillings per member of the society per annum. In 1889 there were 580 members, which meant a subvention of £198.[42] None of this could have

---

40. See the share stubs (Modern Records Centre, University of Warwick, MSS.420/RP/2/2) and the minutes of the directors' meeting, October 3, 1886, and Managers Report, October 1889 in MSS 420/RP/2/1. 420/RP/2/1 is the key document for the economics of the *Brewing Trade Review*, comprising a large ledger containing the minutes of all the Annual General Meetings and reports of the Brewing Trade Review Company, 1886–1964 (from 1900 the company was known as the Review Press Limited). The pages are unnumbered throughout.
41. Ordinary General Meeting Minutes, October 25, 1886, MSS 420/RP/2/1. The "editorial expenses" in Figure 4.3 must refer to commissioned work.
42. Finance Committee Meeting, February 6, 1889, MS 420/CB/1/1/5.

been guessed from a reading of the *Review* alone, where it appears that the entire subscription went to funding the periodical.

Adding together the figures in Figure 4.3 for advertising under "Receipts" and "Assets" (that is, what advertisers still owed the *Review*) the result is £1,200 (and almost £1,300 if discounts and "bad debts" are also added). This amount overshoots by less than 7 percent the content analysis estimate of £1,113, a figure acceptable for a rough calculation. Greater caution over claims to the reliability of content analysis is suggested, however, by how the estimate of advertising income for 1891 (£1,221) is over £200 less than the figure of almost £1,485 given in the Manager's Report for 1891.[43] We can conclude, therefore, that quantitative analysis of column inches may allow us to make guesses about the economics of a periodical, but we must not treat them as anywhere close to reality.

Yet the balance sheets and reports are themselves not entirely transparent either. In this case, they need to be read with the discursive accounts of the minutes of the County Brewers Society. From those we learn that the paper made a loss in its first year and only when Danvers Powers took over as manager in the second did it start to make a profit. We also learn that the *Review* was only one arm in what today would be called a communications strategy by the society, aimed at lowering taxation and reducing regulation of the industry. The *Review* may have been, as repeatedly described in the minutes of the annual general meetings of the Society, "of much assistance to the society as containing a permanent printed record of all matters relating to Brewers, and as a monthly medium of communication between the executive and members of the society," but its pages do not record, as the minutes do, how the society also placed letters in the local and national press, courted journalists and members of Parliament, subscribed to what the minutes call "Kindred Societies" (including the Individualist, laissez-faire Liberty and Property Defence League), and, not least, assiduously lobbied government ministers. The debits and credits of a periodical, like its pages, only tell part of the story about the kinds of economic relationships that it is designed to promote.

There is certainly a good deal about the sources of income and the production and distribution costs of periodicals and newspapers I have had to omit here, from the prices of different inks and paper or the different wages of country and London printers[44] to the standard mode of binding weekly issues into monthly parts and then into six-monthly or annual volumes, each with a greater mark-up than the previous. My intention has been less to cover all the ground than to alert researchers to possible questions raised by the topic and to sketch some of the methods by which these questions can be answered. I have tried to show how numbers on their own are unstable, misleading, and open to sins of omission and commission. In a study of periodical economics, we need to attend not only to questions of quantitative accuracy but, crucially, also to the human relationships that numbers represent. While hardly supporting a return to the determining substructural role attributed to economics by classical Marxism, the several methods of economic analysis I have been exploring here offer great potential for further critical understanding of nineteenth-century periodicals and newspapers.

43. Ordinary General Meeting Minutes, October 26, 1891, MSS 420/RP/2/1.
44. On the different "'stab" (established) wages of printers, see Crisp, *Printers*, 30.

Section II

CONTRIBUTORS AND CONTRIBUTIONS

5

WRITING FOR PERIODICALS

Linda H. Peterson

When the major reviews and magazines of the nineteenth century were founded—the *Edinburgh Review* in 1802, the *Quarterly Review* in 1809, *Blackwood's Edinburgh Magazine* in 1817, the *New Monthly Magazine* in 1821, the *Westminster Review* in 1824, and *Fraser's Magazine* in 1830, to name the earliest and most prominent—these new publications offered substantial payments to writers and thereby made it possible to pursue authorship as a professional career. While reviews had existed in the eighteenth century, they had attempted the impossible (full coverage of all new books) and paid little (or nothing). The *Edinburgh Review* changed the literary scene by selecting only books it deemed important, allowing reviewers to treat books as launching points for their own ideas, and remunerating contributors well (at least ten guineas per sheet, typically £25–£40 per article). Other periodicals followed suit, even if they paid at slightly lower rates. As a result, according to Lee Erickson, "Young men seeking their fortune in London and Edinburgh soon could afford to become professional journalists and could make enough money to live as gentlemen."[1]

Many early contributors to the reviews were gentlemen by birth who practiced other professions and did not really need payment to support themselves—for example, Francis Jeffrey (1773–1850), the *Edinburgh*'s first editor, who trained as a lawyer; Henry (later Lord) Brougham (1778–1868), who practiced law and held political office; and Sydney Smith (1771–1845), who served as a clergyman. These men turned to periodicals more to promulgate their political and philosophical views than to launch their careers as authors, and they aligned themselves with periodicals that shared their politics (Whig for the *Edinburgh*, Tory for the *Quarterly* and *Blackwood's*, and Radical for the *Westminster*). With regular payment for contributions, however, many talented, university-trained men found that they could support themselves solely by the pen and thus consider themselves authors by profession. Early in the century, Robert Southey (1774–1843), poet laureate from 1813 to 1843, wrote regularly for periodicals because he needed the income to support his family; typically, he received £100 for an essay published in the *Quarterly Review* and thereby added £600–£700 per year to his income.[2] Thomas Carlyle (1795–1881), educated at the University of Edinburgh, became a

---

1. Erickson, *Economy*, 72.
2. Ibid., 84.

tutor after receiving his degree and in his spare time published on German literature, including a translation of Wolfgang von Goethe's *Wilhelm Meister's Apprenticeship* (1824) and an original biography, *The Life of Schiller* (1825). Yet because these books yielded little profit, Carlyle turned to periodical writing, placing important essays in the *Edinburgh Review*, the *Foreign Quarterly Review*, and *Fraser's Magazine*. Later in the century, George Henry Lewes (1817–78) started his literary career by contributing to the *Westminster Review*; later wrote for the *British and Foreign Review*, the *Foreign Quarterly Review*, and *Fraser's Magazine*; and eventually assumed the editorship of the *Leader*. Although all three authors published books, a substantial portion of their income was derived from periodical writing.

About this professional arrangement, some authors were ambivalent—Carlyle the most so, Lewes the least. When Carlyle moved to London to pursue a literary career, he was initially pleased that "two or three magazine men [were] chirping to me with open arms," and he admitted his pleasure in placing his work in the *Edinburgh*: "There is no periodical so steady as the *Edinburgh Review*, the salary fair, the vehicle respectable."[3] Yet he also complained that "*Fraser's Magazine* gives the most scurvy remuneration of any Periodical extant" and vowed "it should have no more stuff of mine."[4] *Fraser's* did, in fact, get more "stuff" from Carlyle because it published several additional essays and then, in 1833–34, ran his masterpiece, *Sartor Resartus*, in eight installments when no book publisher would buy his manuscript for adequate remuneration. Carlyle's larger complaint about periodicals was that they often were not the best medium for expressing an author's ideas: "One *has* no good vehicle," he told his brother, "you must throw your ware into one of those dog's-meat carts, such as travel the public streets, and get it sold there, be it carrion or not."[5]

In contrast, G.H. Lewes celebrated the rise of periodicals as the catalyst for transforming authorship into a middle-class profession. In an important article published in *Fraser's* in 1847, Lewes declares, "Literature has become a profession. It is a means of subsistence almost as certain as the bar or the church."[6] Lewes cites £300 per year as a baseline for a professional literary income (suggesting a range from "1,000 down to two hundred a-year").[7] Much of his essay details the relative payments to English and European writers for different kinds of work—for example, twenty guineas (£22) per sheet in English periodicals versus 250 francs (£10) in French, £200 for an average novel in England versus one-tenth that fee (£20) for a novel in Germany. In his analysis of national differences, Lewes attributes the success of the professional author in England to the proliferation of periodicals: "The real cause we take to be the excellence and abundance of periodical literature. It is by our reviews, magazines, and journals, that the vast majority of professional authors earn their bread; and the astonishing mass of talent and energy which is thus thrown into periodical literature is not only quite unexampled abroad, but is, of course, owing to the certainty of moderate yet, on the

---

3. Thomas Carlyle to Jean Carlyle, December 25, 1831, and to John A. Carlyle, January 21, 1831, *Carlyle Letters Online*.
4. Thomas Carlyle to John A. Carlyle, January 21, 1831, *Carlyle Letters Online*.
5. Thomas Carlyle to John A. Carlyle, January 10, 1832, *Carlyle Letters Online*.
6. [Lewes], "Condition," 285.
7. Ibid., 286.

whole, sufficient income."[8] For Lewes, periodical writing brought in more income than book writing—hence, his more positive view.

Throughout the nineteenth century, authors debated the pros and cons of periodical versus book publication. Better ready money for periodical writing was not the only factor to consider. With books, authors had the possibility of maintaining copyright of their intellectual property—an asset, if the book was successful, that might yield significant income over a lifetime. Another factor, as Carlyle pointed out, was intellectual: books allowed an author to sustain inquiry of a subject over two hundred, three hundred, or more pages, in contrast to the typical twenty to forty pages of a magazine article. In cultural terms, moreover, books had greater prestige and possessed an aura of permanence that periodicals lacked. Indeed, even within periodicals, frequency of publication influenced status: the hierarchy went from quarterly reviews at the top, to monthly magazines, and then to weeklies.[9] Finally, whether rightly or wrongly, throughout the century books were considered "literature," connoting genius and erudition, whereas periodicals were deemed "journalism"—that is, presenting the "business of the day" or "saying a thing of the hour in the manner in which a clique of the hour wishes to have it said."[10] Despite the fact that Carlyle published a significant number of periodical essays, he believed that writing for the reviews reflected the unfortunate self-consciousness of the age. In "Characteristics," published in the *Edinburgh Review* in 1831, he proclaimed, "Nay, is not the diseased self-conscious state of Literature disclosed in this one fact, which lies so near us here, the prevalence of Reviewing! . . . By and by it will be found that all Literature has become one boundless self-devouring Review; . . . Thus does Literature also, like a sick thing, superabundantly 'listen to itself.'"[11]

Not all authors cared about producing Literature (with a capital L). Some, including many women, preferred periodical writing because it gave them a venue for addressing the "business of the day," whether the topic was cultural, educational, political, or economic. Harriet Martineau (1802–76), for example, submitted articles anonymously to the *Monthly Repository*, a Unitarian periodical, because she wished to address pressing issues of women's education and achievement. Her first publication, "Female Writers on Practical Divinity" (1822), not only discussed prominent women writers of the past century but also analyzed the possibilities for women in the contemporary literary marketplace. Her next submission, "Female Education," explored the values and uses of women's education. For Martineau, making money or earning status was not the primary reason for publishing these articles; indeed, she received nothing beyond the pleasure of expressing her ideas and seeing them in print. As she later explained in her *Autobiography* (1877), "My business in life has been to think and learn, and to speak out with absolute freedom what I have thought and learned. The freedom is itself a positive and never-failing enjoyment to me, after the bondage of my early life."[12]

---

8. Ibid., 288.
9. See Brake below, p. 238
10. [Oakley], "On Commencing Author," 90.
11. Carlyle, "Characteristics," 369.
12. Martineau, *Autobiography*, 1:101–2.

Martineau's career provides a good example of how a woman writer might use periodical writing to promulgate her views, create a voice in the public sphere, and eventually earn a substantial income from her efforts. Martineau followed a common pattern, beginning with anonymous publication in the *Monthly Repository*; establishing a continuing relationship with that periodical, including professional advice from its editor; and developing a similar relationship with a book publisher, on whom she could count to place her longer manuscripts. As Alexis Easley explains, "Periodical journalism [was] attractive to women authors [because of] the policy of anonymous publication associated with most journals, magazines, and reviews until the 1860s. Anonymous publication provided women with effective cover for exploring a variety of conventionally 'masculine' social issues. It also allowed them to evade essentialized notions of 'feminine' voice and identity."[13] Martineau had less desire to evade publicity about her identity than many women, but anonymity allowed her to prove her worth without gender bias.

Other women writers of Martineau's generation used periodicals to launch their careers, supplement their income, and speak out on important public issues. Mary Howitt (1799–1888) began by publishing poetry with her sister in a Staffordshire weekly, the *Kaleidoscope*, and collaborating with her husband William on travel writing for another regional paper, the *Mercury*. Although she and William published many books, they relied on periodicals—including *Chambers's Edinburgh Magazine* and Dickens's *Household Words*—for public expression of their progressive views and for a steady source of income. With the desire of spreading education and political reform to the working and middle classes, in the mid-1840s the Howitts initiated their own magazine, *Howitt's Journal*, to which Mary contributed articles on education issues, reform movements, women's concerns, literary authors, and artists. As Brian Maidment notes, "This periodical, wrought out of evident support for the intellectual and cultural development of the working classes, combined William's political enthusiasm with Mary's concern for the social inclusion of women and children."[14]

In the next generation, Marian Evans (1818–80), later known as George Eliot, moved to London to pursue a literary career and work with John Chapman as editor of the radical *Westminster Review*. While editing the *Westminster* during the 1850s, Evans published her own essays in the journal, most famously "The Natural History of German Life" (1856), in which she argues for realistically representing the "people as they are," and "Silly Novels by Lady Novelists" (1856), in which she calls for higher standards in women's fiction and admonishes "women of mediocre faculties . . . to abstain from writing."[15] Writing book reviews allowed her to champion philosophical views she endorsed, such as R. W. Mackay's theory of progressive revelation in *The Progress of the Intellect*, which argued that divine revelation is "co-extensive with the history of human development, and is perpetually unfolding itself to our widened experience and investigation."[16] Only when she entered into a common-law marriage with G.H. Lewes did

---

13. Easley, *First Person Anonymous*, 1.
14. Maidment, "Works in Unbroken Succession," 23.
15. Eliot, *Selected Essays*, 110, 162.
16. Quoted in Ashton, *George Eliot*, 75.

Evans begin, with his encouragement, to write fiction and turn to book publication—though her fiction, including *Scenes of Clerical Life* (1857) and *Romola* (1862), often appeared serially in periodicals before publication in book form.[17]

When Marian Evans launched her career as a novelist in 1857, she published "Scenes of Clerical Life" anonymously in *Blackwood's Magazine* and then used a pseudonym, George Eliot, for the book version. She would continue to publish under this signature in books and periodicals. By the mid-1860s "signature"—that is, signing one's name to reviews and articles—became an innovative practice (though never a universal norm) and offered an opportunity to build a literary reputation by means of one's name. The *Fortnightly Review* introduced the practice to combat the abuses of anonymous reviewing and, in the words of its prospectus, "to remove all those restrictions of party and of editorial 'consistency' which in other journals hamper the full and free expression of opinion."[18] In its first number, the *Fortnightly* enacted this new practice by publishing a signed excerpt from *The English Constitution* by Walter Bagehot; an article, "The Influence of Rationalism," by George Eliot; "Personal Recollections of Abraham Lincoln," by M.D. Conway; "On Atoms," by John Herschel; and the opening chapters of Anthony Trollope's new novel, *Belton Castle*. As this partial list reveals, signature had effects other than boosting the writer's individual reputation; it allowed the periodical to advertise its high quality by publishing the names of distinguished contributors.

By the end of the nineteenth century, writing for periodicals and signing one's work had become a standard feature of professional authorship. Signature enabled authors to accrue fame by means of their periodical columns, articles, reviews, and tales; in turn, it allowed periodicals to attract readers who admired these authors. In *The Pen and the Book* (1899), Walter Besant, founder of the Society of Authors, describes the "kind of life led daily by the modern man of letters" and shows this man—"or this woman, for many women now belong to the profession"—going "into his study every morning as regularly as a barrister goes to chambers."[19] Like a barrister with a variety of briefs, the professional author takes up a variety of literary tasks: "Two or three books waiting for review: a MS. sent him for an opinion: a book of his own to go on with—possibly a life of some dead and gone worthy for a series: an article which he has promised for a magazine: a paper for the Dictionary of National Biography: perhaps an unfinished novel to which he must give three hours of absorbed attention."[20] Besant's description includes at least two tasks that involve periodicals—reviewing and article writing—and it is likely that the "unfinished novel" would appear first in serialized form in a magazine. The professional man or woman of letters would invariably write for periodicals.

Contributing Fiction

The nineteenth-century reviews—the *Edinburgh*, *Quarterly*, *Foreign Quarterly*, *Westminster*, and others—were periodicals that, as their titles indicate, focused on reviewing and evaluating

---

17. Ashton, *George Eliot*, 172–87.
18. Quoted in Nash, "What's in a Name," 57.
19. Besant, *Pen and Book*, 24.
20. Ibid., 24–5.

books. In distinction, the magazines—*Blackwood's Edinburgh Magazine*, *Fraser's Magazine*, the *Monthly Magazine*, and, after mid-century, a host of others, including Dickens's *Household Words* and *All the Year Round*, as well as the *Cornhill*, *Macmillan's*, *Belgravia*, and *Temple Bar*—made fiction and narrative non-fiction an essential component of their offerings. This distinction emerges in the editorial prospectus for *Blackwood's*, which refers to itself as a "Repository of whatever may be supposed to be most interesting to general readers,"[21] and in its table of contents, which lists "Tales and Anecdotes of Pastoral Life" along with original poetry, antiquarian anecdotes, analytical notices, and reviews of new publications. Indeed, the term "magazine," which originally referred to a "storehouse for goods or merchandise," eventually came to mean figuratively a "store or repertoire" of resources within a periodical.[22]

The proliferation of magazines provided aspiring and established fiction writers with new outlets for their work. When Charles Dickens (1812–70) turned from parliamentary reporting to literary writing, he submitted "sketches" to the *Monthly Magazine*, a periodical that published his work but paid him "nothing for his contribution, as was the practice with amateurs."[23] Once Dickens landed a regular position as a reporter for the *Morning Chronicle* and proved his worth, he negotiated extra payment for his "Street Sketches," a series in the *Morning Chronicle* launched in 1834 that combined his vast knowledge of London with his ability to imaginatively enter the lives of characters he observed. These sketches, like the "Sketches of London" he initiated for the *Evening Chronicle* in 1835, were an amalgam of the essay and the tale, a combination of acute observation of London life (omnibuses and coaches, the Old Bailey and Greenwich Fair) and sympathetic engagement with the lives of London's inhabitants. Signed "Boz," they allowed him, in Kathryn Chittick's words, to "remove the sketch-writer from the ranks of anonymity" and give "his way of writing a trademark."[24]

Of all Victorian novelists, Dickens was the most astute in using innovative publishing formats to distribute his work, enrich his income, and advance his reputation. Book historian Simon Eliot observes that Dickens adapted the working-class form of the monthly part when issuing his early novels: *The Pickwick Papers* (1836–37), *Nicholas Nickleby* (1838–39), *The Old Curiosity Shop* (1840–41), *Martin Chuzzlewit* (1843–44), and *Dombey and Son* (1846–48); doing so allowed readers to buy fiction in affordable segments rather than as costly hard-cover books.[25] Dickens also serialized his novel *Oliver Twist* (1837–39) in a shilling monthly, *Bentley's Miscellany*, and later featured *Hard Times* (1854) in the two-penny weekly magazine he edited, *Household Words*. He would again showcase one of his own novels, *Great Expectations* (1860–61), in *All the Year Round*, another periodical he edited.

Although not all novelists enjoyed the same level of success that Dickens achieved, they learned important lessons from his techniques: how to use periodicals to advance their careers, earn extra income, and establish enduring relationships with publishers. Margaret Oliphant

---

21. "Prospectus," n.p.
22. *Oxford English Dictionary* online, s.v. "magazine," 1, 5, 6b.
23. Chittick, *Dickens and the 1830s*, 44.
24. Ibid., 57.
25. Eliot, "Business of Victorian Publishing," 44.

(1828–97), for instance, began publishing fiction in a mode common at mid-century: she sent full manuscripts of her novels to firms known for their popular novels (Colburn, Blackwood, Hurst and Blackett), accepted a lump-sum payment for copyright, and saw her work issued in book form. Yet she, too, began publishing her work serially. As early as the 1820s, one of her publishers, John Blackwood, introduced the practice of serializing novels and then issuing them in book form.[26] He used this dual-publication approach with Oliphant's Scottish historical novel *Katie Stewart*, which ran from July to November 1852 in *Blackwood's Magazine* and then appeared as a book in 1853. Although Oliphant continued to sell novels to Blackwood, she more frequently contributed reviews, essays, and travel articles to "Maga," as it was called, in the 1850s, becoming its chief (anonymous) reviewer and "general utility woman" until her death in 1897.[27] Only at a moment of family and financial crisis in 1861 did she dash off a short story, "The Rector," specifically for the magazine. It appeared in September 1861, followed by a longer story, "The Doctor's Family," which ran from October 1861 through January 1862; then *Blackwood's* ran three more novels in the "Chronicles of Carlingford" series, as they came to be called. All appeared subsequently in book form. Such dual publication resulted in dual payment—first for magazine publication, then for the copyright of the book.

It is difficult to generalize about the income that periodical fiction generated for writers. We know that George Eliot received £52 10s. (roughly twenty guineas per sheet) for "Amos Barton," the first story in "Scenes of Clerical Life" to appear in *Blackwood's Magazine*; two other "Scenes," "Mr. Gilfil's Love Story" and "Janet's Repentance," were paid at a similar rate for a total of £263 for the eleven installments.[28] When Blackwood proposed issuing the stories in book form, he first offered £120, eventually agreeing to £180.[29] In 1857, Eliot sorely needed the combined £450 for magazine and book publication, as she and Lewes were not only supporting themselves but also his sons and often Agnes Lewes, his estranged wife. These earnings were nothing like the offer that the publisher George Smith made for serializing Eliot's *Romola* (1862–63) in the *Cornhill Magazine*—a stupendous £583 6s. 8d. for each of the twelve parts, with a total of £7,000 for dual publication in magazine and book form. In comparison, Oliphant (who, as a widow, also needed funds to support her children) was paid standard rates for her novel, *The Athelings*, which was serialized in *Blackwood's* in some of the same numbers as Eliot's *Scenes*. When Oliphant hit her stride in the Carlingford series during the early 1860s, she found it remarkable that Blackwood offered £1,500 for the copyright of *The Perpetual Curate* (1864). A decade later, the *Graphic* would offer her £1,300 for a six-part serialization of an as-yet-unwritten story, "The Innocents."[30]

The payments made to Eliot and Oliphant, both popular novelists, surpassed those received by ordinary writers of periodical fiction. In *The English Common Writer*, Nigel Cross notes the mere 1s. per page paid in 1825 to George Barrow for hackwork on *Celebrated Trials* and

---

26. Finkelstein, *House of Blackwood*, 9.
27. Oliphant used this phrase to describe herself in *Annals of a Publishing House*, 2:475.
28. Haight, *George Eliot*, 246.
29. Ashton, *George Eliot*, 186–7.
30. Oliphant, *Autobiography*, 66, 94.

only half that amount to Hannah Maria Jones for popular fiction issued in penny and sixpenny parts. In contrast, Chapman and Hall offered Dickens nine guineas a sheet (12s. per page) to write *The Pickwick Papers* in 1836.[31] Cross adds the example of Julia Pardoe, famous in her day for the *Romance of the Harem*, who was paid £50 for a novel in the 1850s by Hurst and Blackett, the publisher who took Margaret Oliphant's second-tier work for often ten times as much.[32] Popular novelists who worked the dual-publication system were more likely to garner a livable income—as did Harriette Maria Smythies in the 1850s when she wrote serial fiction for *Cassell's Family Magazine*, the *London Journal*, and the *Ladies Treasury* and then sold copyrights of her serials to Hurst and Blackett for publication as three-volume novels.[33]

By the end of the nineteenth century, the proliferation of British periodicals (up from 3,597 in 1887 to 4,914 in 1901), the emergence of American periodical markets, and the US agreement to observe international copyright law allowed even minor writers to increase their incomes significantly.[34] The young sensation novelist Mary Cholmondeley (1859–1925) had, at the start of her career, sold the copyright of *The Danvers Jewels* (1887) and *Sir Charles Danvers* (1889) for £50 each to Bentley and Son.[35] With their success, George Bentley offered £250 for serial publication of *Diana Tempest* (1893) in his magazine *Temple Bar* and £150 for book publication, adding a £100 bonus after the novel went into a fifth edition.[36] After Cholmondeley published her best-selling *Red Pottage* (1899), she contracted with the *Lady's Realm* for a story of 5,000 words, and in 1906 she serialized *Prisoners (Fast Bound in Misery and Iron)* in the same periodical. On the highbrow end, she placed "The Pitfall" with Henry Newbolt in the *Monthly Review* (1901), warning him that it "is what I believe is called 'advanced.'"[37] In her negotiations over payment, she explained that she was asking less than usual (£50 for 8,500 words instead of her customary £40 for 5,000) because "that particular story had to be placed where it would reach a cultivated reader. In ordinary magazines I am most certain it would have failed to make the impression I desired."[38] As if hinting that she was offering Newbolt a deal, she added that her American agent had sold the serial rights for a short story of 4,000 words for the sum of £50.[39] These payments for periodical fiction were not enormous, but they reflected an increase from the 1850s, when Eliot's forty-three-page, 24,000-word "Amos Barton" garnered just over £50—roughly the fee Cholmondeley collected for 8,500 words.

In the eighteenth century, Samuel Johnson quipped, "No man but a blockhead ever wrote, except for money."[40] Yet, like many of her fellow writers, Cholmondeley cared about more

---

31. Cross, *Common Writer*, 175–6.
32. Ibid., 182.
33. Ibid., 189–90.
34. Eliot, "Business of Victorian Publishing," 48.
35. Oulton, *Let the Flowers Go*, 43, 51.
36. Peterson, *Becoming a Woman of Letters*, 211.
37. Mary Cholmondeley to Henry Newbolt, October 15, 1901, Wolff 1213b, Harry Ransom Center, University of Texas.
38. Ibid.
39. Peterson, *Becoming a Woman of Letters*, 217.
40. Boswell, *Life of Johnson*, 292.

than financial gain; she also cared about establishing her literary worth and securing a publisher who respected her work. When she published with Bentley in the 1880s and early 1890s, George Bentley enthusiastically praised her first novel *The Danvers Jewels* as "your bright and humorous story" and urged her "to continue to give me the benefit of such papers."[41] The Bentley archive reveals a cordial correspondence between author and publisher. When Bentley retired and sold out to Macmillan, she lost this relationship—including the opportunity for advance serialization in a popular magazine—and had to seek a new publisher for what turned out to be her best work, *Red Pottage*. Although she eventually settled in with John Murray, she never regained the professional and popular status that her alliance with *Temple Bar* and Bentley's publishing firm had provided.

Such ongoing relationships were crucial to the careers of novelists such as George Eliot, Margaret Oliphant, William Makepeace Thackeray, Anthony Trollope, and Thomas Hardy. As Peter L. Shillingsburg notes, "During the years of struggle to establish himself as a writer, Thackeray can hardly be said to have 'had a publisher.'"[42] Once he established a relationship with Smith, Elder, Thackeray could count on dual publication in the *Cornhill Magazine* and in three-volume (triple-decker) format and thus could rely on the secure income these publication formats provided. Interestingly, when George Smith wrote the contract offering Thackeray the editorship of the *Cornhill* and publication of "1 or 2 novels of the ordinary size" in the magazine, he stipulated that Thackeray must cease selling his work to other periodicals during the life of the contract—not even to *Punch*, to which Thackeray had been a regular contributor. As Shillingsburg notes, "George Smith obtained the services of one of the day's two foremost writers of fiction for his magazine," while Thackeray gained a highly lucrative income of £300 a month.[43] More important, Thackeray secured a respected periodical venue for his future fiction and non-fiction writing.

Placing Poetry in Periodicals

Of all periodical genres, poetry has been the least studied, and poets' motives for periodical publication have been the least understood. This neglect has resulted, in part, from the decision of the editors of *The Wellesley Index to Victorian Periodicals* to exclude poetry, thus leaving scholars without a bibliographic record of poets' periodical verse or an understanding of common editorial practices for soliciting poetry and remunerating poets. As Linda K. Hughes observes, the *Wellesley*'s decision presumed a predominance of sentimental verse in newspapers and magazines and an "association of poetry with 'filler.'"[44] It failed to account for major

---

41. Peterson, *Becoming a Woman of Letters*, 211.
42. Shillingsburg, *Pegasus in Harness*, 69.
43. See Shillingsburg, who notes that the contract, as originally written, would have yielded £300 per month, but Thackeray's amendments, most specifying more time for writing his fiction, produced averages from £214 in the first six months to £297 with the editorial work to £422 at the height. Shillingsburg, *Pegasus in Harness*, 105.
44. Hughes, "What the *Wellesley* Left Out," 92. *The Periodical Poetry Index*, edited by Natalie Houston, Lindsy Lawrence, and April Patrick, indexes poems published in Victorian periodicals in a searchable online database, http://www.periodicalpoetry.org.

poems first published in periodicals and for the significance of occasional verse in which poets engaged the questions of their day. Nonetheless, from studies of individual poets we can glean some patterns and motives that encouraged poets to write for periodicals: making a debut, earning income, and speaking out on important public issues.

For aspiring young poets, periodical publication allowed a venue for making a literary debut—for testing whether an editor would print a submission, watching for positive response from readers, and using publication to advertise themselves and their work (once signed publication became the norm). Mary Howitt, as noted earlier, first published poetry in a Staffordshire weekly newspaper; Anne Brontë, writing as "Acton Bell," placed two poems in *Fraser's Magazine* before she turned to novel writing; and Christina Rossetti, writing under the pseudonym Ellen Alleyn, published her work in the Pre-Raphaelite journal, the *Germ*. Robert Browning published dramatic monologues, "Porphyria's Lover" and "Johannes Agricola in Meditation," in the *Monthly Repository* under the rubric "Madhouse Cells." Algernon Charles Swinburne, who had already published a volume of poetic drama as he left Oxford University, turned to two leading periodicals, the *Spectator* and *Once a Week*, to launch his professional career as a poet and literary critic. And Oscar Wilde began his literary career with poems in two Irish journals, *Dublin University Magazine* and *Kottabos*.

Perhaps the most famous case of using periodicals to make a literary debut is that of Laetitia Landon, "L.E.L." Landon had been a rhymester since childhood, and when she was in her late teens, her proud, ambitious grandmother sent samples to their neighbor William Jerdan, editor of the *Literary Gazette*. The *Gazette* regularly featured an "Original Poetry" column, with some verses by known authors but most submitted by readers, amateurs, and aspiring poets. Landon fell into the last category. Her first poem in the *Gazette*, "Rome," appeared on March 11, 1820—not with the initials "L.E.L." but simply signed "L," not as a featured poet but merely as a "correspondent." Later in the year, the *Gazette* published other poems by "L" of varying quality and on different subjects: "To a Michaelmas Daisy" (March 18, 1820), "A West Indian Anecdote" (August 5, 1820), and a "Fragment" (August 26, 1820). This fourth poem, set in a quiet grove, a scene of "pensive loveliness," expresses the "blighted feelings, hopes destroyed" of a young woman whose hopeless love ends in early death.[45] In this poem, Landon found her subject matter (the joys and woes of love) and a successful mode of self-presentation (as a modern-day Sappho). Yet to make a successful debut, she also needed a signature that distinguished her from other contributors and transformed her from a "correspondent" into an acknowledged poet. Thus, she adopted the initials "L.E.L." in a series of "Poetic Sketches" launched in January 1822, which announced their subject: "A Woman's whole life is a history of the affections."[46] In her rise to fame as a poetess, Landon's choice of periodical, signature, and subject matter were all crucial. As Bulwer Lytton recalled in 1831, he and his fellow college students would "rush every Saturday afternoon for the 'Literary Gazette,' [with] an impatient anxiety to hasten at once to that corner of the sheet which contained the three

---

45. L. [Landon], "Fragment," 556.
46. L. E. L. [Landon], "Poetic Sketch the First," 27. Landon's "Poetic Sketches" appeared between January 12 and February 16, 1822.

magical letters L.E.L. And all of us praised the verse, and all of us guessed at the author. We soon learned it was a female, and our admiration was doubled, and our conjectures tripled."[47]

It is unlikely that Landon, or the young poets cited above, received a fee for their early periodical poetry (with the possible exception of Swinburne, who had already published verse when he made his debut in the *Spectator*). Yet income was a strong motive for publishing in newspapers and magazines, and some poets received substantial fees for their periodical publications. As a well-established poet, William Wordsworth received one hundred guineas in 1829 for five poems solicited by the *Keepsake,* a literary gift book published annually.[48] Samuel Taylor Coleridge received £50 for five poems in the same periodical, claiming that this amount was "more than all, *I* ever made by all my Publications."[49] Literary annuals typically paid high fees to famous poets whose names they wished to feature, but they could not be relied upon for a regular source of income as the editors tended to solicit verse to accompany themes depicted in the large-plate illustrations that made these gift books desirable.

Magazines like *Blackwood's*, however, and later the *Cornhill Magazine, Macmillan's Magazine,* and the *Fortnightly Review,* did pay regularly, even handsomely, for poetry. Paula R. Feldman has traced the profits that Felicia Hemans accrued between 1823 until her death in 1835 for poems published in *Blackwood's Magazine* and the *Monthly Magazine*: £227 1s. 6d. for the former and £280 16s. 1d. for the latter, together representing over 20 percent of her income for this period.[50] Moreover, Hemans took advantage of the dual publication system by collecting her magazine verses and new work in books of poetry, including *The Forest Sanctuary* (1828), *Songs of Affections* (1830), and *Scenes and Hymns* (1834), for which she made £100 per edition.[51] This system held sway well into the 1860s when Christina Rossetti, who would become the greatest devotional poet of the century, placed short lyrics in *Macmillan's Magazine*. In January 1861, she submitted her first poems, "Uphill" and "A Birthday," to editor David Masson and saw them in print that spring; happy to receive the standard guinea fee, she wrote to Alexander Macmillan, "You may think whether I am not happy to attain fame (!) and guineas by means of the Magazine," adding, "I am in great hopes of being able to put a volume together."[52] Macmillan issued her now-famous *Goblin Market and Other Poems* in 1862.

Many nineteenth-century poets placed verse in periodicals less for income than for political and ideological purposes. Elizabeth Barrett Browning wrote "The Cry of the Children" after reading Richard Hengist Horne's "Report on the Employment of Children and Young Persons in Mines and Factories" and published it in *Blackwood's Magazine* in August 1843 to protest appalling work conditions. Alfred Tennyson's "The Charge of the Light Brigade," which commemorates the bravery of soldiers in a disastrous battle of the Crimean War and mocks the blundering of the generals in charge, appeared in the *Examiner* on November 18, 1865, after

---

47. [Bulwer], "Romance and Reality," 546.
48. Feldman, *Keepsake*, 20.
49. Ibid., 21.
50. Feldman, "Poet and the Profits," 73.
51. Ibid., 89.
52. Marsh, *Christina Rossetti*, 269–70.

which he had 2,000 quarto pamphlets printed for the soldiers at Sebastopol.[53] Swinburne's sonnets on Louis Napoleon, printed in the *Fortnightly Review* in 1869, with others appearing in the *Examiner* in 1873 after the emperor's death, offer direct commentary on European politics and excoriate the French emperor for the sufferings he inflicted on humankind:

> If haply, or ever its cursed life have ceased,
>   Or ever thy cold hands cover his head
> From sight of France and freedom and broad day,
>   He may see these and wither and be dead.[54]

Alice Meynell, a nominee for poet laureate after the death of Tennyson, published "A Father of Women" in the *Observer* to mourn the "crippled world" after World War I yet also to underscore women's contributions to the war effort: "Approve, accept, know them as daughters of men, / Now that your sons are dust."[55] These poets and many others used periodicals to have their say on contemporary political, economic, and social questions. Like the review writers who used the *Edinburgh* and *Quarterly* at the beginning of the century to advance their views on British politics, Victorian poets throughout the century wrote for magazines and newspapers to engage the pressing issues of their day.

---

53. Ledbetter, *Tennyson and Victorian Periodicals*, 126.
54. Swinburne, *Poems*, 2:323.
55. Meynell, *Poems*, 147.

6

EDITORS AND THE NINETEENTH-CENTURY PRESS

Marysa Demoor

What did nineteenth-century editors do and why did they pursue this line of work? How were they chosen to serve in editorial roles and what was expected of them? Answers to these questions differed widely from sector to sector of the press and from the beginning of the nineteenth century to the end. In 1899, the conservative *Blackwood's Edinburgh Review Magazine* accused editors of being merely salesmen who prioritized circulation figures above quality.[1] In 1831, Leigh Hunt regarded them as unwilling participants in literary puffing, forced to play a commercial game by their proprietors, or, if they were part-proprietors, by those who had a dominant share in the business.[2] Two years earlier, the radical *Westminster Review* had portrayed them as hard workers in the engine of constant improvement,[3] and in 1832 *Tait's Edinburgh Magazine* regarded the "influence of a few of the London editors over public affairs" to be so great "that they must enter into every question of Government" even though they were anonymous and were paid just £500 a year (except *The Times* editor, who received £1,000).[4] Apart from the irascible *Blackwood's* article, most periodicals portrayed editors as selfless, urbane, clubbable professionals who were committed to the ideals of taste and integrity and were attentive to aesthetic and political concerns. That this notion was distinctly gendered and classed is made clear in an 1860 piece from the *London Review*, which described editing as depending on "gentlemanly and candid feelings . . . towards everyone, and on every subject and occasion."[5] This gender and class position was reproduced in one of the first modern volumes devoted to nineteenth-century editors, *Innovators and Preachers*, edited by Joel Wiener in 1985. However, even before Barbara Onslow pointed out that earlier studies of editorship silently confirmed nineteenth-century masculine bias,[6] considerable academic work had been done, and has been done since, on women editors such as Charlotte Yonge, Christian Isobel Johnstone, Eliza Cook, Mary Braddon, Ellen Wood, Florence Marryat, Ella Hepworth Dixon, Annie Swan, and, of

1. [Whibley], "Sins of Education."
2. [Hunt], "Success of Periodicals."
3. [Merle], "Newspaper Press."
4. "Botheration of the 'Personal,'" 290.
5. [Mackay], "Town and Table Talk," 8.
6. Onslow, *Women*, 1.

course, Marian Evans.[7] Many of these editors are discussed elsewhere in this volume. But it would be too facile and triumphalist to focus on women editors here. Marianne Van Remoortel has shown in her analysis of census reports that although women were active in the publishing trade as publishers, editors, contributors, compositors, and, predominantly, newsagents, men dominated the editorial field.[8] We have to accept that nineteenth-century editors were overwhelmingly male and middle class; thus, this chapter, while not seeking to replicate past elisions of female editors, must acknowledge and reflect the gendering and social classification of the nineteenth-century editor.

Patten and Finkelstein, in their study of the editorship of *Blackwood's*, distinguish three types of editorships: the "big-name" editor, the "hands-on" editor, and the publisher-proprietor.[9] These types overlap, which makes it difficult to assign any given editor to a single category (Dickens is a case in point), but the categories remain useful because they hint at the editor's many responsibilities. This classification scheme informs my thinking about the editorial role in this chapter, but at the same time I pay some attention to the differences between newspaper and periodical editors—roles which also sometimes overlap—and shall briefly examine the position of sub-editor.

The careers of celebrity editors have been dealt with in the many biographies devoted to eminent Victorians such as Dickens, Thackeray, Trollope, and Eliot. In the past, these writers were studied first and foremost as novelists. Despite some isolated work, such as Lehmann's collection of letters from Dickens to his sub-editor, only quite recently have these writers been treated as editors and journalists.[10] As John Gross points out, for many years journalism was considered a career and literature a vocation, and thus the two were treated and prioritized differently.[11] Research into the editing responsibilities of authors thus only started in the second half of the twentieth century.

What Editors Did

The anonymity of most editors meant that for contemporaries the editorial process was considered mysterious, even intriguing. As the September 16, 1882 issue of *Chambers's Journal* put it,

> Newspaper editors are personages with whom, in the mind of the public at large, there has always been associated a certain degree of mystery. There is no class of men whose work passes so directly and so constantly before the public eye; yet there are few with regard to whose real position and functions more vague, confused, or erroneous notions are entertained, even on the part of persons otherwise well informed. This is no doubt largely due to the anonymity which is preserved in the newspaper press of this country.

---

7. See Palmer, *Women's Authorship*; Beetham, *A Magazine of Her Own?*; Easley, *First-Person Anonymous*; Fraser, Green, and Johnston, *Gender and the Victorian Periodical*; Dillane, *Before George Eliot*; Fehlbaum, *Ella Hepworth Dixon*.
8. Van Remoortel, *Women, Work, and the Victorian Periodical*.
9. Patten and Finkelstein, "Editing *Blackwood's*," 150–1.
10. Lehmann, *Dickens as Editor*.
11. Gross, *Rise and Fall*, 37.

> Readers come to identify the opinions of a particular organ more with the sheet of printed paper, and with its distinctive name and features, than with the individual or individuals by whom it is directed, and of whom, it may be, they know nothing.[12]

The impersonal, decorporealizing anonymity associated with the newspaper editor was also characteristic of editors associated with other types of periodicals, especially the venerable quarterlies. However, at the lower-status end of the market, especially from the 1840s, it was not uncommon for periodicals to exploit the name of a celebrity author/editor, such as Eliza Cook, Douglas Jerrold, or G.W.M. Reynolds. The duties of editors also varied widely according to the type and popularity of the periodical they were responsible for, ranging from those few periodicals (such as the short-lived *Original*) which were written entirely by one person,[13] to periodicals where the editor was the only regular staff member (with most content being provided by penny-a-liners and reader-contributors or cut and pasted from other publications by compositors), and at the other end of the spectrum, to papers with a large editorial staff, such as *The Times*.

Editors, as a rule, wrote very little about their own practices or work routine. Dallas Liddle postulates that only by the middle of the nineteenth century had "audiences [begun] to understand the term 'editor' as denoting the authoritative central intelligence of a periodical."[14] There are, however, sporadic publications by editors and contemporaries which provide (sometimes oblique) commentary on the nature of editorial work. The index to Palmegiano's annotated bibliography of *Perceptions of the Press* provides a wealth of material, and occasionally the odd relevant article can be found in various nineteenth-century periodicals databases. Gibbons Merle, for example, writing in the 1829 *Westminster Review*, is unusually clear about what was involved in London morning newspaper editing, focusing specifically on its seasonal (as well as daily) news cycle:

> The editor's duty begins, strictly speaking, with the publication of the evening newspapers. He has to read their leading articles, and support or refute their arguments. He remains at his post until a late hour, prepared to write comments on the foreign newspapers as they arrive (a duty in which he is generally assisted by his sub-editor) and to direct, in a leading article, attention to any topic of interest before the public. During the sitting of parliament he is compelled to remain at the office until two or three o'clock in the morning. . . . It is not rare to see a leading article of nearly a column written at two o'clock in the morning on some subject which had been discussed an hour or two previously in the House of Commons.[15]

Most articles on the subject, however, generally promise more than they give. For example, "The Life of an Editor," published in the monthly *Rambler* in 1854, is really only an expatiation on the problems an editor encounters: grievances of contributors, complaints and wishes of publishers, the angry reactions of authors reviewed in the journal, and the "minor troubles" of

---

12. "Newspaper Editors and Their Work," 585.
13. See King, "Thomas Walker's *The Original*."
14. Liddle, *Dynamics of Genre*, 87.
15. [Merle], "Newspaper Press," 225.

an editor's life, "correcting proof-sheets, and other similar trifles."[16] The article concludes by comparing a periodical issue to a procrustean bed of five, six, or seven sheets into which one expects the editor to bring together a huge quantity of material that comes from various quarters. The writer probably never realized that the metaphor turns the editor into the murderous Procrustes himself rather than his victim.

A nineteenth-century editor is usually envisioned finding contributors and then bullying and/or cajoling them into writing in specific ways on specific topics, before correcting and altering their manuscripts to fit his vision of the character of the periodical. He is a Procrustes indeed but with the honeyed skills of Aphrodite's attendant, Peitho, the goddess of rhetoric and persuasion; he must make contributors *want* to fit the bed he will chop them into, a task that could easily meet with resistance. Both aspects of the job are legible in one of the most famous relations between an editor and contributor: Dickens and Elizabeth Gaskell. Dickens initially called her his "Scheherazade" and consulted her on all significant changes to her submissions to *Household Words* (one of the most famous being his graceful deletion of a complimentary reference to himself).[17] They later fell out over the editing of *North and South* (1854–55) when it was serialized in *Household Words*. Gaskell did not like how Dickens condensed her novel or divided it into episodes; they nonetheless maintained a working relationship, and Gaskell continued to contribute for some time. It is relatively easy to find examples of high-profile contributors reflecting—often unhappily—on their experience of being edited. Thomas Carlyle's complaints of the "light editorial hacking and hewing"[18] perpetrated by Francis Jeffrey of the *Edinburgh Review* (1802–1929) is but one example. At the same time, it must be acknowledged that Jeffrey, at least according to Walter Bagehot, "invented the trade of editorship," and his editorial work helped to establish the eminence of the *Edinburgh*'s collective "we."[19]

The job of sub-editor had, if possible, an even lower profile than the editor's, yet it could be just as exacting. W.H. Wills's work as Dickens's sub-editor of *Household Words* demonstrates how editorial responsibilities were sometimes divided. Dickens oversaw every aspect of the publication, but it was Wills who assumed the mundane tasks of revising the contributions, writing the business letters, visiting contributors, taking care of the finances, and sometimes doing research for Dickens's other projects. Newspaper sub-editors also played an instrumental role in day-to-day editorial operations. Gibbons Merle gives a specific account of what a metropolitan morning newspaper sub-editor did in the late 1820s, and there is no reason to think these responsibilities changed for much of the century:

> The duties of a sub-editor on a morning paper commence about the middle of the day—at this time he arranges for the printer the original communications which have been laid before his superior, and which have obtained his approbation, and revises any report which may at that time have been sent for insertion. He then makes his selections

---

16. "Life of an Editor," 516.
17. For a thoughtful account of Dickens's editing of *Cranford* in *Household Words*, see Recchio, *Elizabeth Gaskell's Cranford*, chapter 1.
18. Thomas Carlyle to Macvey Napier, November 23, 1830, *Carlyle Letters Online*.
19. Bagehot, "First Edinburgh Reviewers," 276. See Shattock, "Reviews and Monthlies."

WHILE THE EDITOR IS AT LUNCH.
OUR TYPIST: I say! Are you fond of figures? I detest them:
THE YOUNG SUB: Well—er, I'm awfully gone on yours!

Figure 6.1 "While the Editor Is at Lunch," *Judy: or The London Serio-Comic Journal* 70 (November 1, 1905): 519. Reproduced from *British Periodicals* with permission from ProQuest LLC, www.proquest.com.

from the provincial papers which are sent to the office; and when the evening papers are published, extracts from them also, and arranges his extracts for publication—occasionally writing an original paragraph on some subject of interest. From that time, until the paper is sent to press, which may be at one, two or four o'clock in the morning, he is occupied in overlooking the different reports or communications as they arrive, and in selecting from them such as he thinks worthy of insertion.[20]

When William Duncan retired as sub-editor of the *Newcastle Chronicler* in 1891, a short piece appeared in the *Blackburn Standard and Weekly Express* which claimed that the sub-editor was "responsible for all errors, and is supposed to know everything."[21] He has to find a balance between the wishes of the contributors and reporters and the demands of the printer; he has to decide which letters to print and which to leave out, which articles should get priority and which can wait. The overview concludes, "It is often imagined that the editor is the presiding genius and governing spirit of a newspaper; but practically it is the sub-editor who is the

20. [Merle], "Newspaper Press," 224–5.
21. "A Sub-Editor's Duties and Difficulties," 5.

Deus et Machina [sic]."[22] By the early twentieth century, jokes could be made at the expense of sub-editors, as Figure 6.1 suggests.

If there are few accounts of editing and sub-editing beyond considerations of big names such as Dickens, whose letters survive, research can still seek to reconstruct editorial practices by a variety of other means, including the close analysis of edited texts. Kate Jackson, for example, has explored George Newnes's editorial persona in *Tit-Bits* through a discussion of his textual choices, while Lynne Warren has shown how, as editors of *Woman*, Arnold Bennett and Fitzroy Garrett tried to limit the interpretive possibilities of texts by answering and altering readers' questions.[23]

Big Names as Editors: Dickens and Trollope

If editing was hard work, it also meant a steady income, and journalists and authors were in general eager to obtain such a position. Dickens, even after achieving celebrity status, went from one editorship to another, each time negotiating better conditions and a higher salary, and always dissatisfied, resenting interference of any kind and seeking absolute control over the periodicals he edited. He repeatedly renegotiated the deal over his first editorial adventure, *Bentley's Miscellany* (1837–68), with his salary adjusted in March 1837 to £10 for each monthly number that sold 6,000 copies, with £5 extra for every additional 500. He ended his editorship in 1839 despite a final offer of £40 a year, "just for the use of his name."[24] Despite his increasingly large remuneration, he fought to retain editorial control with increasing fervor.[25] With the launch of the weekly *Master Humphrey's Clock* by Chapman & Hall in 1840, Dickens's financial future looked positively rosy since he was now offered £50 a week and a share in the profit of the magazine over five years. This allowed him to break away from Bentley's interference. *Master Humphrey's Clock* was the product of his own quirky imagination and was, as John Drew has demonstrated, deliberately conceived as being unlike any existing category of periodical publication.[26] Dickens himself contributed all of the periodical's content and published it in weekly, monthly, and biannual numbers. As he noted, these unusual decisions were "intended to baffle the imitators and make it as novel as possible."[27] *Master Humphrey's Clock* came to a premature demise at the end of 1841, partly because Dickens realized that weekly serialization of his fiction did not give him enough time to develop and finish plots to his satisfaction. He became the editor of the *Daily News* in January 1845, having been offered the large sum of £2,000 a year and a share in the paper's profits.[28] But his enjoyment of the post was short-lived; realizing he had no time to write fiction and exasperated once more by the proprietor's interference, he resigned after seventeen issues. Naturally, all of this experience was valuable for his full-blown editorial career conducting the weekly *Household Words* (1850–59) and its sequel *All the Year Round* (1859–70). *Household Words* was owned and published by Bradbury and Evans, and this led to tension when they refused to

---

22. Ibid.
23. Jackson, "George Newnes"; Warren, "Women."
24. Patten, *Charles Dickens and His Publishers*, 75–83.
25. Ibid., chapter 4.
26. Drew, *Dickens the Journalist*, 48–9.
27. Dickens to Cattermole, January 13, 1840, Dickens, *Letters* 2:7.
28. Drew, *Dickens the Journalist*, 71.

overtly take his side in his acrimonious separation from his wife. Dickens would brook no further interference and set up *All the Year Round*, assuming the role of both editor and proprietor.

Dickens's skill at securing favorable terms for his editorial work and his understanding of the economics of journalism were just as apparent to his friends at the time as they are to us today. His colleague Mark Lemon sought his advice in March 1853 when he wanted to strengthen both his position and his income as *Punch* editor by asking for a share in the magazine's ownership. A draft of his letter to *Punch*'s proprietors demonstrates how editors used qualities of clubbability, urbanity, and "candid" integrity to their advantage:

> My dear B[radbury] and E[vans].
>
> I address this business letter to you as the Firm, in the perfect certainty that you will not misconstrue a word of it. I beg you to understand that I am truly sensible of having always received the most generous, manly and honorable treatment from you. I never can hold it in a more lively remembrance than I do now.
>
> You know whether I have endeavoured to deserve your confidence by a thorough devotion of myself to Punch, and a complete relinquishment of any private convenience, occupation, or desire, that could possibly interfere with it. I will not say another word on that point.
>
> My time of life, my family, and my close and long connexion with you, all taken into account, decide me, after much anxious consideration, to ask you whether you think you can give me some share in Punch. I do not seek a large one—my expectations are modest, I hope—but if I could have some little proprietorship in Punch that could be made an Editorial one, so that the share and the Editorship should be inseparable and my present position thus rendered superior to any chances and changes that may lie beyond ourselves, it would be a relief a comfort and an encouragement to me that I cannot possibly express.
>
> But you are not to consider that, I know. You can only ask yourselves—a little influenced perhaps by your unvarying friendship and consideration for me, which I gratefully acknowledge—whether I have rendered any faithful services in my sphere of action, that give this application some color of reason. If you can think so, I gladly and hopefully leave the rest in your hands.
>
> I have made the purport [of] this letter known to no one but C.D. Without any request on my part, he has answered "that as your friend and mine, if there is any impartial part he can take in the matter, or any confidence he can receive, or any trust he can execute, or any friendly office he can discharge, his services are more than ready."[29]

Lemon had clearly sought Dickens's advice about his career plans and invoked his name as leverage. In general, there seems to have been a feeling of collegiality among editors: they were beginning to recognize themselves as a professional group that defined itself against publishers and proprietors on the one hand and the generators of content on the other.[30] For the publisher,

---

29. Mark Lemon to Bradbury and Evans, April 1, 1853, in Dickens, *Letters* 7:57, n1.
30. This assumption is confirmed by the correspondence of W.H. Dixon. Mark Lemon had received a complaint about Dixon and forwarded it to him, attempting to warn a fellow editor of a potential problem. Unnumbered manuscript in the possession of Ghent University. See Pattijn, "Editing the Correspondence," 78–9.

it was crucial to choose the right editor to minimize the firm's financial risks. The editor translated that risk into cultural terms by making decisions about what to publish and when—after all, it was he who lost his job if the popularity of the periodical or newspaper diminished.

Anthony Trollope provided a great deal of commentary on the mechanics and finances of periodical journalism. He resigned from the Post Office in 1867 when offered the editorship of James Virtue's monthly *Saint Paul's Magazine* at £1,000 a year.[31] As in Dickens's case, the author's name was used to market the periodical and thus was printed on the front page along with the name of the illustrator, J.E. Millais. Editors were appointed partly for their literary connections, and, indeed, Trollope was able to secure a large number of eminent writers for the magazine, including Leslie Stephen, Eliza Lynn Linton, Austin Dobson, G.H. Lewes, George MacDonald, and Margaret Oliphant. Eager for autonomy, Trollope set his own editorial agenda and made the magazine his own.[32] As explained in his *Autobiography*, his aim was

> firstly, that I should put whatever I pleased into the magazine, or keep whatever I pleased out of it, *without interference*; secondly, that I should, from month to month, give to him [Virtue] a list of payments to be made to contributors, and that he should pay them, allowing me to fix the amounts; and, thirdly, that the arrangement should remain in force, at any rate, for two years. To all this he made no objection; and during the time that he and I were thus bound together he not only complied with these stipulations, but also with every suggestion respecting the magazine that I made to him.[33]

Virtue sold the title in May 1869 to Alexander Strahan, and Trollope resigned the following year. His experiences gave him material for "An Editor's Tales," which, along with his *Autobiography*, provide insight into the editing profession. Following the new codes that were coming to define a professional editor, Trollope insisted that he would read all manuscripts sent to him and that he would try to judge them impartially.[34] He also recognized the tensions in the editor's mediating position between authors and publishers. According to him, the best editors of periodicals were actually the publishers themselves since they were less "soft" than professional authors: "Nothing certainly has ever been done better than *Blackwood's*. The *Cornhill*, too, after Thackeray had left it and before Leslie Stephen had taken it, seemed to be in quite efficient hands—those hands being the hands of proprietor and publisher. The proprietor, at any rate, knows what he wants and what he can afford. . . . I did not so sin very often, but often enough to feel that I was a coward. 'My dear friend, my dear friend, this is trash!' It is so hard to speak thus—but so necessary for an editor!"[35] This reference to *Blackwood's Edinburgh Magazine* is important. The magazine was named for its owner, William Blackwood, who acted

---

31. *Saint Paul's* ran from 1867 to 1874, though Trollope resigned in 1870 after it was sold to Alexander Strahan in 1869.
32. See Turner, *Trollope and the Magazines*, 188. For background on Trollope, manliness, and the professions, see King "Army, Navy, Medicine, Law."
33. My emphasis. Trollope, *Autobiography*, 320.
34. Ibid., 166.
35. Ibid., 323.

and was occasionally identified as its editor, In 1822, an entirely different editor, "Christopher North," assumed the editorship of *Blackwood's*. However, the man behind that pseudonym, John Wilson, was never really the magazine's editor. This lack of clarity afforded the team behind *Blackwood's* (chiefly Wilson, J.G. Lockhart, James Hogg, and William Maginn) license to misbehave in print, while the owner (and, in reality, the editor), William Blackwood, could deny full responsibility for its contents.[36]

Editing the *Athenaeum*

The weekly *Athenaeum* (1828–1921) was one of the most successful, influential, and enduring periodicals of the nineteenth century. Unlike most periodicals of its time, the *Athenaeum* preserved editorial notes that reveal the identities of its anonymous contributors.[37] In addition, because of the high status of both the periodical and its owners (for a long time, the Dilke family), there is quite a lot of archival material, including a small collection of letters to and from William Hepworth Dixon (editor from 1853 to 1869) in the Ghent University Library.[38] Bearing out Trollope's reasoning, the longevity and status of this weekly seems to lie in the fact that the proprietors were involved in editing the journal.[39]

The *Athenaeum*'s first two years (1828–30) are difficult to reconstruct, but following the arrival of editor Charles Wentworth Dilke in 1830, its history comes into focus. At the same time he assumed his post as editor, Dilke acquired a main share in the *Athenaeum*, obtaining total control over the paper.[40] His vision was to establish the paper as the most prestigious and authoritative critical periodical of its day. He overtly rejected the practice of "puffing" and made sure specialists wrote the book reviews published in the magazine. During the sixteen years of his editorship, he was so involved with the editing that, according to Tuckwell, "he withdrew altogether from general society."[41] After his resignation in 1846, he was succeeded by T.K. Hervey and later, in 1853, by William Hepworth Dixon, but the Dilke family retained ownership.

Dixon, a controversial figure, is sometimes accused of bringing about the *Athenaeum*'s loss of prestige at a time when the owner, the second Charles Dilke, was decidedly disengaged. As an editor, Dixon was thoroughly disliked. As the elder Dilke put it, "Everybody seems to rejoice in the opportunity of showing a personal dislike to the man."[42] Letters addressed to Dixon in his editorial capacity promise to provide a glimpse of his working life, yet they offer little insight. The letters do, however, demonstrate how an editor could simply decide to change a policy introduced by a previous editor. Log-rolling, which the first Dilke had worked so

---

36. See Morrison, "William Blackwood," 22.
37. This so-called "marked file" is kept at City University Library, London.
38. This has been transcribed and edited by Pattijn in "Editing the Correspondence."
39. The management of the *Athenaeum* has been described on several occasions by literary historians and students of Victorian periodicals. See Marchand, *Athenaeum*, and Demoor, *Their Fair Share*.
40. Tuckwell and Gwynne, *Life of Dilke*, 1:4.
41. Ibid.
42. Marchand, *Athenaeum*, 80, n211.

hard to abolish, returned, and Dixon was not averse to accepting bribes, such as cigars, from publishers whose books were scheduled to be reviewed.[43] He of course also corresponded with authors who were unhappy with notices of their work and demanded to be put in touch with the reviewer. This demonstrates that the editor assumed a gatekeeping role in the publishing network, providing work for writers and at the same time protecting them from retribution. Dixon obviously knew the rules of the game but somehow did not play his part in a sufficiently covert or professional way. This is what led to his bad reputation.

The third Sir Charles Wentworth Dilke inherited the *Athenaeum* in 1869 and, groomed by his grandfather, hoped to return the magazine to its former glory.[44] The young Dilke prepared the ground well before he actually inherited the paper by writing to Dixon about reviews that had appeared in the magazine, potential topics he might pursue, and methods he might use to chastise the staff if they failed to live up to his expectations. Before he became the *Athenaeum*'s owner, the young Dilke had developed a close friendship with Dixon. They went together to the United States and to Russia, and both wrote books about their travels. Dixon published his on America first and thus stole Dilke's thunder. But when Dixon attempted to repeat this preemptive approach when publishing his volume on Russia, Dilke thought he had gone too far, and as soon as he inherited the *Athenaeum*, he dismissed Dixon. Dilke gave himself some time to look for an appropriate editor by first appointing a regular trustworthy contributor, John Doran, as an interim, but then, in 1870, he appointed a good friend from university, Norman MacColl. MacColl was a hands-on editor who devoted his life to the weekly, dying soon after retiring early in December 1904.[45] Dilke's choice of MacColl seems to underscore the importance of university connections in landing influential editorial positions.

MacColl was the best kind of interventionist editor. He often invited potential reviewers to lunch and convinced them to contribute knowledgeable reviews and articles. One can only conclude that an unknown person like MacColl was a better editor than many of his celebrity counterparts because he was so dedicated to his work. Indeed, choosing a celebrity author as editor was not a guarantee of success, and one wonders why publishers continued to ask them to serve. Every editor endured pressure from the proprietor to sell a good product. This responsibility was a heavy weight, especially for a novelist like Dickens but for other authors as well, including Trollope and Thackeray, who wanted the freedom to act without interference. Unlike Dickens, many opted out when the sales of a periodical declined.

Conclusion

The owner and/or publisher of a periodical had the power to select the editor, and in many cases it was this team that jointly determined the political profile of the journal and its

---

43. This occurred prior to the publication of Edward Dicey's *Cavour: A Memoir*. The book was subsequently favorably reviewed in the *Athenaeum* by the editor himself. See "Cavour: A Memoir."
44. See also Marchand, *Athenaeum*, 84. It was not unusual for editorships to be dynastic; *Blackwood's Edinburgh Magazine* and the *Lancet* were also family affairs.
45. From the summary of MacColl's farewell speech, as given in the *Bookman*, we learn that he was given complete support by Dilke and generous assistance by his contributors. See "News Notes," 172.

publishing policy. A change of team usually meant a change of policy and ideological stance. Hence, to characterize a periodical merely by its identity at one particular moment of time of its run is misguided. Likewise, though editors sometimes chose contributors to suit their own ideological perspectives, thus creating something close to a homogenous publication, it is dangerous to assume that any journal was monolithic in its views.

Towards the end of the century, the job of the editor was no longer as mysterious an occupation as it had been at the beginning. Besides Trollope's "An Editor's Tales," other illuminating accounts were published, including sketches of two nineteenth-century editors, Frank Hill of the *Daily News* and Philip Harwood of the *Saturday Review*, in George Saintsbury's *A Last Scrap Book*. Equally interesting is a page of portraits of editors published in W.T. Stead's *Review of Reviews* in May 1891 (Figure 6.2). It is unclear why the magazine included this page or why the particular editors were selected. Yet the editors chosen were clearly celebrities, an interesting mix of nine men and two women (L.T. Meade of *Atalanta* and Mme Adam of the *Nouvelle Revue*), confirming that, although clearly a minority, women editors were present in the public consciousness— a point that Stead, an editor who was well known for his political interventionism and who actively promoted the women's movement in the *Review*, was no doubt keen to make.[46]

Of course, at the fin de siècle women editors still received negative press. Women celebrities, then as now, were easy targets. For instance, the *Bookman*, in its March 1897 "News Notes" column, argues that contributors always receive the worst and most discourteous treatment from women editors.[47] Yet even with such negative press, some women were able to succeed in a male-dominated field. For example, Rachel Beer (*née* Sassoon) was the first woman editor of a British national paper. Born in Bombay in 1858 into a wealthy family of Baghdadi Jews, she married a financier who inherited the weekly *Observer*. She contributed articles and from 1891 began editing the paper. In 1894 she bought and edited the penny *Sunday Times* while continuing her editorship of the *Observer*. Her acceptance of the *Sunday Times* editorship caused gossip and speculation about "many startling things which it is hardly necessary to say have not happened,"[48] yet the independent views the paper expressed under her editorship caused its circulation to increase. Beer was a well-known member of the Institute of Journalists and the Society of Women Journalists, and it was she who arranged to have a conversation with Count Esterhazy during which he confessed to forging hundreds of letters in the Dreyfus case. She published the sensationalist confession in the *Observer*. Esterhazy retaliated with a libel case against her, but in the end he was court-martialled, Dreyfus was pardoned, and she claimed the moral victory. Her wealth and outsider status seem to have given her unusual acuity and drive. After her husband's death in 1903, however, her family conspired to have her certified insane and the newspapers she edited were sold. She survived until 1927. Until recently she has been neglected in newspaper history, often mentioned with more than a hint of ridicule.[49]

---

46. See Easley, "W.T. Stead," and the rest of the volume, *W.T. Stead, Newspaper Revolutionary*, edited by Brake, King, Luckhurst, and Mussell.
47. "News Notes," 164.
48. Billington, "Leading Lady Journalists," 103.
49. Koren and Negev's *First Lady* is the first biography of Beer.

Figure 6.2 "Some Magazine Editors," *Review of Reviews* 3, no. 17 (May 1891): 508.

Direct discussion of editing in nineteenth-century periodicals, though infrequent, often assumes a tone of either humor or resignation—feelings with which a researcher might sympathize. No publication could survive without an editor, yet the comparative lack of material available to researchers concerning the practice of editing renders this scholarly task extremely difficult. The case of Rachel Beer is testament to the need to investigate and interrogate pre-existing narratives of editing and to methodically evaluate the status of individual editors as well as the editorial profession in general over the course of the nineteenth century.

7

ILLUSTRATION

Brian Maidment

To undertake the study of nineteenth-century periodicals without consideration of the importance of illustration is now unimaginable. The proliferation of illustrative media was driven by successive advances in the use of new or reinvented technologies of reproduction, including wood engraving, lithography, and the use of stereotyping (which facilitated reprinting) and photomechanical developments later in the nineteenth century. Many Victorian magazines not only embraced opportunities for incorporating illustration and other graphic elements but were, in many cases, branded through and constructed by their visual content.

Wood engraving was supported by a rapidly expanding cohort of highly competent entrepreneurs, who often combined printing and publishing activities with the production of blocks for illustrations. This provided a cheap, rapid, and versatile mechanism for illustrating periodicals from the 1820s on. It is hardly surprising that wood engraving, despite some initial anxieties over its historical associations with vernacular or "low" culture, became overwhelmingly the most common reprographic method used throughout the century, even after photoreprographic techniques became widely available. Because wood engravings could be assimilated into the typeset page, they enabled the production of innovative and attractive magazine designs throughout the Victorian period. The wood-engraved image, built out of (but not confined by) small boxwood blocks, could take any shape on the printed page. The dialogue between the traditionally unframed edges of the small-scale, wood-engraved vignette and the possibilities available for framing the page or the image with various rules also presented designers with endless opportunities to construct a distinctive and visually satisfying page.

One of the pleasures of studying Victorian periodicals is encountering images that are conceived and shaped as physical expressions of a text rather than as accompaniments or explanations. The suggestive sharpness of H.G. Hine's image for the *Illuminated Magazine* (1843–45), for example, has been cut back to fit the typeset page. The hanging, half-obscured view under the bridge, the frail capital "N" made up of reed-like fronds, and the almost childlike blocked lettering in the title give some sense of the extent to which the wood engraving could, in the right hands, form an eye-catching and expressive textual element within a magazine (Figure 7.1). Here, the shape-shifting potential of the wood engraving literally wraps its meanings around the text.[1]

---

1. Maidment, "*Illuminated Magazine*," 30–8.

Season of mists and mellow fruitfulness!
  Close bosom friend of the maturing sun;
Conspiring with him how to load and bless
  With fruit the vines that round the thatch-eaves run;
To bend with apples the mossed cottage trees,
  And fill all fruit with ripeness to the core;
    To swell the gourd and plump the hazel shells
With a sweet kernel; to set budding more
  And still more, later flowers for the bees,
  Until they think warm days will never cease,
For Summer has o'erbrimmed their clammy cells.

Who hath not seen thee oft amid thy store?
  Sometimes whoever seeks abroad may find
Thee, sitting careless on a granary floor,
  Thy hair soft-lifted by the winnowing wind;
Or on a half-reap'd furrow sound asleep,
  Drowsed with the fume of poppies, while thy hook
Spares the next swath and all it's twinèd flowers;
And sometimes, like a gleaner thou dost keep
  Steady thy laden head across a brook;
  Or by a cider press, with patient look,
Thou watchest the last oozings, hours by hours.

Where are the songs of Spring? Ay, where are they?
  Think not of them, thou hast thy music too,
While barrèd clouds bedeck the dying day,
  And touch the stubble plains with rosy hue;
Then in a wailful choir the small gnats mourn
  Among the river sallows, borne aloft
  Or sinking, as the light wind lives or dies;
And full-grown lambs loud bleat from hilly bourn;
  Hedge-crickets sing; and now with treble soft,
  The red-breast whistles from a garden croft,
And gathering swallows twitter in the skies.—KEATS.

THE MONSTER CITY

BY THE REV. ROBERT JONES.

NOVEMBER'S sun, red and large, was fast sinking into a gorgeous resting-place of clouds, and a thin mist, gradually condensing as the day declined, floated through the air, as I sailed in my tiny skiff against the stream of a broad and glorious river. The burning clouds were mirrored in the waters, converting them into an estuary of molten gold.

Impelled, as it were, by some invisible power, I found myself approaching a mighty and colossal city, whose endless palaces and minarets were bounded only by the clouds. As I neared its domes, ships of gigantic stature skirted the banks of the river, from whose tall tapering masts broad crimson pennons, like fragments of clouds, were floating on the breeze. Through their spars and cordage, on either side, I could distinctly trace the outline of mighty storehouses for merchandise, or granaries large enough to contain the harvests of nations.

My little barque and myself seemed mere atoms amidst the surrounding vastness, and yet, despite our insignificance, our progress was rapid and powerful. A flowing breeze bore us onward. We passed many a tower and tapering spire, whose height was lost in the clouds; and many a temple whose space would have sufficed for a world to worship at its shrine. Passing and repassing us were mighty steamships vomiting their lurid flames on the air, and beating the waters around them into a very storm—huge amphibious monsters, whose powers seemed derived from all the lightnings of heaven being condensed in their furnaces.

Figure 7.1 H.G. Hine, wood-engraved illustrations for "The Monster City," *Illuminated Magazine* 3 (September 1844): 286.

A relatively small number of periodicals—notably specialist trade journals or metropolitan quarterlies like the *Westminster Review* (1814–1914) and *Edinburgh Review* (1802–29)—used the absence of illustration as a badge of their intellectual seriousness. Many others saw illustration as a necessary mechanism for coaxing in readers through the offer of visual pleasure. For every *Chambers's Edinburgh Journal* (1832–1956), which shunned illustration on its multi-columned and densely printed page,[2] there was many a *Saturday Magazine* (1832–44) and *Penny Magazine* (1832–45) which believed in the necessity of the visual as a means of engaging with newly or barely literate readers. Visually interesting paratextual elements were also widely understood to be an extremely important component of a successful magazine. The incorporation of graphic elements into the design of distinctive mastheads, title pages, indexes (in the case of *Punch*), and other visual emblems of self-identification was a crucial means of characterizing, individuating, advertising, and selling a periodical title (Figure 7.2).

The centrality of a readily identified and long-lasting masthead to a journal's identity can be gauged by the evident wear on the masthead blocks visible in successive years of the *Illustrated London News* (1842–1989) caused by persistent reuse. Each issue of *Figaro in London* (1831–39), a relatively long-running satirical weekly, was announced by a widely-known image of Figaro by Robert Seymour. The printer continued to use the original blocks, presumably to avoid the expense of re-engraving, even though they showed an immediately visible white line running between them (Figure 7.3). Further evidence of the importance of the visual appeal of the title

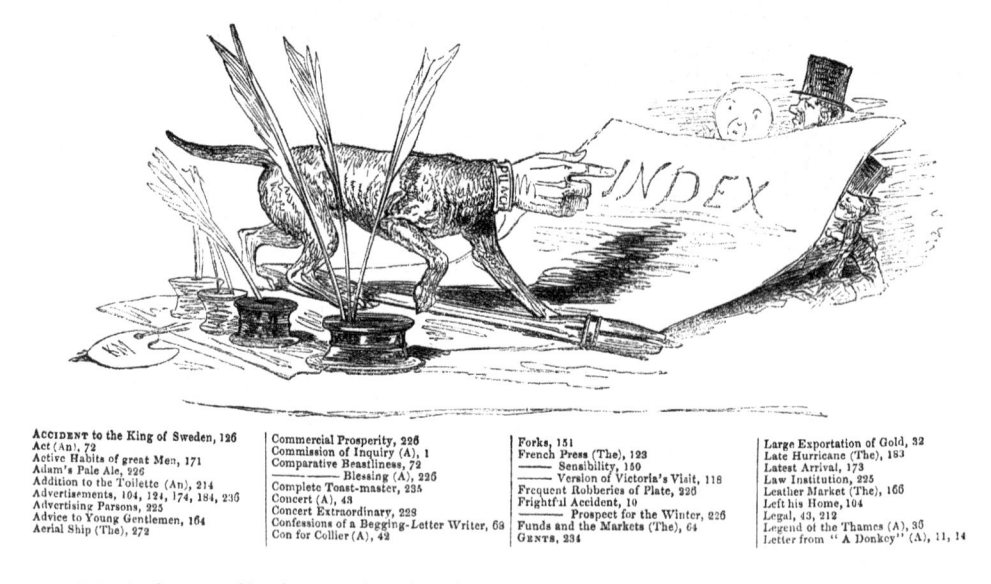

Figure 7.2 Wood-engraved headpiece to the index of *Punch* 5 (1843). Courtesy of Special Collections and Archives, Liverpool John Moores University.

2. It did so in order to foreground the presumed dedication of its readers (the self-improving artisan classes) to print.

ARO IN LOND

> Satire should like a polish'd razor keen,
> Wound with a touch that's scarcely felt or seen.—LADY MONTAGUE.

aricatures are parts (though humble ones,) of Political History. They supply of public men, which cannot be found elsewhere."—CROKER'S NEW WHIG GU

Figure 7.3 Robert Seymour, detail from the wood-engraved masthead for *Figaro in London* 5, no. 239 (July 2, 1836): 105.

page can be found in the sequence of different wrapper designs that characterized early issues of *Punch*, a sequence finally stabilized through Richard Doyle's second design adopted in January 1849.[3] While color printing was expensive and impractical to reproduce on a regular basis, some Victorian periodicals nonetheless offered colored lithographs, often of an ambitious size

3. Spielmann, *History of "Punch,"* 42–9.

and aesthetic sophistication and frequently in the form of free give-away supplements to special issues, associated almanacs, or, as in the case of the large-scale *British Workman*, as striking glossy glazed covers to volume reissues. Tipped-in (pasted in) engraved or lithographed fashion plates were also commonly used in journals aimed at women readers.

The titles of many well-known magazines made their dependence on illustration quite clear, either explicitly (the *Illustrated London News* or *Cassell's Illustrated Family Magazine*, 1853–67) or implicitly (the *Graphic*, 1869–1932). While throughout the century there was some sense that illustration was at odds with high seriousness (heavyweight quarterlies like the *Westminster Review* remained illustration-free), the successful use of illustration for comic purposes (*Punch* and its many imitators) and for topical reportage (*Illustrated London News* and its rivals) in middlebrow journals founded in the 1840s gave visual content at least a semblance of respectability. Literary monthlies such as *Once a Week* (1859–80), *Good Words* (1860–1911), and the *Cornhill Magazine* (1860–1975) offered aesthetically ambitious plates to complement the poetry, articles, and serialized fiction that comprised their printed content, which furthered the claims of illustration to seriousness as well as aesthetic ambition. Such magazines began to employ art editors like the Dalziel Brothers, and their visual content was often developed with the possibility of later republication in volume form. *Dalziel's Bible Gallery* (1881) is a successful example of the ways in which periodical illustrations, in this case those first published in *Good Words*, could be reworked as a book. The introduction of a wide variety of illustrative modes later in the century (based on photographic reprographic processes) suggested an increased authenticity and verisimilitude in the representation of events, gave additional authority to the status of illustration, and vastly increased the palette of reprographic effects.[4]

Despite the centrality of illustration to the development of Victorian periodicals, there is no recent general history of periodical illustration or of wood-engraved periodical illustration available, with Mason Jackson's *The Pictorial Press* from 1885 still serving as the most useful survey.[5] The discussion of the history of periodical illustration can certainly be widely found in specialist period and generic studies, including several surveys of "black and white" illustration in periodicals of the 1860s[6] or in Celina Fox's *Graphic Journalism in England during the 1830s and 1840s*,[7] and, increasingly, in studies of particular periodicals, a line of study substantially inaugurated by Peter Sinnema's study of the first ten years of the *Illustrated London News*.[8] Gerry Beegan's *The Mass Image* offers a valuable history of the impact of photomechanical reprographic processes on later Victorian periodicals.[9] There are also several useful collections of essays on various aspects of periodical illustration which give a strong sense of the increasingly sophisticated ways scholars are approaching the topic.[10] Surveys of the history of wood engraving and lithography widely acknowledge the importance of periodicals in publicizing

---

4. Beegan, *Mass Image*, 1–31.
5. Jackson, *Pictorial Press*, 219–363; Anderson, *Printed Image*.
6. See Goldman, *Victorian Illustration*; Suriano, *Pre-Raphaelite Illustrators*; Kooistra, *Poetry, Pictures*.
7. Fox, *Graphic Journalism*.
8. Sinnema, *Dynamics of the Printed Page*.
9. Beegan, *Mass Image*.
10. Brake and Demoor, *Lure of Illustration*; Cooke and Goldman, *Reading Victorian Illustration*.

the technical and aesthetic resourcefulness with which images might be made available to mass readerships. While specific discussion of periodical illustration generally forms a sideshow in broad-based studies of nineteenth-century illustration,[11] scholarly interest in periodical illustration has progressed far enough to lay out an ambitious agenda for future research.

Wood Engraving: The Representational, Pictorial, or Comic

It is easy enough to see the appeal of wood engraving to editors, publishers, and booksellers. Wood engravings could be produced with remarkable speed, especially when an image was divided up between a number of engravers. The long-lasting nature of wood blocks allowed for massive print runs, their shape and size could be endlessly varied, and, best of all, they could be easily situated amidst circumambient text to form a close alliance between text and image, resulting in a visually satisfying page. During the 1830s and 1840s, wood engravers rapidly assembled in London and were often employed in workshops overseen by engraver-entrepreneurs. Working in these shops, they helped to fulfill the voracious demands of the periodical marketplace, and it was through their skill that some semblance of tonal and compositional sophistication was able to disguise the representational limitations inherent in the wood engraving. The preponderance of wood-engraved illustration as a central element in the design and construction of periodicals does little to resolve the difficulties of evaluating the nature and purpose of the graphic content to be found in magazines. Indeed, the very term "illustration" seems to assign it to a subordinate role in the printed text. To invoke "visual pleasure" is hardly sufficient as a starting place for trying to suggest the range of purposes, modes, and functions that Victorian periodical illustration assumed. In a recent book on mid-Victorian illustration, Paul Goldman and Simon Cooke lay out what they see as the central complexities of periodical illustration.[12] They stress the need for multidisciplinary approaches to what they describe as a "dynamic and evasive medium."[13] Studying illustration requires first of all an awareness of the physical relationship between type and image on the printed page and an understanding of the ways illustration comments on, re-enacts, or rewrites the text which it accompanies. But further, Goldman and Cooke argue, illustrations "mirror and critique" the culture that produces them.[14] They therefore must be understood within the particular history of the aesthetic, economic, and reprographic history of image-making for a mass public, which might well include knowledge of the relationship between mass-circulation illustration and painting. It is fair to say that until very recently such an ambitiously cross-disciplinary approach has not been applied to the study of the illustrations found in periodicals.

In this context, it is useful to think a little about the importance of recognizing the complexities of wood engraving as an illustrative medium, especially given its seeming "naturalness" as a presence in the Victorian reading experience. The omnipresence of wood engraving, not just in periodicals but more broadly in Victorian visual culture, tends to blur the range of

---

11. Twyman, "Illustration Revolution"; Houfe, *Dictionary of British Book Illustrators*, 13–202.
12. Cooke and Goldman, *Reading Victorian Illustration*, 1–32.
13. Ibid., 11.
14. Ibid.

functional categories that illustration often simultaneously occupied. At the broadest level, these categories might be defined as representational, pictorial, or comic. The concept of a wood engraving as potentially representational depends on an assumption, shared by both editors and readers, that the medium was unproblematically naturalistic—a tall order given that wood engraving was essentially a monochrome and linear medium poorly suited to tonal complexity and was long associated with vernacular and popular culture, where simplified images were the rule. Yet for Victorians, wood engraving, despite its limitations and simplifications, was widely accepted as a truthful representational medium and, thus, the best mechanism for representing the appearance and texture of the material world. Wood engraving established itself as an expository and informative medium by means of widespread use in the cheap information miscellanies of the 1820s, which included such significant technical journals as the *Mechanic's Magazine* (1823–72) and the *Lancet* (1823–), as well as more entertaining magazines like the *Mirror of Literature* (1822–47). Informational journals were aimed at a broadly expanded readership ten years later through the innovative presence of the *Penny Magazine* (1832–45) and *Saturday Magazine* (1832–44) (Figure 7.4). They also became crucially associated with reportage early in the Victorian period, an association rendered widely visible after the establishment of the *Illustrated London News* in 1842 and imitators like the *Illustrated Times* (1855–72) that rapidly followed.

It remains hard to accept the apparently unworried ease with which Victorians accepted wood engraving as an essentially naturalistic and representational medium. The famous triumphalist statement from the opening number of the *Illustrated London News* asserted the power of wood engraving to represent the world accurately: "We do hold it as triumphant that WE are, by the publication of this very newspaper, launching the giant vessel of illustration into a channel the broadest and widest that it has ever been dared to stem. . . . The public will have henceforth under their, and within their grasp, the very form and presence of events as they transpire."[15] Looking now at the black and white wood engravings used in early issues of the *Illustrated London News*, the notion that they represent the "very form and presence" of the natural world seems an unlikely one, although it has not prevented many scholars from offering such images as unmediated depictions of nineteenth-century reality (Figure 7.5).

There were obvious limits to the ability of wood engraving to depict the world naturalistically, even for generations of Victorian readers well acquainted and at ease with its formal qualities. In order to describe an increasingly complex and technocratic society to an ever-growing audience often lacking much formal education, the wood engraving was necessarily forced to use simplified visual codes in order to inform and explain. Such a drive towards the informative meant that many, perhaps most, wood-engraved illustrations were more diagrammatic than representational in their pursuit of an expository way of describing the world—that is, they provided a simplified, non-naturalistic account of the structure of things in order to offer information translated into visual forms that explained as well as represented their subjects (Figure 7.6). Clearly, too, expository and informative wood engravings were as amenable as words in defining and explaining the world in terms that were not ideologically neutral. The

---

15. "Our Address," 1.

Saturday Magazine.

Nº 20.   OCTOBER 27TH, 1832.   {PRICE ONE PENNY.

UNDER THE DIRECTION OF THE COMMITTEE OF GENERAL LITERATURE AND EDUCATION,
APPOINTED BY THE SOCIETY FOR PROMOTING CHRISTIAN KNOWLEDGE.

THE PEAK CAVERN, DERBYSHIRE.

THE Peak of Derbyshire, in which this stupendous cavern is situated, gives name to a large tract of hilly country in the county of Derby, between the Derwent and the Dove, and is separated from Staffordshire by the last named river. This district is a region of bleak barren heights and long-extended moors, interspersed with deep valleys through which many small streams take their course. The High Peak is peculiarly liable to violent storms, during which the rain descends in torrents, and frequently occasions great damage. The country abounds in mines of lead, iron, coal and antimony.

On the summit of an almost inaccessible rock is seated the little town of Castleton, so called from a very ancient castle, the ruins of which remain. From some of the ornaments still remaining in one of the walls, it is supposed to have been a Norman structure, and is said to have been built by William Peveril, the natural son of William the Conqueror. Its historical interest has been revived by Sir Walter Scott, in his novel of *Peveril of the Peak*; but it was not, as might be inferred from that work, in the possession of the family of the Peverils, at so late a period as the Restoration. At the base of the huge rock on which stands this curious remnant of antiquity, is the mouth of the celebrated Peak Cavern, commonly called the Devil's Hole.

The entrance is situated in a gloomy recess, between two ranges of perpendicular rocks, having on the left, a rivulet, which issues from the cave, and pursues its foaming course over broken masses of limestone. A vast canopy of rock overhangs the mouth of this stupendous cavity, forming a low arch, 120 feet in width and 42 in height.

VOL. I.

At the first entrance, the spectator is surprised to find that a number of twine-makers have established their residence and manufactory within this tremendous gulf, and the combination of their rude appearance and machines, with the sublime features of the natural scenery, impresses the mind with an indescribable emotion of awe. After proceeding about ninety feet, the roof becomes lower, and a gentle descent conducts by a detached rock to the inner entrance, where the blaze of the day wholly disappears, and all further researches must be pursued by torch-light.

The passage now becomes extremely confined, and the visiter is obliged to proceed about twenty yards in a stooping posture; but on his arrival at a spacious

Interior of the Cavern.

Figure 7.4 Wood-engraved title page for the *Saturday Magazine* 1, no. 20 (October 27, 1832): 153.

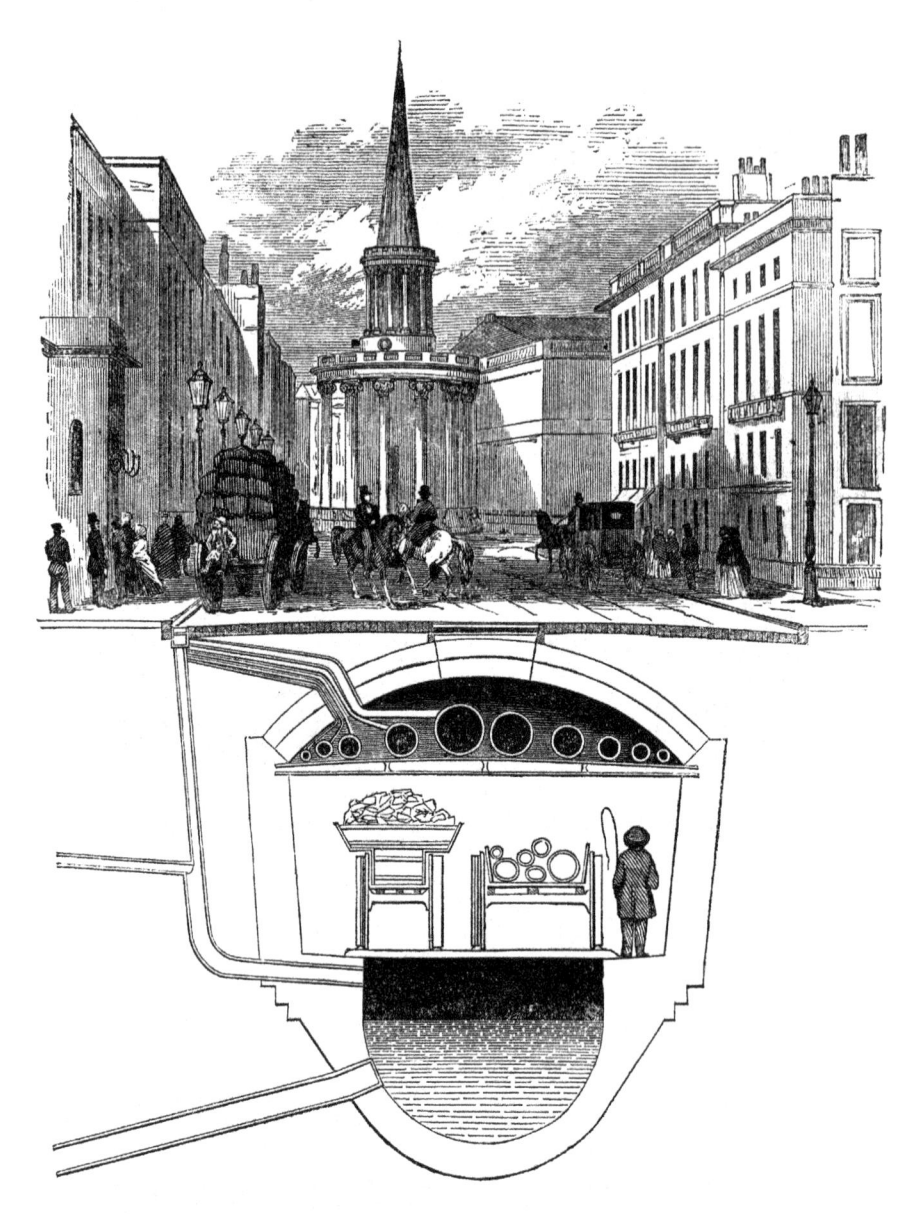

PROPOSED METROPOLITAN SUBWAY FOR SEWAGE, AND GAS AND WATER SUPPLY.

Figure 7.5 Wood engraving showing a "Proposed Metropolitan Subway," *Illustrated London News* 23 (October 29, 1853): 367. Courtesy of Special Collections and Archives, Liverpool John Moores University.

ownership, deployment, and definition of what constituted "information" was highly contested in the early Victorian press, and images were no less implicated in these contests than words.

Further complexity in the definition of categories comes from the evidently pictorial qualities of many Victorian periodical illustrations. Commercial, aesthetic, and practical reasons

THE
WEEKLY VISITOR.

Number XCVIII.] TUESDAY, AUGUST 19, 1835. { PRICE ONE HALFPENNY.

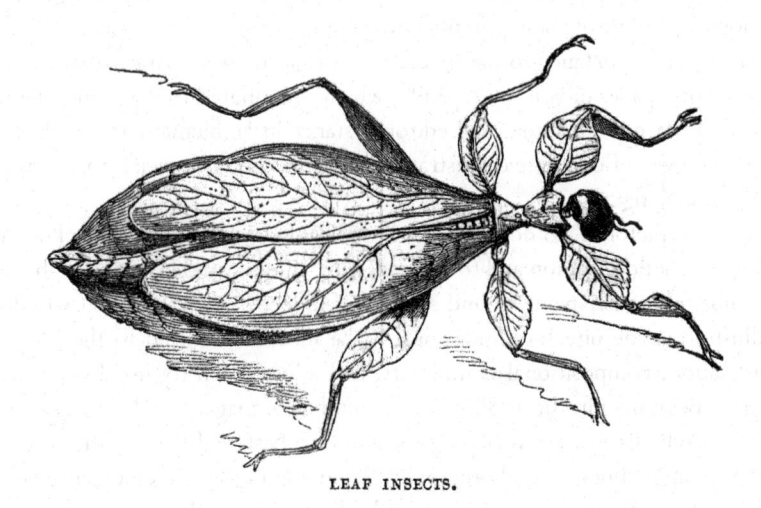

LEAF INSECTS.

LEAF-INSECTS.
"Crushed before the Moth."

Destined as are the insect tribes to be the food of birds and beasts, and indeed of each other, (for the insect kingdom has its lions and its tigers,) still are they not left utterly destitute of means of self-protection. Such a law would be an isolated exception to the general system and order of things, which it has pleased the Almighty to establish. That insects should exist in myriads, is essentially necessary, for they are needed as food; that they should be destroyed by myriads, is as equally necessary, otherwise they, in their turn, would depopulate the earth, and destroy every "green thing." The multitudes that are this year devoured by birds or beasts, or swept by the winds into lakes, rivers, and the ocean, there to become the food of aquatic animals, will have their places supplied, the next year, and so on. And if we examine attentively we shall find that each individual possesses in common with its fellow, some mode of self-protection, some means of escape, some plan of eluding adversaries, so that the destruction of a race shall never be complete; but that survivors of the havoc of one season, shall remain to produce a progeny, whose numbers shall fill up the vacuum. But what means of defence, what plan of escape can beings so feeble, so exposed, so incapable of effective resistance, employ? Few indeed that are active, many that are passive. We have not time or space to enumerate each peculiar device, each instinctive artifice; but there is one so immediately proclaiming the Almighty Architect, and so nearly connected with the very existence of the insect beings themselves, that we cannot overlook it. We allude to a resemblance to the objects near or upon which, under ordinary circumstances, they are to be found. This is the case with multitudes. "One of our scarcest British weavils," (*curculio nebulosus*) say Kirby and Spence, "by its grey colour, spotted with black, so closely imitates the soil, consisting of white sand, mixed with black earth, on

VOL. II.   2 P

Figure 7.6 Wood-engraved illustration to "Leaf Insects," *Weekly Visitor* 2, no. 98 (August 19, 1835): 297.

for including illustrations in magazines are obvious enough. Images situated alongside or even within text (thanks to the versatility of the wood engraving) performed the traditional function of explaining, extending, reinterpreting, or reiterating the verbal content they accompanied. Such illustrations were particularly well adapted to the needs of serialized fiction, adding visual pleasure and readily grasped expository depth to the narrative (Figure 7.7). Other illustrations were essentially decorative, producing an arresting and pleasing visual impact on the page or the double-page spread. One important consideration in printing images of this kind was an acknowledgement of their potential afterlife as scraps or decorative elements in the home. Of particular importance to the success of a magazine were paratextual elements such as mastheads or title pages of volume reprints, which contributed to the brand identity of the periodical and displayed its content and editorial stance in emblematic form. Portraits were another central strand of decorative illustration, which offered a crucial way to acquaint the public with its public figures.

Using the term "pictorial" to describe this broad category of illustration acknowledges its relationship to aesthetic ambition and to the codes, techniques, and graphic vocabulary of fine art images, most obviously painting and sculpture. Indeed, much Victorian wood-engraved magazine illustration, despite the limitations of the medium, aspired to the level of finish, tonal sophistication, compositional complexity, and allusive density usually associated with fine art images. Beginning in the 1830s, a large number of magazines dedicated considerable space to the reproduction of artworks, a process much hastened later in the century by the increased reprographic fidelity of photography. Beginning in the late nineteenth century, this self-consciously aesthetic tradition of black-and-white image-making was a central point of interest for collectors and commentators, especially those who were attracted to the periodical contributions of artists such as John Everett Millais, Edward Burne-Jones, and Aubrey Beardsley. The democratization of fine art images for the edification and enjoyment of a mass reading public informs many discussions of Victorian magazine illustration. Such a relentless concentration on the aesthetic achievements of Victorian periodical illustration, however, has perhaps been conducted at the expense of recognizing the variety and quality of much work published outside the culturally ambitious pages of the mid-Victorian monthlies or the knowingly aesthetic magazines of the fin de siècle.

The term "pictorial" also rather misleadingly suggests that the primary generic dialogue that structured ambitious decorative and aestheticized periodical illustration took place between fine art and the wood-engraved image. In practice, magazine illustration drew energy from many other sources—among them the tropes of Gothic melodrama found both on the stage and in illustrated down-market sensational fiction, as well as within portraiture, caricature, and the vernacular broadside tradition (Figure 7.8). In turn, magazine illustrations were themselves assimilated into a variety of related visual traditions. Of particular importance was the reuse of periodical images in decorating transfer-printed pottery and Staffordshire portrait figures. The gestural vocabulary for the illustration of magazines was heavily dependent on the stylized presence of theatrical stereotypes as well as fine art images. Engraved and etched portrait and topographical prints similarly provided a basis for many periodical illustrations. Despite the aspiration of magazines like the *Illustrated London News* to offer authentic eyewitness accounts of the events they depicted in their pages, it is clear that many illustrations were

EVAN HARRINGTON; OR, HE WOULD BE A GENTLEMAN.
BY GEORGE MEREDITH.

CHAPTER IX.
THE COUNTESS IN LOW SOCIETY.

By dint of stratagems worthy of a Court intrigue, the Countess de Saldar contrived to traverse the streets of Lymport, and enter the house where she was born, unsuspected and unseen, under cover of a profusion of lace and veil and mantilla, which only her heroic resolve to keep her beauties hidden from the profane townspeople, could have rendered endurable beneath the fervid summer sun. Dress in a foreign style she must, as without it she lost that sense of superiority, which was the only comfort to her in her tribulations. The period of her arrival was ten days subsequent to the burial of her father. She had come in the coach, like any common mortal, and the coachman, upon her request, had put her down at the Governor's house, and the guard had knocked at the door, and the servant had informed her that General Hucklebridge was not the governor of Lymport, nor did Admiral Combleman then reside in the town, which tidings, the coach being then out of sight, it did not disconcert the Countess to hear; and she reached her mother, having, at least, cut off communication with the object of conveyance —cast salt on her many traces, as it were.

The Countess kissed her mother, kissed Mrs. Fiske, and asked sharply for Evan. Mrs. Fiske let her know that Evan was in the house.

"Where?" inquired the Countess. "I have news of the utmost importance for him. I must see him."

"Where is he, aunt?" said Mrs. Fiske. "In the shop, I think; I wonder he did not see you passing, Louisa."

The Countess went bolt down into a chair.

"Go to him, Jane," said Mrs. Mel. "Tell him Louisa is here, and don't return."

Mrs. Fiske departed, and the Countess smiled.

"Thank you, Mamma! you know I never could bear that odious, vulgar little woman. Oh, the heat! You talk of Portugal! And, oh! poor dear Papa! what I have suffered!"

Flapping her laces for air, and wiping her eyes for sorrow, the Countess poured a flood of sympathy into her mother's ears, and then said:

"But you have made a great mistake, Mamma, in allowing Evan to put his foot into that place. He —beloved of an heiress! Why, if an enemy should hear of it, it would ruin him —positively blast him—for ever. And that she loves him I have proof positive. Yes; with all her frankness, the little thing cannot conceal that from me now. She loves him! And I desire you to guess, Mamma, whether rivals will not abound? And what enemy so much to be dreaded as a rival? And what revelation so awful as that he has stood in a—in a—boutique?"

Mrs. Mel maintained her usual attitude for listening. It had occurred to her that it might do no good to tell the grand lady, her daughter, of Evan's resolution, so she simply said, "It is discipline for him," and left her to speak a private word with the youth.

Timidly the Countess inspected the furniture of the apartment, taking chills at the dingy articles she saw, in the midst of her heat. That she should have sprung from this! The thought was painful; still she could forgive Providence so much. But should it ever be known she had

Figure 7.7 Charles Keene, wood-engraved illustration to George Meredith's *Evan Harrington*, *Once a Week* 2, no. 38 (March 17, 1860): 243. Courtesy of Special Collections, Liverpool John Moores University.

Figure 7.8 "The Demon Shows Theresa to Faust," wood-engraved illustration for G.W.M. Reynolds's *Faust*, *London Journal* 2, no. 32 (October 4, 1845): 49.

derived from existing sources or, indeed, entirely from the imagination of their draughtsman. The interpenetration and cross-pollination of graphic traditions and visual codes brought an energy and range of cultural reference to magazine illustration that gives complexity to even the most utilitarian, simply drawn images.

Comic images were ubiquitous in the Victorian press, even in magazines whose central interest was topical reportage, such as the *Illustrated London News*. This was one outcome of the failure of the single-plate etched and engraved caricature to maintain its cultural prestige into the Victorian period. It is notoriously difficult to define the "comic"; here I use the term to refer to works that produce a humorous, pleasurable response, perhaps (but also perhaps not) suggesting satirical commentary. *Punch* has been taken to typify this kind of illustration, but as I shall show later, we need to attend to other sources as well.

Of the three categories of wood-engraved illustration defined above—representational, pictorial, and comic—it is the representational tradition that has been least explored in recent scholarship. Nonetheless, two key studies provide an important agenda for writing a fully informed history of Victorian periodical illustration. Celina Fox's *Graphic Journalism* offers a well-researched overview of key developments in the relationship between periodicals and their graphic content in the early Victorian period. The structure of her survey remains persuasive. The opening chapter comprises an account of the status of wood engraving that acknowledges the delicate distinctions in cultural levels that existed between various genres of periodical literature. She suggests that the dominance of wood engraving as a reprographic medium for magazines did not happen without difficulty or challenge. She then argues that the rise of new forms of wood-engraved political satire in the early 1830s gained considerable popularity in ways that owed much to the traditional freedom from legislation and censorship that caricature had enjoyed in Britain. Fox thus sees the arrival in the 1830s of mass-circulation, informative, illustrated magazines aimed at self-improving artisans as largely a reaction to the specter of a "radical" satirical press, rather than the inevitable recognition by socially progressive reformers of the need for an "improving" and politically neutral illustrated press. Equally challenging is her view that serialized fiction in magazines derived its major impetus from the genre of police gazettes, which brought together, through the medium of narrative, elements of the "old broadside tradition, . . . useful knowledge and middle class concern, . . . working class politics and satire, . . . [and] the growth of popular literature and illustrated news journalism."[16] This emphasis on tradition (in this instance, illustrated crime reporting), new and innovative responses to a vastly changed socio-political situation, and the influence of new reprographic technologies also informs Fox's account of the rise of graphic reportage, as epitomized by the founding of the *Illustrated London News* in 1842.

Patricia Anderson's *The Printed Image* focuses on the role of illustration in cultural negotiations between classes associated with the emergence of mass literacy between 1790 and 1860. Anderson is anxious to avoid crude generalizations and assumptions about the socio-political affiliations and reading habits of particular social groups among the less well-off, and, like Fox, she acknowledges (if in less detail) the origins of many Victorian textual formations in popular culture of the late eighteenth century. But her focus is in many respects canonical, relegating the little-known outsiders, hack artists, and anonymous engravers that populate Fox's study to continued obscurity. Anderson's "canon," comprised of the *Penny Magazine*, followed by the *London Journal* (1845–1928), *Reynolds's Miscellany* (1846–69), and *Cassell's Illustrated Family Magazine* (1853–67), has become something of a route map for scholars of Victorian illustrated journalism as they make their way through a mass of material, searching for key titles.

Both Anderson and Fox provide important ways of approaching the illustrative traditions of the later Victorian press. Anderson focuses on the cultural politics of visual information, showing how the diagrammatic account of reality offered by wood engravings in mass-circulation journals between 1830 and 1860 is implicated in a cultural conflict over the nature of what should be disclosed to a mass reader as "useful knowledge." Subsequent research has led to an increasingly sophisticated approach to the significance of scientific and technological information in Victorian periodicals.[17] Fox constructs a convincing narrative of the origins of the documentary impulse that characterized so much mid- and late Victorian periodical illustration. In particular, she stresses the importance of the comic tradition as a source for social observation and reportage and suggests the weight of the vernacular tradition as an influence on later graphic traditions. She also suggests that the later Victorian press was rooted in the illustrated diversionary and "unimproving" literature of Regency culture. Recent scholars, such as Peter Sinnema, have begun to bring more sophisticated theoretical models to bear on discussions of

---

16. Fox, *Graphic Journalism*, 158.
17. Cantor, Dawson, Gooday, Noakes, Shuttleworth, and Topham, *Science in the Nineteenth-Century Periodical*.

the representational assumptions of the documentary wood engraving, showing how "reality" is mediated through the complex visual codes and traditions of the medium.[18]

As already suggested, the ambitious pictorial illustrations found in Victorian periodicals, many of them accompanying texts commissioned from major writers, have long been valued, collected, and celebrated as a major artistic achievement of the Victorian period. Using traditional art historical categorization, a "school" of British black and white illustrators was established by connoisseurs and collectors like Forrest Reid and Gleeson White in the late nineteenth and early twentieth century.[19] Reid and White were particularly attracted to illustrated middlebrow monthlies and weeklies like the *Cornhill Magazine*, *Good Words*, *Quiver*, *Argosy*, and *Once a Week*. Although they extended their interest to books, magazines remained the premier locale for their interest. Alongside the work of well-known painters like John Everett Millais, Dante Gabriel Rossetti, Ford Madox Brown, and Edward Burne-Jones, Reid and White also celebrated a number of outstanding, if rather less well-known, illustrators who worked primarily for magazines—including G.J. Pinwell, Arthur Boyd Houghton, and Josiah Whymper. Subsequent scholarship has endorsed and deepened understanding of the quality of line and composition employed by these artists in their contributions to magazines. The work of Paul Goldman and Simon Cooke, in particular, has sustained the high status accorded to the black and white pictorialists. In his influential *Victorian Illustration*, Goldman distinguishes three major schools of ambitious black and white illustrators working across both volume and periodical media in the mid-Victorian period—the Pre-Raphaelites, the Idyllic School, and the High Victorians. His book is based on the study of fifty illustrated magazines, ranging from successful literary monthlies like *Good Words* to more specialist publications like *Every Boy's Magazine* (1862–66) and then to periodicals like the temperance *British Workman* (1862–68), which aimed to attract artisan readers through spectacular visual content (Figure 7.9). Since 2000, more complex scholarly models for the relationship between image and text in periodicals have been developed, notably by Linda Hughes,[20] which has led to broader understanding of the range of illustrated texts to be found in periodicals and the possible interests and tastes of readers. Recent research has also begun to reshape the Victorian literary landscape by focusing on the remarkable ways in which periodicals served as the primary site for the consumption of poetry, a focus that was driven by illustration.[21]

Goldman's study of Victorian illustration runs from 1855 to the 1880s and thus excludes the aesthetically self-conscious and experimental "little" magazines of the 1890s, which strove to express a cohesive aesthetic in every aspect of their content and appearance. Periodicals like the *Yellow Book* (1894–97) and the *Dome* (1897–1900) were deliberately founded to expound aesthetic philosophies linked to modernity and the avant-garde, thus uniting interest in such topics as Celtic patterns, European symbolist art, and experimental graphics employing art

---

18. Sinnema, *Dynamics of the Pictured Page*; Fyfe, "Illustrating the Accident."
19. White, *English Illustration*; Reid, *Illustrators*.
20. Hughes, "Inventing Poetry and Pictorialism."
21. Kooistra, *Poetry, Pictures, and Popular Publishing*.

Figure 7.9 John Gilbert, "The Ship on Fire," wood-engraved title page illustration for the *British Workman* 107 (November 1863): 425. Courtesy of Special Collections, Liverpool John Moores University.

nouveau motifs. Rossetti and Burne-Jones were among the celebrated artists who joined W.B. Yeats, Laurence Housman, and other modernist figures in the pages of the *Dome*, while the *Yellow Book* depended heavily on Aubrey Beardsley's illustrations to advertise its avant-garde and experimental credentials.

Humor and Illustration

Scholarly interest in the continuing stream of brilliant *Punch* cartoonists—including John Leech, Richard Doyle, John Tenniel, Charles Keene, and George du Maurier—has to some extent hindered awareness of broader traditions of comic and humorous periodical illustration in the Victorian period. While the prodigiously successful formulations of graphic content developed by *Punch* were hugely difficult for its rivals to evade—it is quite hard to visually differentiate some imitators such as the *Puppet Show* (1848–49) from *Punch*—there were, nonetheless, important and innovative, if relatively unknown, comic and satirical artists working across a range of humorous periodicals. Several such magazines sought to build their brand identity out of the regular presence in each issue of a large-scale illustration by a named artist who was closely allied to both the periodical's design and its editorial stance. *Punch* provided the model for competing publications, including the *Man in the Moon* (1847–49), *Joe Miller the Younger* (1845), the *Puppet Show*, and, later in the century, *Fun* (1861–1901) and *Judy* (1867–1910) (Figure 7.10). The principal illustrators for such magazines, while less well-known than *Punch* artists like Leech, Doyle, and Tenniel, were nonetheless named by their respective publications and were important in establishing their brand identities. John Procter at the *Man in the Moon* and *Judy*, William Boucher at *Judy*, and Matt Morgan and Frank J. Sullivan at *Fun* were all extremely capable and productive cartoonists working in the *Punch* tradition. Some satirical journals tried hard to find an original graphic format for their cartoons, with magazines like the *Tomahawk* (1867–70) employing a named illustrator, Matt Morgan, to draw spectacular double-page, two-color, wood-engraved images in order to arrest the reader's attention. Late in the century, the strip cartoon (already well established in Europe and the United States as a popular feature of periodical literature) became a staple feature of British comic periodicals. This was due to the emergence of Ally Sloper, a character originally figured as a faux-naïve adventurer in single-plate images for *Judy* by Charles Henry Ross. In 1884, he became the protagonist in his own graphic magazine, *Ally Sloper's Half Holiday* (1884–1916), drawn successively by Ross, Marie Duval (Ross's wife), W.G. Baxter, and W.F. Thomas.[22]

Punch's overwhelming influence in establishing the dominant graphic modes for enacting visual humor in Victorian periodicals was more the outcome of a brilliant synthesis of available and emerging potentialities than any major innovation. The "big cut" was a full-page cartoon on a political or socio-cultural topic that anchored each issue of *Punch* in its immediate historical moment. This feature was derived from a sequence of less than successful attempts to adapt the eighteenth-century single-plate etched or engraved caricature to a periodical or serial form. From the 1830s, periodicals attempted to adapt single-plate political caricature to a more

---

22. Bailey, "Ally Sloper's Half-Holiday"; Sabin, "Ally Sloper."

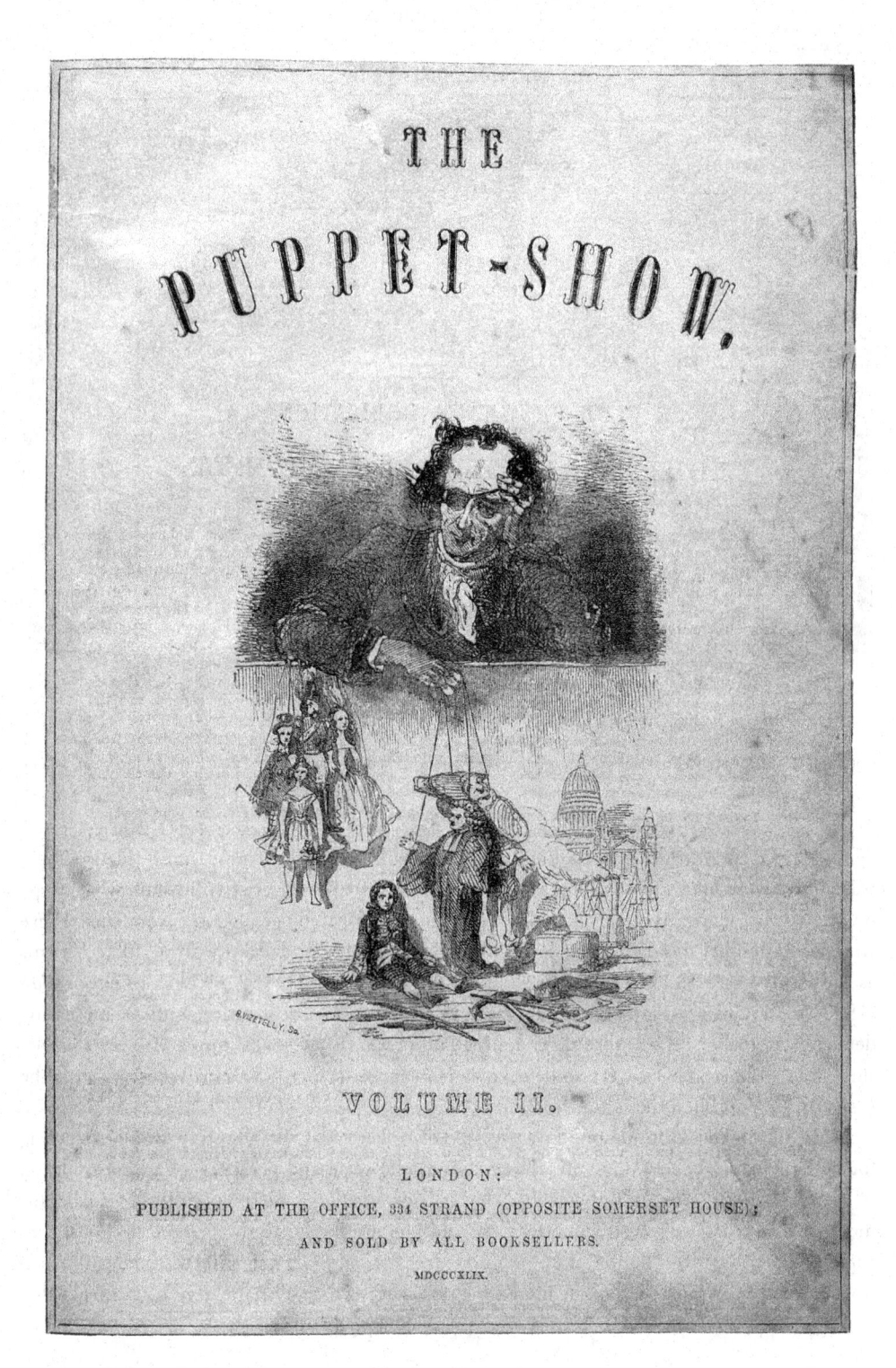

Figure 7.10 Engraved title page to volume 2 of the *Puppet Show* (1849).

Figure 7.11 C.J. Grant, "The Irish Schoolmaster and His Pupils," *Political Drama, No. 128* (London: Drake, c. 1834).

democratized and fun-seeking marketplace. C.J. Grant's lengthy *Political Drama* (Figure 7.11) was innovatively John Doyle's long series of lithographed *Sketches*, drawn in somewhat wispy outlines, were innovatively produced as a series of eye-catching, gigantic woodcuts. There were also attempts to adapt large-scale lithographed political caricature to periodical forms as early as the mid-1820s,[23] but it was only in the 1830s that Thomas McLean's *Looking Glass* (1830–36) found a way to combine traditional graphic political satire with an increasing demand for smaller-scale, more diversionary humorous visual "jokes" into a viable magazine; since lithographic images were expensive and not easy to integrate into typeset pages, the *Looking Glass* published them as inserts.

Punch solved these limitations in an extremely clever way, by adopting wood engraving for its large-scale weekly "big cut," thus retaining the scale and presence of a long tradition of graphic political satire and then separating out the smaller-scale socio-cultural visual commentary into wood-engraved vignettes that could be dropped into the printed text either to support articles or to function as autonomous freestanding jokes. For these smaller illustrations, *Punch* drew upon the rapidly increasing popularity of small-scale humorous images that

---

23. Maidment, *Comedy, Caricature and the Social Order*, 47–110.

were beginning to populate a wide range of print cultural forms in the 1830s and early 1840s. Many of these publications, such as the *Comic Offering* (1831–35), were produced as annuals or as Christmas gift books, but the comic small-scale wood engraving invaded or even conquered the marketplace for visual humor in the 1830s, finding its way into play texts and song books as well. In the 1830s, the wood-engraved comic vignette was also increasingly used by artists like George Cruikshank as a relatively naturalistic aspect of early social exploration. Cruikshank illustrated texts from the 1820s and 1830s, such as *Sunday in London* and *Mornings in Bow Street* (which offered a comic but acutely observed account of low-life London), inspired *Punch* artists to take street life and the comedy of manners as their subject. It is possible that the roots of realism in Victorian visual arts and fiction may well lie in the comic vignettes of the 1830s and 1840s rather than any more self-consciously aesthetic source. Further evidence of *Punch*'s eclectic and inspired gathering of available visual resources can be found it its use of tiny silhouette jokes and decorative capitals to begin articles or to act as introductions to each letter in the index. All these varied resources are shown to best advantage in what may well be *Punch*'s finest visual achievement, the early years of the annual *Almanack*.

These comic graphic forms together established the vocabulary for comic illustration, leading to the emergence of the comic strip in the last years of the century. In his magisterial *History of the Comic Strip*, David Kunzle argues that the comic strip was a major vehicle for serially published visual humor in the nineteenth century, but he is implicitly rather dismissive of the British comic press of this time.[24] His argument serves as a useful reminder that the tradition of illustrated humorous periodicals was startlingly different in Britain than in continental Europe or North America, where lithography had much more success and where the comic strip was rapidly developed. It also suggests the distinctiveness, if not necessarily the insularity, of nineteenth-century British periodical illustrative traditions in general. It was only late in the century that a truly oppositional voice to Mr. Punch, the proletarian droll Ally Sloper, began to exploit a more truly democratic audience for visual comedy.

The introduction of "process" reprographic techniques towards the end of the century formed another major shift in how the physical world was visualized. Process methods used photography to project original images onto metal plates. Once they were etched, these plates enabled photographs to be printed alongside typeset material. As Gerry Beegan points out, photomechanical reproduction made the visual content of late nineteenth-century newspapers and magazines "more abundant, complex, and increasingly hybrid."[25] He concludes that the "introduction of photomechanical technologies destabilized reproduction and representation so that the discrete categories of photograph, wood engraving, and drawing took on a new fluidity."[26] The use of half-tone engraving, in particular, explains the increasingly naturalistic and "photographic" look of late nineteenth-century magazines and newspapers (Figure 7.12). The half tone was, despite some presence in book illustration, primarily the province of magazines and newspapers, where its ability to render detail was particularly useful. By the end

---

24. Kunzle, *History of the Comic Strip*, 18–24.
25. Beegan, *Mass Image*, 9.
26. Ibid.

the fair. Pity he did not get the chance. He'd have nailed him. Everyone says that Markson has made an awful mull of it, and now the fellow has got clean away, no one knows where. Who's the best man now? You can't say much for your side, Tom."

As I watched him stride away towards the park, I thought: "Yes, but thank God, Smollett did *not* get the chance."

Figure 7.12 "A.P.," process-engraved illustration for "Why He Failed," *Strand Magazine* 2 (July 1891): 30. Courtesy of Special Collections, Liverpool John Moores University.

of the century, illustration, largely carried out through photomechanical means, had become commonplace in almost every magazine, except for specialist scholarly journals.

The study of the illustration of Victorian periodicals has been dominated, until relatively recently, by the desire to establish aesthetic hierarchies foregrounding such high points as the comic inventiveness of the *Punch* illustrators, the literary pictorialism of the "black and white" artists who worked for the middlebrow monthlies of the 1860s, and the aesthetic adventurousness of "art" magazines in the 1890s. A number of factors have, however, brought a new potentiality to the study of periodical illustration, not least the increasing recognition that periodicals research forms a relatively autonomous field for academic study, a field that is, because of the nature of the source material, inevitably cross-disciplinary in its approach. The relationship between word and image in the Victorian periodical press is now understood to be something far more complex than the term "illustration" immediately suggests. In order to be fully understood, the study of illustration requires close attention to the reading practices employed by consumers of the Victorian press and thus to the complex iconographical sources of nineteenth-century illustration, as well as to the strengths and limitations of wood engraving as a reprographic medium. There is now a widespread recognition that illustration may not necessarily be primarily "illustrative"—that is, a visual mechanism for confirming or authenticating a statement primarily made by a text. The study of Victorian periodical illustration must also acknowledge the pleasurable as well as the socio-political, aesthetic, and cultural claims made by images on our attention. The staggering wealth of visual resources made available by major digitization projects (such as Cardiff University's *Lost Visions* illustration archive) should ensure that the study of periodical illustration will continue to expand as a necessary means of understanding the discourses of the Victorian periodical press.

8

POETRY

Linda K. Hughes

In May 1809, Rudolph Ackermann's *Poetical Magazine* (1809–10) announced a distinctly new periodical feature: rather than publishing "Collections of Miscellaneous Poetry" gathered by booksellers, it would "contain such productions alone, as have never appeared in print, or are but little known; and [present] itself as a receptacle to inoffensive poetic compositions of every kind, and from every Muse."[1] The magazine also announced that it would publish two colored engravings per monthly issue to accompany poetic contributions, thus establishing a precedent for the publication of illustrated original poetry in popular periodicals. Best known today for its humorous illustrated serial poem *The Schoolmaster's Tour* (later *The Tour of Dr. Syntax*), written by William Combe and illustrated by Thomas Rowlandson, the *Poetical Magazine* also established that poems, not just novels, could be successful serials and that periodical poetry could enter cultural memory. Later examples include John Keats's "Ode on a Grecian Urn," first issued in the *Annals of the Fine Arts* (January 1820); Elizabeth Barrett's "Cry of the Children," first published in *Blackwood's Edinburgh Magazine* (August 1843); and Rudyard Kipling's "Danny Deever," first printed in the *Scots Observer* (February 22, 1890). Poetry was an essential feature of the nineteenth-century periodical press. Every decade, across titles, class formations, and political orientations, thousands of poems were published in magazines and newspapers. In this essay, I will first assess the scale of periodical poetry and then turn to its multiple functions, forms, conventions, and effects, including its relation to ephemera and the democratization of authorship. In the process, I will raise questions for future research and propose methods for investigating poetry in the periodical press.

No exact count of the number of poems published in periodicals is available. A search for poems in just one digitized database of periodicals, 1800–1900, yields 142,755 hits.[2] Andrew

---

1. [Ackermann], "Introductory Address," i.
2. ProQuest *British Periodicals I & II*, accessed November 7, 2013. The results of this search among 587 periodicals displayed the greatest number of hits in the 1820s (18,107) and 1870s (18,581), with the fewest published in the 1850s (7,231). Since North's *Waterloo Directory* includes 50,000 titles but anticipates documenting 125,000 titles in all, my sampling of the ProQuest database represents only a portion of the total number of periodical poems. There are many digital projects focused on nineteenth-century poetry, including the *William Blake Archive* (www.blakearchive.org), the *Periodical Poetry Index* (www.periodicalpoetry.org), and the *Rossetti Archive* (www.rossettiarchive.org).

Hobbs has estimated that the local press, including provincial papers, published five million poems throughout the century, most of them original productions by local writers.[3] Ackermann's *Poetical Magazine* also took a democratic approach, publishing the work of some two hundred poets in its brief run.[4] Periodicals used poetry as filler and also excerpted verse in reviews, fiction, essays, and accounts of parliamentary speeches. In addition, since poems first published in periodicals were not protected by copyright, an inestimable number of reprintings occurred in Great Britain, North America, and throughout the British Empire.[5] Aside from niche magazines such as Ackermann's or *Poet's Corner*, at the century's end (1899–1907) poetry customarily occupied only a small portion of the pages or columns of a given issue. Yet its pervasiveness and cumulative presence underscores its cultural and commercial importance.

Poetry and the News Cycle

Periodical poetry participated in the news cycle insofar as it appeared in date-stamped issues with contents defined by their currency. In addition, poems were often specifically wedded to news events, from royal births, deaths, and weddings to accidents or even the weather. As Natalie Houston has shown, "Poetry was one way that individuals participating in the communal, nation-defining experience of reading the newspaper described by Benedict Anderson were guided toward emotional and aesthetic interpretations of different national events."[6] Given the blending of journalism and poetry, it is important for researchers to consider what poetry can do that news reports cannot and vice versa. What interactive relationships are set up between a column devoted to, say, a shipwreck and a descriptive lyric printed in close proximity to it? Or how are multiple poems written in response to a single event shaped by the celebrity (or anonymity) of the poet, the modulation of public opinion, or the editorial policy and political orientation of the periodical publishing context? How does reading laterally across poems relativize any single poem, suggest the value of poetry as editorial, or expose the commodity value of brief verse that could augment attention to debates or events capturing widespread interest?

For example, when it was proposed that a Lake District railway line be extended near Ambleside in 1844, William Wordsworth protested by publishing a signed sonnet with an appended note in the October 16 *Morning Post*. Both sonnet and note were reprinted in the October 19, 1844 *Examiner* amidst news and gossip and again in the November 1, 1844 *Critic*, which gave the reprinted opinion poem higher production value by placing it at the head of "Gleanings, Original and Select" and surrounding the poem with more white space than in the *Examiner*.[7] The *Examiner* then published "Projected Railways in Westmoreland. In answer to Mr. Wordsworth's Late Sonnet," which treated the mixing of the "harsh steam-car with the cataract's shout" as inevitable and extolled the importance of giving laborers the opportunity

---

3. Hobbs, "Five Million Poems," and personal communication, July 12, 2013. See also Chapman and Ehnes, introduction.
4. Ellis, "Poetical Magazine," 349.
5. Ledbetter, *Tennyson and Victorian Periodicals*, 2; Van Remoortel, "New Contexts," 75–86.
6. Houston, "Newspaper Poems," 241.
7. Wordsworth, "On the Projected Kendal and Windermere Railway," 660; rpt. *Critic*, 162.

for Sunday visits to the Lake District, thus enabling them to "read" the scenery "by light of thine [Wordsworth's] own lays."[8] This lyric, signed "R.M.M.," reflected the reformist bent of the *Examiner* but also indicated the reputation of Richard Monckton Milnes, a minor bard whose work did not merit full signature. War likewise inspired poetry embedded in the news cycle. Tennyson's "Charge of the Light Brigade," published in the *Examiner* on December 9, 1854, is perhaps the most famous, but the Napoleonic Wars, the Sepoy Rebellion, and the Boer War likewise elicited periodical poetry from multiple perspectives.[9]

Memorial verses were also tied to the news cycle, serving as counterparts to obituaries insofar as they announced deaths and highlighted the salient achievements or qualities of the deceased. After the death of Princess Charlotte and her stillborn child on November 6, 1817, the *Gentleman's Magazine* not only featured a six-page account of her death and funeral (largely "extracted" from a newspaper) in its November issue but also published numerous poetic memorials ranging from the anonymous "To the Memory of the Princess Charlotte," reprinted from the *Glasgow Courier*, to poems by Thomas Campbell, John Mayne, John F.M. Dovastan, and, in the December number, Mrs. Eliza Smith. Such poems circulated national news but also invited readers to participate in patriotic mourning. If this poetry was ephemeral, it was also simultaneously allied to the genres of elegy and epitaph, which were meant to have lasting appeal; it offered the sonorities, rhythms, and evocation of feeling usually missing from obituaries.[10] When paired with common or hymn meter (as with Mayne's "All the People Mourning!"), a lyric could enable far-distant readers to participate in the simulacrum of the memorial service. By adopting elevated language and encomium to suggest high seriousness, such work could parallel the memorial moment of silence in which an anonymous public is asked to pause, reflect on the life of the departed, and remember the burden of mortality for all.

When the deceased person was a writer, the composition of memorial verse posed specific challenges. In order to embed the memorial poem in the same news cycle as the obituary, poets had to write quickly yet also maintain sufficiently high poetic standards to demonstrate the importance of poetry and to sustain their own reputations. The elegy has long been seen as a contestatory genre in which the surviving elegist competes with the departed bard when crafting a poem. But the elegist's agonistic relationship is distinctly different in a periodical context, for in this case the poet is also a rival poet-journalist (no matter how enduring the resulting poem) who competes with other surviving poets to be first to publish a tribute. Mapping poetic tributes to the dead (e.g., to Tennyson in 1892) along a timeline, making note of the use of signature, can thus illuminate rivalries between poets and competing journals.[11]

For example, Wordsworth quickly composed "Extempore Effusion, on reading, in the *Newcastle Journal*, the news of the death of the poet, James Hogg," which was then published in

---

8. R.M.M. [Richard Monckton Milnes], "Projected Railways in Westmoreland," lines 2, 8.
9. For Tennyson, see Ledbetter, *Tennyson and Victorian Periodicals*, 121–7; for Romantic-era war poems in periodicals, see Bennett and Smith, *British War Poetry*; for discussion of the Sepoy Rebellion periodical poems, see Hughes, "What the *Wellesley Index* Left Out," 100, 107–8; and for Boer War periodical poetry, see Smith, *Drummer*.
10. See Scodel, *English Poetic Epitaph*; and Demoor, "From Epitaph to Obituary."
11. For issues in signed or anonymous periodical poetry, see Easley, *First-Person Anonymous*, 153–73.

the December 12, 1835 issue of the *Athenaeum*.[12] Hogg died on November 21, and the poem is dated November 30. Wordsworth's "extempore" composition is documented in the poem's paratext, yet Wordsworth positions his tribute to Hogg in a higher philosophical register as well. He reviews the sequence of great writers lately dead, from Scott and Coleridge to Lamb and Crabbe, leaving him to contemplate "Who next will drop and disappear?"[13] Speedy composition is also evident in the title and subtitle of Algernon Swinburne's "A New Year's Eve. Christina Rossetti died December 29, 1894," published in the *Nineteenth Century*, February 1895.[14] His memorial verse underscores the importance of paying attention to gender issues in tributes to writers. Swinburne at first emphasizes Rossetti's "sweet" soul and song, waiting until the second page to declare that "there is none to sing as she sang upon earth, not one."[15] Likewise, Wordsworth's 1835 memorial to Hogg did not include a stanza on the recent death of Felicia Hemans, though he dedicated a few lines to her in a later version of the poem.[16] Further work needs to be done to determine how many memorial verses were allocated to women poets within the news cycle and how many women contributed signed memorial verses to newspapers and periodicals.

Periodical Poetry and Politics

Any poem that commented on legislation or newly announced governmental policy participated in the news cycle. For example, the anonymously published "Mr. Disraeli's Speech at the Mansion House, August 4, 1875" satirically represented Benjamin Disraeli crowing over his legislative victories.[17] Likewise, light verse in *Punch* and *Fun* mocked political overreach or foolishness—their humor serving not only to leaven the sting of criticism (and evade libel) but also to cut the powerful down to size. An alternative, and very serious, body of periodical poetry was integral to radical politics, serving as a vehicle for democratic, anti-monarchical activism inspired by the French Revolution, the Chartist movement of the 1830s and 1840s, the nascent internationalism and socialism of the 1850s, and the socialist and communist movements of the century's final decades. As Stephen Behrendt argues, poetry's ability to engage the emotions and elicit reader participation "in the 'making' of the work" not only lessened the distance between poet and audience but also involved readers in actively producing radical content so that the "text becomes verification, not suggestion."[18] Anne Janowitz emphasizes the links of poetry to a people's tradition of oral forms and common meter—a point echoed

---

12. Wordsworth, "Ettrick Shepherd" ["Extempore Effusion"], 930–1. The *Athenaeum* affixed a title to the poem, "The Ettrick Shepherd"; this was removed when it was reprinted in the December 27 issue of the *Examiner*. Both periodical poems lack the stanza on the death of Felicia Hemans that Wordsworth added later.
13. Wordsworth, "Ettrick Shepherd," line 28 (930).
14. Swinburne, "New Year's Eve," 367–8.
15. Ibid., lines 5, 24.
16. Wordsworth added lines 37–40 on Hemans when the "Extempore Effusion" was included among "Epitaphs and Elegiac Pieces" in the 5th edition of *Poems* (1836–37).
17. "Mr. Disraeli's Speech at the Mansion House," 913.
18. Behrendt, "British Women Poets," 89; see also Scrivener, *Poetry and Reform*.

by Elizabeth C. Miller in her work on late-century radical poets, for whom "poetic tradition" could signify a "pre-capitalist formation."[19] Mike Sanders contends that poetry's intrinsic role in Chartism was the "transformation of consciousness" made possible by exposing readers to new ideas and by affording affect and pleasure that elicited the desire for "further, similar, sensations."[20] Equally crucial was poetry's "ability to imagine things differently"—to envision and create a new order of power relations in an aesthetic medium that implicitly countered utilitarian or laissez faire politics.[21]

Appeals to sensuous experience are evident in the opening lines of George Dyer's "Ode to Liberty" in the 1795 *Tribune*, edited by fellow radical (and poet) John Thelwall:

> HAIL! More refulgent than the morning star,
> Gay queen of bliss, fair daughter of the sky,
> I woo thee, Liberty! and hope from far
>   To catch the brightness of thy raptur'd eye.[22]

Modulating into utopianism, the poet declares that, should liberty not come to Britain, he will flee elsewhere:

> I would hasten to some happier soil,
>   Where tyrants had no rule, no slaves obey.
> There would I woo thee, goddess, heav'nly fair;
>   Sing my wild notes to thee, where'r I roam;
> Britons no more the muse's praise should share,
>   Tyrants abroad and miscreants at home—
> E'en Britain's friend would publish Britain's shame;
> While barb'rous tribes should hear, and scorn a Briton's name—[23]

A fearless radical, Dyer signs his poem, though its abstractness offers him cover.[24] In contrast, an earlier lyric in the same journal accusing "Pitt and his crew" of "effac[ing]" liberty is signed only "Juvenis."[25] Possibly the pseudonym disguises the authorship of Thelwall himself, but signature or its absence in radical verse should always be considered in relation to politics and threats of arrest or libel. In addition, it should be examined in relation to the editorial aims, house style, and role of celebrity in its periodical publishing context.

Joseph Radford's signed poem "The War-Cry," published in the *Northern Star* in 1840, hails the "pealing thunder" sweeping across Scotland, Wales, England, and Ireland that embodies

---

19. Janowitz, *Lyric and Labour*, 26; Miller, *Slow Print*, 168.
20. Sanders, *Poetry of Chartism*, 13.
21. Ibid., 19.
22. Dyer, "Ode to Liberty," lines 1–4 (147).
23. Ibid., lines 153–60 (148).
24. Janowitz, *Lyric and Labour*, 69.
25. Juvenis, "Impromptu," 236.

"tyranny's funeral knell" and the people's unified voice demanding "The Charter" beneath the "banner of freedom."[26] Radford's decision to sign his work was brave given that the poem mentions John Frost, a radical who had been charged with high treason when two dozen men died during a Chartist insurrection at Newport.[27] More circumspectly, a Scottish contribution signed "Amicus" immediately below Radford's lyric celebrates the release of two other Chartist leaders: "May White and Collins bravely move / The cause that soon will make them shine."[28]

By the 1880s, when communism and anarchism had not yet attracted a mass following and middle-class Britons such as Walter Crane and William Morris were gravitating toward socialism, it was perhaps safer for poets to sign their incendiary lyrics. Yet, as before, radical poetry continued to move readers to feel, think, and act: promoting group solidarity, de-centering governmental authority through attack, and imagining a rupture with the present that would instate a new order. Elizabeth Miller surveys the formal as well as ideological interventions of poetry in a range of socialist, anarchist, and communist journals, which usually included at least one poem per issue.[29] Yet signature remained uneven. Edith Nesbit, a house poet for *To-day*, the "monthly magazine of scientific socialism," often signed her work E. Nesbit but also published under the initials E.N.[30] Miller also recovers the working-class Leeds poet Tom Maguire, who published numerous poems as "Bardolph."[31] However, signed or unsigned, radical poems and periodicals were interventions from the margins. Research tracing the reception of radical poetry in the mainstream press would enhance scholarly understanding of its broader impact.

Groups desiring to change laws or the ideological status quo represent another political formation that found expression in periodical poetry. Elizabeth Gray examines poems supporting suffrage in the *Women's Penny Paper* and *Herald*.[32] The *Chameleon*, a short-lived Oxford magazine published in 1894, boldly represented same-sex desire, most famously in Lord Alfred Douglas's lyric "Two Loves" ("the love that dare not speak its name"). Receiving notice in the mainstream press, however, spelled disaster for the *Chameleon*, which ceased publication after a single issue.[33] Charlotte Boyce examines campaigns in the *Illustrated London News* and other middle-class illustrated newspapers during the 1840s focused on eliciting support for the amelioration of hunger.[34] Elizabeth Barrett Browning's "The Cry of the Children" in *Blackwood's Edinburgh Magazine* and Thomas Hood's "Song of the Shirt" in *Punch* similarly mobilized support for government action to relieve suffering even though the poems did not demand that readers themselves take action. As Alison Chapman demonstrates, expatriate women's poetry during

---

26. Radford, "War-Cry," 3.
27. Sanders, *Poetry of Chartism*, 87; see also 129, 138.
28. Amicus, "Lines to Messrs. White and Collins," 3.
29. Miller, *Slow Print*, 167–220.
30. See, for example, E.N., "Richborough Castle," 157–8.
31. Miller, *Slow Print*, 212.
32. Gray, "Poetry and Politics," 134–57.
33. Hyde, *Chameleon*, 1.
34. Boyce, "Representing the 'Hungry Forties,'" 421–49.

the late 1840s promoted the Italian Risorgimento while also forging solidarity among women and imparting agency to poets who were excluded from political power or editorial influence in Britain.[35]

Some nineteenth-century political poetry anticipates what would later be called identity politics: the belief that one's identity confers knowledge that can help advance social change and that those excluded from power must play an active role in liberating themselves.[36] This was also true of many working-class women's poems published in newspapers and periodicals. As Florence S. Boos has shown, poems published in periodicals such as the *People's Journal*, *Ben Brierly's Journal*, and the *Glasgow Penny Post* enabled workers to articulate the conditions and experiences of their lives in their own voices and idioms.[37] For example, in Ellen Johnston's "The Last Sark. Written in 1859," a famished mother of two contemplates pawning her husband's last shirt to stave off absolute starvation for the family. Johnston depicts social injustices as well as the physical and affective toll of unemployment or low-wage work in terms that would be recognized by other worker-readers. As Boos notes, such poetry has received less attention than Chartist verse, yet it was equally political in the sense that it enabled workers to affirm their talents and register their social and economic positions.

Sanctities: Home, Nation, Faith

If political poetry resisted or critiqued the status quo, an immense body of poetry sanctified inviolable domesticity, nationhood, and religious faith. Many of these lyrics recycle time-worn thoughts or images. For example, the opening stanzas of three poems, published 1829–79, rely upon a common store of images and themes:

"Home"(1829)

Home of my youth! Though thy pleasant shades
    I never more may see;
And many years have pass'd away
    Since last I gaz'd on thee:
Yet memory fondly loves to trace
    Each well-remember'd scene,
And lingers, as in childhood's hour,
    Among thy meadows green.

"The Old Home"(1859)

The old home, it was sanctified by many a joy and care,
By all the lights and shadows each passing day will wear;

---

35. Chapman, "Poetry, Network, Nation," 275–85.
36. Alcoff and Mohanty, introduction, 2.
37. Boos, "Homely Muse," 255–85, and *Working-Class Women Poets*.

'Twas sanctified by many a hope, though buried now it be;
For brightly shone each landmark forth, seen from the household tree.

"My Cottage Home"(1879)

In a little fairy valley,
    Where the oak and maple twine,
Where a silver streamlet wanders,
    Is this pretty home of mine.
Where the wild flowers bloom the sweetest,
    And the robins love to come,
And the brightest sunbeams linger,
    Is my little cottage home.[38]

Not surprisingly, each poem was signed with initials only. The indistinguishability and abundance of such poems point to their performative function: their rehearsal of values already known and embraced but needing daily reaffirmation. It is not surprising that such poems assumed the function of prayer, sermons, and hymns; the verities of home and faith were often intertwined, revealing continuity between domestic periodical poetry and the expression of general, non-doctrinal piety. Dismissal of such work as "filler" misses an opportunity to consider why editors so often featured such lyrics and why readers desired them, especially when the surrounding white space demanded by poetry could have been filled with more prose or even adverts. One approach is to view sentimental or pious poetry as mediating the modernity and ephemerality of periodical publication by redirecting attention to abiding communal values and the realm of the sacred.[39]

The close association of religion and poetry provided further justification for the printing of pious lyrics.[40] Caley Ehnes argues that in *Good Words*, a religious Sunday magazine, poetry was used to instigate and sustain weekly devotional practices and "shape the rhythms of ideal readers' lives."[41] Moreover, lyrics such as Dora Greenwell's "Pencil Marks in a Book of Devotion," published in *Good Words* in 1860, modeled the reading of periodical poetry within a religious frame.[42] In contrast to *Good Words*, which sought a broad audience, other periodicals used poetry to shore up specific religious doctrines or to fuel sectarian dispute. For example, "The Suffering Christian," published in the *Wesleyan-Methodist Magazine*, presumably recapitulated the Methodist belief in grace as "all-sufficient":

Jesus, my Lord, my God,
    Thy promise I embrace;

---

38. H., "Home," lines 1–8; F.J.C., "Old Home," lines 1–4; C.P., "My Cottage Home," lines 1–8.
39. Hughes, "What the *Wellesley Index* Left Out," 99.
40. According to John Henry Newman, "With Christians, a poetical view of things is a duty." Newman, "Review," 169.
41. Ehnes, "Religion," 470.
42. Ibid., 472–3.

> And hail, beneath the Father's rod,
>   Thy all-sufficient grace.[43]

An untitled lyric in the *British Magazine*, a periodical aligned with the Oxford Movement, is more disputatious in glancing toward Calvinism, Presbyterianism, and Roman Catholicism in its final stanza:

> Geneva, Scotia, is thy temple built
>   In fashion as thou wilt?
> Untemper'd mortar daubs thy holier dome,
>   Self-honor'd Rome![44]

New research that compares poetry in sectarian periodicals to those in broadly Christian, family, or literary magazines would illuminate poetry's functions in multiple venues and might reveal whether religious poems, like many hymns, could travel across denominations and unite multiple communities.

Gender analysis of religious and domestic periodical poetry is already well advanced. F. Elizabeth Gray examines women's poetry in the evangelical, middle-class *Christian Ladies' Magazine*, edited by Charlotte Elizabeth Tonna. In addition to reconfirming the continuum between religion and domesticity for women, Gray's study demonstrates that women could stake an indirect claim to biblical exegesis, a customary male preserve, by aligning themselves with Tractarianism and deftly manipulating biblical allusion and imagery. Kathryn Ledbetter's study of women's periodicals traces the continuum of religion and domesticity in L.E.L.'s conflation of "poetry with morality, religion, empire, and feminine ornamentation" and in an 1842 conduct book that urged women to read poetry: "If it be true poetry, it is the twin-sister of religion."[45] Both scholars emphasize women's empowerment through domestic, sentimental, and religious poetry within a cordoned-off domain consistent with the ideology of separate spheres.[46] Gray and Ledbetter observe that affective or pious poetry was hardly confined to women or women's magazines. How men's and women's domestic and religious verse compared across decades or periodical titles merits further study.

Patriotic verse praises the nation rather than God or home, but it, too, brings diverse readers into an imagined community of shared allegiance. As Tricia Lootens notes of "The English Boy," first published by Felicia Hemans in *Blackwood's Edinburgh Magazine* in 1834, "In focusing local reverence for the literal and symbolic remains of patriotic heroism . . . heroes' graves not only unified distinct national folk communities but also bound those communities to the rest of the world by evoking the universal love and sorrows of liberty."[47] Unlike war poems, which were tied to the news cycle, patriotic verse might invoke historical events such as Cressy,

---

43. Henwood, "Suffering Christian," lines 1–4.
44. H., untitled poem, lines 23–6.
45. Gray, "Beatification," 262–4; Ledbetter, *British Victorian Women's Periodicals*, 1.
46. Ledbetter, *British Victorian Women's Periodicals*, 13.
47. Lootens, "Hemans and Home," 247.

as Hemans does in "The English Boy," or celebrate British liberty, as J.H. does in concluding "Liberty: An Ode" (1849):

> Modern Liberty's first-born,
> My country! Rise, and greet the morn!
> Let ancient Britain lead the van
> In the high progress of immortal Man![48]

If the verses themselves were transient, periodical poems that repeatedly enforced the verities of home, nation, and faith figured significantly in nineteenth-century periodicals and deserve further theorization and analysis.

Entertainment

Poetry literally lightened up periodical pages with its surrounding white space; humorous, light, and romantic verse also "lightened" periodical pages with entertainment. Natalie Houston suggests that light verse in newspapers provided a "kind of relaxation for the mind wearied of data" by offering "easily-processed meter and rhyme."[49] In addition to *The Schoolmaster's Tour* in the *Poetical Magazine*, numerous other humorous verse serials and series appeared, including Thomas Hood's *Miss Kilmansegg and Her Precious Leg* in the *New Monthly Magazine* (September 1840–February 1841). Most, however, were brief *jeux d'esprit*. In Winthrop Mackworth Praed's "My Partner," an aspirant tries vainly to create a spark with the daughter of a wealthy aristocrat on the dance floor. While he tries out one conversational ploy after another, she talks only of the weather, until the speaker ruefully considers,

> But to be linked for life to her!—
>   The desperate man who tried it,
> Might marry a Barometer,
>   And hang himself beside it![50]

The poem becomes topical when the dancer tries to discuss recent fiction—"'Vivien Grey' / Was positively charming . . . / And 'Frankenstein' alarming"—providing a fascinating snapshot of literary gossip.[51] A principal outlet for humorous poems was *Punch*, founded in 1841, followed by the more downmarket *Judy* in 1867. Many of these poems offered political satire or commentary, but others deflated pretensions or laughed at contemporary fads. May Kendall's "Lay of the Trilobite," published in the January 24, 1885 issue of *Punch*, targets human presumption. A man contemplating a fossil lauds the "providential plan" whereby it "should be

---

48. Hemans, "English Boy," line 19; J.H., "Liberty: An Ode," lines 251–4.
49. Houston, "Newspaper Poems," 236.
50. [Praed], "My Partner," lines 93–6.
51. Ibid., lines 13–14, 16 (353–4).

a Trilobite, / And I should be a Man!" until the trilobite speaks and exposes the man's hasty self-congratulation.[52]

Like religious or patriotic verse, humorous poetry also served to create and sustain community. According to Salvatore Attardo, research tends to highlight humor's "positive aspects," including its "collaborative, gregarious, community-building aspects."[53] In assuming consensus about what was and wasn't done or was laughable rather than outrageous, periodical poetry most often enforced middle-class frames of reference, as in the Praed lyric cited above or, late in the century, the verse of Frederick Locker and Austin Dobson, which demanded a readership able to appreciate allusion, complex verse forms, or subtle laughter.[54]

Love is one of poetry's abiding themes, hence the thousands of love poems published in nineteenth-century periodicals. While poems often centered on divine or domestic love rather than erotic passion, the recurrence of romantic love poetry functioned as the verse complement to love plots in periodical short stories and novels, providing readers the chance to contemplate love in a different register and, with the aid of rhyme and rhythm, to recall lyrics long after a first reading. Eliza Cook's "Love On," first published in the *New Monthly Magazine*, strikes two of the most familiar notes in periodical love poetry: the imperative of love ("Love on, love on, the soul *must* have a shrine") and love's loss ("though we may live to see / The dear face whiter than its circling shroud").[55] The yoking of desire and loss expressed yet also safely regulated passionate feeling. Narrative love poetry provided some of the same pleasures as prose love tales and could likewise appear serially. "The Bayadere" by L.E.L., a tragic oriental tale, appeared in three parts in the *Literary Gazette* (August 30–September 13, 1823), and James Hogg, writing as the Ettrick Shepherd, described the genesis and decline of love in a three-part poem in *Fraser's Magazine* ("Love's Legacy," October–December 1834). Later in the century, William Allingham's two-part neo-medieval verse tale, "Mervaunee," appeared with illustrations in the *Cornhill Magazine* (July–August 1876), and the two-part classical verse tale "Procris," by Graham R. Tomson, was likewise illustrated in the *Universal Review* (May–June 1890).[56]

A final role for periodical love poetry was to accent themes in concurrently published serial fiction. During the October installment of Thomas Hardy's *Far from the Madding Crowd* in the *Cornhill Magazine*, editor Leslie Stephen placed Augusta Webster's poem "My Loss" ahead of Hardy's tale with only an intervening article on Sir Edwin Landseer between them. Her poem echoed the subject matter of Hardy's chapter, which featured Fanny's death and Troy's apparently suicidal swim from shore. Webster's lyric likewise shifts from burgeoning red roses in a "green nook" evocative of "love's delight" to a "soddened plot I know, / Blackening in this chill and misty air," and the speaker is left to moan, "Ah, my folly! Ah, my loss, my pain!"[57]

---

52. [Kendall], "Lay of the Trilobite," lines 14–16.
53. Attardo, "Preface: Working Class Humor," 121.
54. See, for example, Dobson's "Dilettant," 425–6.
55. Cook, "Love On," lines 17–18.
56. The University of Florida Rare Books has digitized Allingham's hand-corrected proofs of the *Cornhill* verse tale, providing an indication of the publishing process for such work. Allingham took care to indicate the number of parts at the head of each installment.
57. Webster, "Swallows," 80, and "My Loss," 474.

Webster's poem thus introduces and encapsulates the emotional trajectory readers would encounter in Hardy's text a few pages on.

Poetry and Special Features

Although "Passage of the Mountain of Saint Gothard" by Georgiana, Duchess of Devonshire, in the January 1800 *Scots Magazine*, was no doubt welcome simply because a duchess wrote it, her widely reprinted lyric is one of many verse analogues of travel writing.[58] Matthew Arnold's "Stanzas from the Grande Chartreuse" (*Fraser's Magazine*, April 1855) is in part an alpine travelogue, as well as a mid-century *cri de coeur* about faith's decline. Late in the century, Mathilde Blinde's "Ave Maria in Rome" (*Magazine of Art*, January 1894) marks a traveler's impression while also providing an occasion for the illustrations of John Fulleylove. Verse travelogues were not always signed, as was the case with "The Pyramids," published in the *Monthly Magazine* (October 1841), or J.S.B.'s "Marathon," which appeared in the May 1854 issue of *Blackwood's*. Given the intensive scholarly interest in nineteenth-century travel writing in recent decades, it would be useful to have a fuller account of poetry's role in this cultural formation.

A feature relevant to current global and classical studies is the publication of poetry in translation. Translations from classical literature on the one hand confirmed cultural elites who had completed schoolboy translations from Latin or Greek and could appreciate the finesse and accuracy of verse translations. Yet classical translations also democratized poetry by bringing classical materials to readers denied educational opportunities due to class or gender. Translations from French or Italian might mark out cosmopolitan travelers or skilled poets fluent in classical and modern languages, such as Algernon Swinburne. Because middle-class women were typically instructed in French, French-language literature could also fall within the purview of women's accomplishments, and for those who, like Miss Pinkerton in *Vanity Fair*, hadn't quite mastered the tongue, translations enabled them to feign knowledge of the originals. Since Cook's tours and Baedeker guides often catered to British travelers on the Continent, interest in contemporary literatures brought closer through translation increased as well. Some representative translations for 1800–1840 include "Song, Translated from the French," by Alpheus, in the *Lady's Monthly Museum* (May 1821); "To Minna, Translated from the German of Schiller," by O., in the *Literary Chronicle* (June 8, 1822); "The Death of Orpheus and Eurydice: Translated from the Fourth Book of Virgil's *Georgics*," by H.S. Boyd, in the *Gentleman's Magazine* (November 1815); "Sonnet, Translated from Petrarcha," by A.S., in the *New Monthly Magazine* (January 1824); and "Ode, Translated from the Persian of the Poet Hafez" in the *New Universal Magazine* (August 1814). A two-part translation from Sanscrit, entitled "The Story of Nala and Damayanti," by Charles Bruce, appeared in *Fraser's Magazine* (December 1863–January 1864), while later in the century a spate of translations of Heinrich Heine and Goethe appeared, 116 of them in *Blackwood's* alone, 1877–78.[59] Since translation as an act of original

---

58. Though this was not its earliest printing, the *Scots Magazine* version appeared two years before the first London edition was printed and had obvious celebrity appeal.
59. Houston, Lawrence, and Patrick, "Bibliographic Databases," 72.

creation and cultural interchange has received increasing attention in the last decade, mapping periodical poetry's role in this practice would enlarge studies of periodicals and print culture.

Another poetry feature, seasonal or "month" lyrics, were important adjuncts to marking the temporality of periodicals. The tradition is as old as the opening lines of Chaucer's *Canterbury Tales*, but in an era of mass-circulating periodicals, such lyrics doubly marked the date of a periodical issue and celebrated the publishing cycles that demanded the ever-new production of texts. The first stanza of an unsigned lyric in the *London Journal* is representative:

> July is here; the lakelet clear
>   In slumb'rous calm reposes;
> The sunbeams fly across the sky,
>   Or linger in the roses.[60]

Such poetry confirmed habitual seasonal associations yet also elevated diurnal temporality by linking it to poetic rhythm and imagery. Christmas was another occasion for the proliferation of lyrics, and it is worth recalling that Dickens incorporated Adelaide Procter's verse narratives into five of his extra Christmas numbers from 1854 to 1859.

Like all other genres, poetry participated in the explosion of visual images in nineteenth-century periodicals. *The Schoolmaster's Tour*, as previously noted, was an early illustrated original poem. George Cruickshank illustrated T.H.S.'s "The Temptations of St. Anthony" in *Bentley's Miscellany* more than a quarter century later.[61] This value-added feature expanded rapidly during the "golden age" of Victorian illustration in the 1860s, beginning with *Once a Week*, when some of the most prominent Victorian artists contributed illustrations to periodicals.[62] Lorraine Janzen Kooistra has pioneered methods of reading poetry and illustrations as sometimes complementary, sometimes competing media.[63] Other factors to consider in investigating illustrated poems include layout, the narrative properties of illustrations, the relationship between illustrated poems and other content in a given periodical issue, the interrelationship between illustrations in a single issue, and the link between an artist's paintings and periodical contributions.[64] Additional research is needed on the relative function of illustration for poetry and for fiction, especially since the relation between word and image was more intimate in poetry due to its compression and iconicity, which is enhanced by surrounding white space.

Throughout this essay, I have approached poetry as a component of popular mass media, but there is much to be gained by situating the complex aesthetic strategies of major poets within a periodical context. Not only did many canonical poets publish original signed work in periodicals, but some niche periodicals also multiplied opportunities to read and publish experimental or avant-garde poetry, for example, the Pre-Raphaelite magazine the *Germ* (1850),

---

60. "July Is Here," lines 1–4.
61. T.H.S., "Temptations of St. Anthony" (1838).
62. Goldman and Cooke, *Reading Victorian Illustration*, 1–3; Hughes, "Inventing Poetry," 41–72; Ehnes, "Navigating the Periodical Market," 96–112.
63. Kooistra, *Artist as Critic*, 5, and *Poetry*, 22–5, 29–33.
64. See Hughes, "Inventing Poetry," 43–51; Leighton and Surridge, "Plot Thickens," 67.

the *Oxford and Cambridge Magazine* (1856), or *Dark Blue* (1871–73), which published Swinburne's "The End of the Month," illustrated by Simeon Solomon. Also ripe for furthur analysis are the *Yellow Book* (1894–97), in which John Davidson's "Thirty Bob a Week" first appeared (July 1894), and the *Scots/National Observer* (1889–94), which published some of editor W.E. Henley's free verse lyrics, as well as Kipling's *Barrack Room Ballads* and poems by W.B. Yeats. The *Fortnightly Review* published original poems by D.G. Rossetti, Swinburne, Arnold, Morris, and Verlaine, and the Roman Catholic *Month* published John Henry Newman's "The Dream of Gerontius" in two parts (April–May 1865). These periodicals featured poetry qua poetry, thus anticipating modernist little magazines and their postmodern heirs.

In addition to addressing the questions raised in this essay, future scholarship should include the transnational reprinting and circulation of poetry.[65] Original poetry was a massive presence within nineteenth-century periodicals, and the field of periodical poetry offers exciting opportunities and fruitful terrain for further research.

---

65. See Van Remoortel, "New Contexts"; Hack, "Wild Charges"; and Chapman, "Transatlantic Mediations."

9

PROSE

Beth Palmer

Prose of varying length, tone, purpose, and style made up the vast majority of periodical content throughout the nineteenth century. It was a vehicle for conveying news; offering personal opinions; entertaining readers; and assessing cultural, political, and social events. The variety of competing prose discourses in nineteenth-century periodicals provides a rich field for research, but it is not always the easiest terrain to navigate. Structuring an analysis of these prose forms inevitably gives rise to questions about readership and precedence. We find ourselves asking how we should read across these competing voices, how we should prioritize, and how nineteenth-century readers did so as well. Which is more important: the editorial that allows us to determine the periodical's political outlook, the cryptic "Notice to Correspondents" that advises an individual in difficulties, or the serialized fiction that attracts the eye of the casual reader? Furthermore, is it right to say that these different pieces of prose within an issue of a periodical are competing with one another for attention and survival, or does such Darwinian language gloss over connections and correspondences between an issue's separate units? A scholarly analysis of prose forms in nineteenth-century periodicals cannot recreate the reading practices of previous centuries, nor can it hope to trace all the connections or contradictions that exist between the pieces of prose in a particular run of periodicals. It can, however, explore the most prominent prose forms in the nineteenth-century press and give a sense of how they fit into the larger context of the periodical issue and the publishing world.

The first half of this chapter covers fictional prose forms, and the second half examines non-fiction. This is perhaps the most obvious distinction to make amongst prose forms, but we can also see porosity between fact and fiction, for example when Charles Reade's serial novels rely on factual reportage of contemporary criminal cases or when George Augustus Sala's special reports take on the imaginative vibrancy of his stories and novels. Individual issues of nineteenth-century periodicals contained a heterogeneous mixture of competing prose forms that provided readers with a complex, multimodal, and individualized reading experience.

Fiction

Anthony Trollope's often-quoted introduction to *Saint Paul's Magazine* (1867–74) confidently asserts, "Now in this year at which we have arrived, it is hardly too much to say that,—exclusive of the political and critical newspapers—the monthly periodicals afford to the reading public the greatest part of the modern literature which it demands."[1] Trollope can be forgiven for a little hyperbole here; fiction was, of course, also read widely outside the monthly magazines. Volumes were bought from stalls and borrowed from circulating libraries, and the weekly and daily press often published fiction. But by 1867, when Trollope began editing *Saint Paul's*, the periodical press and fiction serials were indeed booming. For most early and mid-Victorian readers, especially those who could not afford a three-volume edition, consuming the latest novel would have been a piecemeal process. Indeed, even circulating libraries allowed readers to take home only one volume at a time. By 1867, the price of volume editions for novels had decreased significantly from 31s. 6d. to a much more affordable 6 shillings, but the periodical serial retained a tight hold on the publishing industry throughout the century. Encountering novels in weekly or monthly periodical installments that were surrounded by a miscellany of other texts and images, nineteenth-century readers experienced fiction in different ways than we do.

The serial novel played a role in periodicals beginning in the early nineteenth century. In the 1820s, *Blackwood's Edinburgh Magazine* (1817–1980) transformed magazine culture by introducing serial fiction, such as John Galt's *The Ayrshire Legatees* (1820–21) or *The Steam-Boat* (1821), which met with enthusiastic reader response. Scottish readers particularly enjoyed the local settings and frequent use of first-person narration, which imbued Galt's work with some of the qualities of the oral tale told around the hearth. In England, Frederick Marryat's seafaring novels, such as *Peter Simple* (*Metropolitan Magazine*, 1832–33), appealed to a wide audience; he even used the magazine to preview forthcoming volume publications with sample chapters. In the following decades, cheaper magazines such as the *Penny Novelist* (1832–34) or the *Penny Story-Teller* (1832–37), aimed at the working classes, serialized novels on a weekly basis with great success. Titles like G.W.M. Reynolds's *The Wehr-Wolf* (*Reynolds's Miscellany*, 1846–47) or Alexandre Dumas's translated *Monte Cristo* (*London Journal*, 1844–45) attracted considerable readerships with their labyrinthine plots. These sorts of works were closely related to the "penny bloods" or "penny dreadfuls" that were sold during the early Victorian period as weekly issues. While not magazines as such, these part issues usually contained advertisements and sometimes other content, too, so they echoed the format of the weekly miscellany. Once a "penny dreadful" tale proved popular, ingenious authors could spin it out for years. Reynolds's *The Mysteries of London* began its serialization in 1844 and continued for over a decade. Repetitious plotting or inconsistent characterization did not matter in this sub-genre; readers seem to have relished the piling up of victims week after week. Works like these were undoubtedly influenced by the French *roman feuilleton*, thrilling novels published twice weekly in newspapers such as Eugène Sue's *Les Mystères de Paris*, serialized in the *Journal des Débats*, which had inaugurated the genre in 1842–43.

In 1856, the *Saturday Review* (1855–1938) took a patronizing view towards these penny weeklies and the novels they serialized, despite their wide readership: "The Family Herald, the London Journal, Reynolds's Miscellany, Cassell's Illustrated Paper and a great many others give, every week, at the small cost of a penny, column on column of stirring and spirited

---

1. Trollope, "Introduction," 2.

romance.... These stories are not very like real-life, but they depart from it in a way that is not much to be regretted. Melodramas are not altogether unwholesome food for the half-educated mind."[2] Charles Dickens helped to invigorate the part-issue form of serialization with the incredibly successful *Pickwick Papers* (1836–37) and later with serials in *Household Words* (1850–59), followed by *All the Year Round* (1859–93). Both of his magazines derived their appeal from serialized fiction, and Dickens paid well for respected novelists like Wilkie Collins and Elizabeth Gaskell. The serialization of novels such as *Great Expectations* (1860–61) and *The Woman in White* (1859–60), published under Dickens's validating editorial authority, meant that weekly serial prose fiction became acceptable reading for the middle and working classes. The *Dickens Journals Online* project has made the content of both Dickens's major magazines, including all their serial fiction, freely available online. This and other digitization projects render it much easier for modern scholars and students to gain a sense of each installment as part of a continuum, not just of the novel itself but of the magazine in which it was embedded.

When new monthly periodicals such as *Macmillan's Magazine* and the *Cornhill Magazine* began courting a middle-class reading audience (in 1859 and 1860, respectively), serialized prose fiction cemented its role in determining the success of periodical ventures. The *Cornhill* even used a single-column format that resembled the pages of a novel. Other shilling monthlies, such as *Belgravia* (1867–99), *St. James's Magazine* (1861–1900), *London Society* (1862–98), and Trollope's *Saint Paul's Magazine* followed in their tracks, and some quickly began offering two novels per issue (totaling over sixty pages of serial fiction). This tactic meant that even when one serial came to an end, the reader would already be halfway through another, and would, the editors hoped, maintain their subscription indefinitely. Fans of Mary Elizabeth Braddon were particularly well served by *Temple Bar* (1860–1906) when her *Aurora Floyd* ran concurrently for several issues with her next novel, *John Marchmont's Legacy* (1862–64). Several magazines also followed the *Cornhill*'s cue by employing an established novelist (in this case, W. M. Thackeray) as editor of the magazine and serializing his or her latest fiction in the magazine. This had the double benefit of bringing a novelist's existing readers to the periodical and attracting other quality fiction. Indeed, literary monthlies were often founded by publishers that were keen to utilize their novelists in new ways. Some novelists followed Dickens's example by seeking proprietorial control over a magazine and serializing much of their own work in it. For example, Sheridan Le Fanu bought the *Dublin University Magazine* in 1861 and ran his supernatural stories in it for nearly a decade, while Ellen Wood owned and wrote much of the *Argosy* for twenty years.

Serializing prose fiction in magazines also made successful novelists acutely aware of the revenue streams that could be generated by a single novel. As John Sutherland puts it, "Serialisation broke the rules [and] ... rendered the old ceiling payments irrelevant."[3] At the height of his fame, a novelist like Thackeray could command several hundred pounds per installment. Graham Law has discussed how profits could also come from volume sales, international distribution, and newspaper syndication.[4] British novelists frequently sent their work abroad.

---

2. "Weekly Romance," 365.
3. Sutherland, *Victorian Novelists and Publishers*, 22.
4. Law, *Serializing Fiction*.

Rudyard Kipling's *Kim*, for example, was serialized almost concurrently in *Cassell's Magazine* in Britain and *McClure's* in America between 1900 and 1901, while Thomas Hardy favored the *Graphic* in his home country and *Harper's Weekly* across the Atlantic. British magazines had long been open to foreign fiction, and the lack of international copyright laws throughout most of the century meant that unscrupulous editors sometimes published foreign fiction without authorial acknowledgement or remuneration. Even when a serial was legitimately acquired, different markets often required changes to the original text. Nathaniel Hawthorne's *The Scarlet Letter* was abridged for the *Englishwoman's Domestic Magazine* between 1857 and 1858, while William Dean Howells must have regretted that Charles Reade had not altered his bigamy novel *Griffith Gaunt* for its publication in the *Atlantic Monthly* where its scenes of sexual jealousy caused more controversy in the United States than in Britain.

Serials did not just appear in cosmopolitan magazines; newspapers began serializing fiction in the eighteenth century when a loophole in the 1712 Stamp Act was exploited by printers, who used fiction to fill extra space when they ran out of news.[5] According to Graham Law, sensation novelists such as Wilkie Collins and Mary Elizabeth Braddon were among the first writers to take full advantage of this new method of publication.[6] The involvement of Braddon's partner, John Maxwell, in the early days of novel syndication (along with her own canny business sense) explains her enthusiastic adoption of this publishing mode.

The serial novel was a successful and long-lived publishing format, but some nineteenth-century critics worried about its effects on writers and readers. Margaret Oliphant, for example, when reviewing Wilkie Collins's *The Woman in White*, complained of the "violent stimulation of serial publication—of *weekly* publication, with its necessity for frequent and rapid recurrence of piquant situation and startling incident."[7] Serial novels were often lengthy and had plot-driven narratives, with frequently deployed recaps and cliff-hangers at the beginning and end of each installment. If serialization commenced while writing was still in process, there was no opportunity for an author to correct inconsistencies that might have become apparent as the work developed. Serialization was a complex and taxing publishing strategy; Marryat warned that the "author dare not flag" from month to month.[8] Some novelists coped better than others with its demands. Anthony Trollope, for example, was well known for expertly and methodically managing his serial contributions to fill the space his editors wanted.[9] Walter Besant was even confident enough to write the conclusion to *Blind Love* that appeared in the *Illustrated London News* after Wilkie Collins's death. George Eliot, on the other hand, did not enjoy the experience of serializing *Romola* (1862–63) for George Smith's *Cornhill* and never again wrote a serial for the periodical press.[10] Elizabeth Gaskell's resistance to Dickens's editorial advice while writing *North and South* (1854–55) for *Household Words* has been well documented, as have the effects of editorial prudishness on Thomas Hardy's *Tess of the*

---

5. See Vann, *Victorian Novels*, 1.
6. See Law, *Serializing Fiction*.
7. [Oliphant], "Sensation Novels," 568.
8. Quoted in Vann, *Victorian Novels*, 3.
9. See [Shand], "Literary Life of Anthony Trollope," 186–212.
10. Martin, *George Eliot's Serial Fiction*, 123–81.

d'Urbervilles when it was first serialized in the *Graphic* in 1891.[11] Graham Law's work on serialization, however, argues that the most consistent pressure on the serial novelist in the later part of the century was generic, not stylistic, pushing novelists towards sensation, detective, and action-filled genres.[12]

Most of the best-selling novels of the nineteenth century were published in serial form in the periodical press. From Newgate novels, such as Harrison Ainsworth's *Jack Sheppard* (*Bentley's Miscellany*, 1839–40), to Charlotte Yonge's religious fiction (often serialized in her own *Monthly Packet*), and from social-problem novels like Charles Kingsley's *Yeast* (*Fraser's Magazine*, 1848) to adventure yarns like H. Rider Haggard's *She* (*Graphic*, 1886), any genre could lend itself to serialization. While individual case studies of serialized novels have significantly enhanced our understanding of the interrelationship between press contexts and fictional texts, work on the serial novel has also realigned scholarly understanding of the novel form more broadly, particularly what Rachel Malik calls the "dispersed and disrupted/ive character of the narrative and the incursion and incorporation of popular genres and discourses, embedded as it is amongst numerous co-texts."[13] In the 1890s, the *Gentlewoman* took this dispersal of the novel to an extreme by commissioning twenty-four writers to contribute each part of the serial *The Fate of Fenella* (1891–92) with no forward planning of style or content. Serial novels, like other forms of prose published in periodicals, also led an "independent and vigorous literary existence" outside of their original serial settings.[14] Most of the serials mentioned above were published in volume form soon after their serial publication; they also spawned prequels, sequels, spin-offs, images, related articles, and advertisements. The serialization of novels in newspapers was also systematized and legitimized after 1873 when W.F. Tillotson began selling novels for syndication in local newspapers. Serial fiction was a prolific and productive aspect of the nineteenth-century press; studying it in its various periodical settings often challenges conventional definitions of the literary novel.[15]

The series of interconnected short stories was another important periodical genre. Looking back at the success of his most famous literary creation, Arthur Conan Doyle wrote, "It had struck me that a single character running through a series, if it only engaged the attention of the reader, would bind that reader to that particular magazine."[16] He felt that this format of fresh but interconnected stories would avoid the difficulty that serials faced when readers dropped off after having missed an installment of a complex plot. The "Adventures of Sherlock Holmes," running from July 1891 in the *Strand Magazine* until 1927, did ensure contemporary readers bought George Newnes's new publishing venture in the thousands. Conan Doyle's detective had already appeared in other journals—"A Study in Scarlet" in *Beeton's Christmas*

---

11. For discussions of these episodes, see Hughes and Lund, *Victorian Publishing*, and Hardy, "Candour in English Fiction."
12. Law, *Serializing Fiction*, 200.
13. Malik, "Stories Many, Fast and Slow," 480.
14. Beetham, "Towards a Theory of the Periodical," 24–5.
15. For more on the ways in which reading a serial in a periodical challenges the dominance of the novel in book form, see Turner, *Trollope and the Magazines*, 7–4, 227–40.
16. Conan Doyle, *Memories and Adventures*, 95.

Annual for 1887 and "The Sign of Four" in *Lippincott's Magazine*—but it was in the *Strand* that his series became popular. Critics have attributed this success to Newnes's expertise in constructing a reading community brought together by a shared national identity and the enjoyment of culturally and morally healthy literature. Christopher Pittard further suggests that the magazine had a "symbiotic" relationship with the detective genre, reassuring readers that the threat of crime was contained following the solution of a case.[17] Other contributors to the *Strand Magazine* during the 1890s, including Bret Harte, Grant Allen, and Walter Besant, also worked to build a community of loyal readers. Of course, other magazines quickly emulated the *Strand*'s emphasis on the series, but not with the same success. For example, the adventures of the female detective Loveday Brooke, by Catherine Louisa Pirkis, were not successful enough to make the *Ludgate Magazine* a serious competitor to the *Strand*.

Conan Doyle was not the first writer to create a series of interlocking stories. During the 1840s, Edgar Allan Poe's amateur detective M. Dupin appeared in "The Murders in the Rue Morgue," "The Purloined Letter," and "The Mystery of Marie Rogêt." However, they were published in separate American periodicals and were therefore not as cohesive as the Holmes *Strand* series. The "Recollections of a Police-Officer," published in *Chambers's Edinburgh Journal* (between 1849 and 1853) under the pseudonym "Thomas Waters," were another significant forerunner. Short fiction series did not just focus on detection and mystery. During the 1860s and 1870s, Ellen Wood published the "Johnny Ludlow" series in the *Argosy*, the monthly magazine she edited from 1867 to 1890. Written anonymously by Wood, the series was narrated by the lovable Johnny, who fell into scrapes each month in what amounted to a disjointed bildungsroman chronicling his journey to becoming a good, Christian man. Johnny's story resonated with many of Wood's readers, who wrote to the magazine offering advice to the fictional protagonist. The poet Tom Hood, for example, praised the "healthy" tone of the stories he took to be memoirs.[18] George MacDonald, more famous for his fantasy fiction, also wrote a short series for the *Argosy* narrated by a young woman, Jane, who recounts the exploits of a worldly male family friend. Spoken at the bedside of Jane's ill sister, the domesticity of the frame narrative makes the foreign and fairy-tale settings of the inset narratives seem cozy. As in many series, there is some ambivalence about how to categorize the short story series as a prose genre. MacDonald's narrator asks herself whether she is writing "a short—short—essay? paper? article?—article, that's it—indefinite article, that's better."[19] In a shifting landscape of editorial demands and tight economic constraints on magazine production, contributors could not be sure that any series they began writing would last beyond a few connected stories.

Unlike the serial or the series, a reader owed a short story no loyalty; a single episode had to work hard to grab the reader's attention amongst the many other features of the magazine. The short story genre has always been a difficult one to define. The term "short story" was coined in 1884, but the genre was also known as the single-episode tale, prose tale, short

---

17. Pittard, "Cheap, healthful literature," 4. See also Jackson, *George Newnes and the New Journalism*.
18. Tom Hood to "Johnny Ludlow," February 7, 1873, Robert Wolff Archive, Harry Ransom Research Center, University of Texas.
19. MacDonald, "Journey Rejourneyed," 63.

narrative, or sketch.[20] It is almost impossible to generalize about a genre that led some writers to use appealing clichés and well-worn tropes and others to experiment with content and style. However, nineteenth-century short stories often employed first-person narrators and incorporated motifs from romantic novels, comic papers, travel writing, and Gothic tales. An 1849 issue of the *Ladies' Cabinet of Fashion, Music, and Romance* (1832–70), for example, includes a story named after its heroine "Ellen Allardyce" that is set on board a ship and demonstrates its heroine's modesty, beauty, and familial duty. It is written anonymously and told by an unnamed male narrator, who rescues the female passengers when the ship founders. It praises Ellen's fulfillment of feminine conventions in sentimental tones and implicitly promises romance between the narrator and heroine. It was the sort of story that might have appeared in any number of weekly or monthly periodicals of the period. Thirty years later, the high-end *Savoy* (1896) carried a short story of the same name by Rudolf Dircks (a woman writer better known for her translation of Schopenhauer). It focuses entirely on the title character's interiority and reveals her slowly dawning epiphany that she wants to retain the independence of single life but will only be truly fulfilled by having a child. The story sounds very much like the work of George Egerton and highlights, as much New Woman writing did, the double bind constricting women's lives. The *Ladies' Cabinet* and the *Savoy* were magazines aimed at very different audiences, but these contrasting "Ellen" stories provide a sense of the plasticity of the short story form in the nineteenth-century periodical press.

The single-episode tale was an important revenue stream for many working writers of the nineteenth century. Conan Doyle, when recounting his early attempts at literary press work, writes, "When a paper sent me a woodcut and offered me four guineas if I would write a story to correspond I was not too proud to accept."[21] Here it seems that Conan Doyle's editor makes the letterpress secondary to illustration, reversing the kind of hierarchy we might expect in a literary magazine. Conan Doyle's experience was not uncommon; some writers saw the short story as a training ground leading to more "significant" work. Several, particularly late-century magazines, offered evidence against such perceived inadequacy in the short story form. The *Strand*, as we have seen, achieved great success with its serial tales, but it also showcased short stories from writers like Rudyard Kipling, Grant Allen, and later D.H. Lawrence and Evelyn Waugh. The *Savoy*, which was proud of short stories like Dircks's "Ellen," aimed to "present Literature in the shape of its letterpress, Art in the form of its illustrations."[22] Similarly, the *Yellow Book* (1894–97), the periodical most closely associated with fin de siècle decadence, places Henry James's "The Death of the Lion" in the first position in its first number, marking the prominence of the short story in its aesthetic. *Cosmopolis* (1896–98) included stories published in English, German, and French, and George Gissing and James were among its high-profile contributors. Short stories were also a key feature of periodicals written for children and young people, including titles such as *Aunt Judy's Magazine* (1866–85), the *Boy's Own*

---

20. For an exploration of short fiction in the early nineteenth century, see Killick, *British Short Fiction*. Later examples are examined by Bowen in "Collins's Shorter Fiction," 37–49.
21. Conan Doyle, *Memories and Adventures*, 74.
22. Symons, "Editorial Note," 1.

Paper (1879–1967) and *Girl's Own Paper* (1880–1956), and the specially extended Christmas numbers of many weeklies and monthlies, which attempted to attract readers with stories, whether heart-warming or spine-chilling.

Non-Fiction Prose

As Anne Humpherys has shown, the division between "fact" and "fiction" in the press may seem obvious, but the division between the two journalistic discourses is more porous than it seems, with much fiction and non-fiction prose "shar[ing] narrative characteristics, including a beginning, a middle, and an end, and plotting strategies for linking separate phenomena."[23] The prose features that I discuss in the second half of this chapter often utilize strategies associated with fictional works to engage readers. Reviews frequently used fictional texts as catalysts for polemics, while news reports sometimes adopted the language and tone of sensation fiction. Correspondingly, the sections in the second half of this chapter are not as neatly divided as those in the first half.

"'The news' as we understand it is a nineteenth-century creation," according to Lucy Brown.[24] The century certainly saw huge changes in the way news was gathered and presented due to technological developments in printing, engraving, photography, railways, and telegraphs, which allowed for speedier reporting and dissemination. Many metropolitan and regional newspapers separated the news into shorter sections such as "Home," "Foreign and Colonial," "Police," "Court," and "Parliamentary," which allowed readers to navigate what, to modern eyes, appears to be dense columns of prose. While *The Times* had a reputation for sturdy continuity (the paper was described by Matthew Arnold in 1863 as an "organ of the common, satisfied, well-to-do Englishman"),[25] the *Illustrated London News* (1842–1989) was the first paper to break up columns of news writing and remove advertisements from the front page; instead, it invested in large, attention-grabbing engravings and used three rather than the four, six, or eight columns favored by other papers. The *Illustrated Police News* (1864–1938), following the format of the *Illustrated London News*, moved even further towards what we would now call the tabloid press by emphasizing crime narratives. For example, "Extraordinary Escape of a Woman from Indians" (an article reported from the Kansas correspondent of the *New York Times*) is illustrated with a startling image of a woman's throat being cut by a group of Native Americans, and the accompanying text reflects the excitement of the story in language that seems novelistic. The escape of the resourceful Sarah Jane Luster from her captors is favored by a "dark and stormy night, when both dogs and savages were within doors."[26]

While Thomas Carlyle reportedly recommended a "journal with the maximum of news and the minimum of editorial comment" as the best recipe for success in the periodical press, not all nineteenth-century editors agreed.[27] Several news-based publications were strongly aligned

---

23. Humpherys, "Popular Narrative and Political Discourse," 34–5.
24. Brown, *Victorian News and Newspapers*, 1.
25. Arnold, "Function of Criticism," 22.
26. "Extraordinary Escape of a Woman from Indians," 1.
27. "Suggestions for the Licensed Victuallers," 825.

with their editor's political opinions. For example, *Reynolds's Weekly Newspaper* (1850–1967), reporting on "Lord Brougham's Vagaries," makes G.W.M. Reynolds's republicanism abundantly clear. Lord Brougham is roundly rebuked for his "wild and extravagant" remarks during a parliamentary discussion of the reduction of foreign ambassadors' salaries. The article concludes, "We tell Lord Brougham that before long not only the relatives of dukes and marquises will be compelled to work for their bread, but even these dukes and marquises themselves shall be taught, to them a bitter lesson, that they must produce before they will be permitted to consume."[28] *Cobbett's Political Register* (1802–36) similarly maps the shifting opinions of its radical editor, William Cobbett, alongside news reporting of "Proceedings of Parliament" and other newsworthy items. When the *Register* details the progress of the petition presented to Parliament to repeal the additional duty on printing paper, Cobbett weighs in with his own editorial opinion, justifying his rationale for why "I, who purchase no inconsiderable quantity of printing paper, have refused to sign the petition."[29] Open letters and signed editorials were an important feature of Cobbett's publication, stamping it with his own personality and political orientation.

Close attention to the editorial section of a newspaper sometimes reveals power struggles behind the front pages. In March 1849, the Chartist *Northern Star* bore evidence of a conflict between its editor, George Julian Harney, and the Chartist leader Feargus O'Connor. Harney opines that "Mr. O'Connor so plied the office with editorial matter that there was, generally, no room for anyone else to say a word."[30] Managing his paper but not writing leaders, Harney grew frustrated and began publishing correspondence pieces under a nom de plume, a strategy that O'Connor found underhand and which he denounced in the paper's own correspondence pages.

Reviewing as a periodical practice was also often marked by personal and political tensions (see especially pages 188–9 below). Reviews of publications and public events made up a significant portion of the prose published in periodicals, and the practice was associated, at least in the early decades of the nineteenth century, with the quarterly reviews. The *Quarterly Review* (1809–1967) competed with the *Edinburgh Review* (1802–1929) for the cultural and moral authority that would ensure readers' loyalty and trust. Both were intellectual heavyweights that covered broad scientific, historical, and cultural terrain, and both were aimed at a well-educated, well-off readership. Their contributors were experts, scholars, and literary gentlemen (all of whom published anonymously), such as William Hazlitt, Charles Lamb, Walter Scott, and John Keble. The significant difference was that the *Edinburgh* was aligned with the Whig party, and the *Quarterly* was associated with the Tories. In 1823, Hazlitt was confident that the review format was the healthiest of literary endeavors, while for Thomas Carlyle the prevalence of reviewing in the press was symptomatic of a sick and parasitic literary culture.[31] Despite Carlyle's opinion, Lamb's essays published under the pseudonym "Elia" in the *London*

---

28. [Reynolds], "Lord Brougham's Vagaries," 2.
29. Cobbett, "Duty on Printing Paper," 11.
30. Harney, untitled editorial, 5.
31. See Shattock, *Politics and Reviewers*, 2.

Magazine (1820–25) were incredibly popular. His works broke from essayistic conventions to assume an anecdotal and digressive structure. The essays rambled elegantly around subjects from chimney sweeps to Sidney's sonnets and gave a strong impression of the writer's individual personality. Hazlitt was equally influential as an essayist, and he, too, published in the *London Magazine* (*Table-Talk*, 1821–22), but his conversational style was marked by an "acidity which was palliated by Lamb's dreaminess."[32]

Reviews were not always inflected by personality or politics. Edward Dowden, for example, writing in an August 1872 issue of the *Contemporary Review* (1866–1988), is allowed twenty pages for his knowledgeable and enthusiastic review of George Eliot's fiction and poetry.[33] By this time, the *Contemporary Review* was only publishing twice yearly and was not trying to compete with the monthlies or weeklies by offering timely reviews of the latest works. It understood the review as a larger, broader, and longer publishing venue that allowed works of literature to accumulate over a period of time so that each could be reviewed in relationship to a wider oeuvre by an expert in a relevant field. Eliot herself was a reviewer and essayist for the *Westminster Review* (1824–1914), which she edited with John Chapman. Some of Eliot's most important ideas are worked out in reviews of individual writers or works. The typical structure of these review essays moves from the particular to the general: her review of the writings of Madame de Sablé (October 1854), for example, moves from the individual's work to its wider bearing "on the culture of women in the present day."[34] The French writer and her fellow female nationals were admitted to a "common fund of ideas" from which, Eliot argues, her own British contemporaries are excluded.[35] Such a review, with its commanding final assertion, "Let the whole field of reality be laid open to woman as well as to man," would not have been out of place in one of the feminist publications that sprang up in the 1860s.[36]

Not all authors received such intellectually or politically engaged appraisals in the periodical press. Outside of the quarterlies, books would usually receive a brief and often descriptive review, frequently with substantial quotations from the text. Many magazines and papers devoted a section to reviews of new publications entitled "Our Log-Book" (*Argosy*), "Literary Intelligence" (*Publisher's Circular*), or "Our Library Table" (*Athenaeum*). In these formats, reviewers wrote anonymously, so S.A. Frost had no opportunity to respond when her book *How to Write a Composition* received a brief but fatal critique, which misidentified her as a man and claimed that the book's topics were ill-chosen, that its arrangement was illogical, and that its "more appropriate title ... would be—'How *not* to Write a Composition.'"[37] Such reviewers saw themselves as "cultural police responsible for protecting public standards and taste" and were most stinging when they felt a text endangered public morality.[38]

---

32. Killick, *British Short Fiction*, 27.
33. Dowden, "George Eliot."
34. [Eliot], "Madame de Sablé," 36.
35. Ibid.
36. Ibid., 37.
37. "Our Library Table," 119.
38. Thompson, *Reviewing Sex*, 12.

In 1865, the *Fortnightly Review* (1865–1954) began a new policy of signed reviewing, explicitly stating in its prospectus that the reviews would represent the opinion of the individual rather than the periodical or its editorial team. It was hoped that this practice would give the reviewer more freedom and protect authors and readers from personal bias.[39] Signature would also offer some protection to the editor, who was often a journal's only named authority and, as such, was exposed to the ire of those who felt slighted by its content, especially reviews. The recipient of an unenthusiastic appraisal in the *Quarterly Review*, for example, displaced his anger from the anonymous reviewer onto the public figure of the editor, saying, "I shall ever consider the new Editor [John Taylor Coleridge], to be as great a B— as the annoying slanderer who wrote [the review]."[40]

Other important prose genres in periodicals included features, tit-bits, fillers, and interviews. Some early nineteenth-century magazines focused on celebrities, including *La Belle Assemblée* with its series of "Biographical Sketches of Illustrious Ladies," which began with a portrait of Queen Charlotte in February 1806. However, it was during the second half of the nineteenth century that the *Fortnightly Review*'s move towards signature was taken up by other periodicals, and from this point onwards we can trace a growing interest not just in signature but also in celebrity and personality through many prose features of the periodical press.[41] Raymond Blaythwayt was perhaps the best-known interviewer in the late nineteenth-century press; his "Celebrities at Home" features for the *World* proved he could charm his way into the lives of numerous personalities. The celebrity interview became a regular feature in late-century popular magazines, including the *Strand* and the *Windsor Magazine*, although the interviews, particularly those of women, often emphasized the domestic over the professional in their life stories. For example, in an interview in the November 1892 issue of *Hearth and Home*, an interviewer encourages novelist Edna Lyall to talk about her struggle for literary recognition and her attitude toward female suffrage, but the narrative of female professionalization is set within the comfort of the successful author's "ivy-covered parsonage" and is further displaced by discussion of Lyall's fragile body and ill health.[42] When editors could not find subjects willing to be interviewed, they managed to cater to (or create) public interest with features like "Portraits of Celebrities at Various Points of their Lives" (*Strand Magazine*), "Children of Notable People" (*Windsor Magazine*), or even "The Dogs of Celebrities" (*Strand Magazine*). In features like these, prose often takes up a somewhat secondary function, explicating images and photographs. *Our Celebrities: A Portrait Gallery* (1888–95) provided an entire magazine dedicated to celebrity life, and even the *Athenaeum* had an "Our Weekly Gossip" column. Prose writers in the press sometimes became celebrities in their own right, creating and perpetuating their public image through multiple channels of publication. George Augustus Sala may have begun his career writing anonymously, but his distinctive prose style, marked by flights of fancy and a personal tone, soon gave him a distinct identity as "GAS" and led

---

39. See Nash, "What's in a Name?," for more on whether such hopes were fulfilled.
40. Quoted in Wyland, "John Taylor Coleridge," 229.
41. See, for instance, Easley, *Literary Celebrity*, and Ledbetter, *Tennyson*.
42. "Chat with 'Edna Lyall,'" 890.

him to work as a special correspondent for the *Daily Telegraph*, amongst other press positions. Sala and other buccaneering journalists, such as Henry Morton Stanley, placed themselves as characters, or even protagonists, in the narratives they told. They capitalized on their prose contributions by editing their journalistic reports into book-length volumes and touting their expertise on lecture tours.[43]

At the other end of the journalistic spectrum, many prose pieces were reappropriated without attribution in newspapers and periodicals. Such practices were inevitable in a system where intellectual property was not well protected, and "scissors-and-paste" journalism was common practice. A number of articles in *Chambers's Edinburgh Journal* purported to expose the behind-the-scenes workings of the press, including practices used by unscrupulous editors, such as rejecting a story from a freelance writer and then publishing it as a letter to the editor, thereby avoiding payment to the freelancer. The depiction of the press office in these articles is vivid: "By the side of the sub-editor's chair is an enormous waste-paper basket, which is full to the brim, the floor all around it being covered with letters, proofs, papers, and other rubbish which have escaped from the 'Balaam-box' of the establishment."[44] The "balaam-box" was a holding place for any bits and pieces of prose that might need to be pressed into duty to fill space when the issue came to be printed; its proximity to the waste-paper bin was not accidental. The article also describes how the sub-editor's assistants were "dexterously using their scissors to disembowel" various pieces while the sub-editor himself was cutting up the work of penny-a-liners (freelance journalists whose rate of pay encouraged prolixity) in order to turn their verbose articles into compact items.[45] Prose was by no means sacred in the nineteenth-century periodical press; as a commodity, its value depended on where it was sold and to whom.

All these bits and pieces of prose could be dizzying to the average reader, and enterprising editors and publishers brought out new periodicals that promised to sift the best from the rest. W.T. Stead's *Review of Reviews* (1890–1936) aimed to provide a "readable compendium of all the best articles in the magazines and reviews," as Stead put it, gesturing to Arnoldian ideas of culture as the "best thoughts of the best men."[46] Useful to busy professionals, who were unable to make time to read widely, or to those living abroad, who wanted a digest of the cultural and political scene, the *Review of Reviews* was a great success and spawned numerous imitators. Periodicals such as *Tit-Bits*, *Answers to Correspondents*, and *Sketch* all ran with the idea that busy readers needed help to wade through the deluge of print culture. They assumed the average reader's attention span was short, so they included puzzles, jokes, letters, anagrams, popular sayings, and anecdotes alongside brief news items. *Tit-Bits* itself gave rise to numerous offshoot publications in the twentieth century, from joke books to story collections. The inquiry column alone was incredibly popular, producing its own offshoots such as *1,000 Answers to 1,000 Questions* (1884).

---

43. See Waters, "Much of Sala," and McKenzie, "Paper Heroes," for more on Sala's style and his place amongst other self-publicizing special correspondents.
44. "Scissors and Paste," 1.
45. Ibid.
46. Stead, "Programme," 14.

The everyday social life of nineteenth-century Britain was reflected in the prose of obituaries, recipes, correspondence, police reports, shipping news, stock market reports, birth and marriage announcements, job and personal advertisements, and numerous other elements of the press which provide glimpses of forgotten individuals and their connections to the larger life of the nation. As one early-century writer suggests, "It is a newspaper which shows life in all its varied shades and colours."[47]

Prose might be the largest constitutive element of the vibrant and various nineteenth-century periodical, but it is not contained by the form in which it was published. As Margaret Beetham puts it, "These genres [fiction, articles, letters pages] often lead an independent and vigorous literary existence" outside the pages of the press: in volume form, in readers' scrapbooks, in their memories, and now in new digital repositories.[48] Prose is a form that lends itself to remediation; consequently, researchers should be sensitive to the movement of a prose work in and out of the press, as well as its potentially shifting place within a specific periodical context.

---

47. Janet, "On Newspaper Reading," 219.
48. Beetham, "Towards a Theory of the Periodical," 24–5.

Section III

GEOGRAPHIES

10

EMPIRE AND THE PERIODICAL PRESS

Michelle Tusan

The story of empire continues to preoccupy British historians and literary critics. In recent years, scholars have increasingly turned their attention to the nineteenth-century press. Historians, to be sure, have always gleaned information from reports in newspapers and periodicals about the British Empire. But today more and more researchers understand that press reports produced by and about the empire are themselves worthy of historical study. Scholars now read the periodical press as much for what it says about a particular idea, person, or event as for what it can tell us about British imperial culture more broadly. This chapter traces the evolution of this new approach to writing about empire and the press, highlighting the theoretical methods that have helped to integrate these fields of inquiry.

Studies of empire and the press reflect current trends in the broader field of imperial history and literature that situate the colony and metropole in one analytic frame. Methods drawn from cultural history, perhaps more than any other subfield, informed the earliest iterations of the New Imperial History and have changed the ways that scholars approach the study of newspapers, periodicals, and journals related to empire. Postcolonial studies, led by the groundbreaking work of Edward Said, has influenced current understandings of imperialism as an uneven, ideologically driven process that made and sustained modern empires.[1] This has opened up a space to analyze the structural and ideological role of the press in determining imperial relationships. The study of journalists, editors, and periodicals and their readers in imperial contexts explains how the press helped forge connections and create divisions among imperial subjects at home and abroad. Scholars generally find themselves divided into two camps: one focused primarily on exploring the press's role in mediating the relationship between colonized and colonizer, the other asking how the imperial press affected metropolitan culture.[2] Both approaches, however, remain focused on exploring the nature of the relationships forged through imperial ties.

At the same time, scholarly work on empire and the press continues to draw upon familiar themes and theoretical approaches that inform other subfields of periodical studies. Issues of

---

1. Said, *Orientalism*.
2. This debate is best illustrated in the work of Antoinette Burton, who argues for the centrality of empire in the shaping of the colonial metropole, and in the work of Bernard Porter, who argues against this position, claiming that empire mattered very little to Britons. See Burton, *After the Imperial Turn*, and Porter, *Absent-Minded Imperialists*.

community, nation, power, and the public sphere undergird the study of empire and the press. Benedict Anderson's notion of imagined community remains useful in determining how the press functioned to create connections between colony and metropole in colonial contexts.[3] The imperial press could forge strong bonds of kinship among Britons and the colonies or among the subjects of colonial rule. Scholars starting with the concept of an imperial public sphere find that it usefully explains the development of a culture of politics centered on imperial matters within the empire itself. The proliferation of imperial publics and counterpublics through the medium of the press during the height of the British Empire has led to new ways of seeing the imperial process.[4] Within this context, the study of the press has focused attention on relationships of power forged by and through the media. No longer do scholars study the press as a neutral site where information is printed, distributed, and conveyed to readers. The press instead has emerged as a distinct space for the production of cultural representation and power.[5]

Improved access to periodicals produced by and about the empire has helped facilitate research. When J. Don Vann and Rosemary VanArsdel published *Periodicals of Queen Victoria's Empire* in 1996, many of the periodicals discussed in chapters on India, New Zealand, South Africa, and other outposts of the British Empire, such as Malaya, Cyprus, and Malta, were difficult to find without traveling to research libraries around the world.[6] The editors noted that their "exploratory" collection represented an "initial step" in opening up the diverse world of periodicals published in the empire, and they encouraged researchers to move beyond familiar accounts of the English press.[7] The continued digitization of major collections of periodicals means that scholars can now study an increasing number of both obscure and well-known papers from their desktops. This offers new opportunities and challenges for researchers.[8] Though still expensive and largely available only at large university libraries, these collections published by Gale Cengage, ProQuest, Adams Matthew, and others include newspapers such as the *Times of India* and many lesser-known regional, religious, feminist, missionary, and nationalist publications from all over the British Empire. This makes it possible to take a regional or issue-based approach to studying the press in the colonies. It also means that comparative studies of the press across the empire and the metropole can have greater depth in terms of the number and types of periodicals included in a particular investigation. The study of communities of publishers, journalists, and readers now easily extends beyond London-based periodicals and newspapers to those published in Johannesburg, Wellington, Toronto, Accra, Cairo, Delhi, Dublin, Sydney, and beyond.

---

3. Anderson, *Imagined Communities*.
4. Habermas, *Structural Transformation of the Public Sphere*, and Calhoun, *Habermas and the Public Sphere*.
5. Curran, *Media and Power*; Bailey, *Narrating Media History*; Hampton, *Visions of the Press*; and Chalaby, *Invention of Journalism*.
6. Canadian periodicals have been studied by scholars due to their relatively widespread availability, but other periodicals, particularly those from former colonies in Africa, have been more difficult to find and thus study. Vann and VanArsdel, *Periodicals of Queen Victoria's Empire*, 5–6.
7. Ibid., 3–4.
8. Bingham, "Digitization of Newspaper Archives," 226–7.

The study of empire and the periodical press has undergone significant change in recent years. The regional approach of *Periodicals of Queen Victoria's Empire* has been largely superseded by a focus on questions of identity, community, and nation. Chandrika Kaul's collection *Media and the British Empire*, for example, attempts to understand the relationship of the press to empire by analyzing points of contact between the mother country and the empire. In the remainder of this chapter, I will examine divergent ways of looking at the British Empire through the lens of the press within recent scholarship. One group of researchers is interested in understanding the press as a means of forging connections between those who share a common sense of Britishness. They adopt what Simon Potter has called the "British world" approach that primarily attempts to understand the relationship of the white dominions and colonists to the metropole.[9] Another set of scholars has taken what I call an "Imperial world" approach, which explores how colonized peoples used the press as a vehicle for resistance that enabled them to create new forms of community and identity within the confines of the British Empire.

British Identities and Empire

The press is a good a place to start when investigating Britain's relationship with its colonies during the late nineteenth and early twentieth centuries. In *News and the British World*, Simon Potter reconstructs the economic and political ties forged by a press system that helped create the "British world." Looking beyond the cultural studies turn in imperial history, Potter puts economic relations back at the center of historical inquiry. At the same time, his work uses a center/periphery framework to analyze changes that came to define the relationship between Britain and her white dominions. This approach focuses on the production, reception, and transmission of news, offering a complex picture of the Victorian press within a larger imperial system. Here British identities are forged and reinforced by media across the empire.

Potter reconsiders the question asked by Benedict Anderson: What makes a nation? Nationalism emerges as a positive force in forging regional identities, which work in concert with the core values of the imperial metropole. This topic is further explored in Potter's edited collection, *Newspapers and Empire in Ireland and Britain*, which demonstrates how the imperial press system helped to constitute and consolidate empire. As dominions came to understand their distinctiveness, they also found themselves tied more closely to the imperial center, particularly in terms of economic relations. The process simultaneously operated in reverse: Britons came to rely on the relationship with white settler colonies for economic prosperity at home. The notion of an imagined kinship further strengthened ties between these regions. British identity thus emerged as the product of interactions between colony and metropole.

Not surprisingly, Scotland, Wales, and Ireland had a complicated relationship with the British Empire. As part of "Greater Britain" they assumed the role of colonizer; at the same time, England's conquest of these regions through war and acts of union made them colonies within the empire. This ambiguous relationship shaped the way the Scottish, Welsh, and Irish press represented the British imperial mission. The Irish press is the best-studied case in this regard.

---

9. Potter, *News and the British World*.

Ireland's semi-colonial status necessarily raised the question of whether or not Ireland was a part of "Greater Britain." The representation of the Irish in the British press, as Michael de Nie demonstrates, revealed the liminal status of the Irish in British imaginings of itself.[10] The study of British opinion on imperialism, through the lens of the press, offers a way of understanding the complex relationship between Irish and British identity as it was contested and reshaped during the late nineteenth and early twentieth centuries.[11]

Nationalism looms particularly large in accounts of the Irish press. In his work on Irish journalists, Ian Sheehy argues that nationalists exploited the pro-empire sentiment during the late nineteenth century to support the Home Rule movement. Journalists like T.P. O'Connor claimed that integrating white dominions into a close-knit network of economic and political relationships would strengthen the empire.[12] Studies of the Irish nationalist press demonstrate the complexity of Ireland's colonial relationship to Britain. Patrick Maume's research on the pro-nationalist and anti-imperialist *Irish Independent* has demonstrated how the paper served imperialist commercial interests while at the same time arguing for Irish self-government.[13] Felix Larkin demonstrates how the *Freeman's Journal* used imperial questions to further nationalist claims.[14]

At the imperial center, the press promoted a common sense of British national identity around the idea of empire. John MacKenzie's *Propaganda and Empire* demonstrates the important role played by the empire in constructing a sense of imperial Britishness at home. According to MacKenzie, many of the values considered Victorian were rooted in the idea of empire that was promoted in the music halls, cinema, radio, exhibitions, textbooks, literature, social institutions, and political organizations.[15] Many images of empire consumed in Britain came in the form of press advertisements for products that came from the colonies. Anandi Ramamurthy's *Imperial Persuaders* examines images of Africa and Asia in British advertising, highlighting the mechanisms of colonial control at work in representations of the empire while revealing the web of economic and cultural ties that bound Britain to its colonies.[16]

Control and spread of information within the metropolitan press played an important role in connecting the colonies to the imperial center. But membership in this broadly construed imperial nation described by Potter and others was limited primarily to white settlers living in New Zealand, Australia, Canada, and South Africa.[17] There was, of course, more to the empire than these white dominions; in recent years, scholars have begun to interrogate the role played by the press in other colonial contexts. Chandrika Kaul's *Reporting the Raj* demonstrates the role of the British press in facilitating empire in India. For the Raj, information management

---

10. De Nie, *Eternal Paddy*.
11. De Nie, "British Conceptions of Ireland and Irishness," 4.
12. Sheehy, "View from Fleet Street."
13. Maume, "*Irish Independent* and Empire."
14. Larkin, "The Dog in the Night-time."
15. Popular imperialism, according to MacKenzie, supported ideas and institutions that promoted an enduring sense of Britishness that included reverence for royalty and support of the military. *Propaganda and Empire*, 3–12. See also MacKenzie, *Imperialism and Popular Culture*.
16. Ramamurthy, *Imperial Persuaders*, 11–20.
17. Lester shows how this works in the latter case in *Imperial Networks*, 5–8.

meant imperial control.[18] The press played a central role in Indian politics while reinforcing a common sense of purpose among Anglo-Indians and Britons at home. India's importance to the study of media and empire has been further demonstrated in two essay collections: David Finkelstein and Douglas Peers's *Negotiating India in the Nineteenth Century Media* and Julie Codell's *Imperial Co-Histories: National Identities and the British and Colonial Press*.[19] These studies address the question of whether or not there were two "nations" made up of Anglo and non-Anglo subjects during the age of imperialism. Whether it came from the colonies or the metropole, all news came to be regarded as "British news" which unified the empire. However, the importance of regional identities cannot be underestimated, particularly outside of the white dominions. Research on the press and empire forces scholars to reconsider what is meant by "nation" in imperialist contexts in the first place. The study of the press in the colonies offers a productive arena of research for media historians interested in the relationship between national and political identity.

Bringing the Empire Home

Another way to explore the relationship between the press and the British Empire is through investigating the work of those who made writing about the empire a career. Well-known nineteenth- and early twentieth-century journalists and writers, including Rudyard Kipling, Arthur Conan Doyle, Evelyn Waugh, and J.A. Hobson, wrote extensively about empire. Lesser-known journalist Lady Henry Somerset also wrote about what she cast as British imperial interests. Her writing on the Armenian massacres in the Ottoman Empire for the feminist *Woman's Signal* (1894–99) made the case for British responsibility for protecting minority civilians.[20] Through her columns, she raised money and awareness about the effects of the killings on widows and orphans in Eastern Anatolia in the late nineteenth century.[21] Other writers, such as Joseph Conrad, were heavily influenced by journalism, particularly the work of foreign correspondents. According to Matthew Rubery, "Conrad's perception of the world was influenced as much by the daily press as by serious literature."[22] Today, Conrad's fictional writing on empire is often considered alongside the work of those who reported on atrocities in the Congo around the time he was writing *Heart of Darkness* in the late nineteenth century.[23] Inspired by the crusade against Belgian rule in the Congo under King Leopold II, in 1909 Arthur Conan Doyle wrote his own exposé called *The Crime of the Congo*. The daily press, led by *The Times*, joined the conversation on empire, publishing a series of articles on the Congo around the same time. Other writers who exploited the relationship between media, literature, and empire included Mark Twain, Roger Casement, George Washington Williams, and E.D. Morel.

---

18. Kaul, *Reporting the Raj*, 24–5. Bayly examines the importance of communication in facilitating empire in *Empire and Information*.
19. Finkelstein and Peers, *Negotiating India in the Nineteenth Century Media*, and Codell, *Imperial Co-Histories*.
20. Tusan, "Humanitarian Journalism," 104–6.
21. Ibid.
22. Rubery, *Novelty of Newspapers*, 141.
23. Ibid., 141–58.

The work of war correspondents has received increased attention by scholars. J.A. Hobson's *Imperialism*, penned after his stint as a reporter during the Boer War, exposed the corrupt relationship between capitalism and British imperialism in Africa. *Waugh in Abyssinia*, a reprint of Evelyn Waugh's exploits during the Italo-Abyssinian War of the mid-1930s, sheds light on the origins of the relationship between journalists and the fickle demands of the commercial news media. Part journalistic handbook and part travelogue, the book offers a contrarian account of Italian aggression in modern-day Ethiopia during a period of continued Western expansion in East Africa. Writers like Hobson and Waugh wore many hats as journalists, travelers, and imperialist observers. For journalist and reformer Henry Nevinson, reporting news about injustice and human rights was a duty that he embraced in his role as a war correspondent.[24] Writers like Waugh felt no such humanitarian responsibility; Waugh complained of boredom, personal discomfort, competition between reporters for stories, and a lack of "real" news upon which to report. These experiences, when placed in contrast to the demand of the commercial press for titillating news stories, reveal the difficulty of producing news in an imperial context. For journalists like Waugh, who idly waited for something to happen on the eve of the Italian invasion of Ethiopia in 1935, the war appeared as a joke ripe for satirical treatment. Those affected by its tragedy certainly understood it as something much more than Europe flexing its muscles in a seemingly insignificant imperial outpost in Africa.

Victorian journalists brought stories of the empire home to an increasing number of readers. The end of the taxes on knowledge in the 1850s and the rise of a free, mass-market press created new opportunities for reporters to represent and comment upon Britain's formal and informal imperial projects. Reportage on the Crimean War, the Indian Mutiny, and the Boer Wars regularly appeared in the press of the day. Controversial topics like the Eastern Question, which informed British foreign policy in the Near East, also received increasing attention in the periodical press during the second half of the nineteenth century.[25] The Crimean War (1853–56), the first foreign conflict to receive full media coverage, brought Britain's role in the Ottoman Empire home for readers in a new way.[26] Coverage of the war in *The Times* also revealed the growing power of the press in shaping public opinion and exerting influence over the political careers of men like Lord Palmerston.[27] The 1857 "Indian Mutiny" was also widely covered in the mid-Victorian press.[28] Jill Bender's work demonstrates that Irish press coverage of the mutiny offered competing visions of Ireland's role as both colonized and colonizer.[29] The conflict represented a turning point in the debate over Irish nationalism because it brought to light both the advantages and disadvantages of having connections with the world's most powerful empire.[30] Úna Ní Bhroiméil turns the nationalist gaze outward in her work on the *Irish World*. This American paper provided

---

24. John, *War, Journalism and the Shaping of the Twentieth Century*.
25. Tusan, *Smyrna's Ashes*, 16–18.
26. Markovits, "Rushing into Print," 559–62.
27. Fenton, *Palmerston and the Times*, 131–3.
28. Palmegiano, "The Indian Mutiny in the Mid-Victorian Press."
29. Bender, "Mutiny or Freedom Fight?" Lowry's work on the coverage of the South African War further highlights this ambiguity.
30. Lowry, "Nationalist and Unionist Attitudes to Empire."

a platform for criticism of British and American imperial ambitions at the turn of the century. It voiced concern over America's too-cozy relationship with Britain while offering a larger critique of American imperial aspirations during the Spanish-American War.[31]

For British readers, news about the empire also came from the missionary press. Scholars have long mined missionary periodicals as sources of information on religious, imperial, and cultural history. As historical documents, these often well-indexed and increasingly accessible publications have provided a treasure trove of information. Each major Victorian church organization that engaged in missionary activities had its own periodical; taken together, this amounted to several hundred titles in total.[32] Periodicals such as the Church Missionary Society's flagship journal the *Gleaner* (1841–70, 1874–1921), *Female Missionary Intelligencer* (1854–99), *Daybreak* (1886–1918), and *India's Women* (1881–1957), for example, specifically targeted female audiences and employed British women journalists in order to drum up support for missionary work abroad. Church-based magazines run by organizations like the Church of England, the Quakers, and the Methodists likewise contained extensive accounts of missionary work.[33]

Specialized missionary periodicals provide excellent material for research on empire and the press. Feminist periodicals, as the case of Lady Somerset illustrates, often reported on women's issues in Britain and the empire.[34] Study of the missionary press thus has the potential to highlight the important role women writers played in representing the empire to readers at home. As Anna Johnston notes, editors, writers, and church proprietors of missionary periodicals created new ways of connecting readers to the project of mission work by incorporating features associated with the mainstream press, such as human interest stories, high-quality illustrations, and serialized fiction.[35] In addition, missionary journals supplied much of Victorians' geographical knowledge and sparked "popular interest in the empire."[36]

Empire and Colony

Understanding the role of the press in British imperialism requires either reading extensively in the indigenous press or reading British colonial periodicals against the grain. Either approach can be challenging given the inaccessibility of source material and the difficulty of uncovering the views of indigenous peoples due to the mediating influence of print and the colonial archive.[37] The question asked by G. Spivak, "Can the Subaltern Speak?" has particular resonance in the case of the press.[38] How to read mediated sources is a continual challenge faced by historians who study indigenous and anti-colonial newspapers. Power dynamics within the

---

31. Bhroiméil, "The Irish-American Press and the South African War."
32. *Missionary Periodicals Database*, accessed October 23, 2008, http://research.yale.edu:8084/missionperiodicals/index.jsp.
33. Tusan, "Gleaners in the Holy Land."
34. Tusan, *Women Making News*.
35. Johnston, "British Missionary Publishing," 22–5.
36. Altholz, *Religious Press in Britain*, 123. See also Johnston, *Missionary Writing and Empire*.
37. Burton, *Archive Stories*.
38. Spivak, "Can the Subaltern Speak?"

colonial relationship complicate understanding the production, readership, and reception of these periodicals. The missionary press is a case in point. Read by some as agents of empire that helped secure British authority and claims over the empire, missionary publications can also provide information about local and indigenous issues, including statistics on church membership, chronicles of daily life, and descriptions of missionary activities in local communities. In addition, the popularity of missionary periodicals among Victorian readers suggests that such publications deserve closer examination by scholars.[39]

Feminist periodicals provide another opportunity to read empire against the grain. Beth Baron's work on women's periodicals in Egypt, for example, reveals the rich world of writing by and about women in the late nineteenth century.[40] Antoinette Burton's important work on Victorian feminism and India also uses the press to analyze colonial relationships.[41] Her reading of the role of the British women's periodicals in representing the relationship between Indian and British women offers an important critique of the maternal character of Victorian feminism. The feminist press, as demonstrated in my own work, was active in promoting legislative reforms for women in the early twentieth century, thereby providing a link between Indian and British feminists.[42] The *Vote*, the organ of the Women's Freedom League, and *Stri Dharma*, the voice of the Women's India Association, published the news and happenings of the women's movement in India and Britain, respectively.[43]

The press also provides an important entry point for interrogating Victorian understandings of race in the empire. Damon Salesa's examination of representations of race in the New Zealand press during the 1860s offers a rare glimpse into how mixed-race peoples used the media to protect their interests. News coverage of the so-called "Paper War," for example, pitted indigenous rights against colonial interests in a discursive battle over authority.[44] Wars of the pen as well as the sword, these conflicts gave voice to indigenous interests. The eventual acceptance of "half-castes" in colonial New Zealand undermined settler authority by making it hard to draw stark lines between sides. Such resistance to either-or racial ideology revealed the ways in which the British colonial system could be undermined by its subjects.

Reading visual representations of empire against the grain can also promote understanding of the imperial world. Anandi Ramamurthy, for example, analyzes advertising images of black subjects, demonstrating how advertisers exploited racial stereotypes to serve commercial interests. As this study and others have shown, images were particularly powerful in determining the construction of racial categories of difference.[45] Photographers played a part in this construction of empire by producing visual representations of the colonial project.[46] Importantly,

---

39. In "Imperial Emotions," Haggis recently argued for the important cultural role played by missionary periodicals in creating "affective communities."
40. Baron, *Women's Awakening in Egypt*.
41. Burton, *Burdens of History*.
42. Tusan, "Writing *Stri Dharma*," 623–7.
43. Tusan, *Women Making News*, 265.
44. Salesa, *Racial Crossings*, 213–27.
45. Ramamurthy, *Imperial Persuaders*, 6–11.
46. Ryan, *Picturing Empire*.

while photographic images and advertising served to reinforce the mechanisms of colonial control, they also opened up possibilities for colonial subjects to talk back to the colonial project through the production of subversive counter-narratives that, as Paul Gilroy has shown, had the ability to undermine racist stereotypes.[47]

The interconnectedness of imperial and domestic concerns during the height of the British Empire is best represented in Chandrika Kaul's edited collection, *Media and the British Empire*. Here themes of nation, identity, and resistance come to the fore in a series of wide-ranging essays addressing diverse imperial settings. The focus is on what Kaul calls "communication media power," which "helped create and sustain imperial power."[48] The time period of the collection spans from the end of the Napoleonic Wars to the eve of decolonization, offering a long view of how the media's function changed over time. Studies of individual newspapers and periodicals published in Britain and the empire show how the media maintained and sometimes served to undermine British control. The implications here move beyond media studies theory and use the media to explain historical events and processes including the beginning and ending of British rule in India

The investigation of imperial narratives in combination with media and press history has produced a number of important new studies. It also suggests possibilities for future research. As recent scholarship has shown, the press provides the researcher interested in colonial responses to empire with opportunities to contribute to the growing field of imperial studies. The themes of community and resistance that have guided this scholarship rely on understanding the political and economic forces at work in the making of empire as well as the representation of the empire itself in the press. To help facilitate research in these areas, more periodicals published in and about the empire need to be made available either online or on microfilm. This is particularly true of periodicals originally published outside of Britain. Access to these periodicals would give researchers another way to hear the voices of peoples affected by British rule who lived outside of the colonial metropole. An index of imperial publications that updates the work of Vann and VanArsdel would also help facilitate research. At present, scholars interested in empire and the press must dig through indexes of other collections and scan press bibliographies, hoping to find periodicals with subject matter related to the British Empire and imperialism.

What has the current focus on empire added to press history? It has provided important historical perspective on the power of pro- and anti-imperialist discourses and processes. Avenues for research in periodicals are wide open and becoming broader as the field of British imperial studies continues to develop. Media scholars, historians, and literary critics now have access to new source material that will facilitate future research connecting press and empire. The inclusion of empire in histories of the nineteenth-century media has the potential of offering new analytic tools for understanding how the process of imperialism functioned.[49] Researchers have shown that indigenous peoples relied on colonial structures and liberal discourse to

---

47. Gilroy, "There Ain't No Black in the Union Jack."
48. Kaul, *Media and the British Empire*, 5.
49. See essays in Bailey, *Narrating Media History*, and DiCenzo, *Feminist Media History*.

create a press of their own. Future scholarship should continue the work of researchers who have examined the local press for imperial connections in Ireland, Africa, India, and Britain's informal empire in the Middle East. Such work would provide a clearer foundation for the discourse on decolonization in the late twentieth century, when nationalists in the colonies had greater access to media technologies. This will provide an important vantage point from which to gain a fruitful understanding of the reach and influence of the British Empire on peoples and institutions across the globe.

11

TRANSATLANTIC CONNECTIONS

Bob Nicholson

The history of transatlantic relations is punctuated by moments of rupture and connection. Columbus's arrival in the Americas in 1492 and the voyage of the *Mayflower* in 1620 are still commemorated in American culture as watershed moments in the country's history—symbolic points at which new connections were established between the Old World and the New. By contrast, the Boston Tea Party and the signing of the Declaration of Independence are celebrated as events in which political, cultural, economic, and emotional ties with Britain were severed—moments of rupture which set the tone for a new period of Anglo-American disconnection. An equally symbolic, though now much less celebrated, moment in transatlantic relations occurred on August 5, 1858, when the first transatlantic telegraph cable established a physical link between the high-speed communications networks of Europe and America. While it had once taken over a week to carry information from Britain to the United States, the first official message to be sent along the cable was transmitted in approximately thirty-five minutes. "Europe and America are united by telegraph," it ran, "Glory to God in the Highest; on earth peace, good will towards men."[1]

The transatlantic press had no doubt as to the profound significance of the event. Articles forecasting the dawn of a new age in Anglo-American relations were published by newspapers on both sides of the Atlantic. Under the eye-catching headline "The World Revolution Begun," the *New York Herald* confidently proclaimed that the arrival of the cable marked the "starting point of the civilization of the latter half of the nineteenth century."[2] "Since the discovery of Columbus," declared the leading article of the London *Times* on the same day,

> nothing has been done in any degree comparable to the vast enlargement which has thus been given to the sphere of human activity. . . . Distance . . . is annihilated. For the purposes of mutual communication and of good understanding the Atlantic is dried up, and we become in reality as well as in wish one country. . . . [The cable] has half undone the Declaration of 1775, and gone far to make us once again, in spite of ourselves, one people. To the ties of a common blood, language, and religion, to

---

1. Herald, "Atlantic Telegraph," 7.
2. "World Revolution," 4.

the intimate association in business and a complete sympathy on so many subjects, is now added the faculty of instantaneous communication, which must give to all these tendencies to unity an intensity which they never before could possess.[3]

"THERE IS 'NO MORE SEA'!" shouted the Boston *Liberator*, quoting Revelation 21:1, a passage referring to the arrival of the New Jerusalem: "ENGLAND AND AMERICA FACE TO FACE!"[4]

Editors on both sides of the Atlantic were quick to highlight the role that journalism would play in mediating this new age of transatlantic communication. "The first revolution will be made in the press," argued the *New York Herald*. "We look confidently forward to the time when the *Herald* will contain, besides its local and city intelligence and advertisements, nothing but a mass of faithful telegraphic reports of the events in the whole world of the previous day."[5] Similarly, *The Times* forecast that "within a very short period we shall be able to present to our readers every morning intelligence of what happened the day before in every quarter of the globe."[6]

Eight years later, when a more reliable cable was established, a Kansas paper reiterated the importance of the periodical press in mediating transatlantic discourse: "The ocean is spanned; storms cannot delay nor calms retard the thoughts which one continent speaks to another; we shall hereafter read in the morning papers at breakfast the news of events transpiring in Europe the day before; the two great Nations speaking the same language have annihilated space and time, and will henceforth talk to each other as friends standing side by side."[7] Here, in the predictions of editors, we begin to see the power of the press as a bridge between British and American discourse, a connecting force that enabled millions of readers on one side of the Atlantic to keep in touch with the daily pulse of life on the other. However, for all its dramatic symbolism, the completion of the Atlantic cable did not establish a new golden age of transatlantic media relations overnight. Over the course of the nineteenth century, a series of social, cultural, political, economic, and technological forces gradually drew the periodical networks of Britain and America into an increasingly entangled ecosystem. By the end of the period, readers of British periodicals were treated to a regular diet of imported American news stories, financial bulletins, foreign correspondence, sports coverage, serialized fiction, joke columns, gossip, and thousands of other miscellaneous snippets clipped from the pages of US newspapers and magazines. At the same time, a similar traffic flowed in the opposite direction and helped to embed elements of British culture within the everyday reading experiences of millions of Americans. These textual borrowings were accompanied by a range of stylistic and professional exchanges. Editorial techniques developed in the New York press soon found their way to London and vice versa—often via the transatlantic migration of journalists and editors themselves. Together these developments allowed newspapers and periodicals to become the

---

3. Leader, *Times*, August 6, 1858, 8.
4. "The Greatest Human Achievement," 3.
5. "World Revolution," 4.
6. Leader, *Times*, August 6, 1858, 8.
7. "Great Triumph!," 2.

nineteenth century's most pervasive "contact zone" between British and American culture, a channel through which words, texts, people, and ideas from one country entered the cultural bloodstream of the other.

This chapter outlines the ways in which scholars have begun to map these important new connections. The opening sections track the current state of research on transatlantic press history and highlight areas for further development. The closing sections of the chapter make links to the broader field of transatlantic studies and argue that the digitization of nineteenth-century periodicals presents new methodological possibilities for exploring the entangled history of British and American print culture.

An Anglo-American Invention

Media historians have become increasingly attuned to the fact that journalism did not develop independently on both sides of the Atlantic but was, in the words of Jean Chalaby, an "Anglo-American invention."[8] As a result, they have begun to consider the history of Anglo-American periodicals within a range of new comparative and connective contexts.[9] This body of scholarship is still relatively small and remains ripe for further development. Nevertheless, a handful of landmark events and a few distinctive periods have already emerged. Firstly, it is important to stress that the history of transatlantic media relations predates the nineteenth century. Historians of the early modern Atlantic world have mapped out a complex web of connections between Europe, Africa, and the Americas and have tracked the "kaleidoscopic movements of people, goods, and ideas" that began in this period.[10] Periodicals were certainly part of this transatlantic traffic. Historians and literary critics have long recognized the role played by literary periodicals in the formation of a transatlantic republic of letters during the eighteenth century, and these connections are currently being analyzed in more detail by scholars working within the field of transatlantic literary studies.[11] A detailed survey of this literature lies beyond the scope of this chapter, but Carla Mulford's essay on Benjamin Franklin and his work as a transatlantic literary journalist provides a useful introduction to the subject and points to a number of areas which require further research. Historians of the nineteenth-century press would do well to acquaint themselves with this scholarship. At present, there is a tendency to compartmentalize the early modern period and regard its print culture as part of an entirely separate system from what emerged during the age of the telegraph. The telegraph did not, however, eradicate older channels of exchange. In order to fully understand the history of the press as a transatlantic contact zone, it is necessary to track how connections and networks established by the eighteenth-century press continued to operate and evolve across later periods.

---

8. Chalaby, "Journalism."
9. For a recent collection of essays in this area, see Ardis and Collier's *Transatlantic Print*.
10. Armitage and Braddick, *British and Atlantic*, 1.
11. For useful introductions to the field of transatlantic literary studies, see Manning and Taylor, *Transatlantic Literary Studies*, and Bannet and Manning, *Transatlantic Literary Studies*.

The most significant event of the eighteenth century for the history of transatlantic media relations was, of course, the Revolutionary War. Paradoxically, a conflict that was driven by a desire to sever political ties between Britain and America actually increased the volume of journalistic traffic between the two countries and strengthened links between their periodical networks. The acrimonious build-up to the war and the years of conflict that followed provided British newspaper readers with regular opportunities to consume fragments of American culture, encounter some of the country's leading voices, and vicariously explore the landscapes captured by war reports. While periodicals have long been used by historians to explore British responses to the revolution, the best and most recent history of the subject is Troy Bickham's *Making Headlines*. Bickham shifts the battlefield of the revolution away from the war-ravaged New York frontier and transplants it into the vibrant coffee houses and book clubs of London, Birmingham, and Edinburgh. The press, he argues, fuelled a sustained national debate in which everybody, from London-based politicians to provincial blacksmiths' wives, engaged in hotly contested discussions over the shortcomings of Congress, the merits of George Washington, and the morality of enlisting American Indians. Crucially, this was not a temporary phenomenon. The information networks and journalistic practices discussed by Bickham continued to shape Anglo-American relations long into the new century.

The role played by periodicals in shaping Britain's relationship with the United States during the first half of the nineteenth century has received relatively little scholarly attention. This is a shame, for the period witnessed important developments in both the history of journalism and transatlantic relations. In particular, the role played by periodicals in negotiating the aftermath of the revolution and the gradual transition to a new age of Anglo-American cordiality needs to be mapped in more detail. The relationship between America and the Chartist press is also deserving of greater attention. As Thomas Scriven has pointed out, Radical editors of the 1830s and 1840s looked admiringly towards America and reappropriated elements of its popular culture for their own publications.[12] While the Chartist movement itself was relatively short-lived, its editors pioneered forms of transatlantic cultural exchange that would later become part of the mainstream press. Columns of imported American newspaper jokes, for example, appeared in Chartist periodicals in the 1830s, such as *Cleave's Gazette* (1834–36) and the *Northern Liberator* (1837–40), long before they became a characteristic feature of New Journalism.[13] Finally, some attention has also been paid to the role of the press in shaping British responses to the American Civil War.[14] However, much of this research uses periodicals as a source of public opinion rather than as objects of study in their own right. For my own part, I have recently begun to track how reports from the American Civil War acted as vehicles for the transatlantic movement of American culture, particularly slang terms such as "skedaddle."[15] There is a great deal more work to be done on how the intense burst of press coverage during the early 1860s reshaped British ideas about the United States.

12. Scriven, "Jim Crow Craze."
13. Nicholson, "Jonathan's Jokes," 36.
14. See Grand, *American Civil War*; Blackett, *Divided Hearts*; and Campbell, *English Public Opinion*. Wiener's *Americanization*, discussed in more depth later in this chapter, also includes a section on the American Civil War.
15. Nicholson, "Looming Large," 4.

The end of the American Civil War marked the beginning of a transformative period in transatlantic media relations. When in April 1865 Abraham Lincoln was assassinated in a Washington theater, it took nearly two weeks for news of his death to reach newspaper readers in Britain. Sixteen years later, when President Garfield was shot by a deranged office-seeker, the relationship between America and the British press had changed significantly.[16] This time, news of the attempted assassination reached Britain within hours.[17] As Garfield's life hung in the balance, regular updates on his pulse, temperature, and respiration were telegraphed to British newspaper offices. A president's death, while generating a predictable surge of interest, was only part of a wider journalistic phenomenon. Each morning the latest news stories from "across the pond" appeared in newspapers throughout Britain. Accounts of a political speech in Washington, a devastating fire in Nevada, a gruesome murder in Chicago, a gunfight in Indiana, and the closing prices at the New York stock exchange were printed by British provincial and metropolitan newspapers hours after being published in America. While it would be misleading to claim that Britain and America were now, in the words of the *New York Herald*, "moved simultaneously by the same thought," both the speed and the volume of transatlantic exchange had increased markedly.[18]

Press Interest in America

Digital archives allow us explore these developments from a quantitative perspective. Figure 11.1 shows the results of a keyword search for "Americ*" or "United States" across a sample of twenty-nine British papers published between 1850 and 1896.[19] While it would be unwise to place too much interpretative weight on a rudimentary form of "culturomics," the pattern is worth noting.[20] As we might expect, references to America increased dramatically during the early 1860s as British papers reported on the progress of the Civil War. In the late 1860s, as the conflict gradually receded from view, references to America experienced a slight decline. Interestingly, the opening of the first commercially viable Atlantic cable in 1866 does not appear to have stimulated a significant upsurge in American coverage; the new technology, for all of its apparent promise, did not appear to have an immediately transformative impact upon the fabric of British newspapers. References to America increased steadily during the 1870s before spiking dramatically between the years 1879 and 1881. In 1881, references to America were 41 percent higher than they had been in 1878. Unlike the 1860s, this increase in

---

16. For the media response to Garfield's assassination, see Menke, "Media."
17. See, for example, "Notes of Latest News," 7.
18. "World Revolution," 4.
19. The "*" symbol searches for variations on the base word, such as "American" or "Americanisation." The newspapers selected were the *Aberdeen Journal, Blackburn Standard, Bristol Mercury, Bury and Norwich Post, Daily News, Derby Mercury, Dundee Courier, Era, Essex Standard, Glasgow Herald, Hampshire Telegraph, Huddersfield Chronicle, Ipswich Journal, Jacksons Oxford, Leeds Mercury, Leicester Chronicle, Liverpool Mercury, Lloyds, Manchester Times, Morning Post, Newcastle Courant, North Wales Chronicle, Nottinghamshire Guardian, Reynolds's, Royal Cornwall Gazette, Sheffield Independent, Southampton Herald, Trewman's Exeter,* and *York Herald*.
20. For a more detailed discussion of this culturomic research, see Nicholson, "Counting Culture" and "Digital Turn."

Figure 11.1 Full-text search for "Americ*" OR "United States" in twenty-nine British newspapers. Results displayed by year.

Source: selected from *19th Century British Newspapers*, Gale Gengage.

coverage cannot be explained by an obvious external factor; in fact, historians have generally treated the years between the Alabama Claims (early 1870s) and the Spanish-American War (1898) as a relatively uneventful period in Anglo-American relations. However, this apparently quiet period in transatlantic political history seems to have been accompanied by a significant increase in cultural exchange that was driven, at least in part, by the press.

There are a number of ways in which this apparent increase in press coverage of American affairs might be explained. On a commercial level, the introduction of new transatlantic telegraph lines led to a significant increase in capacity and a marked decrease in rates. As a result, the daily serving of financial intelligence supplied to British papers by Reuters' transatlantic business service increased from a few brief lines stating the price of gold and cotton to lengthy columns summarizing the previous day's business on the New York Stock Exchange. Similarly, it was now financially viable for major metropolitan papers, such as the *Standard*, to receive lengthy daily reports from dedicated American correspondents. In June 1881, the first installment of the new American coverage in the *Standard* (1827–1916) was devoted to a strike among New York brewers, but it included incidental asides on the drinking habits of the city's German population, the celebration of Whit Monday, and the similarities between American lager beer and London stout. Once this story had been concluded, the correspondent moved on to describe a strike among railroad laborers, the construction of New York's underground railway, the proceedings of a sensational divorce case, the results of a senatorial election, a summary of an editorial published by the *New York World*, and the indifferent response exhibited by the American public to news of troubles in Ireland.[21] The message was sent from New York on a Wednesday evening and appeared on the shelves of British newsagents the next day. The day after, a fresh bulletin appeared featuring news about senatorial debates on international copyright, the unmasking of a man who had successfully impersonated the brother of a British lord, the latest developments in the aforementioned divorce case, the increased availability of bank loans, and a gang of fraudsters operating on Wall Street.[22] It was now possible for British readers to keep in touch with the daily rhythms of life in metropolitan America—to consume the latest news and gossip hours after it had circulated in the clubs and reading rooms of New York. By 1881, the press began to operate as its editors had predicted in the 1850s—as a transatlantic contact zone that enabled British and American readers to "talk to each other as friends standing side by side." However, with the exception of prominent figures such as George Augustus Sala, we currently know relatively little about the foreign correspondents who facilitated these daily conversations or the ways in which they represented American life to British newspaper readers.[23]

Alongside this high-speed news traffic, the final quarter of the nineteenth century also witnessed a series of stylistic, typographical, and rhetorical exchanges as journalistic techniques pioneered in one country became commonplace in the other. This process has recently been mapped out in impressive detail by Joel H. Wiener. His latest monograph, *The Americanization of the British Press, 1830s–1914*, argues that the development of the popular press was a collaborative transatlantic project.[24] As the title indicates, Wiener suggests that America was the leading player in this process. "While popular journalism in Britain pioneered the retailing of gossip and the use of pictures," he argues, "most of the key transformations in journalism occurred a little earlier and had a greater impact in America."[25] Interviews, human interest stories, sensational cross-heads, a culture of speed, and the adoption of what Martin Conboy terms a "commercial vernacular" are all highlighted by Wiener as American innovations that were subsequently employed by British editors such as W.T. Stead, George Newnes, T.P. O'Connor, and Alfred Harmsworth.[26] These exchanges were in turn facilitated by the transatlantic movements of editors and journalists themselves. Wiener argues that these developments occurred in response to shared social, cultural, and political changes, including the evolution of representative forms of government, the development of new communications networks, and increasing literacy rates. The result, he argues, was the emergence of a shared

---

21. "United States (By Telegraph)," June 9, 1881, 5.
22. "United States (By Telegraph)," June 10, 1881, 5.
23. Blake, "George Augustus Sala."
24. Wiener, *Americanization*. The core thesis underpinning this study was foregrounded by Wiener in an earlier article of the same name. Wiener has also edited a useful collection on *Anglo-American Media Interactions* with Mark Hampton.
25. Wiener, *Americanization*, 4.
26. Conboy, *Language of Newspapers*, chapter 5, "A Message from America: A Commercial Vernacular," 95–112. It should be noted that Wiener himself emphasizes terms such as "democratic" and "popular" in place of "commercial" when describing the relationship between popular newspapers and their readers. See Wiener, *Americanization*, 5.

transatlantic print culture in which popular newspapers on both sides of the Atlantic courted the attention of an emerging mass readership by drawing on a shared repertoire of journalistic techniques.

Wiener's study makes a vital contribution to our understanding of Anglo-American media relations. However, as a roundtable by several critics on his work has suggested, it also leaves room for further investigations and theoretical refinement (particularly around a loaded term like "Americanization").[27] For example, Wiener, by his own admission, gives a "disproportionate emphasis to the journalism of London and New York."[28] He gives a brief nod to the "increasing importance of the provincial press" in this period but argues that "London, dominant in so many ways, was, clearly, a forcing ground for journalistic creativity."[29] However, as Andrew Hobbs has demonstrated, the provincial press was a vibrant and influential component of Victorian popular culture and equally capable of fostering journalistic innovations. For example, provincial weekly papers such as the *Hampshire Telegraph* (1803–99) and the *Newcastle Weekly Courant* (1711–1902) introduced regular "Yankee humour" columns long before their metropolitan rivals.[30] Far from being parochial in outlook, these papers played an important role in shaping readers' understanding of the wider world and carried fragments of Americana into the most rural corners of Britain. Their independence of the metropolis was also enabled by news agencies like Reuters, which made it possible for provincial papers to publish items of American intelligence on the same morning as their London rivals. We should not assume, in other words, that Anglo-American media exchanges were always channeled through London and New York.

Transatlantic Exchanges

Periodicals were not the only point of contact between nineteenth-century Britain and America. Scholars working within the burgeoning field of transatlantic studies have identified a range of contexts in which the two countries encountered and explored each another. Firstly, improvements in the speed, safety, affordability, and comfort of transatlantic steamship travel significantly increased opportunities for Victorians to visit America in person. Between 1871 and 1900, the gross migration to the United States from England, Wales, Scotland, and Ireland was just under four million.[31] These passengers were joined by thousands of British tourists, businessmen, writers, and traveling performers who took temporary tours of the United States before returning home. A remarkable number of these travelers felt compelled to publish their impressions of America in travelogues.[32] Historians and literary scholars have focused a great deal of attention on this body of literature, particularly on prominent examples of

---

27. Mayhall, Collier, Silberstein-Loeb, and Wiener, "Roundtable."
28. Wiener, *Americanization*, 7.
29. Ibid.
30. Nicholson, "Jonathan's Jokes."
31. Nugent, *Crossings*, 46. For other studies on transatlantic migration, see Van Vugt, *Britain to America*, and Wyman, *Round-Trip*.
32. For a comprehensive list of these texts, see Nisbet, *British Comment*.

the genre such as Dickens's *American Notes* (1842), Alexis de Tocqueville's *Democracy in America* (1835, 1840), Frances Trollope's *Domestic Manners of the Americans* (1832), Anthony Trollope's *North America* (1862), Matthew Arnold's *Civilization in the United States* (1888), and James Bryce's *American Commonwealth* (1888). While the views of these well-known figures are certainly worth studying, they are an imperfect tool with which to analyze wider Victorian public opinion. Recent explorations of Anglo-American travel literature have drawn upon a broader range of commentary, but representativeness still remains a problem.[33] Simply by visiting America, British travel writers entered into an atypical relationship with the country, for the vast majority of their countrymen never crossed the Atlantic and were compelled to engage with the United States at a distance. In order to fully understand the Victorian relationship with America, it is necessary therefore to move beyond the familiar commentaries of canonical authors, politicians, cultural elites, and transatlantic travelers and go in search of a more popular response. Periodicals provide a promising new source for these kinds of investigations.

British citizens were not, of course, the only travelers to cross the Atlantic. Every steamship that sailed to the New World returned a fortnight later with a corresponding cargo of American migrants, travelers, performers, texts, and commodities. Historians have explored America's presence in Victorian Britain from a range of perspectives. Some have examined the experiences of American immigrants, with a particular focus on canonical writers such as Henry James and the glamorous "Dollar Princesses" who married into the British aristocracy.[34] Others have explored the experiences and responses of American travelers.[35] While these studies provide valuable insights into transatlantic relations, it is important to stress that the number of Americans in late Victorian Britain was always quite small. Outside central London or major port cities such as Liverpool, personal encounters with American travelers would have been rare, particularly in rural regions. Newspapers, on the other hand, carried fragments of America into the most remote areas of Britain on a daily basis.

While the number of American citizens visiting late Victorian Britain was relatively small, some of these travelers commanded significant press attention. Humorists such as Mark Twain and Artemus Ward delivered lectures to packed theaters, and a range of lesser-known actors, musicians, and humorists appeared in the country's theaters and music halls.[36] Performing cowboys, such as Buffalo Bill, reached large audiences in Britain during the 1880s and 1890s. However, while touring performers played an important role in shaping British conceptions of

---

33. For key studies of British commentary on America, see Mulvey, *Anglo-American Landscapes*; Mulvey, *Transatlantic Manners*; Frankel, *Observing America*; Prochaska, *Eminent Victorians*; and Lewis, *Early Encounter*.
34. See McWhirter, *Henry James*, and Zwerdling, *Improvised Europeans*. Gabin criticizes the androcentric nature of Zwerdling's study and explores the experiences of female expatriates in *American Women*. For work on Anglo-American marital relations, see Burke, *Old World*, chapter 7; Davis, "We Are All Americans Now!"; Brandon, *Dollar Princesses*; Montgomery, *Gilded Prostitution*; Cooper, "Informal Ambassadors"; and Woolf, "Special Relationships."
35. Lockwood, *Passionate Pilgrims*; Mulvey, *Anglo-American Landscapes*; Mulvey, *Transatlantic Manners*; Seed, *American Travellers*; Ziff, *Return Passages*; Stow, *American Abroad*; Bendixen, *Cambridge Companion*; Kennin, *Return*; and Wright, "Britain." For a bibliography of American travel literature, see Smith, *American Travellers*.
36. Featherstone, "Artemus Ward."

the United States, it is important to recognize that these blockbuster events were not in themselves part of the fabric of everyday life. Despite their remarkable popularity, the majority of Victorians never attended one of Twain's lectures or witnessed Buffalo Bill's legendary marksmanship. However, many of them were offered an opportunity to engage with these figures through press coverage. Extracts from Twain's work and reviews of his lectures were printed and recirculated in the British press, as were articles devoted to Buffalo Bill and his retinue of Wild West performers. There is, indeed, much more work to be done on the relationship between the periodical press and other forms of Victorian popular culture—particularly the role it played in remediating theatrical performances and amplifying their reach.

Periodicals also played an increasingly important role in mediating the transatlantic literary marketplace. The work of North American authors began to circulate widely in Britain from the 1830s but intensified in the 1850s following the success of Harriet Beecher Stowe's *Uncle Tom's Cabin*. Andrew King has demonstrated the popularity of American female authors such as E.D.E.N. Southworth, Harriet Lewis, and Fanny Fern, whose stories were serialized in mass-market weekly magazines such as the *London Journal* (1845–1928) and the *Family Herald* (1843–1940).[37] While the Anglophone nature of the transatlantic marketplace allowed American texts to be imported more freely than French or German literature, King identifies other forms of translation at work. American locations and characters in many of these repackaged stories were jettisoned for more familiar British equivalents: New York became London, the Adirondacks were relocated to Wales, and slaves were transformed into servants. Stephan Pigeon has uncovered similarly de-Americanizing modifications in works of American didactic fiction in the British *Ladies' Treasury* (1858–95), while my own work on the transatlantic circulation of American newspaper humor demonstrates how these jokes were sometimes divested of their Yankee features before circulating in British newspapers.[38]

Other literary imports were, however, celebrated for their distinctively American character. Thomas Chandler Halliburton's *The Clockmaker*—a collection of comic stories about a wise-cracking Yankee named Sam Slick—was an early favorite with British audiences. These sketches were initially published in 1835 in a Canadian newspaper called the *Novoscotian*, but soon came to the attention of London publisher James Bentley, who printed a pirated collection in 1837. Following the success of this venture, Bentley entered into a formal agreement with Halliburton and published additional installments of Sam Slick's "saying and doings" in the 1830s and 1840s.[39] Pieces by Halliburton also appeared in the literary periodical *Bentley's Miscellany* (1837–68) and were regularly reprinted in British newspapers, demonstrating the fluid relationships that existed between the newspapers, periodicals, and books of the period. Crucially, the commercial and critical success of Halliburton paved the way for other American humorists to cross the Atlantic. Mark Twain's experiences in England have been recounted by biographers, and the British response to his work has been debated by a number of scholars.[40]

---

37. King, *London Journal*.
38. Pigeon, "Anglo-American Cultures"; Nicholson, "You Kick the Bucket."
39. Enkvist, *American Humour*.
40. Powers, *Mark Twain*, 319–35; Baetzhold, "Mark Twain," 328–46; Lee, "International Twain"; and Budd, *Mark Twain*.

Dennis Welland has contributed a detailed study of Twain's relationship with his British publishers, and John S. Batts has explored his influence on Jerome K. Jerome.[41] Victorian responses to other leading American humorists, such as Artemus Ward and James Russell Lowell, have also received consideration, though Nils Erik Enkvist's *American Humour in England before Mark Twain*, published in 1953, remains the only broad treatment of the subject. Indeed, the role played by the press in circulating the work of these well-known American humorists has thus far received little attention. When one of Twain's humorous anecdotes was clipped out and reprinted in a popular metropolitan paper such as *Lloyd's Weekly News* (1842–1931), it had the potential to reach more British readers in a single day than his books did during his entire lifetime. In the absence of robust transatlantic copyright legislation, these acts of literary piracy occurred on a mass scale and carried the work of American writers across the Atlantic and into the hands of millions of British readers.

Transatlantic media exchanges were also facilitated by formal business arrangements. Tillotsons, a syndication agency, had offices in Bolton and New York and successfully sold the work of Wilkie Collins, Mary Braddon, Rider Haggard, and other British novelists to American newspaper publishers.[42] This market became particularly lucrative following the passing of the Chase Act of 1891, which granted British authors copyright protection in the United States, but well before that, periodical publishers had sought out new international markets. *Harper's Monthly Magazine* launched a European edition in 1881, published in London by Sampson Low. The same year, the *Detroit Free Press* introduced a weekly London edition composed largely of short stories and American humor. It lasted until 1898 and at its peak sold more than 100,000 copies a week.[43] In a similar vein, W.T. Stead helped found American and Australian editions of the London *Review of Reviews* (1890–1936), though these papers remained independent of one another in editorship and appearance. A number of smaller periodicals, such as the *Anglo-American Times* (1865–96), the *British and American Journal of Commerce* (1873), and the *London American Register* (1875–1915), were founded with the intention of addressing both British and American audiences.[44] While these transatlantic business ventures played an important role in shaping the emergence of a new Anglo-American public sphere, they have received relatively little attention from historians. In order to fully understand the workings of this inter-textual, transatlantic culture of reprinting, we need to look beyond the texts themselves and uncover the business relationships and dissemination pathways that underpinned their circulation.

The Digital Transatlantic

The recent digitization of nineteenth-century periodicals offers new opportunities for the study of transatlantic history. In purely practical terms, some of the barriers that once made this research difficult have now been lifted. While Wiener appears to have conducted most of his research by personally traveling back and forth between archives in London and New York,

---

41. Welland, *Mark Twain*; Batts, "American Humour."
42. Law, *Serializing Fiction*.
43. Bradshaw, "*Detroit Free Press*."
44. Miller, *America and the British Imaginary*, 65–79.

scholars building on his pioneering work will doubtlessly make most of these journeys online. This is not to suggest that digital archives have entirely replaced their paper counterparts; thousands of periodicals are yet to be made available online, while other important sources that help map their production or the movements of journalists are only available in physical repositories. Nevertheless, the new methodological possibilities presented by digital archives are pushing databases into the foreground of new research practices and enabling new topics. In particular, the ability to keyword-search large archives of periodicals has made it possible to track the transatlantic movement of people, goods, texts, and ideas in ways that were hitherto impossible. The culturomic research mentioned earlier in this chapter promises to help us read the press from a distance and quantify broad cultural changes in ways that would not have been possible using paper and microfilm sources.

This is an exciting time to study transatlantic connections. Wiener's book, published in 2012, was the first monograph to focus explicitly on Anglo-American media interactions during the nineteenth century, and the number of conferences and discussions now devoted to the subject, together with a handful of promising new doctoral projects, suggest that more will soon follow in its wake. As a result, it is difficult to predict where the field might be in even five years' time. However, one thing seems certain: the number of connections and exchanges that have recently been uncovered between the periodical cultures of nineteenth-century Britain and America means that we can no longer study them in isolation. As the editors of these papers pointed out in their response to the Atlantic cable, the press was capable of transcending national boundaries and making connections between two geographically distant peoples. It is now time for historians to do the same.

12

TRANSNATIONAL CONNECTIONS

Jane Chapman

Connections between Britain and non-Anglophone countries have always been strong. Authors, publishers, advertising agents, and other generators and transmitters of popular culture were well aware of their role in the global marketplace. Newspaper press directories, for example, facilitated the placement of advertisements for British goods in a wide range of foreign newspapers and periodicals. Recent scholarship has emphasized these global connections.[1] For instance Louis James has examined the importance of French literature in the British literary marketplace during the 1840s, and Eugenia Palmegiano has studied British views of continental European journalism in forty-four nineteenth-century periodicals.[2] Many other studies have mined periodicals in order to illuminate transnational themes, including trade, science, design, and fashion. Much work has been done in these areas in general, but there is still much to do, especially in the field of periodicals research, where the comparative study of British and non-Anglophone periodicals is still relatively new. This chapter cannot cover the entirety of the field; instead, I will suggest a few potential areas for further exploration, focusing on Germany, France, and Japan. Rather than denying the value of periodicals as repositories of historical data, I will revisit the areas mentioned above—trade, science, design, and fashion—to suggest how they might be researched further using a transnational comparative approach.

Transnational Comparisons: Advantages and Hindrances

By the advent of the twentieth century, various technologies were influencing the nature and presentation of information and the extent and the speed by which it was transmitted globally. As these systems were developed, newspapers and periodicals acknowledged that different parts of the world were being drawn together in new ways, even though the production and consumption of periodicals was not uniform across the globe. Until quite late in the century, periodicals were forms of communication limited to literate, urban, industrial, and mainly Western societies.[3] If they appeared elsewhere, they were usually imported as part of the

---

1. *Sell's* details how and where to advertise internationally from 1883; *Mitchell's* and *Deacon's* from 1886.
2. James, *Fiction for the Working Man*, 159–69; Palmegiano, "First Common Market."
3. See King, "Magazines, International," 2748 and "International Histories of Magazines." 1–5 at *Greenwich English Prof* http://blogs.gre.ac.uk/andrewking/.

colonial apparatus, as Vann and VanArsdel's *Periodicals of Queen Victoria's Empire* demonstrated twenty years ago. It is important to remember, however, that there were also non-colonial contexts in which British periodicals were circulated; hence, in this chapter, I focus on continental Europe and Japan.

In past decades, scholars have excluded non-Anglophone contexts from periodicals research due to linguistic barriers, even though we knew these connections were important. We were aware, for example, that both France and Germany heavily influenced the Anglophone world of ideas during the Enlightenment and the Romantic era. We also knew that French was, in the nineteenth century, the lingua franca of diplomacy and that its publishing industry was international in its outlook. Yet attempts to compare Continental and Anglophone periodicals remain rare. Whether this will change with the advent of online tools such as Google Translate remains to be seen; for the moment, researchers still need to have competence in two or more languages. With the welcome advent of the European Society for Periodical Research (ESPRit) based in the Netherlands—whose lingua franca is English—we may begin to make transnational comparisons, even though at present many papers given at ESPRit conferences are focused on periodicals in discrete countries.[4]

Comparative methods are defined by what Mahoney and Rueschemeyer call a "concern with causal analysis, an emphasis on processes over time, and the use of systematic and contextualised comparison" of similar and contrasting cases.[5] By employing a coherent and rigorous framework, researchers are able to ask big questions and achieve ambitious outcomes. In the social sciences, comparative historical analysis has a distinguished tradition of identifying commonalities and similarities, as well as pinpointing specificities and differences using these frameworks.[6] While this may sound like a rigidly schematic approach, what it means at root is that researchers need to ensure that their comparisons are justified. A comparative approach also allows researchers to test theoretical propositions in ways that are not possible when focusing on a single case study. Transnational comparative content analysis is likely to reveal differences in attitudes towards how periodicals operate in the literary marketplace, including the identities of their contributors based on occupation, gender, class, sexuality, "race," education, ethics, and religion. Such an approach could reveal new links between texts and audiences and could provide insight into economic relations in various markets or countries. It could also demonstrate to what extent periodicals in different countries assumed similar formats or published advertisements by the same companies. These adverts might also help us compare the wealth, style, or trends in different countries at different times. Other areas that need to be examined in a comparative light include systems of marketing; communal uses of periodicals in cafés, coffee houses, reading societies, or schools; and, more broadly, publishing and economic systems that promoted or impeded the print trade.

---

4. See http://www.ru.nl/esprit/welcome/about_esprit/.
5. Mahoney and Rueschemeyer, *Comparative Historical Analysis*, 6.
6. Ibid., 3. The authors also usefully remind us of classic theoretical formulations of the comparative approach by Park, "Reflections on Communications"; Deutsch, "Growth of Nations"; and George, "Quantitative and Qualitative Approaches."

There are many advantages to a comparative approach to media history, particularly since it engages with so many facets of the nineteenth-century culture industry. However, it is not without its difficulties. Comparative data is often difficult to access when studying national markets, economic sectors, or individual periodicals. The researcher's choice of cases in a comparative analysis can be easily open to criticism and always needs to be justified. It is possible to stretch comparisons beyond the limits of credibility or to be overly selective in the choice of case studies which may not be representative. There is also the risk that comparative statements can become too simplistic, tenuous, or generalized.[7] This is why a rigorous and transparent framework is essential: the researcher not only needs to be systematic and clear about what exactly is being compared but also must pay careful attention to the context of each item analyzed.

While most periodicals research is nationally focused, two recent studies offer models for how to construct coherent frameworks and justifiable comparisons. Felicity Jensz compares two Moravian Church periodicals from different countries—the British *Periodical Accounts* and the German *Missions-Blat*—and analyzes their different target audiences and purposes. Thoralf Klein focuses on a historical event, the Boxer War, and explores similarities and differences in how it is represented in German, British, and American periodicals, as well as in one periodical he terms "international" (the *China-Bote*, a German-language interdenominational journal that cooperated widely with missionary groups from many countries). Both researchers are careful to point out similarities and dissimilarities between the periodicals they study, not only their treatment of topics but their historical development, production, and readership.[8]

German Resources and Transnational Science

After the Napoleonic Wars ended in 1815, it was easier to import foreign printed material into Britain, even though it was still subject to a hefty tax. Limitations on the accessibility of foreign intelligence was one of the reasons for the establishment of the *Foreign Quarterly Review* (1827–46), which focused on material that had not yet been translated into English.[9] By the second half of the nineteenth century, the transnational flow of ideas was more relaxed. The publication of Samuel Scudder's *Catalogue of Scientific Serials of all Countries* (1879) demonstrates the increased level of interest in international exchange within the scientific community. Suzanne Zeller points out that in Canada it was hoped that the exchange of ideas with scientists in other countries would encourage "public pride, prestige, confidence resulting from scientific achievements" and bridge "cultural and political divisions"—a view that Elizabeth Tilley, in her study of the *Dublin Penny Journal*, believes could equally be applied to Ireland.[10] By 1900, the internationalization of academic disciplines, led by German, French, and British institutions, had accelerated rapidly, leading to the founding of the International Association of Academies, which met for the first time in 1901. Such cooperation was also reflected in the establishment of

---

7. Chapman, *Comparative Media History*, 2.
8. Jensz, "Diverging Reports"; Klein, "Protestant Missionary Periodicals."
9. See Houghton, *Wellesley Index*, 2:129–38.
10. Zeller, *Inventing Canada*, 8; Tilley, "Science, Industry, and Nationalism," 142.

the *Internationale Wochenschrift für Wissenschaft, Kunst und Technik* (International Weekly for Science, Art, and Technology) in 1907.[11] However, the desire for the exchange of knowledge beyond national borders precedes the fin de siècle. Like the *Foreign Quarterly Review*, the British *Academy* (1869–1916) demonstrated what Gillian Beer refers to a "wonderfully inclusive ideal of free intellectual movement between disciplinary forms and across national boundaries."[12] Its founding editor, Charles Edward Appleton, was profoundly influenced by the German commitment to research and its dissemination across borders. He was inspired particularly by the *Literarisches Centralblatt für Deutschland* (1850–1944), which was set up to provide a "vollständige und schnelle Übersicht über die gesammte literarische Thätigkeit Deutschlands" (a fully continuous and rapid survey of the whole of Germany's literary activity) at a time when "Deutschland" in political reality comprised a set of independent states.[13] Even more ambitiously, Appleton aimed for the *Academy* to survey the whole of European literary and scientific activity *despite* national differences between French, German, and British ideals of intellectual endeavor—a subject that surely calls for more comparative research in the relevant periodical literature.

Although scholars have shown interest in the late nineteenth-century popularization of science, this interest has not necessarily led to the increase in comparative analyses that one would have hoped for: most studies remain nationally oriented.[14] The *Science in the Nineteenth-Century Periodical* online index, for example, only includes periodicals published in Britain. A few scholars have begun to catalogue the history of science publishing in Europe, but they have not yet focused on periodicals.[15] Some researchers, however, have studied science periodicals in a comparative way. Janet Browne and Susan Sheets-Pyenson, for example, have compared periodicals in London and Paris in order to explore the emergence of a "low" scientific culture.[16]

British press directories are helpful for finding information on non-Anglophone periodicals from the 1880s onwards (particularly *Sell's*, *Mitchell's*, and *Deacon's*). The online *Western European Studies Section* (WessWeb) is also a useful initial port of call for studying European periodicals. This resource is divided into sections based on language group and century of publication. It includes indexes, guides, websites, and annotated bibliographies. Divisions within language sections reveal the wealth and diversity of material provided by this resource. For example, the nineteenth-century German-language periodicals category (in "Old News: Historical Newspapers") is subdivided into Austrian, German, and German-Jewish periodicals.[17]

---

11. When the International Association collapsed in 1914, it was considered a catastrophe (von Ungern-Sternberg, "Scientists," 129). The current International Council for Science (founded in 1931) regards the International Association as its parent organization (see http://www.icsu.org/about-icsu/about-us/a-brief-history).
12. Beer, "*Academy*," 182.
13. Editorial Note, 1.
14. See, for instance, Cantor and Shuttleworth, *Science Serialised*, and Henson, Cantor, Dawson, Noakes, Shuttleworth and Topham, *Culture and Science*.
15. See Gascoigne, *Historical Catalogue*; Meadows, *Development of Science Publishing*.
16. Browne, "Darwin in Caricature"; Browne, "Squibs and Snobs"; Sheets-Pyenson, "Popular Science Periodicals." See also Broks, *Media Science*; and Fyfe, "Periodicals and Books Series."
17. http://wessweb.info/index.php.

Access to several periodical titles is also available through *Zefys*, the German-language national historical newspaper digitization project, which also makes available German-language material published not only in Germany and the German states but also elsewhere in the world, including titles such as the *Deutsch-Ostafrikanische Zeitung* (German-East African Times, 1899–1916), published in Daressalam.[18] The union catalogues for Austria and for different regions of Germany are worth consulting: further information on these can be found in *Info Connect*'s "Union Catalogues in Europe"[19] and at the Deutsche Nationalbibliothek.[20] Also useful is Dominique Baudin's German union catalogue of French periodicals and the *Bibliotheksdienst* (the periodical of German bibliographies), which publishes articles about the latest digitization projects.[21] Finally, the British Library has quite a large collection of German periodicals published in London.[22] These include illustrated periodicals; newspaper supplements; trade journals; market reports; and bilingual and trilingual journals, which provide commentary on the London social scene. In present-day holdings and nineteenth-century publishing contexts, language and country do not necessarily coincide, even in Anglophone countries where a single language is assumed to dominate. Comparative studies must therefore pay attention to different publishing systems, each with its own legal, technological, political, social, and economic contexts.

French Periodicals and Transnational Fashion and Caricature

Paying close attention to context is also important when studying nineteenth-century French-language periodicals, which might have been published in Belgium, Algeria, "Cochin-China" (now part of Vietnam), Great Britain,[23] or France. French-language periodicals, like their English- and German-language counterparts, have a rich publication history outside the metropolis, though Paris had by far the highest number of periodical publications. During the second half of the nineteenth century, Paris consolidated its position as the global capital of art and fashion, as exemplified in the pages of the influential literary and artistic periodical *La Revue Blanche* (1889–1903), a complete run of which is available online through *Gallica*, the digitization project sponsored by the Bibliothèque Nationale de France (BNF).[24] Haute couture developed using a system pioneered by an Englishman based in Paris, Charles Worth,[25] who was mentioned frequently in fashion magazines such as *Le Magasin des demoiselles* (1844–96), *La Mode illustrée* (1860–1937), and *Le Moniteur de la mode* (1808–92). Early in the century, French

---

18. For the general page, see http://zefys.staatsbibliothek-berlin.de. Available numbers of *Deutsch-Ostafrikanische Zeitung* can be accessed at http://zefys.staatsbibliothek-berlin.de/.
19. www.lwrw.org/union_catalogs_Eur.htm.
20. http://www.dnb.de/EN/Home/home_node.html.
21. Back issues (to 1996) can be consulted free online at http://digital.zlb.de/viewer/!toc/019591853/0/LOG_0000/.
22. http://www.bl.uk/reshelp/findhelprestype/news/germanlanguagenews/index.html.
23. The *Courrier de l'Europe* was published in London 1843–84 as the equivalent of the Parisian English-language *Galignani's Messenger*.
24. See *Gallica*, http://gallica.bnf.fr. There is also a printed bibliography by Jackson, *La Revue Blanche*.
25. Villette and Hardhill, "Paris and Fashion," 466.

fashion plates were copied in expensive British fashion magazines such as *La Belle Assemblée* (1806–47). From the 1860s, they penetrated the penny-weekly market, appearing in periodicals such as the *London Journal* (1845–1928) and *Bow Bells* (1862–97).[26] Studies of fashion tend to be conducted through the prism of transnational movements, concepts, and theories, such as modernity or the gendered body, with magazines providing merely an evidential contribution. For example, in "The Development of Consumption Culture and the Individualization of Female Identity: Fashion Discourse in the Netherlands, 1890–1920," Delhaye does not engage in comparative study of the periodicals themselves. There are some comparative studies of fashion journals published in the same language.[27] However, despite the fact that the theoretical basis for transnational research in fashion history is well established, few scholars have taken the intrepid step of comparing fashion periodicals published in different languages.

French archives are plentiful and easy to access, either online or in major libraries, and the choice of periodicals to research is extensive. In fact, French historians have done an excellent job of identifying and assessing holdings, not just those in major collections, such as the BNF, but also in provincial, private, and academic archives. The indexing of the French periodicals market began as early as 1898, when the *Répertoire Bibliographique des Principales Revues Françaises*, edited by Daniel Jordell, was launched. The first edition registered 146 publications, but by the following year there were 257. The British Library maintains an excellent list of reference works for French periodicals and newspapers, as well as print, CD-ROM, and microfiche versions of bibliographies, such as those published by the BNF periodicals department and standard texts such as Hatin's *Bibliographie historique et critique de la presse périodique française* and Bellanger, Godechot, Guiral, and Terrou's *Histoire générale de la presse française*.[28] For background information on new bibliographies, digital projects, and academic articles about bibliographic issues, researchers can consult the *Bulletin des Bibliothèques de France* (BBF), which provides much useful information, including the entire back catalogue of the *BBF revue* since its beginnings in 1956.[29] Place and Vasseur's valuable bibliography covers the years 1840–1930 for a select number of both famous and lesser-known French literary periodicals, with facsimiles of cover pages, an introduction to each journal, and full bibliographic descriptions, which include information about the editors, contributors, and physical characteristics of each periodical, along with a table of contents for each issue. It also includes an invaluable index of names cited which allows researchers to trace networks. The *Bibliographie de la littérature française de 1800 à 1930* by Hugo Thieme (1933) is still useful: it lists, for example, a contemporary bibliography for learned societies by de Lasteyrie published between 1888 and 1918. Another useful finding aid is *Système universitaire de documentation* (SUDOC),[30] an online union catalogue of French university libraries. It includes *Myriade*, a union catalogue of 250,000 periodical titles in French libraries and archive centers, comprising 2,000 non-university institutions, such as municipal

---

26. King, *London Journal*, 155–67, 218–22.
27. For example, see Mackie's study of early eighteenth-century periodicals, *Market à la Mode*.
28. See http://www.bl.uk.
29. See http://bbf.enssib.fr.
30. See http://www.sudoc.abes.fr.

libraries. The most useful online resource for researchers is probably *Gallica*, which includes many periodicals. In addition, *Gallica* links up to other digital holdings, such as the *Bibliothèque numérique de Roubaix* (an online local history archive), and provides brief background information on individual daily newspapers as well as periodical and press history.

Probably the most fruitful area for comparative study of Anglophone and French periodicals derives from the period itself. After the French Revolution, many countries followed political events in France closely. This interest is reflected in the British Library's periodical manuscript holdings, which comprise some 20,000 caricatures and illustrations produced in France and Germany during the Franco-Prussian War (1870–71) and the Commune that followed.[31] Such events were extensively reported—and sketched—in British newspapers and periodicals such as the *Illustrated London News*: there is much work to be done in comparing images of the same reported events in French and Anglophone periodicals.

Satiric magazines also offer fertile ground for comparative analysis of caricature. One of France's strongest contributions to nineteenth-century publishing history is its political satire. As the century progressed, so too did satirical and humorous denunciations of power in journals such as *Le Charivari* (1832–1937), Philipon's *Le Journal pour rire* (1848–55), and later *Le Tam-tam* (1835–45), *Le Chat noir* (1881–95), *Le Courrier français* (1888–1913), *Gil Blas* (1879–1914), or the many other publications that developed significant, faithful readerships, despite constant battles with the censor (even after the liberal press law of 1881). *Gil Blas* epitomized the modernist spirit, aiming, as its masthead declared, to "amuser les gens qui passent, leur plaire aujourd'hui, et recommencer le lendemain" (amuse people passing by, please them today, and begin again tomorrow). Such an approach was intended to provide an immediate connection with readers, according to Schiau-Botea.[32] Besides their British analogues, such French periodicals merit comparison with popular German satiric papers such as *Fliegende Blätter* (1845–1944) and *Simplicissimus* (1896–1967), both of which had circulations of almost 100,000 by the end of the century.[33]

Japanese Women's and Expatriate Periodicals

The role of periodicals as agents of transnational cultural transmission needs to be situated within broad conceptual fields of inquiry, such as studies of orientalism and the origins of European modernism. *The Modernist Journals Project* online, based at Brown University and the University of Tulsa, only includes English-language periodicals,[34] and while the *Oxford Critical and Cultural History of Modernist Magazines* does cover Britain, the United States, and continental Europe, countries and languages remain strikingly divided by volume and section. This leaves plenty of scope for more in-depth work into the origins of European modernism in the transnational periodical press.

---

31. See http://www.bl.uk/reshelp/findhelpregion/europe/france/france/france.html.
32. Schiau-Botea, "Performing Writing," 28.
33. There is a digital version of *Simplicissimus*: http://www.simplicissimus.info/.
34. *Modernist Journals Project*, http://www.modjourn.org/.

Japan is now one of the most literate societies in the world, with an exceptionally high consumption of print and online materials, but periodical publishing in Japan is a relatively recent development. The government encouraged the growth of the newspaper industry during the Meiji period (1868–1912), which, as James Huffman has shown, shifted rapidly from small craft to industrial models of production. This might seem to undermine comparisons with the West, where the shift was much less sudden. Although the comparative historian may well try to identify similarities between national examples, it is not axiomatic that the countries should be at the same state of development.[35] Japan modernized and opened up to Western influence at a rapid pace during the Meiji period, but the flow of cultural knowledge was by no means transmitted by a one-way current. While the study of late nineteenth-century *japonisme* in Europe is well established in the West, and orientalist depictions of Japan in the Western press have also come under scrutiny,[36] less is known about the effect of the West on Japan. Meiji thinking aimed "to re-conceptualise Japanese culture and Japanese notions of civilization, not slavishly explore Western culture and society as though it were the non-negotiable model toward which Japan must be transformed,"[37] and this is reflected in contemporary periodical publishing. A comparative study of cross-cultural influences between Japan and the West based on English-language publications and secondary scholarship is feasible, depending on the choice of topic.

The early Meiji period witnessed a flowering of women's self-expression and education, prompting, for example, discussion of women's work opportunities and their position in society. Some educated Japanese women traveled to Europe, followed Western literary and religious discourses, organized their own literary societies and other networks, and used periodicals to communicate the new ideas that they acquired. They revered Millicent Fawcett and other Western women and noted England's success in combining Enlightenment ideals with economic, military, and intellectual prowess. The leaders and formative years of the women's movements in Japan have been well researched contextually,[38] but the periodicals produced by these communities have been neglected. We do know, however, that girls used journals as vehicles for self-publishing and that periodicals published excerpts and reviews of influential foreign literary texts. They also served as forums for discussion and information sharing on developments abroad, as well as for political and social discourse.

When researching Japanese periodicals, the *Meiji Shinbun Zasshi Bunko* at the University of Tokyo is particularly useful. The library collections include 2,030 newspapers and 7,550 periodicals, in addition to original prints and earlier editions from the Meiji era.[39] The other major database is the *Scholarly and Academic Information Navigator* (CiNii), which includes articles, books, and periodicals.[40] Given the poor quality of translation software where

---

35. See, for example, Chapman, *Comparative Media History*; Chapman, *Gender, Citizenship, and Newspapers*.
36. See, for example, Yokoyama, *Japan in the Victorian Mind*.
37. Swale, *Meiji Restoration*, 95.
38. Patessio, *Women and Public Life*; Walthall, *Weak Body*; Patessio and Ogawa, "To Become a Woman Doctor"; Anderson, *Place in Public*.
39. The database can be found at http://www.meiji.j.u-tokyo.ac.jp/. Though Google Translate may prove helpful, researchers will most likely need the assistance of a Japanese translator to navigate this site successfully.
40. http://ci.nii.ac.jp/info/en/cinii_outline.html.

non-Indo-European languages are concerned, access to Japanese material is difficult without knowledge of the language. However, comparative work can still be carried out using contemporary observations from non-Japanese perspectives, such as those of Alice Mabel Bacon, originally published in 1902.[41] The University of Hawai'i at Mānoa has compiled a list and chronology, derived from a Japanese website,[42] of English-language periodicals for foreigners that often reported on controversial articles in Japanese-language publications, the response they received, and whether or not they had been censored.[43]

According to Adam Geczy, "Meiji Japan was deeply complicit in demarcating specific associations and in customizing its cultural aesthetic for Western consumption in which gender and objects were intertwined. In their march to modernization, the Meiji went to great lengths to define the role of women."[44] The classic image of this is the family photograph in which women wear kimonos and men wear Western suits. Yet during the 1880s, upper-class Japanese women emulated Paris fashions, and impressions of British male sovereignty were formed that contributed to what Geczy calls "obverse orientalism" whereby the Japanese came to feel that the West was superior.[45] Periodicals were pivotal in the birth of Japanese couture and the gradual domination of the Japanese fashion industry by the West. Comparative work on Japanese and European women's periodicals—for example, how they were distributed and marketed—would pay ample dividends.

Japan's influence on the arts in Europe and America is visible in many Western periodicals which featured Japanese dress in articles; images; reviews of works such as Pierre Loti's *Madame Chrysanthème* (1887); and fiction such as Zola's *Au Bonheur des dames* (run in *Gil Blas* in 1882). Triangulation between European and Japanese trade, consumerism, and periodicals would yield interesting results, for despite many studies of cross-cultural influence,[46] the role of periodicals in this exchange has not been seriously considered. By the end of the nineteenth century, Liberty, a department store which traded in *japonisme*, could claim a virtual monopoly on taste-making across Europe.[47] It encouraged designers and artists, and supported various oriental cultural societies, such as the Japan Society (founded 1891). Loose Liberty dresses, with their kimono influences, were often featured in journals, including *Aglaia* (1893–94), the organ of the Healthy and Artistic Dress Union.[48] There were many other importers of Japanese goods into Europe, such as the German art dealer Siegfried Bing. Following his launch of the Maison de l'Art Nouveau in Paris, which featured the Japanese arts he had been importing

---

41. Bacon, *Japanese Girls and Women*.
42. See http://guides.library.manoa.hawaii.edu, derived from the Japanese-language *Eiji Shinbun Shi* (*English Newspaper History*), which has some reproductions and links to basic material on other nineteenth-century Japanese English-language newspapers (see http://homepage1.nifty.com/samito/JThistory4.htm).
43. An interesting research project would be to compare expatriate periodicals in various countries such as James Gordon Bennett's *Paris Herald* (1887–) and *Galignani's Messenger* (1814–95) in France.
44. Geczy, *Fashion and Orientalism*, 123.
45. Ibid., 117.
46. See, for example, Checkland, *Japan and Britain*, and Sato and Watanabe, *Japan and Britain*.
47. Checkland, *Japan and Britain*, 109.
48. Cunningham, *Reforming Women's Fashion*, 123–5.

since 1870, Bing started his own magazine, entitled *Le Japon Artistique* (1888–91). The scale of such transcontinental trade is evident in periodicals such as the *Gazette des Beaux-Arts* (1859–2002), which mentions other traders, such as the Sichel brothers, who in one year alone imported 5,000 objects from Japan.[49]

It is clear from the *Japan Gazette Hong List and Directory* (1875–81) that adverts by furniture brokers and furniture depots aimed at collectors and importers were numerous, and that the trade in the manufacturing and supply of Japanese art and carved cherry-wood curios was providing ample employment for wood carvers.[50] Yokohama was the hub of trade and Western influence, with a strong business community of British expatriates, which has received some attention from scholars.[51] However, a comparative study of their lifestyles could be conducted through the prism of English-language newspapers such as the *Japan Weekly Mail* (1870–1950) or Hansard's *Japan Herald* (originally the *Nagasaki Shipping List and Advertiser*, 1861–). Comparison with the French-language *L'Echo du Japon* (1875–80) would provide another perspective.

One of Yokohama's most interesting long-time residents was the satirist and artist Charles Wirgman, who in 1862 established, wrote, and illustrated the *Japan Punch* to relieve the boredom of foreigners living in Tokyo and Yokohama. Wirgman depicted himself as Mr. Punch, using anecdotes, stories, and features full of puns, satire, and caricatures of his friends and others, including the editors of English-language newspapers. His monthly picture news sheet continued somewhat sporadically through to 1887 and was republished in 1976 as a ten-volume set. His drawings were carved in wood by Japanese carvers, printed on thin local paper, and then compiled into a string-tied booklet that was woodblock printed until 1883, when production converted to lithograph printing.[52] It was precisely through his employment of Japanese engravers that his style entered the Japanese visual aesthetic and was eventually translated into twentieth-century manga.

As these examples show, there is clear evidence that scholars of nineteenth-century periodicals should attempt to escape the confines both of national markets and monolingualism. Language barriers can be overcome, but researchers must be willing to work within varying national and cultural contexts. While this process of self-education may well constitute the biggest impediment to fostering a transnational comparative method, it nonetheless offers many rewards to the diligent researcher.

---

49. Ibid., 117.
50. Several issues of the *Japan Gazette* are available through Google Books.
51. Cortazzi and Daniels, *Britain and Japan*; Blum, *Yokohama in 1872*; Hoare, *Japan's Treaty Ports*; Pedlar, *Imported Pioneers*.
52. Wirgman was also a painter who trained and influenced a number of Japanese artists, becoming "almost a god-like figure to Japanese painters intent on learning Western style painting." Rogala, *Genius of Mr. Punch*, 224.

13

PERIODICALS IN SCOTLAND

David Finkelstein

In 1776, Samuel Johnson commented sardonically to his shadowing biographer James Boswell that "no man but a blockhead ever wrote, except for money."[1] Johnson's comment came at the end of an era marked by the expansion of work in London's Grub Street, a world where authors without wealthy patrons churned out words for one-off payments, and printer-publishers could use and dispose of copyright as they pleased. The landmark trial of Donaldson v. Becket in 1774, when a Scottish bookseller successfully challenged the London book trade's monopoly on reprint and copyright matters, created a legal precedent for the development of a new literary economy and new opportunities for authorship, particularly in the Scottish periodical and newspaper press.

Such opportunities were fuelled by efforts of Scottish businessmen, intellectuals, and print culture specialists in the wake of the late eighteenth-century Scottish Enlightenment. In the early nineteenth century, the founding of innovative literary periodicals transformed Edinburgh into the second literary city in Great Britain, a role diminished only by the fallout and subsequent reorganization and consolidation that followed the English stock market crash of 1826. Key figures in the early development of the Scottish periodical press included Archibald Constable, Walter Scott's publisher and backer of the *Edinburgh Review* (1802–1929); William Blackwood I, founder of *Blackwood's Edinburgh Magazine* (1817–1980); and William and Robert Chambers, creators of *Chambers's Edinburgh Journal* (1832–1956). These publishers realized that material designed for leisure reading could boost the sale of journals and newspapers, as well as serve as useful advertising for their firm's "brand" of fiction and non-fiction. The use of serialized material from the 1840s onwards became ubiquitous in both periodicals and newspapers; this created a market in which texts (either pirated or legally purchased) could be serialized and circulated internationally. As Johnson-Woods notes, "Stories from New York, fashion from France, information from Australia filled the democratic pages of the mid nineteenth-century miscellany," including those produced in Scotland.[2] Similarly, advances in technology, infrastructure, and modes of distribution—public and subscription libraries, railway stalls, and bookshops, as much as steam-powered transport—allowed print and periodical

---

1. Boswell, *Life of Johnson*, 292.
2. Johnson-Woods, "Virtual Reading Communities," 355.

literature to transcend the local. Edinburgh publications increasingly traveled beyond Scottish borders, reaching international audiences. As a result, their contents often became identified as "British" rather than "Scottish."

With that in mind, it is hardly surprising that the print culture of nineteenth-century Scotland was so vast and so pervasive that it cannot be described in a single chapter. Consequently, this chapter narrows its focus to five literary periodicals published in Edinburgh that are most often cited in secondary sources. Many of these periodicals are freely available online through Google Books, ILEJ (Internet Library of Early Journals), the *Internet Archive*, or the subscription database *British Periodicals I & II*. *Blackwood's Edinburgh Magazine* and the *Edinburgh Review* (1802–1929) were amongst the first Scottish periodicals to be indexed and to receive dedicated studies; for this reason, they are often considered canonical in the study of Scottish and British journalism.[3] The others focused on here, *Tait's Edinburgh Magazine* (1832–61), *Good Words* (1860–1911), and *Chambers's Edinburgh Magazine* (1832–1956), follow *Blackwood's* and the *Edinburgh Review* at a distance but are now almost as well known.[4] This restricted focus of the chapter is indicative of the great deal of work that remains to be done on Scottish newspaper and periodical history, despite the excellent work of researchers such as Bill Bell, Joanne Shattock, Laurel Brake, and Padmini Murray.[5] More research needs to be done, especially large-scale quantitative studies, as discussed in Chapter 16, but also scholarship on the Edinburgh legal and medical press, the Glasgow political newspaper press, and the non-metropolitan Scottish press, as briefly discussed below.[6]

The *Edinburgh Review* and the Rise of the Literary Journal

One of the signal events in the development of the Scottish periodical press was the launch of the quarterly *Edinburgh Review* in 1802. Founded in Edinburgh by four disaffected Whig lawyers and bankrolled by Archibald Constable, the *Edinburgh Review* focused on publishing lengthy review essays. Another innovation was its editorial policy of providing regular payment for contributions. It also adopted a policy of publishing unsigned contributions, a practice that was associated with earlier literary miscellanies and remained almost universal in British literary periodicals until the 1860s.

The *Edinburgh Review*'s authoritative style, along with its emphasis on publishing lengthy reviews and philosophical disquisitions, proved sustainable, and the standards and parameters by which it operated were soon emulated. Its preeminence ensured that the critical essay, for

---

3. *Blackwood's Edinburgh Magazine* and the *Edinburgh Review* were included in the first volume of Houghton's *Wellesley Index* in 1966. See also Cutmore, *Conservatism* and *Contributors*, and Shattock, *Politics and Reviewers*. Dameron and Palmer's *Index* covers *Blackwood's*.
4. See Mitchell, "*Good Words*"; and Srebrnik, *Alexander Strahan*; Easley, "*Tait's Edinburgh Magazine*"; Fyfe, *Steam-Powered Knowledge*; and Thomas, *Chambers's Journal, 1854–1910*.
5. Bell's *Edinburgh History of the Book* includes essays by Shattock ("Reviews and Monthlies"), Brake ("Popular 'Weeklies'"), and Murray ("Newspapers").
6. MacDonald's *Negotiated Knowledge* only covers the Scottish medical periodical up to 1832. The *Scotsman* (1817–) is one of the few Scottish newspapers to have been the subject of a full-length study. See Morris, *Scotland's Paper*.

about twenty years, was a dominant literary form and a highly marketable literary commodity in reviews and magazines of the period. As Walter Bagehot famously declared in 1855, British literary reviews owed their existence to the new style of journalism that had sprung from the pages of the *Edinburgh Review*. "Review-writing," he noted, "is one of the features of modern literature. Many able men really give themselves up to it."[7] However, he suggested that the *Edinburgh Review*'s popularity was in part due to modern reading habits, for "people take their literature in morsels the way they take their sandwiches on a journey."[8] Reviewers were crucial guides, for the "modern man must be told what to think—shortly, no doubt—but he *must* be told it. The essay-like criticism of modern times is about the length which he likes. The *Edinburgh Review*, which began the system, may be said to be, in this country, the commencement on large topics of suitable views for sensible persons."[9] Francis Jeffrey was the lead editor of the *Edinburgh* between 1803 and 1829. In 1802, he met with his like-minded collaborators Henry Brougham, Francis Horner, and Sydney Smith at Buccleuch Place, Edinburgh, to discuss their new venture. During this meeting, they declared that their prospective journal should offer commentary only on select books of the moment. More importantly, as the opening number made clear, what would drive their journal was quality:

> Of the books that are daily presented to the world, a very large proportion is evidently destined to obscurity, by the insignificance of the subjects, or the defects of their execution. . . . The very lowest order of publications are rejected, accordingly, by most of the literary publications of which the Public are already in possession. But the contributors to the Edinburgh Review propose to carry this principle of selection a good deal further; to decline any attempt at exhibiting a complete view of modern literature; and to confine their notice, in a very great degree, to works that have either attained, or deserve, a certain portion of celebrity.[10]

For initial inspiration, the *Edinburgh* drew on long-standing eighteenth-century traditions of Scottish debate on philosophy, politics, economics, evolution, and revolution, while consistently upholding the superiority of Scottish educational and legal systems.

Byron and other contemporaries were quick to note the Scottish flavor of the *Edinburgh Review*. In "English Bards and Scotch Reviewers," published in 1809, Byron retaliated against attacks that had been lodged against him in the *Review*, insinuating that Scottish smartness was symptomatic of a lack of literary talent. Scottish reviewers might be good critics, he claimed, but they lacked creativity: "I could not say Caledonia's Genius, it being well known there is no Genius to be found from Clackmannan to Caithness."[11] It is no wonder that Byron felt defensive given the prominence of Scottish authors and reviewers in the British periodical industry. One of the most important Scottish literary figures of the period was Walter Scott,

---

7. Bagehot, "First Edinburgh Reviewers," quoted in Shattock, "Culture of Criticism," 77.
8. Ibid.
9. Ibid.
10. Advertisement, *Edinburgh Review* 1, n.p.
11. Byron, *Works*, 4:198.

who ultimately abandoned the *Edinburgh Review* and successfully lobbied John Murray to establish the London-based Tory *Quarterly Review* (1809–1967) in 1809. Later, Scott's son-in-law, the Glaswegian John Gibson Lockhart, served as its editor (1826–53). Other important figures in the Edinburgh literary landscape included William Blackwood, John Wilson, and James Hogg, whose literary hijinks marked the early days of the Tory monthly *Blackwood's Magazine*, founded in 1817. Three years later, Aberdonian John Scott founded the monthly *London Magazine* (1820–29), which for a time was *Blackwood's* chief rival.

Chief among the Scottish-led monthly productions that followed in the wake of the *Edinburgh Review* was *Blackwood's Edinburgh Magazine*, established in April 1817 by William Blackwood I. Blackwood subsequently played a key role in both the periodical and book-publishing field, revitalizing the older Edinburgh tradition of the publishing house as a literary gathering place. From the outset, he encouraged emerging writers to make his place of business a center of literary society. When the firm moved to new premises on 45 George Street in 1829, he established the "Old Saloon"—an oval room where portraits of literary men stared down upon an oval table and where confirmed "Blackwoodians" gathered for decades. *Blackwood's* is famous now as the flagship periodical of the firm, but it was initially edited with lackluster effort by James Cleghorn and Thomas Pringle. Consensus at the time suggested that the *Edinburgh Monthly Magazine*, as it was first known, was planned by Blackwood to be a Tory alternative to his rival, the *Edinburgh Review*. Revisionist scholarship has since shown that it was originally intended to rival the "ailing monthly *Scots Magazine* [1839–], which Blackwood had identified as a weak spot in Constable's stable of literary periodical productions."[12]

The first few issues of *Blackwood's* were anything but exciting. Blackwood terminated Pringle's and Cleghorn's contracts after six months and relaunched the journal in October 1817 as *Blackwood's Edinburgh Magazine*. He revitalized the magazine by seeking editorial input and contributions from members of his literary coterie, including John Gibson Lockhart, John Wilson ("Christopher North"), and James Hogg. The first issues established the magazine's reputation by featuring personalized satire, attacks on local and national literary figures, and a heterogeneous mix of fiction, poetry, political essays, and literary reviews. The lawsuits brought against the firm for its libelous approach brought welcome publicity, even if such litigation frightened off some of its trade connections. Baldwin, Cradock & Co. (Blackwood's London agents) and Oliver & Boyd (Blackwood's printers) severed their connections because of the furore.

Bringing home the first number of his relaunched journal, William is said to have presented it to his wife with the words, "There's ma Maga-zine."[13] In affectionate parody, the journal became known to future generations of contributors and readers as "Maga." Maga's rising reputation and sales swiftly outpaced the *Scots Magazine*, while at the same time attracting competition from the *London Magazine*. Its editor John Scott characterized his magazine as being in direct competition with *Blackwood's* and often made a point of attacking his rival's approach and content. The hostility between the monthlies culminated in Lockhart challenging John Scott to a duel in 1821. In what may be considered the most extreme conclusion to a literary

---

12. Finkelstein, "Periodicals, Encyclopaedias," 204. See also Milne, "The 'Veiled Editor' Unveiled," 89.
13. Tredrey, *House of Blackwood*, 51.

quarrel in the nineteenth century, G.H. Christie faced Scott in Lockhart's place and mortally wounded him with his second shot. Future "Blackwoodians" confined themselves to attacks on such luminaries as William Wordsworth, John Keats, William Hazlitt, and Samuel Taylor Coleridge. It is a curious paradox that while to outsiders the duel between men from Edinburgh and London magazines might appear to represent Scotland and England, the combatants, Scott and Christie, were both Scottish.

Blackwood consolidated his initial success by using the journal to attract a core of established writers to the firm. These included Irishmen William Maginn and Samuel Ferguson, as well Scottish journalists John Galt, Douglas M. Moir ("Delta"), and Thomas De Quincey. The magazine also featured occasional reviews by Walter Scott, fiction by Samuel Warren and Susan Ferrier, and essays by Samuel Taylor Coleridge. Maga was used both as a showcase for new talent and as a method of attracting potential contributors to the firm's book lists. A technique pioneered by Blackwood was the volume publication of works first serialized in the magazine, an innovation that predated similar remediations by Henry Colburn and Richard Bentley. Works featured in this way included John Galt's *The Ayrshire Legatees* (1820–21), Douglas M. Moir's *The Autobiography of Mansie Wauch* (1824–28), and Susan Ferrier's *Marriage* (1818) and *Inheritance* (1824).

Under the editorship of John Blackwood (1845–79) and his nephew William Blackwood III (1879–1912), *Blackwood's* consolidated its position in British literary culture as a leading representative of male-centered Tory intellectual culture, though its status certainly declined towards the end of the century. Nonetheless, it continued to publish significant lengthy works by writers such as Anthony Trollope, F. Marion Crawford, Joseph Conrad, and Neil Munro, as well as shorter works by Oscar Wilde, R.D. Blackmore, Thomas Hardy, Arthur Conan Doyle, and John Buchan. *Blackwood's* also featured both anonymous and signed works by significant Victorian women writers, including George Eliot and Scottish author Margaret Oliphant. After the serialization of her first novel, *Katie Stewart*, in 1852, Oliphant became a stalwart of the magazine. Of Oliphant's significant role as literary critic, Henry James would later begrudgingly remark in his obituary notice, "I should almost suppose in fact that no woman had ever, for half a century, had her personal 'say' so publicly and irresponsibly."[14] Other Scottish women writers who were inspired to break new ground in a variety of periodical and literary genres included Constance Gordon-Cumming, an irrepressible traveler who published over sixteen books and thirty-six articles during her lifetime based on her journeys across Asia, North America, and the Pacific; Charlotte Dempster, whose novels and articles would cover fine art, Continental fiction, philosophy, and religion; and Christian Isobel Johnstone, whose work as co-editor of several Scottish journals (the *Edinburgh Chronicle*, *Inverness Courier*, and *Johnstone's Edinburgh Magazine*) and whose contributions to monthlies such as *Blackwood's* and *Tait's Edinburgh Magazine* would challenge the political, social, religious, and sexual mores of contemporary society.[15]

---

14. James, *Notes and Novelists*, 358.
15. Gordon-Cumming is discussed by Guelke and Morin, "Gender, Nature, Empire," though more work on her journalism remains to be done. There is even less on Charlotte (Louisa Hawkins) Dempster: see the entry on

Chambers and the Mass-Market Periodical

A significant publishing phenomenon spurred on by developments in cheap printing technology was the mass-market periodical aimed at a working-class audience. Intellectual aspirations amongst the lower classes, mockingly referred to by contemporary critics from 1827 onwards as the "march of intellect," were, in fact, a reflection of and a response to the opportunities and challenges presented by an increasingly industrialized society. Some saw this as a threat to social order, particularly in the wake of the politically charged Chartist Movement or the Reform Act of 1832. Thomas Carlyle, in the December 1831 issue of the *Edinburgh Review*, thundered, "What, for example, is all this that we hear, for the last generation or two, about the Improvement of the Age, the Spirit of the Age, Destruction of Prejudice, Progress of the Species, and the March of Intellect, but an unhealthy state of self-sentience, self-survey; the precursor and prognostic of still worse health?"[16] By 1845, however, as one English commentator noted, the sea change in cultural presumptions, encouraged by mass-market print consumption, was now firmly entrenched and unstoppable, with "light postage, quick transit, cheap Bibles, and cheap Periodicals, for the Millions of England!"[17]

Chief among the pioneers who aimed to produce "improving" reading material for the masses were William and Robert Chambers, who built up a formidable publishing enterprise from meager circumstances.[18] Their work was founded on the ideals of civic responsibility and self-improvement: publishing inexpensive reading material was, they felt, crucial to allowing others to achieve success in the public realm through faith, self-reliance, and self-education. In February 1832, these ideals formed the cornerstone of the firm's most significant venture: the weekly *Chambers's Edinburgh Journal*. As William noted in his autobiography, "I resolved to take advantage of the evidently growing taste for cheap literature, and lead it, as far as was in my power, in a proper direction."[19] In 1863, he was joined by his brother Robert, who co-edited the magazine and wrote the bulk of its weekly content, which included a mixture of essays; biographies of well-known individuals; reflections on science, nature, and history; and instructive, morally-grounded works of fiction and poetry. Retailing at the low price of three halfpennies, the magazine's aim at the start was to offer affordable, entertaining knowledge on a mass scale. As he announced in the first issue of the journal, "The principle by which I have been actuated is to take advantage of the universal appetite for instruction which at present exists; to supply to that appetite food of the best kind, in such form and at such price as must suit the convenience of every man in the British dominions."[20]

Although *Chambers's Edinburgh Journal* was a radical and risky experiment in mass publishing (no previous journal had attempted to reach such a wide audience with such a broad-ranging

---

her in Gifford and McMillan, *History of Scottish Women's Writing*, 218. Johnstone has enjoyed more attention: see, for example, Easley, *First-Person Anonymous*, ch. 3.
16. Carlyle, "Characteristics," 365.
17. John Campbell, as quoted in Howsam, *Cheap Bibles*, xiii.
18. See Fyfe, *Steam-Powered Knowledge*.
19. Chambers, *Memoirs*, 233.
20. Chambers, "Editor's Address," 1.

menu), its formula proved a success. From the start, its circulation was a vigorous 30,000 per issue; by 1834, circulation had risen to 50,000; and after the addition of a London agent that facilitated a wider circulation across the United Kingdom, circulation rose to a peak of 90,000 per week in 1840.[21] Six weeks after the launch of the journal, a London imitator arrived in the shape of Charles Knight, who with the backing of the Society for the Diffusion of Useful Knowledge, began publishing the *Penny Magazine* in late March 1832. It was less expensive, and while it did not feature fiction or poetry, its pages, unlike those in *Chambers's*, were embellished with woodcut illustrations. For a time, the *Penny Magazine* rivaled the popularity of *Chambers's Edinburgh Journal*, achieving a circulation of 200,000 in its first year.[22] By 1846, however, it ceased publication, a victim of high costs and a declining readership due to its unvarying diet of dull, didactic text.

The Chambers firm was not the only Scottish periodical publisher to aim for a mass-market readership. William Tait, an Edinburgh bookseller, started the monthly *Tait's Edinburgh Magazine* in 1832, shortly after the launch of *Chambers's Edinburgh Journal*. Tait was determined to rival both *Blackwood's* and *Chambers's* as a key Edinburgh-based publication. His journal soon became heavily invested in promoting legal reforms, publishing new works by Catherine Gore and Harriet Martineau, and attracting star contributors such as J.S. Mill, Leigh Hunt, John Galt, and Thomas De Quincey. At its height, it reached an estimated circulation of 4,000 per month. Under the editorship of Christian Isobel Johnstone from 1834 to 1846, it reduced its price to one shilling and it soon became a key shilling monthly in British periodical culture.[23]

Monthly Periodical Activity

By the 1860s the periodical landscape in Scotland had changed. Sales statistics offer insight into the exponential rise in readership of Scottish monthlies at the expense of the longer-established quarterlies. *Blackwood's Magazine*, for example, saw sales rise from about 3,700 in 1820 to 5,000 in 1826 and then 9,000 by 1832, before dropping down to a stable average of 6,500 in the 1860s and 1870s; its rival, the *Quarterly Review*, went from a print run of 14,000 in 1818 to 10,500 in 1829, and then to an average of 9,000 by 1849; the *Edinburgh Review*, on the other hand, had a circulation of around 12,000 a quarter in 1818 but dropped to half that in 1828 and then fell to about 3,000 from 1845 onwards.[24] From the second half of the century, new Scottish periodicals were founded aimed at new reading groups. Among these were religious-influenced journals such as *Good Words* (1860–1911) and *Good Words for the Young* (1868–77) published by Alexander Strahan. *Good Words* first appeared as a sixteen-page weekly priced at 3½d. before switching format in January 1861 to become a sixty-four-page sixpenny monthly. It was edited by the prominent Church of Scotland minister Norman Macleod until his death in 1872, when the editorship passed on to his brother Donald. Focused

---

21. O'Connor, "*Chambers's Edinburgh Journal*," 106.
22. Taunton, "*Penny Magazine*," 486.
23. Shattock, "*Tait's Edinburgh Magazine*," 613–14.
24. Finkelstein, "Selling *Blackwood's Magazine*," 81; Finkelstein, *House of Blackwood*, 165–6; Shattock, *Politics and Reviewers*, 97–99; Quarterly Review *Archive*; Bennett, "Revolution in Thought," 236.

predominantly on content that combined religious instruction with stories and articles, it attracted contributions from prominent figures such as Anthony Trollope, Thomas Hardy, Lord Alfred Tennyson, William Gladstone, and J.A. Froude. Its circulation during the 1860s and '70s was quite high, averaging between 80,000 and 130,000 copies per issue, a popularity it sustained until finally ceasing publication in 1911.[25] Its corollary, *Good Words for the Young*, an illustrated monthly aimed at a younger constituency, also priced at six pennies per issue, was less successful, despite attracting contributors such as Charles Kingsley, W.S. Gilbert, and Dinah Craik.[26]

Other journals worth mentioning from this period include the quarterly *North British Review*, founded in 1844 by members of the Free Church of Scotland, with contributors drawn from the evangelical wing of the church, from the legal profession in Edinburgh, and from academic circles throughout Scotland. By 1846, it had achieved a modest circulation of about 3,000, but under the editorship of Alexander Campbell Fraser, 1850–57, it became a serious rival to the *Edinburgh* and the *Quarterly* reviews, both in terms of the quality of its literary reviewing and its recruitment of significant contributors such as Charles Kingsley, Thomas De Quincey, W.R. Greg, Herbert Spencer, David Masson, and David Brewster.[27] Also notable were the illustrated weekly *People's Journal* (1858–1990) and the monthly family miscellany *People's Friend* (1869–), both of which had been founded by the Dundee-based John Leng (1828–1906) for the purpose of attracting a working-class readership. Both publications were great successes, especially the *People's Journal*, which reached a circulation of 220,000 by the 1890s.[28] A study of Leng as newspaper and periodical publisher is long overdue. He was originally from Hull and at age nineteen began working for the *Hull Advertiser*. In 1851, he became the editor of the *Dundee Advertiser*, where he established himself as an influential journalist, and in 1889, he went into politics, serving a lengthy term as MP for Dundee. In addition to illuminating the contributions of individual journalists, future research on Scottish journalism might also compare Dundee as a publishing hub to other provincial centers such as Wrexham in Wales, which Peters has recently investigated.[29]

Late-Century Developments

The New Journalism championed by London-based newspaper and journal editors such as W.T. Stead and George Newnes[30] provided new competition for Scottish periodicals at the fin de siècle. Newnes riposted that the appeal of miscellanies like his own *Tit-Bits* lay in being light, wholesome, but also serious enough that "many of those readers may be led to take an interest in higher forms of literature."[31] Aspirational readers also found great pleasure in the

---

25. Lloyd, "*Good Words*," 254.
26. Lloyd, "*Good Words for the Young*," 254.
27. Shattock, "*North British Review*," 457.
28. Fraser, "*People's Journal*," 489. See also Donaldson, *Popular Literature*.
29. Peters, *Politics, Publishing, and Personalities*.
30. It was dismissed as "feather-brained" by Matthew Arnold in "Up to Easter," 638–9.
31. Quoted in Pound, *Mirror of the Century*, 24–5.

fare offered in journals such as Newnes's *Strand Magazine* (founded 1890), which included a mix of interviews, articles, illustrations, and light fiction. The rise of these new periodicals hastened the demise of the Scottish-led, essay-based periodical, acidly characterized by Mark Pattison as "those venerable old wooden three-deckers, the *Edinburgh Review* and the *Quarterly Review* [which are] still put out to sea under the command, I believe, of the Ancient Mariner."[32]

Yet in the early years of the century, Scottish periodicals and journalists played a dominant role in shaping British literary culture. Journals such as the *Edinburgh Review*, *Blackwood's Magazine*, and *Chambers's Edinburgh Journal* had, through being preeminent in their niche arenas of textual space, shifted literary interests and journalistic formats irrevocably. They laid the foundations for a brand of popular literary reviewing now taken for granted in print titles such as the *London Review of Books* or the *New Yorker*. That literary periodicals and newspapers still pay writers to produce fiction and poetry and to review books and contemporary culture is an aspect of cultural production that owes a great deal to the literary revolution begun in Scotland over two centuries ago.

32. Pattison, "Books and Critics," 663.

14

WELSH PERIODICALS AND NEWSPAPERS

Lisa Peters

The study of nineteenth-century periodicals and newspapers in Wales requires particular knowledge and understanding. While command of the Welsh language is helpful, an appreciation of the specific social, cultural, industrial, and geographical divisions and developments of Wales over the period is even more important. The country's rugged geography had long meant poor communication and cultural differences between north and south; in the nineteenth century these differences manifested themselves as a mainly rural and Welsh-speaking middle and north, and a rapidly growing, industrializing, and increasingly anglicized south. Between 1841 and 1901, Wales's population doubled to just over two million, the largest growth being in the southern county of Glamorgan, whose population leapt from 178,500 to 866,250.[1] While the north did develop its own industrial areas,[2] towns in the southern coal valleys and their ports saw dramatic rises in population as immigrants poured in from elsewhere in Wales, as well as from England, Europe, and other locales.[3] Fortunes were made and an industrial class of English-speaking mine owners and managers joined the established English-speaking gentry, while an immigrant Anglophone working class largely supplanted the southern Welsh peasantry. Religion, however, remained a more constant class divide. Throughout the century, the lower classes remained mainly Nonconformist (especially Methodist), while the gentry was Anglican.

In the eighteenth century, the Reverend Griffith Jones's Anglican circulating schools taught nearly half of the population to read Welsh.[4] Despite this, in 1847, the three-volume *Reports of the Commissioners of Enquiry into the State of Education in Wales*,[5] produced by three non-Welsh-speaking commissioners, condemned the Welsh as lazy and ignorant due to their inability to speak English. The *Report* and the succeeding English government's enforcement of the use of English in schools generated a powerful backlash, resulting in an increase in periodicals and

---

1. Williams, *Digest*, 1:41.
2. For a detailed discussion of the industries of north Wales, see Dodd, *Industrial Revolution*.
3. The port of Cardiff, for example, grew 1,600 percent in sixty years. Williams, *Digest*, 1:63.
4. Yalden, "Association, Community, and the Origins of Secularisation," 306; Williams, *Religion, Language, and Nationality*, 207–8.
5. These are known in Wales as *Brad y Lyfrau Gleision*—"Treachery of the Blue Books."

books in Welsh.[6] Indeed, the period between 1860 and 1890 has been described as the "golden age" of Welsh-language publishing.[7]

The First Periodicals and Newspapers

Welsh-language periodicals began very tentatively in the eighteenth century. Only one issue of *Tlysau yr Hen Oesoedd* (Gems of Past Ages, 1735) was published. Late eighteenth-century journals were all short-lived—*Trysorfa Gwybodaeth* (Treasury of Knowledge, 1770); *Cylch-grawn Cynmraeg* (Welsh Magazine, 1793); the *Miscellaneous Repository* (1795, written in Welsh, despite its English title); and *Y Geirgrawn* (the Magazine, 1796). In 1799, the first of Wales's many religious journals appeared: *Y Trysorfa Ysprydol* (the Spiritual Treasury, 1799–1827) aimed at Calvinist Methodists. Its publication history was almost as fraught, with its first avatar ending after two years, only to be revived in 1809 before finally ceasing publication in 1827.[8]

Whilst Welsh periodicals were dominated by various religious denominations, politics drove Welsh newspapers. Even though Hammond in 1850 recorded a 50/50 split in the number of Conservative and Liberal papers,[9] Liberal support dominated the market in terms of numbers sold. Welsh Conservatives became more concerned with newspapers mainly in a rear-guard action after the 1868 general election when, for the first time, Wales returned more Liberals than Conservatives to Parliament. Nonetheless, *May's Press Guide* of 1876 still lists only eight Conservative newspapers in Wales compared to twenty-seven Liberal, four Liberal-Conservative, and fourteen "Neutral."[10]

Like their English, Scottish, and Irish counterparts, Welsh newspapers suffered from the "taxes on knowledge" and experienced a similar explosion in numbers after their repeal. Unlike periodicals, newspapers limited their circulation to a defined locality in order to lessen distribution problems over a mountainous terrain. The comparatively late arrival of the Welsh press, relative to England, can be attributed to poor communications, a sparse, predominantly rural population, and, of course, the existence of two languages. Poor communications meant that it was difficult to gather and disseminate local news and that the arrival of London newspapers containing the latest national and foreign news took time. Similar factors affected the supply of stamped papers, which printers were obliged to keep in excess supply. This tied up capital and rendered the economics of newspaper production correspondingly less flexible and responsive. Another difficulty came from English-language newspapers published in cities close to the Welsh border, such as Bristol and Chester.

---

6. Walters, "Welsh Language," 363.
7. Williams, *Y wasg Gymraeg*; and Williams, "Cyhoeddi llyfrau Cymraeg." However, in "Golden Age Reappraised," Jones argues that this "golden age" was a myth.
8. It was revived again in 1830 as *Y Drysorfa* (the *Treasury*) and ended in 1968.
9. *Hammond's List*, 14.
10. *May's*, ix.

Although Thomas Jones, a native of Corwen residing in Shrewsbury, may have produced the first Welsh-language newspaper in 1705,[11] the first known newspaper published in Wales was the Swansea-based, English-language *Cambrian* (1804–1930). The *Cambrian* was followed by the *North Wales Gazette* (1808–)[12] in Bangor and the first Welsh-language newspaper, *Seren Gomer* (Star of Gomer, 1814–15). Like the *Cambrian*, *Seren Gomer* was published in Swansea, but unlike the English-language newspaper, it aimed to be a national newspaper.[13] Jones blamed stamp duty and distribution problems for its failure,[14] whilst Rees pointed to its inability to attract English-language advertising (for English speakers were more likely to have spare cash for advertised goods).[15] This was an early indication that it was the English-language press that would be dominant in Wales.[16]

Politics and the Newspaper Press

Between 1804 and 1855, forty-two newspapers appeared in south Wales: seven in Welsh, thirty-three in English, and two bilingual.[17] Welsh-language newspapers tended to be short-lived. The fortnightly *Gwron Cymraeg* (Welsh Hero, 1852–56) was the longest-surviving pre-1855 Welsh-language newspaper in the south;[18] more typical was *Y Papyr Newydd Cymraeg* (the Welsh Newspaper, 1836–37) published in Caernarvon. There was, however, a noticeable exception, *Yr Amserau* (the Times, 1843–59),[19] which was published not in Wales but in Liverpool, a city with a substantial Welsh immigrant population. Initially a fortnightly, it became a weekly in 1848, when publication was transferred for a few months to the Isle of Man where the stamp duty did not apply. *Yr Amserau* failed to adapt to the post-1855 environment, and by 1857 *Yr Herald Cymraeg* (the Welsh Herald, 1855–1937), based in Caernarvon, had become the most popular Welsh-language newspaper, with a circulation of over 9,000.[20] Meanwhile, *Yr Amserau* was sold in 1859 to Thomas Gee, who merged it with his newspaper *Baner Cymru* (Banner of Wales, 1857–59) to establish *Baner ac Amserau Cymru* (Banner and Times of Wales, 1859–1971), an "intensely political" newspaper which "became the leading Welsh-language organ of radical Nonconformity for the remainder of the century."[21]

---

11. Wiles, *Freshest Advices*, 16.
12. From 1827, it was titled the *North Wales Chronicle*.
13. Jones, *Newsplan*, 37.
14. Ibid.
15. Rees, "South Wales," 305.
16. The first Welsh-language newspaper to run for a significant period (four years) was *Y Newyddiadur Hanesydd* (the Historian's Newspaper), which ran from 1836 to 1839 and was published in Mold. It was later titled *Cronicl yr Oes* (Chronicle of the Age).
17. Defined as the counties of Breconshire, Glamorgan, Cardiganshire, Carmarthenshire, Monmouthshire, and Pembrokeshire.
18. Rees, "South Wales," 301–3.
19. See Jones, "*Yr Amserau*," for further information on this title.
20. Thomas, "Hen Gefndir yr *Herald Cymraeg*," 11.
21. Morgan, *History of Wales*, 50; and Jones, "*Yr Amserau*," 99, respectively.

Sixty-nine newspaper titles were launched in the 1850s and one hundred in the 1880s, the vast majority in English. Twenty new Welsh-language titles were launched in the 1880s, but the number fell in later decades.[22] With their large and rapid population growth, the towns and cities of south Wales were ripe for new titles. Aberdare serves as an excellent case study. Thomas Jones, an Independent minister, initially established *Y Gwron Cymreig* in Carmarthen, taking it with him when he moved to Aberdare in 1854. He later founded *Y Gweithiwr* (the Worker, 1858–60) before the much more successful English-language *Aberdare Times* (1861–1902). *Tarian y Gweithiwr* (the Worker's Shield, 1875–1934) was a much more radical weekly which attacked English mine owners, Tories, and the Church of England. Its readers were coal miners as well as tin and iron workers of the south, and it had weekly sales of 15,000.[23] *Y Gwladgarwr* (the Patriot, 1858–84) was another weekly Aberdare newspaper which opposed the Tories and the Church of England but was of a more temperate viewpoint, having been established by a number of prominent men in the town.[24] As immigrants poured into the valleys, however, English-language newspapers overtook their Welsh-language equivalents and became the norm. For example, Merthyr Tydfil, which was the largest town in Wales in 1851, had only four Welsh-language newspapers as opposed to fifteen in English.

In the north of the country, Bangor was the main newspaper center, followed by Caernarvon, Denbigh, and Wrexham. Bangor was home to the first newspaper in the north—the *North Wales Gazette*—and was also home to a number of Welsh-language newspapers, including *Y Cymro* (the Welshman, 1848–56); *Cronicl Cymru* (the Chronicle of Wales, 1866–72); *Llais y Wlad* (Voice of the Country, 1874–84); *Y Chwarelwr Cymreig* (the Welsh Quarryman, 1893–1902), which was aimed at those working in the slate industries; and the influential *Y Celt* (the Celt, 1878–1906). Caernarvon was the home of *Gwalia* (Cambria, 1881–1921) and the Liberal-supporting *Carnarvon Herald* (1831–36; later the *Carnarvon & Denbigh Herald*, 1836–), which was often to be found in conflict with the Conservative *North Wales Chronicle*. Newspapers came relatively late to Wrexham in the northeast of the country; newspapers from nearby Chester, often with "North Wales" in their subtitles, hindered the development of a local press. It was not until 1848 that a monthly newspaper was established in the town, although by 1870 it had three weekly newspapers. The Liberal-supporting *Wrexham and Denbigh Advertiser* (1850–1958) had a particularly acrimonious relationship with its Conservative rival, the *Wrexham Guardian* (1869–1954). Denbigh was home to Thomas Gee and his newspapers, including *Baner ac Amserau Cymru*, the most important and widely read Welsh-language newspaper[25] and perhaps the closest thing to a national newspaper in Wales during the Victorian era (see Figures 14.1 and 14.2).

Swansea produced Wales's first daily newspaper, the *Cambrian Daily Leader* (1861–1930), and by 1893, it was able to support a second, the *South Wales Daily Post* (1893–1932). Both

---

22. Jones, "Welsh Newspaper Press," 5.
23. Stephens, *New Companion*, 704.
24. Ibid., 296.
25. Jones, "Welsh Newspaper Press," 7.

Figure 14.1 Baner ac Amserau Cymru 43, no. 2276 (October 10, 1900): 1.

wtitles were priced at a halfpenny by 1900.[26] Cardiff also had two daily newspapers from the 1870s—the *Western Mail* (1869–) and the *South Wales Daily News* (1872–1928)—while the daily evening press was established in Cardiff in the 1880s—the *South Wales Echo* (1884–1930) and the *Evening Express* (1887–1917).[27] The north, by contrast, looked towards Liverpool to supply its daily newspaper, primarily in the form of the *Daily Post* (1855–).

The 1868 general election saw for the first time more Liberal than Conservative MPs returned to Westminster for Welsh seats. The Conservative party responded by establishing

26. *Mitchell's*, 1900, 186–7.
27. Ibid., 182.

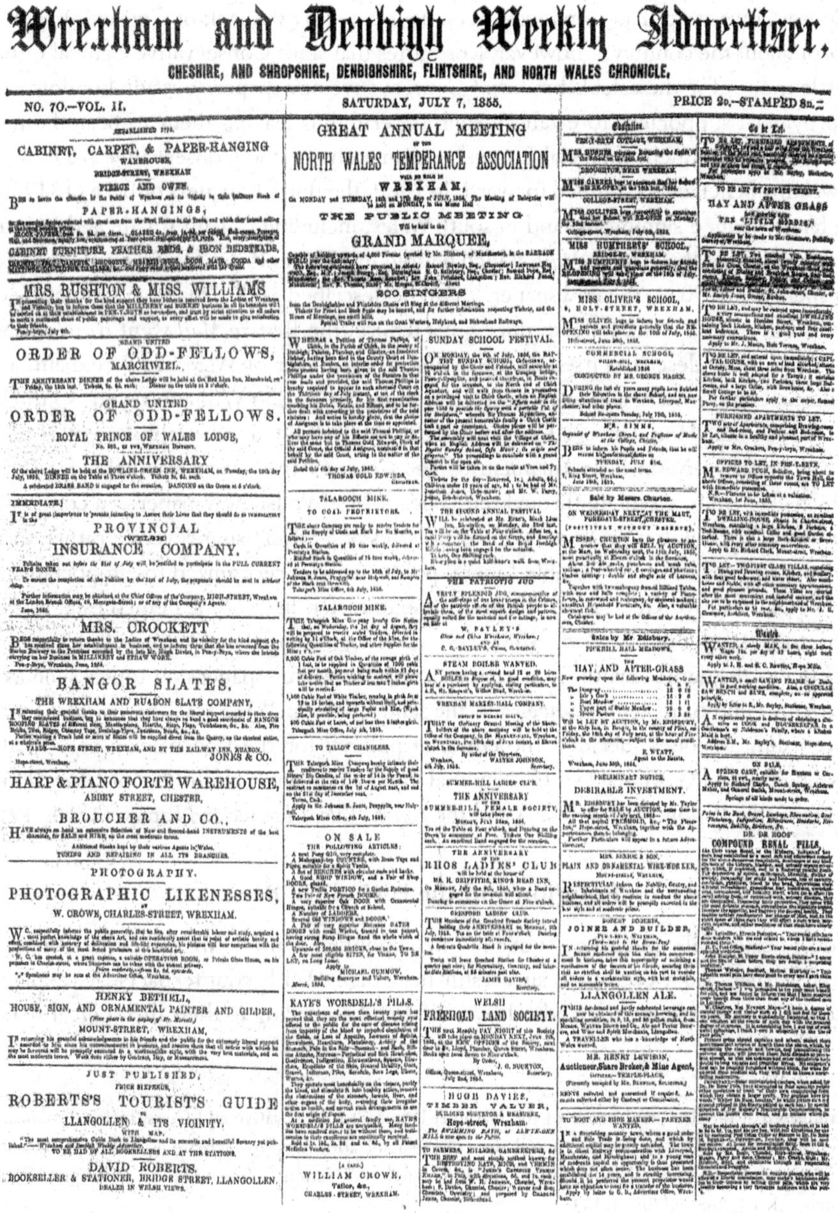

Wrexham and Denbigh Weekly Advertiser.

CHESHIRE, AND SHROPSHIRE, DENBIGHSHIRE, FLINTSHIRE, AND NORTH WALES CHRONICLE.

NO. 70.—VOL. II. | SATURDAY, JULY 7, 1855. | PRICE 2D.—STAMPED 3D.

CABINET, CARPET, & PAPER-HANGING WAREHOUSE,

PIERCE AND OWEN.

PAPER-HANGINGS,

CABINET FURNITURE, FEATHER BEDS, & IRON BEDSTEADS,

MRS. RUSHTON & MISS. WILLIAMS

GRAND UNITED ORDER OF ODD-FELLOWS, MARCHWIEL.

GRAND UNITED ORDER OF ODD-FELLOWS.

ROYAL PRINCE OF WALES LODGE,

THE ANNIVERSARY

PROVINCIAL (WELSH) INSURANCE COMPANY.

MRS. CROCKETT

BANGOR SLATES.

THE WREXHAM AND RUABON SLATE COMPANY,

JONES & CO.

HARP & PIANO FORTE WAREHOUSE,

ABBEY STREET, CHESTER,

BROUCHER AND CO.,

PHOTOGRAPHY.

PHOTOGRAPHIC LIKENESSES,

W. CROWE, CHARLES-STREET, WREXHAM.

HENRY BETHELL,

HOUSE, SIGN, AND ORNAMENTAL PAINTER AND GILDER,

MOUNT-STREET, WREXHAM,

JUST PUBLISHED,

ROBERTS'S TOURISTS' GUIDE TO LLANGOLLEN & ITS VICINITY,

DAVID ROBERTS,

BOOKSELLER & STATIONER, BRIDGE STREET, LLANGOLLEN.

GREAT ANNUAL MEETING OF THE NORTH WALES TEMPERANCE ASSOCIATION

WILL BE HELD IN WREXHAM,

THE PUBLIC MEETING

GRAND MARQUEE,

800 SINGERS

TALACRE MINE.

TO COAL PROPRIETORS.

TALACRE MINE.

TO TALLOW CHANDLERS.

ON SALE

THE FOLLOWING ARTICLES:

MICHAEL GUMMOW,

KAYE'S WORSDELL'S PILLS.

WILLIAM CROWE,

Tailor, &c.,

CHARLES-STREET, WREXHAM.

SUNDAY SCHOOL FESTIVAL.

THE SECOND ANNUAL FESTIVAL

THE PATRIOTIC JUG

STEAM BOILER WANTED.

WREXHAM MARKET-HALL COMPANY.

THE ANNIVERSARY

SUMMER-HILL FEMALE SOCIETY,

RHOS LADIES' CLUB

WELSH FREEHOLD LAND SOCIETY.

HUGH DAVIES,

TIMBER VALUER,

Hope-street, Wrexham.

Scholastic.

MISS HUMPHREYS' SCHOOL,

MISS OLIVER'S SCHOOL,

COMMERCIAL SCHOOL,

Sale by Messrs. Churton.

Sales by Mr. Edisbury.

HAY, AND AFTER-GRASS

DESIRABLE INVESTMENT.

JOINER AND BUILDER,

LLANGOLLEN ALE.

To be Let.

HAY AND AFTER GRASS

FURNISHED APARTMENTS TO LET.

OFFICES TO LET, IN PEN-Y-BRYN.

Wanted.

ON SALE,

COMPOUND RENAL PILLS.

Figure 14.2 *Wrexham and Denbigh Weekly Advertiser* 2, no. 70 (July 7, 1855): 1.

Conservative-supporting newspapers in both north and south Wales and in both languages. The Conservative party had previously been concerned by the lack of Conservative newspapers throughout the country;[28] however, Koss notes that since Conservative Central Office had very little money for the establishment of Conservative newspapers outside London, it relied upon provincial supporters to establish such papers, thus leaving them to bear the financial burdens and the frequent financial losses.[29] Fortunately for the Conservative party in Wales, some wealthy benefactors stepped forward. In 1869, the third Marquess of Bute (1847–1900), whose family owned significant land in south Wales, including Cardiff Castle and Bute Docks in Cardiff, founded the *Western Mail*, which he sold in 1877 to its editor, Henry Lascelles Carr, having spent £50,000 on the newspaper.[30] Carr is described as the "man who established daily journalism in Wales,"[31] and indeed, during his tenure, the *Western Mail* went from strength to strength and today describes itself as the national newspaper of Wales. In Wrexham, a group of prominent landowners and aristocrats, including Sir Watkin William-Wynn, sixth baronet (1820–85), and the Hon. George Kenyon (1840–1908), funded the establishment of the *Wrexham Guardian* (later *North Wales Guardian*).[32] The Conservatives were also behind *Y Dywysogaeth*, which claimed to circulate throughout Wales.[33] Most Welsh newspapers, in contrast, were supporters of the Liberal party and relied on sales and advertising revenue rather than rich aristocratic supporters. One notable Liberal politician who recognized the importance of the press was David Lloyd George, the future prime minister. In 1888 he helped establish *Udgorn Rhyddid* (the Trumpet of Freedom, 1888–98), even suggesting the title himself. He also wrote articles under the name "Brutus" for various north Wales newspapers on topics such as disestablishment, education, temperance, and the land question.[34] He was the company solicitor and, according to Jones, decided the editorial policy[35] for the Caernarvon-based Cwmni'r Wasg Genedlaethol Gymraeg (Welsh National Press Company), publishers of *Y Genedl Gymreig* and *Y Werin* (the People, 1885–1937) and the *North Wales Observer and Express* (1884–1937).

Religion and the Periodical Press

Religious periodicals published outside metropolitan centers in England and Scotland appeared earlier and were more successful than their Welsh counterparts. As explained in Chapter 26 below, religious periodicals were defined according to their theological stance and

---

28. As reflected at the first conference of the National Union of Conservative and Constitutional Associations in November 1867, when one of the stated aims of the association was "to increase and multiply the influence of the Conservative press throughout the United Kingdom." National Union Minutes, November 12, 1867; quoted in Koss, *Rise and Fall*, 1:184.
29. Koss, *Rise and Fall*, 1:178.
30. Cayford, "Western Mail," 54.
31. Ibid., 55.
32. A history of the *Wrexham Guardian* during its period of Conservative ownership can be found in Peters, "Troubled History."
33. Advertisement for *Y Dywysogarth* in the papers of Lewis Jones, National Library of Wales, 6402D.
34. Owen, *Tempestuous Journey*, 51.
35. Jones, "Welsh Newspaper Press," 11.

often included lighter entertainments such as essays, reviews, and poetry. Roberts claims that "for the vast majority of literary Welshmen these periodicals were the regular and staple bill of fare," and this was probably true.[36] Often produced in the Welsh language, such periodicals were used by religious leaders "to sustain and develop communities of belief."[37] Their numbers are impressive and bear witness to the zeal with which denominational differences were sustained.

After the Calvinist Methodist *Y Trysorfa Ysprydol* first appeared in 1799, Wesleyan Methodists produced *Yr Eurgrawn Wesleyaidd* (the Wesleyan Magazine), which became the longest-running Welsh religious periodical (1809–1983). The main organ of the Baptists was *Y Gwir Fedyddiwr* (the True Baptist, 1842–44), later retitled *Y Bedyddiwr* (the Baptist, 1844–68), marketed as a religious and literary monthly. Baptists were also responsible for *Y Greal* (the Miscellany, 1858–1919) and the *Seren Gomer* (Star of Gomer, 1818–1983), which was unusual in that its contents were not limited to religious issues only.[38] The Independents (Congregationalists) produced two very long-running journals: *Y Dysgedydd* (the Instructor, 1821–1968) and *Y Diwygiwr* (the Reformer, 1835–1911), primarily for congregations in south Wales. The Church of England, which, despite its minority status, was the established church in Wales at the time, produced *Yr Haul* (the Sun, 1835–1981) and *Yr Eglwysydd* (the Churchman, 1847–64).[39] One of these denominational magazines still exists today—*Yr Ymofynydd* (the Inquirer)—which was established by the Unitarians in 1846. Walters has shown that these journals did not always practice what they preached, as demonstrated by the ferocious dispute between the editors of *Yr Haul* and *Y Diwygiwr*, David Owen ("Brutus") and David Rees.[40] The mapping of such disputes between people, words, and deeds is certainly an area ripe for future research.

In addition to producing periodicals which aimed to circulate over a large area, if not all of Wales, religious denominations produced local periodicals to serve a particular area or parish. Examples include the *Newport Presbyterian* (1895–96); *Y Cenadydd* (the Messenger, 1876–77), for the Coedpoeth Wesleyan Methodist circuit; *Yr Arweinydd Annibynol* (the Independent Leader, 1878–80),[41] for Independents in the Rhondda; and the *Llandaff Diocesan Magazine* (1899–1919), for the Church of England's Llandaff diocese. Usually these magazines were short-lived. Whilst religious denominations created a flourishing periodical trade in Wales, particularly in terms of Welsh-language titles, the cultural dominance of the religious press seems to have led to the trade's over-dependence on them and consequent vulnerability.[42]

---

36. Roberts, "Welsh Periodicals," 78.
37. Jones, "Print, Language, and Identity," 229.
38. *Seren Gomer* was originally a newspaper. It was relaunched as a fortnightly magazine by Joseph Harris ("Gomer") in 1818 due to the financial pressures of a weekly newspaper. Jones, "Print, Language, and Identity," 229. According to Walters, it "became known as the voice of the Baptists" but was not officially affiliated with the religion until 1880. *Llyfryddiaeth Cylchgronau Cymreig, 1735–1850*, xxiii.
39. See Jones, "Welsh Church Periodical Press."
40. Walters, "Periodical Press," 201.
41. This title continued as *Yr Arweinydd* (the Leader) from 1879.
42. Walters, *Llyfryddiaeth Cylchgronau Cymreig, 1735–1850*, xxxi.

The cultural productivity of religion in Wales can partly be explained by the fact that ministers of religion comprised the largest profession in Wales.[43] They were the natural choice to serve as editors of denominational periodicals and indeed often edited, published and even founded secular periodicals. Ministers were educated and literate, and they came from the same social background as their readers.[44] Some ministers were not satisfied with editing one journal. For example, William Williams ("Caledfryn"), an Independent minister, edited eleven, and Owen Jones ("Meudwy Môn"), a Calvinist Methodist, edited five or six.[45] However, ministers usually shied away from the more demanding editorship of weekly newspapers. Jones has described the role of an early Victorian newspaper editor in Wales as a writer of leading articles, collector and writer of news items, corrector of proofs, accountant (for sales and advertising sales), printing supervisor, and arranger of distribution.[46] The responsibilities associated with editing a smaller newspaper would have been similar to the duties Richard Richards claimed he assumed as de facto editor of the *Wrexham Advertiser*—endless cutting and pasting material from other newspapers.[47]

Wales's denominations involved themselves in the newspaper trade primarily as distributors through their Sunday schools, chapels, or churches. This included the Independent *Y Tyst Cymreig* (the Welsh Witness, 1867–70); the Calvinist Methodist *Y Goleuad* (the Illuminator, 1869–); the Wesleyan Methodist *Y Gwyliedydd* (the Sentinel, 1870); and the Baptist *Seren Cymru* (the Star of Wales, 1851–), "arguably the best-produced weekly Welsh-language newspaper in the nineteenth century."[48] Church of England periodicals, meanwhile, struggled to overcome their weak market position caused by the limited size of their paying audience.[49] The four Welsh Anglican dioceses issued a report in 1879 called *The Welsh Church Press*, which discussed the need to establish two Welsh-language newspapers—one in the north and one in the south—to oppose growing calls throughout Wales for the disestablishment of the Church of England in Wales.[50] Only the northern *Y Llan* (the Church, 1881–84) was founded in response to this call.[51] A successor to the Conservative *Y Dywysogaeth* (the Principality, 1870–81),[52] *Y Llan* united

---

43. According to the occupation tables in the census reports, Wales had 2,243 ministers of religion in 1851 and 4,025 in 1891. See Jones, "Nineteenth Century," 162.
44. Walters, "Periodical Press," 207.
45. In the introduction to *Llyfryddiaeth Cylchgronau Cymreig, 1735–1850*, Walters states that Jones edited five periodicals (xxv), but in "Periodical Press," he names six (207). This uncertainty is indicative of the amount of work that still remains to be done on the Welsh press.
46. Jones, "Newspaper Press," 211.
47. "A Reporter," 4.
48. Jones, "Print, Language, and Identity," 234.
49. Jones, "Welsh Church Periodical Press," 92.
50. See Jones, *Press, Politics and Society*, 123–4, on the Anglican report. Although Wales was predominantly Nonconformist, the Church of England remained the official or "established" church, which led, for example, to farmers, regardless of their religion, paying a tithe (usually 10 percent of their crop) to the local church, in addition to supporting their local Nonconformist chapel. Disestablishment was the prime demand of the Welsh nationalist movement from the late nineteenth century until it was finally achieved in 1920 by the Welsh Church Act of 1914.
51. Jones, "Print, Language, and Identity," 234.
52. Untitled, *Y Dywysogaeth*, 1.

politics and religion, later making its political content more obvious with a title change to *Y Llan a'r Dywysogaeth* (the Church and the Principality, 1884–1955).

Religious denominations also supported temperance periodicals. The temperance movement, discussed in Chapter 25 below, enjoyed significant support throughout Wales, particularly in the 1830s and 1840s. Fifteen temperance periodicals were founded between 1835 and 1850, most notably *Yr Athraw* (the Teacher, 1836–45), *Y Dirwestydd* (the Abstainer, 1836–39), and *Y Dirwestydd Deheuol* (the Southern Abstainer, 1840–41).[53] In the 1870s, temperance organizations turned to newspapers, several of which were published in the northern town of Wrexham, home to thirteen breweries.[54] However, the temperance newspapers of the 1870s were less successful than the temperance journals of the 1830s and 1840s: the *Wrexham Temperance Messenger* lasted for only one issue in 1873, whilst the *Good Templar Advocate and General Intelligencer* (1873), later the *Templar of Wales*,[55] lasted less than a year.

Targeted Audiences

Thomas Gee—the owner, publisher, and printer of the *Baner ac Amserau Cymru*—was one of the most important figures in Victorian journalism in the widest sense.[56] He realized that if Welsh were to survive, it needed periodicals that could discuss the latest advances in knowledge.[57] In 1845, he established the quarterly *Y Traethodydd* (the Essayist, 1845–),[58] which soon became the best-known and most widely read secular periodical in Victorian Wales. It led public opinion on literary as well as religious issues, surpassing literary magazines such as *Y Beirniad* (the Critic, 1859–79) and *Y Llenor* (the Litterateur, 1895–98).[59] Its importance has been recognized by the *Welsh Journals Online* project, which included it as one of only four Victorian journals selected for digitization. One of the first joint editors of *Y Traethodydd* was Lewis Edwards (1809–87), a Calvinist Methodist preacher. His education at Edinburgh University and his decision to base *Y Traethodydd* on English-language Scottish quarterlies, such as the *Edinburgh Review* and *Blackwood's Magazine*,[60] raises the question of whether or not there was a strategic alliance between Scotland and Wales. This possible connection deserves further research.

The latter half of the nineteenth century saw the appearance of several Welsh-language periodicals which sought to follow the example of *Y Traethodydd*. The first Welsh-language, mass-market monthly periodical—*Y Geiniogwerth* (the Pennyworth)—appeared in January 1847.

---

53. Walters, *Llyfryddiaeth Cylchgronau Cymreig, 1735–1850*, xxv.
54. Williams, *Encyclopeadia of Wrexham*.
55. These two newspapers were owned by the International Order of Good Templars, which arrived in Wales in 1871. Lambert, *Drink and Sobriety*, 103.
56. Humpherys's entry on Gee in *Welsh Biography Online* describes him as taking a "prominent part, both on the platform and in the committee room, in the political, educational, and religious movements of the day." Humpherys, "Gee."
57. Jones, "Two Welsh Publishers," 175.
58. For a history of *Y Traethodydd*, see Williams, "Hanes cychwyn Y Traethodydd" and "Hanes Y Traethodydd."
59. Stephens, *New Companion*, 730.
60. Stephens, "Y Traethodydd," 594.

Eschewing illustration, it comprised twenty-eight octavo pages. Given its title, it is surprising that *Y Geiniogwerth* does not seem to have been modeled on the *Penny Magazine* or later popular miscellanies. It only lasted until December 1851 and was followed by the even shorter-lived *Y Gwerinwr* (the Common Man, 1855–56). The economies of scale that English-language cheap weeklies enjoyed were unavailable to Welsh-language publications, and it was only from the 1880s that there were various attempts to break into English. The use of English was growing, not only due to instruction in the schools, but also because of immigration from England into such areas as the north Wales coastal resorts and the south Wales coalfields.[61] One of the earliest attempts was the *Red Dragon* (1882–87), whose subtitle daringly claimed that it was the "national magazine of Wales." It included literature, serialized novels, Welsh history, and portraits of famous Welshmen, and unlike its Welsh counterparts, it avoided religious and theological discussions. In this sense, it has been described as a "calculated attempt to reach out to a new public literate in English but unschooled in a knowledge of Wales."[62]

The desire to educate can also be seen in the development of Welsh children's periodicals. Many of these journals were produced by religious groups and were marketed through Sunday schools. Several ran for over a century and continued well into the twentieth century, making them some of the longest-running Welsh periodicals. Examples include *Yr Athraw i Blentyn* (a Teacher for Children, 1827–1918), *Y Winllan* (the Vineyard, 1848–1965), *Tywysydd yr Ieuainc* (Guide for Young People, 1837–51), and *Y Cyfaill Eglwysig* (the Ecclesiastical Friend, 1862–1957). The most popular was the monthly *Trysorfa y Plant* (the Children's Treasury, 1862–1966). Though it was produced by Calvinist Methodists, it was nonetheless popular amongst children of all denominations. By 1881 it was selling 40,000 copies a month,[63] and in 1911 its editors claimed that over 1.5 million copies had been sold.[64] The religious denominations controlled the children's periodical market until the appearance of *Cymru'r Plant* (the Children's Wales, 1892–1987), which took Welsh children's periodicals into a new era with illustrations and a wide range of engaging content.

Newspapers were mainly aimed at men, and women were corralled, as in England, into ladies' columns and pages.[65] There was a handful of Welsh-language periodicals for women. Although the first Welsh women's journal, *Y Gymraes* (the Welshwoman, 1850–52), was founded by a man, Evan Jones ("Ieuan Gwynedd"), later women's journals were edited by women. *Y Gymraes* contained advice on housekeeping, as Jones believed that women should be encouraged in their role as wives and mothers.[66] *Y Frythones* (the British Woman, 1879–91) was edited by Sarah Jane Rees ("Cranogwen") (1839–1916), a schoolteacher and founder of the Temperance Union of the Women of South Wales.[67] Rees was also the chief columnist for a

---

61. See Pryce, "Language Areas," and Jones, "Welsh Language."
62. Matthias, *Lonely Editor*, 9. A detailed study of the *Red Dragon* can be found in Ballin, *Welsh Periodicals*, 10–22.
63. Walters, *Llyfryddiaeth Cylchgronau Cymreig, 1735–1850*, xxxv.
64. Walters, *Y Wasg Gyfnodol Gymreig*, 19.
65. See, for example, the *Wrexham Advertiser* from 1881.
66. Walters, *Llyfryddiaeth Cylchgronau Cymreig, 1735–1850*, xxxiii.
67. More information about Rees can be found in Jones, *Cofiant Cranogwen*.

later *Y Gymraes* (1896–1934), which took as its theme the moral duties and responsibilities of women and sought to promote women's education and their role in local politics.[68]

Whilst both Anglophone and Welsh-language journals sought to educate readers, their different content demonstrated the divergent cultural needs of the two groups. Welsh-language journals wrote about the outside world, whilst English-language journals aimed to educate monoglot English speakers about Wales. As Roberts explains, "English journals were intended to express an awareness and definition of Welshness which is non-linguistic and mainly antiquarian. . . . Welsh periodicals have . . . a deeper awareness of an external world."[69] Many of these English-language journals were published by learned societies, the most prestigious being *Archaeologia Cambrensis* (1846–), the journal of the Cambrian Archaeological Association, published in London. Several other early English-language journals were published in England and attracted an audience along the border, including the *Archaeological Magazine of Bristol, Bath, and South Wales* (1843–44) and *Collections Historical and Archeological Relating to Montgomeryshire* (1867–). In London, Welsh exiles founded the Honourable Society of Cymmrodorion, which produced *Y Cymmrodor* (1877–1951) and the *Transactions of the Honourable Society of Cymmrodorion* (1892–). Attempts were made, particularly in the 1870s by John Roose Elias ("Y Thesbiad"), to produce a Welsh-language antiquarian magazine, but such efforts proved fruitless.[70] As the English language increased in strength over the nineteenth century, the educationalist Owen M. Edwards (1858–1920) sought to encourage use of the Welsh language through several literary and popular magazines, most notably *Cymru* (Wales, 1891–1927). He also produced an English-language counterpart, *Wales* (1894–97), which aimed to inform the Welsh about the history, literature, and culture of their own country.

As the Welsh immigrated to new lands in the Americas and Australia, they established periodicals there. In 1865, Welsh settlers established a Welsh colony in Patagonia in South America. Since one of the main reasons behind this enterprise was to protect the Welsh language, it is not surprising that the colony produced several Welsh-language periodicals, most notably the newspaper *Y Brut* (the Chronicle, 1868) and the magazine *Y Dravod* (the Discussion, 1891–1961). Further north, Welsh emigrants grouped around the coal and slate mining areas of Wisconsin, Illinois, and Pennsylvania, creating sizeable Welsh-speaking communities with chapels, societies, newspapers, and magazines. As in Wales, the successful periodicals were those published in support of a particular religious denomination, such as *Y Cyfaill o'r Hen Wlad yn America* (the Friend from the Old Country in America, 1838–1933), produced by the Welsh Calvinistic Methodists. The Independents and Baptists followed by successfully producing both religious and children's periodicals.[71] The short-lived *Yr Ausytalydd* (the Australian, 1866–72) and *Yr Ymwelydd* (the Visitor, 1874–76) were founded to serve Welsh-speaking colonies in Australia.

---

68. Stephens, *New Companion*, 303.
69. Roberts, "Welsh Periodicals," 72.
70. Walters, *Llyfryddiaeth Cylchgronau Cymreig, 1735–1850*, xlv, xlvii.
71. Ibid., li. For more information on US titles, see Owen, "Welsh American Newspapers."

Primary and Secondary Sources

Wales is fortunate to have produced many scholars of the periodical press. For studying Victorian journals, the first reference source should always be the excellent two-volume bibliography of Welsh periodicals by Huw Walters, published by the National Library of Wales.[72] The first volume contains an essay on bibliographical sources, whilst the second offers a comprehensive bilingual essay on the Welsh periodicals market from 1735 to 1900. Some of the information from the introductory essay can be found on the website of the National Library of Wales. The bibliography lists periodicals (excluding newspapers) published in Wales and periodicals published outside the Principality but relating to Wales.

The main source for Welsh newspapers is *NEWSPLAN Wales / Cymru*, which is published both online and in book form.[73] The aim of this project is to supply holdings information on Welsh newspapers in either print or microfilm. Both the book and the website contain a brief introductory essay on Welsh newspapers. Like Walters's work, *NEWSPLAN Wales / Cymru* contains information on newspapers published in Wales and those published outside the Principality but relating to Wales. A number of important Welsh periodicals have also been digitized by the National Library of Wales / Llyfrgell Genedlaethol Cymru, which hosts the *Welsh Journals Online* website.[74] Unfortunately, of the forty-four titles so far digitized, only four date from the Victorian era. The National Library also hosts *Welsh Newspapers Online*,[75] which is an ongoing project to digitize Welsh newspapers and newspapers relating to Wales held at the National Library. The newspaper coverage is currently from 1804 to 1919; as its title coverage expands, it will become a vital tool not only for studying the Victorian press in Wales but for investigating the history of periodical journalism more generally.

Several books and articles have been produced on Welsh periodicals in general and also on particular ones, as my notes demonstrate. Several MA theses and doctoral dissertations on individual titles, editors, and journalists, both in English and Welsh, are available through the Theses Collection Wales on the National Library of Wales website. As the internet opens up access to Welsh periodicals, opportunities for researching this area of Welsh literature will increase. Single titles can be studied, as can topics such as children's periodicals or religious titles and, of course, publishing centers.[76] There is still much research to be done on the Welsh diaspora, including how periodicals were used to maintain links to the homeland. Although there have been several studies of *Y Frythones*, there is still more to be discovered about how periodicals reflected the nineteenth-century Welsh woman.[77]

Within Wales, studies of English-language and Welsh-language periodicals can reveal much about how the concept of Welsh national identity changed during the Victorian era. Welsh periodicals are a fertile area for comparative studies: for example, studies of women's or temperance

---

72. Ibid. and *Llyfryddiaeth Cylchgronau Cymreig, 1851–1900*.
73. See http://www.newsplanwales.info; Jones, *Newsplan*.
74. See http://welshjournals.llgc.org.uk
75. http://papuraunewyddcymru.llgc.org.uk.
76. See, for instance, Peters, *Politics, Publishing, and Personalities*.
77. See Williams, "Swyno merched ein gwlad allan o'u hogofau," and Williams, "Y Frythones."

periodicals in England and Wales or investigations of periodicals on the same topic, such as *Cymru* and *Wales*, which were published in Wales but in different languages and were therefore aimed at different audiences. Future researchers might also compare nationalist periodicals such as *Cymru Fydd* or *Young Wales* to analogous titles in Scotland, Ireland, or even the smaller nations of Europe. Whilst such work would rely on the ability to read Welsh and possibly other languages as well, it would place Wales and its literature within a wider European, and even worldwide, framework.

15

PERIODICALS IN IRELAND

Elizabeth Tilley

When researching nineteenth-century Irish periodicals, historians face several challenges, including the persistence of an oral culture in Ireland long after the introduction of print and the difficulty of establishing accurate literacy rates (reading and writing beyond the ability to produce a signature).[1] The 1841 census, the first reliable source available, indicates huge geographical variations in the levels of reading and writing ability—from 85 percent in Ulster to approximately 15 percent in Connaught. Until about 1850, Irish was the language of the majority, particularly outside Dublin, though English, rather than Irish, was the first language most new readers learned, and the foundation of the national school system in 1831 ultimately cemented the predominance of the English language.[2] The market for periodicals in Ireland was always relatively small; indeed, circulation figures for many magazines included the sale of issues to Irish communities living abroad. With such a small audience in mind, the listing of some 4,000 Irish periodical titles between 1800 and 1900 in the *Waterloo Directory of Irish Periodicals* testifies to the continuing optimism of editors and proprietors of Irish journals.

Dublin was the center of periodical production and consumption, and consequently, the assumed audience for most periodicals during the century was an urban one. Raw data indicates that of the four regions of Ireland, Leinster (Dublin) showed the greatest activity, followed by Ulster (Belfast), Munster (Cork), and Connaught (Galway). It should be noted, however, that literary and antiquarian societies in all of these areas were involved in producing journals dealing with aspects of local history and that both regional and national newspapers were available in most areas, including Galway.[3]

Political issues in Ireland influenced the availability and variety of periodicals in all parts of the country. For instance, the Act of Union, which came into effect in 1801, ushered in a new set of legal barriers to the reprint industry that had flourished in Ireland in the eighteenth century. The extension of English copyright legislation to Ireland meant that cheap reprints could no longer

---

1. This essay concerns English-language periodicals in Ireland. The circumstances surrounding Irish-language titles necessitate a separate study. It should be noted, though, that many English-language titles included articles on Irish language and history, which were often set in Irish type.
2. See Ó Ciosáin, "Oral Culture, Literacy, and Reading" 174; see also Cunningham and Kennedy, *Experience of Reading*.
3. See Cronin, "Provincial Publishing."

be produced there with impunity, and some measure of protection was now available for English as well as Irish authors whose work was first published in England. Copyright was also available now for those Irish authors who chose to publish at home. The union of Britain and Ireland also meant that the Irish parliament was dissolved and Irish MPs moved to London. The knock-on effect of this was that jobbing printing, the backbone of any firm, declined sharply after 1801 and the number of printing houses operating in Ireland consequently decreased. Though newspapers and schoolbooks continued to be printed, there were few lucrative contracts to produce legal and government documents since most of this material was now published in London. On the other hand, political and social crises in Ireland were often accompanied by an increase in titles published. A small bubble of activity, primarily newspaper and pamphlet publishing, occurred during the ten-year period encompassing the Irish Rebellion in 1796, but by 1820 a general depression seems to have settled over the country. Around 1830, the domestic output of print increased in response to a new interest in antiquarian study, the strengthening of Royal Irish Academy serial publications, the foundation of mechanics' institutes, and the publication of new Irish language titles following Catholic Emancipation in 1829. Daniel O'Connell's repeal of the union movement in the 1830s and the Young Ireland movement in the 1840s were both highly dependent on an increasingly literate and politicized audience. The tithe war in the 1830s and the disestablishment of the Church of Ireland in 1869 each formed a locus around which pamphlets and short-lived journal titles were published. The land war, along with the home rule movement under Charles Stewart Parnell in the 1880s, again produced a flurry of activity. There is, of course, a pattern here. Periodicals are by their very nature topical and volatile. It is no accident that the number of titles increased during these years, even if most periodicals were short-lived.[4]

Religious controversy was usually a spur to the appearance of new periodicals. In Ireland, the arrival of the *Catholic Penny Magazine* in February of 1834 was swiftly followed by the first issue of the *Protestant Penny Magazine* in June of the same year; the two clashed, as Robin Kavanagh has noted, using the most up-to-date technology of the day.[5] Front-page wood engravings for both magazines were frequently inflammatory, each accusing the other of blasphemy and paganism. Each paper employed illustrations as "elaborate mechanisms . . . to shape attitudes and to define power relationships within Irish culture."[6] By 1836, both penny papers had faded away, though they were soon replaced by a number of similar titles from both sides of the religious divide.

The penny magazine format was also used for less combative purposes. George Petrie's *Dublin Penny Journal* (1832–36) broke new ground in focusing on articles about Ireland's history, language, antiquities, and resources. Though Petrie edited the journal for only one year, it remains a remarkable achievement.[7] Eschewing the generality that characterized English

---

4. The small number of exceptions proves the rule. Periodicals that lasted more than a few years were usually allied to a special interest group, including the *Dublin University Magazine* (1833–77), the *Irish Ecclesiastical Journal* (1840–52), the *Christian Examiner and Church of Ireland Magazine* (1825–39), and the *Irish Builder* (1859–1979).
5. See Kavanagh, "Religion and Illustrated Periodicals," 343.
6. Ibid.
7. Caesar Otway was co-editor in 1832, but it seems clear that Petrie produced the bulk of the paper. In 1833 Otway helped found the *Dublin University Magazine*.

versions of penny magazines, along with the overbearingly "worthy" image of *Chambers's* and other titles sponsored by religious groups or philanthropic societies, The *Dublin Penny Journal* solicited the opinions of a wide range of local correspondents, whose letters were published and commented on in the pages of the journal. Its extracts from John O'Donovan's translation of the medieval Irish chronicles, *Annals of the Four Masters*, foregrounded the importance of the Irish language to the editors. Similarly, a series on the history of Irish surnames established a link with an illustrious past. Petrie's involvement with the Ordnance Survey, and John O'Donovan's work on the derivation and history of Irish place names as part of the historical sections of the Survey, brought about an extraordinary coupling of colonial expediency and nationalism that crossed class boundaries, as well as religious and linguistic barriers.[8] However, the exuberance and pride that characterized the first year of the *Dublin Penny Journal* faded with the departure of Petrie, and under the control of Philip Dixon Hardy (from 1833 to 1836) the magazine lost its identity. Petrie made another venture into journalistic publishing with the *Irish Penny Journal* in 1840, noting in his opening address that, unlike England, Ireland had no penny magazines.[9] Though the *Irish Penny Journal* employed the talents of Samuel Lover, Charles Lever, Mrs. S.C. Hall, and William Carleton, it was ultimately unsuccessful and folded in June of 1841. In the final number, the editor wrote ruefully that more copies had been sold to the Irish population in England than to the Irish at home.[10]

The Young Ireland movement of the 1840s, with its emphasis on education, nationalist reading rooms, and the recovery of Irish history, ushered in another period of activity. The *Nation* newspaper, under the leadership of Thomas Davis, Charles Gavan Duffy, and others, stressed the power of poetry in its political appeals to readers. Poems and songs formed a substantial amount of the material appearing in each issue, and the literary portions of the newspaper were repeatedly collected and republished both as stand-alone volumes and in serial parts with titles such as *The Spirit of the Nation*. Young Ireland responded quickly to political events, and the newspaper format, with its cheapness and topicality, was crucial to the success of the movement. There were no monthly or quarterly (and thus more leisurely) outlets for the Young Ireland message beyond the cheap serial reprints of material from the *Nation*. At mid-century, most Irish periodicals were largely concerned with niche or "family domestic" markets.[11]

The following two case studies are intended to demonstrate recent approaches to investigating the Irish periodical press. The first example uses existing primary and secondary sources to gather elusive information about the establishment and purpose of a niche magazine. The second example points out the interdependence of various publishing genres in the periodical marketplace, emphasizing how this informed the reputations of editors and contributors.

---

8. See Andrews, *A Paper Landscape*, 156.
9. See Clyde, *Irish Literary Magazines*, 105.
10. "To Our Readers," 416.
11. Hayley lists a number of mid-century titles coming from publisher James Duffy. She describes Duffy as purveyor of a "new kind of cosy family Catholicism." See Hayley, "A Reading and Thinking Nation," 42.

The *Citizen* (1839–43)

The starting point for investigation of the *Citizen*[12] is Stephen Brown's short note in *The Press in Ireland*.[13] Brown singles out the title because it fits his criteria for quality: it was written by Irishmen and produced in Dublin, it was nationalist in flavor, and it contained an interesting series of supplements entitled "The Native Music of Ireland," complete with accompanying scores. The printers/proprietors were listed on the title page of the first volume as R. Groombridge in London and James Philip Doyle and John Cumming in Dublin. By the third volume, only the Dublin publisher, Samuel J. Machen of D'Olier Street in Dublin, was listed.

The assumed readership of the *Citizen* was disgruntled and politically aware. The editors were brothers Henry and William Elliot Hudson; Henry was a dentist and collector of Irish music, and William was a lawyer. Both were Dubliners. The talents of the brothers were exhibited in the contents of the journal, from Henry's painstakingly reproduced sheet music, to William's long articles on negligent landlords and the abuse of the judicial system. The excerpt below, taken from an article entitled "Grand Juries," exemplifies the generally combative tone of their work:

> What does it signify, that the contractor happened to be the natural son of the subsheriff, who lent Mr. Mortgage 2,000*l.*? or, that Sir Frederick discovered that he could raise his rents to a considerable extent, by getting persons of ingenuity to discover works that were indispensably necessary, and in whose construction he could employ his tenantry; thus enabling them to pay more rent, and enabling him to improve his property, at the country's expense. Who's to blame for this?—you, fellow-citizens, you; who see such things doing daily, and never do any thing but grumble, and pay for it. Don't mind getting into a passion now, and crying, in ill-humoured laziness, "How can we help it? 'tis all the fault of the aristocracy." 'Tis not all the fault of the aristocracy; they occupy a false position; they are suffered to squander away our money, by a foolish and irrational system,—a system that corrupts them while it plunders us; which weighs down the agricultural and municipal prosperity of the country; which, in the long run, injures the aristocracy themselves.[14]

In articles like this one, the *Citizen* concentrated on political decisions from the past that seemed to exclude the vast majority of Irish citizens from participating in the national government. The remedy was always reasoned reform of the legal system and proper representation of the ratepayer.

Another article in the same number related the experience of an Irish traveler amongst the great houses of England; he noted with approval the Duke of Devonshire's constant

---

12. The full range of titles is as follows: the *Citizen: A Monthly Journal of Politics, Literature and Art* (November 1839–February 1841); the *Citizen: or, Dublin Monthly Magazine* (March 1841–December 1841); the *Dublin Monthly Magazine; Being a New Series of The Citizen* (January 1842–December 1842); the *Dublin Magazine and Citizen* (January 1843–April 1843). See Clyde, *Irish Literary Magazines*, 103–4.
13. Brown, *Press in Ireland*, 65, 110.
14. "Grand Juries," 24.

improvements to his property using stone quarried by his tenants on his own estate. The writer then contemplated the impossibility of observing a similar scene in Ireland: "I sighed when I thought to myself, that if our great Irish landed proprietors wanted to build, they would import Portland stone from England, or send to Scotland for granite, sooner than be indebted to a native quarry."[15] Again, the means of persuasion in these articles was primarily moral and legal, rather than militant, though the indignant tone was constant. The *Citizen* often included less inflammatory material, such as reviews of Irish books. Similarly, an article on the Dublin Mechanics' Institute pictured a meeting during which the members voted for self-government. In the same article, two men of differing political and religious views are imagined sitting together in amiable conversation over the puzzling out of a mathematical problem—all animosity forgotten in the free environment of the Institute. The article then lists the contents of the Institute's library as an example of a balanced menu for the working class:

> "Information for the People," "Chambers' Journal," "Penny Magazine," "Civil Engineer's Journal," "Mechanics' Magazine," "Railway and Mining Journals." There are lighter books. "Bentley," "The New Monthly," "Nickleby." But are all those well-dressed, respectable young men, who crowd the tables, mere workmen? They are. They have the proper pride of appearing well at the room in the evening. They also can dress for an evening party, for the acquisition of knowledge, not for the false dust-raising whirlwind of waltzing and ices. The register's desk is surrounded by a mass of men, who exchange books at the lending library. Is it Jack Sheppard, or Lady Blessington's last novel they enquire for. [sic] Alas! In Dublin we are behind in the world; at least, we poor members of the Mechanics' Institute cannot appreciate the poetry of disgusting vice.[16]

On literature in general, the *Citizen* favored the worthy over the salacious, especially in libraries meant for the working classes, though a long article that attacked *Bentley*'s serialization of *Jack Sheppard* spoiled its own moral somewhat by reproducing some of the best bits.

The emphasis in the journal on native Irish music appears to have come about as a result of an insulting attack on Irish composer Michael Balfe, whose operatic works were declared derivative by a reviewer who signed himself "Observator." The review was reprinted in the *Musical Library: Monthly Supplement* in 1836.[17] The first article on Irish music was therefore a furious counter-attack on the spurious allegations made about Balfe. Entitled "National Music and Musicians," the article ended with an explicit appeal to musicians to examine the native music of Ireland for inspiration. This project in the *Citizen* exhibited the contemporary zeal of Petrie and others like him to collect, classify, and ultimately revitalize Irish arts: "It is evident,—it lies upon the surface of the history of music,—that the more composers have

---

15. "Recollections of Derbyshire," 35–6.
16. "The Mechanics' Institute," 204.
17. A review of *The Siege of Rochelle* reads, "In short, Sir, I deny that Mr. Balfe has any right to be criticised as the composer of an original opera, *inasmuch as he has not only borrowed the subject of the drama of the Chiara de Rosenberg, but the musical ideas, from the overture to the finale*" (italics in original). "Review," 32.

consulted national music—the music of the people—the more have the beauties and attractions of their style been enhanced."[18] The articles on music and other topics in the *Citizen* are often used by scholars as evidence of a new pride in home-grown culture during the 1840s, and the fierce defense of the country in general by the Hudson brothers was picked up by Young Ireland in their own publications.[19] In other words, the *Citizen* is today seen primarily as a source of historical information; the beauty of its own format, along with details regarding its staff and connections, are still to be investigated.

Charles Lever and the *Dublin University Magazine* (1833–77)

There is now a considerable amount of information available about the *Dublin University Magazine* (Figure 15.1), starting with the long introduction in the *Wellesley Index* and continuing with fairly recent book-length studies of the journal. Though often attacked by the nationalist press, *Dublin University Magazine* never ceased to be regarded as an Irish production. It was published in Dublin for the vast majority of its thirty-three-year run, and its editors were invariably Irish. This section suggests ways in which the magazine, usually seen as one of the last bastions of Anglo-Irish conservative opinion in Irish culture, is nonetheless part of an intricate web that stretches across titles, formats, and political allegiance.

Charles Lever is often singled out as one of the more successful editors of the *Dublin University Magazine*, as circulation rose to about 4,000 copies per month during his tenure. His 1842 agreement with publisher James McGlashan stipulated that each monthly issue would include a serial from the editor, or more properly, from his alter-ego, Harry Lorrequer. In fact, it was this Harry Lorrequer who addressed the public in the magazine's first "editorial": "I shall endeavor to show, that while we of Ireland are the acknowledged staff of periodical literature in England, we are able, and, better still, are willing to unite, to obtain for our national journal, the same proud position in public estimation, that Scotsmen have won for their magazine before the eyes of Great Britain."[20] The idea that the *Dublin University Magazine* spoke for the nation, that its vision of Ireland and of the Irish character was universally held, had already been put to the test elsewhere in the press. In Charles Gavan Duffy's *Thomas Davis: The Memoirs of an Irish Patriot* (1890), Thomas Davis is quoted as saying that the magazine "was more habitually libellous of the Irish people than the *Times*."[21] Such comments were a serious blow to the reputation of the *Dublin University Magazine* in Ireland and were ultimately detrimental to Lever's fame. Lever held the position as editor until 1845, though attacks on him were frequent from 1841 on.

From March of 1840 to November of 1841, Lever's novel *Charles O'Malley* appeared in monthly installments in the *Dublin University Magazine*. The novel was also published in 1841 as a two-volume edition with steel engravings by H.K. Browne. At the same time, Lever's publisher, William Curry, offered the public a monthly stand-alone version using the same engravings as in the two-volume edition (two per part) but distinguished by a pink-colored,

---

18. "National Music and Musicians," 196.
19. See Vallely, *Companion to Irish Traditional Music*; and Deane, *Field Day Anthology*.
20. "Introduction," 423–4. The reference is to *Blackwood's Magazine*, the model for the *Dublin University Magazine*.
21. Quoted in Tilley, "Periodicals," 157.

Figure 15.1 Cover of *Dublin University Magazine* 36, no. 212 (August 1850).

wood-engraved paper cover, also designed by Browne. Lever was, of course, taking advantage of the sort of market saturation that Dickens had specialized in following the great success of *The Pickwick Papers*, and in fact Lever and Dickens were frequently paired in both the Irish and the English press. The employment of Browne would have underscored the popular conception of Lever as the Irish Dickens. Seeing these correspondences, the nationalist press was quick to complain (ironically echoing Lever's own views) that Ireland's best authors, poets, and actors were being appropriated by England. The organ of the Young Ireland movement, the *Nation*, had earlier placed Lever alongside Charles Robert Maturin, Maria Edgeworth, John Banim, and William Carleton, as national treasures. The *Dublin University Magazine*, despite its "very bad politics," was similarly declared by the *Nation* to be "equal to any, and superior to most, of the English periodicals of the same class."[22] Contemporary reviews of *Charles O'Malley* were generally positive in the English press. For example, *Fraser's Magazine*, with a certain amount of condescension, declared that Lever was the "best of the mere monthly writers, but no more."[23]

The initial serialization of *Charles O'Malley* in the *Dublin University Magazine* meant that the novel was beyond the reach of those unable to pay the 2s. 6d. for each monthly issue. The general editorial tone and conservative politics of the magazine also meant that it would be unlikely to penetrate much beyond the Anglo-Irish professional class in Dublin and general readers in England. However, at 1s. per monthly part, the part-issue version of the novel in pink wrappers took its place in the bookseller's window beside Dickens's green, Thackeray's jaundiced yellow, and Samuel Lover's rather garish orange issue covers; all were aimed at the same target audience.

As a stand-alone novel extracted from its original context in the *Dublin University Magazine*, *Charles O'Malley* (and other serials like it) no longer had to compete for readers' attention with the highbrow articles published in each issue of the magazine, and it no longer had to align itself with the magazine's conservative politics. By the same token, the satiric portrayal of Irishmen in the stand-alone edition of *Charles O'Malley* was divorced from its original publishing context, which might have formed a neutralizing buffer zone between author and outraged reader. For instance, the first part of *Charles O'Malley* as it appeared in the *Dublin University Magazine* was sandwiched between a biography of Swift (part of the magazine's "Illustrious Irishmen" series) and an article on the history of the celibacy statute at Trinity College Dublin. In contrast, the first part of *Charles O'Malley* as a stand-alone edition was introduced to the reader through Browne's cover illustration (see Figure 15.2). An examination of Browne's design and its reception in the nationalist press might help explain the decline in Lever's status in Ireland during the 1840s as well as the solidification of nationalist hostility to the *Dublin University Magazine*. The illustration thrusts itself before the viewer, forcing us to contemplate it before observing the text and therefore asserting its prominence in any subsequent combined discourse. As we look, just as we read, from left to right, the prospective buyer of *Charles O'Malley* would first see the figure of the ragged Irishman facing away from the viewer, identifiable by his pipe, hidden hands, large head, squat body, air of defiance, and broken hat (sprouting with what appear to be shamrocks). In short, he exemplifies the popular stereotype of the Irish idler. The figure's dominance of the scene includes authority over the paraphernalia of war: the flag, sword, gun, battle helmet, bugle, and two drums (one marked with what may or may not be an Irish harp). In the center is a child with facial features Browne habitually reserved for the working class. Freehand drawing, rather than letterpress, has been used for the text on the cover, and the text itself is obscured in two places by the illustration. The figure on the left and the whole tableau is focused on a pasted-up bill which is peeling off the wall. The lettering on this bill is fanciful, sloppy, carefree, fairly primitive, and somewhat anarchical,

---

22. "English Appropriation of Irish Intellect," 106.
23. Maginn, "Charles O'Malley and Jack Hinton," 449.

Figure 15.2 Paper issue cover of Charles Lever. *Charles O'Malley, the Irish Dragoon* (Dublin: William Curry, 1841).

as the letters spelling out "The Irish Dragoon" seem to resist confinement. Lever's pseudonym stands in place of his real name, making it seem as if no one takes responsibility for the novel. The note identifying the illustrator, on the other hand, appears almost exactly in the middle of the page, emphasizing his importance.

The plot of Lever's novel is rather convoluted, but one of its central strands focuses on the courageous behavior of O'Malley during the Peninsular War. The wood engraving, however, contradicts this plot line. If we agree with Maidment that "images do not represent reality, but are ideological formations 'shaped' by culture," Browne's depiction here of the "typical" Irishman gains extra importance.[24] The fairly crude wood engraving with an Irishman disrespectfully turning his back on the reader has more to do with an English attitude towards Ireland than it does with the plot of Lever's novel. To be fair, Lever had been voicing concerns about this sort of work from Browne as far back as 1839. In a letter to his publisher, James McGlashan, Lever wondered, "Has Phiz any notion of Irish physiognomy? For this is most important."[25] Lever had also complained that Browne had made the character of O'Malley look exactly like Nicholas Nickleby. But before we decide that the fault for misrepresentation lay entirely with Browne, we should note that Lever suggested Browne study the features of O'Connell's supporters in the Repeal Movement in order to improve his accuracy. As Lever said, "He can have nothing better, if not too coarse for his purpose."[26]

Such visual material acted as an advertisement and enticement but perhaps even more importantly as a form of genre coding: comedy or tragedy, domestic or exotic. For the domestic market, the stereotypical representation of the Irish was anachronistic and offensive. The presence of this figure on the cover of Lever's novel in the form of a wood engraving sent a clear signal to readers, especially an English audience. It certainly clashed with the tone of the *Dublin University Magazine* regarding all things Irish. And it clashed badly with the reforming, educational zeal of 1840s movements like Young Ireland, whose *Nation* newspaper had so recently praised Lever as part of a group of Irish notables.

Between June and September of 1843, Charles Gavan Duffy and William Carleton (a contributor to the *Dublin University Magazine*) denounced Lever as a hack, plagiarist, and stranger to Ireland and its culture. This attack unfolded in three articles published in the *Nation*, including a long piece in the June 10, 1843 issue that singled out Browne's engraving for criticism. Duffy noted that the novel itself contained

> not one national character in the entire series to which we have ever met a corresponding man or woman in real life; while the majority have exactly the same relation to the actual people among whom we live that the scarecrow, intended to represent an Irishman on the cover of *Charles O'Malley*, bears to a Meath or Tipperary peasant, as you find him at his labour or in his sports. The same spirit of exaggeration is at work everywhere, engrafted upon a monotony of character which argues,

---

24. Quoted in Thomas, *Pictorial Victorians*, 17.
25. Downey, *Charles Lever*, 110.
26. Ibid.

not merely a poverty of invention, but an utter ignorance of human nature. There is no anatomy—no contrast—no shade—no repose.... Having established these facts beyond dispute, perhaps there will be less difficulty hereafter in proving that he [Lever] is not the most competent person, morally or intellectually, to paint the national character of a people.[27]

Painting the national character accurately was, according to Young Ireland, the main purpose of the press in Ireland during the 1840s. Notions of Irishness, they contended, were constructed as much through reading domestic periodicals as they were through a generally hostile English press. It is tempting to see the crudity of Browne's work on the cover of *Charles O'Malley* as a result of his inexperience or perhaps simply the inexperience of his engraver.[28] This argument would explain the vehement reaction of the *Nation* to the wood engraving on aesthetic grounds. However, the ideological project of the Young Ireland movement demanded that their objections go beyond the aesthetic, forcibly drawing attention to Lever's false delineation of the Irish subject through new technologies of wood engraving, which provided a shortcut to the plot and characters in the serial.[29] The *Nation* had expended great energy trying to alter the popular conception of the Irish character by sponsoring reading rooms, publishing expository articles in the paper, and by issuing their own in-house publications designed to provide suitable reading material for a newly energized population. The last thing they wanted presented to a reading public, especially an English reading public, was another depiction of the fecklessness of the Irish, which seemed to be offered as truth by one of their "national treasures."

Lever's serial novel was certainly full of stereotypes, yet if it had remained in the pages of the *Dublin University Magazine* these depictions would have gone relatively unchallenged. It was the publication of the serial in stand-alone form with a prominent and offensive wood engraving on its cover that drew ire. It posed a vital threat when it was offered as an Irish export—a text that seemed aimed at instructing others about Ireland and its people. Clearly, members of the Young Ireland movement could not ignore the dialogue between text and image, which led them to completely reject a writer whose works they had held up as examples of Irish excellence just one year before.

The response to *Charles O'Malley* illustrates the collision of different publishing formats, as well as the collision of art and text, text and politics, fiction and truth. The recovery of such ephemera, studied in conjunction with the publishing format and editorial stance of the periodical to which it is allied, demonstrates the influence of modes of representation both on private reading experiences and the construction of public reputations. It is often claimed that W.B.Yeats and others overhauled the Irish canon at the end of the nineteenth century and that Lever was deliberately excluded in the process. Evidence derived from the periodical record

---

27. Duffy, "Mr. Lever's 'Irish' Novels," 554.
28. The engraver was Edward Evans not Edmund Evans, as is commonly assumed. Edmund Evans was only a teenager at the time.
29. The association of wood engraving with penny magazines, especially those sponsored by religious and philanthropic societies, was well established by this time.

and its offshoots suggests that the campaign to expel Lever began almost as early as his first published novel in 1839 and that his expulsion was virtually complete long before Yeats's time.

Source Material for the Study of Periodicals in Ireland

Book and periodical history as a discipline in Ireland is most often allied to university English and history departments. Scholars tend to approach periodicals (newspapers and journals) as a source of information in order to illuminate questions about politics or culture. The forms and functions of the periodicals themselves receive less critical attention, though this is changing. While detailed information about the history of Irish periodical publishing is often difficult to come by, there are nineteenth-century sources that provide a starting point for modern studies. For example, Richard Robert Madden (1798–1886) published *The History of Irish Periodical Literature, from the End of the Seventeenth-Century to the Middle of the Nineteenth-Century* in 1867. Madden originally intended to publish three volumes of his *History* but only two appeared, both of which dealt with Irish newspapers. The third volume was to have focused on the "History of Irish Magazines and Reviews, Periodical Essays, and Miscellanies of all kinds—Literary, Political, and Polemical."[30] Since this volume was never published, Madden's history ends with the *Freeman's Journal* around 1800. However, the notes that Madden intended to use in writing the third volume are held in various libraries in Dublin.[31]

Ten years after Madden's *History*, the *Irish Builder*, a long-running trade journal, began a twenty-two-part series (July 1877–June 1878) entitled initially "The Caxton Celebrations" and continued, after its first five parts, as "Notes on the Rise and Progress of Printing and Publishing in Ireland." Written by Christopher Clinton Hoey, the series offered a highly biased yet entertaining account of the trials and tribulations of famous Irish publishers and periodical editors from the beginning of printing in Ireland in 1551 to about 1860. Hoey had a poor estimation of the health of the industry during his own time, as is reflected in his argument that the literary trade declined rapidly after the 1848 rebellion.

Bibliography, broadly conceived, has a long history in Irish research. *The Irish Book Lover: A Monthly Review of Irish Literature and Bibliography* (1909–57) is one of the best sources for highly detailed information about printing and publishing in Ireland, both in Dublin and in other regions. No publishing firm, no matter how small or how short-lived, seemed to escape the notice of long-time editor J.S. Crone. Irish printers were equally well served as the *Irish Book Lover* dealt with typography (Roman as well as Irish-language type), publishing trends, and anecdotes about the eccentrics and success stories in Irish publishing. As the entire run of the *Irish Book Lover* has been digitized by the HathiTrust, it is easily available for research.

In 1987, Barbara Hayley, Enda McKay, and the Association of Irish Learned Journals published a collection of introductory essays on Irish language periodicals and little magazines, as well as Irish literary, historical, trade, and scientific magazines, with material stretching from

---

30. Madden, *History of Irish Periodical Literature*, 82.
31. There are Madden papers in the National Library of Ireland, Trinity College Library, the Royal Irish Academy, and Pearse Street Public Library (all in Dublin).

the eighteenth to the twentieth century. Its appearance should have sparked an explosion of published work on Irish titles, but very little research followed. Nevertheless, Hayley and McKay's book is still very important as a starting point for researchers in the field.[32] More recent studies of Irish periodicals include general histories and compilations of essays, many of them in collections edited by English scholars. A number of doctoral dissertations have focused on both periodical production and the influence of individual periodical titles on Irish politics and society. A healthy increase in the number of specialist conferences and publications is indicative of a resurgence of interest amongst Irish and other European scholars of the press; however, Irish periodicals are still being studied primarily as a repository of knowledge. There is much more work to be done on the function and dynamics of periodicals within the larger cultural history of Ireland.

32. Hayley and McKay, *Three Hundred Years*. See also Tilley's "Periodicals" for general historical background.

16

PROVINCIAL PERIODICALS

Andrew Hobbs

From the 1830s to the 1890s, the majority of English periodicals and newspapers were published outside of London. Sales figures for individual titles may have been lower than for their London counterparts, but from the early 1860s until the 1930s, the total sale of provincial publications was greater than for those emanating from London. When this more dispersed, less London-centric, media geography is acknowledged, it changes many aspects of current scholarship, not least the implicit cultural hierarchy that privileges a metropolitan minority over a provincial majority. We need to appreciate how provincial periodicals were qualitatively different in form and content from their metropolitan rivals. They catered to distinctive and complex local markets; represented places and people known personally to most readers; and appealed to readers' sense of place and local identities. Likewise, when remediating and republishing content from elsewhere, they used distinctively local selection criteria.

Why have provincial newspapers and periodicals received so little scholarly attention? One might argue that they were not produced or read by anyone of significance. If so, the scholarly decision to focus instead on the minority of periodicals produced and read by culturally and politically powerful individuals in London should always be explicit and explained. Another barrier may be what seem to be impenetrable local references. But this local context can be quickly acquired and more than repays the effort.

Paradoxically, provincial periodicals are more "national" than London publications, whilst capturing regional distinctiveness.[1] Using provincial publications as sources for almost any nineteenth-century topic, literary or historical, produces a genuinely national picture, often quite different from work based on narrowly metropolitan sources. Republished material can reveal a great deal about reader reception (for instance, the popularity of particular poets or poems). At one time or another, the provincial press was probably the most significant publisher, in terms of volume of material, for many literary and journalistic genres, including fiction, poetry, history, geography, and dialect literature.[2] Many local papers published original book reviews written by staff reporters; nearly all reprinted reviews and excerpts from

---

1. Hobbs, "When the Provincial Press"; Miller, "Problem with *Punch*."
2. For fiction, see Law, *Serializing Fiction*; for poetry, see Hobbs and Januszewski, "How Local Newspapers."

London periodicals. Simple mathematics means that most readers, particularly in the second half of the century, probably encountered this type of literary material via their local paper.

Definitions

"Provincial," "metropolitan," "local," "regional," and "national" are all distinct concepts. I use "provincial" in opposition to "metropolitan" to mean "published outside of London," rather than "narrow and uncultured."[3] A "local" publication reported on and was distributed within a small area, such as a town and its market area, or in a district of London; a "regional" paper or magazine might be based in a large city such as Manchester but would cover events and be sold across North West England. For most of the nineteenth century, London dailies such as *The Times* (1785–), *Telegraph* (1855–), or *Standard* (1827–) were regional publications, with most of their sales and content confined to the South-East of England.[4] The twenty-first-century term "national newspaper" (with significant sales across the country and containing news from around the nation) was virtually unknown in the nineteenth century and could be applied to very few titles, such as the *Northern Star* (1837–52, a provincial national paper) or the *Illustrated London News* (1842–1989).[5] While "provincial" and "metropolitan" are mutually exclusive, "local," "regional," and "national" are not; national culture and life are not synonymous with metropolitan culture. Equally, national culture can have local and regional variation.

The difficulties of defining "newspaper," "magazine," "journal," and "periodical" are more acute for provincial publications. Apart from morning papers, most provincial newspapers contained more magazine-style content than their London counterparts, while some provincial titles moved from one side of the magazine/newspaper divide to the other. Some small local papers began life as monthly magazines, shifting to weekly publication as readership grew.[6] Conversely, some provincial weekly news miscellanies changed their form and content rather than their frequency, transforming from newspapers to magazines towards the end of the century.[7] The distinction between newspapers and magazines has been maintained by digital publishers of nineteenth-century material, even when inappropriate and misleading.[8] Researchers must immerse themselves in the publications they study (digital, microfilm, or paper) to discern their form and content, rather than trusting digital metadata or other scholars' fleeting impressions.

This chapter deals mainly with newspapers, the dominant form of provincial periodical. Throughout the century, more newspaper titles were produced in the provinces while more magazine titles were produced in London (Figure 16.1). In 1800, there were twice as many provincial newspapers (approximately 100) as metropolitan papers (approximately 50), but there were five times more London magazines than provincial titles (roughly 150 to 30). By 1900,

---

3. See, for example, Matthew Arnold's use of the term "provincial" in "Literary Influence."
4. Brown, *Victorian News*, 255–7.
5. Hobbs, "When the Provincial Press."
6. Peters, *Politics, Publishing, and Personalities*, 20–1.
7. Law, *Serializing Fiction*.
8. Brake, "Half Full," 227.

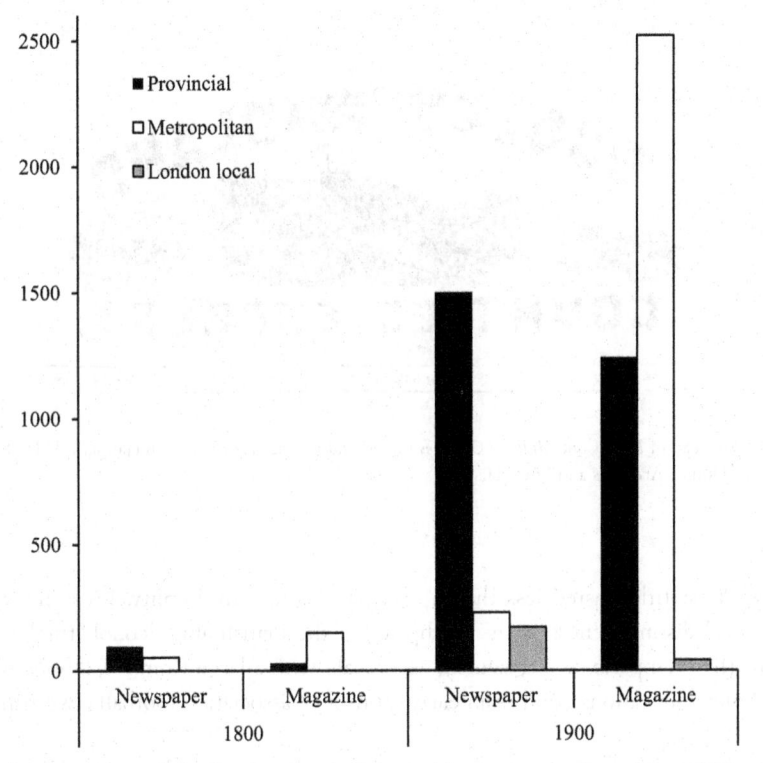

Figure 16.1 Approximate numbers of metropolitan and provincial newspapers and magazines, 1800 and 1900. *Source:* North, *Waterloo Directory* (1900 figures extrapolated from 10 percent sample).

the overall number of English publications had increased tenfold, with growth in titles mainly in the provinces. At century's end, there were three times more provincial than London newspapers (approximately 1,500 to 400, the latter figure including 170 local London titles such as the *Acton & Chiswick Gazette*, 1871–1939), and twice as many metropolitan magazines as provincial ones (2,500 to 1,200). These figures, taken from the *Waterloo Directory*, are underestimates.[9] Regardless, they show that London was by far the most important single publishing center, but the production of newspapers and (to a lesser extent) periodicals became increasingly decentered.

Characteristics of the Provincial Press

The rich profusion of provincial print is best conveyed by local case studies. For example, in Preston, Lancashire, at least fifty titles were published during the nineteenth century. This included four long-running weekly newspapers, some of which became bi-weeklies; three attempts at evening papers; a brief morning daily; and numerous weekly and monthly

---

9. My thanks to Professor John North for providing access to the *Waterloo Directory*.

Figure 16.2 Masthead of *Dudley and Midland Counties Express and Mining Gazette*, no. 16 (January 2, 1858). Courtesy of Dudley Archives and Local History Services.

magazines. Most titles lasted less than a year, and as for any locality, Preston's press conveyed its local distinctiveness as the birthplace of the British anti-alcohol "total abstinence" movement (five temperance magazines), as a locale with a large Roman Catholic population (four Catholic publications), and as an early sponsor of association football (two papers in the 1880s).

Place adds an extra dimension to our understanding of nineteenth-century life and culture, highlighting diversity and conveying the different mentalities and textures of life in each place. For example, the masthead of the *Dudley and Midland Counties Express and Mining Gazette* (1857–58) does what its metropolitan equivalent cannot: it segments its readership by place rather than class, gender, or special interest (Figure 16.2). Meanwhile, the three vignettes celebrate Dudley's distinctiveness, evoking pride in local history, symbolized by its ancient castle, and in its booming industries of mining and iron founding. In the rival *Dudley Weekly Times* (1856–58), a poem advertising Mence & Co.'s boots and shoes includes many local references:

> No wet will penetrate your sole
> From Brierley Hill to Bumble Hole.
>
> . . . .
>
> None can repent who spend their tin
> Next to the Old Malt Shovel Inn.
> This was the sign, but now, alas!
> They've drunk the ale and left the glass.
> A glazier bold the Inn has taken
> And cooked the Old Malt Shovel's bacon.[10]

---

10. Advertisement for Mence & Co, 8.

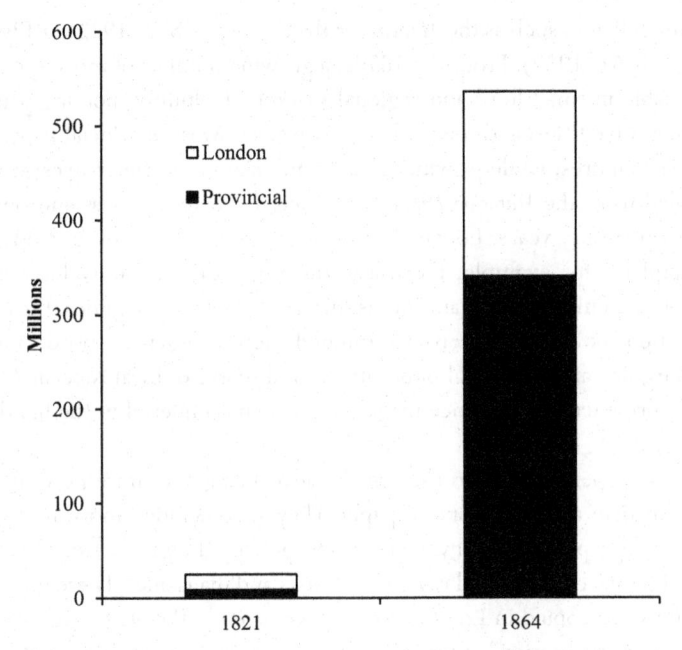

Figure 16.3 Metropolitan versus provincial annual newspaper sales, 1821 and 1864.
Source: Stamp Duty returns; Baines, *Extension*, 22.

Such references, which saturate every provincial publication, celebrate and elevate the ordinary, lending the prestige of print to places far from the centers of cultural power.

Cataloguing hundreds of provincial titles is only part of the story; we also need to quantify sales and readership. Total sales of London publications were far higher than sales of provincial titles until 1855 when the newspaper stamp duty became an optional postage charge rather than a compulsory tax. From then on, provincial newspapers took the lead. By 1864, they sold nearly twice as many copies as London papers, selling 340 million and 195 million copies per year, respectively (Figure 16.3). By contrast, metropolitan magazines generally sold more than provincial magazines throughout the century. From the 1870s, no provincial title could compete with the most successful London papers, such as the *Daily Telegraph* (which achieved a circulation of 241,000 in 1882), or Sunday papers like *Reynolds's* (1849–1967, which sold 300,000 or more copies per annum in the 1880s). However, the bigger provincial dailies overtook some London papers. In 1890, *The Times* and the *Manchester Guardian* (1821–) both sold 41,000 copies, while a dynamic evening paper like Middlesbrough's *North-Eastern Daily Gazette* (1859–) sold 61,000 in 1894, half as much again as *The Times*'s 38,000 circulation. Weekly provincial news miscellanies such as Sheffield's *Weekly Telegraph* (1884–1951) sold about 100,000 copies per issue.[11]

Provincial publications came in many forms. Newspaper genres included evening papers; traditional weekly newspapers; bi-weekly papers; morning dailies modeled on *The Times*; and

11. Berridge, "Popular Sunday Newspapers"; Hobbs, "Deleterious Dominance."

weekly news miscellanies such as the *Manchester Weekly Times* (1842–1922) or Plymouth's *Western Weekly News* (1861–1939). From the 1870s, a growing number of more specialist newspapers became viable in small local and regional markets, including sporting papers; socialist, labor, and cooperative titles; and regional Sunday papers. Most provincial papers were short-lived commercial failures, while provincial magazines had even briefer lives, with 30 percent of those sampled from the *Waterloo Directory* running for a year or less and only 20 percent lasting more than twenty years. Longer-lived titles were usually published outside the commercial marketplace; for example, the transactions of local or county learned societies or the publications of membership organizations such as temperance societies. Provincial publishers, like their metropolitan counterparts, imitated successful genres, producing literary and satiric magazines, unstamped radical publications, and scores of local *Notes and Queries*. Other genres, such as provincial temperance magazines (which numbered in the hundreds), had no metropolitan model.[12]

Provincial newspapers tended to carry more advertising and more news from across the United Kingdom than a typical London paper. They also included more non-news content: poetry, history, geography, biography, jokes, maps, gossipy "London letters," train timetables, travel writing, literary extracts, and reviews of books and magazines. These non-news features proliferated and were copied in London daily papers such as the *Daily Mail* (1896–), leading to the gradual "magazinification" of the newspaper towards the end of the century. From mid-century, the most dynamic provincial weeklies began to publish "literary supplements," an extra four or eight pages of magazine-style content. They also gave away full-page portraits, local views, and sheet almanacs.

Provincial newspapers and magazines were published in almost identical ways to metropolitan titles, with the crucial difference being that provincial publishing practices were tailored to smaller, less differentiated markets. Most provincial newspapers were weeklies. Bi-weekly papers were also common, while evening papers had multiple editions from mid-morning until early evening. All papers would issue special editions and/or temporarily accelerate their frequency (from weekly to daily, for example) during election campaigns, wartime, or other "newsy" periods. Before telegraphy, print times were influenced by the arrival time of mail coaches from London carrying the latest news. The telegraph enabled provincial papers to offer local readers more up-to-date news sooner than London papers. They often had complex and fluid publishing structures: titles combined, produced spin-offs, or varied their publishing practices in different parts of their circulation areas. The only digitization project to have addressed such complexities is the *Nineteenth-Century Serials Edition*; even digitized papers have their own "offline penumbra" of forgotten editions.[13]

Publishers with ambitions beyond their immediate market had two choices: move their operations to London (as did the *Northern Star* and *Tit-Bits*, 1881–1956) or stay put and produce variant titles or editions for each discrete geographical market. Some did both. For example, Andrew Carnegie and Samuel Storey created a syndicate of eighteen daily and weekly

---

12. Harrison, "World of Which."
13. Leary, "Googling the Victorians."

papers from 1881 to 1885. The successful *Catholic Herald* (1888–1947), located in London, likewise published dozens of locally named editions.[14] Watts, Knight, Cassell, and Eglington created a similar structure, printing whole pages of identical content from London on one side of the paper and then sending the pages to hundreds of printers around the country, who added local news and advertising on the other side of the sheets and gave the finished product a local name. This approach was copied by the Derby-based *Parish Magazine* (1859–1918), which left blank outer pages for local parishes to fill with local content—a model that quickly became the best-selling format for religious magazines.[15] All these practices created publications that were simultaneously national and local. They were also used on a smaller local/regional scale in newspaper chains and local editions.

Readerships

Publishers segmented readerships by class and gender but mainly by place. Textual clues such as advertisements, cover price, content (including readers' letters), and style of address reveal the "implied reader"; however, evidence of historical readers in correspondence, diaries, memoirs, sociological surveys, lists of titles taken in reading rooms, and even oral history reveal two important points.[16] First, reading aloud meant that illiteracy was no barrier to the consumption of print; second, any title reached a wider audience than those it directly addressed, as female or working-class readers and listeners "eavesdropped" on publications produced for middle-class men.[17]

The most common type of provincial publication, the general weekly newspaper, was, in the first half of the century, written for men of the middle and upper classes, with a minority of radical papers from the 1820s onwards targeting working-class readers, such as the *Manchester and Salford Advertiser* (1828–48). More working-class readers were catered for by unstamped papers in the 1830s and Chartist papers in the 1840s. The close alignment between political and denominational divisions produced an early segmentation of local markets along political and religious lines. As newspaper prices fell after the 1830s, particularly after 1855, these local weeklies began to treat working-class readers as "us" rather than "them." Before the growth of public newspaper-reading facilities, the local weekly was the only reading matter for many working-class consumers, another reason for its broad range of content.[18] The provincial morning papers of the 1850s onwards were aimed at a middle-class readership that was more likely to read widely, but new working-class publications such as the weekly news miscellany or the evening paper were still the only printed matter seen by many readers, particularly the semi-literate.[19] The news miscellanies were aimed equally at men and women, with some material for children.

---

14. Hendrick, *Life of Andrew Carngie*, 226–34; Wall, *Andrew Carnegie*, 430–41; Allen, "Catholic Herald."
15. Platt, "Sweet, Saintly, Christian Business?"
16. For advertising and implied readers, see Toplis, "Ready-Made Clothing Advertisements."
17. Hobbs, "Reading the Local Paper."
18. "Newspaper Literature."
19. Hobbs, "Reading the Local Paper," 193–4.

Theoretical Models

The provincial press is under-theorized. The stimulating work of Lee, Brown, Jones, and Law has not led to further theoretical speculation; instead, more recent newspaper history ignores local and regional serials or assumes they can fit into metropolitan models. Literature on provincial nineteenth-century magazines is virtually non-existent. Beetham, Powell, and Wyke have looked at some Manchester publications,[35] and Gunn and Jones have investigated urban satiric magazines of the 1870s.[36] Otherwise, research in this area is thin.

Many wider currents affected provincial periodicals, particularly changes in government attitudes to working-class reading, the related growth of literacy, and the more formalized organization of local political parties. Political movements such as the reform campaign of the 1830s, as well as Chartism and the anti-Corn Law movement in the 1840s, used the local press. Scores of social and cultural movements were reflected in serial print, especially the legitimized Roman Catholic Church and its opponents; the temperance movement from the 1840s; dialect literature from the 1850s; amateur science and history from mid-century; and association football from the 1880s. The introduction of elected local councils in 1835 (1855 in London) and the secret ballot in 1872 had an impact, as did urbanization, which created new local markets capable of supporting new publications. Also important were technological changes, such as the telegraph, cheaper paper, increasing automation of printing, and the growth of the railway network. Provincial newspapers benefited greatly from the nationalization of the telegraph companies in 1870. These larger forces are explored in the best scholarly literature, but new connections are waiting to be traced in the memoirs of publishers, journalists, and activists. Another approach would be to track individuals and their publications across disciplinary boundaries in secondary literature and primary sources.

Victorian Britain changed rapidly, but one constant was the desire of readers to see their own locale in print. Joyce believes place was more important than class as an identifier, and evidence from libraries, reading rooms, and other sources shows that local and regional newspapers were preferred by all but the elite in the second half of the century after prices fell.[37] Publishers responded to readers' sense of place and local patriotism with techniques that were similar in every part of the country, but which produced locally and regionally distinctive content.[38] The techniques could be as banal as including the town's name in the newspaper's title; reporting on the local council or cricket team; or publishing dialect poetry, local history, or the doings of a famous local son or daughter. The assumption that provincial publications are about place, while metropolitan ones are not, deserves to be challenged. It is also useful to consider whether there were placeless places or overshadowed places. Was the soil of certain *terroirs* tilled more, in Lancashire or Scotland, for example, than in the London suburbs?

A changeable mixture of economic and ideological motives drove the launch, acquisition, and continuation of provincial papers and magazines. In the early decades of the century, printers

---

35. Beetham, "*Ben Brierley's Journal*"; Powell and Wyke, "Manchester Men."
36. Gunn, *Public Culture*; Jones, "'Dart'and the Damning."
37. Joyce, *Visions of the People*; Hobbs, "Reading the Local Paper," chapter 9.
38. Hobbs, "Reading the Local Paper," chapters 6–7.

used weekly papers to support local patriotism; advocate for particular political and religious viewpoints; advertise London periodicals and patent medicines; promote their own printing and book publishing operations; and champion the belief that a local paper was essential civic infrastructure. There are examples of purely ideological and economic purposes, but most publications occupied a middle ground. Political publications such as Alaric Watts's Tory local papers of the 1820s and 1830s or the radical unstamped titles of the 1830s were subsidized by activists, but most hoped to break even or even make a profit. Pressure-group publications or those produced for members of societies, such as temperance magazines or scholarly transactions, were intended to promote a cause, unite a movement, or share learning, and thus were funded from charitable or membership subscriptions. Subsidies from political parties and campaign movements continued throughout the century.[39] It is harder to find examples from the other extreme—publications produced purely as a business. Even local "advertisers," the Victorian forerunner of the free newspaper, that became viable after the 1833 reduction in advertising duty, consisted mainly of advertising but also some original content demonstrating a commitment to literature or local culture.

The history of the professional provincial journalist has yet to be written, but is likely to challenge current narratives based on metropolitan evidence. Amateur contributors were more significant in provincial papers and magazines than in London publications; this included aspiring writers such as George Eliot, Branwell Brontë, William Makepeace Thackeray, and W.T. Stead. In provincial magazines, local contributors sometimes outnumbered readers. The final issue of the *Bolton Literary Journal and Weekly Miscellany of Entertaining and Useful Knowledge* (1830–31) found it "somewhat mortifying that while the Subscribers to the Journal have been diminishing, the Contributors have been gradually increasing."[40] Amateur journalists included poets, dialect writers, and district correspondents; scholars of history, geography or the sciences; experts in chess and draughts; or secretaries of local sports clubs, who submitted Saturday's scores and brief match reports. This porous aspect of the local paper makes it easily the largest nineteenth-century publishing platform for many kinds of amateur writing and challenges received ideas about authorship as professional identity rather than a pastime for all classes.

Primary Sources and Methodology

Quantitative methods are necessary to make accurate generalizations about the tens of thousands of provincial titles. Numbers of titles can be compiled from the *Waterloo Directory*, the British Library catalogue, and, after mid-century, from commercial sources such as *Mitchell's Newspaper Press Directory*. Sales and readership numbers are relatively straightforward for newspapers until 1855, thanks to government records of compulsory tax stamps purchased by each newspaper, now available digitally via the House of Commons Parliamentary Papers.[41]

---

39. For example, see Buckley, "Search."
40. Untitled, *Bolton Literary Journal*, 126.
41. Wiener's "Circulation and the Stamp Tax" provides a guide to this source and see above, Chapter 4, p. 66, note 27.

After 1855, there are no systematic sales or readership figures until 1931, so we must rely on unverifiable claims by publishers, counter-claims by rival publications, and more modest and reliable figures found in court proceedings, company histories of individual titles, or published commentary on the provincial press.

Original and microfilmed copies of thousands of provincial papers and magazines are preserved by local English libraries, the British Library, and major US research libraries, with growing numbers digitized in commercial databases and free-access services, such as the *Internet Archive*.

Nineteenth-century commentary on the provincial press was widespread in books, newspapers, and magazines (including specialist titles such as the *Printers' Register*). These can be found through searches of digitized texts, the British Library catalogue, indexes of individual publications, and Palmegiano's *Perceptions of the Press*. Publishers' archives are rare, but a few survive in record offices around the country (see the National Archives online catalogue).[42] Company histories and anniversary supplements of individual titles are valuable for researching an insider's view.

Online searching is invaluable, but browsing is still essential. For example, the unwritten rules of newspaper layout have changed, and only intimate knowledge of particular publications and publishing genres can tell us how important a particular article was thought to be or how editors expected readers to behave. In order to understand the time and place in which a publication was produced and what made it distinctive, scholars should avoid focusing on a specific title, assuming that it is typical of its genre. Individual issues of newspapers and periodicals are best understood through comparison with other titles published in the same town, or earlier and later issues of the same title. It is also useful to compare titles produced in other regions with different traditions, including those produced in London. Studying rival publications in any local market is useful, especially for naming personnel who are anonymous in the publication itself. Digital searches allow us to follow individuals between different titles. Biographical approaches to authorship are useful, but other methods, such as prosopography, are required to deal with hundreds of anonymous contributors. Scholars can quickly gain a sense of local context by reading local histories, relevant volumes of the *Victoria County History*, trade directories, and the publications themselves. They can discover how readers used the provincial press by collecting individual accounts of reading, and by counting quantitative sources such as lists of publications taken in libraries and reading rooms. Geographical methods can bring out the meaning of place and help researchers construct the national from the local. For example, they can use maps to track the movement of specific material, genres, or personnel; to identify radial patterns of core and periphery; or to discern more decentered networked structures (by employing network analysis).

Scholars have not made great strides in counting provincial periodicals, perhaps because it is time consuming. For example, it took a full day to compile the ten numbers in Figure 16.1. Yet content analysis, such as counting books advertised or reviewed in a selection of local papers, allows us to identify trends over time and to move beyond impressionistic assertions.

---

42. http://discovery.nationalarchives.gov.uk/.

But content analysis still requires the judgment of what to count.[43] Magazine launches per year emphasize change, while length of run emphasizes continuity. How should we express the figures we record? While parliamentary news increased in column inches in some late-century local papers, it decreased as a percentage of content when papers grew. Which titles should we analyze? Digitization obviates many difficult choices over representative or typical titles, enabling us to analyze everything digitally available. Where the "raw text" of digitized titles is available, it can be "mined" via corpus linguistics programs such as Wordsmith to identify and quantify choice of vocabulary, discourses, preoccupations, writing styles, or even author attributions. Finally, we must be clear about what is included and what is excluded in our counting: for example, stamp duty figures exclude most magazines. Skepticism and a nose for unconscious assumptions and unexamined defaults are essential. Cross-checking different types of sources strengthens scholarly conclusions. Journalists are skilled in telling a good story—but is the story true? Is it promoting a particular agenda?

There is scope for further work in almost every part of this field, but the priority is to develop a big-picture narrative that straddles current periodizations (particularly the 1836 and 1855 watersheds) and that acknowledges links between provincial and metropolitan publishing, and between newspapers, magazines, and books. Surprisingly, digitization of provincial titles has not changed the easy recourse to well-known metropolitan publications.[44] Insights from the spatial turn in history and from material culture may help (a thing has to be in a particular place, after all). Present concerns over the future of the provincial press may encourage more historical interest: for example, the study of towns without papers or the "bundling" of editorial and advertising.

We need an overview of provincial publishing economics. The commonest business trajectory, for example, seems to have comprised inadequate start-up capital, a short period of losses, followed by closure. We know something about provincial morning papers and weekly news miscellanies, but more work is needed on other publication types. Within each publication, there are scores of literary and journalistic genres to be studied, including advertising and illustration. Some of this material was local and original, but much was republished from elsewhere; this culture of reprinting deserves further study. The history of each genre is likely to be rewritten once the role of the provincial press has been incorporated—as is the history of New Journalism. The history of reading and the emotions has much to offer as well.

Two questions loom large. First, why did England, like Scotland, Ireland, and Wales, have such vibrant provincial newspapers in comparison with many other countries? Second, why were there so few successful provincial magazines? In answer to the latter question, we might speculate that perhaps the more hybrid provincial newspaper trespassed on magazine territory or that each local and regional market was smaller and less viable than the national market served by metropolitan magazines. This vast field offers marvelous opportunities. Its low status requires that future work be of a high standard to gain acceptance, but its relative neglect promises new insights and the toppling of many narratives and theories drawn from the minority of periodicals published in London.

43. Beetham, "Towards a Theory."
44. Hobbs, "Deleterious Dominance."

Section IV

TAXONOMIES

17

MARKETS, GENRES, ITERATIONS

Laurel Brake

The primary model of the nineteenth-century press was the daily, weekly, or bi-weekly newspaper which, by including news, was subject to special taxation from the early eighteenth century to 1861.[1] The newspaper was the media format against which other print formats, notably periodicals, were defined as "class" or "specialist" papers rather than as miscellanies that privileged news. Indeed, special-format publications of all sorts, including illustrated newspapers and comic papers, were normally identified as class publications and thus free from the obligation to pay stamp duty. The twelve chapters that follow examine periodicals and newspapers that attracted readers defined by content targeting particular gender, age, and interest groups. Given the limits of the franchise, it is no surprise that political news was usually gendered masculine, while many of the titles discussed below were more gender ambiguous or inclusive, focusing on religion, theater, science, sport, women, children, family, leisure, or professional performance. By way of introducing these chapters, I want to suggest that besides content there are three additional structural categories that characterize the organization of the press in general and "class" periodicals in particular: frequency, location, and price. These categories are just as essential to the definition of a periodical as the nature of their contents or target audience. First, it is necessary to think through the origins and consequences of the division of the field of nineteenth-century media history into the categories "periodical" and "newspaper" before considering the implications of emphasizing alternative categories—frequency, price, and geography—and why we should also consider periodicals and newspapers as remediated iterations.

Periodical versus Newspaper

The contents-oriented taxonomy distinguishing newspapers from class journals—as stamped and unstamped publications, respectively—was just one of a number of competing models for the press during the nineteenth century. When *Mitchell's*, the first sustained annual newspaper

---

1. However, throughout the nineteenth century, it was unclear which papers were subject to taxation. Definitions were contested by editors, and the government unevenly applied criteria for the tax status of individual titles, a practice exposed by those campaigning for repeal. For discussion of these campaigning tactics, see Hewitt, *Dawn of the Cheap Press*, 48–58.

(1817–1980) and *Fraser's Magazine* (1830–82), contributed regularly to a range of papers, including, over time, the *Representative* (1826), the *Standard* (1827–), the *Age* (1825–43), *John Bull* (1820–92), the *Telescope* (1824–26), and the *Literary Chronicle and Weekly Review* (1819–28).[7] Several large nineteenth-century firms, such as Chambers, Cassell's, Constable, Bradbury and Evans, Lloyd's, and Harmsworth, maintained hybrid publishing lists, which included various combinations of books, newspapers, magazines, prints, and cheap serials. Newspapers routinely used copy from other newspapers, in addition to cutting and pasting content from periodicals, such as fiction, poetry, gossip, feature articles, opinion pieces, book reviews, and political cartoons. Newspapers also included original material in reviews and articles in their arts pages, which echoed weekly magazines such as the *Literary Examiner* (1823) or *Literary Gazette* (1817–63). In 1865, one evening daily, the *Pall Mall Gazette* (1865–1923), stated in a manifesto its intention to combine aspects of magazines, reviews, and the morning press.

Correspondingly, many nineteenth-century periodicals, especially the weeklies, incorporated the sort of time-sensitive content usually associated with the newspaper press. *Punch* (1841–2002), for example, closely followed the weekly news of the daily press in its verbal and visual satire. Weeklies such as the *Leader* (1850–60), *Saturday Review* (1855–1938), and *Spectator* (1828–), which were registered with the Inland Revenue as newspapers, were hybrids incorporating features of both newspapers and magazines, with front and back halves dedicated to politics and the arts, respectively. The news-inflected commentary and analysis of these weeklies closely resembled the extended leader sections in a daily or Sunday newspapers. Weeklies brought together two different generic ancestries. Unlike inclusive, miscellaneous newspapers, which easily accommodated diverse departments, cheek by jowl, the self-alienated weeklies exposed their binary wounds in an unaccommodating split. Writers such as Fitzjames Stephen were habitually employed to bind up this disparate content by writing "middles"—non-political leaders, situated between the political leaders and the book reviews.[8] In short, newspapers and periodicals shared contributors, modes of writing, connections to the print industry, and distribution and communication networks. Their foregrounding of news, whether political or cultural, demonstrates their shared emphasis on the topical and the new. They were also linked by their periodicity, incorporation of serial narrative, mutual dependence on advertising, and competition for readers. They were part of the same cultural industry.

Frequency, Price, Geography

Periodical genres and markets are best understood in relation to frequency, price, and geography, all of which delimit contents and contribute substantially to meaning. Methodologically, this approach reflects a tendency in periodicals research to focus on periodicals themselves rather than exclusively on their editorial content. In addition, it demonstrates the importance of expanding our understanding of content to comprise paratext and metadata. In other words, it draws attention to the kind of periodical in which text appears, including its

---

7. See Latané, *William Maginn*.
8. See Rodensky, "Middles," 411–12.

frequency, politics, price, and location of production and distribution, as well as its material culture (dimensions, paper, design, illustrations, and graphics). It also pays attention to the length, position, and function of any article in the journal and whether it is signed or anonymous. Finally, it studies the format in which the journal is currently accessed in relation to its other formats, past or present.

These factors contribute not only to the detailed meanings of a journal's editorial content but also, more generically, to the range and type of material it could select. That the content of periodicals was often standardized according to genre tends to conceal editorial decisions about what might be selected or excluded from each issue. Such decisions would have been particularly invisible to partisan, enthusiast, or otherwise "interested" readers who shared the same political, leisure, or religious interests as the journal they were reading. The type or prominence of fiction published in a magazine was determined by its periodical genre. For example, the early numbers of *Macmillan's Magazine* (1859–1907) included a serial installment of fiction as the lead item in each monthly issue. By 1859, readers were accustomed to the monthly issue of fiction in both magazines and standalone parts. In the previous generation of the press, the absence of serial fiction in the first crop of nineteenth-century reviews—the *Edinburgh Review* (1802–1929), the *Quarterly Review* (1809–1967), and the *Westminster Review* (1824–1914)—was determined by their quarterly frequency as well as by their ostensible emphasis on reviewing. The presence of fiction in the less weighty, more popular magazines of the same period, such as the *New Monthly Magazine* (1814–84) and *Blackwood's Edinburgh Magazine*, is determined by their monthly publication schedule as much as their "magazine" format.

Early *Macmillan's* serials were usually written by authors whose beliefs mirrored the Christian Socialist ideology of its publisher, a background that was often invisible or unremarked upon. For example, Tom Hughes, whose *Tom Brown at Oxford* was serialized in *Macmillan's Magazine* from 1859 to 1860, was already a successful Macmillan author and a member of the firm's social circle.[9] Hughes's affiliations were available to some readers through personal knowledge, and they and others of a Christian Socialist persuasion might have taken for granted Hughes's presence in the first numbers of the new journal, but for most readers then and now this reason for the selection of Hughes's fiction would have been invisible.

For twenty-first-century researchers, the collective identity of any given periodical can be understood by studying its inclusion or exclusion of particular content as well as its publication format. For example, contemporary readers expected to encounter advertisements as part of the information content of successive issues. However, for latter-day readers, the absence of advertisements (excluded by publishers or binders) in retrospectively bound volumes of periodical issues, whether consulted in print or digital form, might be invisible. This invisibility is in part due to the characteristics of the format. At the time of publication, monthly publications carried timely information to consumers in their adverts; in annual bound reprints destined for the library (and in later retrospective readings), the adverts lost their sales function. Publishers saved money on paper, binding, and shipping by excluding them, and the libraries saved space in storing them without the bulk of extra pages.

---

9. Macmillan's had published Hughes's *Tom Brown's Schooldays* two years earlier.

Genres of nineteenth-century periodicals, then, are closely related to their frequency, just as frequency is related to price and price to market niche. That is, weekly periodicals have affinities with daily newspapers, which shape their content, price, and market niche. However, weeklies could charge more per issue than dailies because readers' expenditure was less frequent; they reflected, reviewed and commented rather than broke the news. Their complex niche assumed a largely news-oriented readership but consisted of more than one type of reader: those with little disposable income, such as many readers of the *News of the World* (1843–2011) or the *Workman's Times* (1890–94), who could not afford a daily paper; those who read dailies but valued the opinion, reviews, and reflections on the news provided by periodicals such as the *Examiner* (1808–81), the *Spectator* (1828–), and the *Saturday Review;* and those readers who followed or participated in campaigns, trades, or professions by reading weeklies such as the *Clarion* (1891–1934), *Northern Star,* [*Church*] *Guardian* (1845–1951), *Methodist Times* (1885–1932), *War Cry* (1879–), *Circular to Bankers* (1828–60), or *Builder* (1843–1966). For readers in this last group, weekly periodicals kept supporters up to date with developments and reinforced bonds. Similarly, the *London: the Conservative Weekly Journal of Politics, Finance, Society and the Arts* (1877-79) probably existed primarily to support its fledging group of literary conservative writers (including Andrew Lang, W.E. Henley, and R.L. Stevenson). Another large cluster of weeklies that primarily offered entertainment, such as humor, fiction, poetry, gossip, serial fiction, general interest articles, and answers to correspondents, often infused with the idea of self-improvement. This included titles such as *Cassell's Illustrated Family Paper* (1853–67; *Cassell's Magazine* to 1932), *Chambers's Journal* (1832–1956), the *Family Herald* (1842–1940), *Household Words* (1850–59), *All the Year Round* (1859–95), the *Illustrated London News* (1842–89), the *London Journal* (1845–1928), *Punch*, *Queen* (1861–1967), *Tit-Bits* (1881–1984), and *Truth* (1877–1957).

Monthlies, while topical, were less tied to news and freer in their choice of material since they had events of the entire month to ruminate and draw upon. Like newspapers, they tended to be miscellaneous in their content, even while serving the special interests of niche markets of readers. Unlike newspapers, which were often founded by printers, monthly magazines were usually affiliated with book publishers, whose works they reviewed, advertised, and serialized. Moreover, their stock format—the leisurely article, essay, or installment—replaced the shorter pieces in newspapers and weeklies, as warranted by their limited pagination and news agenda. Monthly magazines were therefore generally more literary than weeklies, even in cases where their orientation was religious, like the *Monthly Repository* (1806–37); campaigning, like the *Dublin University Magazine* (1833–80); or focused on a niche market, like the *Englishwoman's Domestic Magazine* (1852–79). Some made literary content their primary focus. From early in the century, titles such as Henry Colburn's *New Monthly Magazine* included poetry, short fiction, and, eventually, novels in installments. Monthlies were lengthy, assumed a longer period of consumption by readers, and thus generally cost more per issue than weeklies.

Weeklies required less outlay of cash and fit well with the social and economic rhythm of weekly wages and Sunday leisure. On the whole, monthlies attracted a better-paid demographic than the cheaper papers. The physical bulk of monthlies as well as the disposable cash of their readers attracted advertisers and adverts. This package of longer text, including original writing, reviews of recent books, and current advertisements, warranted circulation to readers abroad, who looked forward to "keeping up" at monthly intervals. Notably, a number of cheap weeklies—such as the *London Journal*, *Household Words*, and *All the Year Round*—were also issued in monthly editions with specially created advertising wrappers targeted at middle-class readers, both at home and abroad.

Sub-genres of weeklies and monthlies varied over time, and consequently, the character of magazines varied throughout the century and accrued shifting degrees of cultural status. In 1820, quarterlies took precedence over magazines for the educated reader, but by 1860 monthly magazines were the prevailing medium. Whilst weeklies for the middle classes were newly invigorated by the establishment of the *Spectator* and the *Athenaeum* in 1828, cheaper popular weeklies for working-class readers appeared across a wider period, from the 1820s through the 1840s. Examples include *Chambers's Edinburgh Journal* and the *Penny Magazine* (1832–45). Such a transformation of the media map over time reflects changes in distribution, education, advertising, taxation, styles of journalism, definitions of acceptable contents, ranges of markets, and printing and communication technology. Scholars need to be alert, then, to the dynamic character of the press and the specific characteristics of a title in a given time period. *Punch* of 1845 is quite distinct from *Punch* in the 1860s since changes in staffing, competition, and journalistic markets required adjustment and advancement.

The nexus between format and time in periodicals is evident if we look at the press of our own day. Readers of daily newspapers expect the content to be timely, even more so in digital formats than print; consumers want the "latest" on a number of fronts, including current events and parliamentary, court, sport, entertainment, business, and international news. That is, an up-to-date miscellany is required, along with editorials, reader correspondence, familiar columnists, weather reports, and broadcast media schedules. The timeliness of digital and print journalism is also expressed through photographs and advertising—a sale scheduled for tomorrow or a new book, gig, or film. Likewise, the contents of print weeklies are geared to the day of the week on which they are published. Published on the weekend, the *Spectator* and *New Statesman* take stock of the week's events in political pages at the front of each issue and the arts in their back pages. The weekly *Economist* and *New Yorker* offer ambitious analysis and independent investigation from a privileged perspective enabled by distance in time from the events described. Specialized popular magazines, such as *Sports Illustrated*, *Private Eye*, or *Vogue* publish contents closely related to their frequency—weekly, fortnightly, and monthly.

The nexus between genre and frequency invisibly determines what kind of content periodicals and newspapers include and how this is inflected by editorial interests. Frequency is one of the important factors in determining the market for press commodities. In our own time, when the purchase of daily print newspapers is diminishing, we are witness to the slow disappearance of printed paper as a medium for news but also to a rapid escalation in the frequency of updates: a daily publication cycle is no longer fast enough. As consumers, we can easily distinguish between the miscellany offered by the daily printed paper, which sifts and analyzes news most readers already know from the radio or the web, and the digital website of the "same" title, updated irregularly throughout the day and night with news, often raw as it comes in. Price may also be hastening the demise of print news. At present, news on the web is either free or comparatively cheap, even though both print and digital versions are accompanied by a significant amount of advertising copy, which in both cases is overwhelmingly the main source of income. Problematically for both formats, the amount of advertising is directly linked to circulation, as measured by sales or clicks. Print, which still largely charges for sales, is likely to lose circulation, and thus advertisers, to free or cheap web news. Lacking a cover price but similarly requiring high circulation, it is forced to fund itself entirely through direct advertising or by collecting information from its readers to sell or use to foster sales of other products.[10] A comparison between print and digital news in terms of consumption and format reveals the importance of price, frequency, market, readership, and geographic location in determining content.

In the nineteenth century, the frequency of news (the news cycle) and the comparative costs of newspapers and periodicals were also important. Frequency of publication with attendant costs was attached to consumption patterns based on class and gender. For at least half of the nineteenth century, until the advent of cheap penny and ha'penny papers in 1855–61, daily papers were not the usual format for working-class readers, who favored weeklies that fit into patterns of weekly pay and leisure. Thus, newspapers targeted at the working classes were often Sunday titles, such as the *Northern Star*, *Reynolds's Newspaper* (1850–1967) or *Lloyd's Weekly* (1842–1931). From the 1840s, working-class men read fiction in the *London Journal*, a popular illustrated penny weekly.[11] Dailies and monthlies tended to attract middle- and upper-class readers who could spend more for a single purchase regularly and whose reading patterns benefited from leisure spread over the week. Magazines were more geared to women than the dailies were; as fiction increasingly appeared in a new generation of monthlies after 1860, middle-class women readers became a more important segment of their target readership. Quarterlies, published less frequently than magazines, were notable for their longer articles and weightier contents. Because they were politically affiliated and expensive, they tended to attract middle- and upper-class male readers of their respective parties: Tory (*Quarterly Review*), Whig (*Edinburgh Review*), and Radical (*Westminster Review*).

Before the repeal of the taxes on print, the regional press was most often weekly. Even after 1861, weekly regional papers published a combination of parliamentary, domestic, foreign policy, law court and "police" news, along with railway and coach timetables, market prices, sport updates, correspondence, and church, parish, regional, and local news. In keeping with the metropolitan weeklies and Sunday papers, they also offered entertainment: stories, tales, jokes, gossip, or light commentary from a local columnist. For local readers, one of the most valuable elements of these papers was their adverts, which promoted all manner of local services, jobs, and events, and functioned both as news and commerce. Local papers in the London boroughs assumed a similar profile.

Of course, regional and local titles carried generic national adverts as well. Like all print media, they relied on advertising as well as their cover price to stay solvent, but even the adverts in metropolitan titles, which had a higher proportion of generic advertising, highlighted their geographical specificity in the publication of local personal, theater, and job notices. Likewise, the local affiliations of London titles were demonstrated by their participation in the

---

10. News organizations foster a symbiotic financial relation between their print and web editions by devising advertising packages that include paper as well as digital publication.
11. King, *London Journal*, 176–88.

infrastructure of the London print industry. Monthly magazines and high-culture weeklies, such as the *Saturday Review*, *Spectator*, and *Athenaeum*, were largely London based, and this was reflected in their advertising pages, which promoted metropolitan monthlies and new books published by London publishers on a monthly basis. The common locale and physical proximity of London periodicals and newspapers figured in the monthly distribution process. On "magazine day" at the end of each month, specially hired "bag men" collected the monthly crop of magazines, books, and part-issues for news agents, who then shipped the monthly orders to clients outside London and abroad.[12] Despite the national or worldwide distribution of these monthly and weekly titles, their local identity and production base were marked by their adverts and imprints.

As noted above, newspaper press directories deployed geography along with frequency as primary organizational categories. This structure was derived from the advertising industry. Mitchell's newspaper directory was a branch of his advertising business; most of his clients were business owners who wanted to advertise in the local press. While some academic studies of the local and regional press take note of locale, few have paid attention to locality in the metropolitan (London) press, a large category of print during the nineteenth century. Our failure to map historic titles geographically may be exacerbated by our use of digital interfaces, which obscure the geographic and bibliographic origins of print.

Remediation Then and Now

So far, my discussion has focused on the frequency—daily, weekly, monthly, or quarterly—associated with the publication of individual issues of periodicals and newspapers. However, the individual issue is only the first of a number of formats and frequencies in the commercial life of a periodical. "Remediation" is the term to describe the migration of a title from one format or medium to another.[13] The afterlives of a single issue vary according to the frequency of the periodical or newspaper. Nineteenth-century dailies and weeklies were often published in multiple editions, all carrying the same date on the masthead but varying in time of publication—for dailies, the time of day and for weeklies, the day of the week. Thus, the earliest edition of dailies and weeklies, sometimes called the "country" edition, was published first so as to be loaded on trains and distributed to readers across the country by the date on the masthead. This allowed for maximum sale of metropolitan papers at provincial destinations, where they were in competition with local papers. These early editions were forced to omit certain information, such as the latest news or stock market prices. Indeed, the "country" editions of weeklies sometimes even reprinted information from the previous week's later editions as news for their weekly country readers.

Some daily newspapers published weekly editions that were digests of the previous week's issues. Weeklies were often gathered into monthly aggregations, sometimes accruing fresh adverts, frontispiece illustrations, paper covers, and tables of contents in the process. Both of

---

12. See Brake, "Magazine Day," 390.
13. See Bolter and Grusin, *Remediation*.

Charles Dickens's weeklies, *Household Words* and *All the Year Round*, followed the pattern of gathering weekly issues into monthly numbers. Where weeklies were often too slight to be sent abroad, monthly aggregations of issues were heftier and could attract foreign or colonial readers and advertisers. Likewise, these compilations attracted middle-class readers and advertisements catering to their needs. Monthlies and quarterlies were often reissued in half-yearly volumes with hard covers for personal, private, and public libraries, while some dailies appeared in bound volumes at monthly or semi-monthly intervals. Publishers offered readers a choice of bindings from cheaper to more expensive designs, creating attractive volumes to tempt collectors and libraries. Many publishers also sold boards for readers to bind their own copies. In addition to reissuing periodicals over the course of a year as a series of products, publishers also produced annual aggregations of periodical issues in volumes, usually called "library editions." However, such series of reprints of their journals in various formats were not the only products publishers generated: popular articles were often reprinted for sale as standalone pamphlets, and complete issues were sometimes reprinted and sold (for example, the *Illustrated London News* guides to the Great Exhibition). Illustrations from issues were also reprinted in order to boost publishers' income. Occasionally, whole runs of periodicals were reprinted after a new series had commenced, as was the case with *Chambers's Journal* and the *Westminster Review*. New series were undertaken to mark a significant change—of editor, format, size, or policy—and to rebrand the periodical with added or revised features.

This process of iteration continues into our own time. Most modern readers encounter nineteenth-century periodicals in digital editions. Although only a small fraction of the estimated total of 50,000 nineteenth-century periodicals and newspapers has been digitized, readers usually focus disproportionately on titles available online due to ease of access. Digitization, more amply explored in Chapter 1 of this volume, constitutes yet another form of remediation, created and distributed by publishers of our own time according to prevailing publishing conventions. Single issues rarely figure in these digital archives; instead, publishers release whole runs of titles reproduced from bound volumes which are most often sold to institutions, such as libraries, rather than to individual readers. New reading practices, such as keyword searching, are facilitated by digital archives, which offer a user interface that is distinctly different from the table of contents and index associated with print. The practice of turning the pages of a codex is transformed into the process of browsing digitized pages. Although it sometimes requires considerable effort, researchers working with online databases may read single periodical issues from cover to cover and may read articles in relation to one another so as to discern the structure of individual issues.

Many other characteristics of periodicals and newspapers may not be readily discernible via online interfaces. Covers, adverts, dimensions, and prices (which change regularly) may all be missing from digitized versions of periodicals and newspapers—as was also the case for old microfilm copies. Pages may be missing as well, so researchers are advised to study multiple copies of a single newspaper or periodical, if possible, and to compare digital copies with print and other digital versions to uncover the partialities and particularities of any single copy to which they initially have access. In the first stages of research on the press, researchers should also consult key reference works. The most recent phase of the *Waterloo Directory*, edited by John North and his team, is available digitally and in print. This guide provides basic information on individual titles and a unique cumulative outline of the immense scope of the nineteenth-century British press. Richard Altick's *The English Common Reader* offers a narrative synoptic overview that is helpful at the early stages of a research project. *The Dictionary of Nineteenth-Century Journalism* comprises short, accessible entries by experts that pinpoint useful sources for further research. One of its most valuable characteristics is that it covers the press as a whole, providing entries on journal titles, journalists, editors, publishers, printers, illustrators, and topics central to the field.

The diversity and size of the nineteenth-century press are such that there are many avenues for future research. Whole categories of the press—such as the trade press or professional titles associated with a single trade or profession, such as printing or law—are available for future research. Digitization has made it possible to compare titles in similar market niches or draw connections between weeklies, monthly magazines, and reviews across the century or the nation. Valuable studies focused on partial runs of single titles have appeared,[14] but digital access makes extended coverage of entire runs more manageable. While the women's press of the period has received serious attention,[15] it remains a rich area for future scholarship. The link between fiction and periodicals has similarly attracted significant scholarly attention,[16] but there is still ample scope for new research. By contrast, scholarly inquiry into the role of poetry in the press has only begun.[17] There has likewise been limited work on press illustration or article genres—travel narratives, leaders, reviews, or court reports. Future research will no doubt also explore the myriad roles writers assumed when working for newspapers and periodicals. Individual war correspondents such as W.H. Russell and Henry Nevinson have been singled out, but whole categories of contributors—for example, special correspondents, columnists, and leader writers—have received little attention. Nor has there been much work on the business or economic history of nineteenth-century publishers. We know very little about individual journalists, male or female. Recent studies of William Maginn, G.W.M. Reynolds, and Frances Power Cobbe provide good examples of how to proceed.[18]

Another potential area for future research is to focus on recovering the journalistic work of celebrities who were well-known novelists, poets, dramatists, or politicians. Recent books on George Eliot, Charles Dickens, Douglas Jerrold, and Oscar Wilde indicate the possibilities within this field of inquiry.[19] Digitization has opened up whole new areas of research,[20] and the large datasets associated with digital archives have suggested new methodologies that fall within the broad category of distant reading. National identity, as formulated through language, is

---

14. See, for example, Christie, *Edinburgh Review*; Demoor, *Their Fair Share*; Leary, *Punch Brotherhood*; and King, *London Journal*.
15. See, for example, Beetham, *Magazine of Her Own?*; Easley, *First-Person Anonymous*; Onslow, *Women of the Press*; and Peterson, *Becoming a Woman of Letters*.
16. See, for example, Turner, *Trollope and the Magazines*; Law and Patten, "Serial Revolution."
17. See, for example, Hughes, "What the *Wellesley Index* Left Out," and Ledbetter, *Tennyson and Victorian Periodicals*.
18. Latané, *William Maginn*; Humpherys and James, *G.W.M. Reynolds*; Mitchell, *Frances Power Cobbe*.
19. Dillane, *Before George Eliot*; Drew, *Dickens the Journalist*; Slater, *Douglas Jerrold*; Stokes and Turner, *Collected Works of Oscar Wilde*.
20. See, for example, Mussell, *Nineteenth-Century Press in the Digital Age*, and see above, Chapter 1.

perhaps the most powerful underlying framework of media research. Most media histories are national—British, American, French, Canadian, Australian, or German—but few monographs, with the exception of Wiener's recent book, have examined the porosity of media within the transatlantic press or the English-speaking world.[21] The European Society for Periodicals Research (ESPRit) is dedicated to studying the press in Europe. Using large databases, they examine newspapers and periodicals produced in different languages and nations that were unified by geography, technology, and the infrastructure of journalism. Like other disciplines, media history has its own history, objects of study, structures, and critical practices. Relatively new, it is still scoping the field and developing its own theory and methodology. Frequency, genre, and iterations are some basic structures for continued study.

---

21. Wiener, *Americanization of the British Press*.

18

MEN AND THE PERIODICAL PRESS

Stephanie Olsen

The nineteenth-century periodical press was a key medium in the articulation and negotiation of gender ideologies. This chapter examines the incorporation of specific "masculine" subject matter, audiences, and authorship within specialist periodical genres and features or subsets of general-interest periodicals.[1] Recent work on women and femininity in periodicals can also help to illuminate the ways in which men were gendered in the journalistic press. It should be borne in mind from the outset that the gendering of men was not a singular process but rather a competing series of narratives that defined individual identities in terms of age and class but also according to other attributes such as character, occupation, marital status, and urban or rural location. The scale, diversity, and rapid proliferation of the periodical press meant that it was an important part of a responsive and dynamic yet often uneven and contradictory process of gender definition.[2]

In recent years, the notion of gender in periodicals research has focused primarily on representations of femininity and on periodicals specifically directed to women. Research on masculinity in periodicals is still nascent. The idea that men were even subject to gender ideology is a fairly recent scholarly realization.[3] The focus on feminine gender in periodicals research has led to a historiographically narrow view that replicates the gender dichotomies within nineteenth-century discourse. Yet the challenge of isolating masculine identity in periodicals is daunting. Unlike periodicals for women, children, or specialized audiences, periodicals for men were not usually designated as such. In fact, if a periodical was not specifically addressed to a particular set of readers, it was assumed to be directed to men. An implicit male audience was targeted across the publishing spectrum, from periodicals of a general, political, or topical nature to those focused on fiction, non-fiction, or a mixture of both; from religious and "secular" (non-denominational or non-sectarian) titles to scientific, medical, and sporting periodicals; from periodicals for professionals to those designed especially for youth; and from those pertaining to upper-class urbanity to those aiming to reach the working man in the provinces.

---

1. The author wishes to thank Justin Bengry for help with queer periodicals, Alexandra Esche and Johanna Rocker for research assistance, and finally Rob Boddice for his useful suggestions.
2. For more on this cultural process in mid-Victorian England, see Poovey, *Uneven Developments*.
3. See, for example, Connell, *Masculinities*, and Tosh, "What Should Historians Do with Masculinity?"

As Margaret Beetham has observed, any given periodical "works by positioning its readers in a particular way."[4] Yet readership is difficult to determine. As I have argued elsewhere, periodicals for boys were sometimes read by men.[5] Even periodicals aimed specifically at women often discussed men, male issues, or male characters and thus may have been attractive to male readers. It is therefore important not to ascribe too much meaning to intended audiences but rather to focus on the often varied and sometimes contradictory content of periodicals. As we shall see, male writers and readers, and the periodicals they contributed to and read varied a great deal.

The goals of the periodical press were as varied as its subject matter: to inform, to entertain, to shape opinion, to foment change, to encourage continuity, or to cater to particular groups or viewpoints. Embedded in these goals, usually implicitly, were constructions of male gender norms, with a stress on conformity or change in national or regional contexts. What was meant, for example, by masculine strength? Was it physical, spiritual, political, stoical, or intellectual? Should a man's identity be associated with place, family, community, work, national or international concerns, intellectual pursuits or class politics? Using these varied lenses, what did it mean to be manly? The periodical press addressed these questions in numerous ways that cannot be explained merely along class or regional lines. For example, there is a regular feature on "Men and Manners" in the *Kaleidoscope or, Literary and Scientific Mirror* (1818–31) published by Egerton Smith (1774–1841), who also established the *Liverpool Mercury* in 1811. And the conservative *Scots Observer* (later the *National Observer*, 1888–97) published a series of articles on "Modern Men" dedicated to "great men," writers, and explorers. The Cardiff *Western Mail* (1869–) included articles titled "How to Make Men Soldiers," "Depression among Public Men," and "Manliness in Politics." The *North Wales Chronicle* (1827–) published an article titled "Professorial Manliness and Generosity," and the *Belfast News-Letter* (1737–) printed a piece titled "True Manliness." In addition, the long-running *Gentleman's Magazine* (1731–1922) provided readers with images of masculinity in articles on a wide range of topics, from commodity prices to poetry.[6]

Not only were representations of masculinities diverse and sometimes contradictory but masculine readership and authorship were also varied. The gendering of Victorian periodical authorship was far from static and stable.[7] Over the course of the nineteenth century, careers in journalism were increasingly accessible to women as well as to men of the lower classes. According to Fraser, Green, and Johnston, "This was a matter of some concern to those who preferred the idea of a more exclusive press."[8] They cite a critic of modern periodicals, blaming the "'reward of money' for having 'tended to reduce the public writer to the level of a tradesman.'"[9] Despite such resistance, writers increasingly came from varied backgrounds and embodied different kinds of masculinity. Authors who relied on writing for their livelihoods

---

4. Beetham, *A Magazine of Her Own?*, 12.
5. Olsen, *Juvenile Nation*, 30.
6. See, for example, "Remarks upon Various Subjects" and "Friendship. A Chapter for Youth."
7. See Fraser, Green, and Johnston, *Gender and the Victorian Periodical*, 6.
8. Ibid., 12.
9. Ibid.

offered different perspectives on work, the professions, sources of knowledge, and other aspects of manhood than those of the gentlemanly lay elite. The implied masculinity of journalistic discourse was also destabilized by the influx of women into the profession.[10] An important factor was the convention of anonymous publication in most periodicals until the 1860s, which allowed women to take on "masculine" subject matter. Of course, as Fraser, Green, and Johnston note, the convention of anonymity also masked masculine gender and "allowed men to enter female preserves, addressing subjects just as conventionally regarded as feminine, enabling a radical refusal of the limits of Victorian identity politics."[11] They further remind us that all members of the household had an impact on the development of the content of periodicals, complicating "relations between the so-called public sphere and the private domestic sphere."[12] While they argue that the periodical press was a "critical mediating agent," which offered a "liminal space between public and private domains," historians of masculinity have tended to question the distinction between public and private experience.[13] Masculinity—whether in an ideal or transgressive form—was never entirely public or private. Articles in the periodical press focused on men's roles in the family as sons, husbands, and fathers—their respective duties in the home and toward family members—just as they focused on more predictable topics like work and politics. Men's public and private roles were mutually constitutive in defining their gender identity.

Class-based Definitions of Masculinity

There were various class-based definitions of masculinity at work within the periodical press. Working-class periodicals such as the *Charter*,[14] *Northern Star*,[15] and *Poor Man's Guardian*[16] provided readers with models of proud, working-class masculinity that were distinct from definitions of middle-class manhood.[17] William Cobbett's weekly *Political Register* (1802–35), known for its radicalism and emphasis on parliamentary reform, was popular among working-class readers, particularly young bachelors, who were the subject of a dedicated column, "Advice to Young Men."[18] Socialist periodicals of various stripes, such as the *Clarion*, the *Labour Leader*, and the *Labour Prophet,* provided idealized examples of working-class masculinity. In the *Labour Prophet*, Robert Blatchford writes, "When you meet a *man* he will tell you to respect *everybody*; but he will also tell you to respect yourself. And he will tell you that unless you respect yourself you will never respect other people. You will only *fear* them. Which is a very different

---

10. See Easley, *First-Person Anonymous*, 1.
11. Fraser, Green, and Johnston, *Gender and the Victorian Periodical*, 17.
12. Ibid., 5.
13. Ibid.
14. See, for example, "To the Noblemen, Gentlemen, and Middlemen."
15. Examples include "Address of the Working Men's Association of Leith" and "To the Men Who Work," "Working Men, Support your Order!"
16. For example, see "To the Unrepresented Seven Millions."
17. For more on working-class masculinities, see Clark, *Struggle for the Breeches*.
18. See Fordham, "Reform, War and Taxes"; "Advice to Farmers, Dealers, and All Parents"; "To Young Men"; "Advice to Young Men"; and "To the Young Men of England."

thing."[19] This sort of instruction, common in the working-class periodical press, was meant to attract and cultivate readers of the "right" stripe.

Working-class newspapers often approached men as class-based political actors but also as heads of families and as intellectually curious readers. News items figured prominently, but they were certainly not gender neutral. According to Andrew King, news "was one of the major signifiers of the gender of the implied reader."[20] The Crimean War, he notes, "opened up the gender exclusivity of 'news.'"[21] Many periodicals published war reportage written from a masculine perspective designed to shape opinion.[22] This included extensive war coverage, embracing discussion of equipment, uniforms, battle strategies, and the politics of diplomacy.[23] Just as importantly, they provided men with models of martial masculinity.

Defining Masculine Identity

Some periodicals, whether lowbrow or highbrow, were more gender inclusive or changed their gendered target reader. For example, as King points out, the *London Journal* (1845–1928) started a "cheap domestic *men's* magazine" that had to manage its news in such a way as to avoid being classed as a publication that carried news. Twenty-five years later, it had metamorphosed into a "space where women feel at home."[24] Indeed, defining and gendering male identity in periodicals often depended on an understanding of their relation to, and distinction from, women. For highbrow periodicals, such gender distinctions were often most vividly and complexly defined in the mainstream literary reviews. For example, in "Men and Women," published in the *Fortnightly Review* (1865–1954), Maria Gray essentializes gender difference, writing, "Modesty belongs as much to a fine-natured youth as to his sister; but it is honoured in her, and laughed at in him, which accounts for the difference between them when they have respectively attained manhood and womanhood."[25] Yet she also depicts them as having some gender traits in common: "Tenderness and its outcome, pity, are as inseparable from true manliness as true womanliness."[26] And she acknowledges that "it is only by taking the average of both that the average man will be found superior to the average woman. If we come to individuals we find that a great many women are indefinitely superior to the average man, and that some women are superior to all but the supremely great men."[27] Working-class, middle-class, and elite periodicals all feature examples and descriptions of ideal men and their characters in diverse life situations.

---

19. Blatchford, "Good and Bad Boys," 65–6.
20. King, *London Journal*, 176.
21. Ibid.
22. See, for example, "War and Its Trophies," "Burdens Entailed on the People by War," "Preparations for War," "Shot-Proof Men-of-War," "Army Reform," and "War—Army Estimates."
23. Examples include "Navy; Its Want of Men," "Progress of the War," and "Bravery of British Troops."
24. King, *London Journal*, 176.
25. Grey, "Men and Women," 677.
26. Ibid., 678.
27. Ibid., 676.

Such disquisitions on male character were frequent but nowhere so much as in the juvenile periodical press. Some targeted a specifically male audience, for example Samuel Beeton's weekly *Boy's Own Magazine* (1855–90), which was one of the first and most often imitated periodicals for boys. These periodicals predated the publishing boom in juvenile periodicals, which included important titles like the successful *Boy's Own Paper* (1879–1967), published by the Religious Tract Society, and the more working-class Amalgamated Press papers, the *Boys' Friend* (1895–1927), *Boys' Herald* (1903–13), and *Boys' Realm* (1912–19).[28] Another magazine with a comparatively long life was *Chums* (1892–1934), published by Cassell and Co. All of these papers, even the commercially driven Amalgamated Press papers, contained moral messages for boys and young men focused on molding their character and conduct. Many were in fact also read by adult men (as well as by women and girls), as letters to the editor frequently attest.

Magazines for women of all classes also defined masculinity in complex terms.[29] In 1818, the *New British Lady's Magazine or Monthly Mirror of Literature and Fashion* published an article titled "Distinction of the Male and Female Character," arguing that women are "tender and weak" and need the support of strong men who have "their heads and their hearts more occupied."[30] Given that men most likely read these articles, they were perhaps equally influenced by the advice provided. Magazines aimed at a more popular audience also defined women in relationship to men.

Men frequently read family magazines, sometimes out loud. As the frontispiece of the *Leisure Hour* suggests, this was promoted as a desirable way to spend time with and instruct wives and children (Figure 18.1).[31] From the 1860s onward, family magazines like the *Leisure Hour*, *Sunday at Home*, *All the Year Round*, and *Cassell's Family Magazine* catered to male readers by publishing "stories of adventure and bravado and . . . scientific news."[32] Yet men most likely read the "feminine" content of these periodicals as well. While there were no popular religious magazines for men only, these "family-centred improving magazines," according to Callum Brown, were also "truly exploratory of male religiosity, for it was in men's relations to the family that the key to issues of their piety and impiety lay."[33] Articles in family newspapers tied manliness to Christian faith and piety. In an article published in the *Liverpool Mercury*, for example, the Reverend John Diggle argued that "godliness is the true seed of manliness, and manliness the natural fruit of godliness."[34] Manliness for a large segment of the religious and even the "secular" press was intertwined with Christian piety and moral conduct.

Other periodicals focused not only on the spirit but on the body and on sport. Sporting periodicals can be viewed as the most obviously "masculine" publications of the nineteenth

---

28. Boyd, *Manliness and the Boys' Story Papers*, 70–1.
29. See, for example, "Men, Women and Gods"; Barrington, "What Are Men without the Vote?"; "Men and Males"; Gwynne, "How Men Protect the Interests of Women"; and "Is Courage an Attribute of Men Only?"
30. "Distinction of the Male and Female Character," 22–3.
31. For further discussion of this image, see Olsen, *Juvenile Nation*, 106.
32. Brown, *Death of Christian Britain*, 113.
33. Ibid.
34. "Godliness and Manliness," 7. See also "Christian Manliness," "Religious and Moral," and "On Humility."

Figure 18.1 Frontispiece to the *Leisure Hour* (1860), detail.

century.³⁵ In its early years, the *Sporting Magazine* (1792–1870) included detailed accounts of bull baiting and dog fights as well as extensive coverage of the aristocratic sport of cockfighting, which went hand in hand with the elite preoccupation with thoroughbred horse racing. As cockfighting and blood sports became vilified in the press, in Parliament, and in "polite" circles during the 1840s, they became associated with a "rough" masculinity that did not fit the new manly ideal. The *Sporting Magazine*, under the editorial control of Robert Surtees, changed its name from the *Sporting Magazine, or Monthly Calendar of the Turf, the Chase, and Every Other Diversion Interesting to the Man of Pleasure, Enterprize & Spirit* to simply the *Sporting Magazine*. It proclaimed that it had "thrown off . . . [its] old cover, and donned a new one—something more characteristic of the times, and to the exclusion . . . of one or two sports that have become antiquated."³⁶ As Rob Boddice argues, "The rhetoric of manliness and Englishness was to be reserved, from then on, only for unimpeachable fox hunters" at the expense of the "rougher" sort.³⁷ Moreover, the whole sporting press was consolidated, with the *Sporting Magazine* becoming identical, after 1846, to the *New Sporting Magazine*, the *Sportsman*, and the *Sporting Review*.

A central point of focus in periodicals and newspapers was the state of British manliness. How was "manly" behavior best defined? And how might boys and men be taught to model these behaviors? The periodical press answered these questions in multiple and sometimes contradictory ways. In 1869, the *Fortnightly Review* published a vigorous debate on manliness between novelist Anthony Trollope and noted historian Edward Augustus Freeman.³⁸ Freeman argued that

---

35. See, for example, Jorrocks, "Thoughts on Hunting"; Deccan, "Life in the Jungle"; Nimrod, "The Life of a Sportsman"; Watt, "Careless Sportsmen"; Ranger, "Life in the Woods"; A.H.B., "The Days of Duels"; and "Field Sports."
36. Quoted in Boddice, "Four Stages of Cruelty?," 194.
37. Ibid.
38. See Freeman, "Morality of Field Sports" and "Controversy on Field Sports"; Trollope, "Mr. Freeman on the Morality of Hunting."

field sports were unmanly, and Trollope responded by championing physical exercise, especially in the context of polite and conversational society, as an essential aspect of masculinity. The debate eventually sparked discussion in a broad array of periodicals and newspapers, including the *Pall Mall Gazette*, *Sporting Magazine*, *The Times*, and *Manchester Guardian*. It was also the subject of two illustrations in *Punch*.[39] Central to the controversy was Trollope's assertion of aristocratic privilege where manly pursuits were concerned (a subject which dominated the sporting press) along with his defense of this brand of manliness against critiques in respectable journals such as the *Fortnightly*, which he had himself helped to found. Freeman's intellectual assault on aristocratic faux manliness ended up as a debate about what kinds of manliness should be represented in the periodical press. Judging by the continuing prosperity of the hunting world and its associated publications, the idea of middle-class, middlebrow, intellectual manliness failed to gain much traction in the periodical press during the mid-Victorian era.

Professional Journals

Professional journals, representing the developing fields of medicine, law, business, and science, provided their own representations of competing masculinities. The *Economist* (1843–), and later the *Financial Times* (1888–), provided commercial, financial, and business news and helped to define men who practiced these professions and trades. They also provided a specialized view of current and international affairs. On November 5, 1870, the *Economist*, for example, described Lord Granville's intervention between France and Prussia as marked by "singular clearness, manliness and precision."[40] That an 1851 letter in the same paper on the value of protectionist relief for agricultural depression could also be referred to as "manly" attests to the intended audience of such a periodical and to the high value of such an epithet in public opinion.[41]

Nature (1869–) provided the general public, gentleman scientists, and "professional" men with a venue not only for scientific exploration but also for gender definition. Though promoting "Lectures to Ladies," it also conveyed opinions, couched in scientific terms, that encouraged the application of observations from the non-human animal world to men and women: "Males are frequently lithe, active, aggressive, gorgeously coloured and decorated. Females are often sluggish, vegetative, passive and soberly coloured."[42] This sort of scientific evidence could serve to preserve and enhance hierarchical gender distinctions. In "The Dulness of Science," for example, *Nature* also defines a hierarchy of men in an ascending scale toward those who understand the value of science. The author decries the "acquisition of gain" at the expense of the acquisition of knowledge.[43] It was not science that was dull but rather types of men—the

---

39. Boddice, "Manliness and the 'Morality of Field Sports.'" See also "Manliness of Speech."
40. "Armistice," 1337.
41. "Value of Protectionist Relief," 613.
42. "Lectures to Ladies," 45–6; P.C.M., "Evolution of Sex," 532.
43. F.R.S., "Dulness of Science," 43.

mentally blind man, the business man, the farmer, or the "affluent and the nobly-born" man who only studies classics.[44] The educated man of science must lead the way.

A similar definition of desirable masculinity through professional and scientific pursuits was communicated in the medical journal *Lancet* (1823–). According to Debbie Harrison, Thomas Wakley, founder and editor for thirty-nine years, "asserted a new and inclusive masculine authority that equated professional status with a self-disciplined and meritocratic vocation that was linked to clinical and scientific expertise rather than to class and wealth."[45] Indeed, she notes, "*The Lancet*'s masculinity was based on a heroic opposition" to that of the gentlemen of the elite and lucrative medical education establishment.[46] It provided verbatim notes of medical classes to those who could not afford to attend in person and defended the rights of working-class men, who were harmed or even killed by the medical establishment's incompetence.[47] Even after Wakley's death in 1862, the *Lancet* continued to provide medical men with a model of professional masculinity and a space to debate medical issues, particularly in the letters to the editor section. It also allowed them to take pride in their work and support the professionalization of medicine.[48]

The exclusively male legal profession attached much meaning to the manliness of both practitioners and the public who came into contact with the profession. The *Edinburgh Review* (1802–) and the *Quarterly Review* (1809–), for example, contained articles on legal topics read by specialists and the educated public, but increasingly practitioners turned to journals that were specifically directed at them and which helped to define the profession and its (male) members. The *Jurist*, founded in 1827, was one of the first professional legal journals to claim that its content was both scientific and designed to reach the public at large.[49] More prominent journals include the *Justice of the Peace* (1837–), the *Law Magazine or Quarterly Review of Jurisprudence* (1828–1915), and the preeminent journal for practitioners, the *Law Times* (1843–1965; continued as the *New Law Journal*). Clients and legal professionals were described as men of "honour, honesty, and truth" whose "manliness" was beyond question, regardless of whether they were on the same or opposing sides.[50] The *Solicitors' Journal* (1856–) had a "Birth, Marriages, and Deaths" section for members of the profession in which one solicitor's death was marked by a tribute to his qualities of the "rarest order," including his "manliness, geniality, courtesy and kindheartedness."[51] Three decades earlier, in 1860, the same publication, in an article titled "Judicial Statistics," decried the increase in violent crime by declaring that it made "us tremble for the ancient manliness of Englishmen, by whom it was held in abhorrence."[52]

---

44. Ibid., 43–4.
45. Harrison, "All the *Lancet*'s Men," 3.
46. Ibid., 16.
47. Ibid., 8.
48. See, for example, "Health of the British Navy," "On Materialism in Men of Science," and "Obligations of the General Medical Council."
49. For an overview of law periodicals, see Vogenauer, "Law Journals," 26.
50. "Privilege of Counsel," 294.
51. "General," 774.
52. "Judicial Statistics," 680.

Fin de Siècle Masculinities

By the last decades of the nineteenth century, conventional definitions of masculinity and femininity were becoming entrenched. For example, in "Silent Men," a 1889 *Leisure Hour* article, James Mason asserts that the "best and most successful men are silent and awkward in company, whereas women are full of chit-chat."[53] Yet such stereotypes were hotly contested and surreptitiously subverted. Several scholars have pointed to the unevenness and subversion of gender categories and roles in this period.[54] For Jeffrey Weeks, sexuality was at the core of the Victorian "battle over appropriate sexual values in a rapidly changing world."[55] According to Elaine Showalter, "What was most alarming to the *fin de siècle* was that sexuality and sex roles might no longer be contained in the neat and permanent borderlines of gender categories."[56] Most articles depicting new masculinities were contradictory in their attitude toward changes in gender roles. An article in the *Leisure Hour*, for example, insisted that the "Ideal Husband" must accompany the New Woman: "Women are to know all, and men are not to be permitted greater liberty and indulgence than women. Thus we have the advent of the new man and the ideal husband, both the creation of the new woman and the feminine spirit of the time."[57] We might think of this article as a modern appeal for men to engage to a fuller extent in family and household affairs, yet the author goes on to argue that it would be tiresome if men sought control over the minutiae of household management and that these duties should be women's responsibility. The essay concludes that the best way to ensure an "ideal husband" is to be an ideal wife.[58]

Men who identified with alternative models of masculinity could find material to draw them into mainstream periodicals, especially when reading against the grain. According to Justin Bengry, "Effeminate and queer men—consumers like anyone else—no doubt read . . . early men's fashion magazines, despite the injunctions against them by editors and contributors. They followed magazines' precepts, and looked to them for guidance to navigate their fashion and style choices."[59] Early papers also included discussions of male physicality and fashion. For example, the *Examiner* (1808–86), a radical weekly paper founded by Leigh and John Hunt, included an 1808 article titled "Male Fashions." The article begins by claiming that real men do not care about such frivolous matters: "The most obscure individual apes his superior in his apparel, and, as far as his finances will allow him, vanity and folly appear to be his leading characteristics."[60] Paradoxically, the article then proceeds to give a detailed account of the sartorial splendor of the Prince of Wales, which men are encouraged to emulate. By the fin de siècle, discussion of fashion was associated with emerging definitions of queer identity.

---

53. Mason, "Silent Men," 51.
54. See, for example, Sinfield, *Wilde Century*; Dellamora, *Victorian Sexual Dissidence* and *Masculine Desire*; Weeks, *Sex, Politics and Society* and *Sexuality and Its Discontents*.
55. Weeks, *Sexuality and Its Discontents*, 73.
56. Showalter, *Sexual Anarchy*, 9.
57. St. Helier, "Ideal Husband," 626.
58. Ibid., 627–8.
59. Bengry, "Courting the Pink Pound," 128.
60. "Male Fashions," 268.

"Effeminate," alternative, and "deviant" models of masculinity associated with fin de siècle culture were explicitly figured in, and partially fashioned by, the periodical press.[61] In the 1880s and 1890s, the *Artist and Journal of Home Culture* (1880–1902) and the *Studio* (1893–1964) featured homoerotic examples of youthful male beauty in articles and illustrations, most likely as a means of catering to a queer, non-hegemonic masculine readership.[62] Likewise, the *Quorum* (1894) promoted tolerance toward an emerging homosexual subculture through coded discussion of male friendship.[63] The homoerotic Oxford undergraduate journal *Spirit Lamp* (1892–93), edited by Oscar Wilde's lover Lord Alfred Douglas, discussed students' sexual allure for both women and men.[64] There was also a large underground trade in homoerotic pornography for men of every taste.[65]

Advertisements

Looking beyond the editorial content of periodicals, advertisements tell us a great deal about the ways masculinity was constructed throughout the century. They also indicate "unmanly" ailments that prevented men from assuming their rightful roles. For example, an advertisement in the *Penny Illustrated Paper and Illustrated Times* (1861–1913) for Dr. Lynn's Fig Remedy asked, "Why are Men Stronger than Women?" and then provided a remedy for restoring men's "natural" dominance.[66] Another advertisement in the same paper promotes the use of galvanic electricity to combat a range of emasculating complaints such as "nervous exhaustion, physical debility, melancholia, or any sign of premature decline of vital energy."[67] Men could not be "real" men with those sorts of emasculating afflictions. Throughout the century, competing versions of masculinity were represented in advertising, opening spaces for readers to figure out what it meant to be a consumer and a man.

Directions for Future Research

Nineteenth-century periodicals were important venues for defining and redefining gender norms and identities. As scholars continue working in this relatively understudied field of inquiry, it will be important to take into account multiple definitions of masculinity and how these manly ideals changed over the course of the century. It will likewise be useful to explore the contradictory messages about masculine roles in periodical texts, even within a single title or issue. The ubiquity of periodicals for men and by men, and the simultaneous invisibility of men as gendered readers and writers, has meant that research on men and masculinity has to

---

61. Bengry, "Courting the Pink Pound," 125.
62. See Brake, "Gay Discourse," and Cook, *London and the Culture of Homosexuality*, 127–9. For a more detailed discussion, see Bengry, "Courting the Pink Pound," 126.
63. Bengry, "Courting the Pink Pound," 146, n16.
64. Deslandes, *Oxbridge Men*, 59–60.
65. For more on the production and reception of obscene publications, see Nead, *Victorian Babylon*, 150–61, 178–84.
66. "Why Are Men Stronger than Women?," 290.
67. "Men Only," 358.

catch up with scholarly work on women and femininity. Future work should consider not only gender but also its intersection with other categories like age, class, politics, and religion. It should also move beyond representations of men and masculinity to enquire how messages in the periodical press for men and women of all classes and ages were appropriated, reappropriated, and altered. This, in turn, would illuminate how the periodical press, in its many forms, changed, and was changed by, cultural, social, and political forms of gendered roles and identities.

19

PERIODICALS FOR WOMEN

Kathryn Ledbetter

For many years, prejudices against women's writing and culture discouraged scholars from cataloguing, archiving, and collecting women's periodicals. Negative judgments of women's magazines and journals as sentimental, oppressively domestic, or unintellectual resulted in unfair and unscholarly marginalization of the genre.[1] Attempts to filter out sentiment, religion, and domestic or bourgeois ideology had the effect of closing an important window to the past. Although looking backward never reproduces an accurate picture of lived reality, traces of Victorian women's lives remain on the pages of periodicals for us to explore. Generalizations about content and readership are somewhat unstable because of the many titles that appeared throughout the century; however, the largest portion of women's periodicals targeted white, heterosexual, middle-class women readers and focused on self-enrichment and the reinforcement of women's conventional roles in society. Publishers experienced varying levels of financial success with women's periodicals, depending on competition and economic conditions, and titles often merged or disappeared after only a few issues. Yet several weathered financial challenges to become popular reading choices for many years.

Women's Interests Valued

Victorian women's periodicals offered a closed space that valued and expanded women's interests. Men, of course, enjoyed far greater opportunities for intellectual enrichment than women did because of their access to clubs, military service, politics, education, and professional opportunities. Yet even in an era heavily imbued with separate spheres ideology, women's periodicals opened paths that otherwise would have been inaccessible. While many titles confirm stereotypical domestic roles by featuring fashion plates, recipes, moral instruction, advice columns, sentimental literature, and needlework patterns, they also aggressively examined topics such as women's work, philanthropy, education, equality, and social issues. Articles on university degrees, job training, and women's rights encouraged women to seek a footing in the world

---

1. For example, in her influential study, Cynthia White implies that Victorian women's magazines are generally "insipid, limited in scope and lacking all mental stimulus, being designed for a new breed of woman whose interests and activities were confined wholly to the domestic sphere." White, *Women's Magazines*, 35.

outside the home. Periodicals also provided women with opportunities to assume roles as writers and editors, thus fulfilling their hopes of professionalization in the literary marketplace.

Expansion of middle-class readerships prompted publishers to diversify their periodical offerings. Before the nineteenth century, only upper-class women had the money, leisure time, and education to justify the purchase of a magazine.[2] Early periodicals for women maintained an elite focus by providing articles of interest to the leisure class, including clever word games suitable for parlor play, gossipy correspondence, and short essays written by authors under satiric pseudonyms. The first women's magazine was reportedly the short-lived *Ladies' Mercury* (1693), a compilation of diverse news and correspondence produced by London bookseller John Dunton. Once publishers caught on to the idea of catering to women readers, the genre evolved from newsy almanac and pocket-book formats such as the *Ladies' Diary* (1704–1840) and the *Female Tatler* (1709–18) into miscellanies such as the *Female Spectator* (1744–46), the *Lady's Weekly Magazine* (1747), the *Lady's Curiosity, or Weekly Apollo* (1752), and the *Lady's Museum* (1760–61).[3] Women's periodicals during this time offered an array of witty fare suitable for bluestocking intellectuals and attempted to compete with periodicals such as the *Spectator*, which was published for a more general readership. One popular eighteenth-century women's periodical became a model for early nineteenth-century titles: the *Lady's Magazine, or Entertaining Companion for the Fair Sex*, which appeared in 1770 and continued until 1832. The table of contents from a 1781 issue indicates the variety of offerings available: poetry, fiction, essays, short features, foreign news, theater and book reviews, essays, correspondence, music scores, embroidery patterns, and court news. Periodicals such as the *Lady's Magazine* also often included copper-plate engravings depicting members of the royal family or illustrating works of fiction (Figure 19.1).

Women's periodicals during the first decade of the nineteenth century maintained this formula, fulfilling expectations for light literature, needlework patterns, correspondence, and the latest fashions. Although more women were literate and had an increasing amount of time and money for leisure activities, women's periodicals for all social classes were not yet available. Fashion plates might allow servants to dream but only after the periodical had drifted downstairs from the lady's dressing room. John Bell's *La Belle Assemblée* (1806–32) became a notable trendsetter for fashion magazines because of its lavish costume illustrations displayed in a larger royal octavo format. Bound in orange wrappers and sold for three shillings, *La Belle Assemblée* included a special section of London and Paris fashions with two engraved fashion plates. It also offered a steady supply of fiction and poetry as well as articles featuring gossip, science, politics, and travel, along with embroidery patterns.[4] The size and elegance of the magazine was powered by advertisements for millinery, dresses, and other consumer goods.

Several popular fashion magazines established in the first half of the nineteenth century maintained strong readerships over many years, including the *Ladies' Fashionable Repository*

---

2. Adburgham reports that the term "magazine" was not applied to a periodical until the third decade of the eighteenth century: "It was the happy thought of a bookseller named Edward Cave to use it in the sense of a storehouse of miscellaneous writings."
3. For fascinating summaries of eighteenth-century women's magazines, see White, *Women's Magazines*; Adburgham, *Women in Print*; and Beetham, *A Magazine of Her Own?*
4. Women viewed embroidery as "fancy work" suitable for ladies; plain sewing instruction never appeared in early women's magazines.

Engrav'd for the Lady's Magazine.

Princess Royal as she appear'd at Court on the Queen's Birth-Day.

Figure 19.1 Copper-plate engraving of the "Princess Royal as She Appear'd at Court on the Queen's Birth-Day," *Lady's Magazine* 12 (February 1781): 62.

(1809–95), the *Ladies' Pocket Magazine* (1825–39), *Blackwood's Lady's Magazine and Gazette of the Fashionable World* (1836–60), the *World of Fashion and Continental Feuilletons* (1824–51), the *Ladies' Gazette of Fashion* (1834–94), *Le Follet: le Journal du Grand Monde, Fashion and Polite Literature* (1846–1900), and *Ackermann's Repository of Arts, Literature, Commerce, Manufactures, Fashion and Politics* (1809–29), which featured at least two hand-colored fashion plates per issue. Textile manufacturers who advertised in *Ackermann's* could send dress fabric samples to promote

Figure 19.2 Frontispiece engraving featuring fabric swatches from textile manufacturers, *Ackermann's Repository of Arts* 12, no. 72 (December 1814).

their newest patterns. For example, a page from the December 1814 issue exhibits swatches of fabrics suitable for December fashions (Figure 19.2).[5]

During the 1830s, literary annuals were a popular periodical genre featuring romantic poetry and fiction illustrated with steel-plate engravings. These annuals were offered for sale during the fall season as expensive Christmas gifts for ladies. Rudolph Ackermann is notable for his role as publisher of the first literary annual, the *Forget-Me-Not* (1823–47). Publishers quickly tapped into the annuals craze by publishing titles such as the *Keepsake*, *Gem*, and *Literary Souvenir*. Like women's periodicals, they appeared in calendared regularity. Publishers attempted to attract women readers by incorporating romantic fiction, elegant engravings of fashionable women, decorative bindings in tooled leather or watered-silk dress fabrics, and other material displays of femininity. Annuals also often boasted celebrated society women authors as editors. The annuals threatened magazine sales for a few years, but competition among annuals diluted demand and quality. Periodicals such as the *Ladies' Cabinet of Fashion, Music and Romance* (1832–70) and the *New Monthly Belle Assemblée* (1834–70) soon dominated the market by offering more literature on an ongoing basis and at a cheaper price. They featured a winning combination of poetry, fiction, short essays, correspondence, reviews, and fashion news illustrated with colored fashion plates (Figure 19.3). Monthly and weekly women's periodicals were slowly becoming a more useful part of the middle-class woman's everyday life.

Like literary annuals, women's magazines often employed literary woman as editors. A brief list of nineteenth-century women authors who edited or owned their own periodicals includes Mary Russell Mitford, L.E.L. (Letitia Elizabeth Landon), Lady Blessington, Caroline Norton, Eliza Cook, Mary Howitt, Annie Swan, Mary Elizabeth Braddon, Camilla Toulmin (Mrs. Newton Crosland), Charlotte Yonge, and Ellen Wood. Mrs. (Margaret Harries) Cornwell Baron Wilson, founder and editor of the *New Monthly Belle Assemblée* until 1844, was a dramatist, novelist, biographer, and poet who published her first book of verse in 1816. She was also a frequent contributor to many literary annuals, such as the *Forget-Me-Not*, *Friendship's Offering*, *Literary Souvenir*, *Keepsake*, and *Book of Beauty*. Henry Fothergill Chorley called Wilson a "large lady, but a small authoress. She displayed [at a literary gathering] rather protuberantly, below the waist of her black dress, a tawdry medal, half the size of a saucer, which had been awarded her by some provincial Della Cruscan literary society."[6] Chorley's depiction of Wilson as a ridiculous relic demonstrates prejudices against the sensual, emotional excesses of the Della Cruscan poetry popular during the early nineteenth century, but it also epitomizes misogynistic attitudes toward women writers as silly beings with silly work to do. Wilson wrote a considerable portion of the text in her monthly periodical. She also employed women contributors who aspired to authorship but would never achieve success beyond the pages of the *New Monthly Belle Assemblée*. Women thus assumed important roles as producers and consumers of women's periodicals. Jeffrey Auerbach notes that of sixty-two bylines that appeared in the

---

5. I am grateful to Brian Maidment for sharing this periodical page with me. Rudolph Ackermann's London shop was a center for printed art of all types.
6. Quoted in Auerbach, "What They Read," 137n.

Figure 19.3 Hand-colored fashion plate, *New Monthly Belle Assemblée* 8 (January 1838): 58.

Ladies' Companion and the *New Monthly Belle Assemblée* during 1851, "women outnumbered men three to one."[7]

Women's periodicals participated in the discourse on gender by upholding notions of propriety and separate spheres ideology in preliminary addresses inaugurating new volumes. Published in 1838, shortly after the young Victoria's accession to the throne, the *New Monthly Belle Assemblée*'s address is typical:

> The PROPRIETORS deem it unnecessary, from the high auspices under which the work is published (it being especially patronized by the most AUGUST MOTHER in the Realm, whose Portrait graces the present number), to direct attention to that *moral tone* pervading its contents, which renders the BELLE ASSEMBLEE so desirable a magazine to place in the hands of the young and virtuous female—while the continuation of the same talent which has hitherto been so efficiently manifested in its editorial department, is the best security they can present to its readers for future literary excellence.[8]

The volume features a frontispiece portrait of the new queen elegantly robed with a rolled paper in her lap, perhaps an edict she is approving or an issue of the *New Monthly Belle Assemblée*. Queen Victoria's profile or engraved image is featured in banners of several women's periodicals as a guiding light of moral decency and a model of nineteenth-century womanhood.

The monthly *Ladies' Cabinet* was similar to the *New Monthly Belle Assemblée* in content but offered four colored fashion plates per issue instead of two, although in a smaller, pocket format. The *Ladies' Cabinet* could easily compete with the celebrity editor of the *New Monthly Belle Assemblée* by boasting two French literary women as editors: the mother-and-daughter team of Margaret and Beatrice de Courcy. The *Ladies' Cabinet* looked like a monthly spinoff from literary annuals except that it offered one or two story-picture engravings instead of the twelve or thirteen featured in most annuals. Proprietors of the *Ladies' Cabinet* expanded its physical format to quarto size in 1845 in order to compete with the *New Monthly Belle Assemblée* and other titles, but fiction continued to be the staple content. According to Auerbach, "Throughout 1851, on the average seventy-six percent of the pages [in the *Ladies' Cabinet*] were devoted to fiction, eight percent to general knowledge or history, thirteen percent to fashion, . . . two percent to poetry."[9] Periodicals and literary annuals became workshops for the development of the short fiction genre, which was still in its formative stages.

After the accession of Queen Victoria in 1837, the moral tone of women's periodicals shifted somewhat due to changing social expectations for women, the expansion of middle-class readerships, and reductions in the taxes on knowledge. This evolution resulted in the concurrent expansion and diversification of the press, enabling the secure establishment of women's

---

7. Ibid., 133.
8. "Address," i.
9. Auerbach, "What They Read," 126.

periodicals as a separate genre. The landscape for women's periodicals profoundly changed during the latter half of the nineteenth century as publishers increasingly issued new titles designed for diverse female readerships such as middle-class housewives, social activists, celebrity hunters, religious reformers, sophisticated intellectuals, working-class women, and hobbyists.

The most successful and influential of British Victorian middle-class women's periodicals was the *Englishwoman's Domestic Magazine* (1852–77), which, as Margaret Beetham points out, "marked a watershed between the exclusive ladies' magazines and the popular women's domestic journals which were to become the staple of the genre from the 1890s. It assumed that women wanted fiction and fashion but it also dealt with the dailiness of readers' lives. Unlike the mother's magazines, however, it secularised those lives, offering the way to domestic happiness rather than salvation."[10] Owned and edited by magazine entrepreneur Samuel Beeton and his wife Isabella, the *Englishwoman's Domestic Magazine* sold 25,000 copies a month within two years of its inauguration, expanding to 37,000 by 1856. By the time Beeton began a new, enlarged series in 1860, the *Englishwoman's Domestic Magazine* claimed 50,000 readers. According to Cynthia White, Beeton "was one of the first to recognise the untapped potential of the middle-class market, and his experiment opened the eyes of other publishers to the rich profits to be reaped by catering to women of all classes, paving the way for the vast expansion in publishing for women which took place at the end of the century."[11]

As proof of his intent to attract and expand middle-class readerships, the magazine initially cost only two pence, thus underselling other monthlies, which typically cost a shilling. Contents for volume one, published in 1852, show a marked variation in articles tailored to the specific, ordinary interests of women at home. Features from this volume include biographies of Maria Edgeworth and Harriet Beecher Stowe, as well as essays on dancing, beauty, idleness, gardening, pets, personal grooming, female education, domestic virtues, and proper dress. Needlework patterns, poetry, cooking recipes, and home remedies for common ailments are juxtaposed with short fiction, correspondence, and "Things Worth Knowing"—household tips for everything from cleaning black lace and killing rats to fixing door squeaks. Throughout the 1850s, the tone and themes of the magazine shifted gradually from sanctification of the domestic woman to commodification of her every need. Issues from the new series beginning in 1860 were much larger than periodicals of earlier years, and colored plates displaying fashions "Expressly Designed & Prepared for *The Englishwoman's Domestic Magazine*" came with each issue, next to an advice column titled "The Englishwoman's Conversazione" (Figure 19.4). The *Englishwoman's Domestic Magazine* shaped notions of middle-class domestic femininity and appealed to the masses instead of a select few. Beeton owned several other women's periodicals, most notably the *Queen: The Lady's Newspaper and Court Chronicle* (1861–1922), which he was forced to sell in 1866 after Isabella died. Yet by this time, as Beetham points out, Samuel Beeton had "thoroughly transformed the middle-class woman's magazine, begun to re-work the conventions of the expensive ladies' illustrated paper and pioneered the magazine for young women."[12]

---

10. Beetham, *A Magazine of Her Own?*, 59.
11. White, *Women's Magazines*, 44.
12. Beetham, *A Magazine of Her Own?*, 60.

Women's Roles Expanded

Examination of Victorian women's periodicals destabilizes stereotypical depictions of Victorian women as voiceless automatons controlled by domestic ideology. Perceptions of femininity evolved throughout the long nineteenth century, and debates about female roles in society appeared in nearly every women's periodical beginning in the eighteenth century, including those strictly focused on fashion. During the 1830s, women were expected to champion middle-class morality in their roles as humble, self-sacrificing wives, sisters, and mothers. Such a model is distasteful to modern readers, but Victorian Christian evangelism was a powerful tool for female radicalism, which defied stereotypes of Victorian women as apolitical and non-opinionated drudges. Victorians believed that the Bible commissioned believers to proselytize, to change the world with the message of Christianity, and to care for those who were physically, morally, and spiritually ill in whatever dank or foreign place they might be suffering. The "Great Commission" justified women's missionary work outside the home, allowing them to observe the lifestyles of different social groups, whether they lived in the slums of London or Bombay.

Religious women's periodicals such as the *Christian Lady's Magazine* (1834–49), the *Christian Mothers' Magazine* (1844–45), and the *British Mothers' Magazine* (1845–55) combined missionary fervor with motherly advice, calls for reform, and devotional literature. As Elizabeth Gray points out, the *Christian Lady's Magazine* insisted that "contributors (and readers) must be *Christian* ladies," but at the same time it paradoxically "both produces that nebulous boundary and produces itself as an arbiter of appropriate spiritual discussion, through its editorial policy, its generous interpolation of editorial comment, and . . . through its inclusion of poetry as an 'appropriate' genre."[13] Gray demonstrates the ways that religious expression through imaginative literature feminized Christian identity. The *British Mother's Magazine*, for example, reported on meetings of the London Central Maternal Association, explicated biblical passages, and reviewed books of Christian interest, but it also featured educational articles on astronomy, natural history, musical instruction, and woman's influence. In July 1845, the periodical reprinted and supportively reviewed a publication arguing that women have a powerful influence on civilization. The reviewer asserts that "power is chiefly exerted in the way of authority; and is, therefore, of necessity limited in its sphere of action: influence has its source in human sympathies, and is, therefore, *practically* boundless in its operation."[14] Maternal power is supreme, but women must cultivate their intellectual powers to realize their full potential. "A vast amount of influence belongs to women, *as women*," but they must be directed by Christian principles.[15]

The civilizing mission informed women's philanthropic and social activism for the rest of the century. Women's periodicals freely discussed social problems such as prostitution, education, poverty, suffrage, unwed motherhood, labor issues, sexual dangers, factory legislation, and the abuse of governesses and seamstresses. When the 1851 census revealed a surplus of

---

13. Gray, "Beatification through Beautification," 264.
14. "Woman's Mission," 439.
15. Ibid., 439.

women in Britain, the resulting debate over how they might be employed became known as "The Woman Question." Although women took their roles as wives and mothers seriously and most Victorian women rejected any hint of radicalism, countless articles in women's periodicals descried the lack of employment opportunities for women who needed to support themselves or yearned for an identity outside the domestic sphere. From the 1850s onward, a few small-circulation periodicals owned or edited by female activists dedicated themselves to women's employment issues and early feminist activism. Inspired by Anna Jameson's call for a collective response to the Woman Question, Bessie Rayner Parkes and Barbara Leigh Smith Bodichon formed the English Woman's Journal Company to promote solutions for the women's employment crisis. Soon Parkes and actress/novelist Matilda Mary Hays inaugurated and edited the first British periodical devoted to feminist issues, the *English Woman's Journal* (1858–63). They published fiction, poetry, biographies, book reviews, updates on laws affecting women, a correspondence forum, and a column titled "Passing Events."[16] Article titles suggest the types of monthly fare available for readers of the *English Woman's Journal*: "The Profession of the Teacher" and "Property of Married Women" (March 1858); "The New Law of Divorce" and "Physical Training" (May 1858); "On the Adoption of Professional Life by Women" (September 1858); "Charities for Women.—Preston Hospital, Shropshire" (December 1859); "What Can Educated Women Do?" and "Letter to Young Ladies Desirous of Studying Medicine" (January 1860); and "Infant Mortality" (February 1861). In 1864, the *English Woman's Journal* became the *Alexandra Magazine & Woman's Social and Industrial Advocate*, which was edited by Parkes until 1866, when Jessie Boucherett became editor and renamed it the *Englishwoman's Review of Social and Industrial Questions*. After leaving her editorial position, Parkes wrote that a journal such as theirs needn't be well written and should "never be taken as a sample of what women can do":

> The sort of sober wisdom acquired by really good women, in practical life, must always be the staple of any extended movement for helping working women, and this sober wisdom will rarely be expressed in the most artistic, or the most incising intellectual manner. . . . It is not a hundred years since the majority of Englishwomen did not know how to spell correctly, and yet they were by no means fools in domestic or social life; and, even now, I consider that a very wide intellectual tolerance is required when sifting the wheat from the chaff in writings upon our movement, and the best writing is not always certain to embody the best sense.[17]

Pauline Nestor notes that the importance the *English Woman's Journal* was not its "contribution of a political theory, and even less a literature, to the women's movement. It resided rather in the very nature of the magazine—a foray by women for women into the world of print,

---

16. For more information on the "Woman Question," the *English Woman's Journal*, *Victoria Magazine*, and the Langham Place Circle, see Dredge, "Opportunism and Accommodation"; Dreher, "Redundancy and Emigration"; Herstein, "Langham Place Circle"; Nestor, "New Departure in Women's Publishing"; Rendall, "Moral Engine"; Robinson, "Amazed at our success"; Schroeder, "Better Arguments"; and Stone, *Emily Faithfull*.
17. Parkes, "Use of a Special Periodical," 259.

Figure 19.4 Two-page spread showing arrangement of the "Englishwoman's Conversazione" feature next to hand-colored fashion plates. *Englishwoman's Domestic Magazine* 9 (November 1864): 288.

principled and political in the broadest sense, and as much actual as metaphorical for the female compositors of the Victoria Press."[18]

Emily Faithfull established the all-woman Victoria Press in August 1859, employing female compositors for the first time in England. The press published the *English Woman's Journal* as well as pamphlets and other materials related to women's issues, including an anthology of literature titled *Victoria Regia* (1861) and a shilling monthly magazine that became the voice of the women's movement, *Victoria Magazine* (1863–80). The *English Woman's Journal* and the *Victoria Magazine* did not achieve large circulations, nor did they feature literature of great quality, but they nevertheless demonstrated a degree of radical female engagement with politics and activism at a time when women had no legal status and few opportunities. The passage of the Married Women's Property Act of 1882 and the repeal of the Contagious Diseases Acts in 1886 marked a significant change in women's self-definition, and feminist periodicals of

18. Nestor, "New Departure in Women's Publishing," 100.

the 1880s, such as the *Women's Penny Paper*, the *Woman's Herald*, and the *Woman's Signal*, took a stand on other pressing social issues such as temperance, socialism, vegetarianism, theosophy, and sexual mores. Periodicals for middle-class and working-class women seeking employment appeared in the 1880s and 1890s, offering a heterogeneous mixture of word games, features on gardening and needlework, and articles on current women's issues such as emigration, education, and employment opportunity.

Women's News Explored

At the same time that women's periodicals began to demarcate a political space in Victorian print culture during the 1840s and 1850s, the quarto-sized, six-penny weekly *Lady's Newspaper* (1847–63) began to experiment with notions of what constituted proper news for women. The frontispiece engraving of the first volume represents women's presumed interests: art, music, fashion, and romantic leisure activities such as horseback riding with a male companion (Figure 19.5). Editor Charles Dance assures women readers that his paper will provide a brand of news that is appropriate for ladies:

> We shall make you acquainted with all the leading events of the day, without fatiguing or disgusting you with lengthy disquisitions. We can tell you that a battle has been won or lost, without shocking your sensibilities by its painful details. We can inform you that a minister has resigned, and yet omit the long dull speeches which preceded his doing so. The prices of bread and meat are useful things to know, and you will find them unencumbered by long articles on the state of the corn and cattle markets.[19]

In spite of this patronizing promise, the paper did provide police news and a measure of hard news from the colonies, along with articles about popular science, travel, and "foreign intelligence" as well as fiction and some poetry. Biographies of women writers, reports on education and emigration for women, news of rebellions and politics in the colonies, and a good supply of needlework patterns rounded out the weekly fare. In his opening address, Dance claims that sensational reportage of "accidents and offences" will be "recorded without heart-rending particulars," but the foreign intelligence column on May 8, 1847 features a sensational story reprinted from an American missionary journal titled "A CIVIL WAR IN CHINA.—ONE HUNDRED AND THIRTY THOUSAND SIX HUNDRED AND THIRTY-EIGHT PERSONS KILLED OR WOUNDED."[20] Foreign news included dispatches from France, Spain, Turkey, India, and the United States. A summary of parliamentary activities along with provincial, metropolitan, and court happenings provided serious news. The first page of any newspaper usually highlights its top story, but what editors and readers of the *Lady's Newspaper* perceived as a top story is unclear. One front page might illustrate a violent tribal war somewhere in the empire, and another might illustrate a London social event, for example the front page of the

---

19. Dance, "Good News for the Ladies," 2.
20. "China," 436.

Figure 19.5 Frontispiece illustration from the first issue of the *Lady's Newspaper* 1, no. 1 (January 2, 1847): 1.

DESIGNS FOR ROMAN EMBROIDERY, MODERN POINT LACE, BRAID AND CROCHET, DRAWN LACE

Figure 19.6 Embroidery pattern from the *Queen* 55 (January 17, 1874): 64. The periodical was folio-sized, and the pattern folded out three times from the center to show the design.

March 18, 1851 issue, which displays a carpet presented by 150 women to Queen Victoria for the Great Exhibition. In some ways, the paper's contents seem like other women's periodicals of the 1840s, with the usual poetry, fiction, correspondence, advertisements, fancy-work patterns, celebrity marriages, theater reviews, fashion illustrations, kitchen tips, and illustrated articles on philanthropic interests. However, the mixture of "feminine" reading matter with politics, police records, and foreign news provided women readers with glimpses of a much wider world than was usually provided by women's periodicals.

When Samuel Beeton purchased the *Lady's Newspaper* in 1861 and merged its title with the *Queen*, he signaled the end of traditional newspaper reportage in Victorian women's periodicals. In a letter to "Victoria" in the *Englishwoman's Domestic Magazine*'s "Englishwoman's Conversazione," he announces that the *Queen* will not be a "ponderous, didactic paper. Common sense and good humour are qualities as rare in the press as learning and satire. Gay, graceful, sensible writing is what the editor of 'The QUEEN' proposes to fill his columns with. Music, the theatre, and all manner of amusements, in-door and out-door, will be largely dealt with."[21] After 1866, Edward Cox, along with his nephew Horace Cox and author-editor Helen Lowe, developed the newspaper into a stunning fashion publication for upper-class educated women. Everything was bigger and better in the *Queen*, including needlework patterns that were occasionally colored and sometimes triple-folded (Figure 19.6). The content of the *Queen* resembled the *Lady's Newspaper* in its mixture of news, needlework, etiquette, fashion, and entertainment, along with news about "The Upper Ten Thousand at Home and Abroad" and a large number of advertisements. By the 1880s, the magazine featured an increasing array of illustrations of art, pets, costumes, fashions, needlework, and foreign scenes. Although some

---

21. "Englishwoman's Conversazione," 264.

issues feature regular domestic columns, such as "The Housewife" or "Cuisine," readers of the *Queen* were defined as being decidedly less concerned with the quotidian details of home management than the particulars of the boudoir and the social scene. A volume of the *Queen* serves up a banquet of material details about upper-class Victorian women's culture unavailable in any other format. According to David Doughan, the "*Queen* reigned supreme over the glossies for more than half a century, until the changing social order and fashions of the 1920s produced a number of rivals, mostly notably *Vogue*, to challenge its supremacy."[22]

Women's Opportunities Developed

The late nineteenth-century woman reader had more power, education, freedom, opportunity, and political savvy than her predecessors, but advertising and editorial content in women's magazines suggest that women continued to see themselves as feminine and domestic. Late-century periodicals—from slick illustrated monthlies, such as Annie Swan's *Woman at Home* (1892–1920), the *Lady's Realm* (1896–1915), and *Womanhood* (1898–1907), to the penny weekly *Home Chat* (1895–1956)—suggest that late Victorian women shared a common interest in material and emotional self-fulfillment. What appears on the page of a periodical is designed for purchase and consumption. Yet regardless of their economic or social status, Victorian women liked to read about love, marriage, children, fashion, hobbies, personal enrichment, and other women. Specific topics and depth of detail may vary, but women's periodicals share a common purpose of binding women to each other.

Hilary Fraser, Stephanie Green, and Judith Johnston discuss the multivocality present in the late Victorian women's magazine, noting its "capacity to encompass ideology and difference within the same textual space. Multivocality can unsettle and affirm prevailing social values. The woman's magazine can appear, for example, to transcend class boundaries by referring to experiences common to all women, but also reinforces stereotypes of women as concerned with trivial subjects such as appearance and gossip."[23] As editor of the *Woman's World* (1887–89), Oscar Wilde attempted to elevate the woman's periodical by putting women's writing, interests, intellectual scope, and cultural significance on display. Wilde wrote to his publisher that he aimed to "take a high standpoint, and deal not merely with what women wear, but with what they think, and what they feel.... [It] should be made the recognised organ for the expression of women's opinions on all subjects of literature, art, and modern life."[24] The second article in Wilde's inaugural issue, Evelyn Portsmouth's "The Position of Woman," proclaims a new "solidarité" among women of all classes and expresses hope that the bond will influence civilization in much the same terms as her sisters expressed in the 1840s:

> May not the time be come when the strength of woman is imperative to make man stronger?—when it is necessary for him that she should be his fitting companion—loyal

---

22. Doughan, "Periodicals by, for, and about Women in Britain," 263.
23. Fraser, Green, and Johnson, *Gender and the Victorian Periodical*, 177.
24. Wilde, *Letters*, 194–5.

but not servile? May not the hour have struck when her own elevation is absolutely necessary to prevent his deterioration? And out of the present may not that future be already preparing which will increase, and not decrease, the physical and mental distance between man and woman?—when she will fully taste the satisfaction, not of her inferiority, but of his superiority, of which every fresh development in her favour now makes her the builder and preserver?[25]

Clearly, at the fin de siècle the reforming spirit was still an irresistibly powerful ideology for women. Periodicals throughout the century articulated this theme through their treatment of beauty, fashion, literature, and feminine intellect.

Future Research

Because of past tendencies to ignore or discount periodicals as important artifacts, the genre is ripe with opportunities for future research. The gaps in our knowledge of the business, readerships, and production of women's periodicals are painfully evident. If correspondence between publishers, editors, and authors of women's periodicals exists, this archival material may not have been catalogued. Financial records may be submerged within accounts of publishers who regarded periodicals as marketing tools for their more profitable book trade. Publishers' archives need to be unpacked and broadly re-indexed before we can evaluate specific author-editor relationships, marketing approaches and costs, and relations with participants at all levels of material production. The process of identifying editors, authors, artists, and other contributors has barely begun. Mining archival material of contributors may further reveal attitudes and business arrangements that would help to contextualize women's periodicals within the larger print culture. However, anonymity was common in women's periodicals, partly because of the nature of the genre and partly because notions about feminine propriety dictated a sense of humility. Many authors may never be identified, and others may not have bothered to keep records, not believing their work to be important. Many women writers worked as prolific contributors to women's periodicals but remain unnoticed; because they were not novelists or poets, scholars may overlook their contributions. In these cases, primary research on minor authors or in provincial archives may be revealing. Other future scholarship might explore how women read periodicals; for example, how they may have interpreted elements such as illustrations, fashion, needlework, word games, fiction, poetry, essays, advertising, and photography. More research on circulating libraries or bookshops, as well as exploration of the diaries of average Victorian women, may help to theorize women's reading and consumption of Victorian commodities. For all of these projects, women's periodicals hold valuable clues toward a revised history of nineteenth-century women's work, culture, and reading.

25. Portsmouth, "Position of Woman," 10.

20

FAMILY MAGAZINES

Jennifer Phegley

The stunning array of successful family magazines that emerged in the mid-nineteenth century complemented the domestic concerns of the era. The emphasis on domesticity was embodied by Queen Victoria, who presented herself as a humble wife and mother though she was the powerful leader of both a nation and an empire. This new magazine genre capitalized on the Victorian worship of home and family by assembling reading materials meant to be shared in the parlor and at the fireside. There were many kinds of family magazines: secular, religious, lowbrow, middlebrow, illustrated, non-illustrated, large format, small format, bound, unbound, weekly, and monthly. Magazines for the family were marketed to the working classes as well as the middle and upper classes and sold for as little as a penny or as much as a shilling.

Family magazines are often assumed to be synonymous with the shilling monthly magazines that emerged in the 1860s. However, while shilling monthlies were usually family magazines, family magazines were not always shilling monthlies. Many of the penny weeklies founded in the 1840s and 1850s set the standard for family magazines and influenced the development of the more prestigious monthlies. While the price points and frequency of publication differed, they shared a common objective: to provide original, entertaining serial fiction at an affordable price printed alongside informative articles, poetry, and sometimes enticing illustrations designed to appeal to men, women, and children.

This sense of inclusivity is evident in the 1851 frontispiece of the two-penny *Family Friend* (1849–70). The central illustration showcases a large, age-diverse group gathered around the paterfamilias, who is presumably reading the *Family Friend* aloud (Figure 20.1). This scene is flanked by young women engaged in domestic arts and crafts. At the bottom of the page, a woman wearing religious garb provides moral instruction to a boy. These images attempted to convey that the magazine would improve family life by occupying readers in constructive activities and moral enlightenment. While family magazines included articles geared toward women's interests, they were not like mid-century women's magazines that focused primarily on fashion, decorating, domestic advice, sewing, cooking, cleaning, and mothering. The content of family magazines was more diverse. "The successful formula," Sally Mitchell explains, "was to provide something for everyone."[1] Yet

---

1. Mitchell, "Forgotten Woman," 31.

Figure 20.1 Frontispiece of the *Family Friend* 4 (January–June 1851).

as Margaret Beetham puts it, "domesticity was both" the family magazine's "subject" and "its destination."[2]

The development of the genre marked a shift away from didactic working-class periodicals such as *Chambers's Edinburgh Journal* (1832–1956) and the *Penny Magazine* (1832–46), a

---

2. Beetham, *A Magazine of Her Own?*, 46.

publication of the Society for the Diffusion of Useful Knowledge intended to educate the masses. Beetham argues that these earlier general interest magazines "assumed the masculine as an unarticulated norm, though they may have been read by women as they were by the middle classes."[3] Despite their secular leanings, *Chambers's* and the *Penny Magazine* were often seen as preachy or dull. The new breed of family periodicals was not only more inviting to women but also reveled in entertaining its readers. Though *Chambers's* included some short fiction and the *Penny Magazine* featured woodcuts of plants, animals, machinery, and architecture, family magazines focused on illustrated serial fiction that would captivate readers and keep them coming back for more. However, they were also careful to avoid associations with the cheap, lurid publications often known as "penny dreadfuls" or "penny bloods." Family magazines walked a fine line between titillation and respectability.

Family magazines in a variety of formats thrived from the 1840s until the 1870s. This trajectory coincides with some key developments in the publishing industry, including the 1855 repeal of the stamp tax. By the 1830s, revolutionary anxieties had dissipated, and views began to shift away from the suppression of information toward the promotion of cheap reading materials as a means of self-improvement for the lower classes. In 1855 and 1861, respectively, the stamp tax and the paper tax were eliminated, thus expanding the market for newspapers and periodicals by substantially lowering costs for consumers. According to Richard Altick, these changes threw the "publishing and printing industries into a happy uproar."[4] With expenses decreasing and technology improving (rotary presses and typesetting machines were introduced at mid-century), "periodical printing became one of the most highly mechanized of all English mass-production industries."[5] Mitchell points out that once "publishers recognized that the same profit could be made by selling a magazine to thirty thousand people at a penny each instead of to three thousand at sixpence," the penny weekly craze of the 1840s was born.[6]

Penny Weekly Family Magazines

The *Family Herald* (1842–1940), the *London Journal* (1845–1928), *Reynolds's Miscellany* (1846–69), the *Leisure Hour* (1852–1905), *Cassell's* (1853–1932), *Bow Bells* (1862–97), and the *London Reader* (1863–1903) were among the penny weeklies that catered to upwardly mobile laborers and the lower-middle classes.[7] Mitchell explains that the readership "crossed class lines defined either economically or socially: the common denominator was the aspiration

---

3. Ibid.
4. Altick, *English Common Reader*, 357.
5. Ibid.
6. Mitchell, "Forgotten Woman," 31.
7. Altick claims that of the 630 magazines published in 1873, 253 were religiously affiliated, though they were often indistinguishable from the secular publications. Altick, *English Common Reader*, 361. Of the magazines listed here, the Religious Tract Society's *Leisure Hour* is the only one that is overtly religious in tone and message, yet its features and fiction were similar to the other penny magazines.

for respectability."[8] Mass audiences for magazines, she notes, included new city dwellers filling "clerical, technical, and supervisory jobs that hardly existed a generation earlier"; these largely urban readers had "changing aspirations, expectations, and opportunities" and were adjusting to new lives away from their families and communities.[9] Working women—including servants, seamstresses, factory workers, shop girls, and teachers—were key members of the penny magazine audience as well. While they had little time to spare, they were often eager to read for escape as well as for knowledge. According to Mitchell, family magazines offered "commonly shared information, attitudes, and emotional reactions that delineate[d] respectability" for readers "living in a milieu which was new to them."[10] The popularity of these publications is attested to by their proliferation: in 1860 there were 17 penny weeklies in circulation, in 1880 there were 83, and by 1900 there were 304.[11] Whereas the *Penny Magazine* and *Chambers's* had achieved average circulations of 30,000–70,000, the new mass-market family publications such as the *Family Herald*, the *London Journal*, and *Reynolds's Miscellany* were reaching 100,000–400,000 readers.[12] Andrew King argues that the circulation of the older miscellanies decreased as the new penny family magazines increased. For example, *Chambers's* sold 86,750 copies a week in 1844, but that number slipped to 23,000 in 1855. Likewise, the *Penny Magazine* declined from 40,000 in 1845 to 25,000 the following year. The *London Journal*, on the other hand, sold around 90,000 copies in 1847, increasing to 500,000 in 1855.[13]

Penny family magazines were dominated by adventurous, melodramatic, and sensational fiction. The standard sixteen-page issue also featured domestic, historical, biographical, and scientific articles as well as poetry. As Wilkie Collins declared in an article exploring the penny weekly, "My eye! What a lot of print for the money!"[14] Reviewers acknowledged that the serials in this new breed of family magazine were of a more respectable nature than the usual cheap fiction. Margaret Oliphant, who notoriously criticized sensation fiction aimed at the middle classes in the shilling monthlies of the 1860s, assessed penny magazine fiction more generously. She notes that the *London Journal* and the *Family Herald* "stand up head and shoulders above the mass of their co-aspirants," including their "severe and edifying" predecessor the *Penny Magazine*.[15] While she says *Reynolds's Miscellany* looks "rather villainous," she maintains that it contains "nothing . . . to offend anybody" and that one could read any of these publications "without fear for our character" since they typically contain "nothing to alarm our conscience."[16] Likewise,

---

8. Mitchell, "Forgotten Woman," 34.
9. Ibid., 33.
10. Ibid., 34.
11. Gerrard, "New Methods," 66.
12. Altick, *English Common Reader*, 394.
13. King, *London Journal*, 82–3. King rightly cautions that circulation figures for nineteenth-century periodicals are somewhat unreliable because they were often used for promotional purposes. Furthermore, several people may have read each issue, and they were often purchased in a variety of formats (weekly issues, monthly bound volumes, reprints, and back issues) that make readership difficult to track (82).
14. [Collins], "Unknown Public," 219.
15. [Oliphant], "Byways of Literature," 203.
16. Ibid., 212.

Francis Hitchman calls the *Family Herald* an "eminently creditable specimen of the penny magazine," while the *London Journal* was "more gushing and sensational" in its illustrations and fiction.[17] Despite containing "plenty of crime and not a little vice," the *London Journal*'s criminals "always came to grief in the end, and virtue was duly rewarded with wealth and titles and honour."[18] An 1866 article in *Macmillan's* argues that although "an impression still remains that the penny journals run riot in pictures of debauchery and crime," in reality "these twelve or fifteen years have wrought a change, and any one who will look at such a periodical as the *London Journal* will be much struck, perhaps a little abashed, by the strong moral tone that pervades the writing. There is no lack of crime and dallying with things forbidden; but . . . the writers always profess to show a crime in order that we may see what a hideous thing it is, and may have our moral principles strengthened."[19] Perhaps Collins, Oliphant, Hitchman, and *Macmillan's* anonymous critic recognized the kinship between these penny periodicals and the shilling monthlies they likely read themselves.

Penny magazines not only featured sensational fiction but also salaciously tantalizing illustrations. The opening image for the *London Journal* serial *Three Women; or the Fatal Passion* by Fairfax Balfour (a pseudonym for playwright, novelist, and illustrator Watts Phillips) is a case in point (Figure 20.2). Complementing the suggestive title of the novel, the illustration reveals a darkly cloaked Lady Agnes de Vere lurking behind a velvet curtain as she witnesses her husband's intimate liaison with an Italian dancer. The illustration alone would have been enough to entice many readers to purchase the magazine even if they had missed out on previous installments of the novel. *Macmillan's* commented on the *London Journal* illustrations with more interest than disapproval:

> Here we see men dogging each other on dark nights, lurking behind trees, and looking round corners; gipsies in woods are entering into mysterious compacts with gentlemen disguised in huge cloaks; burglars with dark lanterns are prowling in houses; assassins are aiming blows at the back of unconscious victims; murderers steal into the chambers of sick men; women wake up startled in their beds and listen; ladies listen at doors; young girls are seen flying on the tops of houses from highly-impassioned pursuers; ladies elope with lovers in the dead of the night . . . and everywhere we see hair flying disheveled in the wind.[20]

These intriguing scenes may have focused on scandalous characters and plots, but they were generally considered harmless. Penny magazine serials were more likely to be criticized for their lack of literary quality. For example, Wilkie Collins complained of their "extraordinary sameness," as if they "might have been produced by the same man."[21]

---

17. Hitchman, "Penny Press," 389.
18. Ibid., 391.
19. "Penny Novels," 97.
20. Ibid., 102.
21. [Collins], "Unknown Public," 221.

Figure 20.2 "Lady De Vere Makes a Discovery," *London Journal* 43, no. 1103 (March 31, 1866): 193.

Another feature of penny family magazines that invited amusement and sometimes derision was the correspondence columns which printed answers to readers' questions on everything from love and etiquette to home remedies and legal advice (Figure 20.3). Teresa Gerrard attests to the popularity of these columns among readers, who in 1870 were submitting about two hundred letters a week to the *Family Herald*.[22] Despite the fact that only the answers to readers' questions were printed (sometimes making them very mysterious indeed), Gerrard argues that editors assumed audiences were reading these columns closely and even saving them for reference since their correspondence frequently alluded to previously published answers.[23] King points out that because "public interaction with the consumer was not a feature found in periodicals of higher symbolic capital at this time," it was considered a bizarre and perhaps even dangerous feature of the penny press.[24] Collins was particularly taken by

22. Gerrard, "New Methods," 56.
23. Ibid., 58.
24. King, *London Journal*, 19.

these "Notices to Correspondents," which he calls the "most interesting page in the penny journals."[25] He declares,

> There is no earthly subject that is possible to discuss, no private affair that is possible to conceive, which the amazing Unknown Public will not confide to the Editor in the form of a question, and which the still more amazing editor will not set himself seriously and resolutely to answer. . . .Young girls beset by perplexities which are usually supposed to be reserved for a mother's or an elder sister's ear only, consult the editor. Married women, who have committed little frailties, consult the editor. Male jilts in deadly fear of actions for breach of promise of marriage, consult the editor. Ladies whose complexions are on the wane, and who wish to know the best artificial means of restoring them, consult the editor. Gentlemen who wish to dye their hair, and get rid of their corns, consult the editor.[26]

Yet as *Macmillan's* acknowledged, the correspondence pages, like penny magazine serials, were "of the most noble and elevating order" since the editors would "not for a moment tolerate any doubtful conduct."[27] Indeed, even the questionable inclusion of matrimonial advertising in these columns is characterized as an entertaining sideshow that complements the "moral tone of the penny novels," each of which may be sensationally "full of horrors" and the "mysteries of crime," but will nevertheless ultimately "ally itself to morality."[28] As Gerrard argues, many correspondents were seeking "to better themselves mentally and intellectually" by writing to the editors, indicating that their "interest in print media was directed by a desire to appear knowledgeable in dealing with others."[29]

Bow Bells was a late-coming rival to the *London Journal* and the *Family Herald* that publisher John Dicks hoped would capitalize on audiences already cultivated by its predecessors. He also aimed to attract a female readership by including features in the magazine's "Ladies' Pages"—such as needlework and dress patterns—that had been pioneered by Samuel Beeton in the *Englishwoman's Domestic Magazine*. *Bow Bells* was essentially a hybrid of the family magazine and the woman's magazine and thus highlights the slipperiness of the boundaries between periodical genres. By 1865, *Bow Bells* was clearly achieving its goals as it claimed an impressive circulation of 200,000.[30] King argues that the *London Journal*'s waning sales figures in the mid-1860s may have been, at least in part, a result of *Bow Bells*'s success.[31]

---

25. [Collins], "Unknown Public," 219.
26. Ibid., 219.
27. "Penny Novels," 98–9.
28. Ibid., 101. For more background on the development of matrimonial advertising in the pages of the penny press, see chapter 3 of Phegley, *Courtship and Marriage*.
29. Gerrard, "New Methods," 62.
30. Humpherys, "*Bow Bells*," n.p. Mitchell estimates that a penny magazine had to sell at least 30,000 copies to break even, so this was a healthy readership that would have made the magazine profitable for Dicks. Mitchell, "Forgotten Woman," 37.
31. King, *London Journal*, 84.

208 THE LONDON JOURNAL. [March 31, 1866.

NOTICES TO CORRESPONDENTS.

Mary Ann.—Free passages are given to female servants to the Australian colonies; the wages average from £15 to £50 per annum. Apply to Mr. Bate, secretary, Colonial Emigration Society, 44, Charing-cross, S.W.

Admirans.—If the occupation franchise in boroughs was reduced to £8 upon the rateable value, it would increase the electors 35 per cent.; if to £6, 69 per cent.; and if to £5, 115 per cent.

George Thompson, a young Scotsman, six feet in stature, wishes to marry an English girl, about seventeen years of age. He has an income of £200 a-year.

Xeranthemum.—Sir John Cass's School was founded in 1709, with an income, then, of the value of £540. The trustees at present have a surplus income, after defraying extravagant expenses of £2,783.

Mililotus.—The sun-flower yields a large quantity of seed, for which poultry will leave almost any other food.

Dewsbury.—Yes; mineral oil mines have just been discovered at Trowbridge, in Wiltshire.

Cleopatra, the daughter of an officer in the army, is anxious to be settled, and have a husband and a home of her own. She is twenty-five years of age, and although short in stature, considered to be very good-looking. She will have no money, so that her husband must have not less than £200 a-year. She would not object to going to India or Australia.

W. W. W.—On New Year's-day there were only sixty debtors in Whitecross-street Prison.

Annie.—The first number of the *Times* appeared on the 1st of January, 1788.

May Morton asks us to hasten that desirable event, her marriage, by informing our bachelor friends that she is nineteen years of age, tall, has a fine figure, small waist, dark eyes, and clear complexion. In disposition she is cheerful. As she will have a little money of her own, her choice must be a tall and handsome young gentleman, of respectable family and fortune.

G. S. C.—1. Flexmore, the clown, died on the 20th of August, 1860. 2. William Farren, the celebrated actor, died on the 24th of September, 1861, aged seventy-five.

Forlorn.—Mr. Algar, of Clement's-lane, City, undertakes the business of inserting advertisements in Canadian and other colonial newspapers.

Cincinnatus thanks the ladies who have favoured him with replies, and would be glad to correspond with either of them. He would give the preference to one of true Christian principles, and who was able to sing and play sacred music.

Minnie.—The colloquial pronunciation of Greenwich is "Grinidge."

American Bowl.—The banking firm of Messrs. Prescott, Grote, Cave, and Co. is now 100 years old, having been first established on the 1st of January, 1766.

B. W. Z., who is twenty-nine years of age, and at present chief officer in the merchant service, passed master, of good family expectations, tall, and well-looking, wishes to correspond with a dark young lady, not more than twenty-five years of age. He would like her to be amiable, and have a small income of her own.

Enamoured.—Gentlemen do not wear engaged rings. Take the lady to a jeweller's, and there will be no mistake on your part.

H. S.—Between the years 1660 and 1756, 869 authors, printers, and sellers of books or engravings, were arrested and thrown into the Bastille, Paris.

Pollie H. does not think she is very pretty; but she has £300 a-year. She wants a sensible, good-natured husband, who is fond of laughing and fun.

C. E. W. B. Y.—"The Jackdaw of Rheims" is one of the "Ingoldsby Legends." The other pieces will be found in almost any modern book of recitation.

Cairo.—The entire amount of coal remaining in Great Britain, down to a depth of 4,000 feet, is estimated at 80,000,000,000 tons, and the extent of our coal-fields at 5,400 square miles.

A Warwickshire Lass would like to marry a midland-county gentleman, not more than thirty, of gentlemanly exterior, a Protestant, and comfortably settled for life. She is twenty-two, well-looking, and well-educated, and will have a fortune.

H. S.—The Forfarshire steamer was wrecked on one of the Faroe Islands, on her voyage from Hull to Dundee, on the 6th of September, 1838. Nine persons were saved by the courage of Grace Darling and her father. Elton, the actor, was among the number drowned.

Julian Young.—The Emperor and Empress of the French visited this country from April the 16th to the 21st, 1855. The Queen and Prince Consort visited Paris on the 18th of August, 1855.

Veritas hopes some fair one will have compassion on him. He wants a wife respectably connected, prepossessing in appearance, and not older than himself. He is twenty-two, has £180 a-year, and good expectations.

W. H. H.—The examinations for the Civil Service are competitive.

Cigarros.—The Manilla cigars imported into Europe do not contain opium.

Deodar.—The coal-fields of America are estimated at 196,000 square miles in extent.

A. A. A., a bachelor, forty-three years of age, and an agriculturist in a large way, is anxious to possess a wife, in the person of a fair lady, with golden or brown hair, of good stature, about thirty, and musical.

An Enquirer.—Marriages between all degrees of cousins are lawful in this country.

Ricardus.—To your very pointed questions, we are entitled to withhold any answer by putting forth the plea of privilege. As editor of this journal, we are placed in the condition of lawyer, physician, and friend, and are requested, in addition, to supply information on many other subjects. In our triune capacity, there is a confidence reposed in us which it is our duty to maintain inviolate. The correspondence submitted to us is sacred—it falls under no cognizance save our own, and when its requirements have been satisfied, the letters are destroyed. You will, therefore, perceive how impossible it is for us to reply to you as you seem to wish. Besides, no one is entitled to pry into the secrets of our editorial desk, the more especially as it contains weekly the photographs of scores upon scores of lives: some warm and youthful, some weak and despondent, others vain, morbid, and selfish, and, alas! some wretchedly criminal. Our task is to endeavour to please, as well as to oblige, all who consult us, and if sometimes our good nature is so heavily taxed, that it comes into collision with our cold and matured judgment, we cannot be censured for giving a little latitude to a kindly feeling which in its exercise injures none, but affords consolation and amusement to countless numbers.

Bernardo.—Peace with Russia was proclaimed April the 19th; thanksgiving-day, May 4; illumination-night, May 29, 1856.

Forget-me-Not, a young lady of the middle stature, with deep blue eyes and rich auburn hair, and told by her friends that she is pretty, wishes to marry a tall and handsome young gentleman, highly educated and respectable. Fortune no object, as she has £800 a-year, and will succeed to a large estate on the death of an aunt.

D. Hogarth.—Lilies of the valley do not like to be removed. They are best planted in a shady place—say a border facing the east—and there let them spread around each other.

Scotsman.—The borough magistrates of Truro had not a single case brought before them between the 8th and the 29th of January.

James will, no doubt, pay due attention to such fair correspondents as "Phillis M.," a blonde of twenty-one; "Emma H.," twenty-three, pretty, and the daughter of a farmer and innkeeper; "A Merry Girl," tall, handsome, eighteen, and entitled to a legacy of £1,000; "Laura," twenty-four, and pretty, whose fortune is her pretty self; "Theresa," twenty, tall, dark, and handsome.

A MOONLIGHT THOUGHT.

Sweet, pale-faced moon, that lookest down
Upon the clover-scented ground,
A magic charm of beauty lending,
Where the majestic river bending
Round the woodland sweeps away;
Down in my darkened bosom falleth
One sad ray, and it recalleth
Memories of an absent day.

Dear, pale-faced moon, thy silvery beam
Brings back to me an olden dream;
One that I hoped had been forgotten—
A simple flower, left untrodden
By the remorseless heel of Time.
And once more the hope-birds sing,
And once more life's tower-bell doth ring,
"Such a dream may not be thine!" E. E. R.

Bullionist.—A woman, although married, having a power of appointment, may make a will.

Mr. Swin.—1. A county-court has no jurisdiction in cases of slander. 2. By the recent retirement of Sir Charles Wood, now Viscount Halifax, Earl de Grey and Ripon is Secretary of State for India.

T. G.—1. Waterloo-bridge was opened on the 18th of June, 1817. 2. The Duke of Wellington was prime minister from 1828 to 1830.

C. C. B., it seems, has won the good opinion of "Helena Floyd," who is twenty-one, fair, blue-eyed, and loving; "Ermina," twenty-one, good-looking, and sure to be a good wife to a good husband; and "Birdie," who wants his *carte de visite*.

E. T. C.—The drawing of carts by dogs was first prohibited by statute on the 1st of January, 1855.

A Scion.—Before any distress can be legally made, the rent must be demanded on the premises; but you may be summoned to the county-court without any demand being previously made, as you were bound to take it when due.

A. G. M.—An executor cannot purchase the property of the testator.

Bertha, a middle-aged widow, with a comfortable home in London, would be happy to share it with a religious gentleman, from forty-five to fifty years of age.

L. L. S.—The accident at the Victoria Theatre took place on the 27th of December, 1858.

D. E.—The new year commences immediately after the clock has struck twelve on the night of the 31st of December.

March.—The employer is not liable for injury caused by the neglect of one servant to another.

Ottoman.—The proportion of depositors in savings-banks has more than doubled since the year 1831.

W. J. R., if really inclined to matrimony, may be able to select a wife from among "Kate," who is eighteen, and candidly says she is no beauty, but has rosy cheeks, fine eyes, and is fond of literature; "Maid of Mona," twenty-two, and good-looking; "W. E. M.," eighteen, rosy-cheeked, and blue-eyed; "M. J. B.," twenty-six, dark, well-educated, and industrious.

Peronne.—In Hungarian, the family name precedes the baptismal; thus "Alexander Petofi" is "Petofi Sandor."

W. P.—For marriage purposes, illegitimate children and legitimate children are considered as relations, and the ordinary rules apply. You could not marry your niece.

P. S. (Belfast).—No; you could not evade the penalty by the means you propose.

East Lynne.—To Cure Warts.—Touch them every night and morning with a drop of strong nitric acid, and pare them carefully every other day. Put a little sweet oil round the base.

S. A. E.—We present to this gentleman's regard notices from "Fanny," a pleasing girl, blessed with sound sense; "Manx Fairy," twenty, and a well-to-do tradesman's daughter; "Dolly," twenty-three, tall, and fine-looking, with black wavy hair, and dark brown eyes; "L. L.," twenty-six, a famous housekeeper, and worth £300; "Ellen," lady-like, and agreeable in person as well as manners; "R. B.," twenty-four, and far from being vain or "flirty;" "Effie," twenty-two, tall, pleasing, and fairly educated; "Laurestina," a good girl, fond of home, and who would like to reside in London.

Duped.—Yes; the illegitimate child can take the property left her by her father's will.

E. B.—No; a man cannot "give his wife money, &c., before he becomes bankrupt," and the creditors can "come down on her" if he does so.

Psyche.—1. Girls at fifteen may fancy they are in love; but as they creep on to seventeen and eighteen, the fond illusion vanishes, and quite a new and more ardent feeling takes possession of their nature. 2. Lord Byron was not an atheist. A true and glorious poet like him could not have "fallen into [that] blind cave of eternal night," even if he had wished it. As a man, he was erratic, frequently sophistical, and self-torturing, but never an atheist. He railed against hypocrisy, and hurled sarcasms against would-be holy men; but in his heart of heart, he loved all things sacred. While in Italy, he had only four books on his study-table, and one of them was the bible.

Lucy.—1. The lady's name was Davenport. She was married. 2. We are not justified in answering.

Chesham, Dr. Heriot, E. G. H., Penelope, and H. Hayes, are all referred to respectable solicitors, their cases being matters for the consideration of a court of justice.

Nellie boldly proposes for "Derry" She is twenty, fair, and admires dark gentlemen.

W. H. B.—To Varnish Drawings.—Boil clear parchment cuttings in water, in a glazed earthern vessel, till they produce a very clear size; strain it, and keep it till required; then give the work two coats of the size, passing the brush quickly over the work, so as not to disturb the colours.

J. B. W.—See our reply to "John Thomas E.," in the present number.

J. L. Y.—A domestic servant cannot lawfully leave without the customary month's notice.

Glossop.—The proportion of paid-up capital and reserved funds in London joint-stock banks to their liabilities is 8 35 per cent.

Britomarte has been eagerly noticed by "An Irish Medical Man," thirty-seven, handsome, and having some property; "Henry C. M.," twenty-seven, and good-looking; he wishes to go abroad; "St. Barnabas," forty, good-looking, healthy, and active; "Frank E. F.," not quite forty, and a clerk who has saved money.

A. B. C. D.—It is a well-known fact that the cat can have hydrophobia; but it is absurd to suppose that the bite of any cat is necessarily dangerous. As a matter of precaution, the wound should be sucked, or caustic applied to it.

Rosamond Vallefort.—All would depend upon the particular circumstances.

An Injured Mechanic.—Only in the event of your being permanently injured could you sustain an action for damages, after having accepted a weekly payment when out of work, by way of compensation.

John Thomas E., Y. O. F., and Z. Z. Z.—Take seven drops of the muriate tincture of iron three times a-day in cold water for three months, and frequently sponge yourself all over with cold water.

Valerian.—One thousand tons of bamboo will give 500 tons of pulp fit for paper-making.

B. L. Y.—Yes; for 200 years Japan was closed against all direct intercourse with Europe.

W. J. A. has received flattering replies from "Harriett," a dark and good-tempered girl; "Rose S.," a farmer's daughter, twenty, handsome, and quite tired of a rough life; "Lizzie Wright," dark, with a good figure, and an excellent temper; "Louise," nineteen, short in stature, and a brunette; "S. J. S.," a tradesman's daughter, twenty-one, and considered handsome.

Jane Skillet and Y. O. F.—Any chymist will readily supply you with a depilatory. We always recommend the constant use of the tweezers in preference.

H. W. C.—The accounts vary as to the number of lives lost in the London; the highest is 240—the lowest, 207.

M. J. J.—Forward the manuscript, and, if possible, obtain an interview with the publisher or manager.

T. H. S.—Members in the House of Commons wear their hats or not, just as they like. The Queen could lawfully marry a commoner.

J. Wilson.—By all means learn French; that language is always useful to a tradesman.

Maynard Higgs.—Jamaica was settled by the Spaniards in 1510, and remained in their possession about 150 years. It was captured on the 3rd of May, 1655, by Admiral Penn and General Venables, who found about 1,500 Spaniards and Portuguese, and about the same number of negroes and mulattoes, on the island; but no trace of any of the aborigines.

Elinor thinks "H. Dion" worthy of her hand. She is seventeen, and of the Grecian type of female beauty.

John S. S.—You will, if you take care of yourself, continue growing in stature until you are twenty-one.

Catamaran.—The publishers will readily furnish you with the information, if you forward a stamped and addressed envelope.

Handwriting.—Minnie (very good)—George Lewis (yes)—Jenny M. (good; the colour of the hair is light flaxen)—F. T. M. (good, and adapted for a lawyer's office)—J. T. S. (good)—Bella S. (good, and lady-like)—Violet L. (very good)—Cigarros (very good).

Letters Received.—Emma E., A. D. E., Ellen, Mary Ann Knight, C. W., Fred Boyd, Emma, Arthur Bedinfield, E. G. W., Alice Linden, Alfred Homer, Jack of the Hills, J. M., Alfred Bright, Amy F., Samuel Albert, C. A. E., Cupid, M. D., Sincerite, Miss E. V., G. C. F., E. H. Laurence, M. B., Annetta, Helena, J. R., Clarence L., M. A. Duke, F. C. J., The Lass of Richmond Hill, Francais, Inquisitive, Y. Z., Aimee, Lilian, Maud, Grace and May, Ricardo, Two Sisters, Marie, Harry F., Minnie Clyde, Lily and Laura, Minnie Roe and Flora Clyden, Tom Brown, W. J. C., Jessie and Ross, Helen Alberto, J. T. D., Alpha, Lizzie M., Philip Bertram, May Isabel, Alice Maud, Emily Munro and Alice Stevens, Belinda Montezuma, Jessie Huntley, A. Chas. J., J. of Australia, T. M. P., Edward Hotspur, Lily of the Valley, Emily Morris, Blanche, Harold, E. M., H. J. Bellerophon (answered in a previous number), D. M. Thomas.

*** We do not guarantee the return of Rejected Manuscripts. As they are sent to us voluntarily, authors should retain copies.

All Letters must be Addressed to the Editor of "The London Journal," 332, Strand, London.

Now publishing, Vol. I. of The Guide, containing the popular tale of "Minnigrey," complete, price 4s. 6d.; also Vols. II., III., and IV., bound in cloth, 4s. 6d. each.

†‡† Now Ready, the Index to Vol. XLII., Price One Penny. Also, Bound in Cloth, Vol. XLII., Price 4s. 6d.

THE BEST FAMILY NEWSPAPER IS
THE WEEKLY TIMES.
PRICE ONE PENNY.

A NEW AND POWERFULLY-WRITTEN STORY OF ORIGINAL AND EXCITING INTEREST, BY
PIERCE EGAN, Esq.,
Author of "The Poor Girl," "Fair Lilias," &c., will shortly appear.

London: Printed at the "Nassau Steam Press," 60, St. Martin's-lane, and Published for the Proprietor by George Vickers, at the Office of "The London Journal," 332, Strand.—March 31, 1866.

Figure 20.3 "Notices to Correspondents," *London Journal* 43 (March 31, 1866): 208.

Bow Bells offered exciting serial fiction and other material Louis James argues was quintessentially suitable for female servants who came from a wide range of backgrounds, were of "ambivalent social position," and were "relatively mobile socially" upon leaving service.[32] James's typical servant, "Betsy," made reading selections that were "fiercely" improving but also escapist, romantic, and violent.[33] *Bow Bells* also regaled Betsy, as well as a wide variety of other working- and lower-middle-class women readers, with regular features on grammar, etiquette, and domestic pursuits as well as philosophical articles about women's roles.

Bow Bells's sensational and sentimental cover illustrations were balanced by the masthead of the magazine, which included images of women in classical robes engaged in various reading, writing, and artistic pursuits (Figure 20.4). These women are arranged around the central image of the tower of St. Mary-le-Bow church, the magazine's namesake and an identifying landmark of London's East End. While the classical figures stand in sharp contrast to the magazine's association with the Cockney center of London, they symbolize a kind of cultural identity that its core audience might have hoped to achieve. Positioning these ancient scholarly women as overseers of a "weekly magazine of general literature" also emphasized its educational purpose even as the serial fiction and illustrations highlighted its entertaining qualities. While the magazine may not have provided the lofty fare its masthead promised, many of *Bow Bells*'s non-fiction articles did promote the importance of reading to women's self-improvement. For example, "Good Reading" describes the activity as the highest "accomplishment" a woman could have since it is useful in so many situations and is not as showy or individualistic as piano playing or singing.[34] Furthermore, it is something that more people have a facility for and can successfully cultivate. Reading well is described as the "natural exponent and vehicle of all good things" and is defined as something that is done in a family setting.[35]

As in the *Family Friend*'s frontispiece, in *Bow Bells* reading is conceived as a communal rather than a private experience: "What fascination there is in really good reading! What power it gives one! In the hospital, in the chamber of the invalid, in the nursery, in the domestic and the social circle, among chosen friends and companions, how it enables you to minister to the amusement, the comfort, the pleasure of dear ones, as no other art or accomplishment does."[36] Even when reading is promoted for more selfish reasons, *Bow Bells* still frames it as beneficial to others. "The Habit of Reading" urges women to read every day to break up the monotony of their work. Though their responsibilities may prevent them from reading in a leisurely manner, the article urges that it is "not the books we finish at a sitting which always do us the most good. Those we devour in the odd moments, half a dozen pages at a time often give us more satisfaction, and are more thoroughly digested."[37] Furthermore, "it is the habit of reading, rather than the time at our command, that helps us on the road of learning. . . . If we make use of spare minutes in the midst of our work, and read a little, if but a page or a paragraph, we shall find

---

32. James, "Trouble with Betsy," 353.
33. Ibid.
34. "Good Reading," 212.
35. Ibid.
36. Ibid.
37. "Habit of Reading," 346.

Figure 20.4 Masthead of *Bow Bells* 4 (February 14, 1866): 49. Reproduced with permission from ProQuest LLC.

our brains quickened and our toil lightened."[38] One can imagine a household servant stealing glances at bits and pieces from *Bow Bells* in this hurried but satisfying manner. *Bow Bells* exemplifies the attitude toward women's reading found in the penny family magazines and anticipates the preoccupation with women's reading and writing practices in the shilling monthlies.

Shilling Monthly Family Magazines

By the 1860s, just about every publishing house had launched its own shilling monthly family magazine for a middle-class audience. These magazines functioned, at least in part, as advertising venues for publishing companies. Barbara Quinn Schmidt points out that while many publishers actually lost money on their shilling monthlies, they maintained them as an essential promotional tool that would draw attention to their newly contracted authors and forthcoming books.[39] These upscale family magazines, much like their lower-level peers, were meant to be entertaining, but they were also self-consciously geared toward providing a higher literary and cultural education that would allow readers to demonstrate their suitability for membership in the industrious and tasteful middle classes. Shilling monthlies featured both realistic and sensational fiction, essays on topics of historical, geographical, and cultural interest, as well as travel narratives, poetry, and, usually, high-quality illustrations.

In addition to *Macmillan's* (1859–1907) and the *Cornhill* (1860–1975), shilling monthlies included *Temple Bar* (1860–1906), *St. James's* (1861–1900), *Tinsley's* (1867–92), *St. Paul's* (1867–74), and *Victoria* (1863–80). Some of these magazines took their names from their publishers, others from areas of London intended to signify their cultural cachet. Exceptions include Emily Faithfull's *Victoria*, which took the namesake of the queen in order to convey the importance of women to literary culture, and Ellen Price Wood's *Argosy* (1865–1901), which was described as a ship full of literary treasures. The cover of the *Argosy* featured the tagline "laden with golden grain" above the image of a man in classical robes rowing an elegantly

---

38. Ibid.
39. Schmidt, "Novelists," 143.

Figure 20.5 Cover of the *Argosy* 23, no. 137 (April 1877).

carved boat (Figure 20.5). It cost 6d. but its format was modeled on the shilling monthly. Like the *Argosy*, many monthlies relied on their association with a famous editor to attract an audience—Mary Elizabeth Braddon at *Belgravia*, George Ausgustus Sala at *Temple Bar*, William Makepeace Thackeray at *Cornhill*, and Anthony Trollope at *St. Paul's*.

By the 1860s the shilling monthly family magazines were a major force in the publishing industry, despite their relatively modest circulation figures in the 20,000–80,000 range.[40] Shilling monthlies were less than half the price of long-standing elite magazines like *Blackwood's* (1817–1980) and *Fraser's* (1830–82), which were a step down from the quarterly reviews but not as family friendly as the newer magazines. In the winter of 1859–60, both *Macmillan's* and the *Cornhill* were launched. The first number of the *Cornhill*, edited by William Thackeray and featuring a novel by Anthony Trollope, sold an astonishing 120,000 copies. Altick proclaims that this was "one of the most heartening events in the whole history of English periodicals, for the *Cornhill*, with its unmatched array of talent . . . was a first-class magazine. That it could attract so many purchasers seemed proof that the audience of serious readers had expanded almost apace with that of the entertainment seekers."[41] While the novelty wore off and many more competitors entered the market, the shilling monthly proved that it could satisfy a middle-class audience hungry for serialized fiction of a higher quality than that offered by the penny periodicals.

Thackeray's description of the *Cornhill* (named for the London street where the publishing house of Smith, Elder was located) exemplifies the tone of most shilling monthlies. In his editorial column, he declares that the magazine will balance fact and fiction, thus offering a healthy literary diet alongside the dessert of its serials: "Novels are sweets. All people with healthy literary appetites love them—almost all women—a vast number of clever, hard-headed men. . . . Judges, bishops, chancellors, mathematicians are notorious novel-readers; as well as young boys and sweet girls and their tender kind-hearted mothers."[42] Yet the boundary between fact and fiction was not as obvious as the difference between roast beef and sweets. Much of the fiction was realistic and much of the non-fiction employed literary devices, including fictional characters and dialogue. Indeed, the ability to discern the educational elements of both fact and fiction was a key characteristic of the shilling monthly reader. As Peter Smith argues, the *Cornhill* offered "opportunities to the intelligent non-specialist to become acquainted with current ideas, whether scientific, literary, or sociological."[43] The middle-class woman reader was the ultimate intelligent non-specialist who would benefit from the wealth of material available in the family magazine.

According to Wynne, the legitimization of sensation fiction as respectable reading for the educated middle classes in family magazines like the *Cornhill* was central to the success of both sensationalism and the family magazine itself. Shilling monthlies, she explains, distanced serial sensation novels from the cheap thrills and shoddy writing associated with the penny weeklies while exploring "anxieties surrounding shifting class identities, financial insecurity,

---

40. Ellegård, "Readership of the Periodical Press," 32–3.
41. Altick, *English Common Reader*, 359.
42. Thackeray, "On a Lazy, Idle Boy," 127.
43. P. Smith, "*Cornhill Magazine*," 31.

the precarious social position of single women, sexuality, failed and illegal marriages, insanity, and mental debilitation, fears of criminality, and perceptions that modernity itself was undermining domestic life."[44] The inclusion of these sensational themes highlights the kinship between the penny weeklies and the shilling monthlies. Though the fiction and non-fiction in the monthly family magazines might have been of a higher aesthetic quality than the prose featured in the penny weeklies, it was perhaps the appearance of the monthlies—the quality and number of illustrations, along with a smaller size, lengthier format, and more expensive paper and bindings—that really set them apart. The *Cornhill*, which featured two serials in each issue, often included a full-page plate for each novel provided by a well-known artist such as Frederick Leighton, George du Maurier, John Everett Millais, or Frederick Walker. These illustrations were typically less sensational than those featured on the covers of the penny weeklies. Walker's illustrations for Thackeray's *The Adventures of Philip* (serialized January 1861–August 1862) are typical of the idealized, somewhat sentimental style that reproduced what Forrest Reid calls the "charming aspects of ordinary domestic life—a pretty girl shelling peas, or an old woman lifting the kettle from the hob," which are set against a backdrop of simple interior spaces or natural outdoor settings.[45] "Laura's Fireside," for example, depicts a pleasantly sentimental family scene without much mystery or excitement (Figure 20.6).

Like penny weeklies, shilling monthlies addressed women as intelligent participants in critical conversations about literary and cultural subjects, and dismissed the idea that reading "low" cultural forms like sensation fiction would have a negative impact on them. Of course, these magazines were simultaneously promoting both kinds of reading—the informative and the exciting—so they had a stake in defending higher and lower literary forms. Mary Braddon used her editorship of *Belgravia* to argue that women could actually become better interpreters of life and literature by reading sensation novels, which would train them to judge characters and people more accurately and to avoid putting themselves into compromising situations. She employed critics like G.A. Sala to link sensationalism with more acceptable literary traditions, such as Greek tragedy and Shakespearean drama, to illustrate that sensational forms had a long, respectable history. Sala and other writers for *Belgravia* went so far as to blame other critics for the corruption of literary taste, thereby turning the tables on those who doubted the value of sensation fiction and the intellectual abilities of women readers. For example, T.H.S. Escott claimed that it was critics rather than women who were in danger of a "habit of slovenliness . . . destructive of all mental improvement and discipline" because they were the readers who believed they could "see everything at once" and "grasp complexity" without missing anything.[46] Yet, he argues, critics are more likely than leisured women to skim and skip and read uncritically precisely because they were reading too much in too little time.[47] Likewise, Sala took away the legitimacy of the critic (and even the father or husband) as an acceptable regulator of women's reading, arguing that "novels are written for grown up women and not

---

44. Wynne, *Sensation Novel*, 3.
45. Reid, *Illustrators of the Eighteen Sixties*, 134.
46. Escott, "Vagueness," 412–13.
47. Ibid., 410.

Figure 20.6 "Laura's Fireside," *Cornhill Magazine* 3 (April 1861): 385.

for babes and sucklings"; therefore, "grown women should be free to choose whatever reading material they desire."[48]

Family magazines, then, were defenders of novels, sensational and otherwise, and of women's abilities to read critically and productively. Family magazines were also, predictably, more welcoming to women writers than were many other periodicals. While this periodical genre and the serial novel dominated the publishing world, women writers were more widely published than ever before.[49] In an early advertisement for the *Cornhill*, Thackeray explicitly invited "pleasant and instructed gentlemen and ladies to contribute their share," though Janice H. Harris's content analysis reveals that between 1860 and 1900 only 20 percent of its contributors were women.[50] While this was a greater number than for many of the more elite periodicals of the day, Thackeray's editorial commentary on the pleading "thorn letters" he received reveals his discomfort with the desperation of women who submitted work to the magazine: "'I am poor; I am good; I am ill; I work hard; I have a sick mother and hungry brothers and sisters dependent upon me. You can help us if you will.' . . . Ah me! We wound where we never intended to strike; we create anger where we never meant harm; and these thoughts are the Thorns in our Cushion."[51] Thackeray was certainly frustrated by the barrage of submissions, but he was also sympathetic to women's eagerness to earn money by writing for periodicals and understood that magazines like the one he edited had opened the floodgates to women writers.

Victoria Magazine addressed women's limited earning opportunities head-on as it set out to transform women from consumers to producers of literary content. The magazine originated with the ladies of the Langham Place Circle, an organization founded by Bessie Rayner Parkes and Barbara Bodichon in 1855 to agitate for the passage of a Married Woman's Property Act. When the act failed in 1857, the women turned their attention toward founding publications that furthered women's social, political, and literary interests and supported organizations that advanced women's education and employment opportunities. Under the direction of Emily Faithfull, the Victoria Press began publishing high-quality literary works and training women to become compositors and printers. The press eventually became Queen Victoria's official printer and produced the magazine that was her namesake. The women of Langham Place also produced the *English Woman's Journal* (1858–64) and the *Englishwoman's Review* (1866–1910), but these were more explicitly focused on women's political rights and social status, while *Victoria* was clearly intended to compete with other family magazines. While promoting feminist literary criticism and feminist business practices was part of *Victoria*'s core mission, it was primarily a literary magazine with Faithfull at its helm and Emily Davies as its chief literary critic. *Victoria* was the first mainstream feminist family magazine featuring the standard serial novels alongside fiction, non-fiction, and poetry. However, since the editors could not afford to attract as many prominent authors as a publication like the *Cornhill Magazine*, it shifted focus slightly to offer more reviews of fiction. Indeed, it reviewed many of the novels serialized in

---

48. Sala, "Cant of Modern Criticism," 54.
49. Phegley, *Educating the Proper Woman Reader*, 8.
50. Quoted in G. Smith, "Our Birth and Parentage," 6; Harris, "Not Suffering and Not Still," 385.
51. Thackeray, "Thorns in the Cushion," 126.

the *Cornhill*. *Victoria*'s reviews supported realist fiction rather than sensation novels, but like the other shilling monthlies, it vigorously defended women readers from the dismissive attitudes of elite critics. Unlike many other family magazines that highlighted sensation fiction, Davies's "Literature of the Month" section praised moral fiction that featured complex and intelligent female characters, paying special attention to works by women writers such as Anne Thackeray, Margaret Oliphant, George Eliot, and Elizabeth Gaskell.[52] As *Victoria* and *Bow Bells* reveal, the boundary between women's periodicals and family magazines was more permeable than has often been acknowledged.[53] Likewise, the boundary between penny weeklies and shilling monthlies is less distinct than is usually recognized. Indeed, *Victoria* incorporated a correspondence column reminiscent of those appearing in *Bow Bells* and other penny family magazines. However, it is Dickens's hybrid periodicals that illustrate the kinship between the weeklies and the monthlies most clearly.

Charles Dickens and the Hybrid Family Magazine

Charles Dickens's *Household Words* (1850–59) and *All the Year Round* (1859–95) were hybrids of the weekly and monthly family magazines that, as Lorna Huett notes, "employed a combination of the publishing practices from both ends of the marketplace."[54] These magazines were published weekly and sold for two pence. They were accessible to the working classes but still attractive to middle-class readers, who would have been particularly pleased with their link to the inimitable Dickens. *Household Words* was modeled after *Chambers's*, an early penny weekly magazine whose assistant editor, W.H. Wills, also helped Dickens edit his journals. Like *Chambers's* and many other penny weeklies, it was printed in double columns with no illustrations. However, it stood apart because it featured higher-quality fiction and harder-hitting investigative journalism and was unified by an engaging Dickensian style of writing that permeated all of its features.[55] Huett argues that "*Household Words* was an oddity: a cheap publication welcomed into the drawing rooms of the middle classes, and into the reading rooms of reputable institutions" by sheer force of the esteemed editor, whose name appeared in the running header on every double-page spread of the magazine.[56] It was "to a great extent responsible for inverting views of the cheap press: rather than being an organ of sedition or revolution, the two-penny paper became an acceptable way for the middle-classes to consume the products of the leading authors of the day."[57] Dickens may well have been attempting to fulfill Collins's prophecy

---

52. For a close analysis of *Victoria*'s feminist reviews of realistic fiction, see Phegley, *Educating the Proper Woman Reader*, 176–84.
53. Samuel Beeton's *Englishwoman's Domestic Magazine* (1852–79) reformulated the woman's periodical at mid-century at about the same time that the family magazine emerged. Like family magazines, the *EDM* highlighted serial fiction; however, it featured more practically oriented articles on household management, sewing, cooking, gardening, arts and crafts, and fashion—elements that *Bow Bells* adapted and borrowed.
54. Huett, "Among the Unknown Public," 76.
55. Drew, "*Household Words*," n.p.
56. Huett, "Among the Unknown Public," 70.
57. Ibid.

in his *Household Words* article "The Unknown Public"—that a "great, an unparalleled prospect awaits . . . the coming generation of English novelists. To the penny journals of the present time belongs the credit of having discovered a new public. When that public shall discover its need for a great writer, the great writer will have such an audience as has never yet been known."[58] Dickens's magazines were perhaps intended to insure that he was the great writer who would unify the penny press and the shilling monthly readers into one audience.

All the Year Round replaced *Household Words* when Dickens had a dispute with his publisher, Bradbury and Evans. Wills stayed on as sub-editor of *All the Year Round*, which also sold for two pence. However, the magazine expanded its audience by privileging high-quality serial fiction and replacing politically oriented topical pieces on education and industrialism with articles on science, history, and travel.[59] By this time, the shilling monthlies had arrived, and *All the Year Round* followed the standard set by these successful magazines. The lower cost and exciting sensation fiction featured in *All the Year Round* likely made up for the fact that it was printed in a "drab" double-column format and lacked the lavish illustrations of the typical shilling monthly.[60] Despite its aesthetic sparseness, *All the Year Round* reached an average of 100,000 subscribers, beating *Household Words*'s average of 40,000 readers. Dickens thus transformed the genre of the family magazine by attempting to appeal to readers at multiple levels of the literary marketplace. However, his efforts to unite the classes in reading his magazines were not successfully imitated. Instead, the 1870s ushered in a new era in which audiences were increasingly fragmented. As a result, family magazines were superseded by niche-market periodicals for men, women, boys, girls, and other more narrowly defined special interest groups.[61]

Wynne compares the Victorian periodical press to the "internet today, where different voices compete for attention within an expanding media which defies boundaries and definitions," noting that it "was forever in a state of flux and transition as various discourses and genres established themselves (or sank into oblivion) through its pages."[62] It was, perhaps, the genre of the family magazine that most changed the periodical publishing industry and that most readily met the needs of the entire sweep of the Victorian reading public: from the servant and the factory worker to the clerk and the shop girl, from the middle-class housewife and the business entrepreneur to the woman author and the clergyman. While many individual family magazines have not been examined by scholars in great detail, it is the study of the intersections among the various kinds of publications within the genre that has been most neglected. In order to advance our understanding of this genre, it will be necessary to study the ways in which seemingly disparate magazines worked with the same basic formula to carve out specific family markets based primarily on class status. In addition, we must look beyond the titles usually studied—the *Cornhill Magazine* or *Household Words*—in order to fully understand this diverse and fascinating genre.

58. [Collins], "Unknown Public," 222.
59. Drew, "*All the Year Round*," n.p.
60. Wynne, *Sensation Novel*, 24.
61. Mitchell, "Forgotten Woman," 30.
62. Wynne, *Sensation Novel*, 167.

21

CHILDREN'S PERIODICALS

Kristine Moruzi

The history of British children's periodicals is inextricably entwined with the changing nature of childhood during the nineteenth century. The Victorians inherited Romantic conceptions of the child as pure, innocent, natural, and wise. Yet there was also a strand of thinking, initiated by John Locke, that the child was essentially a *tabula rasa*, or blank slate. Authors writing in the didactic tradition of the late eighteenth century, such as Maria Edgeworth and Sarah Fielding, depicted children as requiring education and experience to become "acceptable to, and accepting of, society's norms of gender and class expectations."[1] The tension between these conceptions of childhood continued throughout the nineteenth century and became increasingly important as literacy levels improved and children came to be seen as an important market for the publishers of periodicals. As Diana Dixon observes, the fact that there were more than five hundred periodicals for children and young people published between 1866 and 1914 indicates a "recognition by publishers that the juvenile market was ripe for exploitation."[2]

Children's magazines were shaped by a range of religious and commercial interests that shifted along with changing definitions of childhood. Conceptions of childhood found in nineteenth-century children's periodicals tell us as much about the attitudes of middle-class editors and contributors as they do about young readers themselves. The "genre" of children's periodicals is further complicated by their wide-ranging content, which included short stories, serialized novels, poetry, non-fiction articles, illustrations, editorials, and correspondence. The contents of magazines were determined by the influence and control of the editor and the type and variety of contributors, as well as opportunities for reader input. Often changes in magazine style, content, and attitude became obvious only over a period of years. By examining individual issues in relation to a magazine's entire run, researchers can begin to discern opposing viewpoints and detect unusual content.

As Julia Briggs and Dennis Butts have pointed out, the importance of periodicals to the development of children's literature in the nineteenth century "cannot be overemphasized."[3] The market for both books and magazines grew markedly as the century progressed. At the

---

1. Wood, "Angelic, Atavistic, Human," 116.
2. Dixon, "Children and the Press," 133.
3. Briggs and Butts, "Emergence of Form," 163.

beginning of the century, relatively few periodicals were written and published specifically for children. In 1824 there were only five magazines for young people in England, yet in 1900 there were 160.[4] By the turn of the twentieth century, an increase in the number of children's periodicals resulted in a fiercely competitive market that made it difficult for new magazines to establish a brand and attract a sufficiently large readership. The actual readership for many nineteenth-century children's magazines is difficult to determine. Although some publications announced their circulation numbers, particularly when attempting to attract advertisers, those numbers were most likely inflated. Moreover, a lengthy run did not necessarily indicate commercial viability. The long-lived *Monthly Packet* had a relatively scant circulation of approximately 2,000, which suggests that financial motives were less crucial to publishers than the content of the magazine. Children's periodicals with low circulations that lacked such outside funding typically folded.

Over the course of the century, many children's periodicals had runs of a year or less, although the lucky few would last for years or even decades. These long-lived publications have been the focus of most scholarship since short-run periodicals were more ephemeral and less likely to have been preserved in libraries and archives. These latter most likely had a limited readership and low circulation numbers, although the circulation required to keep a magazine in business varied widely. Some weekly magazines had much healthier circulations, such as the *Boy's Own Paper* and the *Girl's Own Paper*, which published 150,000 and 250,000 copies per issue, respectively.

Prior to 1850, children's magazines were predominantly religious in orientation. Two of the earliest were launched in 1824: the evangelical *Child's Companion; or, Sunday Scholar's Reward* (1824–1923) and the Anglican equivalent, the *Children's Friend* (1824–1929). Both emerged out of the Sunday school movement, which was focused on teaching poor and working-class children to read religious texts. The *Child's Companion*, published by the Religious Tract Society, included missionary tales, natural history, and stories reinforcing the need for children to behave piously. The *Children's Friend* was intended as a companion to adult religious magazines edited by the Rev. William Carus Wilson. Both of these early periodicals were monthly, one-penny publications which were intended to guide both boys and girls towards appropriate Christian behaviors.

A series of changes to the duties and taxes related to printing and publishing made children's periodicals more viable after 1850. The duty on advertisements was abolished in 1853, the stamp tax in 1855, and the paper tax in 1861, all of which combined to reduce the price of newspapers and periodicals. The expansion of the periodical press during this period contributed to the improvement of children's literacy in the second half of the nineteenth century. This was further bolstered by the Elementary Education Act of 1870, which introduced mandatory education for all children between the ages of five and twelve. At the same time, children were increasingly seen as a new target market for books and magazines, and publishers correspondingly sought to produce less expensive, higher-quality reading material for a youthful audience. Most children primarily accessed fiction through the periodical press, in

---

4. Dixon, "From Instruction to Amusement," 63.

large part because weekly and monthly magazines were more affordable than books. After 1850 and continuing through to the beginning of World War I, the improved market for children's periodicals and the perceived need to differentiate between periodicals for boys and for girls meant an unprecedented increase in the number of juvenile titles.

The influence of religion on children's periodicals declined towards the end of the century as religious periodicals lost their market share and as publishers attempted to attract a broader, more secular spectrum of readers. Unsurprisingly, publishers such as the Religious Tract Society expressed concern about this shift away from religious content. In 1879, the society launched the *Boy's Own Paper* to counteract the influence of penny dreadfuls, which published stories featuring lurid crime and sensational storylines. Beginning in the 1840s, as Patrick Dunae explains, penny dreadfuls were "based on the traditions of the Newgate Calendar and the Gothic novel: they often featured bizarre, supernatural figures . . . or heinous characters."[5] However, by the latter decades of the century, the term was applied almost exclusively to boys' periodicals of the lowest class. This stratification based on gender and class was particularly apparent in the last decades of the century, when the number of magazines aimed specifically at girls or boys increased markedly.

The earliest nineteenth-century periodicals for children contained few, if any, illustrations, but most titles published later in the century took pride in the breadth and quality of their illustrated content. These illustrations provided children with images of themselves engaged in a variety of different activities and thus reflect shifts in attitudes towards childhood throughout the Victorian and Edwardian eras. This emphasis on illustrations may be owing to the change in children's purchasing power. Early in the century, juvenile periodicals were usually purchased by adults on children's behalf. Later in the century, children could purchase their own periodicals with pin money, which meant magazines above all needed to be entertaining. Children were attracted to serialized fiction, short stories, jokes, puzzles, and poetry. After 1850, most children's periodicals depended heavily on fiction, which could occupy over 50 percent of a given number. They typically included non-fiction articles as well, encompassing biography, history, hobbies, nature, science, and sports. Later in the century, children's magazines often included vibrant correspondence sections and sometimes extravagant promotional campaigns that included prize draws and competitions.

Boys' Periodicals

Boys were eagerly targeted by periodical publishers in the 1850s. One of the first periodicals to achieve lasting success was Samuel Beeton's *Boy's Own Magazine* (1855–74). This thirty-two-page monthly contained useful informational articles as well as exciting fiction by well-known boys' authors such as W.H.G. Kingston and Captain Mayne Reid. Ostensibly Christian in tone, it differed markedly from the penny dreadfuls. Although priced at 2d. and therefore not out of reach for lower-class boys, it nonetheless tended to attract a middle-class readership. The *Boy's Journal* (1863–71) was intended to compete with Beeton's magazine. Its 3d. price per monthly

---

5. Dunae, "Penny Dreadfuls," 133–4.

number (which rose to 6d. in 1864 when the magazine was enlarged and enhanced) meant that it was primarily aimed at a middle-class readership, but it "struggled to compete with the penny weeklies" that appeared after 1866.[6] Contributors included renowned boys' author Captain Mayne Reed as well as Jules Verne, whose serialized story "Journey to the Centre of the Earth" first appeared there in 1870.

Although it was commercially unsuccessful, the *Boys' Miscellany* (1863–64) played a role in redefining the boys' periodical. Aimed at a working-class readership and priced at 1d., it contained numerous penny dreadful serials and was lavishly illustrated. As Christopher Banham points out, it established the "blueprint for boys' magazines" that was later standardized by Edwin J. Brett and the Emmett brothers.[7] He further contends that Brett's *Boys of England* (1866–99) was "arguably the most popular and successful of all Victorian boys' magazines."[8] This one-penny weekly magazine was aimed at the working classes and included attractive cover illustrations combined with fiction, non-fiction, and a popular correspondence column (Figure 21.1). Its "Jack Harkaway" series proved to be immensely popular with boy readers. The magazine would prove to be the industry standard for decades. Brett established a *"Boys of England* Office" in an attempt to distance his publication from his Newsagents' Publishing Company, which was known for publishing penny dreadful fiction.[9] The magazine began to struggle in the 1870s in the wake of stiff competition from Alfred Harmsworth's halfpenny weeklies. It also faced a serious threat from the Emmett brothers, who launched the rival *Young Gentleman's Journal* in 1867.

The weekly *Boy's Own Paper* (1879–1967) was a leading Victorian boys' magazine because of its high-quality content and its Christian ethos. Charles Welsh's survey of children's reading in 1884 identifies the *Boy's Own Paper* as a clear favorite with its intended readership.[10] George Andrew Hutchison, who edited the magazine until 1912, published stories by many well-known authors of boys' fiction, such as R.M. Ballantyne, G.A. Henty, W.H.G. Kingston, Talbot Baines Reed, and Gordon Stables. Although priced at one penny to attract working-class readers, it may have been more successful at appealing to the middle classes. Patrick Dunae points out that it did so by co-opting "some of the violence and nonconformity which had characterized the disreputable papers" and redirecting "the spirit of the penny dreadfuls into acceptable channels."[11] The major competitor for the *Boy's Own Paper*, *Chums* (1892–1934), was founded in 1892, and "after a shaky start it captured a large share of the same [mainly middle-class] audience."[12]

---

6. Banham, *"Boy's Journal,"* 68.
7. Banham, *"Boys' Miscellany,"* 68.
8. Banham, *"Boys of England,"* 69.
9. This practice of differentiating a new periodical from others produced by the same publishing company would later be adopted by the Religious Tract Society when it began publishing the *Boy's Own Paper* and the *Girl's Own Paper* under the auspices of the *"Leisure Hour* Office."
10. The *Boy's Own Paper* was the clear winner with 404 votes. Other boys' magazines received far fewer votes: *Boys' World* (16 votes), *Young England* (11 votes), and *Boys of England* (6 votes). Although this survey is non-scientific, it is interesting as a rough indicator of girls' and boys' reading preferences. See Moruzi, *Constructing Girlhood*, 6.
11. Dunae, "Boys' Literature," 108.
12. MacDonald, "Signs from the Imperial Quarter," 34.

Figure 21.1 Reissue cover of *Boys of England* 19, no. 490 (September 4, 1883).

Even though critics of the press expressed anxieties about the influence of penny dreadfuls on young boys, concerns about their reading habits were less common than anxieties about girls' reading preferences. Hence, much later in the century Alfred Harmsworth was able to achieve success with sensationalist weeklies for boys, such as *Marvel* (1893–1922), *Pluck* (1894–1924), and the *Boy's Friend* (1895–1927). Harmsworth claimed that they contained wholesome fiction, yet many of the stories in his magazines featured criminals and outlaws. His success was based on the cheap halfpenny price of his magazines.

Girls' Periodicals

The earliest girls' periodical was the 1838 *Young Ladies' Magazine of Theology, History, Philosophy, and General Knowledge*. Its short run of less than a year suggests that either girls were not yet interested in consuming content addressed specifically to them or that the content missed its target readership. A more successful girls' periodical was the High Church Anglican *Monthly Packet of Evening Readings for Younger Members of the Church of England* (1851–98), which was edited by Charlotte Yonge until 1893. The religious content of the magazine indicates that its readership was initially composed of girls preparing for confirmation; however, the removal of "Younger" from its title in 1866 suggests the core readership may have been aging.[13]

In the 1860s, there was a significant shift in girls' periodicals (almost a decade later than a comparable shift in boys' periodicals) as commercial publishers began to realize that there was money to be made from girl readers. The one-penny fashion periodical *English Girls' Journal, and Ladies' Magazine: A Weekly Illustrated Book for Every Dwelling* (1863–64) had a relatively short run and was followed by the slightly more successful *Young Ladies of Great Britain* (1869–71). In 1864, Samuel Beeton, already well known for the *Englishwoman's Domestic Magazine* (1852–90), launched the weekly *Young Englishwoman: A Magazine of Fiction and Entertaining Literature, Music, Poetry, Fine Arts, Fashions, and Useful and Ornamental Needlework*, which incorporated black-and-white and later color engravings. Eager to reach a broad audience, Beeton assured parents that it "may be placed without the slightest fear in the hands of girls of tender age."[14] It was initially edited by Beeton and his wife Isabella, who also edited the *Englishwoman's Domestic Magazine* until her death in 1865. Following Beeton's death in 1877, Beeton's *Young Englishwoman* (which had been renamed in 1870) continued as *Sylvia's Home Journal* in 1878 and then became *Sylvia's Journal* in 1892 before ceasing publishing in 1894. These later title changes served to distance the magazine from the youthful audience suggested by the original title, presumably because the publishers wanted to retain readers even after they grew up, married, and had children.

A year after the appearance of the *Boy's Own Paper*, the Religious Tract Society launched a sister publication, the *Girl's Own Paper* (1880–1956), which went on to become the most popular girls' magazine of the century (Figure 21.2). Editor Charles Peters explained that he hoped to "foster and develop that which was highest and noblest in the girlhood and womanhood of

---

13. In an attempt to attract or retain readers who were no longer in their teens, the weekly *Girl's Own Paper* became the monthly *Girl's Own Paper and Woman's Magazine* under the editorship of Flora Klickmann in 1908.
14. McNeely and Hughes, "Young Englishwoman," 695.

Figure 21.2 Cover of the *Girl's Own Paper* 19, no. 970 (July 30, 1898).

England."[15] Priced at one penny and appearing weekly, this popular, long-running magazine offered girls "stories of their own."[16] The content of the *Girl's Own Paper* demonstrates how reading was increasingly defined in gendered terms. For example, Stables contributed articles to the *Boy's Own Paper* on "Boys' Dogs and All about Them" as well as "The Boy's Own Museum;

15. Klickmann, "Editor's Page," 1.
16. Briggs and Butts, "Emergence of Form," 158.

Or, Birds and Beasts, and How to Stuff Them." His contributions to the *Girl's Own Paper* are focused on health and moral virtues, including "Exercise, and How to Benefit By It" and "Work Versus Idleness."

Although periodicals for girls appeared early in the century, the success of the *Girl's Own Paper* demonstrated the financial viability of producing an inexpensive weekly one-penny magazine aimed specifically at girls. A slightly earlier example of a successful girl's magazine is Routledge's monthly *Every Girl's Magazine* (1878–87), edited by Alicia Leith. It was succeeded by *Atalanta* (1887–98), which was edited by popular girls' novelist L.T. Meade and focused on the importance of education for girls. The shorter lived *A.1.* (1888–90), edited by Jane Menzies, was less successful in attracting a readership. In his review of girls' magazines in 1888, Edward Salmon identifies only three girls' periodicals—*A.1.*, the *Girl's Own Paper*, and *Atalanta*—as magazines "that could be placed advantageously before anybody, to say nothing of girls in their teens."[17] Salmon's comment is consistent with an ongoing concern that girls should be encouraged to read high-quality magazines rather than inappropriate, sensational fiction that would make them forget their responsibilities as daughters, sisters, and eventually wives.

The 1890s and early twentieth century saw the appearance of a number of new girls' magazines, including the 6d. monthly *Girl's Realm* (1898–1915), edited by Alice Corkran, and the *Girl's Empire* (1902–04), published by Andrew Melrose, which was intended for "English-speaking girls all over the world."[18] This period also saw the founding of cheaper weekly romantic fiction magazines like the half-penny *Girl's Best Friend* (1898–99),[19] aimed at working-class girls. Proto-feminist magazines like the three-penny *Young Woman* (1892–1915) were aimed at a slightly older audience and, as Emma Liggins notes, managed to address the "strong-minded single woman, offering careers guidance, interviews with female 'breadwinners' and serious articles on living alone."[20] In addition, it incorporated traditional elements of the domestic magazine, such as fashion, recipes, and advice on child care.

Magazines for Boys and Girls

Despite editors' attempts to define their readership based on gender, children read a variety of material that crossed gender lines. An 1884 survey, for example, suggested that girls were reading a wide range of material—whether it was intended for them or not—from the *Girl's Own Paper* and the *Boy's Own Paper* to *Punch* and *Cassell's Family Magazine*.[21] Illustrated family magazines such as *Cassell's* offered flexibility and choice for young readers.

Although many publishers felt that gender differentiation was instrumental to marketplace success, others felt that magazines targeted at both boys and girls would be more successful.

---

17. Salmon, *Juvenile Literature*, 195.
18. Cover, *Girls' Empire* 1 (1902).
19. This title continued as the *Girl's Friend* until 1931.
20. Liggins, "Life of a Bachelor Girl," 217.
21. The *Girl's Own Paper* received 315 votes, many more than the *Boy's Own Paper* (88 votes), *Little Folks* (71), *Good Words* (15), *Aunt Judy's Magazine* (11), and *Every Girl's Magazine* (8). Salmon, *Juvenile Literature*, 23.

One relatively short-lived magazine was the one-penny monthly *Companion for Youth* (1858–61), edited by John and Mary Bennett, which frequently borrowed illustrations and drawings from other periodicals. Its early demise was brought on by fierce competition from boys' magazines. The *Chatterbox* (1866–1953) was the longest running of mixed-gender children's magazines, which Drotner describes as "catering to the whole of the large Victorian nursery."[22] The Rev. Erskine Clarke founded the magazine in reaction to penny dreadful magazines such as *Young Englishman* (1873–79) and *Young Briton* (1869–77). The serial fiction in the *Chatterbox*, *Aunt Judy's Magazine* (1866–85), and other ambitious literary children's magazines typically featured protagonists between the ages of eight and fifteen.

Often children's magazines capitalized on the reputation of the editor. The "Aunt Judy" in the title of *Aunt Judy's Magazine* referred to editor Margaret Gatty's daughter, Juliana Ewing, a notable children's author who wrote numerous serialized stories for the magazine. *Good Words for the Young* (1868–72) similarly relied upon the reputation of its editor, George MacDonald, who was a well-known children's author. Intended as a companion to publisher Alexander Strahan's successful *Good Words*, it contained wholesome literature for children with a broadly Christian outlook. It reinforced its suitability for a wide range of readers with contributions designed to appeal to both sexes, including stories by Hans Christian Andersen, Charles Kingsley, and Dinah Craik.[23] The halfpenny *Our Young Folks' Weekly Budget* (1871–97)[24] took a different approach to attracting and maintaining its readership. Instead of depending on the reputation of an editor, the magazine focused on exciting children's fiction. Inspired by Brett's "Jack Harkaway" series, editor James Henderson published a variety of serials, including Robert Louis Stevenson's *Treasure Island* (1881–82) and later Stevenson's *The Black Arrow* (1883) and *Kidnapped* (1886).

Constructing Gender and Empire

Even though girls and boys often read the same magazines, editors attempted to define their reading preferences in gendered terms. For instance, the first issue of the *Boys' Own Magazine*, published in 1855, explains that "feminine accomplishments" such as knitting and embroidery are "entirely useless, if not distasteful" to boys and assures readers that its pages will contain "matters of interest, amusement, and healthful and moral excitement, calculated at once to produce pleasure and convey instruction."[25] Gendered reading became even more strictly demarcated as the century progressed. The idea that boys should read different material from girls coincided with debates about manliness and women's rights.[26] While boys were typically

---

22. Drotner, *English Children*, 118.
23. The magazine was retitled *Good Things for the Young of All Ages* in 1873. MacDonald severed his association with the magazine in 1874, and it ceased publication in 1877.
24. This periodical went through a series of name changes—first *Old and Young* (1891–96) and then *Folks at Home* (1896–97)—in order to attract a broad spectrum of readers.
25. "Boys' Own Magazine," n.p.
26. Recent scholarship on women's reading includes Flint's *Woman Reader*, Phegley's *Educating the Proper Woman Reader*, and Bilston's *Awkward Age*.

directed towards publications that endorsed heroism, muscular Christianity, and—later in the century—imperialism, girls were directed towards domestic skills and charity work. It was not until the 1880s and 1890s that middle-class girls' periodicals regularly included articles about employment and education. Sally Mitchell proposes that the popularity of girls' magazines for both the middle and working classes was owing to the development of the "new girl" who "occupied a provisional free space" characterized by "new ways of being, new modes of behaviour, and new attitudes that were not yet acceptable for adult women."[27] Regardless of their political persuasion, girls' magazines typically followed trends in the general press by publishing an increasing number of articles discussing the training and demands of newly available occupations for women. However, the fiction that appeared alongside such articles often represented women working only in cases of economic necessity. The tensions between the domestic ideal and the new realities of women's lives were reflected in girls' magazines of the period, thus demonstrating how relevance and topicality were crucial to a magazine's success.

Just as the contemporary issues related to women's rights filtered into girls' magazines, the discourse of empire also played a central role in the development of children's periodicals. Jeffrey Richards, in *Imperialism and Juvenile Literature*, explains how juvenile literature functions "not just as a mirror of the age but an active agency constructing and perpetuating a view of the world in which British imperialism was an integral part of the culture and psychological formation of each new generation of readers."[28] Boys' adventure fiction encouraged strength and heroism beginning in the 1840s with Frederick Marryat's sea stories, which were followed in the 1850s and 1860s by the adventure stories of two popular evangelical children's writers, W.H.G. Kingston and R.M. Ballantyne. Because it was intended to appeal to boys and channel their energies in appropriate directions, adventure fiction influenced the content of boys' periodicals. Patrick Dunae explains that in the 1870s, a "decade regarded traditionally as the watershed of the new imperialism," a number of periodicals were founded that contributed to the imperial project.[29] As MacDonald points out, the success of *Chums* in the 1890s was owing to its "consistent and forthright devotion to imperialism: it discovered . . . that the conquest and defense of the Empire could be presented as an exciting and even sensational drama."[30] Emigration to the colonies became a central concern in the second half of the century and was often presented to boys and girls as an exciting opportunity for adventure and heroism.[31] Adventure fiction did not appear in girls' periodicals until the early twentieth century when adventure novels by Bessie Marchant and Evelyn Everett-Green became popular. Even when domestic fiction continued to dominate girls' periodicals, however, other content reflected the concerns of empire. For example, as Michelle Smith has shown in her examination of the *Girl's Own Paper*, advertising was "inextricably entangled with imperial concerns."[32]

---

27. Mitchell, *New Girl*, 3.
28. Richards, *Imperialism and Juvenile Literature*, 3.
29. Dunae, "Boys' Literature," 106. See also Fulton, "Boys' Adventure Magazines."
30. MacDonald, "Signs from the Imperial Quarter," 34.
31. For discussion of the ways in which the *Girl's Own Paper* promoted emigration to the colonies, see Moruzi, "The freedom suits me."
32. M. Smith, *Empire in British Girls' Literature and Culture*, 33.

Editors and Readers

Strong editorial personae often gave children's periodicals a sense of thematic and ideological cohesiveness. Charlotte Yonge's voice was synonymous with the *Monthly Packet*, a magazine she edited for four decades. Yonge also serialized many of her novels in the magazine, thus forging a connection between the periodical's brand and the editor's High Church beliefs. In contrast, *Atalanta* editor L. T. Meade included little of her own fiction in the pages of her magazine, although she certainly took advantage of her status as a popular writer for girls as a means of attracting high-profile literary contributors such as H. Rider Haggard, Robert Louis Stevenson, Mary Molesworth, Katherine Tynan, George MacDonald, and Charlotte Yonge. Meade was also a strong proponent of women's education and included articles about the various women's colleges as well as some occasional fiction that supported higher education. Likewise, Brett's former involvement with the Chartist movement meant that *Boys of England* "carried undertones of political radicalism."[33]

Even if the editor was a relatively unknown children's author, he or she often tried to establish a connection with the magazine's readers through editorials and correspondence. As the editor for *Kind Words* explains on the final page of the first number in 1866, "We shall always reserve this page for communication between ourselves and our readers; it will bring us into close contact and make us feel an interest in one another. . . . There will be good advice given kindly, useful sayings told pleasantly, and wise ones cheerfully. We intend this page to be bright, and sparkling, and merry."[34] Such editorial addresses were intended to create a bond between editor and reader, a relationship that was reinforced on a weekly or monthly basis. Editors often also reached out to readers for assistance when seeking new subscribers to their magazines. For example, in the May 1886 number of *Kind Words*, the editor writes,

> Our circulation has been most encouraging, but not such as to make us rest satisfied, for we are sure there must be thousands of boys and girls to whom, as yet, we are strangers, and who would be very glad to become acquainted with us. Some of you are at school, others are in situations, but all of you have friends to whom you might introduce us with such confidence as you may be able to feel.
>
> Will you make the effort after reading this? Will you all try and get at least one weekly or monthly subscriber?[35]

Evidently subscriptions improved since *Kind Words* continued until 1879, when it was renamed *Young England*, and remained in print until 1937. However, such appeals to readers were not always successful. The June 1899 issue of the *Monthly Packet* includes a similar appeal, yet the magazine failed to produce any further issues.

As Fraser, Green, and Johnston have noted, periodicals also established a relationship between editor and reader in correspondence pages. Each periodical branded itself by

---

33. Banham, "*Boys of England*," 69.
34. "This Is the Last Page," 8.
35. "To Our Readers," *Kind Words*, n.p.

establishing a "set of standards which it tries to represent as normal and which most nearly represent how that journal wishes to present itself to the public."[36] Both the *Boy's Own Paper* and the *Girl's Own Paper* were known for publishing reader correspondence. For example, the May 31, 1879 issue of the *Boy's Own Paper* addresses reader queries about the difficulty of obtaining a copy of the magazine, noting that "newsagents [are] trying to substitute other periodicals."[37] The second item is the magazine's response to "several correspondents" who asked for instructions on how to construct a telephone.[38] Girls were even more active letter writers, with the correspondence pages in the *Girl's Own Paper* often running across multiple pages. Girls' queries ranged widely, including inquiries about work, education, emigration, hobbies, health, and beauty. For example, in response to a query from "Meg," a victim of parental abuse, the editor suggests that she "consult a doctor" and confide in him the reason for her headaches in the hope that the doctor can explain to her parents that "any blows on the head are dangerous."[39] Indeed, correspondence columns may have provided one of the only venues in which girls could seek out and obtain health information in an anonymous way.[40]

Whether the correspondence in these magazines was written by "real" children or contributed by magazine staff is difficult to determine. As Richard Altick notes, "One suspects that many of the queries [in family magazines], especially the ones which today would be addressed to reference librarians, were concocted in the editorial office."[41] However, the sheer volume and variety of letters to the editor suggest that at least some of the inquiries were genuine. Moreover, it was in each magazine's interest to develop and reinforce a sense of community among readers by printing and responding to correspondence.[42] While some queries may have been strategically inserted to garner attention in a provocative way, the magazine also had a vested interest in responding to readers' inquiries in order to encourage reader identification and the purchase of subsequent issues. Another type of correspondence feature, the exchange column, similarly encouraged reader participation. For example, in the May 1868 "Boy's Exchange," published in Beeton's *Boy's Own Magazine*, a variety of goods are offered in trade, including a "beautiful twenty-keyed German concertina," which A. Bailey of 38 Holywell-street, Oxford, hoped to exchange for a "telescope or revolver."[43]

Editors of children's magazines employed a variety of other strategies to encourage readers to maintain an active interest in their magazines. For example, *Aunt Judy's Magazine* encouraged readers to subscribe to charitable projects by contributing to an 1868 campaign to purchase a cot for the Great Ormond Street Children's Hospital. The appeal was supported by the

---

36. Fraser, Green, and Johnston, *Gender and the Victorian Periodical*, 79.
37. "Correspondence," 320.
38. Ibid.
39. "Answers to Correspondents," 367.
40. For further details on the "fatherly mentor" role editor Charles Peters presented in his response to girls' queries, see Patton, "Not a limitless possession."
41. Altick, *English Common Reader*, 360.
42. For an interesting exploration of the sometimes fractured communities of readers associated with these two girls' periodicals, see Rodgers, "Competing Girlhoods."
43. "Boy's Exchange," n.p.

magazine through the publication of subscriber names and contribution amounts, as well as regular reports from the hospital about the children who slept on it. The success of the "Aunt Judy's Magazine Cot" campaign prompted other magazines to sponsor cots at the hospital as well.[44]

Children were also encouraged to actively contribute to magazines through reader competitions. In *Atalanta*'s "Scholarship and Reading Union," for example, girls were encouraged to pursue a course of reading and to write essays in response to a topic. In the year-end competition, a university scholarship was offered as a prize. Other competitions were less scholarly, awarding prizes for woodworking, painting, drawing, and embroidery. The *Boy's Own Paper* offered a "variety of prizes for essays, solutions to puzzles, anagrams, etc.," beginning with a picture-essay competition in which readers under the age of sixteen were invited to write a story based on an engraving included in the magazine.[45] In May 1868, the *Boy's Own Magazine* printed readers' poems on the importance of industry to a nation's strength. Because periodicals often printed details of entrants' names and ages, these competitions provide valuable data about magazine readership.

Resources and Directions for Future Research

Nineteenth-century children's periodicals have been a topic of research since the early twentieth century. The first twentieth-century study of juvenile magazines was Ralph Rollington's *A Brief History of Boys' Journals, with Interesting Facts about the Writers of Boys' Stories* (1913). It was followed, much later, by Ernest S. Turner's *Boys Will Be Boys* (1948). Both studies focus on boys' periodicals, which Mary Cadogan and Patricia Craig attempted to redress in *You're a Brick, Angela!: A New Look at Girls' Fiction from 1839 to 1975* (1976). Sheila Egoff's *Children's Periodicals of the Nineteenth Century: A Survey and Bibliography* (1951) represents one of the earliest attempts to document the breadth of the field. Kirsten Drotner's *English Children and Their Magazines, 1751–1945* (1988) makes a substantial contribution to the survey of children's magazines, as does the work of Diana Dixon. Sally Mitchell's *The New Girl: Girls' Culture in England 1880–1915* (1995) makes a crucial intervention into ideas of late Victorian and Edwardian girlhood by drawing extensively on girls' periodicals. Other books, such as Terri Doughty's *Selections from* The Girl's Own Paper, *1880–1907* (2004), have helped to increase the visibility of children's periodicals as artefacts of nineteenth-century children's culture.

Scholars of the nineteenth-century children's press will also find useful information in studies of women's writing.[46] In *Women of the Press in Nineteenth-Century Britain* (2000), Barbara Onslow argues that women often edited and wrote for children's periodicals because

---

44. While the network of publications read by children can be difficult to determine, some evidence exists within the magazines themselves. Charlotte Yonge launched a similar charitable appeal in 1871, remarking that "most of the readers of *The Monthly Packet*" are also reading *Aunt Judy's Magazine*. Yonge, "Cumberland Street," 92.
45. "Our Prize Competition," 16.
46. Briggs argues that the connection between women writers and children's books was brought about, in part, by a "coincidence of timing in that women began to take up writing as a profession at about the same time as books specifically written for children began to be published in any numbers" and a "coincidence of interests, in that

they found it "difficult to enter the realms of publishing and editing at national and provincial daily newspaper level."[47] Additional scholarship is needed to explore women authors' careers as writers for children's periodicals, particularly the network of publications to which they contributed.

Working-class children's periodicals have received some scholarly attention, most notably in Kelly Boyd's *Manliness and the Boys' Story Paper in Britain: A Cultural History, 1855–1940* (2003). Boyd examines the definitions of masculinity appearing in mass-market story papers, "which had as their audience the average boy, the lad for whom education ended—and work commenced—early."[48] Like other children's magazines, working-class periodicals are sometimes difficult to locate in archives since they were intended to be read, shared, and discarded. Monthly middle-class magazines were collected and preserved more often than their cheaper weekly competitors, which means that there is a gap in scholarly understanding of publications aimed specifically at working-class children. Researchers need to remember that databases like Gale Cengage's *19th Century UK Periodicals* have digitized only a small subset of children's periodicals and thus provide a stepping stone to further archival research rather than a comprehensive survey of the field.

Another aspect of children's periodicals that has received little attention is their advertising pages. This is partly due to the fact that advertisements were often stripped from weekly and monthly numbers when they were bound into annual volumes. Nonetheless, the advertisements that remain could provide valuable insight into how children of the nineteenth century were targeted as consumers. Children's periodicals are a rich and valuable research tool for historians of nineteenth-century children's literature and culture. They present a vivid portrait of the multiplicities of childhood during this period and reflect changing attitudes toward children across the century. There is much more to be done to explore the kinds of magazines available to children and to investigate their treatment of class, race, gender, and religion.

---

women were committed to the nursery world as mothers, nurses, or governesses in a way that few men were." Briggs, "Women Writers and Writing for Children," 223.
47. Onslow, *Women of the Press*, 1.
48. Boyd, *Manliness and the Boys' Story Paper*, 2.

22

SPORTING PERIODICALS

Yuri Cowan

Like journalism and, indeed, the news itself, sporting literature has its origins in correspondence and record-keeping. Sportsmen like Peter Beckford and Isaak Walton passed on their knowledge and experience of hunting and fishing in the form of dialogues and letters, giving recommendations for likely game coverts and fishing holes, providing notices of meetings, and recounting exhilarating or fruitless days in the field. Although institutions like the Jockey Club and Marylebone Cricket Club kept and sometimes published records,[1] the *Sporting Magazine* (1792–1870) was the first monthly devoted entirely to sport, and it dominated the marketplace in the early part of the nineteenth century. Covering chiefly rural sports but also providing notices of cricket games, boxing matches, and duels ("affairs of honour"), the "Old Magazine," as it was called, filled its pages with the correspondence of enthusiasts who signed their letters with Latinate or neoclassical pen names like "Veritas" and "Acastor," in addition to publishing the work of more celebrated regular contributors. That such a specialized magazine could find a dedicated consumer base at a shilling per issue is not entirely surprising when we consider its readership at the time (the genteel, usually landholding, prosperous male) and the characteristics of sport itself. Sporting literature and reportage are ideally suited to the periodical format, which thrives on the up-to-date, the local, and the anecdotal, conveying information that is contingent and frequently changeable. Sporting journalism has its origins in the conversations of opinionated men who discussed variations in local environment and conditions and were desirous of ready intelligence in their turn. At this early date, the writer on sporting subjects was more likely to be a participant than a spectator, and more likely to present himself as an enthusiastic amateur "gentleman correspondent" rather than, as later in the century, a dedicated paid journalist. The nineteenth century saw the industrialization of print, the professionalization of both sport and authorship, the increasing specialization of sporting magazines devoted to particular fields like cricket, cycling, and football,[2] and the

---

1. John Cheny published his *Historical List* of racing information for the Jockey Club as early as 1727; later in the century the Weatherby family took over publication of the *Racing Calendar*. The earliest cricket score books were not published and were lost in a fire in 1825. Ford, *Cricket*, 21.
2. Huggins counts over twenty papers with "cycling" in the title over the last two decades of the century, most of them apparently short-lived (*Victorians and Sport*, 153).

democratization and urbanization of the audience for sporting activity and spectacle. By 1896, *Pearson's Magazine* guessed that about £1 per head was being spent on sport every year, suggesting its enormous economic as well as social importance.[3] Even if women were increasing engaged in sport, the vast majority of that money was spent by and on men (Figure 22.1 shows only two women towards the thinner side of the figure). We should not be surprised, therefore, by the sporting press's gender bias, which this chapter will reflect. Indeed, besides its gendering, sporting journalism's basis in celebrity admiration and enthusiasm, its drive to communicate and to receive fresh information, and its undaunted sense that it was upholding a particularly English sporting sense of self remained constant.

For these reasons, nineteenth-century periodicals are an indispensable tool for the study of the evolution of Victorian sporting literature and culture. The periodical corpus forms the foundation of, for instance, Adrian Harvey's exemplary study of *The Beginnings of a Commercial Sporting Culture in Britain, 1793–1850*. A similar treatment covering the second half of the century remains to be written, and would likely be a very different enterprise, but it too would necessarily find its clues in newspapers and magazines. The second half of the century saw not only the rise and dominance of spectator sports such as Association football and county cricket, but also increased access to participatory sports in Britain for urban middle-class devotees of sport. Sporting journals also became a venue in which to debate the treatment of animals inherent in the old rural entertainments, or a place to celebrate and to proselytize for the mid-Victorian cultures of hygiene and athleticism. Whether as gamblers, spectators, or participants, sporting enthusiasts in England came increasingly to rely on the authority of a growing stable of paid authors, statisticians, and journalists. In terms of the production of periodicals, the second half of the century brought the rise and spread of more and more specialized magazines, as well as cheaper production costs. It also, following on from what Wakeman has called "the photomechanical revolution," saw an increase in illustration.[4]

Technological improvements informed the industrialization and democratization of both sport and print, which advanced in tandem throughout the century. By 1831, the year in which the *Sporting Magazine* (the "Old Magazine") was supplanted by the *New Sporting Magazine* (1831–70), the old systems of game preservation still persisted and institutions such as fox hunting and horse racing ("The Turf") were still going strong. Rural sports, particularly participatory ones like hunting, shooting, and fishing, remained the focus of the magazine. But the horses and dogs were being bred up to the point that they sometimes had to be reined in to avoid capturing the fox too early, firearms were growing ever more accurate, while the efficiency of the *battue* system meant that a thousand birds or more could be shot in a matter of days, and increased convenience of transportation to the countryside from the towns was soon to change the social environment of sport. Huggins and Tolson, however, warn against over-emphasizing the last, suggesting that the impact of railways should not be overestimated: "Changes in sport were driven much more by increases in leisure time and real wages among some groups from mid-century, by the sporting information which was first passed on by

---

3. Mason, "Money We Spend on Sport."
4. Wakeman, *Victorian Book Illustration*, 119–45.

1000 clubs, with an average expenditure of £250 each.

Of the smaller clubs, averaging an expenditure of £25 per season, we have fully 5000. This gives us a total club expenditure of £435,000.

At least 500,000 cricketers of all grades and classes incur a personal expenditure clearly incidental to the game, to the average amount of £3 per annum, or £1,500,000; and at least 3,000,000 of spectators of matches average one shilling per head of expenditure beyond admission fees, or £150,000. Hence cricket contributes to our total some £2,085,000.

Coming now to Football, and reckoning there are 40 Association clubs whose average annual expenditure is £5,000, also 5,000 other clubs averaging £40 a year, and crediting the Rugby clubs with an expenditure of £200,000, we have a total of £600,000.

Half a million players in both sections of the game will not average less than £2 per head in clothing, boots, travelling, and various incidentals, or £1,000,000. Finally, spectators flock to the great matches in their thousands, and many travel considerable distances. An average expenditure beyond their admission fees of 1s. a head, no one can say is excessive. Putting the number of spectators at three millions, we add on £150,000; and our football bill is £1,750,000.

We have now disposed of what may fairly be called the six major sports of the country, and our figures are: Racing, £10,818,000; hunting, £9,041,000; shooting, £5,700,000; angling, £3,700,000; cricket, £2,085,000; football, £1,750,000; or a total for six months' sport of £33,094,000.

Space does not permit of a similar close analysis of the various branches of sport which still remain; but, bearing in mind the necessity for some discrimination between what may be fairly termed sport, and that which is ordinary recreation, and applying the same broad principles, we arrive at the following additional figures:

Coursing	£400,000
Cycling	1,200,000
Polo	250,000
Yachting	1,000,000
Boating	500,000
Swimming	200,000
Golf	1,000,000
Hockey, bowls, quoits, etc.	100,000
Athletics	500,000
	£5,150,000

In this way we bring up the total cost of British sport to a total of over thirty-eight millions per annum, or about £1 per head of the whole population.

If we added to this gigantic total the various branches of what may be alternatively termed outdoor recreation, such as horse-riding, driving, lawn-tennis, croquet, etc., etc., and the distinct branches of indoor recreations, such as billiards, cards, chess, draughts, dominoes, theatres, concerts, balls, etc., we should obtain a figure which would at least rival, if it did not surpass, the Imperial Revenue.

Who, after this, can say, that we are a melancholy race, or that we take the affairs of life sadly?

The Artist has depicted here the relative sizes of the devotees of the various Sports, if judged according to the money spent upon each particular branch.

Figure 22.1 Page from J. Mason, "The Money We Spend on Sport," *Pearson's Magazine* 1 (May 1896): 534.

electric telegraph in the late 1840s and became a major feature of the popular press from the 1860s, by growing commercialism, and by the development of a more positive attitude to 'manly' exercise, than they were by the railways."[5]

However, Huggins and Tolson also stress that participatory sports like hunting, shooting, angling, and golf were indeed boosted by the railways, especially for "the wealthier minority who could afford first or second-class travel."[6] This explains the persistence of magazines devoted to field sports, especially the *(New) Sporting Magazine* and the even longer-lived *Field*, in an urbanizing society that would by the end of the century adopt a culture of spectatorship that would rival and ultimately supplant the active culture of individual exercise and team sportsmanship eulogized in Hughes's *Tom Brown's Schooldays*, in Newbolt's "Vitaï Lampada," and in the boys' magazines of the early twentieth century.[7] The new transportation and information networks also distributed papers and journals and spread information. *Saturday Night*, the four-page halfpenny football special established in September 1882 in Birmingham, is a striking example of the way in which the periodical form could bring information to the masses regularly and cheaply.[8]

The variety of formats adopted by nineteenth-century sporting periodicals reflects the diversity of ways in which people could appreciate and participate in sport. There was always some variation in terms of the extent to which (for instance) statistics, tips, anecdotes, and narratives were included, and substantial differences among the papers in terms of their price, tone, and style of reportage. The numerous nineteenth-century titles containing the word "sporting" can offer a bewildering array of similar-sounding periodicals (the *Sporting Times*, *Sporting Review*, *Sporting Record*, *Sporting Gazette*, *Sporting Life*, and many others), and yet each of these is as distinguishable from its peers as, say, *Blackwood's*, the *Athenaeum*, and the *Saturday Review* in the field of literature and reviewing. Lambie's history of the *Sporting Life* is a useful example of a biography of a sporting paper based on personal networks of journalists, editors, and publishers, as well as the wider social context. In the format and style of each individual periodical, it is certainly possible to recognize its niche coverage, to discern its intended class of audience, and to position that periodical within or on the pale of received moral rectitude, as pandering to the popular or appealing to exclusivity.

By way of illustration, the *(New) Sporting Magazine* could be said to have balanced itself delicately on the cusp of easy gentility and upstart mercenary brashness when it allotted top billing to its two celebrity contributors, the star writer Charles James Apperley ("Nimrod") and the canny editor Robert Smith Surtees ("the Yorkshireman," "Jorrocks"). Despite occasional satirical sniping by Surtees, the editor was sure always to give Nimrod's easy elegance the upper hand, assuring the triumph of the conservative worldview and maintaining the *New Sporting Magazine*'s genteel tone. Closer to the middle of the road, the *Sporting Chronicle* kept the lower-middle classes supplied with racing news from 1871 to 1983. A five-penny weekly like *Bell's*

---

5. Huggins and Tolson, "Railways and Sport," 100.
6. Ibid., 111, 113.
7. For a more detailed discussion of this athletic culture, see Mangan's *Athleticism*.
8. See McIntyre, "Football Specials;" On the origins of *Saturday Night*, see Mason, *Association Footbal*, 192.

London Life, with its unabashedly broad coverage of sporting subjects, its lurid crime stories, and its advertisements for louche songbooks, could also attract well-known writers such as Dickens and Southey while apparently being read by all classes in spite of its cheap format and sometimes racy tone.[9] As a contemporary wrote of the annual *Guide to the Turf* (1840–) by *Bell's* contributor William Ruff: "If it really be, as the hypercritical assert, The Roughs' Guide, then has the rough of to-day, in spite of occasional grandiloquence, better reading and a more reputable instructor than would have been tolerated or understood by the aristocratic bloods who wrenched off knockers and maltreated watchmen a generation back."[10] Readers were characteristically sensitive to shifts of tone and politeness throughout the century, but especially, as in this case, from the Regency to the Victorian.

The distinctions between sporting periodicals, then, are many and subtle, and any study of them must take their historical moment, format, intended audience, and reception into account. Although it is tempting to see sporting periodicals as in danger of being supplanted by more statistics-oriented specials, there were certain things that the higher-end journals could do that newspapers and specials could not. Harvey describes the balance well:

> From January 1793 *The Sporting Magazine* contained an almanac, detailing forthcoming horse races and the like, as well as listing important dates in the calendar, notably the start and finish of the shooting season. This effectively mapped out the sporting year and was a feature emulated by newspapers. However, the more frequent appearance of newspapers enabled them to carry up-to-date details of forthcoming events, especially pedestrian matches that were spread over a number of weeks, because they could provide regular bulletins. However, although newspapers were able to provide information far more quickly, they were unable to devote as much space, and even their most copious accounts were likely to be overshadowed by those of *The Sporting Magazine*; which would sometimes provide two or more reports of the same event.[11]

The relaying of raw data was but one function of the sporting periodical: anecdote and opinion were devoured readily by readers, especially if they offered some kind of arcane knowledge that might be useful in distinguishing oneself mounted in the field or over cigars at the club, or in gaining the upper hand over one's bookie. Although Harvey suggests that even as early as 1822 the circulation of a journal like the *Sporting Magazine* could be endangered by the more up-to-date information offered by the daily and weekly press,[12] it is also important to note that it was the genteel storytelling manner of Nimrod that saved the "Old Magazine." Whether with regard to rural sport or to team sports, anecdote and storytelling—*narrative*—were key to sport reporting's appeal from the first.

---

9. Richards and Milne, "*Bell's Life in London.*"
10. "Roughs' Guide," 496.
11. Harvey, *Beginnings of a Commercial Sporting Culture*, 36.
12. Ibid., 45.

As a literary phenomenon, sporting periodical literature had its known celebrity authors from the beginning, and work in the field holds a lot of promise for the study of authorship. Besides Nimrod and Surtees, William Hamilton Maxwell, Henry Hall Dixon ("The Druid"), and Pierce Egan emerged in the early and middle years of the century, as well as writers like Hazlitt, who took up the subject only incidentally. In addition, there was a large stable of usually anonymous amateur correspondents who wrangled with and corrected each other on subjects like the origin of the terms "near side" and "off side" when driving a carriage, or the finest breeders of terriers.[13] In the early days, there were only a few paid venues in which the dedicated sporting journalist could shine, and some of these writers (like Maxwell) found their little successes in book form instead. As the periodical press mushroomed around mid-century, however, there were more and more sheets to be filled and ever more ways in which one might make a living covering and announcing sporting events.

In addition to providing narratives of sporting activities and matches, writers could provide tips (including mnemonic rhymes[14]), relay anecdotes of famous sporting characters, and even (as in the case of the *Field*, 1853–) include society gossip. An 1878 piece in the *Saturday Review* suggests some of the essential traits of a popular sporting writer:

> When an author sticks closely to sporting, however graphically entertaining and realistic he may be at first, he is sure to get barren and monotonous after a time. If he hopes to establish himself as a public favourite he must have some measure of cultivation as well as of versatility; he must be able to talk of a picture as of a hound, and must distinguish the delicate perfumes of the boudoir from the more racy scents of the kennel and the stable-yard.[15]

The article is, among its more general observations about sporting authorship, a memorial to George John Whyte-Melville (1821–78), the author, soldier, and sportsman, but the characteristics it notes here are equally applicable to a writer like Nimrod.

It was, of course, possible to write in a racier manner as well. In the 1880s, the *Sporting Times* (nicknamed "The Pink 'Un" after the distinctive color of the paper used in its initial run) associated itself with a jovial, quasi-Bohemian circle of writers whose later memoirs make amusing reading about the great gamblers of the 1840s, the jaunty male journalist world of the Pelican club,[16] and seedy boxing matches in the 1880s at the "School of Arms" in Lambeth.[17]

---

13. "'Near' and 'Off' Side" and "Terriers: Replies to an Inquiry." For the culture of the "gentleman correspondent," including the suggestion that many or most of the letters were written by the editor Surtees himself, see Gregory, "Mr. Jorrocks's Lost Sporting Magazine," and Cowan, "Industrialising Print, Sport, and Authorship."
14. Mason writes that "there was never any doubt in the minds of both newspaper proprietors and editors that racing results and tips sold newspapers" (*Association Football*, 194–5). For rhyming tips, see, for instance, Tate, "Binstead"; the practice is satirized in "Tip Topics."
15. "Sporting Writers," 779.
16. See, for instance, Arthur Binstead's *A Pink 'Un and a Pelican* and J.B. Booth's *Old Pink 'Un Days* and *'Master' and Men: Pink 'Un Yesterdays*.
17. For the shadier associations of sport with masculine misbehavior, see Huggins and Mangan's *Disreputable Pleasures*; Springhall, "Disreputable Adolescent Reading"; and Cohen, Gilfoyle and Horowitz, *Flash Press*.

Finally, although the roll call of nineteenth-century authors appears on the surface to be overwhelmingly masculine, Catriona Parratt has given direction to the study of women's sporting authorship with her outline of sources for female sport in Victorian and Edwardian England, suggesting a wider involvement of women in sports than appears at first glance, spearheaded by school advocates and by writers such as Ada Ballin, the editor of *Womanhood* (1898–1907).

Sport has long been noted by Victorianist scholarship as an important locus for understanding the construction of British masculinities and femininities in the nineteenth century, but there were still deeper class divisions reflected in approaches to team and individual play. Alpine climbing, cycling, and polo, for instance, required a certain amount of financial outlay, and rural pursuits generally had deep roots in the landowning classes. Huggins in the second chapter of *The Victorians and Sport* provides the best introduction to the subject, noting some surprising variations, including for instance that "Rugby union was largely a middle-class game in England and lowland Scotland, but was a mass sport in Wales, and to an extent on the Scottish border."[18] The turf was universally enjoyed by spectators of all classes, while the growth of the football special drew in the working classes. Cricket brought together amateur "gentleman players" like the urbane criminal Raffles (from the short stories of E. W. Hornung) on the same field as "professionals" from the working classes.[19] As Mason puts it, working-class men played to win and their aspirations were often financial.[20]

A study of sporting journals in terms of their readerships also offers rich possibilities, from the aspirational *Badminton Magazine of Sports and Pastimes* (1895–1923) on down to the rough-and-ready football specials. Though these are widely divergent examples, in actual fact the degrees of difference are as subtle as the shadings of class. Thus the *Badminton*'s elegant, clear type and copious photographic illustrations show it to be clearly the swells' choice before the turn of the century, in contradistinction to a grubby and ephemeral racing paper, which the single-sheet *Prophetic Bell* had been in 1871 before it quickly metamorphosed into the more substantial *Sporting Chronicle* (1871–1983), aiming upward to the lower-middle classes.[21] To properly characterize the differences between the target audience of, say, the *Field* and the *Sporting Gazette* in 1862, one also has to take into account aspects such as distribution (national in both cases, and international in that of the former), price (6d. for the *Field* as opposed to 3d. for the *Sporting Gazette*), and coverage (the *Sporting Gazette*'s being somewhat broader, and from a slightly more urban perspective).

The twin processes of telling the periodical's life story and illustrating its social context are further dependent upon close study of the care that went into its design and format, the technique and quality of its illustrations, the quality of its paper, its cover price, and so forth. Much scholarly inquiry into the physical form of sporting periodicals must still be carried out in research libraries such as the British Library, the research center of the National Football Museum, or, in America, the National Sporting Library in Middleburg, Virginia. This is

---

18. Huggins, *Victorians and Sport*, 20.
19. Bateman, *Cricket, Literature, and Culture*, 39–41.
20. Mason, "Sport," 293.
21. Lambie, *Story of Your Life*, 119.

not only because for bibliographical research there is no substitute for viewing periodicals in bound or unbound form, but also because digital surrogates are not as accessible as they could be. Some sporting periodicals are available to very varying degrees on archive.org, ProQuest's and Cengage's periodicals databases, or the British Newspaper Archive. Some, such as *Field*, are still in business, though occasionally under new names and even no longer in print (the *Sporting Life*, for instance, founded in 1859, migrated wholly to the web in 1998).

If the physical format and typography of these periodicals was dictated to a certain extent by their intended reading community, it must have been even more dependent on the nature of the information it conveyed. This information could be graphic in the form of illustration or numerical and statistical tables, all of which required more complicated processes than just the setting of type. The very first issue of the *Sporting Magazine* (October 1792) included an engraving of "His Majesty going out with his stag hounds on [sic] Windsor Forest," and future issues always included engravings in keeping with the developing culture of sporting spectatorship. These illustrations were integral statements that often took on a life of their own, as when *Wisden*'s institution of the five "Cricketers of the Year" developed out of a well-received implementation of photographic portraits in 1888.[22] At all times there was a great demand for satirical illustrative matter, which is often very illuminating about facts on the ground.[23]

That the periodical format has always delighted in numbers can be shown by a glance at (for instance) the *Gentleman's Magazine* of November 1790, with its various tables of Meteorological Diaries, Prices of Grain, Theatrical Register, and Bills of Mortality; Wisden's *Cricketer's Almanack For the Year 1867* comprises a calendar that intersperses the birthdays of famous cricketers with such important dates as the beginning of grouse shooting, the institution of the Victoria Cross, and the date of the Battle of Lewes in 1264, thus placing the game firmly in the context of English history and gentlemanly enterprise. A sustained study of the ways in which the Victorians compiled and arranged the numbers that evoked football and cricket matches and racing results, something like Alan Schwarz's popular book *The Numbers Game* on the history of baseball statistics, would be a fascinating project, especially if it could also take into account the influence of changes in printing technology on the graphic representation of knowledge.[24]

Originally, the most prominent statistics were for the turf, in the form of lists of horse racing stakes, stud books, and sales. The first *Racing Calendar* was published by the Jockey Club as early as 1727, by subscription, and thus was much pricier than most periodicals.[25] From 1773 until its demise in 1912, the Weatherby family published a new *Racing Calendar*, also by subscription, in complementary book and newspaper form. According the *Calendar* for 1847, "The RACING CALENDAR is published by Subscription, commencing on the 1st of January.

---

22. Gutteridge, "History of Wisden." *Wisden's Cricketer's Almanac* began in 1864 and still survives.
23. Huggins's "Cartoons and Comic Periodicals" is particularly illuminating.
24. I would like to thank Alexander Jackson of the National Football Museum for his suggestions on the history of statistics reporting.
25. According to Vamplew, "[John] Cheny funded the calendar by asking subscribers for a seven-year commitment with a half-crown to be paid with the order, 5s. annually for the first six years, and, as a reward for loyalty, only a further half-crown in the seventh year" ("Cheny," n.p.).

The first Number of the Sheet Calendar appears early in January; the Book containing the Races to Come early in February; and the Book containing the Races Past, with the Foals of the year, as soon as possible after the conclusion of the Racing Season."[26] The advertisement goes on to state that the Sheet Calendars and both books could be purchased at £1 15s., while the Sheet Calendars on their own could be subscribed to for £1 5s. The complementary format meant that the books could give the large picture, including the often complex ground rules for each meeting, with long indexed lists of horses and their parentage and ownership, the colors of the riders, the description of the courses, and the stakes of each race, while the more frequent sheets could update the information as horses were added or dropped. And yet even this temporally-layered system of information could not do justice to the shifting environment of the track, where odds and circumstances changed right up to the moment of the post through injury, weather, and luck. There is a complicated relationship between the sporting narratives provided by journalists and the rote publication of data in lists, tables, and graphs: while sporting statistics gave the reader a controllable stockpile of raw information through which outcomes might be predicted, sporting anecdotes offered judgments, opinion, and precedents that prepared one to confront the more unpredictable contingencies of the field that could arise from the interactions of man, beast, and environment. The Victorians' passion for numbers and statistics, however comprehensive in its designs, only gestured at its potential to control the complex world around them; they understood all too well that countable facts were no substitute for the kind of real-world experiences that could be shared with and recounted by journalists, correspondents, and readers.

The migration of this information is another valuable area of future research for the history of sporting news in the Victorian period. Binstead's memoir retails at one point an evocative picture of the racing press-room around the turn of the century:

> Two-thirds of the good fellows in the reportorial cockloft are in the employ of one or other of the big Press Agencies, and, from the time the numbers go up for the opening race until ten or twenty minutes after the last winning jockey has been weighed in, they are so punctiliously busy that only occasionally can they slip out to "oil the machinery." . . . Each of these messages goes to hundreds of different newspapers all over the country, and the man who writes them has only a vague knowledge of their destination, as new papers are constantly being added to, and defunct organs taken off, each service. The journalist who "spreads himself" in the racing page of the big London daily is not more proud of his work than the Press-Agency man, who, going his endless rounds, comes across a "stick" of his own "flowery" in the sporting column of the *Rochdale Evening Sausagewrap*. And so mote it be.
>
> When a sporting reporter's feet wear out, his "proprietors"—for they own him body and soul—buy him a Windsor chair and a gum-pot, and make a sub-editor of him.[27]

---

26. Weatherby and Weatherby, *Racing Calendar*, n.p.
27. Binstead, *Pink 'Un and a Pelican*, 23–4.

The "Press-Agency man" was an essential cog in the mechanisms of mass periodical culture in the late nineteenth century, and his contributions, though hard to quantify or even in most cases to attribute, are evocative of the changing state of the sporting press and the influence of technology. The harried writer in the "reportorial cockloft" is a far cry from the gentleman correspondent in the days of the "Old Magazine." Similarly, the shifting landscape Binstead describes of upstart papers and diverse services, where the author is barely aware of the destination of his brief notices, is a world of steam and speed far removed from the world of the *Sporting Magazine* in which even Melton Mowbray was some days' ride from London.

The rate at which this transmission of information could occur varied over the course of the century depending on the technology used. So, for instance, the October 1830 number of Calcutta's *Oriental Sporting Magazine* gives descriptions of sporting events that were taken with credit from [*Bell's*] *Life in London* from May 16 and June 13, followed by other material from the *Spectator* and the *Liverpool Albion*.[28] The lapse of just four months between the articles' publication in the English papers and their appearance in the Calcutta periodical is informative, and yet, within a few years, Thomas Waghorn's innovative Overland Route would cut the lag significantly. Using quantitative computing methods, it should soon be possible to trace the geographical movement and adaptation of these kinds of borrowed entries, both in terms of the ways in which they were reused in different provinces or overseas locations and in terms of the variations in the amount of time that process took. Warner provides one such model with his animation of "The Boston Committee's correspondence with the towns of Massachusetts" in which the correspondence is shown to radiate geographically outwards across the colony over the course of two weeks, from November 20 to December 3, 1772.[29]

This migratory character of dispersal, repetition, and reprinting, whether through the press agencies, through correspondence, or through acknowledged or unacknowledged borrowing from other periodicals, is characteristic of news in general but especially of sporting information. If the earliest sporting news had appeared in the form only of brief mentions in "Country News" or society news, by the end of the nineteenth century the growth of sporting sections in newspapers like *The Times* had begun to legitimate sporting news as news.[30] Not only did sporting information travel from one variety of publication to another, but columns and narratives in periodicals might be recast in collected form in books, as when Surtees first turned his Jorrocks stories into a loose novel. The volume of collected journalism has a long history in nineteenth-century literature; and, for sporting journalists like Nimrod, Frederick Gale, and Henry Hall Dixon, publishing their work in single volumes was a way of re-capitalizing on their completed work and of keeping their names before the public eye. In the field of sporting literature, reuse and repetition did not always stale for the reader; rather, it seems to have had a comforting effect, especially with regard to the conservative rural sports, with their sense of history and custom.

---

28. See *Oriental Sporting Magazine* 1 (October 1830): 53, 56, 56–61.
29. Warner, *Protocols of Liberty*.
30. According to Huggins, "*The Times* featured nineteen different sports in 1874, and twenty-seven by 1901, and included far more articles on individual sports" (*Victorians and Sport*, 6).

Periodical literature thus simultaneously worked to mirror, embrace, and dispel the sense of disorientation attendant on the speedy institutional and technological changes felt by the nineteenth-century sporting world. At the beginning of the century, writers like Nimrod and Surtees brought a worldly attitude to bear on a largely rural sporting milieu that was coming to grips with technological innovations and beginning to find itself invaded by the urban middle classes. Later in the century, periodicals found ways to cash in on the growing appetite for public spectacle in the form of team sports like football and cricket, and to cater to the needs of those who took advantage of their newfound leisure time to enjoy participatory, often expensive sports like golf, cycling, and even motoring.[31] The self-image of the reader must also have changed accordingly. Muscular Christianity and the culture of athleticism in the public schools made the male body a site for scientific improvement every bit as much as the rod, the rifle, and the thoroughbred horse.[32] We see the female reader appealed to equally innovatively in the changes that Ada Ballin made to *Womanhood*, advocating sport as part of a hygienic regimen. At the beginning of the century, the potential reader of sporting literature might most readily have been imagined as Nimrod's Frank Raby, the hero of *Life of a Sportsman* (1842), a young gentleman with an allowance and copies of the *New Sporting Magazine* in his rooms at Oxford; by century's end, it might equally have been one of the working men in Robert Tressell's novel *The Ragged-Trousered Philanthropists* taking a break from painting in order to form a syndicate, "each member contributing threepence for the purpose of backing a dead certainty given by the renowned Captain Kiddem of the Obscurer."[33]

At the turn of the twentieth century, the audience for sport had multiplied. It now had eclectic tastes that went well beyond the field sports of the early century. It was more democratic, even if not all sections of it were always as active as the earlier one had been in participating. The new audience had more leisure and spare cash to watch professionals play the roles that amateurs had in the past, and advertising clamored for the attention of enthusiasts with disposable income to purchase golf clubs, bicycles—and more papers. This consumer market of readers formed part of a complex media ecology that employed ever more authors and editors; offered opportunities for specialized sporting journals to sprout, wither, or grow; and further fed back into the environment to fuel the growth of spectator and participatory sports. It was in the character of sporting journalism to feed on and to enable this process of media modernization: in the same way that sportsmen themselves had always had to be open to change in order to succeed in the field, sporting periodicals had to adapt to changing cultural conditions in order to flourish in the marketplace.

---

31. On the latter, see Shepherd, "British Press."
32. Mangan, *Athleticism*.
33. Tressell, *Ragged-Trousered Philanthropists*, 10.

23

COMIC/SATIRIC PERIODICALS

Craig Howes

As Donald J. Gray and J. Don Vann have noted, the first challenge for any researcher interested in nineteenth-century British comic and satiric periodicals is defining the subject.[1] Vann helpfully explains that a "Victorian comic periodical typically contains jokes, comic verse, riddles, parodies, caricatures, puns, cartoons, and satire," with most "published weekly and sold for a penny, although a few were monthly and prices ranged up to sixpence and occasionally a shilling."[2] Gray declares that "it is easy enough to recognize . . . the central tradition of the comic journalism of the century," which he maps out with the three weeklies *Figaro in London* (1831–39), *Punch, or the London Charivari* (1841–2002), and *Ally Sloper's Half-Holiday* (1884–1923).[3]

But what of the monthlies? Or the substantial comic or satiric components of such publications as *Blackwood's* (1817–1980), *Fraser's* (1830–82), or *Vanity Fair* (1864–1914)? Or the constant presence of a "journalism of scandal and ribaldry"?[4] Or the scores of regional publications—evidence that every town with a printing press wanted its own *Figaro*, *Punch*, *Jackdaw*, or *Satirist*? Complicating matters further is the huge amount of contemporary critical and theoretical commentary about comic and satiric periodicals, often highly prescriptive or self-justifying, that has influenced subsequent scholarship—for instance, Donald J. Gray's identification of *Figaro in London*, *Punch*, and *Ally Sloper's Half-Holiday* as turning points: "Victorian comic journalism developed from an association in its beginnings with slander and ribaldry to an association at the end of the century with what Victorian journalists and literary critics called light literature."[5] To a greater degree than with most categories of periodicals, new directions in scholarship on comic/satiric periodicals may require an interrogation of dominant assumptions that the producers of periodicals themselves wanted us to make about the relative merits of various publications and about the history of their production. Because so many later critics have followed these leads, earlier critical and theoretical texts will appear prominently in this overview.

---

1. Vann, "Comic Periodicals"; Gray, "List of Comic Periodicals."
2. Vann, "Comic Periodicals," 278.
3. Gray, "List of Comic Periodicals," 2.
4. Ibid., 4.
5. Ibid., 4.

Though descriptions of the nineteenth century as a time when satire disappeared or became domesticated are pervasive in literary histories, the essentials of the argument can still be accessed in Stuart M. Tave's *The Amiable Humorist* (1960) and Robert Bernard Martin's brief critical appendix to Tave, *The Triumph of Wit* (1974). Tave argues that during the Restoration and earlier eighteenth century, Juvenalian, Hobbesian satiric wit was dominant in the writings of Dryden, Pope, Swift, and others, but by the early nineteenth century this angry impulse had been softened into a good-natured comic impulse, perhaps derived from Sterne. Martin agrees with this narrative but argues that by the latter half of the Victorian period wit had returned, articulated notably in George Meredith's *An Essay on Comedy and the Uses of the Comic Spirit* (1897).

Many studies of satire and comedy take this assessment for granted. "The great age of satire was roughly 1660 to 1800," Dustin Griffin writes, which may explain why his historical overview of English satire jumps from the eighteenth century to the twentieth.[6] Studies of the early nineteenth century make their own arguments for satire's disappearance, which often coincides with the death of Byron, or of that irresistible target, George IV. Marcus Wood declares this thesis in the title of his important book, *Radical Satire and Print Culture 1790–1822* (1994), and raises two crucial considerations for conducting research on nineteenth-century comic and satiric periodicals: politics and genre. Scholars and historians of political rhetoric during this period, such as J.R. Dinwiddy, Ann Hone, Olivia Smith, and William Hardy Wickwar, all deal extensively with these periodicals.[7] But this age loosely marked out by the French Revolution, the Napoleonic Wars, and the First Reform Bill also offers scholars of comic and satiric periodicals a full range of publications dedicated to attacks and mockery. Jon P. Klancher identifies the major satiric and comic periodical writers as William Cobbett, Thomas Wooler, Richard Carlyle, and William Hone.[8] The periodicals range from such conservative publications as George Canning and William Gifford's the *Anti-Jacobin* (1797–98) or Theodore Hook's *John Bull* (1820–92), to radical responses that invoke Edmund Burke's dismissal of the uneducated classes as the "swinish multitude" in their titles, such as Daniel Isaac Eaton's *Politics for the People; or Hog's Wash* (1794–95), or Thomas Spence's *Pig's Meat; or, Lessons for the Swinish Multitude* (1793–96), or to the indictments of inequities and injustices found in Cobbett's *Political Register* (1802–35), Wooler's *Black Dwarf* (1817–24), and Hone's *Reformists' Register* (1817).

These texts have all drawn critical attention; however, other publications more explicitly identified themselves as comic and satiric. Substantial, often conservative serials such as the *Satirist* (1808–14), *Scourge* (1811–15), *Busybody, or Men and Manners* (1816–18), *Dublin Satirist* (1809–10), *English Spy* (1825–26), and *New Bon Ton* (1818–21) appeared monthly, featuring long articles and colored, full-page prints. Popular weekly papers included *Bell's Life in London, and Sporting Chronicle* (1822–66), whose March 17, 1822 subtitle promised to combine "with the News of the Week, a rich Repository of Fashion, Wit, and Humour, and the interesting incidents of High and Low Life." The various papers and serials written and edited by Leigh Hunt, including the *Examiner* (1808–86) and the *Liberal* (1822–23), have received a great deal

---

6. Griffin, *Satire*, 1.
7. Dinwiddy, *From Luddism*; Hone, *For the Cause*; Smith, *Politics of Language*; Wickwar, *Struggle for the Freedom*.
8. Klancher, *Making of English Reading Audiences*.

of critical attention, partly because of his illustrious cast of writers, including Byron, and partly because of Hunt's own comic and satiric activities, which led to his conviction and imprisonment for libeling the Prince Regent in the *Examiner*.

This history raises issues of politics and aesthetics. In his landmark book *Radical Underworld: Prophets, Revolutionaries, and Pornographers in London, 1795–1840* (1988), Iain McCalman refers to a "long and intricate overlap between the allegedly separate spheres of 'respectability' and 'roughness'" that parallels similar, supposedly dichotomous relationships between the "literary" and the "vulgar," "seditious," "blasphemous," "libellous," or the "sub-literary."[9] Focusing his attention on "long-term carriers of 'rough' political and cultural traditions," McCalman concludes that the "bawdy and satirical literary traditions of Regency radicalism are supposed to have disappeared during the 1820s, but a mass of related populist-style material continued to flow from radical presses throughout the twenties and thirties."[10] This claim is borne out by several historical studies, including his own, but their authors seem to assume that radical politics and a popular readership rendered pointless the literary study or close examination of the publications themselves as visual art—a spur, perhaps, to more recent scholars, such as David Kuntzle and Brian Maidment, who are doing precisely this.[11] Comic and satiric publications of the 1830s often get mentioned within historical studies of the taxes on knowledge and the resulting flood of unstamped penny papers that resisted such censorship and suppression. Patricia Hollis's *The Pauper Press: A Study in Working-Class Radicalism of the 1830s* (1970), James A. Epstein's *Radical Expression: Political Language, Ritual, and Symbol in England, 1790–1850* (1994), and Joel Wiener's *The War of the Unstamped: The Movement to Repeal the British Newspaper Tax, 1830–1836* (1969) offer valuable insights into satiric periodicals. For example, Wiener notes that in the spring of 1832, more than eighteen unstamped satiric papers were published in London, with others cropping up in Liverpool, Glasgow, and Sheffield.[12] But Hollis observes that those enforcing the stamp act described papers like the *Penny Magazine*, *Literary Gazette*, *Crisis*, and *Figaro* as "either merely or harmlessly amusing, or more really instructive" and therefore "should be very reluctant to enforce the law against them."[13]

Some impressive recent work has focused primarily upon the visual aspects of comic and satiric papers of this period. Partly in response to the notion that the 1830s was an "aesthetic black hole of market-driven, trivial, and visually uninteresting graphic production that filled a cultural gap,"[14] Brian Maidment, in *Comedy, Caricature and the Social Order, 1820–1850* (2013), offers a thorough and informative overview of how changes in print technology and readership affected the form and impact of such publications, most notably

---

9. McCalman, *Radical Underworld*, 3.
10. Ibid., 221.
11. Kunzle, *History of the Comic Strip* and "Between Broadsheet"; Maidment, *Comedy, Caricature and the Social Order*.
12. Wiener, *War of the Unstamped*, 177–9.
13. Hollis, *Pauper Press*, 158. Hollis is quoting words attributed to Alley, a stamp office lawyer, in response to Cowie, the publisher of the *Church Examiner*. From *True Sun*, September 1, 1832.
14. Maidment, *Comedy, Caricature and the Social Order*, 4. Here Maidment is summarizing David Kunzle's conclusion in *History of the Comic Strip*.

by creating new relationships between text and image.[15] Radical political content and the new forms of visual production come together most closely in *Figaro in London* (1831–39), Donald J. Gray's first time-marker and a very important comic periodical, largely because of its staff. Robert Seymour, a comic illustrator second only to George Cruikshank in reputation, was the artist. Maidment gives the best account of Seymour's work for *Figaro* and his entire oeuvre. The writers and editors included Gilbert À Beckett and Henry Mayhew. Both would figure prominently in *Punch*, and the history of Victorian journalism more generally—À Beckett with a host of comic publications and the *Illustrated London News*, and Mayhew with the famous *Morning Chronicle* series that became *London Labour and the London Poor* in 1851. Both writers have been the subject of biographical and critical studies beginning soon after their deaths, suggesting a general and continuing public interest. À Beckett's son, Arthur William, compiled *The À Becketts of Punch: Memories of a Father and Sons* (1903), and Mayhew's son, Athol, concocted *A Jorum of "Punch" With Those Who Helped to Brew It* (1895). Appearing much later were Anne Humpherys's *Travels into the Poor Man's Country: The Work of Henry Mayhew* (1977), and Leslie Yeo and E.P. Thompson's edited collection, *The Unknown Mayhew* (1971). *Figaro in London* served as a template for the Victorian comic paper. Its weekly tabloid format, with political cartoons and other comic illustrations, along with jokes, gossip, parodies, theater reviews, and running commentary on political and social matters, became the publishing standard.

Weekly publications co-existed with, and often fed, comic monthlies and annuals as well as collections of comic cuts.[16] George Cruikshank was the gold standard for such collections for decades, but Thomas Hood's *Comic Annual* (1830–42), Louisa Sheridan's *Comic Offering* (1831–35), and Gilbert À Beckett's and the *Figaro* staff's *Comic Magazine* (1832–34) also gathered humorous poetry, prose, and sketches into book-length publications. Robert Seymour, John Doyle (who signed his work "HB"), and C.J. Grant issued collections of their caricatures. For an overview of the interplay between image and text in these publications, see Celina Fox, *Graphic Journalism in England During the 1830s and 1840s* (1984); Louis James's "Cruickshank and Early Victorian Caricature"; Richard J. Pound's dissertation on "Serial Journalism and the Transformation of English Graphic Satire, 1830–36" and his essay on C.J. Grant; and chapter three of Maidment's *Comedy, Caricature and the Social Order*. For biographical studies, see Robert L. Patten's magnificent two-volume *George Cruikshank's Life, Times, and Art* (1991, 1996), John Cowie Reid's *Thomas Hood* (1963), John Clubbe's *Victorian Forerunner: The Late Career of Thomas Hood* (1968), and Sara Lodge's *Thomas Hood and Nineteenth-Century Poetry: Work, Play, and Politics* (2007).

Running parallel to the comic/satiric weeklies and annuals, however, was what Donald J. Gray labels "early Victorian scandalous journalism."[17] These long-lived, often conservative, and highly personal satiric publications, which included Theodore Hook's *John Bull* (1820–92), Charles Molloy Westmacott's *Age* (1825–43), Barnard Gregory's *Satirist* (1831–49), and

---

15. Ibid., 5.
16. For an account of the comic monthlies, see Gray, "List of Comic Periodicals," 4.
17. See Gray, "Early Victorian Scandalous Journalism."

Renton Nicholson's the *Town* (1837–42), provided "not an amusing or denigrating addition to the news" but rather "an invitation to a dark reading of the news itself."[18] For excellent accounts of such publications, see David E. Latané's "Charles Molloy Westmacott and the Spirit of the *Age*" (2007) and *William Maginn and the British Press* (2013).

Punch and Its Competitors

As the Victorian age began, then, comic and satiric periodicals might contain fierce attacks on political champions of the people; amusing, clever frolics; knowing commentaries on British politics and society; or exposés of the dark, corrupt lives of the wealthy and powerful. *Punch, or the London Charivari* and its many imitators united these qualities in publications catering to an emerging, and soon to be dominant, British middle class. First appearing in July 1841, *Punch* swiftly became the most successful and famous of all British comic periodicals, and, not surprisingly, a primary subject of critical interest. As early as 1875, Joseph Hatton published a series of articles titled "The True Story of 'Punch.' An Historical, Biographical, and Critical Gossip." At the turn of the century, long-time *Punch* contributor and editor F.C. Burnand published "'Mr. Punch.' Some Precursors and Competitors" (1903). However, it is M.H. Spielmann's massive, authoritative *History of Punch* (1895) that remains the principal source of information about the first fifty years. Subsequent studies include R.G.G. Price's *A History of Punch* (1957) and Arthur Prager's *The Mahogany Tree: An Informal History of Punch* (1979).

Two recent critical works deal with *Punch*'s first twenty-five years: Richard D. Altick's *Punch: The Lively Youth of a British Institution, 1841–1851* (1997) and Patrick Leary's *The Punch Brotherhood: Table Talk and Print Culture in Mid-Victorian London* (2010). Altick's *The English Common Reader* (1957), *The Shows of London* (1978), and *The Presence of the Present: Topics of the Day in the Victorian Novel* (1991) are still major resources for those researching comic and satiric periodicals, and his book on *Punch* provides a detailed history of how the staff developed strategies for dealing with the political, cultural, and aesthetic issues of the day. Leary draws upon the *Punch* archive, the diaries and letters of its contributors, and especially the Henry Silver diary (a detailed record of the weekly *Punch* staff meetings) to provide important information about *Punch*'s production, its staff/owner relations, its significance within the London literary scene, and the heated internal debates about its direction and purpose. Leary also supplies a fine overview of the critical literature on *Punch*. Gale Cengage and Liverpool John Moores University have recently completed the online *Punch Historical Archive*, which identifies *Punch* contributors from 1843 to 1919.

Biographical scholarship has shed light on many of these contributors, including Douglas Jerrold, the prolific comic writer of the 1830s, 1840s, and 1850s. His son Walter published *Douglas Jerrold and "Punch"* (1910) and *Douglas Jerrold, Dramatist and Wit* (1914), and more recently Michael Slater produced his valuable study, *Douglas Jerrold, 1803–1857* (2002). Gordon N. Ray's two-part biography (1955, 1958) of William Makepeace Thackeray supplies a wealth of information about early *Punch* contributors, as does Arthur Adrian's biography of

---

18. Ibid., 327.

Mark Lemon (1966), who emerged as *Punch*'s principal editor. George Somes Layard's *A Great "Punch" Editor: Being the Life, Letters, and Diaries of Shirley Brooks* (1907) tells the story of a prolific and highly influential contributor and editor, but Patrick Leary's chapter on Brooks is far more insightful and informative.[19] *Punch* illustrators have also been the subject of revealing studies. John Leech is discussed in Frederick G. Kitton's 1884 biography and in Henry J. Miller's "John Leech and the Shaping of the Victorian Cartoon: The Context of Respectability" (2009). Frankie Morris's *Artist of Wonderland: The Life, Political Cartoons, and Illustrations of Tenniel* (2005) explores John Tenniel's long association with *Punch*; T. Martin Wood's *George du Maurier: The Satirist of the Victorians* (1913) deals with an equally venerable artist; and Leonée Ormond's *Linley Sambourne: Illustrator and Punch Cartoonist* (2010) details the life of another prominent contributor to *Punch*.

Punch's success and its critical history have made it the litmus test for evaluating virtually all satiric and comic periodicals. Donald J. Gray writes that "by the middle of the century the character of a comic periodical had been clearly established by the success of *Punch*,"[20] and the staff was aware and proud of this achievement. Henry Silver claimed that at one *Punch* dinner, "Lemon said *Punch* had blotted out the *Age* and *Satirist*, 'and other vile publications,' which before *Punch* existed, were the only amusing journals of the day."[21] Donald J. Gray agrees, writing, "By the mid 1840s scandalous journalism as Westmacott, Gregory, and Nicholson practised it was just about finished,"[22] and James Hannay, a mid-Victorian writer with a strong interest in satire, argued that the humorous magazine in general "was not catering for men with political purpose, and certainly not for the isolated genius; it was dealing with the Great British Public and the wholesome British family."[23] *Punch* not only assumed the most prominent position in the nineteenth-century comic and satiric pantheon but also took credit for defining the genre's tone and purpose, and for the most part, later critics have agreed with this assessment. For a detailed account of this transition, see Frank Palmeri's "Cruikshank, Thackeray, and the Victorian Eclipse of Satire" (2004).

While this genealogy might be accurate, its prescriptive nature has undoubtedly created incentives for, and obstacles to, further research. In his landmark *Fiction for the Working Man* (1963), Louis James notes but does not praise the shift in comic tone during the Victorian era, declaring that by the 1850s, comic publications "were beginning to share the fate of much out-of-date fiction, and became juvenile literature."[24] Much of *Punch*'s published history also conforms to what Patrick Brantlinger has described as the "heroic myth of the bourgeoisie" that Thomas Babington Macaulay celebrated as the stabilizing force lying between a "narrow oligarchy above," corrupted by the "vices engendered by power," and an "infuriated multitude below," suffering from the "vices engendered by distress."[25] But as early as 1833, the *Poor Man's*

---

19. Leary, *Punch Brotherhood*, 110–32.
20. Gray, "List of Comic Periodicals," 5.
21. Quoted in Fox, *Graphic Journalism*, 238.
22. Gray, "Early Victorian Scandalous Journalism," 340.
23. Quoted in Fox, *Graphic Journalism*, 247–8. For more on Hannay, see his *Satire and Satirists*.
24. James, *Fiction for the Working Man*, 44.
25. Quoted in Brantlinger, *Spirit of Reform*, 18.

Guardian was already describing members of the middle class as "occupying an intermediate position between the workman and the aristocrat—employing the one and being employed by the other, they insensibly contract the vices of both tyrant and slave."[26]

The bourgeois, triumphalist narrative, with its accompanying celebration of the gentleman, often informs readings which interpret early *Punch* and the comic periodicals that preceded it as products of the vulgar, the ignorant, or the adolescent; depict *Punch*'s early rivals as the work of ill-bred or immoral hacks; and characterize the younger generation of comic publications produced during the 1850s and 1860s as the scribblings of Bohemian decadents. Speaking of 1830s periodicals in *English Caricaturists and Graphic Humourists of the Nineteenth Century* (1893), Graham Everitt, for instance, remarked that the "only excuse . . . for this sort of thing is to be found in the fact that comic journalism being then in its infancy, personal abuse was mistaken for satire" and that writers felt themselves "superior to the rules of literary courtesy."[27] And in 1907, George Somes Layard made the same claim about Shirley Brooks and *Punch* itself: "In common they started life with rude and unmannerly jibes, as most professional jesters do. At first they shot folly with a blunderbuss as it flew. Later they learned that to tickle it with a feather was just as effective. The older they grew the more they laughed, the less they sneered. The older they grew the more they sympathised, the less they despised. They found that love, kindness, goodwill were more worthy of cultivation than hate, indignation and cynicism."[28]

As noted above, Frank Palmeri has referred to this shift as the "Victorian eclipse of satire," though, as Robert Patten has observed, this sense of civility did not necessarily extend beyond the circle of class and nationality: "While middle-class readers of *Punch* were comforted by the gentle cartoons of themselves supplied by Leech and Doyle, they approved of altogether more hostile representations of the Irish as vagrants, ruffians, and anarchists—in short, as apes."[29] But Leary, Altick, and many other *Punch* historians have recorded how this ethos led to the flight or banishment of some of *Punch*'s most important early writers. According to E.P. Thompson, Henry Mayhew was an early casualty not only because he felt that the "satirist and the social investigator were necessary to each other" but because he "never suffered from this kind of middle-class moral halitosis."[30] What "unites the Mayhew of the *Comic Almanac* and of the *Morning Chronicle* investigation is contempt for the values of the 'highly respectable man.'"[31] Douglas Jerrold shared Mayhew's opinion, and the *Punch* staff returned frequently to the subject of Jerrold's politics and vulgarity long after his death.[32]

The most loathed former *Punch* contributor, however, was Albert Smith. In addition to writing for and editing many comic and satiric publications, Smith was a popular performer who enacted gripping accounts of adventures in the Alps and served as a literary older brother to a cluster of comic journalists who espoused Bohemian values and an antipathy to the now-establishment

---

26. Quoted in Stedman Jones, *Languages of Class*, 146.
27. Everitt, *English Caricaturists*, 224.
28. Layard, *Great "Punch" Editor*, 225.
29. Palmeri, "Cruikshank, Thackeray"; Patten, *George Cruikshank's Life*, 2:188.
30. Thompson in Mayhew, *Unknown Mayhew*, 45–6.
31. Ibid., 46.
32. Leary, *Punch Brotherhood*, 24–6, 30–2, 74, 123–4.

Punch.[33] Though Edmund Yates and George Augustus Sala were the most visible members of this group, there was an army of young writers and illustrators, including Robert Brough, Matt Morgan, and even W.S. Gilbert, who produced a formidable number of comic texts and images from the mid-1840s to the 1870s in *Judy* (1867–1907), *Toby* (1867–68), *Puck* (1844), the *Man in the Moon* (1847–49), the *Puppet Show* (1848–49), the *Tomahawk* (1867–70), and scores of other short-lived publications. Robert Brough's *Marston Lynch* (1860) is an autobiographical fiction about this literary Bohemia. For an account of perhaps *Punch*'s most successful rival, published from 1861 to 1901, see Edward S. Lauterbach's "*Fun* and its Contributors: The Literary History of a Victorian Humor Magazine." Memoirs of Yates (1884) and Sala (1894, 1896) were followed by a series of fine critical studies, Ralph Straus's *Sala: The Portrait of an Eminent Victorian* (1942), P.D. Edwards's *Dickens's "Young Men": George Augustus Sala, Edmund Yates, and the World of Victorian Journalism* (1997), and Christopher Kent's essays "British Bohemia and the Victorian Journalist" (2000) and "The Idea of Bohemia in Mid-Victorian England" (1973).

As Richard Altick notes, rail travel increased the market for topical papers with brief articles and pictures, making *Punch* and the *Illustrated London News* the "most characteristic periodicals of their time."[34] Railway passengers also served as an audience for "comicalities," miscellanies produced by Augustus Mayhew, Douglas Jerrold, Edmund Yates, and G.A. Sala.[35] Altick observes that these later miscellanies had none of the earnestness and seriousness of the *Penny Magazine* and its 1830s relatives.[36] Publisher Henry Vizetelly confirmed this in his 1893 autobiography, deploring the contemporary popularity of "shilling shockers, penny and halfpenny comics, and 'tit-bits' and 'short cuts' to amuse and confuse us during our uncomfortable journey."[37]

As the audience for entertaining, ephemeral reading continued to grow from the 1860s onward, so did the variety of satiric and comic periodicals. Contemporaries and later critics have represented this publishing landscape as a broad middle country occupied by *Punch* and its imitators, flanked by comic sheets for lower-middle-class or juvenile audiences as well as by scandal sheets and surveys of fast life in the city that sometimes claimed to be satiric monitors. One of the constants in these middle-class offerings was comic and parodic verse on the issues of the day. W.M. Praed and Thomas Hood led the way early in the century, and *Punch* produced an endless stream of such poetry, which was imitated in such publications as *Judy* and even improved upon in what became W.S. Gilbert's "Bab Ballads," featured in *Fun* during the last half of the 1860s.[38]

Cheap comic and salacious publications occupying the flanks of the literary marketplace were cartoon, joke, and anecdote grab bags, such as the *Novelty* (1882–85), *Funny Bits* (1883–85), and *Nice Bits* (1884–85). These titles began to flourish in the 1880s, and papers with even more cartoons, or comic "cuts," flooded the market in the 1890s. Such publications were often explicitly juvenile, even if the readership wasn't. *Ally Sloper's Half-Holiday* (1884–1923)

---

33. For information on Smith, see Fitzsimons, *Baron of Piccadilly*.
34. Altick, *Presence of the Present*, 21.
35. Altick, *English Common Reader*, 299.
36. Altick, *Presence of the Present*, 133.
37. Vizetelly, *Glances Back*, 1:117.
38. Altick discusses poetry and topicality as a source for humor in *Presence of the Present*, 31.

declared itself to be a "Selection, Side Splitting, Sentimental, and Serious, for the Benefit of Old Boys, Young Boys, Odd Boys Generally, and Even Girls." It was the most prominent of a slew of such penny and half-penny dreadfuls as the *Coloured Comic* (1890–1906), *Comic Cuts* (1890–1953), *Funny Cuts* (1890–1920), the *Joker* (1891–97), *Nuggets* (1892–1905), *Pictorial Comic Life* (1898–1928), and the *World's Comic* (1892–1908).

As *Comic Cuts* proclaimed, such papers offered "One Hundred Laughs for a Halfpenny" and often published sensational murder stories surrounded by cartoons parading various racist and gender stereotypes. *Ching Ching's Own* (1888–93), for instance, featured a Chinese "Melly" man along with crude caricatures and rollicking adventure stories driven by contemporary British attitudes about race and empire. Such content had been around for decades. As L. Perry Curtis Jr. explains, "By the 1860s no respectable reader of comic weeklies—and most of their readers were respectable—could possibly mistake the simous nose, long upper lip, huge, projecting mouth, and jutting lower jaw as well as sloping forehead for any other category of undesirable or dangerous human being than that known as Irish."[39] African and American blacks, Asians, Jews, and many other familiar butts of xenophobic humor appeared frequently in *Punch* and other middle-class publications, but these stereotypes especially proliferated in the later penny comics as easy sources of laughs. As for gender, the first major history of *Punch* by Spielmann confidently declared that "women, as a rule, are humorists neither born nor made."[40] According to Spielmann, women "can make, we are told, but they cannot take, a joke; at any rate, they are usually out of their element in the comic arena."[41] Small wonder, then, that the demands of women towards the end of the century for education, the franchise, or emancipation often provoked whimsical and brutal humor—or that a certain class of satiric publications was devoted to the lives of prostitutes or adulterous women in high life. As for the dirtier flank of salacious gossip, Donald J. Gray notes that a number of periodicals during the 1870s and 1880s revived the scandal-mongering tradition which had flourished in the 1820s.[42] Adolphus Rosenberg published a number of such sheets, including *Town Talk* (1878–85), *Quiz: The Satirist* (1879), *Rosenberg's Little Journal* (1886–87), and *Tittle Tattle* (1888); other comic journals of the period defined themselves through contrast. For example, in May 1882 Liverpool's *Halfpenny Owl* firmly rejected the idea that the "mass of the people can only be entertained in their moments of leisure by invented tales and insinuations implying slanderous imputations on public and private character."[43]

Future Research

"The histories of most Victorian comic periodicals have yet to be written,"[44] wrote J. Don Vann in 1994, and this largely holds true today, although steadily increasing access to online

---

39. Curtis, *Apes and Angels*, 29.
40. Spielmann, *History of "Punch,"* 392.
41. Ibid.
42. Gray, "Early Victorian Scandalous Journalism," 344.
43. "Expansion," 1.
44. Vann, "Comic Periodicals," 289.

primary resources will make many more histories possible.[45] Future research on such publications must, however, also interrogate the many self-evident truths pervading our current critical understanding. Whether emerging from Dublin, Liverpool, Manchester, Glasgow, or the Isle of Man, regional humor and satire need to be studied carefully, and the dynamics of class in comic offerings published in the second half of the century require close attention. What ideological work do the cuts and bits papers perform? We also need more information on how other vehicles of comic performance—pantomime, music hall, stage comedy, the club scene, Judge and Jury performances—intersected with print sources focused on laughter and criticism. And we would certainly benefit from developing a more supple vocabulary for describing the hybrid forms these publications take. As Brian Maidment argues in *Comedy, Caricature and the Social Order*, very little scholarship effectively discusses the interplay between text and picture or between writers, artists, engravers, printers, and publishers. Maidment himself is starting to rectify this situation, and Patrick Leary has made an excellent start with his study of *Punch*'s early years. Finally, because of their topicality, which arose from the constant pressure to produce more jokes for the moment, nineteenth-century British comic and satiric publications should also be examined as formative influences upon our own period. Today, television and social media create an even greater flow of humorous yet cutting commentary—and at a much greater frequency than once a week.

---

45. For a brief overview of current directions in digital access to nineteenth-century British publications, see Maidment, *Comedy, Caricature and the Social Order*, 16.

24

SOCIAL PURPOSE PERIODICALS

Deborah Mutch

> The sacred call: it rose up on the wing
> Of the great echo Gutenberg invented.[1]

Social purpose periodicals aimed to create a unified society, to encourage harmony and so establish a safe, peaceful, and happy nation. A typical strategy would be to identify the problem preventing harmony and peace, present it to the reader along with the remedy, and clearly set out the benefits of accepting the vision. The difficulty with this benignly educative motivation for publication—a clear outcome of Enlightenment principles—was that there was no single social problem to be addressed by a single solution: one person or social group's solution was another's problem that also needed to be addressed through a periodical; the harmony proposed to one periodical's imagined community was the oppressive order to be resisted through another. Social purpose periodicals were so numerous and heterogeneous that selection is therefore essential. For the purpose of this chapter, I have selected the wide-ranging issues of class politics, temperance, religion, and gender as most usefully representative because they were debated across the nineteenth century and overlapped with one another. Other chapters in this *Handbook* are devoted to periodicals concerned with temperance, religion, and gender. This chapter, by contrast, aims to show their interaction with each other and with class politics. With that in mind, while the headings here are intended to help orient the reader, they should by no means be considered as exclusive categories which separate them out from the other issues.

Class Politics

The association of print with social issues and control began in Britain with broadsides. Focusing on "religion and politics,"[2] Leslie Shepard notes that "in the sixteenth century . . . a street ballad was a better indicator of public sentiment than a State Paper."[3] The power of printed matter has long been understood, and hegemonic groups have often attempted to control content,

---

1. Engels, "On the Invention of Printing."
2. Shepard, *Broadside Ballad*, 51.
3. Shepard, *History of Street Literature*, 122.

readership, and ownership. An early example of the intent to control content was the 1543 Act for the Advancement of True Religion, which was designed to suppress radical broadsides and booksellers by restricting sales to religious books and tracts.[4] Later, the 1816 Seditious Publications Act and the 1819 "Six Acts" effectively restricted reading and ownership to the rich.[5] The resultant "taxes on knowledge" added 3d. to every pound of paper, constrained revenue by taxing advertisements, taxed reportage on current affairs through the stamp duty on newspapers, and demanded that newspaper proprietors provide a £300 bond on start-up as surety against any possible fines or convictions for libel.[6] The modes of publication that made the dissident periodical dangerous simultaneously benefited periodicals that promoted the status quo. Regularity of publication served to continuously present certain ideas to the reader, maintain a constant vision of the better life, and create a community of readers. "The regularity and public nature of these issue days," Laurel Brake notes, "created numerous and large communities of readers, all of whom were reading the same publication at roughly the same time all over the country."[7] The different cycles of publication—daily, weekly, monthly, and quarterly—might have caused what Brake terms a "cacophony of printed serials,"[8] but within this noise readers could develop their own identities by selecting certain periodicals. As James Mussell has argued, "Newspapers and periodicals interpellated readers into social configurations and, in turn, readers defined themselves in certain ways by choosing to purchase or read a particular publication."[9] A specific periodical became a form of social bond that united readers and created a "community of readers all engaged in the same activity"—and that community of readers might be persuaded to maintain or challenge the status quo.[10]

Periodicals such as the *British Workman* (1855–1921), subtitled *and Friends of the Sons of Toil, Dedicated to the Industrial Classes by their Sincere Friend The Editor*, sought to convince worker-readers of the benefits of their position through the social bond of reading.[11] Founded by Thomas Bywater Smithies and supported by philanthropists such as the Earl of Shaftesbury and Samuel Morley, its mission was to promote the "Health, Wealth, and Happiness of the Working Classes."[12] In an 1851 article titled "The Canker of Discontent," G. Mogridge offered an example of how this mission would be actualized. He encouraged the acceptance of social position through vignettes of discontented workers, such as the fishboy who wished he were a butcher's boy. The fishboy was advised that "it will be better to make the best of your present calling than to render it worse by giving way to discontent."[13] The highly illustrated pages and the full front-page picture, which from 1861 became the *British Workman*'s hallmark, visually

---

4. Ibid., 54.
5. James, "Working-Class Literature," 874.
6. Fyfe, *Steam-Powered Knowledge*, 16; King and Plunkett, *Victorian Print Media*, 82.
7. Brake, *Print in Transition*, 11.
8. Ibid., 30.
9. Mussell, *Nineteenth-Century Press*, 41.
10. Turner, "Periodical Time," 188.
11. Murray, "*Band of Hope Review*," 80. See also Mountjoy, "Thomas Bywater Smithies."
12. "Health, Wealth and Happiness," 1.
13. Mogridge, "Canker," 1.

Figure 24.1 "I'll Go Back, I'll Not Pledge the Clock," *British Workman*, no. 98, February 1863: 1. Courtesy of the Working Class Movement Library, Salford.

reinforced the necessity of accepting one's social position.[14] Many of the illustrations extolled the benefits of prudence and sobriety and gave clear advice on how the workman should conduct his life. For instance, the illustration on the front page of the issue for February 1863 (Figure 24.1), entitled "I'll Go Back, I'll Not Pledge the Clock," juxtaposes the visible benefits of temperance with the poverty of intemperance. The reader is thus provided with both written and visual advice on the benefits of temperance, work and thrift.

While periodicals such as the *British Workman* aimed to maintain the status quo by representing the working classes as compliant and peaceful, others sought to promote social change. One of the earliest periodicals to criticize the class system was William Cobbett's *Political Register* (1802–35). The year the Seditious Publications Act was passed was also the year Cobbett deliberately addressed the needs of "Journeymen and Labourers" by reducing the price of the *Political Register* from 1s. to 2d.,[15] which increased its circulation dramatically (40,000–70,000 in 1816 and 1817).[16] Cobbett used the *Political Register* as a platform for expressing his concerns about the national debt, unemployment, and parliamentary reform, presenting these problems as a "confrontation between the ideal and the 'real,' between the way things should be and the way they were."[17] Consequently, in the hands of the political dissident, the *Political Register* worked for material social change. The young Friedrich Engels acknowledged the revolutionary potential of the press in his poem "On the Invention of Printing" (1840), which provides the epigraph to this chapter.

After Cobbett fled to America to avoid imprisonment for sedition, the reform issue was taken up by Thomas J. Wooler's *Black Dwarf* (1817–24) and Richard Carlile's *Republican* (1819–26). Both avoided the 4d. newspaper tax by publishing less frequently than the twenty-eight-day minimum mandated in the act and by raising their prices.[18] Radical and dissident periodicals continued to be published, but their potency was restricted by infrequency and cost. Henry Hetherington was imprisoned for refusing to pay the stamp duty on his penny weekly *Poor Man's Guardian* (1831–35) during his campaign for both the extension of the franchise and the removal of the taxes on knowledge.[19] Although the 1832 Reform Act was a bitter disappointment to Hetherington and others who had campaigned for the working-class vote, their fight against the duties on print was more successful: the periodical tax was reduced by the Whig government in 1836.[20]

The working-class reader not only benefited from reductions in cost but also from advancements in mechanical printing (which increased the speed of production) and the spread of railways (which increased the speed of distribution).[21] Nevertheless, the working-class readership was still closely associated with political dissent. Paul Thomas Murphy has noted that

---

14. Murray, "British Workman."
15. Murphy, *Toward a Working-Class Canon*, 36.
16. Nattrass, *William Cobbett*, 3.
17. Wilson, *Paine and Cobbett*, 99.
18. Murphy, *Shakespeare for the People*, 63–4.
19. King and Plunkett, *Victorian Print Media*, 85–8.
20. James, "Working-Class Literature," 874.
21. Fyfe, *Steam-Powered Knowledge*, 35–8, 103–5.

the "overall readership of working-class periodicals did not rise gradually between 1816 and 1858. Rather, it rose or declined in close correspondence with fluctuations in working-class political activity."[22]

As Malcolm Chase observes, the creation of a network of periodicals for spreading Chartism throughout the United Kingdom "situated [the Chartist movement] on the cusp of the transition from a largely oral to a mainly print-based popular culture."[23] The national *Northern Star* (1838–52) had the highest sales figures of all of the Chartist periodicals despite having to pay the stamp duty, which raised its price to 4½d. However, it was still subject to the fluctuations of interest in working-class politics. Murphy illuminates these ebbs and flows with a count of the *Northern Star*'s stamp returns: "[Its] circulation was much greater between 1838 and 1842 and again in 1848 (the years three national Chartist petitions were presented to Parliament) than at any other time."[24] Even so, the overlap of oral and print culture meant that multiple working-class readers consumed any given individual copy. The numbers of readers accessing a periodical issue were considerably higher than sales figures alone would suggest. Chase gives examples of issues being shared, temporarily borrowed, and read aloud to friends and work colleagues.[25]

Between 1855 and 1880, a series of events significantly increased working-class interest in the periodical. The removal of the taxes on knowledge was completed in 1861 when the paper tax was lifted; the education acts of 1870 and 1880 widened an already highly literate working class; and the extension of the franchise through the 1867 Reform Act further politicized the working classes. Socialist activists, like the Chartists before them, recognized the importance of the press in spreading their ideas, yet the publications associated with both movements revealed internal fault lines. Just as the *Chartist* (1839–40) encouraged moral force rather than the physical force advocated by Feargus O'Connor's *Northern Star*, so the foundations for many of the later socialist periodicals lay in disagreement. E.P. Thompson argues that one of the primary reasons William Morris and others resigned from the Social Democratic Federation (SDF) in December 1884 was their objection to the power wielded by Henry Mayers Hyndman in his role as founder and chairman of the organization and as owner and editor of the group's periodical, *Justice* (1884–1925).[26] After their departure, Morris and the other defectors founded the Socialist League, and one of their first actions was to publish the *Commonweal* (1885–94). Shortly afterwards, SDF member Henry Hyde Champion began publishing *Commonsense* (1887–88), casting the new periodical as a challenge to Hyndman's revolutionary turn.[27] The fissiparous nature of British socialists, when combined with advancements in the technology for producing and selling cheap periodicals, meant that British socialism was projected through a bewildering array of periodicals.

22. Murphy, *Working-Class Canon*, 10.
23. Chase, *Chartism*, 45.
24. Murphy, *Working-Class Canon*, 10.
25. Chase, *Chartism*, 45.
26. Thompson, *William Morris*, 347–50.
27. Barnes, *Socialist Champion*, 86.

Temperance

While another chapter in this volume focuses on temperance publications specifically, these periodicals must be mentioned here as well, for concerns about the working class, whether framed as encouragement of acceptance or as motivation for change, were often tied to arguments for temperance. Responsibility was synonymous with sobriety; both needed to be taught. Smithies's *British Workman*, for example, was preceded by his temperance periodical for children, the *Band of Hope Review and Sunday Scholars' Friend* (1851–1937). After 1862, this popular periodical was publishing a quarter of a million copies.[28] On the first page of the first issue, Smithies urges the child-reader to "form Temperance Bands of Hope in every city, town, and village, and let us unite in one great army, and never rest until Intemperance falls before our onward march."[29] Before directing its efforts towards children, the temperance movement, in its early years, focused on middle-class consumption since "reformers wanted their own class to set an example for the 'lower orders,'" but the focus soon shifted to the working-class drinker.[30] A slew of temperance periodicals appeared during the nineteenth century, including the *Temperance Magazine and Review* (1832–33); the *Star of Temperance* (1835–36), published for the Manchester and Salford Temperance Association; *Onward* (1865–1909); and the *Temperance Worker and Band of Hope Conductor* (1873–1901). In the early years of the movement, temperance was presented as an alternative to political action, but later in the century, as the franchise expanded, the movement became associated with the Liberal party.[31] The United Kingdom Alliance, in its periodical *Alliance News* (1854–1991), claimed that Richard Cobden would have supported the 1869 Permissive Prohibitory Liquors Bill, thus appropriating the Liberal statesman to its cause, despite his avowed free-trade principles.[32] After the repeal of the stamp tax in 1855, the retitled *Alliance News* began incorporating news reports, which increased its circulation to 14,000–15,000 in 1859, making it one of the most important and influential temperance periodicals.[33] However, arguments for temperance were also included in radical periodicals since sobriety was promoted as necessary in the fight for class equality.

As early as 1819, before the temperance movement had become fully established in Britain, Thomas Wooler's *Black Dwarf* had advocated abstinence from alcohol. During the celebration of Cobbett's return from America, Henry Hunt praised those assembled: "He congratulated them, also, that among so large an assembly he did not see a single bottle of wine, a circumstance which gave reasonable hope that they should not be charged with drunkenness among their other crimes.—(*Laughter.*)—He trusted they would adhere to this temperance."[34] Later, the Chartist movement developed teetotalism as an "integral element," according to Malcolm

---

28. Murray, "*Band of Hope Review*," 37.
29. Smithies, "To the Boys and Girls of All Nations," 1.
30. Shiman, *Crusade against Drink*, 9.
31. Harrison, *Drink and the Victorians*, 162.
32. Ibid., 288.
33. Ibid., 236.
34. "Return of Mr. Cobbett," 801.

Chase.[35] Adherents included Henry Vincent, Henry Hetherington, and John Cleave, owner of the *English Chartist Circular and Temperance Record* (1841–43). In an editorial titled "Temperance Record," Cleave wrote, "We hail with unbounded satisfaction the progress of the temperance movement."[36] His aim was to create a body of temperance Chartists, "as a portion of the CIRCULAR will be regularly devoted to this great object."[37] Indeed, the *English Chartist Circular* was second only to the *Northern Star* in popularity and sales.[38] Feargus O'Connor took advantage of this popularity and contributed, despite his criticism of teetotal Chartism as a dilution of the political message.[39]

The tension between left-wing politics and temperance was also characteristic of the socialist movement later in the century. Keir Hardie advocated voluntary total abstinence while arguing through his *Labour Leader* (1888–1986) that the poverty of the working classes could not be blamed entirely on their consumption of alcohol. In 1897, Hardie asked, "If the spending of ninety millions by the workers [on drink] can be alleged as the cause of their poverty, how much more must the abstraction of £730 millions be as a cause?"[40] Hardie fostered the image of the Independent Labour Party (ILP) as moral, sober, and religious in opposition to the atheist, immoral drinkers of the SDF, which allowed bars in its clubhouses. Hyndman, like Feargus O'Connor before him, believed temperance was a diversion from the cause of socialism,[41] and, like Engels and Blatchford, he was concerned about the lack of alternative leisure activities.[42]

Hardie's concern about the working-class consumption of alcohol stemmed from his own lifelong teetotalism, which was reinforced by his embrace of religion through the Congregationalists. But temperance advocacy was not restricted to Nonconformism; in the 1860s and 1870s, the Church of England Temperance Society prospered, leading to the publication of the *Church of England Temperance Magazine* (1862–72).[43] Temperance periodicals capitalized on the association between temperance and religion and used the pulpit to deliver their message. The *Temperance Worker and Band of Hope Conductor*, edited by the Rev. Frederic Wagstaff, included a regular column entitled "Temperance Work in the Pulpit" which suggested biblical chapters and verses to promote teetotalism. For instance, Wagstaff suggested Acts 19:24–29 ("and the whole city was filled with confusion") as an analogy for the battle against the alcohol trade.[44] He thus presented readers with material they could use to write and deliver a weekly temperance sermon.

---

35. Chase, *Chartism*, 171.
36. Cleave, "Temperance Record," 6.
37. Ibid.
38. Chase, *Chartism*, 171.
39. Chase, "Feargus Edward O'Connor," 467.
40. Hardie, "Temperance Question," 125
41. Waters, *British Socialists*, 34.
42. Blatchford addressed this issue in *Merrie England*, first serialized in the *Clarion* in 1893.
43. Harrison, *Drink and the Victorians*, 281, 282.
44. Wagstaff, "Temperance Work."

Religion, Class, and Gender Issues

While the improvement of the working-class experience through religion was central to the temperance movement, the concerns of Christian groups were not limited to alcohol. Periodicals covering the range of worship within the established Church of England—from the ultra–High Church *British Critic and Quarterly Theological Review* (1792–1853), through the moderate *Church of England Quarterly Review* (1837–58) to the Evangelical *Record* (1828–1949)—raised concerns that the poor were either unwilling or unable to attend services regularly.[45] In the early part of the century, there were calls for churches to be "built in areas where the poor lived and where the poor could get themselves to a church, sufficient seating had to be provided, and the clergy must welcome them."[46] The periodicals promoting Church of England issues would often remind middle- or upper-class readers of their responsibilities and warn of the dangers of disillusioned working-class worshippers converting to one of the dissenting sects. Although historians such as Elie Halévy, E.P. Thompson, and Eric Hobsbawm have argued that Wesleyanism and Methodism, in the first half of the nineteenth century, were characterized by their political and social conservatism, later historians have argued that Nonconformism had a greater destabilizing effect than previously thought: "There is now widespread agreement that the remarkable growth of Evangelical Nonconformity in the period 1790–1830 substantially undermined the Established Church, religious deference, and traditional systems of dependency, which had been at the heart of the old order in church and state."[47]

Dissenting groups used periodicals to differentiate between schisms and to create a sense of group identity over a wide geographical area.[48] Methodist groups aimed to imitate the success of Wesley's *Arminian Magazine* (1778–1969), which achieved a high circulation and worked "to unite [Wesley's] scattered followers, provide them with models of behavior, stimulate them to greater effort, and defend them against embittered Calvinists."[49] Similarly, publications such as the *Protestant Journal* (1831–37) and the *British Protestant* (1845–64) sought to challenge the threat to Protestant domination presented by Catholic emancipation.[50] Later periodicals shifted focus, combining religious instruction with entertainment: "Magazines such as *Good Words*, the *Quiver*, the *Hive*, *Our Own Fireside*, and many others were often edited by popular ministers and clergymen, and contained well-written articles by public figures and writers."[51] The later *Nonconformist* (1841–1900) also included political protest against the Church of England,[52] but the radical press had already addressed the overlap of religion and politics.

---

45. Rochelson, "*Church of England Quarterly Review*," 118.
46. Connors and MacDonald, *National Identity*, 88.
47. Paz, *Religious Traditions*, 131.
48. Billington, "Religious Periodical," 116.
49. Ibid., 115.
50. Connors and MacDonald, *National Identity*, 70.
51. Billington, "Religious Periodical," 128.
52. Burke, "*Nonconformist*," 456–7.

The Chartist movement distinguished between the teachings of Christianity—which they claimed were advanced through Chartism—and the practice of many who declared themselves Christians. For instance, Douglas Jerrold, in the *English Chartist Circular*, mused on the hypocrisy of the rich, who "come to church to keep up the farce that their worldly brethren, with themselves, agree to act; they congregate to perform a ceremony, and that over, the week lies fair before them. . . . As the weekly hypocrites come and go, the devil stands in the porch and counts them."[53] Feargus O'Connor was similarly critical of "Church Chartists" and the division fostered by religious groupings, writing, "Christian Chartism, though apparently all-embracing in its meaning, carries with it exclusion of all other sects from whom we expect political aid."[54] O'Connor's opinion was rejected by the *Northern Star*, but the potential for factional division and patronage of the working classes is evident in Charles Kingsley and F.D. Maurice's *Christian Socialist: A Journal of Association* (1850–52). Despite the proclamation that the journal was "conducted by Several of the Promoters of the London Working Men's Associations," the LWMA was only responsible for the *Gazette*, a report on the meeting of the central board and various associations across the country. The rest of each issue was written by commentators promoting the acceptance of one's social position while working to improve conditions. A letter from "A Working Man" illustrates Chartist (and later socialist) concern about religious division and passivity. He writes, "If we, the toiling masses, are to be saved from practical atheism and its consequences, it must be done by ministers of religion. . . . It is quite true that we, the workmen, have many—ay, a great many faults. We have also a great deal yet to learn."[55] The letter's author denies any potential class equality by deferring to others for guidance and accepting the "faults" of the working classes.

Socialists had similar concerns about the distraction of religion. John Trevor, who "disliked the condescending attitudes that seemed to him to be held by church leaders," founded the Labour Church, "where workers could chart their own destiny, occasionally assisted by middle-class sympathisers," and published the *Labour Prophet* (1892–1901).[56] The Labour Church, like some of the earlier Chartists, sought to align Christianity with socialism. Trevor declared that the "Labour Movement is a Religious Movement,"[57] and Unitarian minister and economist Philip Wicksteed[58] argued that the "Labour movement and the Labour church . . . gives warning to all 'classes,' that they have no right to exist except so far as they serve the masses and make their life fuller and greater."[59] The Labour Church was usually associated with the Independent Labour Party since many members came to socialism through a Liberal, Nonconformist route; Social Democratic Federation members were more likely to have found socialism through Marx or materialist arguments and thus mostly rejected the association of Christianity with socialism. Nonetheless, as Karen Hunt has noted, while "some SDFers

---

53. Jerrold, "Church Pews," 17.
54. "Church Chartism," 4.
55. Working Man, "Some Last Words," 109.
56. Waters, *British Socialists*, 87.
57. Trevor, "Labour Church," 16.
58. Steedman calls Wicksteed an "enthusiastic adherent to the Labour church movement." "Philip Wicksteed," n.p.
59. Wicksteed, "Is the Labour Church a Class Church?," 1.

were atheists . . . religion was recognised as a matter of conscience for the individual party member. Similarly within the ILP there was a diversity of opinions."[60] Such diversity was evident in Robert Blatchford's *Clarion*, the periodical often preferred by ILP members to Keir Hardie's official ILP periodical, the *Labour Leader*. In a review published in the *Clarion*, Blatchford declared that Haeckel's *The Riddle of the Universe* "demolishes the entire structure upon which the religions of the world are built" and that the "case for science is complete."[61] This prompted angry responses from readers, but he welcomed the opportunity to hold an open debate on religion and thus published their opinions and responded to their letters in the pages of the *Clarion*.

Mainstream concerns about religion extended beyond class to include gender. Margaret Beetham and Kay Boardman, discussing the range of periodicals addressing women's religious involvement, note that "many, such as *The Mother's Friend* and *The British Mother's Magazine*, were aimed at working-class women but a significant number, such as *The Christian Lady's Magazine*, were aimed at middle-class women. Almost all had denominational backing and so were pre-eminently non-commercial ventures, but they were significant because they were so pervasive."[62] While an emphasis on Christian morality in defining female behaviors and attitudes was characteristic of all women's periodicals, their content showed differentiation between classes. The *British Workwoman* (1863–96) and the *Servant's Magazine* (1838–69) focused on domestic and religious life while the middle-class periodicals "assumed a relationship of equality between editor and reader" that was absent in working-class periodicals.[63] Attitudes toward the non-religious aspects of life were also differentiated according to class. The working-class *Mothers' Magazine* (1834–62) advocated the general silencing of women—"the first rule we should prescribe to ourselves will teach us not to talk too much"[64]—while upper- and middle-class periodicals such as the *Christian Lady's Magazine* (1834–49) included current affairs, albeit humorously characterized as "Politics made easy or every woman her own representative."[65]

After the newspaper taxes were lifted and the costs of production decreased, the working-class woman presented a greater potential market. Gender, rather than class, defined the reader in women's periodicals. For example, "H.R.H. The Princess of Wales, and the Young Prince George," published in the March 1870 issue of the *British Workwoman* aligned women through motherhood rather than social position. When female labor was addressed in the *British Workwoman*, it was still overshadowed by the emphasis on motherhood as, for instance, in the article and illustration entitled "The Harvest Field: Maternal Love" published in September 1872 (Figure 24.2). The article places labor in the masculine realm: "George Hartley, his wife and son—*he*, the strong man, who, from his appearance, as we look at him, has learned

---

60. Hunt, *Equivocal Feminists*, 14.
61. Blatchford, "In the Library," 3.
62. Beetham and Boardman, *Victorian Women's Magazines*, 45.
63. Ibid.
64. "Hints to Young Ladies." (1838), quoted in Beetham and Boardman, *Victorian Women's Magazines*, 103.
65. Quoted in Beetham, *A Magazine of Her Own?*, 36.

Figure 24.2 "The Harvest Field: Maternal Love," *British Workwoman*, no. 107 (September 1872): 88. Courtesy of the Working Class Movement Library, Salford.

that, 'by the sweat of his brow, he should live.'"[66] Female labor is only indicated by the mother's question to the elder child as she returns to her baby after working in the field alongside her husband and son: "Has he been pretty good? You are sure he has not cried at all?"[67]

Towards the end of the nineteenth century, as the debate surrounding women's roles grew, a greater diversity of attitudes and representations of women were both promoted through and reflected in periodicals. Kristine Moruzi notes the appearance of the New Woman alongside the "Ruskinian model" of femininity during the 1860s: "The traditional model of femininity is presented beside a modern incarnation, revealing the extent to which the *Young Woman* (1892–1915) engages with different perspectives of girlhood."[68] The middle-class periodical may have recognized changing attitudes, but the new image of womanhood or girlhood was presented alongside the older, more conservative models of femininity. *Atalanta* (1887–98) published conflicting images of educated women, while the *Girl's Own Paper* (1880–1956) promoted female exercise that would not threaten decorum. Sometimes change was driven by the reader, as in Charlotte M. Yonge's *Monthly Packet* (1851–98) where readers began "to articulate a modernity at odds with Yonge's ideal of control and containment within the church and the family."[69]

Women were not only consumers of and targets for periodicals but also contributors and producers. Paul Thomas Murphy notes that three early nineteenth-century female journalists were associated with Richard Carlile: his wife, his sister, and his mistress.[70] The latter, Eliza Sharples, was editor of *Isis* (1832), which was an exceptional position for a woman.[71] Sharples combined her political radicalism with feminism as she, like others, recognized the connection between the two: "Some men may ask, why do women make it their business? Our reasons are two: first, because Englishmen have neglected theirs; and, secondly, because our interests are inseparably connected with the welfare of men and, being so, we are bound to co-operate with them for the general good."[72] Male editors did not often allow women direct communication with their readers but some forms of reporting inadvertently gave women a voice, albeit enclosed within the male editor's quotation marks. For instance, Wooler's *Black Dwarf* published a sympathetic report of an address by the Female Reformers of Blackburn in its July 5, 1819 issue. Although the address is given to the Chairman to read to the audience, the words of the reformers travel through written and oral delivery to speak directly to the reader: "We, the Female Reformers of Blackburn, therefore, earnestly entreat you and every man in England, in the most solemn manner, to come forward and join the general union, that by a determined and constitutional resistance to our oppressors, the people may obtain annual parliaments, universal suffrage and election by ballot, which alone can save us from lingering misery and premature death."[73] Women's deferral to men (or male expectation of this

---

66. "Harvest Field," 88.
67. Ibid.
68. Moruzi, *Constructing Girlhood*, 148.
69. Ibid., 114, 106, 40.
70. Murphy, *Toward a Working-Class Canon*, 29.
71. Beetham, *A Magazine of Her Own?*, 35.
72. Potter, "Declaration," 51.
73. Ibid., 456.

deference) was also reflected in the Chartist movement and its periodicals, as the "majority of male Chartists saw women as fulfilling a subaltern role in the movement."[74] John Watkins might have argued in the *Chartist Circular* that single women and widows "have an equal stake in the land they live in" since they "pay rates, cesses, and taxes," but female politicization was only acceptable when external political forces threatened the home.[75] Similarly, when Thomas M. Wheeler called for female assistance in the Chartist cause, it was not activism he wanted but rather for them to "animate us in the glorious struggle; cheer us by your approbation, enliven us by your presence."[76]

Parts of the socialist press were similarly dismissive of feminism: June Hannam and Karen Hunt warn against accepting the view that the Independent Labour Party was more open to the Woman Question than the Social Democratic Federation.[77] Hyndman, chairman of the SDF, considered the suffrage campaign a "means to an end and not an end in itself"; *Justice* editor Harry Quelch and contributor Ernest Belfort Bax considered the issue a distraction.[78] Yet both the SDF's *Justice* and the ILP's *Labour Leader* published significant numbers of articles by female socialists. Dora Montefiore and Eleanor Marx wrote for *Justice*; Katherine Bruce Glasier and Isabella Bream Pearce published in the *Labour Leader*; and "Julia Dawson" (the pseudonym of Mrs D.J. Middleton-Worrell) and Caroline Martyn contributed to Blatchford's *Clarion*. All three periodicals dedicated a separate column to women's issues, which had the effect of focusing the debate on the Woman Question while simultaneously separating the topic from the rest of the journal. Female socialists had to wait until the publication of the *Woman Worker* (1907–10) for a periodical of their own. The *Woman Worker* perpetuated the close connections with its readership that made its parent paper, the *Clarion*, so successful—a strategy that had previously been associated with middle-class women's periodicals.

Social Purpose Periodicals in the Internet Age

The advent of the internet has, in theory, provided access to Victorian periodicals previously only available to researchers with the time, money, and opportunity to travel to specific libraries, archives, and repositories. Large databases hold digital images of tens of millions of pages of newsprint which are now accessible with just a click. Several political periodicals discussed in this chapter, for example, are available through Gale Cengage's *British Library Newspapers* and *19th Century UK Periodicals*. While James Mussell argues that the reader/user of the digital text needs to be proficient in reading the media of digital resources, he recognizes the potential liberation provided by the digital form from the constraints of the printed edition.[79] By removing the costs of hard-copy printing, digital access also removes the cost-based necessity of selecting parts of the periodical for thematic, chronological, or author-based collections.

---

74. Chase, *Chartism*, 43.
75. Watkins, "Address," 49.
76. Wheeler, "Address," 133.
77. Hannam and Hunt, *Socialist Women*, 5.
78. Hunt, *Equivocal Feminists*, 165, 41.
79. Mussell, *Nineteenth-Century Press*, 18–19, 115.

Nevertheless, the digital age has not heralded a periodical-reading utopia. The first—and most important—hurdle for individual researchers to overcome is the cost of online access. Neither Gale Cengage nor ProQuest currently provides subscriptions for individuals, instead charging subscription fees to institutions. Individual readers are advised by Gale Cengage to "contact your library and enquire about online access to our products," which presupposes access to a library with a subscription.[80] The British Library's *British Newspaper Archive* does offer individual subscriptions at £12.95 per month or £79.95 annually (February 2016), but this assumes that the reader has these sums available for use of the site. Without funds for institutional or individual subscriptions, researchers are in the same position they were in before digitization.

Even with institutional access to subscription databases, researchers are only able to access those periodicals chosen for digitization. For instance, apart from the digital copies of the *British Women's Temperance Journal/Wings* (1883–1900) included in *19th Century UK Periodicals*, there is a dearth of temperance periodicals available digitally (as the chapter on temperance periodicals confirms), and while a range of Chartist periodicals has been digitized, the only socialist periodical available in digital form is *To-Day: A Monthly Magazine of Scientific Socialism* (1883–89), which is part of ProQuest's *British Periodicals* database. And even within this periodical there is restricted access to George Bernard Shaw's *Cashel Byron's Profession* (1885–86) due to copyright restrictions.[81] The open-access *Nineteenth-Century Serials Edition* provides unrestricted access but only to a limited selection of titles (which fortunately includes the *Northern Star*). The *Marxists Internet Archive* provides some transcribed *Justice* articles (one per issue) listed by author 1884–1924. This includes pieces by William Morris, Belfort Bax, and editor Harry Quelch. The same site lists and transcribes selected articles from the *Clarion*, and the *William Morris Internet Archive* provides links to transcriptions of Morris articles and poetry available on the *Marxists Internet Archive*. Thus, despite advances in twenty-first-century technology, the ability of modern readers to access many nineteenth-century social purpose periodicals is beset with the same problems encountered by their original readers: prohibitive costs and limited access to anything beyond mainstream periodicals.

---

80. "The Times Digital Archive," http://gale.cengage.co.uk/times.aspx/.
81. Fortunately, Shaw's *An Unsocial Socialist* (1884) is fully accessible in the *British Periodicals* database.

25

TEMPERANCE PERIODICALS

Annemarie McAllister

In terms of circulation, innovation, and contemporary importance, temperance periodicals certainly claim attention, as indeed does the social, cultural, and political influence of the movement they represented. Alcohol use and abuse remain very topical today: enormous amounts of money are being spent on what the UK government and media consider a serious social problem.[1] Temperance periodicals have nonetheless been neglected by scholars because few titles are available in digital form and their content is often considered propagandist or unfashionably pious. However, as access to digitized temperance periodicals increases and scholars make use of these titles in studies of popular nineteenth-century social and cultural movements, scholarly interest in temperance history will undoubtedly increase.

The Temperance Movement

Concerns about the abuse of alcohol in the early nineteenth century led to the formation of temperance societies in the United Kingdom, with members largely drawn from the middle classes. Influenced by developments in the United States, these societies advocated for abstinence from gin and other distilled liquors, along with moderation in the consumption of all alcoholic beverages. By 1830, there were approximately 127 temperance societies in England with a total membership of about 23,000, mostly located in the manufacturing districts of the north. Government action galvanized the nascent temperance movement with the passing of the Beer Act in 1830, which encouraged the opening of thousands of outlets selling beer. In Liverpool, for example, "there opened more than fifty additional beer shops a day for several weeks."[2] Government initiatives had initially encouraged the production of gin in the late seventeenth century in order to make use of surplus grain and to avoid import duties on foreign spirits. After a century of public concern about the influence of cheap gin, the aim of the 1830 Beer Act was to encourage beer drinking as a healthy alternative. Once again the measure proved misguided. Especially in the overcrowded industrial conurbations, beer was now consumed at unprecedented levels, and drunkenness was rife. Historian James Nicholls sums

---

1. For the latest news, see the website *Alcohol Policy UK*, http://www.alcoholpolicy.net/.
2. Webb and Webb, *History of Liquor Licensing*, 124.

up the effect of this social change on public perceptions: "By leading to a dramatic increase in beer sales, the Beer Act increased public anxiety over not just spirit drinking, but alcohol consumption per se."[3] Such anxiety was no longer just a middle-class concern about working-class behavior: workers in the industrial northwest promoted the revolutionary concept of total abstinence—the notion that any consumption of alcohol was a potential danger.

Preston was an industrial town with a history of radicalism. After the 1830 act, it suffered from increased and widespread drink-related public disorder, despite flourishing temperance societies for adults and young people. A more radical strategy for deterring excessive alcohol use was clearly needed. In August 1832, seven men from Preston, including local activist Joseph Livesey, signed a pledge to abstain from all alcoholic beverages, and on September 1 they held a meeting to formalize their vow. Contemporary medical practice advocated alcohol as a remedy for many conditions, so early pledges specifically referred to alcohol taken as a beverage, leaving open the possibility of taking it upon medical advice. This movement to change individuals, and therefore society, was largely led by Livesey. Teetotalism, as total abstinence was also known from 1833, began as a movement of working people taking action to change their own lives, and it certainly sprang from criticism of the existing social and political order. Livesey had little time for upper-class patrons, whom he saw as well-meaning but lazy dabblers. Many other radicals deplored the part alcohol played in the enslavement of working people. For example, social reformer Richard Cobden wrote to Livesey, "The Temperance cause really lies at the root of all social and political progression in this country."[4] The Chartist and temperance movements were linked in important ways: the *Northern Star* "routinely reported temperance activities," and the *English Chartist Circular and Temperance Record* was founded in 1841.[5] For large numbers of working people, the movement offered not just personal salvation but social transformation. It was fundamentally empowering in that they could bring about change for themselves and society. Teetotalism liberated workers by enabling them to keep their wages rather than handing them over to publicans and brewers, and, of course, women and children also benefited. The fiery total abstinence pioneers welcomed the unrespectable poor who, after conversion to teetotalism, sometimes achieved respectability. For many families, the future could now be faced with optimism. As the movement grew, middle-class members began to gain prominence, and some organizations, like the Church of England Temperance Society, founded in 1862, allowed individuals to join on a separate, non-teetotal basis, recalling the older "moderationist" approach. By the mid-nineteenth century, businessmen like Thomas Cook (the founder of the international travel company), John Cadbury (of chocolate bar fame), and John Cassell (to be discussed below) all showed that profit and temperance were by no means antithetical. The movement might have become more respectable and, like many reforming creeds, more rigid and bureaucratic, but it maintained a strong base of support among working-class people. At mid-century,

---

3. Nicholls, *Politics of Alcohol*, 139.
4. Richard Cobden to Joseph Livesey, October 10, 1849, quoted in Morley's *Life of Cobden* and Livesey's *Life and Teachings*, cxvi.
5. Chase, *Chartism*, 122, 147.

the definition of "temperance" had changed: groups which advocated moderation were few, and total abstinence had become the policy of most temperance societies. By the end of the nineteenth century, it was estimated that a tenth of adults were teetotallers. Temperance remained an important social and cultural force until and during World War I, when it was depicted as a patriotic action. King George V, for example, answered Lloyd George's appeal to take the pledge by making a public statement that no alcohol would be served in the royal household for the duration of the war.

Significant temperance organizations included the Independent Order of Rechabites, founded in Salford in 1835, which claimed three million members by the end of the nineteenth century. Two others were founded in the United States: the Sons of Temperance, which was set up in the UK in 1846, and the Independent Order of Good Templars, which was established in 1868. The United Kingdom Alliance for the Suppression of the Traffic in all Intoxicating Liquors (known as the Alliance) was founded in 1853 in Manchester to campaign, ultimately, for prohibition, but also lobbied for legal restrictions on alcohol throughout its existence. Following the radicalism of the Anti-Corn Law League, it attempted to create pressure through shaping public opinion and agitating for change, which would then influence legislators. After its first three years, the Alliance had 30,000 members, and in the 1870s it had considerable influence on the Liberal party; it formed a significant constituency at elections although this undermined its radical claims. The organization was renamed the United Kingdom Temperance Alliance in 1942 and in 2003 became the Alliance House Foundation.

Women were involved in all of these temperance groups, either as regular members or as participants in women's sections, but the first exclusively female organization, the British Women's Temperance Association, was not formed until 1875. The group was fractured by debates about whether to concentrate solely upon alcohol-related issues, such as prohibition, or to support women's suffrage and wider intervention in social policy. In 1893, two new groups formed: the Women's Total Abstinence Union, focusing only upon temperance, and the National British Women's Temperance Association, campaigning on a wider platform. In 1926, they were united by the National British Women's Total Abstinence Union, which in 1993 became the White Ribbon Society. There were hundreds of smaller, specialized temperance groups with local affiliations as well as a variety of national groups, such as the armed services, transport workers, and, of course, the medical profession. The children's movement, the Band of Hope, was founded in 1847; although it was not the first such grouping for young people, it became an outstandingly successful temperance organization. Space forbids anything like a full history or exploration of its significance, but a couple of indicative details are suggestive. The Band of Hope has operated for well over 150 years, changing its name in 1995 to Hope UK. It numbered three and a half million by its zenith in the early twentieth century (when the school-age population numbered only six million), and its periodicals achieved much higher circulations than those for adults, which were in themselves considerable.[6]

---

6. For more information on the Band of Hope, see Shiman, *Crusade*, and McAllister, *Demon Drink?*

Scholarship on Temperance Periodicals

This brief survey should indicate the vast scale of the temperance movement. It flourished at a period (ca. 1840–1920) when developments in production, distribution, literacy, and public interest in self-education made periodicals a key part of organizational strategy. Brian Harrison suggests that the temperance movement, like similar popular pressure groups, had three main functions: to inspire, to inform, and to integrate.[7] Periodicals were vital for all three tasks. Yet, unfortunately, scholars have paid relatively little attention to the influence of individual temperance periodicals or the interrelationships between them. Harrison has published three key sources on temperance journalism, and Olwen C. Niessen's recent work on the topic provides an excellent general survey based on groundbreaking work that deserves to be better known.[8] Although recent studies by McAllister and Olsen explore the significance and use of temperance periodicals, relatively little work on these publications has emerged since Niessen's survey of twenty years ago.[9] Josef Altholz, in *The Religious Press*, briefly surveys temperance periodicals as part of a chapter on "movements," and Kirsten Drotner briefly considers those for children in *English Children and their Magazines*. There have been references to individual periodicals in *Social History of Alcohol and Drugs*, the journal of the Alcohol and Drugs History Society, and its annual bibliographies of work in this area, as well as its blog, *Points*.

Temperance Periodicals: Mapping the Field

Temperance periodicals have several characteristics which make them a particularly useful resource for researchers in Victorian literature, music, education, politics, art history, and popular culture, as well as media, social, and cultural history. A particular feature in many cases is their longevity. The United Kingdom Alliance began publication of the *Alliance Weekly News* in 1855 as a penny weekly. It had a circulation of 20,000 by 1859 and in 1862 was renamed the *Alliance News*. It lasted until 1991 as a monthly. This campaigning periodical was widely read by the temperance movement and endured, although in monthly form in later years, until 1991. Joseph Livesey began publication of the *National Temperance Advocate and Herald* in 1843, which, in turn, became the *British Temperance Advocate*, the official journal of the British Temperance League from 1850 to 1949. Two children's monthlies, the *Band of Hope Chronicle* (1878–1980s, interrupted) and the *Band of Hope Review* (1851–1937), similarly maintained substantial runs.

Allied to longevity are high circulation figures. In 1860–61, for example, the three main weekly temperance newspapers had a combined circulation of 25,000, and the two main quarterly temperance reviews had a joint circulation of 10,000 a month, while the *Band of Hope Review* achieved a circulation of over 250,000.[10] Like the titles published by religious, missionary, and other charitable groups, temperance periodicals had particular patterns in funding, publication, and distribution. Readers obtained a personal, as opposed to a shared, copy of a

---

7. Harrison, "Press and Pressure Group," 282.
8. Niessen, "Temperance."
9. McAllister, *Demon Drink?* and "Picturing the Demon Drink"; Olsen, *Juvenile Nation*.
10. Harrison, *Drink and the Victorians*, 308.

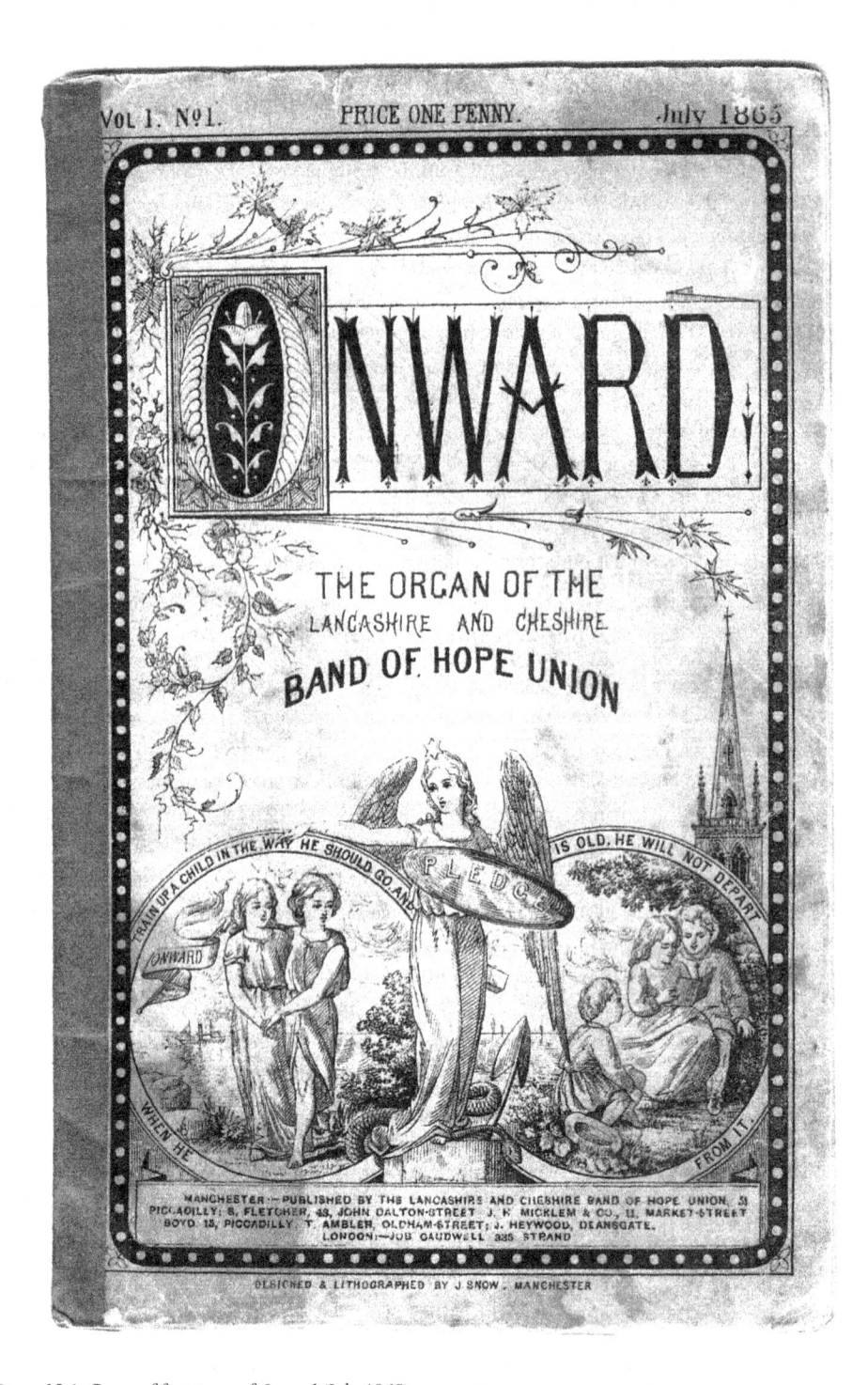

Figure 25.1 Cover of first issue of *Onward* (July 1865).

title by one of three main methods: subscription, free distribution, or purchase of individual copies on the open market. Our assumptions about free distribution need to be examined carefully, since this method of circulation was often a temporary expedient rather than a permanent or viable means of support in the marketplace. It is also important to note that free distribution did not indicate that a title was unpopular. In 1843, at an early stage in the national spread of the temperance movement, Livesey's monthly *National Temperance Advocate and Herald* claimed that it distributed 4,000 free copies out of its total circulation of 9,500. Once a periodical became more successful, free distribution of commercially available titles was unusual. Publishing records, such as those documenting the history of *Onward* (1865–1910; see Figure 25.1), reveal that free distribution was a tactic used at the beginning of publication. For example, in 1867, the Band of Hope sent fifty copies with a speaker to distribute "in the South of England."[11] However, the substantial financial losses which free distribution would involve could not be sustained for long periods: in October 1857 the *British Workman* (1855–1921) was freely distributed in large numbers by the London City Mission in the poorest districts of the city; by 1862, the paper was circulating in excess of 250,000 copies monthly, but the main means of distribution was now through subscription.[12] Brian Harrison's detailed study of the finances of the United Kingdom Alliance's weekly periodicals between 1853 and 1875 shows a pattern of rising costs associated with free distribution and consequent annual financial losses.[13]

Large-circulation publications such as the *British Workman* and its stablemate the *Band of Hope Review* were available on newsstands; their large format and handsome lithographed covers were designed to attract the attention of consumers. Nonetheless, subscription was the usual method of purchase. In many cases, membership of a particular group, such as the Church of England Temperance Society, the Good Templars, or the United Kingdom Railway Union included subscription—in the latter case, a periodical with the sprightly title *On the Line* (1882–1963). The millions of children attending Band of Hope meetings paid a halfpenny for each weekly meeting, if they could afford it, and this covered membership with associated medals, awards, and excursions, along with a monthly penny Band of Hope magazine (usually either the *Band of Hope Review* or *Onward*). Such promotion was undoubtedly a key factor in the high circulation of temperance titles. Some titles included local material in inserts or on covers, providing groups with publications that were unique to them. Most copies of nineteenth-century publications were circulated widely and could expect more than one reader, but some temperance titles intended for voluntary workers contained material that was designed from the start to be reproduced many times. Recitations, songs, lectures, and suggested lessons were printed as resources for working with adults and children.

The scale of the temperance movement and its publications was so vast that it is impossible to list more than major titles or examples of trends in the limited space available. Temperance

---

11. Minutes of Executive, Lancashire, and Cheshire Band of Hope and Temperance Union, May 1867 (unpaginated manuscript in Manchester Central Library, Special Collections).
12. Murray, "*British Workman*." Large temperance societies, however, could afford to publish at a loss since they could count on subscriptions and legacies from well-off members.
13. Harrison, "World," 154.

periodicals can be categorized in many ways: for example, by frequency of publication, by publishing organization, or by focus and policy. However, here they will be considered in two main divisions: those for adults and those for children.

Adults

The periodicals intended for adult consumption share something of a common address, whether directed to men, women, workers, social activists, religious groups, or particular occupational fields. Joseph Livesey, a gifted publicist, realized the importance of periodical publication in inspiring social reform. He published the *Moral Reformer* (1831–33) and continued this work with dedicated temperance publications such as the *Preston Temperance Advocate* (1834–37), the *Progressionist* (1852–53), and the *Staunch Teetotaller* (1867–68). It is evident that he also felt the importance of creating a sense of identity and support in his publications if groups were to survive.

Temperance journal titles changed and developed over the course of the century, as did the temperance organizations which published them. Over time, new temperance groups such as the women's and church-linked societies emerged, and new publications were founded. The *British Women's Temperance Journal* (1883–92) was the journal of the British Women's Temperance Association, reborn as *Wings* in 1892. But when the majority of the committee abandoned single-issue campaigning in 1893, the *Wings* title remained with the suffragist and reforming Women's Total Abstinence Union, while the new National British Women's Temperance Association, focusing solely on temperance, set up the *White Ribbon* (1896–). Although confusing, the periodical history in this case draws attention to one of the most important debates in temperance campaigning for women and illuminates a key point of social history. To read the pages of *Wings* between 1892 and 1893 is to see a violent debate on beliefs and policy dramatically played out. The *Church of England Temperance Magazine* (1862–73) and its successors, the *Church of England Temperance Chronicle* and then the *Temperance Chronicle*, became one of the most widely read temperance periodicals in the later nineteenth century, and its changed incarnations reflect changes in policy and even class-based attitudes to teetotalism. There were also many smaller and shorter-lived periodicals whose pages, filled with advertisements, slogans, and news items, can also provide insight into the way the temperance message was spread.

Just as most villages by 1900 could boast a temperance hall and most towns also had one or more temperance hotels and coffee shops, most districts published temperance periodicals. The longest-running regional title was the *Bristol Temperance Herald* (1836–59), which became the *Western Temperance Herald* (1859–1957), but the Norwich-based *Temperance Monthly Visitor* (1858–1920) and the Derby-based *Temperance Bells* (1890–1945) also claimed impressive longevity. The regional focus of both titles ensured that they could draw on local interest but also a broader readership. Indeed, the *Western Temperance Herald* boasted that it had a national and international circulation. Many smaller, more local temperance periodicals lasted for a year or less; however, as with national periodicals, those aimed at young people were often more successful at maintaining readership. The *Hull Band of Hope Advocate* was based solely in Hull, yet it ran from 1875 to 1910 (having changed its name to the *Hull Band of Hope Journal*). The three main national organizations, all non-denominational, produced the most widely circulated

THE
TEMPERANCE MIRROR.

REMINISCENCES OF A CRAB SUPPER.
By MAGGIE FEARN, *Author of "The Pledged Eleven," etc.*

TIME—nine o'clock on an evening in the warm summer of 188—; place—a pleasant room in a comfortable house in a small fishing village situated upon the western coast of England. A party of six were seated round a supper-table, which looked inviting enough from any point of view. All this the bare outline of fact which any chance observer

Figure 25.2 Cover of the *Temperance Mirror* 7, no. 81 (September 1887): 193.

temperance publications. In addition to the long-running *Alliance News* and *British Temperance Advocate* mentioned above, the London-based National Temperance League (incorporated into the British National Temperance League in 1952) published a variety of titles such as the *National Temperance Chronicle* (1848–56), followed by the *Weekly Record of the Temperance Movement* (1856–69), the *Temperance Record* (1870–1907) and the *Temperance Mirror* (1881–1907; see

Figure 25.2). As indicated above, the tendency for periodicals to be continued under changed names presents a challenge for researchers. Where a periodical remains largely unchanged in mission, approach, and publishing team, it can be considered the same title, but such a determination requires much careful research and raises interesting methodological problems about the periodical identity.[14]

The Rechabites published a range of local periodicals, starting with the *Isle of Man Guardian and Rechabite Journal* (1836–38), but the *Rechabite and Temperance Magazine* (1870–1900) became the national publication. Similar societies, such as the Sons of Temperance and Good Templars, also used periodicals to communicate, inspire, and create fellowship, with the latter, for example, publishing the *Templar* (1871–77), *Templar and Templar Journal* (1877–78), *Templar Journal and Treasury* (1879–80), and the *Good Templar's Watchword* (1874–1965). Temperance organizations in the army and navy, as well as occupational groups such as transport or health workers, and those working in temperance hotels, taverns, and coffee houses, all produced their own periodicals. The *Coffee Tavern Gazette and Journal of Food Thrift* (1886–87) became the *Temperance Caterer*, which, from 1887 to 1923, provided advice, support, and a specialized advertising platform. The market for temperance publications was also supplied by religious denominations, including Methodists, Baptists, and Congregationalists, with the *Methodist Temperance Magazine* (1868–1906) being a lively and long-lived example. The Church of England Temperance Society had originally, in its earlier, teetotal incarnation, produced the *Church of England Temperance Magazine* (1862–72); however, with the adoption of "dual form membership" (teetotal or moderationist), the official organ became the *Church of England Temperance Chronicle* (1873–88) and later the *Temperance Chronicle*, 1888–1914. As Brian Harrison points out, this was one of the most influential temperance publications which ranked alongside the *British Temperance Advocate* and the *Alliance News*.[15] As alcohol was often used in medical treatment, it was considered particularly important to influence medical professionals. Hence, at an early stage journals appeared that argued for the pernicious effects of alcohol on the body, such as the *Temperance Lancet* (1841–42). The National Temperance League published the quarterly *Medical Temperance Journal* (1869–92), the *Medical Pioneer* (1892–97), and the *Medical Temperance Review* (1898–1907). With the establishment of the British Medical Temperance Association in 1876, such journals proliferated, with some featuring academic papers, such as the quarterly *British Journal of Inebriety* (1903–46). Similarly, *Meliora* (1858–69), a quarterly journal of social science published by the Alliance, aimed to provide a platform for academic and policy debates on various social amelioration projects, including temperance.

Apart from temperance organizations, individuals and companies were a significant source of temperance publications. Thomas Bywater Smithies (1817–88) edited the *British Workman* (1855–1921) and *Band of Hope Review* (1851–1937) until his death, shaping their values

---

14. Many US temperance organizations had similar names to those in the UK, including the National Temperance Society and Publishing House (1865–1915). This, in addition to the preponderance of US temperance information on the internet, can make the study of the British temperance movement a minefield for the unwary researcher.
15. Harrison, "World," 140–1.

through design and format as much as through content. The bookseller, printer, and publisher William Tweedie (1821–74) was one of the honorary secretaries of the National Temperance League who distributed almost all of its publications, in addition to many more temperance periodicals, through his premises on the Strand. It was Tweedie who supplied the 1861 circulation figures given above based on his stable of temperance newspapers and magazines for adults and children. The company of printer and publisher Samuel Partridge (1810–1903), S.W. Partridge & Co., in turn, shaped the approach, content, design, and even size of temperance periodicals. Many publishers who would later find fame through other endeavors began with temperance publications. For example, the first editorial project G.W.M. Reynolds (1814–79) undertook was the *Teetotaler* (1840–41); and John Cassell (1817–65) began his publishing career with the *Teetotal Times* (1846–49) and the *Teetotal Essayist* (1847–49), which was retitled the *Teetotal Times and Essayist* (1849–51). Cassell, who at this time was a tea and coffee merchant as well as an agent for the National Temperance Society, used space in the publications to advertise his own grocery products as well as to promote his total abstinence convictions.

Children

Younger members of the temperance community were informed, entertained, and sustained through reading material, which united them in a shared identity and reinforced their membership in the group. As mentioned above, most members of Band of Hope, Cadets of Temperance, Juvenile Rechabite, or Junior Church of England Temperance Society groups (who numbered well over three million by 1900) received magazines by subscription as part of their membership, making these publications arguably the most widely read of the period. *Onward*, which circulated nationally and was printed in London and Manchester, claimed that its monthly circulation, when combined with its companion publication the *Onward Reciter*, had reached half a million by 1895.[16] The format of very early children's temperance publications, such as the *Youthful Teetotaler* (1836), seems like heavy reading to a modern eye. Its dense letterpress would have been unsuitable for the children streaming into the Band of Hope movement, many of whom were illiterate or had very poor reading skills. A revolution in such magazines occurred when in 1851 Thomas Smithies, publisher of the *British Workman*, founded the *Band of Hope Review and Sunday Scholar's Friend* (*Band of Hope Review* from 1861), which provided magnificent woodcut illustrations, including full-page cuts and a more lively page design (influenced by the newer illustrated miscellanies of the 1840s, such as *Reynolds's* and the *London Journal*) than existing offerings for children in the movement. It offered young readers recitations, short articles, improving stories, and Bible mottos, and its association with the already successful Band of Hope was a good marketing strategy.

The desire to present young readers with a less overtly religious message offered an opportunity for another entrepreneurial publishing house. In 1865, the Lancashire and Cheshire Band of Hope Union set up *Onward*, a northern rival with a policy of even more lively content

---

16. *United Kingdom Band of Hope Annual Report*, 48.

featuring songs, jokes, serial stories, and even dialect poems. From the third monthly issue, the title of the editorial was changed to "Editor's Chat," and soon children were addressed directly with a letter from Uncle Ephraim. The editor not only answered their letters in his column but also printed their submissions. The *Onward* world was informal, lively, and practical; it is significant that such a temperance publication was the site of innovation where children's engagement with periodicals was concerned.

Margaret Beetham defines the periodical as a mixed genre in which elements are presented and reproduced within a particular template but whose every issue is different, a genre moreover that encourages a certain selectivity in reading.[17] The potential for performativity through songs and recitations was another important dimension of *Onward* and the other temperance magazines that followed its lead. The *Band of Hope Review* responded to *Onward*'s innovations, and by the end of the nineteenth century, there were few differences between the two magazines, with both presenting lively content and engaging with readers by printing their written work or photographs. With lower circulations, the *Juvenile Templar* (1877–1971) and the *Juvenile Rechabite* (1890–1971) were nonetheless long-lived examples of several titles available for young members of adult temperance groups, offering a similar menu of information and entertainment focused on promoting temperance. This had the effect of constructing children as active social agents: the periodicals not only showed them the social and physical results of overindulgence in alcohol but encouraged them to take a protective role towards adult drinkers, and to consider and debate policy issues.

The monthly magazines for voluntary workers, the *Band of Hope Chronicle* and *Workers Onward* (1910–57), also provide fascinating insights into what young members did in meetings and how the temperance message was promoted. As the children attended on a voluntary basis, teachers had to work to maintain their attention. Because they provided informal training for millions of voluntary teachers, temperance periodicals employed child-centered, activity-based, and interactive educational techniques well before such teaching was employed in state-provided educational settings.

Future Directions

It is difficult to reconcile the potential of nineteenth-century temperance periodicals with their current state of scholarly neglect. Suffrage and socialist magazines had similar roles as organs of propaganda in the cause of reform, but they have received considerably more attention, perhaps due to their relative lack of religious and moralizing references which, to modern tastes, may seem intrusive or old fashioned. Yet temperance was the subject of more periodicals than other social concerns; this is hardly surprising given the high membership of temperance societies, which attained over six million by 1900.[18] In May's *London Press Directory and Advertiser's Handbook* for 1871 there are fifteen periodicals classed as temperance magazines, a number exceeded only by those classed as religious titles (by far the largest category) or those

---

17. Beetham, "Open and Closed," 97–8.
18. Rowntree and Sherwell, *Temperance Problem*, 5. This figure includes adults' and children's societies.

categorized as timetables, as the official organs of societies, or as legal, literary, missionary, science, trade, and Welsh-language periodicals. In his 1969 survey, Harrison notes that "it would be wrong to treat [temperance periodical] literature merely as an entertaining by-way: as another absurdity born of 'Victorian' moral earnestness," yet it seems that scholars have fallen into this trap.[19] This may be why temperance titles are not included in surveys, histories, and plans for digitization. Such a scholarly lacuna has greatly complicated research in this important field. Sad to say, in the twenty years since Olwen Niessen's chapter on temperance periodicals, there has been little improvement in cataloguing or access to finding lists and archives.

The Institute for Alcohol Studies, the Livesey Collection at the University of Central Lancashire, and Senate House Library, University of London, hold the three major UK temperance archives, from the UK Alliance, the British National Temperance League, and the Rechabites and other organizations, respectively. All three have long runs of particular temperance periodicals, but exact dates or details are hard to find without an on-site visit. The British Library, the Bodleian Library, and many local and university libraries throughout the United Kingdom hold runs or individual copies of titles. This includes exciting finds, such as the November 1893 issue of the *Railway Signal, or Lights along the Line, a Journal of Evangelistic and Temperance Work on Railways*, which is held in the Bodleian's John Johnson collection (along with first copies of several such titles). Again, an on-site visit is necessary, although if a particular issue or page is required, archivists can sometimes supply material remotely.

Temperance titles have certainly not been among the first titles to be made available through digitization schemes. ProQuest's otherwise excellent *British Periodicals* has no temperance periodicals, although plenty of citations using the word "temperance" or "Band of Hope" appear in other publications, which indicates the popularity and importance of the movement. Similarly, the Gale Cengage *19th Century UK Periodicals* selection contains only one temperance periodical, the *British Women's Temperance Journal* (continued as *Wings*). This may reflect lack of research in the temperance field, but another important factor has been the reluctance of libraries to include temperance materials in subscription databases. Such archives as those at the Institute for Alcohol Studies, the Livesey Collection, and Senate House were donated by temperance organizations on the understanding that they would be freely available, and the curators, rightly so, have been reluctant to see material "locked up" in subscription-only collections. Alternative digitization projects are, nonetheless, under way and should make these collections freely accessible to all within the next few years, honoring the intentions of those who donated the material. The National Library of Australia's service, Trove, has led the way by providing a digitized version of the *Australian Band of Hope Review and Children's Friend* (1856–61, with several changes of title). This was the first title selected for digitization by the Digitisation and Photography Branch of the National Library of Australia and the Australian Newspapers Digitisation Programme team in 2011. It is ironic that, with much greater collections of temperance periodicals in the UK, so few have been prioritized for digitization by the British Library.

19. Harrison, "World," 125.

Assuming that online access will become easier and finding lists and guides will be developed, there are many directions for future study of temperance periodicals. Longitudinal studies, given the long runs of publication, would shed light on cultural change in general as well as print and publishing history in particular. Food and drink historians would find the advertisements, as well as the text, of temperance periodicals deeply interesting. Given the outstanding and innovative quality of design in some titles such as the *British Workman*, the *Band of Hope Review*, and *Onward*, historians of illustration, art, and design would find them a plentiful resource for research.[20] Given the high circulations of temperance periodicals, their content—including articles, lectures, poetry, songs, recitations, jokes, or serial novels by prolific temperance writers such as Clara Lucas Balfour (1808–78)—is surely worthy of further exploration. Temperance discourse overlaps with radical, religious, professional, and social justice concerns, which suggests innovative comparative studies. Given that the movement aimed to influence hearts and minds, its copious educational material and associated teaching strategies aimed at adults as well as children invite scholarly attention. Study of single pages, issues, or annual runs would reveal what thousands of Victorians expected or received from temperance periodicals. Likewise, it would help us understand how temperance campaigners viewed their movement, which has implications for research in cultural, economic, social, and political history. If the recent increased interest in temperance history continues[21] and access to digitized temperance periodicals expands, then it seems likely scholars will make great strides toward illuminating this important category of nineteenth-century British journalism.

---

20. Murray has begun this work with his study of the *British Workman*. Murray, "Often Taken."
21. See Nicholls, *Politics*; McAllister, *Demon Drink?*; and Yeomans, *Alcohol and Moral Regulations*.

26

PERIODICALS AND RELIGION

Mark Knight

In 1861, *Mitchell's Press Directory* recorded that, of the 481 magazines and reviews published in Britain, the largest category was religious periodicals: no fewer than 207 of the 481, 43 percent of the total. Elsewhere in the directories we read that many religious publications had large readerships: the circulation of the *Christian World* (1857–1961), for example, was 100,000, and *Deacon's Newspaper Handbook* in 1886 thought it "very good for advertisements."[1] Certainly its rates were high, which suggests a large demand for advertising space. This simple quantification of readers and numbers of journals suggests that religious periodicals played a substantial role in nineteenth-century British print culture, a point borne out in several chapters in this volume.

Of course, numbers only tell part of the story. What kinds of publications are covered by the term "religious periodicals"? And what sort of role did religious periodicals play in nineteenth-century British culture? One way of answering the first of these questions is by examining whether, and to what extent, periodicals mark their religious orientation in some explicit way. Publications of this sort include those with a clear religious reference in the title, such as the *Christian World*, the *Jewish Chronicle* (1841–), the *Missionary Chronicle* (1813–1967, with various changes of title), and the *Christian Remembrancer* (1819–68). Another strong marker of a periodical's orientation is its relationship to a religious publisher, such as the Religious Tract Society, whose best-known titles are the *Boy's Own Paper* (1879–1967), *Girl's Own Paper* (1880–1956), the *Leisure Hour* (1852–1905), and *Sunday at Home* (1854–1940). Another important religious publisher was the Society for the Promotion of Christian Knowledge, whose *Saturday Magazine* (1832–44) was set up to counter the secular *Penny Magazine* (1832–45). There were also periodicals directly aligned with a religious denomination or movement, including the *Wesleyan Methodist Magazine* (1778–1969), the Roman Catholic *Tablet* (1840–), and *Evangelical Christendom* (1847–99), published by the Evangelical Alliance. These denominational periodicals were often important sites for the consolidation of ecclesial identity, and although their content frequently extended to other subjects, the life of the church was prominent in the material published.

The number of publications that were clearly marked as religious and were likely to have been among those counted by *Mitchell's Press Directory* is enormous, and it is tempting to stop

---

1. *Deacon's Newspaper Handbook*, 96.

here and look no further. But there are numerous other publications that deserve to be considered under the heading of religious periodicals. Periodicals such as the *Quiver* (1861–1926), *Good Words for the Young* (1868–77), and the *British Weekly* (1886–1970), to name just three examples, included material that might be deemed "secular" yet continued to signal a theological orientation through various means. For example, they might include theological forms, such as sermons and devotional pieces; employ recognizably religious editors or contributors; profess a missionary purpose; focus on Sunday reading; promote a cause aligned with a religious group; or consciously translate theological ideas into popular cultural forms. This second category of "religious periodicals" may be as large as the first, prompting the question of how we should delimit its generic boundaries. Should we include periodicals such as *Merry England* (1883–95), which looked like many other non-religious literary periodicals of the period yet focused on Catholic writers? What about periodicals such as the *Argosy* (1865–1901), which, under Ellen Wood's editorship, became known for domesticated sensation fiction written in a broadly Christian tone?[2] Should we think of temperance periodicals such as the *Band of Hope Review* (1851–1937) under the category of religious periodicals given the importance of religious belief to many advocates of temperance? Can we make sense of the periodicals produced by a publisher like Cassell and Co., including *Cassell's (Illustrated) Family Paper* (1853–67) and *Cassell's Magazine* (1867–1932), apart from the religious beliefs of its founder, John Cassell? How about the *Monthly Repository* (1806–37), which still maintained a debt to its Unitarian founders when it pursued a more literary focus under the editorship of W.J. Fox (1827–37)? Is the presence of theologically inclined contributors (for example, Matthew Arnold or Elizabeth Gaskell) in a journal enough to make us think of that periodical as religious? Such questions leave us with a dilemma. Expansive answers risk making the term "religion" so broad that it becomes emptied of meaning, but the opposite move—focusing only on those periodicals that rely on traditional theological forms or ecclesial matters—is equally problematic because it constricts our appreciation of the diverse ways in which religion was mobilized, experienced, and understood.

To think about religious periodicals in the nineteenth century, then, requires careful and ongoing methodological reflection. For a start, we have to decide what we mean by the term religion. When I use the term here I refer to a discourse that extensively and actively draws on one or more of the established theological traditions. In nineteenth-century Britain, that tradition was predominantly Protestant Christian, though Roman Catholicism, Judaism and, to a lesser extent, other world religions were also a significant part of British public life.[3] There were of course also groups with a less conventional sense of what it meant to be spiritual: for example, Theosophy, Swedenborgianism, and Spiritualism. Although the definition of religion I employ here remains broad and contestable, the imprecision of the term is offset by the existence of bodies of knowledge in theology and religious studies that sharpen our understanding of religious belief and practice during the nineteenth century. Turning to these interpretive

---

2. See Palmer, "Dangerous and Foolish Work."
3. For examples of the growing interest in world religions and periodicals research, see Dajani, "*Islamic World*," and Travis, "Both English and Jewish."

communities not only helps us clarify what we mean by the term "religion" but may also help us overcome a related methodological problem: how to read about religious traditions that are largely unfamiliar. There are a number of specialists in the academy who are knowledgeable about religious discourse, in different forms, and who write about it in historically and theoretically informed ways. Yet many scholars know little about religion and lack the tools necessary to interpret theological material from the period.

Scholarship on Religious Periodicals

Recent scholarship provides useful context on religion and the periodical press, including Felicity Jensz and Hanna Acke's *Missions and Media: The Politics of Missionary Periodicals in the Long Nineteenth Century*, Anthony McNicholas's *Politics, Religion and the Press: Irish Journalism in Mid-Victorian England*, and David Cesarini's *The Jewish Chronicle and Anglo-Jewry, 1841–1991*. There is important work in volumes on the nineteenth-century press in general, such as Louis Billington's "The Religious Periodical and Newspaper Press, 1770–1870" or the chapter on "Faith, Religion and the Modern World" in Linda E. Connors and Mary Lu MacDonald's *National Identity*. Aileen Fyfe and John Topham have likewise published important work on religion and science in Victorian periodicals.[4] Religious historians of recent decades, including Owen Chadwick (*Victorian Church*), Timothy Larsen (*People of One Book*), David Bebbington (*Dominance of Evangelicalism*), and Denis Paz (*Nineteenth-Century English Religious Traditions*), regularly include periodicals among their sources, and *Victorian Periodicals Review* publishes the occasional article on the religious press.[5]

Joseph Altholz was the preeminent scholar of Victorian religious periodicals; much of what we know about religious periodicals is indebted to his book *The Religious Press in Britain, 1760–1900*. Altholz provides background on many overtly religious periodicals by devoting specific chapters to groups such as the Evangelicals, the High Church Anglicans, Dissenters, Presbyterians, and Roman Catholics. The book covers an impressive range of publications, making it the single most useful guide to religious publications of the period. Reading about the various types of publications clustered around different denominations reminds us of the diversity of theological perspectives during the nineteenth century. Altholz pays attention to a range of perspectives outside mainstream denominations, including the publications of the Freethought Movement and more theologically orthodox groups that grew up around particular social concerns, such as temperance and abolition. Altholz's book is an excellent guide, but it is not without its limitations. Although his decision to map religious periodicals by denomination is eminently reasonable, it entails a narrow definition of the material we think of as religious. Altholz was well aware that the religious influence on the nineteenth century extended to other aspects of daily life, including debates about the arts, politics, commerce, science, and

---

4. For the contributions of Aileen Fyfe and Jonathan Topham, see Fyfe, *Science and Salvation*; Topham, "*Wesleyan Methodist Magazine*"; and Topham, "Science, Natural Theology, and Practice." See also Cantor, *Quakers, Jews, and Science*.
5. Examples of recent essays on religion in *Victorian Periodicals Review* include: Janes, "Role of Visual Appearance"; Ehnes, "Religion, Readership, and the Periodical Press"; and Janssen, "Embodying Facts."

travel, yet the denominational structure he employs results in a relatively constricted view of what religious periodicals cover.

Since Altholz's death in 2003, scholarship on Victorian periodicals has had some difficulty knowing what to do with religion. The difficulty may be attributed in part to the philosophical commitments that dominate so much work on Victorian periodicals. Most current work on Victorian periodicals is best described as operating within the paradigm of material history. Yet there is an apparent lack of self-awareness among scholars regarding the critical tradition from which this paradigm emerges. William McKelvy is one of the few scholars to examine "Print Culture's Promethean Dream," by which he means the "tradition of scholarship that implicitly affirms that an expanding print culture is inherently heterodox in religion and radical in politics."[6] His point is well made, and the myth he exposes can be tied to a related strand of scholarship, emerging out of Marxism, which sees religion as an opiate of the people, an ideological system in need of exposure rather than a body of belief with any underlying explanatory power.

Reading Religious Periodicals

While few scholars working on print culture explicitly locate themselves in a Marxist tradition, assumptions from that tradition are pervasive. Much scholarship on periodicals is predicated on the belief that capital is the primary driving force in history, an assumption that commercial interests should always trump religious agendas when it comes to interpreting the evidence before us. Faced with periodicals in which religious and commercial interests appear prominent, periodicals scholars tend to ignore the former and concentrate on the latter. Even when scholars do not explicitly employ Marxist critical tools, their training in the critical tradition associated with the Frankfurt School and Michel Foucault, as well as the related tradition of cultural materialism, influences the sort of analysis they undertake. Combined with an often-benign ignorance of religious history, such scholarship continually leaves theological explanations in the background. Periodicals are thought about primarily in terms of advertising, circulation, material production, and the economic interests of publishing houses. And when religious factors do enter the equation, they are rendered subservient to economic and ideological interests.

Scholarly work on missionary periodicals, meanwhile, struggles to get beyond the problem of an imperial ideology. Periodicals researchers think of Christian publishers as only having a concern with the economic consequences of their circulation figures, and they view the experimentation with different written forms in religious periodicals as a secular effort to increase market share at the expense of religious belief. These ideological and material concerns are obviously important, and I am certainly not suggesting that they are irrelevant to the study of religious periodicals, but the dominance of this line of interpretation can blind us to other factors that are also significant.

While no reading is free of interpretive bias, it is still helpful to think about how our methodological commitments skew our reading of religion, especially as such bias often escapes

---

6. McKelvy, *English Cult of Literature*, 26.

critical notice. Consider, for instance, the appearance of advertisements in periodicals and how we think about their meaning. For many, the growth of advertising in periodicals is evidence of print culture's increasingly secular nature. If advertisements are a commercial endeavor, a desire on the part of companies to market products to readers and an attempt by the publishers of magazines to increase their income, then it might seem to follow that advertisements mark the decline of religious influence on periodicals. Yet such an argument fails to acknowledge that there might be a theological rationale for the inclusion of advertisements. Explicitly evangelical publications such as the *Christian Observer* (1802–77) and the *Evangelical Magazine* (1793–1904) regularly included advertisements alongside their devotional and theological material. Their willingness to do so was partly attributable to the economic realities of a modern world and the need for income, but it was also because their religious worldview took seriously the need to promote the message of the Christian Gospel. The emphasis on promoting a particular message created space for thinking about the promotion of other messages, too, so long as the products advertised were not seen as directly opposed to Christian teaching. Although nineteenth-century Christians were aware of the biblical teaching that the love of money was the root of all evil, this knowledge did not prevent them from seeking more positive ways of engaging with the increasingly prominent economic realities of modern life and deploying them for theological ends. As Joseph Stubenrauch puts it, "While evangelicals always criticized the unbridled pursuit of capital, many understood the workings and innovations of commerce as peculiarly well-suited to the development and spread of religious feelings and experiences."[7] The famous Scottish theologian Thomas Chalmers wrote *On Political Economy* (1832), demonstrating that the relationship between God and money in the evangelical tradition was not simply oppositional.

Acknowledging the willingness of religious communities to think about how they promoted their message helps us to see some of the developments in nineteenth-century religious periodicals in a different light. Rather than presuming that technological and commercial developments were motivated by wholly secular concerns, we might explore the theological gloss religious publishers and editors gave to their practices, even if we want to insist that these glosses do not always give us the complete story and are not the only explanations available. Lowering the price of a periodical, for example, could be an attempt to boost sales and increase profit, but it could also be an attempt to reach a wider audience and heed the biblical mandate to spread the teachings of Jesus to all people. Similarly, both explanations could be used to account for dramatic, attention-grabbing headlines in the Salvation Army's weekly magazine, the *War Cry* (1879–), and for the increasingly diverse content that appeared in religious periodicals during the nineteenth century (for example, children's stories, illustrations, poetry, and travel writing). While this increasing heterogeneity might be viewed as evidence of secularism and the decline of religious belief, it might also be explained as the result of a conscious and theologically motivated desire to use the century's publishing developments to promote the Christian Gospel and to help readers see how theological values affected all aspects of their lives.

---

7. Stubenrauch, "Silent Preachers," 548.

Taking theological explanations seriously requires us to rethink our attitude to propaganda. In the twentieth century, the term "propaganda" acquired a largely negative connotation, describing the systematic efforts by which powerful groups disseminated their message and misled the public. It is easy to see how the suffering of two world wars and the destructive effects of totalitarian regimes extended a suspicion towards propaganda that had started to enter people's thinking in the late nineteenth century, and there are often good reasons to apply this suspicion retrospectively and try to see beyond the propaganda of religious publishers. Yet a more positive view of propaganda allows us to consider religious publishers as innovators rather than just manipulators; it encourages us to examine the multiplicity of reasons why they did what they did, and it makes us more likely to pause when we come to the work of religious periodicals and not simply repeat the repetitive mantra that all religious forms are propaganda that needs to be unmasked.

Evangelicals were behind some of the most prominent and creative religious propaganda of the nineteenth century, as the voluminous output of the Religious Tract Society attests, but they were far from being the only religious group to make use of the periodical form as a means of disseminating their ideas. The Quakers made use of periodicals such as the *Friend* (1843–) and the *British Friend* (1843–1914) to get their message out, and the Tractarians, having derived their name from one form of publication, saw the possibilities of another when John Henry Newman and Thomas Mozley edited the *British Critic* (1792–1853) from 1838 to 1843 and used the publication as a platform for promoting their doctrinal contributions to debates about the direction of the Church of England. Spurred on by the conversion of Newman in 1845, Roman Catholics in the nineteenth century also sought to make their voice heard through publications such as the *Dublin Review* (1836–1968), the *Rambler* (1848–62), *Illustrated Catholic Missions* (1886–1914), and the *Month* (1864–1939). Like the propaganda published by other religious groups, Roman Catholic writing had an internal and an external audience, and the priority given to either group helps explain why some periodicals would adopt a more militant style and others a more conciliatory tone.

In addition to variation between religious periodicals, there was considerable variation within specific titles. Commenting on the changing editorial position of the *Month* and its relation to Gerard Manley Hopkins's poetry (including "The Wreck of the Deutschland," which it rejected), Martin Dubois notes that "in the years Hopkins knew it, the *Month* was walking something of a tightrope between readerships inside and outside the Church."[8] Dubois's account is informative, and in some ways his choice of metaphor here is helpful. The "tightrope" alerts us to the nuance of theological thought and reminds us how much could be at stake in the theological discussions that took place in religious periodicals. Yet in another respect the metaphor is misleading, for it exaggerates the view that the audience for Victorian periodicals was strictly divided between those inside the church and those outside it. Encouraged by theories of advertising, then and since, which emphasize market segmentation and the existence of discrete audiences, it is easy to presume that there was always a sharp divide between religious and secular audiences. In practice, however, audiences overlapped, reflecting the diffuse

---

8. Dubois, "*Month*," 299.

nature of belief throughout the nineteenth century and also the fluctuating and mutable nature of individual faith commitments. Given the large number of Victorians who attended church regularly, it makes sense to suppose that many of those who read "secular" periodicals such as *All the Year Round* and the *Cornhill* had some level of religious commitment, and it does not take long to find articles in those periodicals that spoke to those commitments or paralleled the socio-political views heard from the pulpit, albeit in a less theological register. Moreover, given that lay readers of the explicitly religious periodicals lived lives that extended beyond the confines of the church, it seems reasonable to presume that many of the readers of an overtly religious journal were the same readers who also bought a variety of other literary, political, and cultural publications.

Recognizing that audiences were not as segmented as many people assume and that early periodicals such as the *Leisure Hour* provided a hybrid of religious and secular material, the periodical *Good Words* (1860–1911) sought to break down distinctions between Sunday reading and the reading undertaken during the rest of the week. It offered a mixture of different genres, including explicitly theological material, travel writing, review essays, science writing, poetry, and, most prominently, fiction. The inclusion of sermons and theological commentary alongside fiction from writers such as Anthony Trollope, George MacDonald, and Ellen Wood attracted criticism from some quarters, with one theologically conservative Church of England newspaper, the *Record* (1828–1948), complaining about the "'mingle-mangle' . . . of persons, as well as of things" in *Good Words*.[9] Ironically, the same failure to see how religious thought could accommodate different forms and voices is present in subsequent scholarship on this periodical. Scholars insist that in early issues of *Good Words* the balance between religious and secular material is unstable and its shifts in format demonstrate the triumph of the secular and commercial interests of its publisher, Alexander Strahan.[10] What these judgments miss is Strahan's substantial religious convictions and the theological motivation of his evangelical editor, Norman Macleod, who saw the journal as a vehicle for proclaiming the Christian message to as wide an audience as possible. Macleod defended the mix of sacred and secular material in *Good Words* on the grounds that the combination was integral to a Christian vision of life and that it was possible to "yoke" different elements together "without compromise."[11]

Instead of being seen as vehicles for promoting pure transcendence, then, religious periodicals were understood to offer a form of communication through which a community of faith might gloss the divine significance of earthly existence. This work of propaganda and translation could take many different forms and frequently included strong material concerns. In the case of the *Family Herald* (1842–1940), a penny weekly, the mixture of serialized fiction with other content takes on a different hue when we consider that until 1857 its editor was the Reverend James Smith (also known as Shepherd Smith). Smith was a radical whose beliefs were shaped by the legacy of Joanna Southcott; he thus framed all of his work in theological terms.

---

9. *Good Words: The Theology of its Editor*, 5.
10. For examples of the critical tendency to focus on the commercial at the expense of the theological, see Srebrnik, *Strahan*; and Turner, *Trollope and the Magazines*, chapter 2.
11. Macleod, "Note," *Good Words*.

As Andrew King points out, Smith "confessed in a letter in 1849 that he did not read the stories in the periodical at all. He was only interested in what he himself wrote, the essays and answers to correspondents, to convey the message of 'Universal Charity.' The rest was the sugar on the pill or the lure on the line."[12] Although Smith's private remark encourages us to treat his editorial leaders and answers to correspondents as the center of the magazine's religious dimension, it would be a mistake to think that the fiction in the magazine was entirely unaffected by contributors' awareness of the editor's religious stance. Certainly fiction contributed to the *Family Herald* by writers such as Mary Cecil Hay displays the sort of moralistic tone that would have been unimaginable outside the predominantly Christian culture of the period.

Religion versus the Quantitative

There are many reasons why the religious dimension of periodicals tends to slip from critical view. Like the internal motivations of publishers and editors, representations of religious belief are not easily quantified. We can only measure that which we know, and though all aspects of life risk being diminished when they are quantified, the idea of God brings with it particular challenges for quantitative analysis. In making this claim, I am not suggesting that the Christian religion is oriented towards an abstract concept of transcendence. Despite the powerful influence of Christian Platonism, which has historically pushed Christianity towards an abstract and disembodied theology, the Christian God is also understood by the church to be the God who reveals himself in time and space, who brought the people of God out of Egypt and into a promised land, and who was incarnate in the person of Jesus Christ. Yet the Christian faith does hold that there is something beyond the world that we sense and experience, and that something is especially difficult to quantify and grasp. This has consequences for our understanding of how belief in God meshes with the rest of our experience and requires a more provisional epistemology than quantitative analysis allows. As has been evident in this chapter up until this point, theological accounts of developments in the periodical form and/or contributions to it are often one possibility among many, a conjectural line of argument that is encouraged but not proven by the explicitly religious declarations of many of those writing in the nineteenth century.

Religion's resistance to quantitative analysis did not stop some religious groups in the nineteenth century from making widespread use of numbers. The economic vocabulary present in the motto of *Good Words*—"Good Words are worth much and cost little"—recurs in other periodicals, which make repeated reference to the numbers of those converted, tallies of how many people attended religious services, the sales figures of particular publications, and the revenue generated by religious societies. Among the many examples of this tendency is the *Missionary Magazine and Chronicle*, published with the "hope of more widely diffusing Missionary intelligence, and thereby awakening among British Christians a deeper interest in Missions." It was full of numerical facts and tabulated data, including a detailed list of the financial

---

12. King, "Killing Time," 161. More generally on Smith, see Lockley, *Visionary Religion and Radicalism*, chapters 9 and 10.

contributions made to missionary work over the previous month.[13] Although other religious groups made extensive use of numerical data to support their causes, evangelicals were especially likely to use numbers to give credence to their claims, a fact that likely reflects the emergence of the Evangelical Church at the same time as the Enlightenment, which promoted the idea of quantitative knowledge.[14]

Yet numbers do not tell us as much as nineteenth-century evangelicals or modern scholars like to think—and not just because those working in the humanities or for nineteenth-century religious publishing houses lacked access to large clean data sets or did not possess the higher-level statistical training needed to interpret them. Indeed, my own efforts at the start of this chapter to signal the importance of religious periodicals by citing numerical evidence could be critiqued on the grounds that not everything published in the nineteenth century deserves sustained or equal attention. My argument for paying closer attention to religious periodicals is not that a lot of them were published in the nineteenth century, though their numbers do seem high, but rather that it is difficult to imagine the nineteenth century without the religious debates and influences that played such a crucial and extensive role. Periodicals were crucial to this vitality. As the preface to the 1861 issue of the *Christian Observer* (1802–77) explained, "So rapid are the changes of modern life . . . that it is only in a periodical work that they can even be noted down."[15] In an era that saw a great deal of religious change—the rise of Roman Catholicism, the growth of religious dissent, the decline of the Church of England, the emergence of science, a burgeoning plurality of belief, and a host of new perspectives on biblical hermeneutics, democracy, class, women, national identity, the arts, and society as a whole—periodicals offered one of the most important sites for recording and shaping religious discourse.[16]

To try and get at the centrality of religious discourse in the world of nineteenth-century periodicals, we may do better to make quantitative analysis secondary to another mode of reading, one that has long been at the forefront of work on periodicals (though rarely applied to religion directly). The practice of reading different discourses in conjunction with each other—whether we theorize this alternate mode of reading as an exploration of the Bakhtinian notion of heteroglossia, an awareness of periodicals as "sites of simultaneity," a practice of reading "sideways," an application of Walter Benjamin's notion of interlinear reading, or the kind of attentiveness to the periodical medium inspired by the work of Joseph Altholz—allows us to see religion as an important strand within the textual life of the period.[17] There is a larger case to be made about the need for scholars of the Victorian period to recover an appreciation of theology as a living language. My focus here, however, is on religious periodicals, and my argument is that a greater attention to theological language and its place within our intellectual

---

13. See "New Series," *Missionary Magazine and Chronicle*, 1860, 1.
14. See Bebbington, *Dominance of Evangelicalism*, especially chapter 4.
15. "Preface," *Christian Observer*.
16. For an introduction to some of the main contours of nineteenth-century religion, see Chadwick, *Victorian Church*; Parsons and Moore, *Religion in Victorian Britain*; Knight and Mason, *Nineteenth-Century Religion*; Melnyk, *Victorian Religion*; and Larsen, *People of One Book*.
17. On heteroglossia, see Bakhtin, *Dialogic Imagination*, 324. Wynne speaks of "sites of simultaneity" in *Sensation Novel*, 20. See also Hughes, "Sideways!"; Benjamin, "Task of the Translator"; Altholz, *Religious Press*.

conversation offers the more capacious hermeneutic for thinking about religion in the periodical press. We do not have to be completely fluent in theological language to benefit from the approach I am advocating here. To read periodicals with an eye to the presence of theological discourse allows us to dwell on those aspects of Victorian life that we are more familiar with but to do so in the knowledge that religious contributions continually reconfigured their and our interest in different spheres of life. Literature, business, travel, and science are seen differently when brought into conversation with theology. In an article entitled "The Newspaper," a contributor to *Good Words* put it this way: "The infusion of religious life into the newspaper would act like those strong under-currents in the ocean, which bring the warmth and vitality of the latitudes from whence they come, to shores and climates that would remain frozen and sterile without such genial influences."[18] Although the writer's belief in the redemptive possibility of religious discourse is idealistic, the contributor's choice of metaphor, "under-currents in the ocean," acknowledges the fluid interaction between theology and other discourses and encourages us to look for religion throughout the nineteenth-century periodical press rather than just in discrete locales.

18. M.B., "Newspaper."

27

THEATER AND THE PERIODICAL PRESS

Katherine Newey

The theater in the nineteenth century was intense, frenetic, and ingenious. It was a creative industry of quick-silver reactions to contemporary issues, fads, and fashions that was situated at the forefront of modernity. While contemporary critics throughout the century lamented the "decline of the drama," the theater industry continued to offer novelty and experimentation.[1] It adopted new technologies with alacrity, created new genres such as melodrama and burlesque, remade and renewed popular forms such as pantomime, took up Continental work and its innovations with enthusiasm, and set out to represent the modern world in fresh and relevant acting and staging practices. The customary practices of the theater—its close connections with the off-stage world and its reliance on commercial popularity—meant that the industry was extremely sensitive to social and economic change.

There is another story of the British theater at odds with this narrative. In this view, the theater was in decline, and the nineteenth century was an age of bad acting and even worse dramatic writing. This "high critical"[2] view of the theater was that the written drama was risible, formulaic, and adapted from the French by hacks, with an objectionable focus on the vulgar and the indecorous. In short, it was not art. The theater was dominated to its disadvantage by venal managers and new popular audiences, who were given over to the easy pleasures of spectacle and sensation and were blamed for the "decline of the drama" and its commodification. Constrained by the monopoly of the patent theaters until 1843 and subject to the direct censorship of the Lord Chamberlain (until 1968), the British theater in the nineteenth century was a sad shadow of the glories of Shakespeare and his contemporaries. The drama could only become respectable—both morally and aesthetically—when it sloughed off the demands of popular entertainment and offered a new vision of British society through the work of realist playwrights at the end of the century.

These two views of nineteenth-century theater co-existed throughout the period in regular and sometimes heated dialogue. It is an abiding irony of the period that a culture which

---

1. This term was prevalent in the periodical press in the late 1820s and recurred throughout the century. See, for example, "Decline of the Drama," 3. The Report of the 1832 Select Committee into Dramatic Literature introduced the phrase into parliamentary language.
2. Here I am using Christopher Kent's term from "Periodical Critics of Drama," 31.

demonstrated such spectacular theatricality should hold such ambivalent attitudes to the theater itself. The elite critical view that the popular theater was not satisfactory as art was at odds with the evidence of its continued vitality and variety. These debates and conflicting historical accounts of the nineteenth-century theater were played out in the periodical press, specialist theatrical journals, and general newspapers and magazines. Across the century, the press played a significant role in constructing audiences and shaping their "horizon of expectations" (to use Hans Robert Jauss's term) as an active and engaged reading and spectating public.[3] Jane W. Stedman, in her important survey of theatrical journals, notes that more periodicals were "devoted partly, or wholly to the theatre" in the nineteenth century than at any other time.[4] The press provided a stage for debates within and about the theater in essays, reviews, articles, gossip, and news snippets, and many of these publications were as busy and volatile as the theater itself. Journalism created the theatrical world discursively even as it reported on its events and personalities.

The canonical view that the nineteenth-century popular theater is "not art" has been challenged recently, as scholars reassess the records and documents of the nineteenth-century theater through immersion in the archive. A close consideration of periodicals—from daily newspapers to the quarterlies—is key in this revision. Indeed, much recent research on the nineteenth-century theater would be impossible without the rich resources of periodicals, notwithstanding the puffery and gossip through which much of the reviewing in journals was sustained. Digitization of journals and newspapers has enabled a breadth and depth of reference hitherto rarely possible. However, up to this point theatrical journalism has largely served theater historians as a source of information rather than as discourse in its own right. Brian Maidment commented on this general tendency in 1990 when he asked for a "recognition of periodicals as discourse rather than evidence."[5] Of course, theatrical journalism is not only, or simply, discursive; it is also evidential. But an understanding of what Peter Sinnema calls the "complex rules of production and consumption that governed the Victorian press" needs to run alongside the mining of Victorian periodicals for their information about the theater.[6]

Discourses

My focus is on this discursive function of the press in the first half of the nineteenth century as it is here that ideological battles over the social role of the theater began. Debates in the late Romantic period expose fault lines which structure much discussion of the status and achievement of the theater for the rest of the century. Indeed, early nineteenth-century anxieties about the role and status of the theater in society—embodying tensions between its roles as both entertainment and art—still resonate in British cultural policy today. Despite the frequent (and often damning) critique of its current practices, the idea of the theater was considered one of the markers of the state of the nation and a significant national cultural institution. This was in part because the theater's physical presence, material practices, and professional

---

3. Jauss and Bahti, "Alterity and Modernity," 182. See also, Bennett, *Theatre Audiences*, 34–5.
4. Stedman, "Theatre," 162.
5. Maidment, "Victorian Periodicals and Academic Research," 151.
6. Sinnema, *Dynamics of the Pictured Page*, 3.

self-image were regulated by centuries of centralizing state control. At the restoration of the public theaters in 1660, Charles II bestowed a royal patent on theater managers William Davenant and Thomas Killigrew which eventually provided the Theatres Royal at Drury Lane and Covent Garden with monopoly rights for staging the "legitimate" or spoken drama. These rights were considered to cover both new plays and the repertoire of the English drama from the sixteenth century. The Theatres Royal came to represent the national or legitimate drama even though Britain would not have a designated and subsidized National Theatre until the 1950s. State control was reinforced by the 1737 Theatrical Licensing Act,[7] which gave powers of censorship to the Lord Chamberlain and required plays to be submitted to his office for licensing (with the requisite fee attached). The act also attempted to define the nature and limits of allowable performances of "any new interlude, tragedy, comedy opera, play, farce or other part added to any old interlude, tragedy, comedy, opera, play, farce or other entertainment of the stage or any new prologue or epilogue."[8]

By the 1820s, the apparent stability of this definition of legitimate performance was replaced by a more fractured and shifting industry due to the commercial and demographic pressures of population growth, industrialization, and democratization. The theater, like the periodical press, was part of an urbanizing society, and it responded to the pressure of changes in both audience sizes and demographics through frenetic and often chaotic expansion which produced a volatile pattern of financial and aesthetic success and failure. This was driven by entrepreneurial capitalism in a new speculative model, rather than the older oligarchic model of regulation and monopoly.[9] New theaters were established in areas of working-class population growth, such as the south bank of the Thames ("transpontine theaters") and the densely populated East End, but these were the "minor" theaters, without the royal patent. Under the terms of the original royal patent and the 1737 act, such theaters could not stage spoken drama but instead offer only singing and dancing. By the 1820s, this constraint was flouted almost nightly, as theaters such as the Coburg (still in use as the Old Vic), the Surrey, and Astley's Amphitheatre produced melodrama, comedy, farce, and adapted versions of plays by Shakespeare and his contemporaries as fast as audiences could consume their productions. The first five decades of the nineteenth century were spent in a theatrical and political battle between defenders of the monopoly and those who sought to dismantle it.[10] Struggles over theatrical regulation signified more than economic competition; they indicated a cultural and political battle over ownership of and access to national culture. Audiences and theater professionals, however, showed no doubt about their desire for new kinds of plays and performances. If there was a "decline of the drama," it was one created discursively by critics and commentators determined to use their privileged access to the public sphere of debate, largely through the periodical press.

---

7. *Report from the Select Committee on Dramatic Literature*, August 2, 1832.
8. The text of the bill is reproduced in Thomas, *Restoration and Georgian England*, 205–7.
9. For a comprehensive account of the finances of the British theater, see Davis, *Economics of the British Stage*.
10. For detailed analyses of these theatrical politics, see Nicholson, *Struggle for a Free Stage*; and Davis, "Looking Towards 1843."

Urbanization was a complex process. It was not simply a matter of bringing more bodies into London and providing employment, food, and housing for them (for it was largely London's geography and economy that drove the process in the first half of the century). One of the most significant results of urbanization, Shattock and Wolff argue, was to create a mass reading public.[11] In the theater, this became a vocal, physically present, and actively spectating public. Despite the dismissive attitudes of the contemporary cultural elite towards the cognitive powers of popular audiences (Dickens's "Two Views of a Cheap Theatre" is a prime example), it is safe to assume that there was a substantial crossover between these reading and spectating publics, which constituted a new urban citizenry comprised of self-conscious and articulate reading and spectating presences. This is what Benedict Anderson calls the "imagined community" of the nation created through the mass circulation of print culture.[12] In relation to the theater, the tag "national" was ideologically loaded. The spoken drama of the English tradition, as delineated by the 1737 act, was presented as the "national drama" grounded in the inheritance of Shakespeare as "national poet."[13] Yet access to performances of the national poet were limited to the Theatres Royal, places connected to elite culture by tradition, patronage, and cost of entry. The mass circulation of journals that incorporated writing about theatrical matters—including disputes and debates as well as reviews, gossip, news, opinion, and editorial pieces—created a sense of belonging to an informed coterie invested in a set of national cultural values. In documenting and fomenting debate, theatrical journalism operated to create a distinct discursive field.

The vitality of this field was made possible by an explosion of print in the new media age of the 1820s and 1830s. In this period, both the theater and the press were highly visible elements of a new public culture forged out of the combination of radical activity and the more commercially driven pressures of a new print culture, which emerged during a period of recovery from almost thirty years of war against the French. Parallels between the theater and the press suggest that the phenomenon of "cross-platform mass media" is not only a product of late capitalism and the digital age but also a feature of industrial urban culture from its beginnings in the early nineteenth century. Amongst the many new journals produced was a slew of short-lived theatrical and dramatic magazines. Carl J. Stratman notes the start of twenty theatrical or largely theatrical journals in the years 1831 and 1832.[14] This is in accord with the "entrepreneurial energy and commercial volatility" Brian Maidment finds more generally in comic visual culture of this period.[15] Journals worked symbiotically with the entrepreneurial drive towards new entertainments. Together with the nightly playbills, which served as both advertising outside the theater and as programs within it, these journals offered a variety of information—from a bare outline of each night's entertainment with short commentary to ambitious attempts to set the wrongs of the drama to rights. These range from the *Acting Manager; or, The Minor Spy*, which survived for four numbers from May to June 1831, to *Figaro*

---

11. Shattock and Wolff, introduction to *Victorian Periodical Press*, xiv.
12. Anderson, *Imagined Communities*, 6.
13. For an extended discussion of the place of Shakespeare in these debates, see Prince, *Shakespeare in the Victorian Periodicals*.
14. Stratman, *Bibliography of British Dramatic Periodicals*, 21–4.
15. Maidment, *Comedy, Caricature and the Social Order*, 4.

in London (1831–39)—that exuberant and naughty weekly based on the Paris *Figaro*—to the more sober-sounding *Literary Guardian and Spectator of Books, Sciences and Fine Arts, the Drama, etc.* (1831–32), which was published by William Tindall in two volumes with a total of forty-five weekly numbers. Such pamphlets and journals were created quickly from fragments and gossip and thus stirred up the competition. The more edgy and iconoclastic journals, such as *Figaro in London*, *Bell's Life in London* (1822–86) and *John Bull* (1820–92), paved the way for longer-running satiric journals such as *Punch* (1841–2002). They offered a supplement to the established belles lettres journals continuing from earlier in the century, such as Leigh Hunt's *Examiner* (1808–81), the *Gentleman's Magazine* (1731–1907), the *New Monthly Magazine* (1814–84), and later, Robert Rintoul's *Spectator* (begun in 1828). These established journals carried theater reviews and opinions, as well as reviews of published dramatic literature; however, they tended to focus on the Theatres Royal and the "legitimate" drama, as well as published forms of dramatic literature which were often unperformed.

The tone of theatrical journalism, whether in specialist theatrical journals or the theater columns of general periodicals, tended to oscillate between comic performance and combative portentousness. The comic voice of the period, typified by *Punch*, emerges in shorter-lived journals. Its dominant note is of self-congratulation and the enjoyment of insiders' jokes, which the reader can grasp by virtue of his (less likely her) role as consumer. In *Figaro in London*, for example, there is a hilarious sequence of short notices to readers announcing how wonderful Figaro and his readers are: "To the Readers of 'Figaro in London' All over the World."[16] The sheer bravado of this squib is joyous in itself, as later in the year, the *Examiner* carried a report on the insolvency of the editor, Gilbert À Beckett. *Punch* converted Benjamin Webster's "Prize Comedy" competition into a running joke throughout 1843 and 1844, perhaps influenced by Charles Dickens's and Douglas Jerrold's private jokes about Webster's scheme. "My Dear Jerrold," wrote Dickens on June 13, 1843, "Yes. You have anticipated my occupation. Chuzzlewit be damned,—High Comedy and five hundred pounds are the only matters I can think of."[17] *Punch* announced a series of hoax competitions, including the Victoria Theatre's quest for the "most absorbing domestic drama" in which it is "indispensable that every piece sent in should contain a dream for the 'acknowledged heroine,' and a suicide for the 'recognised tragedian.' All the pieces will be submitted to a committee of servant girls, ill-used apprentices, and victims of oppression."[18] There is a "Prize Preface" competition for volume six of *Punch*, and À Beckett presented his own spoof entries in *Scenes from Rejected Comedies* in *The Quizziology of the British Drama*, published by the *Punch* office in 1847. In 1892, the earnest series of articles by leading writers in the *Pall Mall Gazette* (1865–1923) on "Why I Don't Write Plays," spawned a spoof in *Judy* (1867–1910), including the following contribution by "Mr G.R.S*ms": "The reason why I don't write plays is, that it pays me better to write melodramas and burlesques."[19] Late in the century, even William Archer, hardly known as a comic writer, succumbed to the

16. "To the Readers," 87.
17. Dickens, *Letters*, 3:509.
18. "Another Dramatic Prize," 13.
19. "Why I Don't Write Plays," *Judy*, 152.

satirical mode in his championing of Henrik Ibsen's work. His collection of the shocked and scathing responses of London critics to *Ghosts*, assembled in the article "'Ghosts' and Gibberings" for the *Pall Mall Gazette* (April 8, 1891), is presented as groundwork for the book he says he is writing, *Ibsenoclastes; or, An Anthology of Abuse* (of course, not a real project). Archer's satirical review of the reviewers is picked up by George Bernard Shaw, another champion of Ibsen, in his polemical book *The Quintessence of Ibsenism* (1891), and through the influence of these two critics, the critical myth of British resistance to Ibsen was created. The habit of comic journals commenting on theatrical matters throughout the century offers many pleasures for readers and spectators, from the cheekiness of À Beckett and *Figaro* to the thinly disguised bitterness of Archer, but perhaps more importantly, it emphasizes the discursive role of theatrical journalism in the creation of knowledgeable theatrical communities.

Portentousness, however, was never completely absent, particularly in the expression of views on the place of the theater in British culture. Stedman points out that one of the chief themes of theatrical magazines was to encourage the drama by emphasizing its uplifting nature. In order to establish their respectability, editors needed to "simultaneously defend . . . the virtue and validity of the theatre and polic[e] it so that it would behave with propriety, dignity, and morality."[20] In the 1830s, commentators' attempts both to construct and direct public discourse on the "decline of the Drama" made theatrical journals part of an energetic public debate which connected theater with public policy and discourses of nation-making. In 1832, after the passing of the Great Reform Act, MP and playwright Edward Bulwer-Lytton formed the House of Commons Select Committee on Dramatic Literature with a view to removing the monopoly on the "legitimate" drama claimed by the Theatres Royal in London and elsewhere. Voices of the periodical press played an important role in public debate over this significant shift in the cultural landscape. Most notable was the partisan writing of Bulwer-Lytton and his friend and fellow playwright, Thomas Noon Talfourd, in the *New Monthly Magazine*, a literary periodical founded by Henry Colburn in 1814 and edited by Bulwer-Lytton from 1831. From April 1831 until September 1832, Bulwer-Lytton and Talfourd wrote a series of essays on the drama promulgating radical arguments for removal of the patent theaters' monopoly under the guise of reviews of current productions. They pressed home the urgency of the state of decline, starting with the statement that "at no previous moment has the drama stood so deeply in need of the collateral aid of sound criticism to guide, to direct, and to guard it, as it does now; because, never before has its danger of utter degradation been so imminent."[21] Even pompous editorials offer their own melodramatic pleasures.

Opinionated pronouncements on the politics of the drama were not limited to London—although the phenomenon was most noticeable there. The editorial of the *Liverpool Dramatic Journal* in its first number declared,

> A dramatic periodical has long been a desideratum in this town; we shall therefore make no apology for this. It has long been a matter of regret, that we have no faithful and minute report of the style of our actors, and the state of the drama. . . . The

20. Stedman, "Theatre," 167.
21. "Drama," 166.

influence, however, which public representations have over the manners and feelings of the people, is too extensive to remain unlimited in its control: all power which feels no arbiter will become corrupt.[22]

The journal's leading article, reproduced from *Fraser's Magazine*, comments on the major theatrical controversy of the day—the war between "Majors versus Minors" in London—and details the action of the managers of the Theatre Royal, Covent Garden against the City Theatre in Cripplegate. Like many journals, the *Liverpool Dramatic Journal* aimed both to instruct and offer "useful diversion."[23] The instruction came from reviews of current London productions and articles on the history of the theater; the diversion came from gossip and theatrical politics.

This importation of the metropolitan is typical in its view of the London theater as a significant institution of national culture. The reuse of material (we might say "plagiarism") from metropolitan periodicals was commonplace in regional journals and in journalistic practice throughout the nineteenth century. Bob Nicholson charts the complex journeys of what he calls "scissors and paste" journalism as a cultural phenomenon of the period, arguing that such a practice indicates "something significant about the way print culture gave voice to popular tastes and values."[24] In addition to stirring controversy, the *Liverpool Dramatic Journal* acquires urbanity by appearing to be in the know about backstage doings and internecine professional battles in the London theaters. The journalism itself becomes a kind of theatrical presence, moving between front and back stage, performing as a guide to the mysteries of the theater. Access to the backstage world of management, disputes, and gossip offers special status to the critic who is seemingly permitted into that liminal world between the privacy behind the scenes and the public display on stage. Through the act of reading the journal, the consumer acquires this status as well. In the *Liverpool Dramatic Journal*, the reading public is also a theatrical public. It is a theatrical public that is self-consciously national, one which uses the speed of modern communications to connect the regional northwest to the metropolitan center. However, records suggest that the high ideals of the *Liverpool Dramatic Journal* did not meet the desires of the public; according to Stratman, it survived for only two numbers in 1832. In 1834, a new journal appeared, the *Liverpool Dramatic Censor*, which claimed the same high ideals as its predecessor but which, lasting for just one issue, was similarly unsuccessful.

These Liverpool magazines exemplify the many metropolitan and regional theatrical journals that started as speculative ventures and were enabled by cheap printing and the increased mobility of readers, commodities, and information. Their mode of address to prospective readers is typical and recurs throughout the century. In opening editorials, they articulate the values of the journal and begin to construct an ideal or compliant reader. According to Andrew King, this articulation of values was in part a commercial strategy because a new commodity entering the market must "initiate the communicative event it is economically dependent upon. It must make potential purchasers give it an identity and persuade them that it relates

---

22. Editorial, *Liverpool Dramatic Journal*, 1.
23. Ibid.
24. Nicholson, "You Kick the Bucket," 277.

to themselves. In order to do this it has to get the public to differentiate it from competing products while at the same time it must give the appearance of being already well-known to them."[25] The similarity of claims made in opening editorials of new theatrical journals was so widespread that it became a reliable feature of the medium. To potential consumers theatrical journals offered reassurance that readers would receive content that was knowledgeable but unbiased, critical but judicious, entertaining but respectable. The *Liverpool Dramatic Censor* asserts,

> Those who fancy we write merely to abuse, or to gratify a satirical disposition, will find themselves disappointed, our intent is rather to encourage than deteriorate the Drama, every member of which shall find we will fearlessly do our duty both to the Theatre and the Public—and trusting the Managers will not fail in their endeavours to command success, we hope they will do more—"they will deserve it."[26]

Fifty years later in Norwich (where the Theatre Royal was at the center of an active regional touring circuit), the editor of the *Lorgnette* (1883) makes the same claims, in almost the same language:

> "The Lorgnette" is established—as new ventures in Journalism always are—for the purpose of "supplying a long-felt want." If the gentle reader has not personally realised the existence of this particular want, he must nevertheless take our word for it that it did exist. . . . Modesty forbids any self-laudatory reference to the great good our new enterprise is destined to accomplish; but we are happy in the determination that, if we cannot command success, we shall at least deserve it.[27]

In London, three years earlier, the *Green Room* (1880) offered the same hopeful vision to its readers:

> Without any desire . . . to sound a flourish of trumpets, we may be permitted to state that the chief aim of The Green Room will be to deal with all matters relating to the Drama, to Music, and to Art generally, in an honest, fearless, and independent spirit of criticism. Our wishes are to further the interests of the Stage, to assist in the maintenance of its purity, and to raise it in the estimation of the public. We do not believe in the so-called decline of the Drama.[28]

Much to the disappointment of their editors and proprietors, the *Lorgnette* and the *Green Room* were short-lived, running just two numbers at most. They are typical of a plethora of new weekly journals throughout the century, which had high ideals and short lives, offering a vision

---

25. King, "Paradigm of Reading," 81.
26. Editorial, *Liverpool Dramatic Censor*, 1.
27. "Salutatory," 2.
28. Editorial, *Green Room*, 3.

of a cultured life of art and letters to which many young and upwardly mobile men (and some women) aspired. Alongside the idealistic naiveté of these opening addresses, there is an urbanity that is underpinned by a satirical comic voice, sharp and knowing. In the 1830s, this was the milieu from which both *Punch* and Charles Dickens's first incarnation as Boz emerged.

The *Era* (1838–1939)

Out of this ferment—the wonderful energetic mix of gossip, politics, tub-thumping, and an expanding school of opinionated critics and aesthetes—came one of the most long-standing of theatrical periodicals, the *Era*. It began publication on September 30, 1838 and at first did not define itself as a stage or theatrical journal. The first several pages are of political news and then overseas news. It is not until page seven that the drama column appears as part of a general page entitled "Manners and Amusements." The *Era*'s introductory essay on the theater conforms to the pattern of the opening announcements noted above by incorporating a down-to-earth, pragmatic address to its readers:

> In these days, the drama is a difficult and a delicate subject to handle—a subject on which there have been as many pros and cons as upon any which fill the columns of a newspaper. The strange thing is, too, that there is quite as much party spirit thrown into dramatic criticism as there is into politics. It has been the fashion to write up one actor and write down another—to praise one theatre through all its absurdities, and to vituperate the best efforts of its rival. It is this which, while it does not rob criticism of its sting, prevents its utility, either in convincing the public, or improving the stage.
>
> Volumes have been written on the decline of the drama: it has been attributed to a thousand different causes . . . and to a variety of . . . reasons too numerous to name, and too trite to need being named.
>
> The object of "The Era" is not to investigate the causes of its declension, but to look upon the drama as it is—upon the actors as they are; and not, by drawing comparisons to bygone days, and departed genius, to put us out of love with what we have got. Our maxim is, to make the best of the material that is now before the public—to take up authors, actors, and managers, as we find them, and to praise or blame without regard to place or person.[29]

The *Era* was sponsored by the Licensed Victuallers' Association. It developed into an authoritative trade journal, like that other stalwart of professional journalism, the *Builder*. It went from being a publication designed to serve a newly professionalized sector (as in exercising acknowledged expertise) to "one of the most influential illustrated journals of the Victorian era."[30] The pragmatism and sobriety of the *Era* is significant, marking as it does the shift from

---

29. "Manners and Amusements," 7.
30. Richardson and Thorne, introduction to *The Builder*, ix.

Regency scabrousness to pragmatic reportage. Of course, *Figaro*-style publications were still around in 1838. Besides the *Era*, *Actors by Gaslight; or Pencillings in the Pit* also started that year. But *Actors by Gaslight* did not last longer than a couple of years. The *Era* drew upon the spirit of entrepreneurship of the 1820s and 1830s, but it converted this energy into a more solid and respectable product which survived until 1939. Its place was then assumed by the *Stage*, which survives (at the point of writing) as a weekly newspaper whose website proclaims that it is "the world's longest-running publication for the performing arts industry."[31]

Once the *Era* settled into its theatrical role, it was distinguished by a focus on theater almost to the exclusion of other forms of public life. Later in the nineteenth century, the theater started to feature prominently in a number of upmarket periodicals which combined fashion, sport, and theater, such as the *Illustrated Sporting and Dramatic News* (1874–1943), the *Graphic* (1869–1909), and the *Sketch* (1893–1959). The changing content of these journals is instructive; they combine theatrical news with updates on society events and sporting achievements. The linking of theater into this web of celebrity—particularly in its visual presence through lavish illustration of high society beauties and actresses—was not novel. Eighteenth-century print culture established the connection of theater with celebrity in just this gendered way.[32] The focus on hunting and racing in the *Illustrated Sporting and Dramatic News*, for example, connects theater with aristocratic pursuits in ways that *Bell's Sporting Weekly*, in the 1820s, did not, although *Bell's* carried theatrical gossip as well as accounts of boxing and racing. Although these weekly papers demonstrate the established acceptance and respectability of the theater after the 1860s, they never quite match the sense of speedy response and public engagement with controversy shown in the fly-by-night theater journals of the earlier period. It was these journals that offered a taste of the heady days of theater and radicalism and that foregrounded the role of theater in creating a new urban popular culture, inch by column inch.

This discussion of theatrical journalism raises the question of theatrical periodicalism, or seriality. If one of the functions of a periodical in the nineteenth century was to create a reading public and a community of like-minded citizens, then just what counts as a periodical? In the theater and entertainment industry, this could suggest a much wider range of texts and formats than offered by standard daily, weekly, monthly, or quarterly newspapers and magazines. If we are considering periodical publication across the nineteenth century in terms of its discursive construction of culture and its ability to engage diverse audiences, then other kinds of serial publications might be considered within the orbit of the periodical; even if they are not periodicals, they display qualities of periodicalism. For example, Thomas Hailes Lacy published a long series of play texts as separate pamphlets, but he designed them to be bound in named series, such as "Lacy's English Drama."

Playbills are another very visible example of the effects of seriality beyond journals, magazines, and newspapers. The playbill was, for most of the century, the principal means of advertising the nightly program. However, this function disappeared by the mid- to late Victorian period, with the development of the now-familiar multi-page pamphlet carrying advertising

---

31. The *Stage*, http://www.thestage.co.uk.
32. Luckhurst and Moody, *Theatre and Celebrity*; and Perry, *Spectacular Flirtations*.

and information about the production. The playbill provides us with a record of repertoire, performers, and production personnel such as scene painters, choreographers, stage directors, and musicians. This is its data content; however, like the periodical, the playbill has a recognizable form and discursive content.[33] For at least the first half of the nineteenth century, the playbill was a very public way for the theater manager to communicate with his (sometimes her) audience and to develop a public self-image for his theater. The vivid presence of the playbill in the visual culture of the city is to be seen in John Parry's "A London Street Scene" (1834), one of the most striking depictions of nineteenth-century urban visual culture. The final painting of Augustus Egg's trilogy, *Past and Present*, demonstrates another way in which playbills resonated beyond theater buildings, reading as an index of a woman's fall. The flâneur commentator of *The Language of the Walls* (1855) reads the London walls as part of the experience of urban life, commenting that they "frequently draw our attention from every-day objects and concerns of life, to theatrical *stars*, as they flit from one sphere to another."[34] The playbill was also a place for debate and at times provided running commentary on theatrical matters, including theatrical rivalries or local and national disputes.[35] While playbills did not offer reviews—apart from puffs—they paralleled other functions of theatrical periodicals, providing regular yet punctuated communication which defined a theatrical community. The potential for conversion to more conventional periodical status is demonstrated by the 1849 publication of the *Theatrical Programme and Entr'acte*, which consists largely of bills of plays at the major theaters across London, followed by brief reviews and notices and then several pages of "The Stranger's Friend"—a guide to cab fares to and from places of interest in London—including theaters, exhibitions, and galleries. If not strictly periodicals, daily playbills shared with periodicals a dependence on temporality as well as the "seriality and miscellaneity" that James Mussell identifies as an important characteristic of periodicals.[36]

In this gallop through the thickets of theatrical journalism in the nineteenth century, I have been interested to look at the ways in which periodical publication framed popular theater. For it was both the material practices and the discursive construction of the popular which drove much of the debate about the theater in general. This is strikingly evident in any discussion of the decline of the drama. The debates recorded in the periodical press during the 1830s—indeed, often fomented there by writers through the relatively open platform of the press—set the agenda for most of the rest of the century so that even in the 1880s it was thought necessary to state a position on the decline of the drama. The term "popular" is loaded—indeed, over-determined—in all of this. At one level it refers simply to forms of fiction, poetry, drama, and graphics that are cheaply available, quickly produced, widely circulated, and aesthetically accessible.[37] However, even these descriptive terms are loaded with value judgments. "Cheap," "quick," and "popular" can all too easily be read as implying a

---

33. For a general discussion of the discursive analysis of the playbill, see Balme, "Playbills and the Theatrical Public Sphere."
34. Burn, *Language of the Walls*, 36.
35. See Newey, "Shakespeare and the Wars of the Playbills."
36. Mussell, *Nineteenth-Century Press*, 54–5.
37. Maidment, *Reading Popular Prints*, 53.

lack of aesthetic value or skill, or a derivative and repetitive content. The connections between popular and radical forms, as well as the border policing of art and cultural production by both old and new elites, suggest that any simple definition of popular culture begs questions of value and cultural authority. In this respect, definitions of popular culture were produced through debate and need to be understood as discursive rather than as a set of fixed categories.[38] Periodicals played a central role in this discourse, constituting one of the principal ways in which actual and virtual audiences encountered the theater and theatrical sociability.[39]

---

38. Shiach, *Discourse on Popular Culture*, 19.
39. My use of the term "encounter" draws on Laurel Brake and Julie Codell's use of the concept in *Encounters in the Victorian Press*, 1.

28

ART PERIODICALS

Julie Codell

The Victorian art press defined the nature of art, as the nation increasingly became identified with and through its visual culture. A nineteenth-century innovation, art periodicals were not unique to Britain; they also appeared on the Continent and in the US. The British art press defined itself as a suturing mechanism between artists and the public. It was not only concerned with aesthetics but also the role of art in shaping nineteenth-century society and the nation, as well as the relationship between art and commercial interests amid a growing number of galleries, print shops, and museums. The *Art Journal* (1839–1912) and the *Magazine of Art* (1878–1904), the most popular and long-lasting periodicals, began as recorders and cataloguers of international exhibitions, beginning with the Great Exhibition in 1851. With the emergence of a wide-ranging Victorian visual culture that embraced everything from world fairs and museums to department stores and advertising, art periodicals expanded to include commercial and industrial topics, as well as "high" art. The Victorian art press created a public and a market for British art. From its inception, its motives were to increase public support for art by promoting it as a measure of an advanced society, a sign of national prominence, and an expression of Britishness.

Before the nineteenth century, art criticism was spotty in the press and there were few journals exclusively devoted to it. Among early art periodicals was Charles Taylor's *Artist's Repository and Drawing Magazine* (1785–95), which incorporated chalk and line engravings along with essays on architecture, perspective, technique, landscape drawing, and art history. It also included a dictionary of terms, a compendium of colors, and criticism of current books and exhibitions. Other early art periodicals included the *Artist* (1807–09), the *Annals of the Fine Arts* (1816–20), the *Magazine of the Fine Arts* (1821) and the *Library of the Fine Arts* (1831–34). Rudolph Ackermann's *Repository of Arts* (1809–29) contained satiric aquatints by Thomas Rowlandson; scenes of London by Augustus Charles Pugin and Frederick Nash; hand-colored costume plates; and illustrations of architecture, furniture, and interior decoration. It presented a prescient mixture of high art and crafts later revived in the 1860s.[1] Beginning in the 1840s,

---

1. Roberts's "British Art Periodicals" lists 317 art periodicals published between 1774 and 1899. Roberts's pioneering study defined the concept of the art press—periodicals devoting at least one-third of their contents to art, incorporating a rich array of illustrations and reproductions, and/or focusing on the aesthetics of other subjects.

there were architectural periodicals, most notably the *Builder* (1842–1966),[2] as well as periodicals on furniture, crafts, and interior decoration.[3]

There was also a growing literature on aesthetics and art in the eighteenth century. Joseph Addison and Richard Steele wrote about aesthetics in the *Spectator* (1711–12). Painter Jonathan Richardson suggested a rating system of art criticism in two works, *An Essay on the Whole Art of Criticism as It Relates to Painting* and *An Argument in Behalf of the Science of a Connoisseur* (both 1719), where he proposed a hierarchy of values from 1 to 20—"sublimity" being the highest value. Edmund Burke's *A Philosophical Enquiry into the Origin of Our Ideas of the Sublime and Beautiful* (1757) attracted the French critic Denis Diderot and the German philosopher Immanuel Kant, and was admired by the painter and first president of the Royal Academy, Sir Joshua Reynolds, author of *Discourses on Art* (1769–90). Four years prior to Burke, the painter William Hogarth published his aesthetic ideas in *The Analysis of Beauty* (1753). In this period William Gilpin defined aesthetic concepts of the sublime and the picturesque in *Observations on the River Wye, and Several Parts of South Wales* (1782) to help travelers appreciate the English landscape. In the late eighteenth and early nineteenth centuries, Richard Payne Knight, Uvedale Price, and Dorothy Wordsworth also wrote treatises on the picturesque promoting landscape art. During a period with few public museums or galleries, William Hazlitt wrote art criticism for the *Examiner* (1808–81) from 1816, focusing on history painting, portraits, aristocratic art collections, and a few available public collections. The sublime and the picturesque continued to interest Victorians and were among the subjects addressed in John Ruskin's criticism.

The Victorian art press was divided between populist and specialist periodicals, which were differentiated largely by attitudes toward the market. All art periodicals sought to create market niches, but populist magazines overtly reported economic events—sales, auctions, museum acquisitions, artists' remuneration—while specialist magazines appealed ostensibly to aesthetics and to educated middle-class cognoscenti, an audience only possible after decades of a prolific, widely disseminated art press. Inspired by the Pre-Raphaelite Brotherhood's *Germ* (1850), anti-populist "little magazines" from the 1870s gradually overtook the field by the 1890s, as the popular *Art Journal* and *Magazine of Art* declined. Many mainstream periodicals—including the *Nineteenth Century*, *Blackwood's Edinburgh Magazine*, the *Fortnightly Review*, the *Athenaeum*, and the *Contemporary Review*—also contained artists' biographies and reviews of art books and public exhibitions. In addition, art and art-critical reviews were included in the period's many "miscellaneous" periodicals, such as *Academy: A Monthly Record of Literature Learning, Science, and Art* (1869–1916), *Ainsworth's Magazine* (1842–54), and the *Argosy* (1865–1901).

From the 1850s, the press promoted the rising status of artists by inventing the genre of the heroic artist biography, a culture industry that branded artists by repeating epithets: the manly J.E. Millais, cosmopolitan Frederic Leighton, idealist G.F. Watts, and so forth. As circulating commodities, artists became national heroes in serialized biographies that shaped Victorian concepts of art, artist, genius, and aesthetic worth. Biographies reiterated the trope of struggle rewarded by success, insisting that "no man ever became great without working assiduously,"

---

2. Ibid., 6.
3. Ibid., 5.

as economic success became a sign of a work ethic and moral character.[4] The *Art Journal* series "British Artists: Their Style and Character" (1855) was illustrated by engravings of paintings by prominent engravers such as the Dalziel Brothers. These could be removed and placed on parlor walls, further solidifying the bond between artists and the public.

Illustrations served to underscore the art press's mission to strengthen links between artists and their audiences. The first reproductions were engravings (initially copper, then steel plate in the early nineteenth century), but they were overtaken by wood engravings from mid-century, only to be replaced with photographic methods in the 1880s. Just as fiction serials whetted readers' appetites and reinforced intertwined social and aesthetic values, art reproductions and portraits of artists in serial biographies also served a suturing function. Popularity, more than aesthetic achievement, became a sign that artists were united with the British public through shared taste and values.

The art press enjoyed a wide circulation. The *Art Journal*'s monthly circulation increased from seven hundred in 1839 (when it was called the *Art-Union*) to nearly 25,000 in 1851, demonstrating the press's increasing power over cultural matters. Promoting art commerce, editor Samuel Carter Hall wanted the newly commenced *Art-Union* to demonstrate the "commercial value of the Fine Arts."[5] Further, he hoped to demonstrate that "beauty is cheaper than deformity" and that it was sound policy and patriotism "to resort to native artists . . . in every branch of Art-manufacture" and to offer artists higher rates of remuneration.[6] He bragged, "I had to create a public for Art . . . to make the work respected as well as popular" by blending "information and instruction with interesting and useful intelligence" to replace consumers' purchases of Old Masters with their acquisitions of works by living British artists.[7] The *Art Journal* in 1861 asserted, "The power of the British Press has been as great as that of the Royal Academy, and it has been much more abused" because of critics' "unintelligible jargon . . . technical slang" and "empty phrases" of connoisseurship, instead of an art language for middle-class readers who also enjoyed the periodical's popular Christmas and Easter *Art Annuals*.[8] Art annuals entered the market as art objects themselves (the predecessors of coffee-table books) to generate further cultural capital and consumption of art by living British artists that would satisfy buyers' social aspirations.

The *Magazine of Art* began as a short-lived journal published by John Cassell in order to promote working-class education. Cassell published the *Illustrated Exhibitor* (1851–52), an exhibition catalogue for the 1851 Great Exhibition, with costly wood engravings, which appeared weekly for 2d. and in monthly parts for 8d.[9] The first number sold out in a day; reprints sold 100,000 copies the first month.[10] The *Illustrated Exhibitor and Magazine of Art* was retitled the *Illustrated Magazine of Art* in early 1853, its cover illustrated by George Cruikshank and its

---

4. "British Artists," 45.
5. Hall, *Retrospect*, 1:210.
6. Ibid.
7. Ibid., 1:197–9.
8. "Exhibition of the Royal Academy," 161.
9. For the early history of the magazine, see Greiman, "William Ernest Henley," 53.
10. Nowell-Smith, *House of Cassell*, 32.

writers non-specialists who knew little about art. It sold for 2d. weekly but failed in 1856. The *Illustrated Exhibitor* was created to appear during the 1862 London Exhibition, but sales were weak. In 1878, the year of the Paris International Exhibition and following a decade of a flourishing art market for living British artists, Cassell's partners, after his death, began the *Magazine of Art* (1878–1904), which catered to the general public and was cheaper than the more established *Art Journal*. Editor Marion Harry Spielmann (1887–1904) believed in the mutual benefits of linking art and commerce and treated commercial success as a sign of both artistic quality and a national unity of taste.

The *Magazine of Art* was the third and most successful art magazine published by Cassell's. In 1880, it doubled in size to five hundred pages and changed from pen sketches and woodcuts to photogravure frontispieces and high-quality engravings and woodcuts.[11] When Cassell increased the price of the magazine to a shilling in 1881, its circulation was not affected. In 1893, it cost 1s. 4d. and grew to six hundred pages, which included full-page color reproductions.[12] Between 1881 and 1887, editor William Ernest Henley promoted James Abbott McNeill Whistler, the Barbizon painters, and Auguste Rodin and hired knowledgeable art critics (including Sidney Colvin, R.A.M. Stevenson, Andrew Lang, and Cosmo Monkhouse).[13] When Marion Harry Spielmann became editor, the magazine began to emphasize commercial success; the art establishment, especially the Royal Academy; and trade journal topics such as economics and technical matters. He pilloried French art and its English followers and attacked Impressionism as late as 1904.[14] The periodical initiated an advertising trend of employing pictures by academicians. But sales declined from 1897, despite the addition of features to attract readers, such as "Notes and Queries," which encouraged letters to the editor, sensationalist debates, and supplements. Spielmann's eulogy for the magazine cited his motive to take a "line in art-politics" against new movements, but he finally failed to interest the public in such unfashionable views.[15]

Art Production as a Business

The populist art-press endorsement of artists' new celebrity, wealth, and sociability was underscored by its appropriation of New Journalism methods—interviews, hyperbolic advertising language, and gossip columns, such as the *Art Journal*'s "Art Gossip and Reviews"—to induce spectating and buying. Unlike the French avant-garde, Victorian artists did not see an opposition between creativity and commercial success. The art press thus transformed art production into a business whose enterprising artists mirrored middle-class values: a belief in social decorum, the gospel of work, moral character, and the close relationship between high culture and the nation. However, the art press differed from the New Journalism press

---

11. Rumbaugh, "Magazine of Art," 31–2.
12. "'Magazine of Art'—Its Majority," 316–20.
13. The publishers disliked Henley and in 1881 appointed academy-trained Edwin Bale as Art Director, leaving Henley in charge of literature.
14. Codell, "Marion Harry Spielmann," 7–15.
15. "Valedictory," 461.

in endorsing "timeless" ideals of aesthetic value rather than just transient or topical news. The art press never abandoned the educational mission of the old journalism; what it added was a belief that the purchase of British art was important for being both patriotic and commercially successful.[16]

As Pierre Bourdieu argues, art is produced not only by artists but also by art discourses in "reproductions, catalogues, art journals, museums" whose discourses become a "stage in the production of the work, of its meaning and value."[17] All forms of commentary—criticism, catalogues, biographies, cartoons, media, and exhibitions—compete in a "struggle for the monopoly of legitimate discourse about the work of art, and consequently in the production of the value of the work of art."[18] According to this logic, Hall and Spielmann, among other editors and critics, became co-producers of British art.

Critics mediated relationships between artists and the public while gaining their own cultural authority and professionalism in this mediation process. They not only created a bond between artists and public but they also determined the terms on which that bond rested. Critics joined a large circle of art workers that included art publishers, illustrators, engravers, and dealers. Dealers and artists worked together to advertise works, and they invented new exhibition venues dramatizing and hyping single works at dealers' galleries. Exhibitions grew exponentially with the growing number of galleries and societies far beyond the annual Royal Academy exhibition that had dominated the exhibition scene until mid-century. All had to be reviewed in the press.

Art Criticism and Promotion

During the nineteenth century, critic-journalists made careers writing for the press and were often erudite and well-versed in art history, technique, and patronage. Critics used reputations as a form of capital, created markets for themselves and for artists, and influenced consumption by validating the public's social ambitions through notions of proper taste. They gained authority through prolificacy: William Michael Rossetti wrote almost four hundred art essays for British and American periodicals from 1850 to 1878. An artist's biography might appear in multiple places. For example, F.G. Stephens's essay on James Clarke Hook for the *Portfolio* (1871) was expanded for the *Art Journal* (1888) and an *Art Annual* (1888). Critics' biographies for popular series were often published by periodical publishers.[19] Given this prolificacy by a few critics, some artists appeared repeatedly across newspapers, periodicals, books, and print shops, gaining celebrity status as circulating commodities in a network of

---

16. Codell, "Art Press and the Art Market."
17. Bourdieu, *Field of Cultural Production*, 10–11.
18. Ibid., 36.
19. George Newnes published *Newnes Art Library* and the *Strand Magazine*; George Virtue published the *Art Journal*, along with its annuals, biographies, and book biographies; Richmond Seeley published the *Portfolio* and reprinted its biographies as a series, *The Portfolio Artistic Monograph*; Seeley, Jackson, and Halliday published the *Portfolio*'s series as *English Painters of the Present Day* in 1871; Cassell's published the *Magazine of Art* and a biographical series, *Gems of Art*; Otto Limited published biographies from the *Connoisseur*.

information.[20] As Catherine Soussloff notes, "Names and naming in the biographies of artists and the discourse of art history become performative of the process of art making itself."[21] Anthropologist Mary Douglas considers naming part of a system of consumption, which makes art criticism a promotional genre.[22] Critics were often the artist's friends or even relatives. For example, popular military battle painter Elizabeth Butler's brother-in-law, Wilfred Meynell, wrote her biography, and W.M. Rossetti wrote about his Pre-Raphaelite cohorts.

Marion Harry Spielmann's career exemplifies that of a professional critic. He was born in 1858 to Adam Spielmann, head of a prosperous money exchange and banking firm. He was educated as an engineer, then began collecting art in the 1880s while beginning his journalism career writing for the *Pall Mall Gazette*, where he imbibed New Journalism from the *Gazette*'s editor, W.T. Stead. In the *Magazine of Art*, Spielmann continued the practice of seeking controversy by coaxing artists into debates on timely subjects, such as the nude, art nouveau, copyright laws, or the encroachment of photography into the fine arts. He served as editor of the *Magazine of Art* and its supplement, *European Pictures of the Year*, to which Continental critics contributed. He also served as art critic for the *Graphic*; art editor for *Black and White* (1889–1912), which he helped found; and critic for the *Daily Graphic*, *London Illustrated News*, *Westminster Gazette*, and *Morning Post*. He wrote on art education and museum administration for the *Contemporary Review*, *Nineteenth Century*, *New Review*, *National Review*, and *Figaro Illustré*, along with specialist periodicals like the *Book Buyer*, *Bookman*, *Critic*, *Journal of the Society of Arts*, and *Speaker*. He also contributed to American periodicals: *Harper's Bazaar*, *American Architect and Building News*, the *Dial*, and *Scribner's Magazine*. He was art editor of the *Encyclopædia Britannica*'s tenth edition and contributed to subsequent editions. He also served as editor of *The New Art Library* art series and as author of miscellaneous monographs on Chaucer, Ruskin, Shakespeare's portraits, and British and Continental artists, as well as international exhibition catalogues and popular surveys of art. He wrote for the *Dictionary of National Biography*, the *Oxford English Dictionary*, and *Bryan's Dictionary of Painters*, and served on official committees for public memorials, international exhibitions, war funds, and public art collections. He was a member of the Athenaeum and the Arts clubs, lecturer at the Royal Institute, Fellow of the Royal Society of Literature and the Society of Antiquarians, Officer of the Order of the Crown of Belgium (the chevalier order of Leopold, King of Belgium), and an Honorary Associate of the Royal Institute of British Architects.

In the *Graphic*, he tantalized readers with anecdotes and gossip in his column "An Art Causerie". He attacked Aubrey Beardsley, D.G. Rossetti, Impressionism, Post-Impressionism, and Modernism. Yet he defended Simeon Solomon's work, despite its "moral deficiency,"[23] and wrote in the *Jewish World* in 1906 that Solomon would be "remembered and honoured as an artist," despite his "demoralized" skill.[24] He praised artists as much for their modest lives as for their art, describing William Holman Hunt as having "purified and vitalized the art of England"

---

20. Thirlwell, *William and Lucy*, 123.
21. Soussloff, *Absolute Artist*, 35.
22. Douglas, *Active Voice*, 29.
23. Spielmann, "Art Causerie" (1905), 656.
24. Spielmann, "Simeon Solomon," 626.

and stirred the "emotion of the nation" with *The Light of the World*.[25] He admired Leighton, and believed G.F. Watts provided the "moral leadership of British art."[26]

Spielmann validated British institutions and national superiority while at the same time endorsing didactic art and the moral character of artists. He came into conflict with the New Critics, who were sympathetic to Impressionism and art nouveau, both of which Spielmann abhorred.[27] But he also introduced new topics into art criticism by mixing high art and popular illustration, reproducing works in progress, and reporting on activities of societies, museums, and galleries. He demystified art institutions by describing Royal Academy rituals and the workings of the National Gallery, the South Kensington Museum (later the Victoria and Albert Museum), and the Wallace and Tate public collections. He wrote a book on *Punch* (1895) and advocated for artists' professionalization through the creation of honorary degrees, art in university curricula, copyright protection, and a ministry of culture. He linked middle-class buyers with artists, promoting the New Sculpture movement's small bronze sculptures for modest flats. His close relationship with artists was symbiotic: in return for the publicity his work provided, he received insider information about Royal Academy membership voting and the names of Hanging Committee members. Such symbiosis typified critic–artist relationships, as shown in letters to F.G. Stephens as well.[28]

Spielmann's career trajectory was not entirely unique. J. Beavington Atkinson (1822–86), *Blackwood's* art critic and adversary of John Ruskin and the Pre-Raphaelites, wrote for the *Portfolio*, the *Contemporary Review*, *Fraser's Magazine*, and the *Art Journal*.[29] Tom Taylor (1817–80), a *Times* critic from 1857, was a *Punch* editor, and wrote for the *Graphic*, among other journals. In 1863, Taylor promoted art that served "national sentiment . . . national greatness."[30] F.T. Palgrave (1824–97), author of the article "How to Form a Good Taste in Art" in the *Cornhill Magazine* (1868), wrote for the *Saturday Review*. Philip Gilbert Hamerton (1834–94) also wrote for the *Saturday Review* and the *Cornhill Magazine*, in addition to editing the *Portfolio*. Sidney Colvin (1845–1927), Slade Professor of Art at Cambridge and Keeper of Prints and Drawings at the British Museum from 1884, wrote for the *Fortnightly Review*. F.G. Stephens (1828–1907) was art critic and art editor of the *Athenaeum* for forty years (until his dislike of Impressionism ended this career); he also contributed to the *Art Journal* and *Portfolio*, and was Keeper of Prints and Drawings in the British Museum. William Michael Rossetti (1829–1919) was art critic for the *Critic*, the *Spectator*, and the American journal *Crayon*. Emilia Pattison Dilke (1840–1904) wrote for the *Saturday Review* and the *Academy*, where she served as art editor.[31] These critics' art history books, often based on their press articles, tapped into a growing market for art literature.

Critics, like all Victorian spectators, were overwhelmed with the enormous quantity of Victorian art. When reviewing a Royal Academy exhibition of over a thousand paintings, critics

---

25. Spielmann, "Art Causerie" (1904), 472.
26. Spielmann, "G.F. Watts," 42.
27. On moral content in British criticism, see Flint, "Moral Judgement" and "Philistine."
28. Stephens's letters are in the Bodleian Library, Oxford.
29. See his obituary, "Fine-Art Gossip," 574.
30. West, "Tom Taylor," 319.
31. Clarke, *Critical Voices*.

might briefly mention a work or an artist in a sentence or two and then review twenty or thirty works, usually those exhibited "on the line"—that is, those hung roughly at eye level rather than being placed ("skied") in the dark at the top of the wall. Artists frequently invited critics to their studios to see their works before the exhibition, knowing that their works would probably be skied if they were not members of the academy. Critics concentrated on a painting's subject, perhaps comparing it to the artist's previous works, and they rarely discussed technique or quality. Unless attacking particular flaws, critics rarely described visual content—for example, tone, scale, brushwork, or color relationships.

Another kind of art criticism was ekphrastic—meaning that it was written in a self-consciously artistic way. In 1855, a critic writing on Millais's *The Rescue* in *Fraser's Magazine* became overwrought:

> A figure booted and helmeted is descending a staircase, laden with a rich prize—none of your knights of chivalry, none of your free lances, but a hero of this nineteenth century—a soldier of the fire brigade. The prize he has carried off consists of three children . . . . The little ones are struggling to be free to reach the outstretched arms of the mother, who kneels, all in white nightdress. . . . The thin lip tightly pressed against the half-shown teeth, the hectic crimson of the cheek, the wild eye, show that in her breast, the agony of maternal terror has just changed into the ecstasy of joy over her rescued darlings. . . . He holds the children tenderly, for the brave heart is ever kind. . . . A true sense of pathos in this. . . . You see the earliest light of a cheerless dawn upon wet roofs. . . . There is pathos in that contrast too! . . . This is a great picture . . . true to nature and human nature.[32]

William Michael Rossetti further endorsed the firefighter's heroism, likening him to a Crimean War hero: "There is the whole battle of Inkerman in that face."[33] This topical connection was possible because art criticism appeared in the press, where paintings shared pages with current events.[34]

The language of art criticism was gendered and classed, as shown in the previous example. Critics often referred to androgynous male figures, such as those created by Edward Burne-Jones, as "effeminate" and used words like "manly" as a form of praise. By the 1860s, however, many critics, like many artists, no longer felt tied to a moralistic view of art. In 1868, Sidney Colvin and F.G. Stephens argued for beautiful figures without didactic purposes, and a new group called the "New Critics" emerged by the end of the century. New Critic D.S. MacColl defined this movement:

> For what is the New Art Criticism? It is simply the attempt to apply to current art the same standards which we apply to ancient art, to disengage from the enormous

---

32. W.G.C., "On Some Pictures," 709–10.
33. Rossetti, *Fine Arts*, 215.
34. See Codell, *Victorian Artist* and "English School."

stream of picture-producers the one or two contemporary masters who are worthy to be named beside the ancients, the one or two promising talents that may some day deserve the same praise; to refuse steadfastly to confound the very good with the pretty bad, and to take mediocrity at its own estimate.[35]

Although editors used nationalist rhetoric to promote British artists, from the 1860s onwards press attention to Continental and colonial art advocated a pan-European realism—for example, France's Rosa Bonheur, Hungary's Michael Munkacsy, Russia's Ilya Repin, and white artists from Australia, Canada, and South Africa. This enabled critics to further legitimate British academic realism as a global language.

Art Commerce

Ultimately, however, economics saturated art discourse in the populist press and came to signify artists' status as professionals. Attention to economics was consistent with Hall's notion of "art commerce" and marked the *Art Journal* and the *Magazine of Art* as trade journals that would be consumed by both practitioners and the public. They reported on market fluctuations, auction sales, copyright laws, advertising, and new media, including artistic postcards, which combined aesthetics with commercial viability. They regularly published the year's sales, detailing the dates of auctions as well as the prices, owners, and buyers of art objects.[36] The press tallied art's contribution to the national wealth as well as artists' symbolic capital. One author claimed that the 1871 balance of trade was in the black through consumption of "artistic" goods, which elastically included opera glasses, artificial flowers, and other non-art objects.[37]

The press worked in tandem with art markets by publishing gallery advertisements and free exhibition announcements for the Royal Academy and other professional societies.[38] The *Art Journal* advised artists on economics. For example, one contributor recognized an excess of supply over demand in the art market and recommended dividing it into coteries, an approach adopted by new professional societies of artists after 1880. This author also suggested that poor artists avoid the academy exhibitions, which had been the most important exhibition site since the eighteenth century. Instead, he argued, they should pursue mass production since popular audiences preferred common sense and sanity, and were "keenly alive to beauty, simplicity and truth" rather than the "too evident parade of affectation in Art."[39]

Explaining the economics of the art world to the public, the press drew attention to the professional status of artists, who, unlike doctors or lawyers, lacked credentialing mechanisms. Amateurs competed on the market with professional artists, and the public considered itself adequate to judge aesthetic merit, even without expert knowledge. To remedy these

---

35. [MacColl], "Standard of the Philistine," 357.
36. See, for example, Beaver, "Art Sales," and Rowlands, "Art Sales in America."
37. Simmonds, "Art-Aids to Commerce," 296.
38. Fletcher and Helmreich, "Periodical and the Art Market," 323–51.
39. "Business Side of Art," 249.

anomalies, the art press attempted to define artists' professionalism and promoted successful artists who modeled this ideal. The art press promoted collecting art as an investment as well. Once artists became brand names, they endowed their patrons with cultural and symbolic capital. The *Art Journal* noted when the prices of paintings created by its favorite artists rose, almost as if their stock had risen. Treating beauty as a surplus value, one writer insisted that "taste is a marketable commodity, which being of so much value is worth getting honestly, and by fair purchase."[40]

Victorian artists participated directly in the mutually reinforcing categories of culture and consumption. Highly literate, Victorian artists wrote about their work and aesthetic philosophies. They also participated in interviews with critics, which were accompanied by images of their lavish studio homes and their most well-known works. The growing internationalism of the art market after mid-century led to US editions of the *Art Journal* and the *Magazine of Art*, American critics like William Stillman, and periodicals like the *Crayon*, which reviewed exhibitions of British art in the US and in other countries. The American periodical *Scribner's Magazine* ran a series on British artists, as did the French *Revue des Deux Mondes*.

The Specialist Press

Specialist art journals were more diverse and esoteric than mainstream titles, and they were unwilling to advocate for popular taste or the academy. The *Fine Arts Quarterly Review* (1863–67) was edited by B.B. Woodward, published by Chapman and Hall, and dedicated to the memory of Prince Albert. The sixty-five contributors to the first volume included W.M. Rossetti, F.G. Stephens, Tom Taylor, Philip Gilbert Hamerton, G.F. Waagen, A.H. Layard, and R.N. Wornum, as well as an array of museum curators and Continental and US writers. Content was esoteric and technical—including preservation, restoration, illuminated Latin Psalters, Italian sculpture, design theory, and obscure Renaissance artists. The type used an "f" for an "s" in the first volume, reflecting the magazine's antiquarianism. The *Fine Arts Quarterly Review* stressed art history, which was very unusual since the discipline did not exist in any English university until 1870 and had been constructed only a generation earlier by John Ruskin, Lord Lindsay, and Anna Jameson. Aiming at a readership of collectors and connoisseurs, the *Fine Arts Quarterly Review* promised the "historical and critical description of Galleries, Collections, and Special Exhibitions of works of Art," in addition to reviews of books "in every language" and notices of "practical improvements."[41] It took up the cause of the Royal Commission of 1863: the decay of the frescoes painted in the 1840s for the new Westminster palace. Suspicious of dealers and public taste, it was nostalgic for aristocratic patronage of public works, fearing the new "omnivorous" market.[42] It hoped to influence taste by emphasizing landscapes, etchings, sketches, and Burne-Jones's works, while attacking lucrative genres like portraiture. Yet critics for the magazine often expressed a conservative antipathy to French art.

40. Wallis, "Art, Science, and Manufacture.," 245.
41. "Preface," v.
42. Taylor, "English Painting," 2.

The monthly *Portfolio* (1870–94) was founded and edited by Philip Gilbert Hamerton to fill a gap between cheap and expensive art periodicals and to promote British and Continental printmakers. It published scholarly monographs as well as original engravings and etchings, especially by painter-etchers like Whistler. Its sophisticated critical language was based on impressions rather than an a priori belief that art's source and appeal drew on sensations and synaesthesia. Its lengthy serial essays often linked regions and landscape art, for example Hamerton's fifteen-part series on animals (1872), his twelve-part series on Paris (1883), and his eight-part series on modern German art (1878). The journal also published seven essays on Edinburgh by Robert Louis Stevenson (1878), a four-part series on Botticelli by Julia Cartwright Ady (1882), and a three-part series on Benozzo Gozzoli (1883). It also published articles on lesser-known Renaissance artists, and a thirty-two-part series on contemporary artists by Sidney Colvin, F.G. Stephens, and Tom Taylor. *Portfolio* articles were sometimes republished as books, including Hamerton's book on J.M.W. Turner. After 1894, the magazine became an annual series of monographs by leading art critics and scholars. Essays on technique for students and connoisseurs therein appealed to artists, and both its title and its roots in Aestheticism and the French criticism of Diderot, Baudelaire, and Gautier, emphasized the separation of art from morality.

The *Artist and Journal of Home Culture* (1880–1902) began as the *Artist*, an unillustrated 6d. trade literary monthly published by William Reeves, an art supplies retailer. It catered to women by reporting on a "Female School of Art" in the first issue and developed a column called "Art in the House" that was later entitled the "Ladies' Column." The magazine's title in January 1881 expanded to include "*Journal of Home Culture.*" In October 1894, due to editorial changes introduced by a new publisher, Archibald Constable, the title became *Artist: Photographer and Decorator: An Illustrated Monthly Journal of Applied Art*. In January 1897, it changed to the *Artist, An Illustrated Monthly Record of Arts, Crafts and Industries*, indicating how crucial illustration was in the competition among periodicals. From 1898, it was syndicated in New York and Paris.[43]

The *Century Guild Hobby Horse* (1884, 1886–94) was first edited by architect Arthur Mackmurdo, a follower of Ruskin, and later by designer, scholar, and decadent poet Herbert Horne. It was the first post-*Germ* art periodical that included poetry, art, art history, and criticism. Soon more avant-garde periodicals were published, including the *Yellow Book* (1884–87, edited by Henry Harland and Aubrey Beardsley), the *Savoy* (1896, edited by Arthur Symons and Beardsley), and the *Dial* (1889–97, edited by Charles Ricketts and Charles Shannon). The *Century Guild Hobby Horse* was the only London journal published as an organ of an arts and crafts guild. It promoted a proto–art nouveau style and advocated for the treatment of books as objects of art; in addition, it included scholarly essays on the Italian Renaissance, the unity of art and craft, the poetry of the Romantic and Victorian eras, and seventeenth- and eighteenth-century English architecture. In doing so, it anticipated periodicals such as the *Burlington Magazine*, edited by Roger Fry. The *Hobby Horse* initially cost two shillings—double the price of the *Cornhill* or *Macmillan's Magazine*, which signaled its intended readership of cognoscenti and its

---

43. See Brake, "Gay Discourse."

incorporation of high-quality engravings. Contributions included John Addington Symonds's essays on Walter Pater, Pietro Longhi, and Giovanni Battista Tiepolo; Herbert Home's series on seventeenth- and eighteenth-century British architects, including James Gibbs, Christopher Wren, and Inigo Jones; Arthur Galton's work on the Italian Renaissance and Matthew Arnold; William Michael Rossetti's essays on Ford Madox Brown; Oscar Wilde's article on Keats. It also included poems by Christina Rossetti, Ernest Dowson, Lionel Johnson, Wilfrid Blunt, and Katherine Tynan, and art by Simeon Solomon, Edward Burne-Jones, G.F. Watts, Frederic Leighton, Ford Madox Brown, and Dante Gabriel Rossetti. In addition, it published essays on sixteenth-century printers and reprints of Blake's *Marriage of Heaven and Hell*. According to Mackmurdo, the journal's first issue eschewed popular and commercial art, preferring an art "farthest removed from attempted portraiture of external nature," which offered a "more abstract, or mood-made character than the more popular forms of art possess."[44]

The *Studio: An Illustrated Magazine of Fine and Applied Arts* (1893–1918) was edited by Charles Holme (1848–1923), a collector and author of art books who aligned the magazine with middle-class readers, especially women. In addition to featuring many women artists, Holme was active in the importation of Japanese goods. He was among the first Englishmen to visit central Asia and was founder of the Japan Society (1891–), as well as being the recipient of Japan's Order of the Rising Sun. He also owned William Morris's Red House and was a friend of department-store magnate Arthur Liberty. Writers included New Critics and their Impressionist favorites—including Dugald Sutherland MacColl, Norman Shaw, Walter Crane, Aubrey Beardsley, Camille Pissarro, James Abbott McNeill Whistler, Jean-Baptiste-Camille Corot, John Singer Sargent—who offered a range of juxtaposed but often incompatible aesthetic philosophies.

Many guilds and art societies in the provinces also published magazines. The *Quest* (1894–96), published by the Birmingham Guild of Handicraft, included many women illustrators.[45] The *Magazine* was a hand-illustrated quarterly produced by Glasgow students and associates from 1894. In addition, there were many highly specialized journals on antiquities, Japanese art, Indian arts and crafts, and printmaking, as well as annual art almanacs and directories, most notably, the *Year's Art* (1880–1953), written by Marcus Huish (1843–1921) who was editor of the *Art Journal* (1881–93).

Future Directions

Despite Helene Roberts's and George Landow's early scholarship, Trevor Fawcett and Clive Phillpot's *The Art Press: Two Centuries of Art Magazines* (1876), articles in *Victorian Periodicals Review*, and scattered essays by a few scholars, the art press has historically received limited scholarly attention. However, several important works in the field have recently appeared, including Ann Brothers's *A Studio Portrait: The Marketing of Art and Taste, 1893–1918* (1993), Meaghan Clarke's *Critical Voices: Women And Art Criticism In Britain 1880–1905* (2005), Katherine Haskins's *The*

---

44. Mackmurdo, "Guild's Flag Unfurling," 97.
45. Marsh and Nunn, *Women Artists*, 127–9.

Art-Journal and Fine Art Publishing in Victorian England, 1850–1880 (2012), and Anne Helmreich and Pamela Fletcher's edited collection, *The Rise of the Modern Art Market in London, 1850–1939* (2013), which devotes several chapters to the press and the art market. Future studies of the art press might focus on Victorian critical terminology, the gendering of art writings, the relationship between critics and artists, the role of aesthetic politics in the art press, and the development of the colonial art press. Future scholarship might also track the critical reception of individual artists so as to provide a more detailed analysis of aesthetic values as shaped by the art press.

29

MUSIC PERIODICALS

Laura Vorachek

Music held a central place in nineteenth-century British culture, from the rise of the domestic piano and the popularity of brass bands and choral societies, to the lure of the music hall. Music could be heard in opera and concert halls, drawing rooms, and the streets, performed by professionals, middle-class women, and itinerant musicians, respectively. Sales of instruments, sheet music, and instrument method books rose dramatically in the nineteenth century; the number of musicians and music teachers increased six-fold between 1841 and 1901, and concert attendance surged as the century progressed.[1] As consumption of music became more widespread, the publication of music periodicals increased exponentially: about two hundred new titles were introduced during the nineteenth century.[2] Some lasted only a few months, while others, such as the *Musical Times* (1844–) and the *Strad* (1890–), are still producing issues in the twenty-first century.

Following a tradition established in the late seventeenth century, some early nineteenth-century music periodicals consisted solely of music issued serially. The music appearing in these collections sometimes cannot be found elsewhere, making these publications important for those interested in recovering music of the period.[3] Although popular in the eighteenth century, this type of music periodical fell out of favor in the nineteenth century as the demand for musical knowledge and information grew.[4] To meet this demand, some publishers appended relevant literature to their music serials. By the 1820s, enough of an audience for text-only music periodicals existed to make a journal like the *Quarterly Musical Magazine and Review* (1818–30) successful. However, the desire to reach a wider audience led many publishers to combine literature and music in journals with musical supplements that could be

---

1. According to census figures reprinted in Ehrlich, 6,600 people classified themselves musicians and music teachers in 1841, compared with 39,300 in 1901 (*Music*, 236). See chapter 2 of Weber's *Music and the Middle Class* for a discussion of the explosion in the number of concerts between 1830 and 1848.
2. Langley, "Music," 99. Fellinger et al.'s entry on "Periodicals" in *Grove Music Online* lists 205 music periodicals published in Great Britain between 1800 and 1899.
3. Langley, "Music," 105.
4. Langley, "English Musical Journal," 47. For more on music periodicals consisting solely of music, see Krummel, "Searching."

detached and used separately.[5] These two formats, text-only and text with a musical supplement, remained dominant throughout the century.

Music periodicals were published by music publishers and musical organizations, as well as by independent publishers. For music publishers such as Augener, Boosey, Chappel, Cook, Novello, and Wessel and Stapleton, journals functioned as a marketing tool that enabled them to promote their music and books through advertisements and supplemental sheet music, while at the same time encouraging subscribers to consider what else was in their catalogue. Some journals were aligned with certain musical institutions or advocated for a particular point in a musical controversy. For example, the *Monthly Magazine of Music* (1823) supported the newly founded and somewhat contentious Royal Academy of Music, while the *Musical Magazine* (1835) was the organ of the Society of British Musicians.[6] Music journal editors often had other agendas as well, such as educating the public or promoting the compositions of native-born composers.[7]

In addition to periodicals that covered British musical life broadly, special-interest journals were abundant. These periodicals responded to and capitalized on musical currents such as the brass band movement; increased interest in certain instruments, like the violin or banjo; certain types of music production, such as choirs, organs, and orchestras; and particular locations of music production, including school music and music halls. Musicology journals, such as the *Proceedings of the Royal Musical Association* (1874–1944), emerged in the last quarter of the century with the consolidation of musicology as a discipline.[8]

Readers of music periodicals ran the gamut from amateurs to music professionals, from those whose interest in music and musical tastes was developing to those with cosmopolitan and cultivated tastes. According to Leanne Langley, until 1870 there were two types of general-interest music periodicals, "one for the public, or amateur practitioners wanting instruction, guidance, and encouragement . . . and another for the profession—teachers, scholars, tradespeople—who wanted history, comment, and lots of news."[9] This distinction between readerships dissolved in the 1870s as the two groups and their interests became more uniform.[10]

Music periodicals usually included articles on music history, biography, and (for those with a more professional readership) music theory, as well as correspondence, foreign and domestic news, and reviews of new compositions and musical performances. Those aimed at amateurs, such as the *Musical Times* (1844–), *Tonic Sol-Fa Reporter* (1851–1920), *Minim* (1893–1902), or *Magazine of Music* (1884–97), often included articles on music appreciation and instruction, which could range from "How to Play Scales" to "Mozart's Sonatas and How to

---

5. Langley, "English Musical Journal," 51, 53.
6. Ibid., 63.
7. See Johnson-Hill, "Miscellany and Collegiality," and Hughes, *English Musical Renaissance*, on the didactic intent of the *Harmonicon* and *Musical Times*. Hughes's *English Musical Renaissance* and Langley's "English Musical Journal" argue that journals such as the *Musical Journal* and *Musical Times* advocated for British musicians.
8. Fellinger et al., "Periodicals."
9. Langley, "Music," 101.
10. Ibid.

Play Them."[11] Many journals distributed new music through supplements of sheet music, and some, such as the *Magazine of Music, Violin Times* (1893–1907), and *Strad* (1890–) carried fiction with musical themes.

Two of the earliest influential music periodicals were the *Quarterly Musical Magazine and Review* (1818–28) and the *Harmonicon* (1823–33). Both ran for ten years, an extraordinary length of time considering that most music journals during this period had much shorter runs. Indeed, the approximately thirty new music journals launched during the early decades of the century lasted an average of two years and four months.[12] The *Quarterly Musical Magazine and Review* was founded by Richard Mackenzie Bacon, a Norwich journalist and music critic who served as editor-in-chief and wrote most of the material himself, although his daughters Louisa Mary and Mary Anne served as editorial assistants. Modeled after the *Edinburgh Review* and the *Allgemeine musikalische Zeitung*, it was the first music journal to consist solely of writing about music. The goal of the magazine was to "raise the standards of musical education in Britain by setting criteria for the writing of didactic musical treatises and by providing a forum for discussion on the training of professional musicians."[13] The *Quarterly Musical Magazine and Review* contained biographical sketches of composers and performers as well as articles on acoustics, music theory, music history, musical instruments, performance practice, musical pedagogy, and Anglican church music. It reviewed British and Continental music performances, music, and books on music for an audience of educated amateurs and professionals.[14]

The *Harmonicon* (1823–33), a monthly magazine edited and written largely by William Ayerton, also had a didactic intent, an international scope, and a similar range of readers. Issues included biographies of composers, essays on music history or aesthetics, English and foreign musical news, announcements of concerts and operas, reviews of new music and concerts, and reprinted articles in translation from Continental journals. While the *Harmonicon* was directed at educated readers, its vocal and instrumental music supplements were aimed at amateurs and consisted of a variety of current musical styles and works by popular composers.[15]

The next important journal to emerge was the *Musical World* (1836–91), the first music periodical to be published weekly. It was founded in 1836 by music publisher J. Alfred Novello, who sold it the following year. After a rapid turnover of editors and publishers during its first decade, J. W. Davison took the helm in 1843 and remained editor until his death in 1885. The journal included critical essays on music performance, history, and theory; reviews of opera, concerts, provincial festivals, and English musical life; editorials on musical issues of the day; and the annual reports of music institutions such as the Philharmonic Society, the Society of British Musicians, and the Sacred Harmonic Society. Under Davison's editorship, *Musical World*

---

11. M.L.W., "How to Play Scales"; "Mozart's Sonatas and How to Play Them."
12. Langley, "Life and Death," 137.
13. Kassler, *Science of Music*, 1239.
14. Information on the *Quarterly Musical Magazine and Review* drawn from Kassler, *Science of Music*; Kitson, "*Quarterly Musical*"; and Langley, "English Musical Journal." For a list of other contributors to the journal, see Kassler, *Science of Music*, 1239–40.
15. Information on the *Harmonicon* drawn from Johnson-Hill, "Miscellany and Collegiality"; Kassler, *Science of Music*; Langley "Life and Death"; and Snigurowicz, "*Harmonicon*."

championed English opera as well as certain composers in the Germanic tradition, such as Mendelssohn, Spohr, and Sterndale Bennett, while others such as Schumann, Schubert, Verdi, and Wagner received its censure. It included music supplements for one year—1846.[16]

The *Musical World*'s strongest competitor at mid-century was the *Musical Times and Singing Class Circular*. Its forerunner, *Mainzer's Musical Times and Singing Class Circular* (1842–44), was purchased by the Novello publishing firm in 1844, and J. Alfred Novello became its editor under the new title. Published monthly and directed at an amateur audience, the journal originally focused on singing but expanded its coverage over the course of the century to include all aspects of British musical life. Its main concerns, however, were oratorio and choral music, along with English and Continental composers working in this genre. Foreign musical news was not introduced until 1877; other late additions to its pages included reviews of opera and instrumental music as well as letters to the editor. Its music supplements consisted of vocal music, predominantly choral arrangements with piano or organ accompaniment. The *Musical Times* had six editors during the course of the century, most notably Mary Cowden Clarke (Novello's sister), who served from 1853 to 1856, and Henry Charles Lunn, who expanded the journal's breadth and intellectual depth during his tenure from 1863 to 1887.[17]

Other important music titles that appeared at mid-century include the *Tonic Sol-fa Reporter*, *Musical Standard*, *Monthly Musical Record*, and *Musical Opinion and Trade Review*. The *Tonic Sol-fa Reporter* was renamed the *Musical Herald and Tonic Sol-fa Reporter* in 1889 and finally became the *Musical Herald* in 1891. Published by John Curwen and Sons, it promoted John Curwen's notation method of teaching singing, which had nationwide success. Directed at amateur singers and enthusiasts, the journal included lessons, news about tonic sol-fa groups in Great Britain, popular biography, and the occasional historical article. Its musical supplements included choral pieces written in tonic sol-fa notation.[18]

The *Musical Standard* (1862–1933) was one of the few journals not issued by a music publisher or a musical organization, and as a result it claimed to be "unfettered by clique, and narrowed by no party bias."[19] Aimed at Anglican Church musicians and knowledgeable amateurs, the journal focused on organs, organ music, choral festivals, and other matters related to church music, as well as items of broader interest, including reviews of a range of books, musical events, and published music; it also featured musical news from Great Britain, Europe, and North America. Musical supplements became a regular feature of the magazine after 1867.[20]

The *Monthly Musical Record* (1871–1960), published by Augener and Co., included scholarly articles on music history and criticism as well as reviews of British and European music and musical events. While the journal leaned toward German music and musicians, it also favorably reviewed compositions by native-born composers. Its music analyses, articles on keyboard

---

16. Information on the *Musical World* is drawn from Kitson, "*Musical World*," and Langley, "Music." See Kitson's "*Musical World*" for a list of its contributors.
17. Information on the *Musical Times* is drawn from Clinkscale, "*Musical Times*"; Cooper, *House of Novello*; Fellinger et al., "Periodicals"; and Langley, "Music."
18. Information on the *Tonic Sol-fa Reporter* is drawn from Langley, "Music," and McGuire, "Edward Elgar."
19. "Musical Standard," 1.
20. Information on the *Musical Standard* is drawn from Langley, "Music," and Snigurowicz, "*Musical Standard*."

teaching methods, and correspondence contributed to its wide appeal; musical supplements were added as a feature in 1880.[21] The *Musical Opinion and Trade Review* (1877–) was created to meet the needs of those involved in the commercial aspects of music production—music publishers and instrument manufacturers. It focused on news of interest to those in the trade, including patents, copyright, legislation, advertisements, musical inventions, performance rights, court decisions, new instruments, and new music. The journal gradually expanded to include topics of more general interest, such as historical and educational matters and reviews of provincial festivals, but offered little musical analysis.[22]

In the last decades of the nineteenth century, new titles proliferated as interest and access to music became more widespread. The *Minim: A Musical Magazine for Everybody* was one of several new journals that attempted to appeal to a broad audience—in this case, the "student, amateur or professional"—with biographies; musical news; articles on music appreciation and instruction; reviews of performances in London and the provinces; reports from the Royal Academy of Music, the Royal College of Music, and university music programs; and the occasional fictional piece.[23] It also included music supplements on an irregular basis.

The expanding audience for music periodicals also meant an increased market for specialized journals. For example, the periodical press responded to the banjo craze of the 1880s and 1890s with new titles such as the *Banjo World: A Journal Devoted to the Banjo, Mandoline, and Guitar* (1893–1917); *Jo: A Chronicle of Banjo, Guitar, and Mandoline News* (1895–1915), which was renamed the *Troubadour* in 1896; and *B.M.G.: A Journal Devoted to Banjo, Mandoline, and Guitar* (1903–76). Another popular instrument to inspire competing magazines was the violin. Several violin journals were introduced at the end of the century, including the *Fiddler* (1884–88), *Violin* (1889), *Violin Monthly Magazine* (1889–94), *Violin Times*, and *Strings* (1894–98). The most important of these was the *Strad: A Monthly Journal for Professionals and Amateurs of all Stringed Instruments played with the Bow*, which courted an international readership.[24] It included articles on the history of the violin, violin manufacture and performance; advice on purchasing an instrument; and biographies, fiction, reviews, and concert news.[25]

As this brief overview suggests, music periodicals reflect the development of musical culture during the century, including the expanded audience for music and literature about music and the development of increasingly sophisticated and diverse musical tastes. In addition, they reflect the wide range of interests within the field of music—such as choral societies, amateur singing, church music, trade news, particular instruments, and the work of English composers. More extensive descriptive lists of nineteenth-century music periodicals can be found in Imogen Fellinger et al.'s entry on periodicals in *Grove Music Online*; appendix C of Jamie Kassler's *The Science of Music in Britain, 1714–1830*; volume two of Langley's dissertation,

---

21. Information on the *Monthly Musical Record* is drawn from Fellinger et al., "Periodicals"; Hughes, *English Musical Renaissance*; and Langley, "Music."
22. Information on the *Musical Opinion and Trade Review* is drawn from Coover, *Music*, and Langley, "Music."
23. "Introduction," 7.
24. Bashford notes that *Strad* opened publishing offices in the United States, Canada, Australia, New Zealand, South Africa, and Germany in the 1890s and the first decade of the 1900s ("Hidden Agendas," 25).
25. Information on *Strad* drawn from Bashford, "Hidden Agendas," and Langley, "Music."

"A Descriptive Catalogue of English Periodicals Containing Musical Literature, 1665–1845," and her chapter on "Music" in *Victorian Periodicals and Victorian Society*. Additionally, the *Retrospective Index to Music Periodicals* offers online access to an international selection of nineteenth- and twentieth-century music periodicals. The site provides an annotated calendar as well as keyword and author indexes for several nineteenth-century British periodicals, and its online archive contains full-text digitized reproductions of more than one hundred music periodicals of the period, including half a dozen British titles.

Current State of Research

Research on music periodicals published in the past three decades has focused on three areas: studies of individual periodicals, analyses of specific cultural issues, and historical documentation of musical events and attitudes. Leanne Langley was one of the first scholars to devote serious attention to the study of nineteenth-century British music periodicals. Her 1983 doctoral dissertation, "The English Musical Journal in the Early Nineteenth Century," gives an overview of the early history of music periodicals to 1845 and provides in-depth analysis of the two most prominent journals of the early nineteenth century, the *Harmonicon* and the *Quarterly Musical Magazine and Review*. In 1990, the musicology journal *Notes* published an issue devoted to nineteenth-century British music periodicals. Langley's contribution to this issue, "The Musical Press in Nineteenth-Century England," gives a concise overview of music journalism in general, and music periodicals in particular, arguing for their importance to music historians. D.W. Krummel's contribution to the special issue, "Searching and Sorting on the Slippery Slope: Periodical Publication of Victorian Music," offers a rumination on the difficulty of cataloguing music periodicals and includes a select list of periodicals containing only sheet music and those with music supplements published from the eighteenth to the early twentieth century. James Coover rounds out the issue with "Victorian Periodicals for the Music Trade," an examination of two journals aimed at music professionals, the *London and Provincial Music Trades Review* and the *Musical Opinion and Trade Review*.

Since 1990, scholarship has expanded, considering music periodicals as a subject and as an historical resource. Several studies provide sustained analysis of individual music journals, focusing largely on the economics, personalities, intended readership, and musical movements associated with particular journals. The early and influential *Harmonicon* has been the subject of several articles. For example, Langley analyzes the commercial history of this journal in "The Life and Death of *The Harmonicon*: An Analysis." Drawing on publishing firm data, she argues that the journal failed after ten years and multiple restarts because its content, a mismatch between highbrow articles and popular music, made establishing a stable audience difficult. However, Erin Johnson-Hill contends in "Miscellany and Collegiality in the British Periodical Press: The *Harmonicon* (1823–1833)" that the journal's demise corresponded with the rise of specialized concert genres and an emerging hierarchy of musical taste. She argues that the *Harmonicon*'s didactic intent and its coverage of a wide variety of musical genres in articles and supplemental sheet music made it appeal to a broad readership and allowed it to achieve economic success in the years before musical taste became more compartmentalized. Beth Shamgar examines contemporary debates about harmony in her survey of the journal's reviews of new compositions in "Perceptions of Stylistic Change: A Study of the Reviews of New Music in the *Harmonicon* (1823–1833)."

Not surprisingly, given its longevity, the *Musical Times* has also received a good deal of critical attention. Percy Scholes traces the development of musical culture in England through the lens of the *Musical Times* in *The Mirror of Music 1844–1944*, written to commemorate the one-hundredth anniversary of the journal. While Scholes does not engage in critical commentary, his book offers a good sense of the range of topics covered by the *Musical Times*. In his article published on the 125th anniversary of the journal, Nicholas Temperley provides a more scholarly overview of the history, content, and intended audience of the magazine in its first thirty years. Meirion Hughes devotes a chapter of *The English Musical Renaissance and the Press 1850–1914: Watchmen of Music* to the *Musical Times*, analyzing the role music journalism played in promoting new English music in the second half of the century. He ties the renaissance in national music at this time to the expansion of journalism and the support of particular journalists. In her study of the Novello publishing firm, *The House of Novello: Practice and Policy of a Victorian Music Publisher, 1829–1866*, Victoria Cooper compares the *Musical Times* with several other contemporary music and fine arts journals to demonstrate that its publisher and editor, J. Alfred Novello, was courting a readership of amateur musicians. In "'Le roi est mort, vive le roi': Languages and Leadership in Niecks's Liszt Obituary," Anne Widén provides an analysis of a specific *Musical Times* article, Frederick Niecks's 1886 obituary of Franz Liszt.

Only a handful of other journals have received this kind of analysis. In "Novello's 'Neue Zeitschrift': 1883, Francis Hueffer and *The Musical Review*," Langley examines the politics and personalities behind the short-lived *Musical Review*, a weekly magazine published by Novello that was aimed at a more cultivated readership than its other publication, the *Musical Times*. Focusing on a group of specialist journals, Christina Bashford, in "Hidden Agendas and the Creation of Community," surveys violin magazines that originated between 1884 and 1914 in response to a growing interest in the instrument, focusing on the economics and individuals behind the two most successful, the *Strad* and the *Violin Times*. In "British Brass Band Periodicals and the Construction of a Movement," Denise Odello investigates how periodicals that emerged in the 1880s, such as *British Band News* and *British Bandsman*, promoted the development of the brass band movement, shaped its performance practices, and recorded its history.

Some scholars have centered their examination of a particular cultural issue within the context of a specific journal. For example, James Coover's studies of the *Musical Opinion and Music Trade Review* and *London and Provincial Music Trades Review* trace the response of the music publishing industry to the piracy of sheet music. He also demonstrates how these journals can be useful for dating music editions and tracking firms which changed names through partnerships or went out of business.[26] Kieran Daly's study of the Cecilian reform movement in liturgical music in the Irish Catholic Church between 1878 and 1903 relies primarily on the *Lyra Ecclesiastica: Monthly Bulletin of the Irish Society of St. Cecilia and List of Catholic Church Music*. Patricia O'Hara examines the tension between visual images of female music hall performers and the reviews and feature articles that focus on their proper femininity in the *Music Hall and*

---

26. See Coover, *Music Publishing* and "Victorian Periodicals."

Theatre Review in the 1890s. And in *Representing Non-Western Music in Nineteenth-Century Britain*, Bennett Zon surveys evolving attitudes toward non-Western music in several music periodicals published between the 1830s and the 1930s.

However, most scholarship that engages with music periodicals uses them as historical documents which provide facts, opinions, and cultural context for understanding the musical events and concerns of the period. Musicologists and social historians have recognized the importance of music periodicals as a source for investigating a variety of topics, including the Novello publishing firm; the reception of published music; music critic J.W. Davison; the relationship between professional and amateur musicians; composers, such as Mendelsshon and Elgar; performance venues such as the Crystal Palace and provincial music festivals; performers, performances, audiences, and musical societies; and instruments, such as the concertina, violin, and banjo.[27]

Of course, music and musical events were also reported in the general press, and important music journalism appeared in general periodicals, from daily newspapers to quarterly reviews. Some of the more notable critics included George Hogarth, who wrote for the *Daily News*; J.W. Davison, music critic for *The Times* and editor of the *Musical World*; Joseph Bennett, who covered music for the *Daily Telegraph*; Henry F. Chorley, music critic for the *Athenaeum*; George Grove, founder of the *Grove Dictionary of Music and Musicians*, who edited and provided music criticism for *Macmillan's Magazine*; Francis Heuffer and J.A. Fuller Maitland, who covered music for *The Times*; and George Bernard Shaw, whose music criticism appeared in several periodicals. For a review of important early nineteenth-century music criticism, Langley's dissertation remains indispensable. Meirion Hughes discusses the music journalism of Davison, Bennett, and Chorley in *The English Musical Renaissance and the Press*. For an overview of music criticism appearing in *Macmillan's Magazine* during George Grove's editorship (1868–83), see Ann Parry, Rosemary T. VanArsdel, and Ruth Solie. Robert Terrell Bledsoe and Christine Kyprianides survey the treatment of music in *Household Words* and *All the Year Round*, and Sarah McNeely focuses on three female musicians who contributed music journalism to the *Lady's Newspaper*, the *Girl's Own Paper*, and the *Woman's Signal*. In "Italian Opera and the English Press, 1836–56," Langley surveys the reception of Italian opera in sixteen periodicals, one of which is a music journal.

Future Research

Despite increased scholarly attention to music periodicals in the last fifteen years, much remains to be explored. Christina Bashford notes that the "need to investigate periodicals

---

27. For composers, see Eatock, "Crystal Palace Concerts" and *Mendelssohn*; McGuire, "Edward Elgar." For performers and performances, see de Val, "Legitimate"; Davis, "Dancing the Symphonic"; Eatock, "Crystal Palace Concerts"; Richards, *Imperialism and Music*; and Wilson Kimber, "Mr Riddle's Readings." For performance venues, see Musgrave, *Musical Life*, and Drummond, *Provincial Music Festival*. For audiences and instruments, see Hall-Witt, "Representing the Audience"; Gillett, *Musical Women*; and Vorachek, "Whitewashing." For music publishers and published music, see Palmer, *Vincent Novello*; Horton, "British Vocal Album"; Richards, *Imperialism and Music*; and Pelkey, "Music, Memory." For music critics, see Kitson, "James William Davison." For musical societies and relationships between professional and amateur musicians and audiences, see Ehrlich, *First Philharmonic*, and Gillett, "Ambivalent Friendships."

systematically or contextually has been resisted by scholars of nineteenth-century British music, despite the importance—easily demonstrated in other disciplines—of the value of periodicals research for grown-up history."[28] Musicologists are not the only scholars who have neglected this rich source of information on nineteenth-century musical culture. Music journals can provide insight into musical production and consumption by both amateurs and professionals, providing details on what music they were playing and on what instruments, as well as where they performed—whether in concert halls, music halls, private "at homes," or on the street. They can illuminate musical currents, such as the English musical renaissance or the vogue for certain instruments, and they can shed light on publishing practices for a specialized market.

More studies of individual periodicals are needed that extend beyond the *Harmonicon* and *Musical Times*, paying close attention to their content, readers, editors, publishers, contributors, and commercial histories. Additionally, one might consider how music periodicals responded to the New Journalism or other journalistic or social trends. More attention to specialist journals focused on a single instrument or specific aspect of nineteenth-century musical culture would also be welcome. For example, one might consider how the concert news and repertoire promoted in brass band periodicals created a sense of community among participants. Alternatively, analysis of the performers, attractions, halls, and programs in periodicals such as *Musician and Music Hall Times*, *Music Hall Artiste Association Gazette*, *Music Halls' Gazette*, and *Musical Hall and Theatre Review* could give insight into the social forces that shaped the evolution of the music hall in the nineteenth century. The periodical literature generated in response to these important aspects of nineteenth-century musical history has much to tell us.

There is also a dearth of scholarship on nineteenth-century music criticism, as Meirion Hughes has noted. Further work is needed to identify the names of the critics who reviewed music and musical events.[29] Christopher Kent provides a starting point in his two-part list of drama, music, and art critics publishing between 1830 and 1914 in the general periodical press, but no such list for music periodicals exists.[30] Moreover, Kent's work indicates that critics often reviewed for multiple publications, suggesting cross-currents of influence in music journalism worth further exploration. Did critics frame their reviews of the same event differently for different audiences?

Studies of the sheet music distributed in individual magazines or across multiple periodicals are also needed. Johnson-Hill has begun this effort by examining the music supplements in the *Harmonicon*, focusing on the nationality and prominence of composers and the accessibility of the music. This analysis is conducted in the service of her larger point about the miscellaneous nature of the magazine rather than to make a sustained argument about the music itself. For an example of a more in-depth investigation, one might look at Bonny H. Miller's survey of the

---

28. Bashford, "Hidden Agendas," 13.
29. Hughes, *English Musical Renaissance*, 1.
30. His lists include only three critics for music journals: Edward Algernon Baughan, who covered music for the *Musical Standard* in 1909; Havergal Brian, who reviewed the Hallé concerts for the *Musical World* in 1905; and Henry C. Lunn, who covered provincial festivals while editor of the *Musical Times* between 1863 and 1887.

repertory of music published in non-music periodicals, including *Young Ladies' Journal*, *Girl's Own Paper*, *Studio*, and *Quarto*. Bibliographies like Fellinger's *Periodica Musicalia*, which indexes more than two hundred European and British music periodicals between 1798 and 1830, and Krummel's select list of periodicals containing only sheet music and those with music supplements are another place to begin.

Music journal publishers have also been largely overlooked. To date, Langley and Coover offer the only ventures into this area of music periodical history. Langley's "The Use of Private Papers, Correspondence, and Archives of the Publishing Trade in British Music Periodicals Research" indicates the importance of manuscript sources for providing context on the business side of music periodicals and serves as a finding aid for some early nineteenth-century manuscript materials. In "William Reeves, Booksellers/Publishers," Coover provides a history of the William Reeves publishing house, which published music and music periodicals including the *Musical Standard* from 1862 to 1875, and briefly published the *Strad* and the *Orchestra*.

Scholars also would do well to widen their selection of music periodicals when using them as historical documents. Currently, scholars rely predominantly on the *Musical Times* and *Musical World* and, to a lesser extent, on the *Harmonicon*, *Musical Examiner*, *Musical Herald*, and *Quarterly Musical Magazine and Review*. Given the wealth and range of music periodicals from this period, casting a wider net that includes journals with different audiences or editorial policies would draw a broader spectrum of opinion on particular works, individuals, or musical events. Increased research on individual periodicals as well as on music criticism, supplemental sheet music, and music publishers would contribute to our understanding of both nineteenth-century periodical culture and the period's musical culture. Music periodicals are an important and underutilized source for assessing the broader cultural impact of music and musical movements in the nineteenth century.

CHRONOLOGY OF THE NINETEENTH-CENTURY PERIODICAL PRESS

Gary Simons

Not wishing to duplicate the timelines in this volume or those available in works such as Brake and Demoor's *Dictionary of Nineteenth-Century Journalism* or Griffiths's *Encyclopedia of the British Press*, this chronology reflects material contained in this volume and in the back issues of *Victorian Periodicals Review*. It thus references an eclectic selection of periodicals, publishers, editors, and contributors, including less well-known but culturally revealing titles as well as more specialized or ephemeral publications.

Year	Periodical Press
1800	The *Young Gentleman and Lady's Magazine* (1799–1800), an early periodical advocating for women's education, ceases publication.
1801	Provincial weekly papers publish an average of two poems per week, totaling about 10,000 poems annually.
1802	The *Edinburgh Review* (1802–1929), a prestigious, Whig-oriented journal, begins publication.
1803	Sir Richard Phillips, along with John Murray and other London booksellers, founds the *Globe* newspaper to promote the book industry.
1804	The extensive journalistic career of Leigh Hunt begins with "Mr. Town, Jr., Critic and Censor-general," published in the *Traveller*.
1805	Religious dissenters found the *Eclectic Review* (1805–68) to review works of literature, history, theology, politics, science, art, and philosophy.
1806	*La Belle Assemblée* (1806–32), an early women's magazine featuring mathematical and scientific articles as well as reviews of serious literature, begins publication.
1807	The *Oxford Review* (1807–08) is founded but soon fails, partially because it fraudulently claims to have university ties; ten years later the Attic Society publishes a second *Oxford Review*.
1808	Leigh and John Hunt found the *Examiner* (1808–81), a weekly journal espousing radical principles and covering politics, literature, and theater.
1809	During the tenure of its first editor, William Gifford, from 1809 to 1824, the pro-Tory *Quarterly Review* becomes a leading literary periodical.
1810	George Helmbold, in the *Tickler*, a Philadelphia comic paper, writes of Lord Holland, "What a *Cracker*!"
1811	In the *Edinburgh Review*, Francis Jeffrey approvingly reviews Archibald Alison's book *Essays on the Nature and Principles of Taste*, which judges fine art by its train of associations.
1812	New leadership reestablishes the *British Critic* as an organ of the High Church party.

Year	Periodical Press
1813	The *Museum Criticum, or Cambridge Classical Researches* (1813–26) typifies English classical scholarship with linguistic analysis of Greek texts.
1814	Henry Colburn begins the *New Monthly Magazine*, stressing current events and politics, but he soon shifts its emphasis to literature. The *Times* utilizes a steam-powered Koenig cylinder press which can produce 1,000 copies per hour.
1815	In the *Eclectic Review*, James Montgomery contends that Wordsworth's "The Excursion" confuses God with nature. The stamp tax is instituted to curb the proliferation of radical publications.
1816	The *Anti-Jacobin Review* first uses the word "conservative" in an adjectival political sense; later, the *Quarterly Review* (1830) suggests "Tory" should be replaced by "Conservative." William Hazlitt begins to write art criticism for the *Examiner*.
1817	*Blackwood's Edinburgh Magazine* (1817–1980) combines Tory politics, poetry, reviews, and original fiction.
1818	*Blackwood's Edinburgh Magazine* publishes John Lockhart's vitriolic attacks on John Keats and the "Cockney School of Poetry." The *Quarterly Musical Magazine and Review* begins publication.
1819	The inaugural issue of the *Missionary Herald*, a representative missionary periodical, appears. The Newspaper and Stamp Duties Act increases the taxes on newspapers, periodicals, and pamphlets.
1820	Richard Carlile writes for the controversial working-class *Republican* "with an abridged Johnson, Fenning's Spelling Book, an Oxford Encyclopaedia and two copies of the Bible" by his side. The *Literary Gazette* publishes its first poem by Letitia Elizabeth Landon (L.E.L.).
1821	Thomas De Quincey publishes *Confessions of an English Opium-Eater* in the *London Magazine*.
1822	*Blackwood's Edinburgh Magazine* begins publishing the *Noctes Ambrosianae* (1822–35), an innovative series of imaginary literary conversations. The *Law Gazette* (1822–1847), one of the earliest specialist legal periodicals, is founded.
1823	Popular articles by William Hazlitt (*London Magazine*) and Peter George Patmore (*New Monthly Magazine*) foster public awareness of fine art. The *Mechanics' Magazine, Lancet*, and other periodicals utilize wood engraving to produce illustrations economically.
1824	In the new *Westminster Review*, John Stuart Mill declares that periodicals themselves should be subject to systematic criticism. Two children's magazines, the *Children's Friend* and the *Child's Companion; or, Sunday Scholar's Reward* begin publication.
1825	The *Spirit of the Times* (1825–26), an illustrated digest, concentrates "all that is worthy of being preserved from the whole of our periodical literature."
1826	Cambridge students nicknamed the "Apostles" contribute to the short-lived but meritorious *Metropolitan Quarterly Magazine* (1825–26).
1827	C.M. Westmacott assumes control of an ultra-Tory weekly, the *Age* (1825–43) and solicits money from individuals to suppress stories of their scandals.
1828	The *Athenaeum* (1828–1921), arguably the era's leading weekly literary review, struggles at its inception.
1829	In *Blackwood's Edinburgh Magazine* William Johnston makes the case for paternalism.
1830	During the 1830s, *Fraser's Magazine* (1830–1882), under the flamboyant leadership of William Maginn, assumes a central and often outrageous role in political commentary and literary criticism.
1831	The *Poor Man's Guardian* (1831–35), a penny weekly radical newspaper, advocates for the working classes arming themselves against authority.

(Continued)

(Continued)

Year	Periodical Press
1832	Provincial newspapers disseminate the speeches of leaders of political unions and put pressure on Parliament to enact the 1832 Reform Act. The weekly *Chambers's (Edinburgh) Journal* (1832–1956) and the *Penny Magazine* (1832–45) introduce "improving literature" for mass consumption.
1833	Harriet Martineau's "The Achievements of the Genius of Scott" is published in *Tait's Edinburgh Magazine*. Thomas Carlyle's *Sartor Resartus* begins serial publication in *Fraser's Magazine*.
1834	George Walker initiates the first long-running column on chess in a Sunday newspaper, *Bell's Life in London* (1822–1886).
1835	*Cleave's Weekly Police Gazette* (1834–36), a working-class unstamped newspaper, mixes radical politics, sensational crime news, and popular fiction. The *Star of Temperance* (1835–36) recommends abstinence from alcoholic beverages.
1836	*Fraser's Magazine* caricatures Michael Faraday as part of an 1830–38 series of eighty-one portraits of editors, authors, politicians, scientists, explorers, and other figures of note. The duties on pamphlets and almanacs are eliminated, and the duties on paper, advertisements, and newspapers are reduced substantially.
1837	The series "Hints on Reading. To a Young Lady" in the *Christian Lady's Magazine* warns about the dangers of reading fiction.
1838	As editor of *Bentley's Miscellany*, 1837–39, Charles Dickens promotes the magazine, but his editorship ends when he comes into conflict with Richard Bentley. John Henry Newman utilizes the *British Critic* to promote debates about the Church of England.
1839	Samuel Carter Hall initiates the *Art Journal* (originally the *Art-Union*) (1839–1912), a preeminent British art journal. The *Citizen* (1839–1843), an Irish nationalist periodical, begins publication in Dublin.
1840	Newspaper stamp reports provide circulation figures for *The Times*, *Morning Chronicle*, *Morning Herald*, *Morning Post*, *Evening Mail*, and *Evening Chronicle*.
1841	*Punch* (1841–2002), the iconic humor magazine, begins publication; it soon becomes a cultural landmark.
1842	The age of modern illustrated journalism begins with the launching of the *Illustrated London News* (1843–1989). The Copyright Act increases the minimum period of protection on intellectual property to forty-two years.
1843	The *Zoist: A Journal of Cerebral Physiology and Mesmerism, and Their Application to Human Welfare* (1843–56) supports phrenology and hypnotism. Elizabeth Barrett Browning's "The Cry of the Children," a protest against the conditions of child labor, is published in *Blackwood's Edinburgh Magazine*.
1844	A review of J.M.W. Turner's works in the *Athenaeum* claims that it is difficult to appreciate his use of chaos and unorthodox color. G.W.M. Reynolds's penny weekly serial, *The Mysteries of London*, begins.
1845	Anna Jameson's series, "Essays on the Lives of Remarkable Painters" (1843–45), completes its run in the *Penny Magazine* (1832–46), published by the Society for the Diffusion of Useful Knowledge.
1846	William Thackeray's series of comical character studies, "The Snobs of England," appears in *Punch*. *Mitchell's*, the first annual newspaper press directory for advertisers, is published.
1847	G.H. Lewes argues in *Fraser's Magazine* that periodical literature has made authorship a viable profession. The weekly *Lady's Newspaper* (1847–63) provides news for women.
1848	Eva O'Doherty's address "To the Women of Ireland" in the *Nation*, asserts the propriety of women taking up arms in the cause of Irish independence. The *Rambler* (1842–68) is founded as an organ of (relatively) liberal Roman Catholic thought.

Year	Periodical Press
1849	The *Morning Chronicle* begins a series of articles by Henry Mayhew, "London Labour and the London Poor," which expose the horrors of working-class urban life.
1850	*Reynolds's Weekly Newspaper* (1850–1967) is founded as a pro-Chartist newspaper that mixes radicalism with sensationalism.
1851	John Leech's engraving in *Punch*, "This is the Boy who Chalked up 'No Popery' and then Ran Away," highlights the fervor over the so-called "Papal Aggression." Applegarth's vertical rotary press is displayed at the Great Exhibition in cooperation with *The Times* and the *Illustrated London News*.
1852	Samuel Beeton inaugurates the *Englishwoman's Domestic Magazine* (1852–79), which focuses on middle-class domestic issues, fashion, and fiction.
1853	The eight main departments of the *Leader* (1850–60) are "News of the Week," "Public Affairs," "The Leader," "Open Council," "Literature," "Portfolio," "The Arts," and "Commercial Affairs."
1854	Margaret Oliphant begins her long career with *Blackwood's Edinburgh Magazine*. Tennyson's "Charge of the Light Brigade" is published in the *Examiner*.
1855	Samuel Beeton launches the *Boy's Own Magazine*, which includes scientific articles and lively fiction. The penny stamp is abolished as an obligatory duty on newspapers.
1856	George Augustus Sala's twenty-two descriptive sketches of Russian everyday life appear in *Household Words* as travel writing by a "special correspondent." George Eliot's "Silly Novels by Lady Novelists," published in the *Westminster Review*, argues for higher standards for women's fiction.
1857	The Irish *Nation* supports the Great Mutiny; the daily Dublin *Freeman's Journal* supports British imperialism.
1858	The *English Woman's Journal* (1858–64) is founded. The main London dailies outsource much of their overseas news gathering to Reuters.
1859	W.H. Wills and Dickens transition from *Household Words* to *All the Year Round*. One of the first serials to appear in their new magazine is Wilkie Collins's *The Woman in White*.
1860	The *Cornhill Magazine* (1860–1975), one of the era's most successful literary magazines, begins with fiction serials by Thackeray and Trollope. *Good Words* (1860–1911) illuminates poetry's role in devotional culture.
1861	Sheridan Le Fanu purchases *Dublin University Magazine* and uses it as a vehicle for his own supernatural stories.
1862	*Macmillan's Magazine* publishes poems by Caroline Norton, one of its many celebrated female contributors.
1863	George du Maurier illustrates M.E. Braddon's sensation novel, *Eleanor's Victory*, which is serialized in *Once a Week* (1859–80).
1864	The *Cornhill Magazine* serializes Elizabeth Gaskell's novel *Wives and Daughters*, 1864–66.
1865	The *Fortnightly Review* (1865–1954), edited by G.H. Lewes, introduces Continental ideas and forms which challenge the conventions of British periodicals. *Bow Bells* (1862–1897), a hybrid of the family magazine and women's magazine, claims a circulation of 200,000.
1866	The *Englishwoman's Review of Social and Industrial Questions* (1866–1910) provides information, inspiration, and direction for the Victorian women's movement.
1867	Anne Thackeray's realist reinterpretations of fairy tales (1866–74) in the *Cornhill Magazine* foreground contemporary social iniquities.
1868	Eliza Lynn Linton's anti-feminist essay "The Girl of the Period" appears in the *Saturday Review*.

(Continued)

(Continued)

Year	Periodical Press
1869	In "Arguing with Women," the *Saturday Review* contends that a "man arguing with a woman is at a fatal disadvantage. Neither the weapons nor the laws of combat are equal." The *Fortnightly Review* publishes a debate between novelist Anthony Trollope and historian Edward Augustus Freeman on manliness.
1870	(Vickers') *Boy's Journal* (1863–71) serializes Jules Verne's "Journey to the Centre of the Earth."
1871	The *Graphic* (1869–1932) publishes Hubert von Herkomer's breakthrough wood engraving, *Sunday in Chelsea Hospital*.
1872	The *Dark Blue* (1871–73), an avant-garde magazine, publishes works by Dante Gabriel Rossetti, William Morris, Algernon Swinburne, and Sheridan Le Fanu.
1873	Novel serialization in newspapers is systematized and legitimized.
1874	Florence Marryat, the editor of *London Society* (1862–1898), is the central figure in the illustration "A Holiday Dream of London Society."
1875	The *Englishwoman's Review* (1866–1910), committed to examining the "sources whence spring the evils which oppress women," praises a novel by Elizabeth Eiloart that includes characters representative of the New Woman. *Tarian y Gweithiwr* (the Worker's Shield), a radical Welsh weekly, begins publication.
1876	The *Month and Catholic Review* rejects Gerard Manley Hopkins's "The Wreck of the Deutschland."
1877	*Blackwood's Magazine* serializes Charles Reade's novel, *A Woman Hater*, a thinly veiled plea for female physicians.
1878	Henry Du Pré Labouchere's society weekly, *Truth* (1877–1957), attacks Jews as being unstable, boastful, and biologically flawed. The *Magazine of Art* (1878–1904) is founded as a less expensive alternative to the more established *Art Journal*.
1879	The *Sporting Life* (1859–1998), a bastion of British horse racing and sporting culture, claims a circulation of over 230,000.
1880	Articles encouraging working-class girls to seek employment appear in the *Girl's Own Paper* (1880–1956).
1881	*Tit-Bits* (1881–1984) debuts as a weekly sixteen-page patchwork of advice, anecdotes, quips, queries, and reader correspondence. *Harper's Monthly Magazine* launches a European edition.
1882	Wilkie Collins's novel *Heart and Science* is serialized and syndicated in local newspapers throughout England.
1883	The monthly *Portfolio* (1870–94), featuring original engravings and etchings, publishes a twelve-part series on Paris.
1884	The *Northern Chronicle*, a Scottish newspaper, expresses confidence in General Gordon (in the Sudan) and lambasts Gladstone.
1885	W.T. Stead's "The Maiden Tribute of Modern Babylon," published in the *Pall Mall Gazette* (1865–1923), attacks the sexual exploitation of children. The Socialist League begins publishing the *Commonweal* (1885–94).
1886	"The Tyranny of Fashion," an article published in *Blackfriars* (1885–90), a magazine for postal workers, attacks elite opinion and urges independence in thought and action. The *Brewing Trade Review* (1886–1972) is founded in response to the increased taxation and regulation of beer and spirits. Berne Convention regarding international copyright comes into force.
1887	Oscar Wilde argues that the title of the *Lady's World* (founded 1886) should be changed to the *Woman's World* (–1890) and should "deal not merely with what woman wear, but with what they think and feel."
1888	The pro-suffrage *Women's Penny Paper* (1888–93) begins publication; it is later subtitled "The Only Paper Conducted, Written, and Published by Women." *Le Japon Artistique* (1888–91) highlights the growing influence of Japanese art and style.

Year	Periodical Press
1889	The nature and ethics of hypnotism are debated in the *British Medical Journal* from 1887 to 1891. The *Newcastle Chronicle* is the first of many British newspapers to utilize Linotype, a major advance in printing technology.
1890	The American *Lippincott's Monthly Magazine* (1868–1915) publishes Oscar Wilde's *The Picture of Dorian Gray*. The *Strad*, a periodical dedicated to the violin, begins publication.
1891	The *Punch* cartoon "The Sterner Sex!" reflects anxieties associated with the clothing, sporting activities, and masculinization of the New Woman. The International Copyright (Chace) Act (in the US) provides some protection for British books and periodicals.
1892	Arthur Conan Doyle publishes *The Adventures of Sherlock Holmes* (1891–93) in the *Strand Magazine* (1891–1950). The *Spirit Lamp* (1892–93), a homoerotic Oxford undergraduate journal, discusses students' sexual allure for both men and women.
1893	*Borderland: A Quarterly Review and Index of Psychic Phenomena* (1893–97) popularizes psychic research.
1894	The *English Illustrated Magazine* (1883–1913) features Elizabeth Banks's account of her undercover experience as a crossing sweeper. The *Yellow Book* (1894–97) advocates for an avant-garde aesthetics.
1895	Elizabeth Robins Pennell, a champion of Impressionism, reviews art for the *Daily Chronicle*, the *Nation*, the *Star*, and *Woman*.
1896	The Irish national literary magazine *Shan Van Vocht* (1896–99) popularizes the nationalistic ideas of Sinn Féin.
1897	The *Music Hall and Theatre Review* (1889–1912) takes up the cause of a performer accused of performing on stage with bare legs.
1898	Eugen Sandow starts *Sandow's Magazine of Physical Culture* (1898–1907), the first body-building magazine. The *Girl's Best Friend* (1898–99) offers romantic fiction for working-class girls.
1899	The *Girl's Realm* (1898–1915) asks readers if they would denounce a poor girl who cheated on a scholarship competition.

BIBLIOGRAPHY

Archival Material

Archives of Richard Bentley & Son 1829–98. Chadwyck-Healey, 1976. Microfilm.
Blackwood Private Letter Book, MS 30372. National Library of Scotland.
Dixon Papers [unnumbered manuscript]. University of Ghent.
F.G. Stephens Correspondence. Bodleian Library, Oxford.
Lancashire and Cheshire Band of Hope and Temperance Union. Minutes of Executive, May 1867. Manchester Central Library, Special Collections.
Lewis Jones Papers. National Library of Wales, 6402D.
Macmillan Archive. British Library, Add MS 55999 (unbound pay sheets for *Macmillan's Magazine* 1889–1907).
Modern Records Centre. University of Warwick, MSS.420/CB UK.
Richard Robert Madden Papers, 1727–1864. National Library of Ireland.
Robert Wolff Archive. Harry Ransom Research Center, University of Texas at Austin.

Databases and Websites

Databases are listed in alphabetical order by title. Open-access databases are marked OA (note that not all those marked will necessarily be open access in all locations). Many of the databases listed below are available only through institutions such as universities or research libraries. Web addresses are only given if (as of February 2016) individual subscriptions are possible.

19th Century British Library Newspapers. Gale Cengage, 2007–.
19th Century UK Periodicals. Gale Cengage, 2007–.
Act of Union Virtual Library. http://www.actofunion.ac.uk. OA.
Alcohol Policy UK. http://www.alcoholpolicy.net/. OA.
Alcohol Research Today. http://alcoholresearchuk.org/. OA.
British Newspaper Archive. British Library and Brightsolid, 2011–. http://www.britishnewspaperarchive.co.uk.
British Newspapers, 1600–1950. British Library and Gale Cengage, 2009–.
The Carlyle Letters Online. Edited by Brent E. Kinser. Duke University Press. http://carlyleletters.dukejournals.org. OA.
Connected Histories. British History Sources, 1500–1900. University of Hertfordshire, University of London, University of Sheffield, 2011–. http://www.connectedhistories.org. OA.

BIBLIOGRAPHY

The Curran Index: Additions, Corrections, and Expansions of The Wellesley Index To Victorian Periodicals. Edited by Eieleen Curran and Gary Simons. Victorian Research Web, 2003–. http://victorianresearch.org/curranindex.html. OA.

Database of Mid-Victorian Illustration. Centre for Editorial and Intertextual Research, University of Cardiff, 2007. http://www.dmvi.cf.ac.uk. OA.

Dickens Journals Online. University of Buckingham, 2012–. www.djo.org.uk. OA.

Dublin Core Metadata Initiative. http://dublincore.org. OA.

Economist Historical Archive, 1843–2007. Gale Cengage, 2007.

Eighteenth Century Ireland Society. 2014. http://www.ecis.ie. OA.

Eirdata (Electronic Irish Dataset). http://www.ricorso.net. OA.

Google Books. 2001–. http://books.google.com. OA.

Hathi Trust Digital Library. http://www.hathitrust.org. OA.

Hayes Manuscript Sources for the History of Irish Civilization and Articles in Irish Periodicals. 2012. https://familysearch.org/learn/wiki/en/Hayes_Manuscript_and_Periodical_Sources_for_Irish_Research.

House of Commons Parliamentary Papers. Proquest.

Illustrated London News Historical Archive, 1842–2003. Gale Cengage, 2010.

Illustration Archive: Illuminating the Past. 2015. http://illustrationarchive.cardiff.ac.uk/. OA.

ImageGrid. Bridget Baird and Cameron Blevins, 2012. http://www.cameronblevins.org/imagegrid. OA.

Internet Archive. 1996–. https://archive.org. OA.

Ireland Illustrated. http://adminstaff.vassar.edu/sttaylor/FAMINE. OA.

Irish Builder and Engineer Catalogue. University College Dublin Digital Library, 2009. http://digital.ucd.ie./view/ivrla:30524. OA.

Irish Resources in the Humanities. Edited by Susan Schreibman. Trinity College Dublin, 1999–. http://irith.org/index.jsp

John Johnson Collection of Printed Ephemera. http://www.bodleian.ox.ac.uk/johnson. OA (UK only)

Lost Visions: The Illustration Archive. University of Cardiff, 2014–. http://lostvisions.weebly.com. OA.

Mapping Texts. University of North Texas and Stanford University, 2010–11. http://mappingtexts.org. OA.

National Archives. http://www.nationalarchives.gov.uk. OA.

National Archives Online Catalogue. http://discovery.nationalarchives.gov.uk. OA.

National Library of Ireland Database for Irish Research. 2007–. http://sources.nli.ie. OA.

Newspaper and Periodical History Forum of Ireland. 2012. http://www.newspapersperiodicals.org.

NewsVault. Gale Cengage, 2011–.

NINES: Nineteenth-Century Scholarship Online. 2003–. http://www.nines.org. OA.

Nineteenth-Century British Pamphlets. Gale Cengage, 2009. http://www.britishpamphlets.org.uk. OA (in UK).

Nineteenth-Century Collections Online. Gale Cengage, 2012–.

Nineteenth-Century Serials Edition. 2008. www.ncse.ac.uk. OA.

Poetess Archive. Edited by Laura Mandell, 2007–. http://idhmc.tamu.edu/poetess. OA.

Points: The Blog of the Alcohol and Drugs History Society. https://pointsadhsblog.wordpress.com. OA.

Proceedings of the Old Bailey Online, 1674–1913. www.oldbaileyonline.org. OA.

Punch Historical Archive. Gale Cengage, 2014.

Quarterly Review Archive. Edited by Jonathan Cutmore. *Romantic Circles*, 2005. http://www.rc.umd.edu/reference/qr/index.html. OA.

Readex Collections.

Retrospective Index to Music Periodicals.

Rossetti Archive. 2000–2008. http://www.rossettiarchive.org. OA.

SciPer: Science in the Nineteenth-Century Periodical. http://www.sciper.org. OA.

Social History of Drugs and Alcohol. http://alcoholanddrugshistorysociety.org/shad-journal. OA.

Society for the Study of Nineteenth-Century Ireland. http://www.ssnci.com. OA

Stage. http://www.thestage.co.uk.

Sunday Times *Digital Archive.* Gale Cengage, 2012.

Times *Digital Archive, 1785–2009.* Gale Cengage, 2002–.

Victorian Fiction Research Guides. Edited by Andrew King. Brighton: Victorian Secrets, 2013–. http://www.victoriansecrets.co.uk/victorian-fiction-research-guides. OA.

Viral Texts: Mapping Networks of Reprinting in 19th-Century Newspapers and Magazines. NULab for Texts, Maps, and Networks, Northeastern University, 2013–. http://viraltexts.org. OA.

Waterloo Directory of English Newspapers and Periodicals, 1800–1900. Edited by John S. North. Waterloo: North Waterloo Academic Press, 1994–2003.

Waterloo Directory of Irish Newspapers and Periodicals, 1800–1900. Edited by John S. North. Waterloo: North Waterloo Academic Press, 1986.

Waterloo Directory of Scottish Newspapers and Periodicals, 1800–1900. Edited by John S. North. Waterloo: North Waterloo Academic Press, 1989.

The Wellesley Index to Victorian Periodicals, 1824–1900. ProQuest, 2006–13.

Welsh Journals Online. 2009. http://welshjournals.llgc.org.uk. OA.

William Blake Archive. 1995–. http://www.blakearchive.org/blake. OA.

World Newspaper Archive. Centre for Research Libraries.

Yellow Nineties Online. Edited by Dennis Denisoff and Lorraine Janzen Kooistra. 2012. http://www.1890s.ca. OA.

Film

Wilson, Doug, dir. *Linotype: The Film: In Search of the Eighth Wonder of the World.* 2012. http://shop.linotypefilm.com/collections/frontpage/products/dvd.

Print and Individual Online Sources

"$5,000,000 Failure in London." *New York Times,* October 11, 1898, 5.

À Beckett, Arthur William. *The À Becketts of "Punch": Memories of a Father and Sons.* Westminster: Archibald Constable, 1903.

A.H.B. "The Days of Duels." *Sporting Magazine* 327 (March 1868): 180–92.

Ackermann, Rudolph, ed. "Introductory Address." *Poetical Magazine* 1 (May 1809): i–iv.

Adburgham, Alison. *Women in Print: Writing Women and Women's Magazines from the Restoration to the Accession of Victoria.* London: George Allen and Unwin, 1972.

"Address." *New Monthly Belle Assemblée* 8 (January 1838): i.

"The Address of the Working Men's Association of Leith, to their Fellow-Men of Whatever Sect, Class, Country, or Colour." *Northern Star,* February 17, 1838, 7.

Adrian, Arthur A. *Mark Lemon: First Editor of "Punch."* London: Oxford University Press, 1966.

Advertisement. *Edinburgh Review* 1 (October 1802): n.p.

Advertisement for *British Workman. Band of Hope Review* 1, no. 50 (February 1855): 104.

Advertisement for the "Linotype" Composing Machine. *Daily News,* July 17, 1889, 7.

Advertisement for Mence & Co. *Dudley Weekly Times*, May 22, 1858, 8.
"Advice to Farmers, Dealers, and all Parents." *Cobbett's Weekly Political Register*, January 28, 1826, 293–4.
"Advice to Young Men." *Cobbett's Weekly Political Register*, April 25, 1829, 535–6.
"Aesthetic Identity in the British Musical Press, 1895–1934." *Musical Quarterly* 91, no. 1/2 (2008): 8–38.
Albarran, Alan B., Sylvia M. Chan-Olmsted, and Michael O. Wirth, eds. *Handbook of Media Management and Economics*. Mahwah, NJ: Lawrence Erlbaum, 2006.
Alcoff, Linda Martin, and Satya P. Mohanty. Introduction to *Identity Politics Reconsidered*, edited by Satya P. Mohanty, 1–9. Gordonsville, VA: Palgrave Macmillan, 2006.
Allen, Joan. "*Catholic Herald*." In *The Dictionary of Nineteenth-Century Journalism in Great Britain and Ireland*, edited by Laurel Brake and Marysa Demoor. Chadwyck-Healey, 2012. http://c19index.chadwyck.co.uk.
Allen, Joan, and Owen R. Ashton. *Papers for the People: A Study of the Chartist Press*. London: Merlin Press, 2005.
Altholz, Josef. *The Religious Press in Britain, 1760–1900*. New York: Greenwood Press, 1989.
Altick, Richard D. *The English Common Reader: A Social History of the Mass Reading Public, 1800–1900*. 1957. Reprint, Columbus: Ohio State University Press, 1998.
———. *The Presence of the Present: Topics of the Day in the Victorian Novel*. Columbus: Ohio State University Press, 1991.
———. *Punch: The Lively Youth of a British Institution, 1841–1851*. Columbus: Ohio State University Press, 1997.
———. *The Shows of London*. Cambridge: Belknap Press of Harvard University Press, 1978.
Altschuler, Sari Beth. "*National Reformer* (1860–91)." In *The Dictionary of Nineteenth-Century Journalism in Great Britain and Ireland*, edited by Laurel Brake and Marysa Demoor, 439. Ghent and London: Academia Press and the British Library, 2009.
"American News for European Readers [Advertisement for W.H. Smith]." *Times*, October 18, 1846, 2.
Amicus. "Lines to Messrs. White and Collins." *Northern Star*, November 21, 1840, 3.
Anderson, Benedict. *Imagined Communities: Reflections on the Origin and Spread of Nationalism*. 1983. Reprint, London: Verso, 1991.
Anderson, Marnie. *A Place in Public: Women's Rights in Meiji Japan*. Cambridge: Harvard University Press, 2010.
Anderson, Patricia. *The Printed Image and the Transformation of Popular Culture, 1790–1860*. Oxford: Clarendon Press, 1991.
Anderson, Patricia, and Jonathan Rose, eds. *British Literary Publishing Houses, 1820–1880*. Vol. 106, Dictionary of Literary Biography. London: Gale, 1991.
Andrews, Alexander. *The History of British Journalism: From the Foundation of the Newspaper Press in England, to the Repeal of the Stamp Act in 1855: With Sketches of Press Celebrities*. 2 vols. London: Bentley, 1859.
Andrews, J.H. *A Paper Landscape: The Ordnance Survey in Nineteenth-Century Ireland*. Dublin: Four Courts Press, 2001.
"The Annuals of Former Days." *Bookseller* 1 (November 1858): 493–9.
"Another Dramatic Prize." *Punch* 5 (July 8, 1843): 13.
"Answers to Correspondents." *Girl's Own Paper* 2 (March 5, 1881): 366–7.
"Applegarth's Vertical Printing Machine, Exhibited by the Proprietors of the *Illustrated London News*." *Illustrated London News*, May 31, 1851, 501–2.
Ardis, Ann, and Patrick Collier, eds. *Transatlantic Print Culture, 1880–1940: Emerging Media, Emerging Modernisms*. Basingstoke: Palgrave, 2008.
"The Armistice." *Economist* 28 (November 5, 1870): 1.

Armitage, David, and Michael J. Braddick, eds. *The British and Atlantic World, 1500–1800*. 2nd ed. Basingstoke: Palgrave, 2009.

"Army Reform." *Reynolds's Newspaper*, February 5, 1871, 8.

Arnold, Matthew. "The Function of Criticism at the Present Time." In *Essays by Matthew Arnold*, edited by Humphrey Milford, 9–36. Oxford: Oxford University Press, 1914.

———. "The Literary Influence of Academies." In *Lectures and Essays in Criticism by Matthew Arnold*, edited by R.H. Super, 232–57. Michigan: University of Michigan Press, 1962.

———. "Up to Easter." *Nineteenth Century* 21 (May 1887): 629–43.

Ashton, Rosemary. *George Eliot: A Life*. London: Penguin, 1996.

Aspinall, Arthur. "The Circulation of Newspapers in the Early Nineteenth Century." *Review of English Studies* 22 (January 1946): 29–43.

———. *Politics and the Press, c. 1780–1850*. Brighton: Harvester Press, 1973.

———. "Statistical Accounts of the London Newspapers, 1800–36." *English Historical Review* 65 (April and July 1950): 222–34, 372–83.

———. "Statistical Accounts of the London Newspapers in the Eighteenth Century." *English Historical Review* 63 (April 1948): 201–32.

Atlas, Allan. *The Wheatstone English Concertina in Victorian England*. Oxford: Clarendon, 1996.

Attardo, Salvatore. "Preface: Working Class Humor." *Humor* 23, no. 2 (2010): 121–6.

Auerbach, Jeffrey A. "What They Read: Mid-Nineteenth Century English Women's Magazines and the Emergence of a Consumer Culture." *Victorian Periodicals Review* 30, no. 2 (1997): 121–40.

Ayerst, David. *Guardian: Biography of a Newspaper*. London: Collins, 1971.

Bacon, Alice. *Japanese Girls and Women*. London: Kegan Paul, 2001.

Baetzhold, Howard G. "Mark Twain: England's Advocate." *American Literature* 28, no. 3 (1956): 328–46.

Bagehot, Walter. "The First Edinburgh Reviewers." *National Review* 1, no. 2 (October 1855): 253–84.

Bailey, Michael, ed. *Narrating Media History*. New York: Routledge, 2009.

Bailey, Peter. "Ally Sloper's Half-Holiday: Comic Art in the 1880s." *History Workshop Journal* 16, no. 1 (Autumn 1983): 4–32.

———. *Popular Culture and Performance in the Victorian City*. Cambridge: Cambridge University Press, 1998.

Baines, Edward. *Extension of the Franchise: Speech of Edward Baines on Moving the Second Reading of the Borough Franchise Bill, in the House of Commons, on the 11th May, 1864*. London, 1864.

Bakhtin, Mikhail. *The Dialogic Imagination: Four Essays*. Edited by Michael Holquist. Translated by Caryl Emerson and Michael Holquist. Austin: University of Texas Press, 1982.

Ballin, Malcolm. *Welsh Periodicals in English, 1882–2012*. Chicago: University of Chicago Press, 2013.

Balme, Christopher B. "Playbills and the Theatrical Public Sphere." In *Representing the Past: Essays in Performance History*, edited by Charlotte Canning and Thomas Postlewait, 37–62. Iowa City: University of Iowa Press, 2010.

Banham, Christopher Mark. "*Boy's Journal*." In *The Dictionary of Nineteenth-Century Journalism in Great Britain and Ireland*, edited by Laurel Brake and Marysa Demoor, 68. Ghent and London: Academia Press and the British Library, 2009.

———. "*Boys' Miscellany*." In *The Dictionary of Nineteenth-Century Journalism in Great Britain and Ireland*, edited by Laurel Brake and Marysa Demoor, 68. Ghent and London: Academia Press and the British Library, 2009.

———. "*Boys of England*." In *The Dictionary of Nineteenth-Century Journalism in Great Britain and Ireland*, edited by Laurel Brake and Marysa Demoor, 69. Ghent and London: Academia Press and the British Library, 2009.

Bannet, Eve Tavor, and Susan Manning, eds. *Transatlantic Literary Studies, 1660–1830*. Cambridge: Cambridge University Press, 2012.

Banta, Martha. *Barbaric Intercourse: Caricature and the Culture of Conduct, 1841–1936*. Chicago: University of Chicago Press, 2003.

Barnes, John. *Socialist Champion: Portrait of the Gentleman as Crusader*. Melbourne: Australia Scholarly Publishing, 2006.

Baron, Beth. *The Women's Awakening in Egypt*. New Haven: Yale University Press, 1997.

Barrington, Kate. "What Are Men without the Vote?" *Woman's Herald* 43, no. 1 (1889): 8.

Barry, Maltman. "The Labour Day." *New Century Review* 6 (October 1899): 296–310.

Bashford, Christina. "Hidden Agendas and the Creation of Community: The Violin Press in the Late Nineteenth Century." In *Music and Performance Culture in Nineteenth-Century Britain: Essays in Honour of Nicholas Temperley*, edited by Bennett Zon, 11–35. Aldershot: Ashgate, 2012.

Bassett, Troy. "Living on the Margins: George Bentley and the Three-Volume Novel, 1865–1870." *Book History* 13 (2010): 58–79.

———. "The Production of Three-Volume Novels in Britain, 1863–97." *Papers of the Bibliographical Society of America* 102 (2008): 61–75.

Bateman, Anthony. *Cricket, Literature, and Culture: Symbolising the Nation, Destabilising Empire*. Aldershot: Ashgate, 2009.

Batts, John S. "American Humour: The Mark of Twain on Jerome K. Jerome." In *The Victorian Comic Spirit: New Perspectives*, edited by Jennifer A. Wagner-Lawlor, 91–114. Aldershot: Ashgate, 2000.

Baudelaire, Charles. "Peintre de la vie moderne." Parts I–IV. *Le Figaro*, November 26, 1863, 1–5. http://gallica.bnf.fr/ark:/12148/bpt6k270260r.

Baudin, Dominique. "Le catalogue collectif national des périodiques allemand." *Bulletin des Bibliothèques de France* 6 (1990): 380–7. http://bbf.enssib.fr/consulter/bbf-1990–06–0380–005.

Bayly, Chris. *Empire and Information*. Cambridge: Cambridge University Press, 1996.

Beaver, Alfred. "Art Sales." *Art Journal*, September 1884, 261–4.

Bebbington, David. *The Dominance of Evangelicalism: The Age of Spurgeon and Moody*. Downers Grove, IL: InterVarsity Press, 2005.

Beckford, Peter. *Thoughts on Hunting, in a Series of Familiar Letters to a Friend*. Sarum: E. Easton, 1781.

Beegan, Gerry. *The Mass Image: A Social History of Photomechanical Reproduction in Victorian London*. Basingstoke: Palgrave Macmillan, 2008.

Beer, Gillian. "The *Academy*: Europe and England." In *Representations of the Sciences in Nineteenth Century Periodicals*, edited by Geoffrey Cantor and Sally Shuttleworth, 181–98. Cambridge: MIT Press, 2004.

Beetham, Margaret. "*Ben Brierley's Journal*." *Manchester Region History Review* 17 (2006): 73–83.

———. "'Healthy Reading': The Periodical Press in Manchester." In *City, Class and Culture: Studies of Social Policy and Cultural Production in Victorian Manchester*, edited by Alan J. Kidd and Kenneth W. Roberts, 167–92. Manchester: Manchester University Press, 1985.

———. *A Magazine of Her Own?: Domesticity and Desire in the Woman's Magazine, 1800–1914*. London: Routledge, 1996.

———. "Open and Closed: The Periodical as a Publishing Genre." *Victorian Periodicals Review* 22, no. 3 (1989): 96–100.

———. "Towards a Theory of the Periodical as a Publishing Genre." In *Investigating Victorian Journalism*, edited by Laurel Brake, Aled Jones, and Lionel Madden, 19–32. Basingstoke: Macmillan, 1990.

Beetham, Margaret, and Kay Boardman, eds. *Victorian Women's Magazines: An Anthology*. Manchester: Manchester University Press, 2001.

Begbie, Harold. "Common Heroes. The Clerk's Wife." *Pall Mall Magazine* 24 (May 1901): 104–5.

———. "Common Heroes. The Curate." *Pall Mall Magazine* 23 (January 1901): 14–15.

———. "Common Heroes. The Journalist." *Pall Mall Magazine* 24 (June 1901): 244–5.

———. "Common Heroes. The Merchant." *Pall Mall Magazine* 23 (March 1901): 322–3.

———. *The Lady Next Door*. Edited with an introduction by Patrick Maume. Dublin: University College Dublin Press, 2006.

Behrendt, Stephen C. "British Women Poets and the Reverberations of Radicalism in the 1790s." In *Romanticism, Radicalism, and the Press*, edited by Stephen C. Behrendt, 83–102. Detroit: Wayne State University Press, 1997.

Bell, Bill, ed. *The Edinburgh History of the Book in Scotland*. Vol. 3, *Ambition and Industry 1800–1880*. Edinburgh: Edinburgh University Press, 2007.

Bellanger, Claude, Jacques Godechot, Pierre Guiral, and Fernand Terrou. *Histoire générale de la presse française*. 5 vols. Paris: PUF, 1969–76.

Benatti, Francesca. "A National and Concordant Feeling: Penny Journals in Ireland, 1832–1842." PhD diss., NUI Galway, 2003.

Bender, J.C. "Mutiny or Freedom Fight?" In *Newspapers and Empire in Ireland and Britain: Reporting the British Empire, c. 1857–1921*, edited by Simon Potter, 92–109. Dublin: Four Courts Press, 2004.

Bendixen, Alfred, ed. *The Cambridge Companion to American Travel Writing*. Cambridge: Cambridge University Press, 2008.

Bengry, Justin. "Courting the Pink Pound: Men Only and the Queer Consumer, 1935–39." *History Workshop Journal* 68 (2009): 123–48.

Benjamin, Walter. "The Task of the Translator." In *Illuminations*, edited by Hannah Arendt and translated by Harry Zohn, 68–82. New York: Schocken, 1968.

Bennett, Betty T., and Orianne Smith, eds. *British War Poetry in the Age of Romanticism: 1793–1815*. New York: Garland, 1976. Electronic revised edition. http://www.rc.umd.edu/editions/warpoetry/about.html.

Bennett, Scott. "The Bibliographical Control of Victorian Periodicals." In *Victorian Periodicals: A Guide to Research*, edited by J. Don Vann and Rosemary VanArsdel, 21–51. New York: Modern Language Association, 1978.

———. "Revolution in Thought: Serial Publication and the Mass Market for Reading." In *The Victorian Periodical Press: Samplings and Soundings*, edited by Joanne Shattock and Michael Wolff, 225–60. Leicester: Leicester University Press, 1982.

———. "Victorian Newspaper Advertising: Counting What Counts." *Publishing History* 8 (1980): 5–18.

Bennett, Susan. *Theatre Audiences*. London: Routledge, 1997.

Berridge, Virginia. "Popular Sunday Newspapers and Mid-Victorian Society." In *Newspaper History: From the Seventeenth Century to the Present Day*, edited by David George Boyce, James Curran, and Pauline Wingate, 247–64. London: Constable, 1978.

Berry, Helen. *Gender, Society and Print Culture in Late-Stuart England*. Aldershot: Ashgate, 2003.

Besant, Walter. *The Pen and Book*. London: Thomas Burleigh, 1899.

Bhroiméil, Úna Ní. "The Irish-American Press and the South African War." In *Newspapers and Empire in Ireland and Britain: Reporting the British Empire, c. 1857–1921*, edited by Simon Potter, 195–216. Dublin: Four Courts Press, 2004.

Bickham, Troy. *Making Headlines: The American Revolution as Seen Through the British Press*. Illinois: Northern Illinois University Press, 2009.

Billington, Louis. "The Religious Periodical and Newspaper Press, 1770–1870." In *The Press in English Society from the Seventeenth to Nineteenth Centuries*, edited by Michael Harris and Alan Lee, 113–32, 231–9. Rutherford, NJ: Fairleigh Dickinson University Press, 1986.

Billington, M.F. "Leading Lady Journalists." *Pearson's Magazine* 2 (July 1896): 101–11.

BIBLIOGRAPHY

Bilston, Sarah. *The Awkward Age in Women's Popular Fiction, 1850–1900: Girls and the Transition to Womanhood*. Oxford: Clarendon Press, 2004.

Bingham, Adrian. "The Digitization of Newspaper Archives." *20th Century British History* 21, no. 2 (2010): 225–31.

Binstead, Arthur M., and Ernest Wells. *A Pink 'Un and a Pelican: Some Random Reminiscences, Sporting or Otherwise*. London: Bliss, Sands, 1898.

Blackett, R.J.M. *Divided Hearts: Britain and the American Civil War*. Baton Rouge: Louisiana State University Press, 2001.

Blake, Peter. "George Augustus Sala and the English Middle-Class View of America." *19: Interdisciplinary Studies in the Long Nineteenth-Century* 9 (2009). http://www.19.bbk.ac.uk/index.php/19/article/view/509.

Blatchford, Robert. "Good and Bad Boys." *Labour Prophet* 2 (July 1893): 65–6.

———. "In the Library," *Clarion*, January 23, 1903, 3.

Bledsoe, Robert Terrell. *Dickens, Journalism, Music*: Household Words *and* All the Year Round. London: Continuum, 2012.

Blevins, Cameron. "Coding a Middle Ground: ImageGrid." *Historying* (blog). July 12, 2012. http://historying.org/2012/07/12/coding-a-middle-ground.

Blocker, Jack S., David Fahey, and Ian Tyrell, eds. *Alcohol and Temperance in Modern History: An International Encyclopedia*. Oxford: ABC Clio, 2003.

Blondheim, Menahem. *News over the Wires: The Telegraph and the Flow of Public Information in America, 1844–1897*. Cambridge: Harvard University Press, 1994.

Blum, Paul. *Yokohama in 1872*. Tokyo: Asiatic Society of Japan, 1963.

Boddice, Rob. "Four Stages of Cruelty?: Institutionalizing Humanity to Animals in the English Media, c. 1750–1840." In *Mediale Konstruktionen in der Fruehen Neuzeit*, edited by Wolfgang Behringer, Milos Havelka, and Katharina Reinholdt, 181–96. Korb: Didymos-Verlag, 2013.

———. "Manliness and the 'Morality of Field Sports': E.A. Freeman and Anthony Trollope, 1869–71." *Historian* 70, no. 1 (2008): 1–29.

Bogart, Dan. "Turnpike Trusts and the Transportation Revolution in Eighteenth-Century England." *Explorations in Economic History* 42 (2005): 479–508.

Bolter, Jay David, and Richard Grusin. *Remediation: Understanding New Media*. Cambridge, MA: MIT Press, 1999.

Bonsor, N.R.P. *North Atlantic Seaway*. Vol. 5. Newton Abbott: David & Charles, 1980.

Boos, Florence S. "The 'Homely Muse' in Her Diurnal Setting: The Periodical Poems of 'Marie,' Janet Hamilton, and Fanny Forrester." *Victorian Poetry* 39, no. 2 (2001): 255–85.

———, ed. *Working-Class Women Poets in Victorian Britain: An Anthology*. Peterborough: Broadview Press, 2008.

Booth, J.B. *"Master" and Men: Pink 'Un Yesterdays*. London: T. Werner Laurie, 1924.

———. *Old Pink 'Un Days*. London: Grant Richards, 1924.

Boswell, James. *Life of Johnson*. Edited by Charles Grosvenor Osgood. New York: Scribner's Sons, 1917.

Botein, Stephen, Jack Censer, and Harriet Ritvo. "The Periodical Press in Eighteenth-Century English and French Society: A Cross-Cultural Approach." *Comparative Studies in Society and History* 23, no. 3 (1981): 464–90.

"The Botheration of the 'Personal.'" *Tait's Edinburgh Magazine* 1 (June 1832): 286–90.

Bourdieu, Pierre. *The Field of Cultural Production*. New York: Columbia University Press, 1993.

Bowen, John. "Collins's Shorter Fiction." In *The Cambridge Companion to Wilkie Collins*, edited by Jenny Bourne Taylor, 37–49. Cambridge: Cambridge University Press, 2006.

Boyce, Charlotte. "Representing the 'Hungry Forties' in Image and Verse: The Politics of Hunger in Early-Victorian Illustrated Periodicals." *Victorian Literature and Culture* 40, no. 2 (2012): 421–49.

Boyd, Kelly. *Manliness and the Boys' Story Paper in Britain: A Cultural History, 1855–1940*. Houndmills: Palgrave Macmillan, 2003.

"Boy's Exchange." *Boy's Own Magazine: An Illustrated Journal of Fact, Fiction, History and Adventure*, n.s., 10 (May 1868): n.p.

"The Boys' Own Magazine." *Boys' Own Magazine* 1 (January 1855): n.p.

Bradshaw, James Stanford. "The *Detroit Free Press* in England." *Journalism History* 5, no. 1 (1978): 4–7.

Bradshaw's Monthly Railway and Steam Navigation Guide. London: W. J. Adams, 1841–1961.

Brake, Laurel. "*The Artist and Journal of Home Culture* (1880–1902)." In *The Dictionary of Nineteenth-Century Journalism in Great Britain and Ireland*, edited by Laurel Brake and Marysa Demoor, 25. Ghent and London: Academia Press and the British Library, 2009.

———. "'Gay Discourse' and *The Artist and Journal of Home Culture*." In *Nineteenth-Century Media and the Construction of Identities*, edited by Laurel Brake, Bill Bell, and David Finkelstein, 271–91. Basingstoke: Palgrave Macmillan, 2001.

———. "Half Full and Half Empty." *Journal of Victorian Culture* 17, no. 2 (2012): 222–9.

———. "Magazine Day." In *The Dictionary of Nineteenth-Century Journalism in Great Britain and Ireland*, edited by Laurel Brake and Marysa Demoor, 390. Ghent and London: Academia Press and the British Library, 2009.

———. "The Popular 'Weeklies.'" In *The Edinburgh History of the Book in Scotland*, vol. 3, *Ambition and Industry 1800–1880*, edited by Bill Bell, 358–69. Edinburgh: Edinburgh University Press, 2007.

———. *Print in Transition, 1850–1910: Studies in Media and Book History*. Basingstoke: Palgrave, 2001.

———. "Stead Alone: Journalist, Proprietor, and Publisher 1890–1903." In *W. T. Stead: Newspaper Revolutionary*, edited by Laurel Brake, Ed King, Roger Luckhurst, and James Mussell, 77–97. London: British Library, 2012.

———. *Subjugated Knowledges: Journalism, Gender and Literature in the Nineteenth Century*. London: Macmillan, 1994.

———. "Walter Pater." In *The Dictionary of Nineteenth-Century Journalism in Great Britain and Ireland*, edited by Laurel Brake and Marysa Demoor, 482–3. Ghent and London: Academia Press and the British Library, 2009.

———. *Walter Pater*. Plymouth: Northcote House, 1994.

Brake, Laurel, and Julie Codell. *Encounters in the Victorian Press: Editors, Authors, Readers*. Basingstoke: Palgrave, 2005.

Brake, Laurel, and Marysa Demoor, eds. *The Dictionary of Nineteenth-Century Journalism in Great Britain and Ireland*. Ghent and London: Academia Press and the British Library, 2009.

———, eds. *The Lure of Illustration in the Nineteenth Century: Picture and Press*. Houndmills: Palgrave, 2009.

Brake, Laurel, Ed King, Roger Luckhurst, and James Mussell, eds. *W. T. Stead, Newspaper Revolutionary*. London: British Library, 2012.

Brandon, Ruth. *The Dollar Princesses*. London: Weidenfeld and Nicholson, 1980.

Brantlinger, Patrick. *The Spirit of Reform: British Literature and Politics, 1832–1867*. Cambridge: Harvard University Press, 1977.

"Bravery of British Troops." *Northern Star*, September 24, 1842, 7.

Briggs, Asa, and Peter Burke. *A Social History of the Media, from Gutenberg to the Internet*. London: Polity Press, 2002.

Briggs, Julia. "Women Writers and Writing for Children: From Sarah Fielding to E. Nesbit." In *Children and Their Books: A Celebration of the Work of Iona and Peter Opie*, edited by Gillian Avery and Julia Briggs, 221–50. Oxford: Clarendon Press, 1989.

Briggs, Julia, and Dennis Butts. "The Emergence of Form (1850–90)." In *Children's Literature: An Illustrated History*, edited by Peter Hunt, 130–65. Oxford: Oxford University Press, 1995.

"British Artists: Their Style and Character, No. II – Edward Matthew Ward, A.R.A." *Art Journal*, February 1855, 45–8.

Broks, Peter. *Media Science before the Great War*. Basingstoke: Macmillan, 1996.

Brooker, Peter, Sascha Bru, Andrew Thacker, and Christian Weikop, eds. *The Oxford Critical and Cultural History of Modernist Magazines*. Oxford: Oxford University Press, 2013.

Brothers, Ann. *A Studio Portrait: The Marketing of Art and Taste, 1893–1918*. Parkville: History Department, University of Melbourne, 1993.

Brough, Robert B. *Marston Lynch; His Life and Times, His Friends and Enemies, His Victories and Defeats, His Kicks and Halfpence: A Personal Biography*. London: Ward and Lock, 1860.

Brown, Callum. *The Death of Christian Britain: Understanding Secularisation, 1800–2000*. London: Routledge, 2001.

Brown, Lucy. *Victorian News and Newspapers*. Oxford: Clarendon Press, 1985.

Brown, Richard. *A History of Accounting and Accountants*. Edinburgh: T.C. and E.C. Jack, 1905.

Brown, Stephen. *The Press in Ireland: A Survey and Guide*. Dublin: Browne and Nolan, 1937.

Browne, Janet. "Darwin in Caricature: A Study in the Popularization and Dissemination of Evolution." *Proceedings of the American Philosophical Society* 145 (2001): 496–509.

———. "Squibs and Snobs: Science in Humorous British Undergraduate Magazines around 1830." *History of Science* 30 (1992): 165–97.

Buckley, Colin. "The Search for 'a Really Smart Sheet': The Conservative Evening Newspaper Project in Edwardian Manchester." *Manchester Region History Review* 8 (1994): 21–8.

Budd, Louis J. *Mark Twain: The Contemporary Reviews*. Cambridge: Cambridge University Press, 1999.

[Bulwer, Edward]. "Romance and Reality. By L.E.L." *New Monthly Magazine* 32 (December 1831): 545–51.

"Burdens Entailed on the People by War." *Lloyd's Weekly*, April 29, 1849, 5.

Burke, Kathleen. *Old World, New World: The Story of Britain and America*. London: Little, Brown, 2007.

Burke, Megan D. "*Nonconformist* (1841–1900)." In *The Dictionary of Nineteenth-Century Journalism in Great Britain and Ireland*, edited by Laurel Brake and Marysa Demoor, 456–7. Ghent and London: Academia Press and the British Library, 2009.

Burn, James Dawson. *The Language of the Walls and a Voice from the Shop Windows*. Manchester: Abel Heywood, 1855.

Burnand, F.C. "'Mr. Punch.' Some Precursors and Competitors." *Pall Mall Magazine* 29 (January–April 1903): 96–105, 255–65, 390–7.

Burns, (James) Dawson. *Temperance History: A Consecutive Narrative of the Rise, Development, and Extension of the Temperance Reform*. 2 vols. London: National Temperance Publication Depot, 1889–91.

Burton, Antoinette, ed. *After the Imperial Turn*. Durham: Duke University Press, 2003.

———, ed. *Archive Stories: Facts, Fictions and the Writing of History*. Durham: Duke University Press, 2005.

———. *Burdens of History*. Chapel Hill: University of North Carolina Press, 1994.

"The Business Side of Art." *Art Journal*, August 1888, 249–51.

Buss, Robert William. *English Graphic Satire, and Its Relation to Different Styles of Painting, Sculpture, and Engraving*. London: Virtue, 1874.

Bussey, Harry Findlater. *Sixty Years of Journalism: Anecdotes and Reminiscences*. London: Simpkin, Marshall, Hamilton, Kent, 1906.

Buzzetti, Dino, and Jerome McGann. "Electronic Textual Editing: Critical Editing in a Digital Horizon." In *Electronic Textual Editing*, edited by Lou Burnard, Katherine O'Brien O'Keeffe, and John Unsworth. New York: Modern Language Association, 2006. http://www.tei-c.org/About/Archive_new/ETE/Preview/mcgann.xml.

Byron, Lord. "English Bards and Scotch Reviewers." In *The Complete Works of Lord Byron with a Biographical and Critical Notice by J. W. Lake, Esq.*, 4:175–223. Paris: Baudry, 1825.

C.P. "My Cottage Home." *London Reader*, March 1, 1879, 412.

Cadogan, Mary, and Patricia Craig. *You're a Brick, Angela!: A New Look at Girls' Fiction from 1839 to 1975*. London: Victor Gollancz, 1976.

Calhoun, Craig, ed. *Habermas and the Public Sphere*. Cambridge: MIT Press, 1993.

Campbell, Duncan Andrew. *English Public Opinion and the American Civil War*. Suffolk: Boyden Press, 2003.

Cantor, Geoffrey. *Quakers, Jews, and Science: Religious Reponses to Modernity and the Sciences in Britain, 1650–1900*. Oxford: Oxford University Press, 2005.

Cantor, Geoffrey, and Sally Shuttleworth, eds. *Science Serialised: Representations of the Sciences in Nineteenth-Century Periodicals*. Cambridge MA: MIT Press, 2004.

Cantor, Geoffrey, Gowan Dawson, Graeme Gooday, Richard Noakes, Sally Shuttleworth, and Jonathan R. Topham, eds. *Science in the Nineteenth Century Periodical: Reading the Magazine of Nature*. Cambridge: Cambridge University Press, 2004.

Carlyle, Thomas. *The Carlyle Letters Online*. Edited by Brent E. Kinser. Durham: Duke University Press. http://carlyleletters.dukejournals.org.

———. "Characteristics." *Edinburgh Review* 54 (December 1831): 351–83.

Carver, Terell. *Gender Is Not a Synonym for Women*. Boulder: Lynne Rennier, 1996.

Cayford, Joanne Mary. "The Western Mail, 1869–1914: A Study in the Politics and Management of a Provincial Newspaper." PhD diss., University of Wales, Aberystwyth, 1992.

Cayley, Seth. "Creating the *Daily Mail Archive*." *Daily Mail Historical Archive, 1896–2004*. 2013. http://gale.cengage.co.uk/images/Creating%20the%20Daily%20Mail%20Historical%20Archive.pdf.

Cecire, Natalia. "The Visible Hand." *Works Cited* (blog). May 3, 2011. http://nataliacecire.blogspot.co.uk/2011/05/visible-hand.html.

Cesarini, David. *The Jewish Chronicle and Anglo-Jewry, 1841–1991*. Cambridge: Cambridge University Press, 1994.

"CG68010—Goodwill: meaning of goodwill." HMRC [Her Majesty's Revenue and Customs]. http://www.hmrc.gov.uk/manuals/cgmanual/cg68010.htm.

Chadwick, Owen. *The Victorian Church*. 2 vols. London: A.C. Black, 1966.

Chalaby, Jean K. *The Invention of Journalism*. Houndmills: Macmillan, 1998.

———. "Journalism as an Anglo-American Invention: A Comparison of the Development of French and Anglo-American Journalism, 1830s–1920s." *European Journal of Communication* 11, no. 3 (1996): 303–26.

Chambers, William. "Editor's Address to His Readers." *Chambers's Edinburgh Journal* 1 (February 4, 1832): 1.

———. *Memoirs of Robert Chambers, with Autobiographical Reminiscences of William Chambers*. Edinburgh and London: W. & R. Chambers, 1872.

Chapman, Alison. "Poetry, Network, Nation: Elizabeth Barrett Browning and Expatriate Women's Poetry." *Victorian Studies* 55, no. 2 (2013): 275–85.

———. "Transatlantic Mediations: Victorian Periodical Poetry and Digital Pedagogy." In *Teaching Transatlanticism*, edited by Linda K. Hughes and Sarah Robbins, 211–24. Edinburgh: Edinburgh University Press, 2015.

Chapman, Alison, and Caley Ehnes. Introduction to the Special Issue on Periodical Poetry. *Victorian Poetry* 52, no. 1 (2014): 1–20.

Chapman, Jane. *Comparative Media History: An Introduction, 1789 to the Present*. Cambridge: Polity Press, 2005.

———. *Gender, Citizenship, and Newspapers: Transnational Historical Perspectives*. Basingstoke: Palgrave Macmillan, 2013.

Chase, Malcolm. *Chartism: A New History*. Manchester: Manchester University Press, 2007.

———. "Feargus Edward O'Connor (1796–1855)." In *The Dictionary of Nineteenth-Century Journalism in Great Britain and Ireland*, edited by Laurel Brake and Marysa Demoor, 466–67. Ghent and London: Academia Press and the British Library, 2009.

"Chat with 'Edna Lyall.'" *Hearth and Home* 3, no. 79 (November 17, 1892): 890.

Checkland, Olive. *Japan and Britain after 1859: Creating Cultural Bridges*. London: Routledge, 2003.

"China." *Lady's Newspaper*, May 8, 1847, 436.

Chittick, Kathryn. *Dickens and the 1830s*. Cambridge: Cambridge University Press, 1990.

Chowdhry, Prem. *Colonial India and the Making of Empire Cinema: Image, Ideology, and Identity*. Manchester: Manchester University Press, 2000.

"Christian Manliness, Specially Written for 'Lloyd's' Readers by the Bishop of Hull." *Lloyd's Weekly*, July 30, 1893, 7.

Christie, William. *The* Edinburgh Review *in the Literary Culture of Romantic Britain*. London: Pickering & Chatto, 2009.

"Church Chartism, Teetotal Chartism, Knowledge Chartism, and Household Suffrage Chartism." *Northern Star and Leeds General Advertiser*, April 3, 1841, 4. Nineteenth-Century Serials Edition. http://ncse-viewpoint.cch.kcl.ac.uk.

Claes, Koenraad. "Towards the Total Work of Art: Supplements and other Paratexts to Little Magazines of the 1890s." PhD diss., University of Ghent, 2011.

Clark, Anna. *The Struggle for the Breeches: Gender and the Making of the British Working Class*. Berkeley: University of California Press, 1995.

Clarke, Meaghan. *Critical Voices: Women and Art Criticism in Britain, 1880–1905*. Aldershot: Ashgate, 2005.

Cleave, John. "Temperance Record." *English Chartist Circular and Temperance Record for England and Wales* 1, no. 1/2 (1841): 6.

Clinkscale, Edward. "*The Musical Times*: Introduction." In *The Musical Times: 1844–1900*, edited by Edward Clinkscale, ix–xv. Ann Arbor: UMI, 1994.

Clowes, W. B. *Family Business, 1803–1953*. London: Clowes and Sons, 1960.

Clubbe, John. *Victorian Forerunner: The Late Career of Thomas Hood*. Durham: Duke University Press, 1968.

Clyde, Tom. *Irish Literary Magazines: An Outline History and Descriptive Bibliography*. Dublin: Irish Academic Press, 2003.

Cobbett, William. "Duty on Printing Paper." *Cobbett's Weekly Political Register*, February 13, 1802, 11–14.

Cockburn, Henry. *Life of Lord Jeffrey. With a Selection from His Correspondence*. 2 vols. Edinburgh: A & C Black, 1852.

Codell, Julie. "The Art Press and the Art Market: The Artist as 'Economic Man.'" In *The Rise of the Modern Art Market in London, 1850–1939*, edited by Anne Helmreich and Pamela Fletcher, 128–50. Manchester: Manchester University Press, 2012.

———. "*The Century Guild Hobby Horse*: 1886–94." *Victorian Periodicals Review* 16, no. 2 (1983): 43–52.

———. "Constructing the Victorian Artist: National Identity, the Political Economy of Art, & Biographical Mania in the Periodical Press." *Victorian Periodicals Review* 33, no. 3 (2000): 283–316.

———. "From English School to British School: Modernism, Revisionism, and National Culture in the Writings of M. H. Spielmann." *Nineteenth-Century Art Worldwide* 14, no. 2 (2015). http://www.19thc-artworldwide.org/summer15/codell-on-modernism-revisionism-and-national-culture-in-the-writings-of-spielmann

———. "*Fine Arts Quarterly Review* and Artpolitics of the 1860s." *Victorian Periodicals Review* 23, no. 3 (1990): 91–7.

———, ed. *Imperial Co-Histories: National Identities and the British and Colonial Press*. London: Fairleigh Dickinson Press, 2003.

———. "Marion Harry Spielmann and the Press in the Professionalization of Artists." *Victorian Periodicals Review* 22, no. 1 (1989): 7–15.

———. "Moderate Praise: Art Criticism of *The Portfolio*." *Victorian Periodicals Review* 20, no. 3 (1987): 83–93.

———. *The Victorian Artist*. New York: Cambridge, 2003.

Coggeshall, W.T. *The Newspaper Record*. Philadelphia: Lay, 1856.

Cohen, Patricia Cline, Timothy J. Gilfoyle, and Helen Lefkowitz Horowitz. *The Flash Press: Sporting Male Weeklies in 1840s New York*. Chicago: University of Chicago Press, 2008.

Colclough, Stephen. "'A Greater Outlay than any Return': The Library of W.H. Smith & Son, 1860–1873." *Publishing History* 54 (2003): 67–93.

———. "'Purifying the sources of amusement and information'? The Railway Bookstalls of W.H. Smith & Son, 1855–60." *Publishing History* 56 (2004): 27–51.

———. "Station to Station: The *LNWR* and the Emergence of the Railway Bookstall, 1840–1875." In *Printing Places: Locations of Book Production and Distribution since 1500*, edited by John Hinks and Catherine Armstrong, 169–84. London: British Library, 2005.

Coleman, D.C. *The British Paper Industry, 1495–1860*. Oxford: Clarendon Press, 1958.

Collet, Collet Dobson. *History of the Taxes on Knowledge*. 2 vols. London: T. Fisher Unwin, 1899.

[Collins, Wilkie]. "The Unknown Public." *Household Words*, August 21, 1858, 217–22.

Colvin, Sidney. "A Note on 'Weir of Hermiston.'" *Cosmopolis* 2, no. 5 (1896): 323–33.

"The Commercial History of a Penny Magazine." *Penny Magazine*, September 28, 1833, 377–84; October 26, 1833, 417–24; November 30, 1833, 465–72; December 28, 1833, 505–11.

Conan Doyle, Arthur. *Memories and Adventures*. Oxford: Oxford University Press, 1989.

Conboy, Martin. *The Language of Newspapers: Socio-Historical Perspectives*. London: Continuum, 2010.

———. *The Press and Popular Culture*. London: Sage, 2002.

Connell, R.W. *Masculinities*. Berkeley: University of California Press, 1995.

Connors, Linda E., and Mary Lu MacDonald. *National Identity in Great Britain and British North America, 1815–1851: The Role of Nineteenth-Century Periodicals*. Farnham: Ashgate, 2011.

Cook, Eliza. "Love On." *New Monthly Magazine* 70 (April 1844): 514.

———. "Newspapers." *Eliza Cook's Journal* 1 (June 16, 1849): 111.

Cook, Matt. *London and the Culture of Homosexuality, 1885–1914*. Cambridge: Cambridge University Press, 2003.

Cooke, Simon, and Paul Goldman, eds. *Reading Victorian Illustration, 1855–1875*. Farnham: Ashgate, 2012.

Cooper, Dana Calise. "Informal Ambassadors: American Women, Transatlantic Marriages, and Anglo-American Relations, 1865–1945." PhD diss., Texas Christian University, 2006.

Cooper, Victoria L. *The House of Novello: Practice and Policy of a Victorian Music Publisher, 1829–1866*. Aldershot: Ashgate, 2003.

Coover, James. *Music Publishing, Copyright, and Piracy in Victorian England*. London: Mansell, 1985.

———. "Victorian Periodicals for the Music Trade." *Notes* 46, no. 3 (1990): 609–21.

———. "William Reeves, Booksellers/Publishers, 1825–." In *Music Publishing & Collecting: Essays in Honor of Donald W. Krummel*, edited by David Hunter, 39–67. Urbana: University of Illinois Press, 1994.

"Correspondence." *Boy's Own Paper* 1 (May 31, 1879): 320.

Cortazzi, Hugh, and Gordon Daniels, eds. *Britain and Japan, 1859–1991*. London: Routledge, 1991.

"Country Brewers Society." *Morning Post*, October 25, 1887, 2.

Cowan, Yuri. "Industrializing Print, Sport, and Authorship: Nimrod, Surtees, and the *New Sporting Magazine*." *Critical Survey* 24, no. 1 (2012): 1–16.

Cox, Howard, and Simon Mowatt. *Revolutions from Grub Street: A History of Magazine Publishing in Britain*. Oxford: Oxford University Press, 2014.

Crane, Diana. *Fashion and Its Social Agendas: Class, Gender, and Identity in Clothing*. Chicago: University of Chicago Press, 2000.

Crane, Diana, and Laura Bovone. "Approaches to Material Culture: The Sociology of Fashion and Clothing." *Poetics* 34 (2006): 319–33.

Cricketer's Almanack for the Year 1867. London: John Wisden, 1867.

Crisp, William Finch. *The Printers' Universal Book of Reference and Every Hour Office Companion*. London: J. Hadron, 1875.

Cronin, Maura. "Provincial Publishing." In *The Oxford History of the Irish Book*, vol. 4, edited by James H. Murphy, 46–87. Oxford: Oxford University Press, 2011.

Cross, Nigel. *The Common Writer: Life in Nineteenth-Century Grub Street*. Cambridge: Cambridge University Press, 1985.

Croteau, David, and William Hoynes. *The Business of Media: Corporate Media and the Public Interest*. 2nd ed. Thousand Oaks, CA: Pine Forge, 2006.

Cunningham, Bernardette, and Máire Kennedy, eds. *The Experience of Reading: Irish Historical Perspectives*. Dublin: Rare Books Group of the Library Association of Ireland and Economic and Social History Society of Ireland, 1999.

Cunningham, Patricia A. *Reforming Women's Fashion, 1850–1920: Politics, Health, and Art*. Ohio: Kent State University Press, 2003.

Curran, James. *Media and Power*. London: Routledge, 2002.

Curran, James, and Jean Seaton. *Power Without Responsibility: Press, Broadcasting, and the Internet in Britain*. 7th ed. London: Routledge, 2010.

Curtis, L. Perry, Jr. *Apes and Angels: The Irishman in Victorian Caricature*. Washington: Smithsonian, 1971.

Cutmore, Jonathan, ed. *Conservatism and the* Quarterly Review: *A Critical Analysis*. London: Pickering & Chatto, 2007.

———. *Contributors to the* Quarterly Review, *1809–25: A History*. London: Pickering & Chatto, 2008.

Dagnall, H. "The Taxes on Knowledge: Excise Duty on Paper." *Library*, 6th ser., 20, no. 4 (1998): 347–63.

Dajani, Amjad Muhsen S. "*The Islamic World*, 1893–1908." *Victorian Periodicals Review* 47, no. 3 (2014): 454–75.

Daly, Kieran Anthony. *Catholic Church Music in Ireland, 1878–1903*. Dublin: Four Courts, 1995.

Dalziels' Bible Gallery. London: Routledge, 1881.

Dameron, J. Lasley, and Pamela Palmer. *An Index to the Critical Vocabulary of* Blackwood's Edinburgh Magazine, *1830–1840*. West Cornwall, CT: Locust Hill Press, 1983.

Dance, Charles. "Good News for the Ladies!" *Lady's Newspaper*, January 2, 1847, 2.

Davies, John, Nigel Jenkins, Menna Baines, and Peredur I. Lynch, eds. *Encyclopaedia of Wales*. Cardiff: University of Wales Press, 2008.

Davis, J.Q. "Dancing the Symphonic: Beethoven-Boscha's *Symphonie Pastorale*, 129." *Nineteenth Century Music* 27, no. 1 (2003): 25–47.

Davis, Jim. "Looking Towards 1843 and the End of the Monopoly." In *The Oxford Handbook of the Georgian Theatre, 1737–1832*, edited by Julia Swindells and David Francis Taylor, 156–73. Oxford: Oxford University Press, 2014.

Davis, John. "Primrose, Archibald Philip, Fifth Earl of Rosebery and First Earl of Midlothian (1847–1929)." In *The Oxford Dictionary of National Biography*. Oxford: Oxford University Press, 2004. http://www.oxforddnb.com.

Davis, Richard W. "'We Are All Americans Now!': Anglo-American Marriages in the Later Nineteenth Century." *Proceedings of the American Philosophical Society* 135, no. 2 (1991): 140–99.

Davis, Tracy C. *The Economics of the British Stage, 1800–1914*. Cambridge: Cambridge University Press, 2000.

de Lasteyrie, Robert, ed. *Bibliographie générale des travaux historiques et archéologiques publiés par les sociétés savantes de la France, dressée sous les auspices du Ministère de l'instruction publique*. Paris: Imprimerie nationale, 1888–1918.

De Nie, Michael. "British Conceptions of Ireland and Irishness in the Nineteenth Century." *History Compass* 3 (2005): 1–6.

———. *The Eternal Paddy: Irish Identity and the British Press, 1798–1882*. Madison: University of Wisconsin Press, 2004.

de Val, Dorothy. "'Legitimate, Phenomenal and Eccentric': Pianists and Pianism in Late Nineteenth-Century London." In *Nineteenth-Century British Music Studies*, vol. 2, edited by Jeremy Dibble and Bennett Zon, 182–95. Aldershot: Ashgate, 2002.

Deacon's Newspaper Handbook and Advertiser's Guide. London: Deacon, Samuel, 1877–94.

Deane, Seamus, ed. *The Field Day Anthology of Irish Writing*. Derry: Field Day Publications, 1991.

Deazley, Ronan. "Commentary on the *Statute of Anne* 1710." In *Primary Sources on Copyright (1450–1900)*, edited by L. Bently and M. Kretschmer. 2008. http://www.copyrighthistory.org/cam/commentary/uk_1710/uk_1710_com_272007105424.html.

———. *On the Origin of the Right to Copy: Charting the Movement of Copyright Law in Eighteenth Century Britain, 1695–1775*. Oxford: Hart Publishing, 2004.

Deccan. "Life in the Jungle: Panther Shooting." *New Sporting Magazine* 11, no. 62 (1836): 110–16.

"Decline of the Drama." *Morning Post*, August 26, 1829, 3.

Delhaye, Christine, "The Development of Consumption Culture and the Individualization of Female Identity: Fashion Discourse in the Netherlands, 1880–1920." *Journal of Consumer Culture* 6, no. 1 (2006): 87–115.

Dellamora, Richard. *Masculine Desire: The Sexual Politics of Victorian Aestheticism*. Chapel Hill: University of North Carolina Press, 1990.

———, ed. *Victorian Sexual Dissidence*. Chicago: University of Chicago Press, 1999.

Demata, Massimiliano, and Duncan Wu, eds. *British Romanticism and the* Edinburgh Review: *Bicentenary Essays*. Basingstoke: Palgrave, 2002.

Demoor, Marysa. "From Epitaph to Obituary: The Death Politics of T.S. Eliot and Ezra Pound." *Biography* 28, no. 2 (2005): 255–75.

———. *Their Fair Share: Women, Power, and Criticism in the* Athenaeum, *from Millicent Garrett Fawcett to Katherine Mansfield, 1870–1920*. Aldershot: Ashgate, 2000.

"Depression among Public Men." *Western Mail*, January 25, 1875, 4.

Deslandes, Paul R. *Oxbridge Men: British Masculinity and the Undergraduate Experience, 1850–1920*. Bloomington: Indiana University Press, 2005.

Deutsch, Karl. "The Growth of Nations: Some Recurrent Patterns of Political and Social Integration." *World Politics* 5 (1953): 168–95.

DiCenzo, Maria, ed. *Feminist Media History*. London: Palgrave, 2011.

Dickens, Charles. *The Letters of Charles Dickens*. Edited by Madeline House, Graham Storey, and Kathleen Tillotson. 12 vols. Oxford: Clarendon Press, 1965–2002.

Dillane, Fionnuala. *Before George Eliot: Marian Evans and the Periodical Press*. Cambridge: Cambridge University Press, 2013.

Dinwiddy, J.R. *From Luddism to the First Reform Bill: Reform in England, 1810–1832*. Oxford: Blackwell, 1986.

Dircks, Rudolf. "Ellen." *Savoy* 1 (1896): 103–8.

"Distinction of the Male and Female Character." *New British Lady's Magazine* 1, no. 1 (1818): 20–3.

Dixon, Diana. "Children and the Press, 1866–1914." In *The Press in English Society from the Seventeenth to Nineteenth Centuries*, edited by Michael Harris and Alan Lee, 133–48. London: Associated University Presses, 1986.

———. "From Instruction to Amusement: Attitudes of Authority in Children's Periodicals Before 1914." *Victorian Periodicals Review* 19, no. 2 (1986): 63–7.

———. "Navigating the Maze: Sources for Press Historians." *Media History* 9 (2003): 79–90.

[Dixon, William Hepworth]. "Cavour: A Memoir." *Athenaeum* 1766 (August 31, 1861): 273–5.

Dobson, Austin. "The Dilettant. Imitated from the Fables of Gellert." *Belgravia* 42 (October 1880): 425–6.

Dodd, A.H. *The Industrial Revolution in North Wales*. 3rd ed. Cardiff: University of Wales Press, 1971.

Donaldson, William. *Popular Literature in Victorian Scotland: Language, Fiction and the Press*. Aberdeen: Aberdeen University Press, 1986.

Doughan, David. "Periodicals by, for, and about Women in Britain." *Women's Studies International Forum* 10, no. 3 (1987): 263.

Doughan, David, and Denise Sanchez. *Feminist Periodicals, 1855–1984: An Annotated Critical Bibliography of British, Irish, Commonwealth, and International Titles*. New York: New York University Press, 1987.

Doughty, Terri. *Selections from the* Girl's Own Paper, *1880–1907*. Peterborough: Broadview, 2004.

Douglas, Mary. *In the Active Voice*. London: Routledge, 1982.

Dowden, Edward. "George Eliot." *Contemporary Review* 20 (1872): 403–22.

Downey, Edmund. *Charles Lever: His Life in His Letters*. Vol. 1. Edinburgh: William Blackwood and Sons, 1906.

———. *Twenty Years Ago: A Book of Anecdote Illustrating Literary Life in London*. London: Hurst and Blackett, 1905.

Downie, J.A. *Robert Harley and the Press: Propaganda and Public Opinion in the Age of Swift and Defoe*. Cambridge: Cambridge University Press, 1978.

"The Drama." *New Monthly Magazine* 33 (April 1831): 166.

Dredge, Sarah. "Opportunism and Accommodation: The *English Woman's Journal* and the British Mid-Nineteenth-Century Women's Movement." *Women's Studies: An Interdisciplinary Journal* 34, no. 2 (2005): 133–57.

Dreher, Nan H. "Redundancy and Emigration: The 'Woman Question' in Mid-Victorian Britain." *Victorian Periodicals Review* 26, no. 1 (1993): 3–7.

Drew, John. "*All the Year Round*." In *The Dictionary of Nineteenth-Century Journalism in Great Britain and Ireland*, edited by Laurel Brake and Marysa Demoor. Chadwyck-Healey, 2012. http://c19index.chadwyck.co.uk.

———. *Dickens the Journalist*. Basingstoke: Palgrave Macmillan, 2003.

———. "Household Words." In *The Dictionary of Nineteenth-Century Journalism in Great Britain and Ireland*, edited by Laurel Brake and Marysa Demoor. Chadwyck-Healey, 2012. http://c19index.chadwyck.co.uk.

Drew, John, and Hugh Craig. "Did Dickens Write 'Temperate Temperance'?: An Attempt to Identify Authorship of an Anonymous Article in *All the Year Round*." *Victorian Periodicals Review* 44, no. 3 (2011): 267–90.

Drotner, Kirsten. *English Children and Their Magazines, 1751–1945*. New Haven: Yale University Press, 1988.

Drummond, Pippa. *The Provincial Music Festival in England, 1784–1914*. Aldershot: Ashgate, 2011.

Dubois, Martin. "The *Month* as Hopkins Knew It." *Victorian Periodicals Review* 43, no. 3 (2010): 296–308.

Duffy, Charles Gavan. "Mr. Lever's 'Irish' Novels." *Nation*, June 10, 1843, 554–5.

Dunae, Patrick A. "Boys' Literature and the Idea of Empire, 1870–1914." *Victorian Studies* 24 (Autumn 1980): 105–21.

———. "Penny Dreadfuls: Late Nineteenth-Century Boys' Literature and Crime." *Victorian Studies* 22 (Winter 1979): 133–50.

Dungan, Myles. *Mr. Parnell's Rottweiler: Censorship and the United Ireland Newspaper, 1881–1891*. Sallins: Irish Academic Press, 2014.

Dunn, William Newton. *The Man Who Was John Bull: Biography of Theodore Hook*. London: Allendale, 1996.

Dyer, George. "Ode to Liberty." *Tribune* 2, no. 21 (1795): 147–8.

E.N. [Edith Nesbit]. "Richborough Castle." *To-day: Monthly Magazine of Scientific Socialism* 36 (November 1886): 157–8.

Easley, Alexis. *First-Person Anonymous: Women Writers and Victorian Print Media, 1830–70*. Aldershot: Ashgate, 2004.

———. *Literary Celebrity, Gender, and Victorian Authorship 1850–1914*. Newark: University of Delaware Press, 2011.

———. "*Tait's Edinburgh Magazine* in the 1830s: Dialogues on Gender, Class, and Reform." *Victorian Periodicals Review* 38, no. 3 (2005): 263–79.

———. "W.T. Stead, Late Victorian Feminism, and the *Review of Reviews*." In *W.T. Stead, Newspaper Revolutionary*, edited by Laurel Brake, Ed King, Roger Luckhurst, and James Mussell, 37–58. London: British Library, 2012.

Eatock, Colin Timothy. "The Crystal Palace Concerts: Canon Formation and the English Musical Renaissance." *Nineteenth-Century Music* 34, no. 1 (2010): 87–105.

———. *Mendelssohn and Victorian England*. Aldershot: Ashgate, 2009.

Editorial. *Green Room* 1 (June 26, 1880): 3.

Editorial. *Liverpool Dramatic Censor* 1 (July 12, 1834): 1.

Editorial. *Liverpool Dramatic Journal* 1 (November 12, 1832): 1.

"Editorial Commentary." *Nineteenth-Century Serials Edition*. 2008. http://www.ncse.ac.uk/commentary/index.html.

"Editorial Note." *Literarisches Centralblatt für Deutschland*, October 1, 1850, 1.

"The Editor's Chair." *Woman Worker*, April 14, 1909, 348.

Edwards, P.D. *Dickens's "Young Men": George Augustus Sala, Edmund Yates, and the World of Victorian Journalism*. Aldershot: Ashgate, 1997.

Egan, Pierce. *Sporting Anecdotes: Original and Selected*. London: Sherwood, Neely, and Jones, 1820.

Egoff, Sheila. *Children's Periodicals of the Nineteenth Century: A Survey and Bibliography*. London: Library Association, 1951.

Ehnes, Caley. "Navigating the Periodical Market: *Once a Week*, Poetry, and the Illustrated Literary Periodical." *Victorians: A Journal of Culture & Literature* 123 (2013): 96–112.

———. "Religion, Readership, and the Periodical Press: The Place of Poetry in *Good Words*." *Victorian Periodicals Review* 45, no. 4 (2012): 466–87.

Ehrlich, Cyril. *First Philharmonic: A History of the Royal Philharmonic Society*. Oxford: Clarendon, 1995.

———. *The Music Profession in Britain since the Eighteenth Century*. Oxford: Clarendon, 1985.

[Eliot, George]. "Madame de Sablé." In *Selected Essays, Poems, and Other Writings*, edited by A.S. Byatt and Nicholas Warren, 8–37. London: Penguin, 1990.

———. *Selected Essays, Poems and Other Writings*. Edited by A.S. Byatt and Nicholas Warren. London: Penguin, 1990.

Eliot, Simon. "The Business of Victorian Publishing." In *The Cambridge Companion to the Victorian Novel*, edited by Deirdre David, 37–60. Cambridge: Cambridge University Press, 2001.

———. *Some Patterns and Trends in British Publishing, 1800–1919*. London: Bibliographical Society, 1994.

Ellegård, Alvar. *The Readership of the Periodical Press in Mid-Victorian Britain*. Götegborg: Göteborg University Press, 1957.

"Ellen Allardyce." *Ladies' Cabinet of Fashion, Music, and Romance*, October 1, 1849, 248–52.

Elleray, Michelle. "Little Builders: Coral Insects, Missionary Culture, and the Victorian Child." *Victorian Literature and Culture* 39 (2011): 223–38.

Ellis, Ted R., III. "Poetical Magazine." In *British Literary Magazines*, vol. 2, *The Romantic Age, 1789–1836*, edited by Alvin Sullivan, 347–53. Westwood: Greenwood Press, 1983.

———. "Victorian Comic Journals." In *British Literary Magazines*, vol. 3, *The Victorian and Edwardian Age, 1837–1913*, edited by Alvin Sullivan, 501–14. Westport: Greenwood Press, 1984.

Engels, Friedrich. "On the Invention of Printing." *Marxists Internet Archive*. http://www.marxists.org.

"English Appropriation of Irish Intellect." *Nation*, November 26, 1842, 106.

"The Englishwoman's Conversazione." *Englishwoman's Domestic Magazine*, n.s., 3 (October 1861): 264.

Enkvist, Nils Erik. *American Humour in England before Mark Twain*. Abo: Abo akademi, 1953.

———. "The Biglow Papers in Nineteenth-Century England." *New England Quarterly* 26, no. 2 (1953): 219–36.

Epstein, James A. *Radical Expression: Political Language, Ritual, and Symbol in England, 1790–1850*. New York: Oxford University Press, 1994.

Erickson, Lee. *The Economy of Literary Form: English Literature and the Industrialization of Publishing, 1800–1850*. Baltimore: Johns Hopkins University Press, 1996.

Escott, T.H.S. "Vagueness." *Belgravia* 5 (May 1868): 407–14.

"The Essayist-Periodical Literature." *American Masonick Record and Albany Literary Journal* 4, no. 6 (March 6, 1830): 44–5.

Estermann, Alfred, ed. *Die Deutschen Literaturzeitschriften, 1815–1850*. 11 vols. Munich: K.G. Saur, 1991.

Everitt, Graham. *English Caricaturists and Graphic Humourists of the Nineteenth Century: How They Illustrated and Interpreted Their Times*. London: Swan Sonnenschein & Co., 1893.

"Exhibition of the Royal Academy." *Art Journal*, June 1861, 161–72.

"The Exhibition of Works in Black and White." *Standard*, June 14, 1880, 3.

"Expansion." *Halfpenny Owl*, May 6, 1882, 1.

"Extraordinary Escape of a Woman from Indians." *Illustrated Police News*, January 5, 1867, 1.

F.J.C. "The Old Home." *Leisure Hour* 9 (October 20, 1859): 672.

F.R.S. "The Dulness of Science." *Nature* 1 (November 11, 1869): 43–4.

Feather, John. *A History of British Publishing*. London: Routledge, 1988.

Featherstone, Simon. "Artemus Ward and the Egyptian Hall." In *Leeds Working Papers in Victorian Studies*, vol. 3, *Platform, Pulpit, Rhetoric*, 37–49. Leeds: Leeds Centre for Victorian Studies, 2000.

Fehlbaum, Valerie. *Ella Hepworth Dixon: The Story of a Modern Woman*. Aldershot: Ashgate, 2005.

Feldman, Paula R., ed. *The Keepsake for 1829*. Peterborough: Broadview Press, 2006.

———. "The Poet and the Profits: Felicia Hemans and the Literary Marketplace." In *Women's Poetry, Late Romantic to Late Victorian: Gender and Genre, 1830–1900*, edited by Isobel Armstrong and Virginia Blain, 71–101. New York: St. Martin's Press, 1999.

Fellinger, Imogen. *Periodica Musicalia (1789–1830)*. Regensburg: Gustav Bosse, 1986.

Fellinger, Imogen, Julie Woodward, Dario Adamo, Silvia Arena, Robert Balchin, André Balog, Georgina Binns et al. "Periodicals." In *Grove Music Online*, edited by Deane Root. London: Oxford University Press, 2006. http://www.oxfordmusiconline.com.

Fenton, Laurence. *Palmerston and the Times*. London: IB Tauris, 2013.

"Field Sports." *Examiner*, August 27, 1815, 557.

"Fine-Art Gossip." *Athenaeum* 3079 (October 30, 1886): 574–5.

Finkelstein, David. *The House of Blackwood: Author-Publisher Relations in the Victorian Era*. University Park: Penn State University Press, 2002.

———. "Periodicals, Encyclopaedias, and Nineteenth-Century Literary Production." In *The Edinburgh History of Scottish Literature*, vol. 2, edited by Ian Brown, Thomas Clancy, Susan Manning, and Murray Pittock, 198–210. Edinburgh: Edinburgh University Press, 2007.

———, ed. *Print Culture and the Blackwood Tradition*. Toronto: University of Toronto Press, 2006.

———. "Selling *Blackwood's Magazine*, 1817–1834." In *Romanticism and Blackwood's Magazine: "An Unprecedented Phenomenon,"* edited by Robert Morrison and Daniel Sanjiv Roberts, 69–86. Basingstoke: Palgrave Macmillan, 2013.

Finkelstein, David, and D.M. Peers, eds. *Negotiating India in the Nineteenth Century Media*. London: Macmillan, 2000.

Fitzsimons, Raymund. *The Baron of Piccadilly: The Travels and Entertainments of Albert Smith, 1816–1860*. London: Geoffrey Bles, 1967.

Fletcher, Pamela, and Anne Helmreich. "The Periodical and the Art Market: Investigating the 'Dealer–Critic System' in Victorian England." *Victorian Periodicals Review* 41, no. 4 (2008): 323–51.

———, eds. *The Rise of the Modern Art Market in London, 1850–1939*. Manchester: Manchester University Press, 2012.

Flint, Kate, ed. *The Cambridge History of Victorian Literature*. Cambridge: Cambridge University Press, 2012.

———. "Moral Judgement and the Language of Art Criticism, 1870–1910." *Oxford Art Journal* 6, no. 2 (1983): 59–66.

———. "The 'Philistine' and the New Art Critic: J.A. Spender and D.S. MacColl's Debate of 1893." *Victorian Periodicals Review* 21, no. 1 (1988): 3–8.

———. *The Woman Reader, 1837–1914*. Oxford: Clarendon Press, 1993.

Ford, John. *Cricket: A Social History, 1700–1835*. Newton Abbot: David & Charles, 1972.

Fordham, G.G. "Reform, War and Taxes." *Cobbett's Weekly Political Register*, March 25, 1815, 380–1.

Fox, Celina. *Graphic Journalism in England during the 1830s and 1840s*. New York: Garland, 1988.

———. "Political Caricature and the Freedom of the Press in Early Nineteenth Century England." In *Newspaper History*, edited by George Boyce, James Curran, and Pauline Wingate, 226–46. London: Constable, 1978.

Frankel, Robert. *Observing America: The Commentary of British Visitors to the United States, 1890–1950*. Madison: University of Wisconsin Press, 2007.

Fraser, Derek. "The Editor as Activist: Editors and Urban Politics in Early Victorian England." In *Innovators and Preachers: The Role of the Editor in Victorian England*, edited by J.H. Wiener, 121–42. Westport: Greenwood Press, 1985.

Fraser, Hilary, Stephanie Green, and Judith Johnston. *Gender and the Victorian Periodical*. Cambridge: Cambridge University Press, 2003.

Fraser, William Hamish. "*People's Journal* (1858–1990)." In *The Dictionary of Nineteenth-Century Journalism in Great Britain and Ireland*, edited by Laurel Brake and Marysa Demoor, 489. Ghent and London: Academia Press and the British Library, 2009.

Freeman, E.A. "The Controversy on Field Sports." *Fortnightly Review*, n.s., 8 (1870): 674–91.

———. "The Morality of Field Sports." *Fortnightly Review*, n.s., 6 (1869): 353–88.

Freeman, Michael. *Railways and the Victorian Imagination*. New Haven: Yale University Press, 1999.

"Friendship. A Chapter for Youth." *Gentleman's Magazine*, n.s., 8 (1837): 328–30.

Fuller, Sophie. "Creative Women and 'Exoticism' at the Last Fin-de-Siècle." In *Music and Orientalism in the British Empire, 1780s–1940s: Portrayal of the East*, edited by Martin Clayton and Bennett Zon, 237–55. Aldershot: Ashgate, 2007.

Fulton, Richard. "Boys' Adventure Magazines and the Discourse of Adventure, 1860–1885." *Australasian Journal of Victorian Studies* 15, no. 1 (2010): 1–21.

Fyfe, Aileen. "Periodicals and Books Series." In *Culture and Science in the Nineteenth-Century Media*, edited by Louise Henson, Geoffrey Cantor, Gowan Dawson, Richard Noakes, Sally Shuttleworth, and Jonathan R. Topham, 71–82. Aldershot: Ashgate, 2004.

———. *Science and Salvation: Evangelical Popular Science Publishing in Victorian Britain*. Chicago: University of Chicago Press, 2004.

———. *Steam-Powered Knowledge: William Chambers and the Business of Publishing, 1820–1860*. Chicago: University of Chicago Press, 2012.

Fyfe, Paul. "Illustrating the Accident: Railways and the Catastrophic Picturesque in *The Illustrated London News*." *Victorian Periodicals Review* 46, no. 1 (2013): 61–91.

Gabin, Jane S. *American Women in Gilded Age London*. Gainesville: University Press of Florida, 2006.

Gagnier, Regenia. *The Insatiability of Human Wants: Economics and Aesthetics in Market Society*. Chicago: University of Chicago Press, 2000.

Gallagher, Catherine. *The Body Economic: Life, Death, and Sensation in Political Economy and the Victorian Novel*. Princeton: Princeton University Press, 2006.

Gardiner, Leslie. *The Making of John Menzies*. Edinburgh: Menzies, 1983.

Gardner, Victoria E.M. "The Communications Broker and the Public Sphere: John Ware and the *Cumberland Pacquet*." *Cultural and Social History* 10 (2013): 533–57.

Gascoigne, Robert. *A Historical Catalogue of Scientific Periodicals, 1665–1900: With a Survey of Their Development*. New York: Garland, 1985.

Geczy, Adam. *Fashion and Orientalism*. London: Bloomsbury, 2013.

"General." *Solicitors' Journal* 34 (October 4, 1890): 774.

George, Alexander. "Quantitative and Qualitative Approaches to Content Analysis." In *Trends in Content Analysis*, edited by I. de Sola Pool, 7–32. Urbana: University of Illinois Press, 1959.

Gerrard, Teresa. "New Methods in the History of Reading: 'Answers to Correspondents' in the *Family Herald*, 1860–1900." *Publishing History* 43 (January 1998): 53–69.

Gifford, Douglas, and Dorothy McMillan. *A History of Scottish Women's Writing*. Edinburgh: Edinburgh University Press, 1997.

Gillett, Paula. "Ambivalent Friendships: Music-Lovers, Amateurs, and Professional Musicians in the Late Nineteenth Century." In *Music and British Culture, 1785–1914: Essays in Honour of Cyril Ehrlich*, edited by Christina Bashford and Leanne Langley, 321–40. Oxford: Oxford University Press, 2000.

———. *Musical Women in England, 1870–1914: "Encroaching on All Man's Privileges."* New York: St. Martin's, 2000.

Gilroy, Paul. *"There Ain't No Black in the Union Jack": The Cultural Politics of Race and Nation*. Chicago: University of Chicago Press, 1991.

Gitelman, Lisa. *Always Already New: Media, History, and the Data of Culture*. Cambridge, MA: MIT Press, 2006.

"Godliness and Manliness." *Liverpool Mercury*, March 28, 1887, 7.

Goldman, Paul. *Victorian Illustration: The Pre-Raphaelites, the Idyllic School, and the High Victorians*. Aldershot: Scolar Press, 1996.

Goldman, Paul, and Simon Cooke. Introduction to *Reading Victorian Illustration, 1855–1875: Spoils of the Lumber Room*, edited by Paul Goldman and Simon Cooke, 1–11. Farnham: Ashgate, 2012.

Goldsworthy, Simon. "English Nonconformity and the Pioneering of the Modern Newspaper Campaign." *Journalism Studies* 7 (2006): 387–402.

"Good Reading." *Bow Bells*, March 27, 1867, 212.

Good Words: The Theology of its Editor and of Some of Its Contributors. 2nd ed. London: Record Offices, 1863.

"Gossip on the Grosvenor." *University Magazine* 94 (July 1879): 65–70.

Grand, Alfred. *The American Civil War and the British Press*. Jefferson: McFarland, 2000.

"Grand Juries." *Citizen* 1, no. 1 (1839): 23–30.

Grant, James. *The Metropolitan Weekly and Provincial Press*. Vol. 2. London: George Routledge and Sons, 1872.

———. *The Newspaper Press: Its Origin—Progress—and Present Position*. 2 vols. London: Tinsley, 1871.

"'The Graphic' at the Paris Exhibition from Our Own Correspondent." *Graphic*, September 15, 1900, 374.

Gray, Donald J. "Early Victorian Scandalous Journalism: Renton Nicholson's *The Town* (1837–1842)." In *The Victorian Periodical Press: Samplings and Soundings*, edited by Joanne Shattock and Michael Wolff, 317–48. Leicester: Leicester University Press, 1982.

———. "A List of Comic Periodicals Published in Great Britain, 1800–1900, with a Prefatory Essay." *Victorian Periodicals Newsletter* 5, no. 1 (March 1972): 2–39.

Gray, F. Elizabeth. "Beatification through Beautification: Poetry in the *Christian Lady's Magazine*, 1834–1849." *Victorian Poetry* 42, no. 3 (2004): 261–82.

———. "Poetry and Politics in *The Women's Penny Paper/Woman's Herald*, 1888–1893: 'One swift, bright fore-gleam of celestial day.'" *Victorian Periodicals Review* 45, no. 2 (2012): 134–57.

———, ed. *Women in Journalism at the Fin de Siècle: Making a Name for Herself*. Basingstoke: Palgrave Macmillan, 2012.

"The Great Exhibition." *Times*, May 8, 1851, 3. "The Great Triumph! Atlantic Telegraph Cable Successfully Laid." *Freedom's Champion*, August 2, 1866, 2.

"The Greatest Human Achievement on Record. Laus Deo!" *Liberator*, August 13, 1858, 3.

Gregory, Troy. "Mr. Jorrocks's Lost Sporting Magazine." *Victorian Periodicals Review* 36, no. 4 (2003): 331–50.

Greiman, Liela Rumbaugh. "William Ernest Henley and *The Magazine of Art*." *Victorian Periodicals Review* 16, no. 2 (1983): 53–63.

Grey, Maria G. "Men and Women." *Fortnightly Review* 26, no. 155 (1879): 672–85.

Griffin, Dustin. *Satire: A Critical Reintroduction*. Lexington: University Press of Kentucky, 1994.

Gross, John. *The Rise and Fall of the Man of Letters*. 1969. Reprint, London: Penguin, 1991.

"Grosvenor Gallery Review." *Punch* 76 (June 21, 1879): 285–7.

Guelke, Jeanne Kay, and Karen M. Morin. "Gender, Nature, Empire: Women Naturalists in Nineteenth-Century British Travel Literature." *Transactions of the Institute of British Geographers*, n.s., 26 (September 2001): 306–26.

Guilhamet, Leon. *Satire and the Transformation of Genre*. Philadelphia: University of Pennsylvania Press, 1987.

Gunn, Simon. *The Public Culture of the Victorian Middle Class: Ritual and Authority in the English Industrial City, 1840–1914*. Manchester: Manchester University Press, 2000.

Gutteridge, L.E.S. "A History of Wisden." Originally published in the *Wisden Almanack*, 1963. http://www.espncricinfo.com/wisdenalmanack/content/story/152762.html.

Gwynne, Isabel. "How Men Protect the Interests of Women." *Woman's Herald* 113, no. 3 (1890): 130.

H. "Home." *Ladies' Museum* 29 (February 1829): 80.

H. Untitled poem. *British Magazine* 15 (January 1839): 26–7.

"H.R.H. the Princess of Wales, and the Young Prince George." *British Workwoman*, March 1870, 229.

Habermas, Jürgen. "The Public Sphere: An Encyclopedia Article (1964)." Translated by Sara Lennox and Frank Lennox. *New German Critique* 3 (Autumn 1974): 49–55.

———. *The Structural Transformation of the Public Sphere*. Translated by Thomas Burger with Frederick Lawrence. Cambridge: MIT Press, 1991.

"The Habit of Reading." *Bow Bells*, October 29, 1873, 346.

Hack, Daniel. "Wild Charges: The Afro-Haitian 'Charge of the Light Brigade.'" *Victorian Studies* 54, no. 2 (2012): 199–225.

Hackwood, Frederick William. *William Hone, His Life and Times*. New York: B. Franklin, 1967.

Haggis, Jane. "Imperial Emotions: Affective Communities of Mission in British Protestant Women's Missionary Publications, 1880–1920." *Journal of Social History* 41 (2005): 691–716.

Haight, Gordon. *George Eliot: A Biography*. London: Penguin, 1985.

Hall, N. John. "Trollope, Anthony (1815–1882)." In *The Oxford Dictionary of National Biography*, edited by H.C.G. Matthew and Brian Harrison. Oxford: Oxford University Press, 2004. http://www.oxforddnb.com.

Hall, Samuel Carter. "The Annuals." *Art Union* 1 (November 1839): 171–3.

———. *Retrospect of a Long Life from 1815 to 1883*. 2 vols. London: Bentley, 1883.

Hall-Witt, Jennifer L. "Representing the Audience in the Age of Reform: Critics and the Elite at the Italian Opera in London." In *Music and British Culture, 1785–1914: Essays in Honour of Cyril Ehrlich*, edited by Christina Bashford and Leanne Langley, 121–44. Oxford: Oxford University Press, 2000.

Hammond, Mary. *Reading, Publishing and the Formation of Literary Taste in England, 1880–1914*. Aldershot: Ashgate, 2006

Hammond's List of London and Provincial Newspapers, Periodicals, etc. London: Hammond, 1850.

Hampton, Mark. *Visions of the Press, 1850–1950*. Urbana: University of Illinois Press, 2004.

Hannam, June, and Karen Hunt. *Socialist Women: Britain, 1880s to 1920s*. London: Routledge, 2002.

Hannay, James. *Satire and Satirists*. London: David Bogue, 1854.

Hardie, James Keir. "The Temperance Question." *Labour Leader*, April 17, 1897, 125.

Hardy, Thomas. "Candour in English Fiction." *New Review* 2 (January 1890): 15–21.

Harney, George Julian. "Notices to Correspondents." *Red Republican*, October 5, 1850, 125.

———. Untitled editorial. *Northern Star*, March 24, 1849, 5.

Harris, Janice H. "Not Suffering and Not Still: Women Writers at the *Cornhill Magazine*, 1860–1900." *Modern Language Quarterly* 47, no. 4 (1986): 382–92.

Harris, Stanley. *The Coaching Age*. London: Bentley, 1885.

Harrison, Brian. *Dictionary of British Temperance Biography*. Sheffield: Society for the Study of Labour History, 1973.

———. "Drink and Sobriety in England, 1815–1872: A Critical Bibliography." *International Review of Social History* 12, no. 4 (1967): 204–76.

———. *Drink and the Victorians: The Temperance Question in England, 1815–1872*. 1971. Reprint, Keele: Keele University Press, 1994.

———. "Press and Pressure Group in Modern Britain." In *The Victorian Periodical Press: Samplings and Soundings*, edited by Joanne Shattock and Michael Wolff, 261–95. Leicester: Leicester University Press, 1982.

———. "'A World of Which We Had No Conception': Liberalism and the English Temperance Press 1830–1872." *Victorian Studies* 13, no. 2 (1969): 125–58.

Harrison, Debbie. "All the *Lancet*'s Men: Reactionary Gentleman Physicians vs. Radical General Practitioners in the *Lancet*, 1823–1832." *Nineteenth-Century Gender Studies* 5, no. 2 (2009): 1–32.

"The Harvest Field: Maternal Love." *British Workwoman*, September 1872, 88.

Harvey, Adrian. *The Beginnings of a Commercial Sporting Culture in Britain, 1793–1850*. Aldershot: Ashgate, 2004.

Haskins, Katherine. The Art-Journal *and Fine Art Publishing in Victorian England, 1850–1880*. Burlington: Ashgate, 2012.

Hatin, Eugène. *Bibliographie historique et critique de la presse périodique française*. Paris: Firmin Didot, 1866.

———. *Histoire politique et littéraire de la presse en France*. 8 vols. Paris: Poulet-Malassis et De Broise, 1859–61.

Hatton, Joseph. *Journalistic London, Being a Series of Sketches of Famous Pens and Papers of the Day*. London: Sampson, Low, Marston, Searle, and Rivington, 1882.

———. "The True Story of 'Punch.' An Historical, Biographical, and Critical Gossip." *London Society* 28 (1875): 49–56, 152–61, 237–46, 341–51, 408–15, 511–17; 29 (1876): 127–32, 253–60, 438–42; 30 (1876): 57–63, 554–62.

Hayley, Barbara. "A Reading and Thinking Nation: Periodicals as the Voice of Nineteenth-Century Ireland." In *Three Hundred Years of Irish Periodicals*, edited by Barbara Hayley and Enda McKay, 9–48. Dublin: Association of Irish Learned Journals, 1987.

Hayley, Barbara, and Enda McKay, eds. *Three Hundred Years of Irish Periodicals*. Dublin: Association of Irish Learned Journals, 1987.

"Health of the British Navy." *Lancet* 2, no. 785 (1838): 865–6.

"Health, Wealth and Happiness of the Working Classes." *British Workman* 1 (January 1855): 1.

Hemans, Felicia. "The English Boy." *Blackwood's Edinburgh Magazine* 36 (July 1834): 65–6.

Hempton, David. "Methodism." In *Nineteenth-Century English Religious Traditions, Retrospect and Prospect*, edited by D.G. Paz, 117–43. Westport: Greenwood Press, 1995.

Hendrick, Burton J. *The Life of Andrew Carnegie*. London: Heinemann, 1933.

Henson, Louise, Geoffrey Cantor, Gowan Dawson, Richard Noakes, Sally Shuttleworth, and Jonathan R. Topham, eds. *Culture and Science in the Nineteenth-Century Media*. Aldershot: Ashgate, 2004.

Henwood, O. "The Suffering Christian." *Wesleyan-Methodist Magazine* 16 (October 1837): 800.

Herald, George. "The Atlantic Telegraph. Letter to the Editor." *Times*, August 18, 1858, 7.

Herstein, Sheila. "The Langham Place Circle and Feminist Periodicals of the 1860s." *Victorian Periodicals Review* 26, no. 1 (1993): 24–7.

Hetherington, Eliza. "The Indexing of Periodicals." In *Index to the Periodical Literature of the World*, vol. 2, edited by W.T. Stead and Eliza Hetherington, 3–7. London: Review of Reviews, 1893.

Hewitt, Martin. *The Dawn of the Cheap Press in Victorian Britain: The End of the "Taxes on Knowledge," 1849–1869*. London: Bloomsbury Academic, 2014.

Hill, J. "Anecdotal Evidence: Sport, the Newspaper Press and History." In *Deconstructing Sport History: A Postmodern Analysis*, edited by M.G. Phillips, 117–30. Albany: SUNY Press, 2006.

Hiller, Mary Ruth. "The *Westminster Review*, 1852–1900." In *The Wellesley Index to Victorian Periodicals*, vol. 3, edited by Walter E. Houghton, 546–53. Toronto: University of Toronto Press, 1979.

Hinks, John, Catherine Armstrong, and Matthew Day, eds. *Periodicals and Publishers: The Newspaper and Journal Trade, 1750–1914*. New Castle: Oak Knoll, 2009.

"Hints to Young Ladies, No. IX. Habits of Conversation." *Mothers' Magazine* 4 (1838): 158–63. Reprinted in *Victorian Women's Magazines: An Anthology*, edited by Margaret Beetham and Kay Boardman, 102–4. Manchester: Manchester University Press, 2001.

Hitchman, Francis. "The Penny Press." *Macmillan's Magazine* 43 (March 1881): 385–98.

Hoare, James, ed. *Japan's Treaty Ports and Foreign Settlements: The Uninvited Guest, 1858–1899*. Folkstone: Japan Library, 1994.

Hobbs, Andrew. "The Deleterious Dominance of *The Times* in Nineteenth-Century Scholarship." *Journal of Victorian Culture* 18 (2013): 472–97.

———. "Five Million Poems, or the Local Press as Poetry Publisher, 1800–1900." *Victorian Periodicals Review* 45, no. 4 (2012): 488–92.

———. "Reading the Local Paper: Social and Cultural Functions of the Local Press in Preston, Lancashire, 1855–1900." PhD diss., University of Central Lancashire, 2010.

———. "Watts, Alaric Alexander." In *The Dictionary of Nineteenth-Century Journalism in Great Britain and Ireland*, edited by Laurel Brake and Marysa Demoor. Chadwyck-Healey, 2012. http://c19index.chadwyck.co.uk/.

———. "When the Provincial Press Was the National Press (c. 1836–c. 1900)." *International Journal of Regional and Local Studies* 5 (2009): 16–43.

Hobbs, Andrew, and Annemarie McAllister, eds. "Local and Regional Newspapers." Special issue, *International Journal of Regional and Local Studies* 5, no. 1 (2009).

Hobbs, Andrew, and Claire Januszewski. "How Local Newspapers Came to Dominate Victorian Poetry Publishing." *Victorian Poetry* 52 (2014): 65–87.

Hobson, Harold, Phillip Knightley, and Leonard Russell. *The Pearl of Days: An Intimate Memoir of the Sunday Times, 1822–1972*. London: Hamish Hamilton, 1972.

Hobson, J. A. *Imperialism: A Study*. Cambridge: Cambridge University Press, 1902.

Hodder, George. *Memories of My Time: Including Personal Reminiscences of Eminent Men*. London: Tinsley Brothers, 1870.

Hoey, Christopher Clinton. "The Caxton Celebrations." *Irish Builder* 19 (July 1, 1877): 183–5; (July 15, 1877): 200–2; (August 1, 1877): 216–8; (August 15, 1877): 234–6; (September 1, 1877): 250–1. Continued as "Notes on the Rise and Progress of Printing and Publishing in Ireland." (September 15, 1877): 266–8; (October 1, 1877): 282–4; (October 15, 1877): 298–300; (November 1, 1877): 314–6; (November 15, 1877): 329–32; (December 1, 1877): 346–8; (December 15, 1877): 362–6; 20 (January 1, 1878): 5–6; (January 15, 1878): 21–2; (February 1, 1878): 34–6; (February 15, 1878): 50–2; (March 1, 1878): 67–8; (March 15, 1878): 91–3; (April 1, 1878): 98–100; (April 15, 1878): 114–5; (May 1, 1878): 135–6; (June 1, 1878): 160–3.

Holcomb, Adele. "Anna Jameson: The First Professional Art Historian." *Art History* 6 (1983): 171–87.

Holley, Rose. "How Good Can It Get?: Analysing and Improving OCR Accuracy in Large Scale Historic Newspaper Digitisation Programs." *D-Lib Magazine* 15, no. 3/4 (2009). http://www.dlib.org/dlib/march09/holley/03holley.html.

———. "Many Hands Make Light Work: Public Collaborative OCR Text Correction in Australian Historic Newspapers." *National Library of Australia*. Canberra: National Library of Australia, March 1, 2009. http://www.nla.gov.au/content/many-hands-make-light-work-public-collaborative-ocr-text-correction-in-australian-historic.

Hollis, Patricia. *The Pauper Press: A Study in Working-Class Radicalism of the 1830s*. Oxford: Oxford University Press, 1970.

Hone, Ann. *For the Cause of Truth: Radicalism in London, 1796–1821*. Oxford: Oxford University Press, 1982.

Horrocks, Clare, Brian Maidment, and Valerie Stevenson. *Punch Re-Rooted—Comedy and the Periodical Press, 1820–1850*. http://www.ljmu.ac.uk/HSS/HSS_Docs/Catalogue_text_only.docx.

Horton, Peter. "The British Vocal Album and the Struggle for National Music." In *Music and Performance Culture in Nineteenth-Century Britain: Essays in Honour of Nicholas Temperley*, edited by Bennett Zon, 195–219. Aldershot: Ashgate, 2012.

Houfe, Simon. *The Dictionary of British Book Illustrators and Caricaturists, 1800–1914*. Ann Arbor: Antique Collectors Club, 1978.

Houghton, Walter E., ed. *The Wellesley Index to Victorian Periodicals*. 5 vols. London: Routledge, Kegan Paul, 1966–79.

House of Commons. "A Bill for the More Effectual Suppression of Societies Established for Seditious and Treasonable Purpose; and for Prevention of Other Treasonable and Seditious Practices." *Sessional Papers, 1798–99*, vol. 121, April 22, 1799, 365–84.

———. "A Bill to Alter and Amend the Laws Relating to the Stamp Duties on Newspapers." *Sessional Papers, 1854–55*, vol. 4.609, March 20, 1855, 1–6.

———. "A Bill to Make Certain Publications Subject to the Duties of Stamps upon Newspapers." *Sessional Papers, 1819–20*, vol. 1.45, December 3, 1819, 1–8.

———. "Copyright Commission. The Royal Commissions and the Report of the Commissioners." *Sessional Papers, 1878*, vol. 24.163, 253, i–lxxxix, 1–409.

———. *Report from the Select Committee on Dramatic Literature: With the Minutes of Evidence*. London: House of Commons, August 2, 1832.

———. "Report from the Select Committee on Newspaper Stamps." *Sessional Papers, 1851*, vol. 17.1, i–xlii, 1–659.

———. "Return of the Number of Newspaper Stamps at One Penny, Issued to Newspapers in England, Ireland, Scotland and Wales, from the Year 1837 to the Year 1850." *Sessional Papers, 1852*, vol. 28.497, 1–48.

———. "Return of the Titles, Names, and Addresses of the Publishers, Weight, and Date of Registration of Every Registered Newspaper, Whereof a Portion Is Stated in the Newspaper Itself to be Published Without Stamps." *Sessional Papers, 1854*, vol. 39.525, 1–6.

Houston, Natalie M. "Newspaper Poems: Material Texts in the Public Sphere." *Victorian Studies* 50, no. 2 (2008): 233–42.

Houston, Natalie M., Lindsy Lawrence, and April Patrick. "Bibliographic Databases and 'The Golden Stream': Constructing the *Periodical Poetry Index*." *Victorian Review* 38, no. 2 (2012): 69–80.

"How to Make Men Soldiers." *Western Mail*, December 29, 1870, 3.

Howes, Craig. "Victorian Periodicals—Comic and Satiric." In *Victorian Britain: An Encyclopedia*, edited by Sally Mitchell, 589–90. New York: Garland Press, 1988.

Howsam, Leslie. *Cheap Bibles: Nineteenth-Century Publishing and the British and Foreign Bible Society*. Cambridge: Cambridge University Press, 1991.

Huett, Lorna. "Among the Unknown Public: *Household Words*, *All the Year Round*, and the Mass-Market Weekly Periodical in the Mid-Nineteenth Century." *Victorian Periodicals Review* 38, no. 1 (2005): 61–82.

Huffman, James. *Creating a Public: People and Press in Meiji Japan*. Honolulu: Hawaii University Press, 1997.

Huggins, Mike. "Cartoons and Comic Periodicals, 1841–1901: A Satirical Sociology of Victorian Sporting Life." In *Disreputable Pleasures: Less Virtuous Victorians at Play*, edited by Mike Huggins and J.A. Mangan, 124–52. London: Frank Cass, 2004.

———. *The Victorians and Sport*. London: Continuum, 2004.

Huggins, Mike, and J.A. Mangan, eds. *Disreputable Pleasures: Less Virtuous Victorians at Play*. London: Frank Cass, 2004.

Huggins, Mike, and John Tolson. "The Railways and Sport in Victorian Britain: A Critical Reassessment." *Journal of Transportation History* 22, no. 2 (2001): 99–115.

Hughes, Linda K. "Inventing Poetry and Pictorialism in *Once a Week*: A Magazine of Visual Effects." *Victorian Poetry* 48, no. 1 (2010): 41–72.

———. "Sideways!: Navigating the Material(ity) of Print Culture." *Victorian Periodicals Review* 47, no. 1 (2014): 1–30.

———. "What the *Wellesley Index* Left Out: Why Poetry Matters to Periodical Studies." *Victorian Periodicals Review* 40, no. 2 (2007): 91–125.

Hughes, Linda K., and Michael Lund. *Victorian Publishing and Mrs. Gaskell's Work*. Charlottesville: University Press of Virginia, 1999.

Hughes, Meirion. *The English Musical Renaissance and the Press, 1850–1914: Watchmen of Music*. Aldershot: Ashgate, 2002.

Humpherys, Anne. "*Bow Bells* (1862–1897)." In *The Dictionary of Nineteenth-Century Journalism in Great Britain and Ireland*, edited by Laurel Brake and Marysa Demoor. Chadwyck-Healey, 2012. http://c19index.chadwyck.co.uk.

———. "Popular Narrative and Political Discourse in *Reynolds's Weekly Newspaper*." In *Investigating Victorian Journalism*, edited by Laurel Brake, Aled Jones, and Lionel Madden, 33–47. Basingstoke: Macmillan, 1990.

———. *Travels into the Poor Man's Country: The Work of Henry Mayhew*. London: Caliban, 1992.

Humpherys, Anne, and Louis James, eds. *G.W.M. Reynolds: Nineteenth-Century Fiction, Politics, and the Press*. Burlington: Ashgate, 2008.

Humpherys, Edward Morgan. "Thomas Gee (1815–1898)." *Welsh Biography Online*. http://wbo.llgc.org.uk/en/s-GEE0-THO-1815.html?query=thomas+gee&field=name.

Hunt, Frederick Knight. *The Fourth Estate: Contributions towards a History of Newspapers, and of the Liberty of the Press*. 2 vols. London: David Bogue, 1850.

Hunt, Karen. *Equivocal Feminists: The Social Democratic Federation and the Woman Question, 1884–1911*. Cambridge: Cambridge University Press, 1996.

[Hunt, Leigh]. "Success of Periodicals." *Tatler* 195 (April 19, 1831): 777–8.

Hyde, H. Montgomery, ed. The *Chameleon: A Facsimile Edition*. London: Eighteen Nineties Society, 1978.

"ILEJ: Final Report." *ILEJ: Internet Library of Early Journals*, 1999. http://www.bodley.ox.ac.uk/ilej/papers/fr1999.

Index to Current Literature: Comprising a Reference to Every Book in the English Language as Published, and to Original Literary Articles of Distinctive Character in Serial Publications. London: Sampson Low, 1859–60.

Inglis, Brian. *The Freedom of the Press in Ireland: 1784–1841*. 1954. Reprint, Westport: Greenwood Press, 1975.

Ingram, Alison. *Index to the Archives of Richard Bentley & Son*. Cambridge: Chadwyck-Healey, 1977.

"Introduction." *Dublin University Magazine* 19 (April 1842): 423–4.

"Introduction." *Minim* 1, no. 1 (October 1893): 7.

"Is Courage an Attribute of Men Only?" *Woman's Herald* 219, no. 7 (1893): 4.

Itzkowitz, David. *Peculiar Privilege: A Social History of English Foxhunting, 1753–1885*. Hassocks: Harvester Press, 1975.

J.H. "Liberty: An Ode." *Tait's Edinburgh Magazine* 16 (January 1849): 19–21.

J.P. "The Daily Press: Its Price and Profits." *Metropolitan Magazine* 49 (August 1847): 433–43.

Jackson, Alex. "Football Coverage in the Papers of the Sheffield Telegraph, c. 1890–1915." *International Journal of Regional and Local History* 5, no. 1 (2009): 63–84.

Jackson, Arthur. *La Revue blanche, 1889–1903: Origine, influence, bibliographie.* Paris: M.J. Minard, 1960.

Jackson, Kate. "George Newnes and the 'Loyal Tit-bitites': Editorial Identities and Textual Interaction in *Tit-Bits*." In *Nineteenth-Century Media and the Construction of Identities*, edited by Laurel Brake, Bill Bell, and David Finkelstein, 11–26. London: Palgrave, 2000.

———. *George Newnes and the New Journalism in Britain, 1880–1910: Culture and Profit.* Ashgate: Aldershot, 2001.

Jackson, Mason. *The Pictorial Press: Its Origin and Progress.* London: Hurst and Blackett, 1885.

James, Henry. *Notes and Novelists.* London: J.M. Dent, 1914.

James, Louis. "Cruikshank and Early Victorian Caricature." *History Workshop* 6 (1978): 107–20.

———. *Fiction for the Working Man, 1830–50.* Oxford: Oxford University Press, 1963.

———. "The Trouble with Betsy: Periodicals and the Common Reader in Mid-Nineteenth-Century England." In *The Victorian Periodical Press: Samplings and Soundings*, edited by Joanne Shattock and Michael Wolff, 349–66. Leicester: Leicester University Press, 1982.

———. "Working-Class Literature." In *Victorian Britain: An Encyclopedia*, edited by Sally Mitchell, 874–5. Abingdon: Routledge, 2012.

Janes, Dominic. "The Role of Visual Appearance in *Punch*'s Early Victorian Satires on Religion." *Victorian Periodicals Review* 47, no. 1 (2014): 66–86.

Janet, Ellen. "On Newspaper Reading." *La Belle Assemblée* 149 (1821): 219–20.

Janowitz, Anne. *Lyric and Labour in the Romantic Tradition.* Cambridge: Cambridge University Press, 1998.

Janssen, Joanne Nystrom. "Embodying Facts: Anxiety About Fiction in the *Christian Lady's Magazine* and Charlotte Elizabeth Tonna's Social Problem Novels." *Victorian Periodicals Review* 44, no. 4 (2011): 327–53.

Jauss, Hans Robert, and Timothy Bahti. "The Alterity and Modernity of Medieval Literature." *New Literary History* 10, no. 2 (1979): 181–229.

Jenkins, Geraint H., ed. *The Welsh Language and Its Social Domains.* Cardiff: University of Wales Press, 2000.

Jenkins, Roy. *Sir Charles Dilke: A Victorian Tragedy.* London: Fontana, 1968.

Jensz, Felicity. "Diverging Reports of European Politics and Imperial Aspiration in the *Periodical Accounts* and in the *Missions-Blatt*." In *Missions and Media: The Politics of Missionary Periodicals in the Long Nineteenth Century*, edited by Felicity Jensz and Hannah Acke, 39–56. Stuttgart: Franz Steiner Verlag, 2013.

Jensz, Felicity, and Hannah Acke, eds. *Missions and Media: The Politics of Missionary Periodicals in the Long Nineteenth Century.* Stuttgart: Franz Steiner Verlag, 2013.

Jerrold, Douglas. "Church Pews." *English Chartist Circular* 1, no. 5 (1839): 17.

Jerrold, Walter. *Douglas Jerrold and "Punch."* London: Macmillan, 1910.

———. *Douglas Jerrold, Dramatist and Wit.* London: Hodder and Stoughton, 1914.

John, Angela. *War, Journalism, and the Shaping of the Twentieth Century.* London: IB Tauris, 2006.

Johnson-Hill, Erin. "Miscellany and Collegiality in the British Periodical Press: The *Harmonicon* (1823–1833)." *Nineteenth-Century Music Review* 9, no. 2 (2012): 255–93.

Johnson-Woods, Toni. "The Virtual Reading Communities of the *London Journal*, the *New York Ledger* and the *Australian Journal*." In *Nineteenth-Century Media and the Construction of Identities*, edited by Laurel Brake, Bill Bell, and David Finkelstein, 350–62. Basingstoke: Palgrave, 2000.

Johnston, Anna. "British Missionary Publishing, Missionary Celebrity and Empire." *Nineteenth Century Prose* 32, no. 2 (2005): 20–47.

———. *Missionary Writing and Empire, 1800–1860.* Cambridge: Cambridge University Press, 2003.

Jones, Aled. "The 'Dart' and the Damning of the Sylvan Stream: Journalism and Political Culture in the Late-Victorian City." *Victorian Periodicals Review* 35, no. 1 (2002): 2–17.

———. "The Newspaper Press in Wales, 1804–1945." In *A Nation and Its Books: A History of the Book in Wales*, edited by Philip Henry Jones and Eiluned Rees, 209–20. Aberystwyth: National Library of Wales, 1998.

———. *Powers of the Press: Newspapers, Power and the Public in Nineteenth-Century England*. Aldershot: Scolar Press, 1996.

———. *Press, Politics and Society: A History of Journalism in Wales*. Cardiff: University of Wales Press, 1993.

———. "Print, Language, and Identity: Newspapers in Wales since 1804." In *Newspapers in International Librarianship*, edited by Sjoerd Koopman, 229–40. Munich: Saur, 2003.

———. "The Welsh Newspaper Press." In *A Guide to Welsh Literature c. 1800–1900*, vol. 5, edited by Hywel Teifi Edwards, 1–33. Cardiff: University of Wales Press, 2000.

Jones, Beti. *Newsplan: Reporting of the NEWSPLAN Project in Wales / Adroddiad ar Gynllun NEWSPLAN yng Nghymru*. Aberystwyth: Wales Regional Library System, 1994.

Jones, D.G. *Cofiant Cranogwen*. Caernarfon: Argraffdy'r Methodistiaid Calfinaidd, 1932.

Jones, Ieuan Gywnedd. "The Nineteenth Century." In *A Nation and Its Books: A History of the Book in Wales*, edited by Philip Henry Jones and Eiluned Rees, 157–71. Aberystwyth: National Library of Wales, 1998.

Jones, J.J. "The Welsh Church Periodical Press." *National Library of Wales Journal* 4 (1945): 92–4.

Jones, Philip Henry. "A Golden Age Reappraised: Welsh-Language Publishing in the Nineteenth Century." In *Images & Texts: Their Production and Distribution in the 18th and 19th Centuries*, edited by Peter Isaac and Barry McKay, 121–41. Winchester: St. Paul's Bibliographies, 1997.

———. "Two Welsh Publishers of the Golden Age: Gee a'i Fab and Hughes a'i Fab." In *A Nation and Its Books: A History of the Book in Wales*, edited by Philip Henry Jones and Eiluned Rees, 173–87. Aberystwyth: National Library of Wales, 1998.

———. "The Welsh Language in the Valleys of Glamorgan, c. 1800–1914." In *Language and Community in the Nineteenth Century*, edited by Geraint H. Jenkins, 147–80. Cardiff: University of Wales Press, 1998.

———. "*Yr Amserau*: The First Decade, 1843–52." In *Investigating Victorian Journalism*, edited by Laurel Brake, Aled Jones, and Lionel Madden, 85–103. Basingstoke: Macmillan, 1990.

Jones, Philip Henry, and Eiluned Rees, eds. *A Nation and Its Books: A History of the Book in Wales*. Aberystwyth: National Library of Wales, 1998.

Jorrocks. "Thoughts on Hunting." *New Sporting Magazine* 3, no. 14 (1832): 99–103.

Joyce, Patrick. *The Rule of Freedom: Liberalism and the Modern City*. London: Verso, 2003.

———. *Visions of the People: Industrial England and the Question of Class, 1848–1914*. Cambridge: Cambridge University Press, 1994.

"Judicial Statistics." *Solicitors' Journal & Reporter* 4 (June 30, 1860): 680.

"July Is Here." *London Journal* 58 (July 26, 1873): 63.

Juvenis. "Impromptu on Seeing the Word Liberty Half Erased from a Wall on Which It Had Been Written." *Tribune* 1, no. 10 (1795): 236.

Kassler, Jamie Croy. *The Science of Music in Britain, 1714–1830: A Catalogue of Writings, Lectures and Inventions*. Vol. 2. New York: Garland, 1979.

Kaul, Chandrika, ed. *Media and the British Empire*. New York: Palgrave, 2006.

———. *Reporting the Raj*. Manchester: Manchester University Press, 2003.

Kavanagh, Robin F. *Irish INC: Images from Periodicals of the Nineteenth Century*. 2008. http://dho.ie/drapier/node/141.

———. "Religion and Illustrated Periodicals in the 1830s." In *The Oxford History of the Irish Book*, vol. 4, edited by James H. Murphy, 342–56. Oxford: Oxford University Press, 2011.

[Kendall, May]. "The Lay of the Trilobite." *Punch* 88 (January 24, 1885): 41.

Kennin, Richard. *Return to Albion: Americans in England, 1760–1940*. New York: Holt, Rinehart, and Winston, 1979.

Kent, Christopher. "The Angry Young Men of *Tomahawk*." In *Victorian Journalism: Exotic and Domestic Essays in Honour of P.D. Edwards*, edited by Barbara Garlick and Margaret Harrison, 75–94. St. Lucia: University of Queensland Press, 1998.

———. "British Bohemia and the Victorian Journalist." *Australasian Victorian Studies Journal* 6 (2000): 25–35.

———. "The Idea of Bohemia in Mid-Victorian England." *Queen's Quarterly* 80, no. 3 (1973): 360–69.

———. "More Critics of Drama, Music and Art." *Victorian Periodicals Review* 19, no. 3 (1986): 99–105.

———. "Periodical Critics of Drama, Music, and Art, 1830–1914: A Preliminary List." *Victorian Periodicals Review* 13, no. 1 (1980): 31–55.

Kidd, Alan J., and Kenneth Roberts, eds. *City, Class and Culture: Studies of Social Policy and Cultural Production in Victorian Manchester*. Manchester: Manchester University Press, 1985.

Kieve, J.L. *The Electric Telegraph in the UK: A Social and Economic History*. Newton Abbot: David & Charles, 1973.

Killick, Tim. *British Short Fiction in the Early Nineteenth Century: The Rise of the Tale*. Aldershot: Ashgate, 2008.

King, Andrew. "'Army, Navy, Medicine, Law, / Church, Nobility, Nothing at all': Towards the Study of Gender, the Professions, and the Press in the Nineteenth Century." *Nineteenth-Century Gender Studies* 5, no. 2 (2009). http://www.ncgsjournal.com/issue52/king.htm.

———. "'Killing Time,' or Mrs. Braby's Peppermints: The Double Economy of the *Family Herald* and the *Family Herald Supplements*." *Victorian Periodicals Review* 43, no. 2 (2012): 149–73.

———. *The London Journal, 1845–83: Periodicals, Production, and Gender*. Aldershot: Ashgate, 2004.

———. "Magazines, International History of." In *The International Encyclopedia of Communication*, vol. 6, edited by Wolfgang Donsbach, 2748–52. Oxford, Blackwell, 2008.

———. "A Paradigm of Reading the Victorian Penny Weekly: Education of the Gaze and the *London Journal*." In *Nineteenth-Century Media and the Construction of Identities*, edited by Laurel Brake, Bill Bell, and David Finkelstein, 77–92. Basingstoke: Palgrave, 2000.

———. "*Reynolds's Miscellany*, 1846–49: Advertising Networks and Politics." In *G.W.M. Reynolds and Nineteenth-Century British Society: Politics, Fiction, and the Press*, edited by Anne Humpherys and Louis James, 53–74. Aldershot: Ashgate, 2008.

———. "Thomas Walker's *The Original* 1835." *Greenwich English Prof* (blog). http://blogs.gre.ac.uk/andrewking/2013/04/29/thomas-walkers-the-original-1835.

———. "International Histories of Magazines." 1–5. *Greenwich English Prof* (blog). http://blogs.gre.ac.uk/andrewking/.

King, Andrew, and John Plunkett, eds. *Victorian Print Media: A Reader*. Oxford: Oxford University Press, 2005.

Kitson, Richard. "James William Davison, Critic, Crank, and Chronicler: A Re-Evaluation." In *Nineteenth-Century British Music Studies*, vol. 1, edited by Bennett Zon, 303–10. Aldershot: Ashgate, 1999.

———. "*The Musical World*: Introduction." In *The Musical World, 1836–1865*, edited by Richard Kitson, ix–xix. Ann Arbor: UMI, 1996. http://www.ripm.org/pdf/Introductions/MWO1836–1865intro English.pdf.

———. "*The Quarterly Musical Magazine and Review*: Introduction." In *The Quarterly Musical Magazine and Review, 1818–1828*, edited by Richard Kitson, ix–xi. Ann Arbor: UMI, 1989.

Kittler, Friedrich. *Gramophone, Film, Typewriter*. Translated by Geoffrey Winthrop-Young and Michael Wurtz. Stanford: Stanford University Press, 1999.

Kitton, Frederick G. *John Leech, Artist and Humourist: A Biographical Sketch*. London: George Redway, 1884.

Klancher, John P. *The Making of English Reading Audiences, 1790–1832*. Madison: University of Wisconsin Press, 1987.

Klein, Thoralf. "Protestant Missionary Periodicals Debate the Boxer War, 1900–1901: Martyrdom, Solidarity and Justification." In *Missions and Media: The Politics of Missionary Periodicals in the Long Nineteenth Century*, edited by Felicity Jensz and Hannah Acke, 187–204. Stuttgart: Franz Steiner Verlag, 2013.

Klickmann, Flora. "The Editor's Page." *Girl's Own Paper and Woman's Magazine* 30 (November 1908): 1.

Knight, Mark, and Emma Mason. *Nineteenth-Century Religion and Literature: An Introduction*. Oxford: Oxford University Press, 2006.

Kooistra, Lorraine Janzen. *The Artist as Critic: Bitextuality in Fin-de-Siècle Illustrated Books*. Aldershot: Scolar Press, 1995.

———. *Poetry, Pictures, and Popular Publishing: The Illustrated Gift Book and Victorian Visual Culture, 1855–75*. Athens: Ohio University Press, 2011.

Koren, Yehuda, and Eilat Negev. *First Lady of Fleet Street: A Biography of Rachel Beer*. London: J.R. Books, 2011.

Koss, Stephen. *The Rise and Fall of the Political Press in Britain*. 2 vols. London: Hamish Hamilton, 1981–84.

Krummel. D.W. "Searching and Sorting on the Slippery Slope: Periodical Publication of Victorian Music." *Notes* 46, no. 3 (1990): 593–608.

Kunzle, David. "Between Broadsheet Caricature and *Punch*: Cheap Newspaper Cuts for the Lower Classes in the 1830s." *Art Journal* 43 (1983): 339–46.

———. *The History of the Comic Strip: The Nineteenth Century*. Berkeley: University of California Press, 1990.

Kyprianides, Christine. "Musical Miscellany in Charles Dickens's Journals, 1850–70." *Victorian Periodicals Review* 47, no. 3 (2014): 398–431.

Lake, Elizabeth. "Medicine." In *The Oxford History of the Irish Book*, vol. 4, *The Irish Book in English 1800–1891*, edited by James H. Murphy, 575–84. Oxford: Oxford University Press, 2011.

Lambert, W.R. *Drink and Sobriety in Victorian Wales, 1820–1895*. Cardiff: University of Wales Press, 1993.

Lambie, James. *The Story of Your Life: A History of the* Sporting Life *Newspaper, 1859–1998*. Leicester: Matador, 2010.

[Landon, Laetitia Elizabeth]. "Fragment." *Literary Gazette*, August 26, 1820, 556–7.

———. "Poetic Sketch the First." *Literary Gazette*, January 12, 1822, 27–8.

Lang, Marjory. "Childhood's Champions: Mid-Victorian Children's Periodicals and the Critics." *Victorian Periodicals Review* 13 (1980): 17–31.

Langley, Leanne. "The English Musical Journal in the Early Nineteenth Century." PhD diss., University of North Carolina, Chapel Hill, 1983.

———. "Italian Opera and the English Press, 1836–56." *Periodica Musica* 6 (1988): 3–10.

———. "The Life and Death of 'The Harmonicon': An Analysis." *Royal Musical Association Research Chronicle* 22 (1989): 137–63.

———. "Music." In *Victorian Periodicals and Victorian Society*, edited by J. Don Vann and Rosemary T. VanArsdel, 99–126. Toronto: University of Toronto Press, 1994.

———. "The Musical Press in Nineteenth-Century England." *Notes* 46, no. 3 (1990): 583–92.

———. "Novello's 'Neue Zeitschrift': 1883, Francis Hueffer and the *Musical Review*." *Brio* 45, no. 1 (2008): 14–27.

———. "The Use of Private Papers, Correspondence and Archives of the Publishing Trade in British Music Periodicals Research." *Periodica Musica* 1 (1983): 12–13.

Larkin, Felix M. "The Dog in the Night-time: *The Freeman's Journal*, the Irish Parliamentary Party and the Empire, 1875–1919." In *Newspapers and Empire in Ireland and Britain: Reporting the British Empire, c. 1857–1921*, edited by Simon Potter, 109–23. Dublin: Four Courts Press, 2004.

Larsen, Timothy. *A People of One Book: The Bible and the Victorians*. Oxford: Oxford University Press, 2011.

Latané, David E. "Charles Molloy Westmacott and the Spirit of the *Age*." *Victorian Periodicals Review* 40, no. 1 (2007): 44–72.

———. *William Maginn and the British Press*. Burlington, VT: Ashgate, 2013.

Lauterbach, Edward S. "*Fun* and its Contributors: The Literary History of a Victorian Humor Magazine." PhD diss., University of Illinois, 1961.

Law, Graham. *The Illustrated London News and the Graphic*. Victorian Fiction Research Guide 29. Victorian Secrets, 2013. http://www.victoriansecrets.co.uk.

———. *Serializing Fiction in the Victorian Press*. Basingstoke: Palgrave Macmillan, 2000.

Law, Graham, and Matthew Sterenberg. "Old vs. New Journalism and the Public Sphere; or, Habermas Encounters Dallas and Stead." *19: Interdisciplinary Studies in the Long Nineteenth Century* 16 (2013). http://dx.doi.org/10.16995/ntn.657.

Law, Graham, and Robert L. Patten. "The Serial Revolution." In *The Cambridge History of the Book in Britain*, vol. 6, *1830–1914*, edited by David McKitterick, 144–71. Cambridge: Cambridge University Press, 2009.

Layard, George Somes. *A Great "Punch" Editor: Being the Life, Letters, and Diaries of Shirley Brooks*. London: Sir Isaac Pitman, 1907.

Leader. *Freedom's Champion*, August 2, 1866, 2.

Leader. *Times*, August 6, 1858, 8.

Leary, Patrick. "Googling the Victorians." *Journal of Victorian Culture* 10, no. 1 (2005): 72–86.

———. *The Punch Brotherhood: Table Talk and Print Culture in Mid-Victorian London*. London: British Library, 2010.

Leary, Patrick, and Andrew Nash. "Authorship." In *The Cambridge History of the Book in Britain*, vol. 6, *1830–1914*, edited by David McKitterick, 173–213. Cambridge: Cambridge University Press, 2009.

"Lectures to Ladies." *Nature* 1 (November 11, 1869): 45–6.

Ledbetter, Kathryn. *British Victorian Women's Periodicals: Beauty, Civilization, and Poetry*. New York: Palgrave Macmillan, 2009.

———. *Tennyson and Victorian Periodicals: Commodities in Context*. Aldershot: Ashgate, 2007.

Lee, Alan J. *The Origins of the Popular Press in England: 1855–1914*. London: Croom Helm, 1976.

Lee, Judith Yaross. "The International Twain and American Nationalist Humour: Vernacular Humour as a Post-Colonial Rhetoric." *Mark Twain Annual* 6, no. 1 (2008): 33–49.

Lee, Nicholas. *Irish Identity and Literary Periodicals, 1832–1842*. Bristol: Thoemmes Press, 2000.

Legg, Marie-Louise. *Newspapers and Nationalism: The Irish Provincial Press, 1850–1892*. Dublin: Four Courts, 1998.

Lehmann, R.C. *Dickens as Editor, Being Letters Written by Him to William Henry Wills His Sub-Editor*. London: Smith, Elder, 1912.

Leighton, Mary Elizabeth, and Lisa Surridge. "The Plot Thickens: Toward a Narratological Analysis of Illustrated Serial Fiction in the 1860s." *Victorian Studies* 51, no. 1 (2008): 65–101.

Lester, Alan. *Imperial Networks: Creating Identities in Nineteenth-Century South Africa and Britain*. London: Routledge, 2001.

"Letters to the Editor." *Times*, March 21, 1829, 3; March 24, 1829, 4; March 25, 1829, 4.

[Lewes, G.H.]. "The Condition of Authors in England, Germany and France." *Fraser's Magazine* 35 (March 1847): 285–95.

Lewis, Arnold. *An Early Encounter with Tomorrow: Europeans, Chicago's Loop, and the World's Columbian Exposition*. Urbana: University of Illinois Press, 1997.

Liddle, Dallas. *The Dynamics of Genre: Journalism and the Practice of Literature in Mid-Victorian Britain*. Charlottesville: University of Virginia Press, 2009.

———. "Reflections on 20,000 Victorian Newspapers: 'Distant Reading' the Times Using The Times Digital Archive." *Journal of Victorian Culture* 17, no. 2 (2012): 230–37.

"The Life of an Editor." *Rambler*, June 1854, 510–19.

Liggins, Emma. "'The Life of a Bachelor Girl in the Big City': Selling the Single Lifestyle to Readers of *Woman* and the *Young Woman* in the 1890s." *Victorian Periodicals Review* 40, no. 3 (2007): 216–38.

Linton, Eliza Lynn. "The Girl of the Period." In *Prose by Victorian Women: An Anthology*, edited by Andrea Broomfield and Sally Mitchell, 356–70. New York: Garland Publishing, 1996.

"Literary Commissions." *Hobart Town Gazette*, August 23, 1823, 2.

Little, Alicia. *Li Hung-Chang: His Life and Times*. 1903. Reprint, Cambridge: Cambridge University Press, 2010.

Liu, Alan. "Imagining the New Media Encounter." In *A Companion to Digital Literary Studies*, edited by Susan Scheibman and Ray Siemens. Oxford: Blackwell, 2008. http://www.digitalhumanities.org/companionDLS.

Livesey, Joseph. *The Life and Teachings of Joseph Livesey, Comprising His Autobiography*. London: National Temperance League, 1885.

Lloyd, Amy. "*Good Words* (1860–1911)." In *The Dictionary of Nineteenth-Century Journalism in Great Britain and Ireland*, edited by Laurel Brake and Marysa Demoor, 254. Ghent and London: Academia Press and the British Library, 2009.

———. "*Good Words for the Young* (1868–1877)." In *The Dictionary of Nineteenth-Century Journalism in Great Britain and Ireland*, edited by Laurel Brake and Marysa Demoor, 254. Ghent and London: Academia Press and the British Library, 2009.

Lockley, Philip. *Visionary Religion and Radicalism in Early Industrial England: From Southcott to Socialism*. Oxford: Oxford University Press, 2013.

Lockwood, Alison. *Passionate Pilgrims: The American Traveller in Great Britain, 1800–1914*. London: Fairleigh Dickinson, 1981.

Lodge, Sara. *Thomas Hood and Nineteenth-Century Poetry: Work, Play, and Politics*. Manchester: Manchester University Press, 2007.

Longmate, Norman. *The Water-Drinkers: A History of Temperance*. London: Hamish Hamilton, 1968.

Lootens, Tricia. "Hemans and Home: Victorianism, Feminine 'Internal Enemies,' and the Domestication of National Identity." *PMLA* 109, no. 2 (1994): 238–53.

Lopatin, Nancy P. "Refining the Limits of Political Reporting: The Provincial Press, Political Unions, and the Great Reform Act." *Victorian Periodicals Newsletter* 31 (1998): 337–55.

Lowry, Donal. "Nationalist and Unionist Attitudes to Empire in the Age of the South African War, 1899–1902." In *Newspapers and Empire in Ireland and Britain: Reporting the British Empire, c. 1857–1921*, edited by Simon Potter, 159–76. Dublin: Four Courts Press, 2004.

Lucas, Peter J. "J.A. Bernard's Challenge: Journalists on Journalism in a Victorian Country Town." *Transactions of the Cumberland and Westmorland Antiquarian and Archaeological Society*, 3rd ser., 7 (2007): 193–213.

Luckhurst, Mary, and Jane Moody, eds. *Theatre and Celebrity in Britain, 1660–1900*. Basingstoke: Palgrave Macmillan, 2005.

M.B. "The Newspaper." *Good Words* 3 (February 1862): 117–20.

M.L.W. "How to Play Scales." *Minim* 2, no. 16 (1895): 56.

[MacColl, D.S.]. "The Standard of the Philistine." *Spectator* 3377 (March 18, 1893): 357–8.

MacDonald, Fiona A. *Negotiated Knowledge: Medical Periodical Publishing in Scotland, 1733–1832*. London: Pickering and Chatto, 2009.

MacDonald, George. "A Journey Rejourneyed." *Argosy* 1 (1865): 53–63.

MacDonald, Robert H. "Signs from the Imperial Quarter: Illustrations in *Chums*, 1892–1914." *Children's Literature* 16 (1988): 31–55.

MacFarlane, Helen, and Paul Mortimer-Lee. "Inflation Over 300 Years." *Bank of England Quarterly Bulletin* 34, no. 2 (1994): 156–62. http://www.bankofengland.co.uk/archive/Documents/historicpubs/qb/1994/qb940201.pdf.

[Mackay, Charles]. "Town and Table Talk." *London Review* 1 (July 7, 1860): 8–9.

Mackenzie, John. *Imperialism and Popular Culture*. Manchester: Manchester University Press, 1986.

———. *Propaganda and Empire*. Manchester: Manchester University Press, 1984.

Mackie, Erin. *Market à la Mode: Fashion, Commodity, and Gender in* The Tatler *and* The Spectator. Baltimore: Johns Hopkins University Press, 1997.

Mackmurdo, Arthur. "The Guild's Flag Unfurling." *Hobby Horse* 1 (1884): 1–13. Reprinted in *Symbolist Art Theories: A Critical Anthology*, edited by Henri Dorra, 96–7. Berkeley: University of California Press, 1994.

Macleod, Norman. "Note by the Editor." *Good Words* 1 (December 1860): n.p. http://www.electricscotland.com/hiStory/goodwords/index.htm.

Madden, R.R. *The History of Irish Periodical Literature, from the End of the Seventeenth-Century to the Middle of the Nineteenth-Century*. London: T.C. Newby, 1867. Reprint, New York: Johnson, 1968.

Maginn, William. "Charles O'Malley and Jack Hinton." *Fraser's Magazine* 26 (October 1842): 447–65.

Mahoney, James, and Dietrich Rueschemeyer. *Comparative Historical Analysis in the Social Sciences*. Cambridge: Cambridge University Press, 2003.

Maidment, Brian E. "Class and Cultural Production in the Industrial City: Poetry in Victorian Manchester." In *City, Class and Culture: Studies of Social Policy and Cultural Production in Victorian Manchester*, edited by Alan J. Kidd and Kenneth Roberts, 148–66. Manchester: Manchester University Press, 1985.

———. *Comedy, Caricature and the Social Order, 1820–1850*. Manchester: Manchester University Press, 2013.

———. "*The Illuminated Magazine* and the Triumph of Wood Engraving." In *The Lure of Illustration in the Nineteenth Century: Picture and Press*, edited by Laurel Brake and Marysa Demoor, 17–39. London: Palgrave Macmillan, 2009.

———, ed. "The Literary Culture of Nineteenth-Century Manchester." Special issue, *Manchester Region History Review* 17 (2006).

———. "The Manchester Common Reader—Abel Heywood's 'Evidence' and the Early Victorian Reading Public." *Transactions of the Lancashire and Cheshire Antiquarian Society* 97 (2001): 99–120.

———. *Reading Popular Prints, 1790–1870*. Manchester: Manchester University Press, 1996.

———. "Scraps and Sketches: Miscellaneity, Commodity Culture, and Comic Prints, 1820–1840." *Interdisciplinary Studies in the Long Nineteenth Century* 5 (2007): 1–25.

———. "Victorian Periodicals and Academic Research." In *Investigating Victorian Journalism*, edited by Laurel Brake, Aled Jones, and Lionel Madden, 143–54. Basingstoke: Macmillan, 1990.

———. "'Works in Unbroken Succession': The Literary Career of Mary Howitt." In *Popular Victorian Women Writers*, edited by Kay Boardman and Shirley Jones, 22–45. Manchester: Manchester University Press, 2004.

Maine, Fanny. "The Literature of the Working Classes." *Englishwoman's Magazine and Christian Mother's Miscellany*, n.s., 5 (October 1850): 619–22. Reprinted in *Victorian Print Media: A Reader*, edited by Andrew King and John Plunkett, 40–3. Oxford: Oxford University Press, 2005.

"Male Fashions." *Examiner*, April 24, 1808, 268–9.

Malik, Rachel. "Stories Many, Fast and Slow: *Great Expectations* and the Mid-Victorian Horizon of the Publishable." *English Literary History* 79, no. 2 (2012): 477–500.

Mangan, J.A. *Athleticism in the Victorian and Edwardian Public School*. Cambridge: Cambridge University Press, 1981.

"Manliness in Politics." *Western Mail*, July 4, 1893, 4.

"Manliness of Speech." *Caledonian Mercury*, April 7, 1858, 4.

"Manners and Amusements. The Drama." *Era* 1 (September 30, 1838): 7.

Manning, Susan, and Andrew Taylor, eds. *Transatlantic Literary Studies: A Reader*. Edinburgh: Edinburgh University Press, 2008.

Manual of Book-Keeping for Booksellers, Publishers and Stationers. By a Bookseller. London: Simpkin Marshall, 1850.

Marchand, Leslie A. *The Athenaeum: A Mirror of Victorian Culture*. Chapel Hill: University of North Carolina Press, 1941.

Markovits, Stephanie. "'Rushing into Print': Participatory Journalism during the Crimean War." *Victorian Studies* 50, no. 4 (2008): 559–86.

Marsh, Jan. *Christina Rossetti: A Writer's Life*. New York: Viking, 1994.

Marsh, Jan, and Pamela Garrish Nunn. *Women Artists and the Pre-Raphaelite Movement*. London: Virago, 1989.

Martin, Carol. *George Eliot's Serial Fiction*. Columbus: Ohio State University Press, 1994.

Martin, Robert Bernard. *The Triumph of Wit: A Study of Victorian Comic Theory*. Oxford: Clarendon Press, 1974.

Martineau, Harriet. *Autobiography*. 2 vols. London: Smith, Elder, 1877.

———. *Illustrations of Political Economy*. 9 vols. 3rd ed. London: Charles Fox, 1832.

Marvin, Carolyn. *When Old Technologies Were New: Thinking About Electric Communication in the Late Nineteenth Century*. Oxford: Oxford University Press, 1988.

Mason, J. "The Money We Spend on Sport." *Pearson's Magazine* 1, no. 5 (May 1896): 530–34.

Mason, James. "Silent Men." *Leisure Hour* 38 (January 1889): 48–51.

Mason, Tony. *Association Football and English Society: 1863–1915*. Hassocks: Harvester Press, 1980.

———. "Sport." In *Victorian Periodicals and Victorian Society*, edited by J. Don Vann and Rosemary T. VanArsdel, 291–300. Aldershot: Scolar Press, 1994.

Matthew, H.C.G. "Gladstone, Rhetoric and Politics." In *Gladstone*, edited by Peter John Jagger, 213–19. London: Hambledon, 1998.

Matthias, Roland. *The Lonely Editor: A Glance at Anglo-Welsh Magazines*. Cardiff: University College Cardiff Press, 1984.

Maume, Patrick. "The *Irish Independent* and Empire." In *Newspapers and Empire in Ireland and Britain: Reporting the British Empire, c. 1857–1921*, edited by Simon Potter, 124–42. Dublin: Four Courts Press, 2004.

May, Frederick. *London Press Directory and Advertiser's Handbook*. London: Frederick May, 1871.

May's British and Irish Press Guide. London: Mays, 1874–89. Continued as *Willing's Press Guide and Advertisers' Directory and Handbook*.

Mayhall, Laura E. Nym, Patrick Collier, Jonathan Silberstein-Loeb, and Joel Wiener. "Roundtable: The Americanization of the British Press." *Media History* 19, no. 3 (2013): 369–83.

Mayhew, Athol. *A Jorum of "Punch" with Those Who Helped to Brew It: Being the Early History of "The London Charivari."* London: Downey, 1895.

Mayhew, Henry. *The Unknown Mayhew*. Edited by Leslie Yeo and E.P. Thompson. New York: Pantheon, 1971.

McAllister, Annemarie. *Demon Drink?: Temperance and the Working Class*. Amazon digital services, 2014. Kindle edition.

———. "Picturing the Demon Drink: How Children were Shown Temperance Principles in the Band of Hope." *Visual Resources* 28, no. 4 (2012): 309–23.

McCalman, Iain. *Radical Underworld: Prophets, Revolutionaries, and Pornographers in London, 1795–1840*. Cambridge: Cambridge University Press, 1988.

McCrorie, Ian. *Clyde Pleasure Steamers: An Illustrated History*. Greenock: Orr, Pollock, 1986.

McDowell, Paula. "Towards a Genealogy of 'Print Culture' and 'Oral Tradition.'" In *This Is Enlightenment*, edited by Clifford Siskin and William Warner, 229–46. Chicago: University of Chicago Press, 2010.

McGill, Meredith L. *American Literature and the Culture of Reprinting, 1834–1853*. Philadelphia: University of Pennsylvania Press, 2003.

McGuire, Charles Edward. "Edward Elgar: 'Modern' or 'Modernist?' Construction of an Aesthetic Identity in the British Music Press, 1895–1934." *Musical Quarterly* 91, nos. 1–2 (2008): 8–38.

McIntyre, Matthew. "Football Specials." In *The Dictionary of Nineteenth-Century Journalism in Great Britain and Ireland*, edited by Laurel Brake and Marysa Demoor, 223. Ghent and London: Academia Press and the British Library, 2009.

McKelvy, William. *The English Cult of Literature: Devoted Readers, 1774–1880*. Charlottesville: University of Virginia Press, 2007.

McKenzie, Judy. "Paper Heroes: Special Correspondents and their Narratives of Empire." In *Victorian Journalism: Exotic and Domestic*, edited by Barbara Garlick and Margaret Harris, 124–40. St. Lucia: Queensland University Press, 1998.

McKitterick, David, ed. *The Cambridge History of the Book in Britain*. Vol. 4, *1830–1914*. Cambridge: Cambridge University Press, 2010.

McNeely, Sarah. "Beyond the Drawing Room: The Musical Lives of Victorian Women." *Nineteenth-Century Gender Studies* 5, no. 2 (2009): n.p. http://www.ncgsjournal.com/issue52/mcneely.htm.

McNeely, Sarah, and Linda Hughes. "Young Englishwoman." In *The Dictionary of Nineteenth-Century Journalism in Great Britain and Ireland*, edited by Laurel Brake and Marysa Demoor, 695. Ghent and London: Academia Press and the British Library, 2009.

McNicholas, Anthony. *Politics, Religion, and the Press: Irish Journalism in Mid-Victorian England*. New York: Peter Lang, 2007.

McQuail, Dennis. *McQuail's Mass Communication Theory*. 12th ed. London: Sage, 2012.

McWhirter, David, ed. *Henry James in Context*. Cambridge: Cambridge University Press, 2010.

Meadows, Arthur. *Development of Science Publishing in Europe*. Amsterdam: Elsevier Science Publishers, 1980.

"The Mechanics' Institute." *Citizen* 1, no. 3 (1840): 203–5.

Melnyk, Julie. *Victorian Religion: Faith and Life in Britain*. Westport: Praeger, 2008.

"Men, Women and Gods." *Woman's Herald* 20, no. 1 (1889): 6.

"Men and Males." *Woman's Herald* 86, no. 2 (1890): 402.

"Men and Manners." *Kaleidoscope* 8, no. 372 (1827): 42.

"Men Only." *Penny Illustrated Paper*, December 3, 1887, 358.

Menke, Richard. "Media in America, 1881: Garfield, Guiteau, Bell, Whitman." *Critical Enquiry* 31, no. 3 (2005): 638–4.

Meredith, George. *An Essay on Comedy, and the Uses of the Comic Spirit*. London: Archibald Constable, 1897.

[Merle, Gibbons]. "Newspaper Press." *Westminster Review* 10 (January 1829): 216–37.

Message, Kylie, and Ewan Johnson. "The World within the City: The Great Exhibition, Race, Class, and Social Reform." In *Britain, the Empire, and the World at the Great Exhibition of 1851*, edited by Jeffery A. Auerbach and Peter H. Hoffenberg, 27–46. Aldershot: Ashgate, 2008.

Meynell, Alice. *The Complete Poems of Alice Meynell*. London: Oxford University Press, 1940.

Miller, Bonny H. "A Mirror of Ages Past: The Publication of Music in Domestic Periodicals." *Notes* 50, no. 3 (1994): 883–901.

Miller, Brook. *America and the British Imaginary in Turn-of-the-Twentieth-Century Literature*. Basingstoke: Palgrave, 2010.

Miller, Elizabeth Carolyn. *Slow Print: Literary Radicalism and Late Victorian Print Culture*. Stanford: Stanford University Press, 2013.

Miller, Henry. "John Leech and the Shaping of the Victorian Cartoon: The Context of Respectability." *Victorian Periodicals Review* 42, no. 3 (2009): 267–91.

———. "The Problem with *Punch*." *Historical Research* 82 (2009): 285–302.

Milne, Maurice. *The Newspapers of Northumberland and Durham: A Study of Their Progress during the "Golden Age" of the Provincial Press*. Newcastle upon Tyne: Graham, 1971.

———. "The 'Veiled Editor' Unveiled: William Blackwood and His Magazine." *Publishing History* 16 (1984): 87–103.

Mineka, Francis E. *The Dissidence of Dissent: The Monthly Repository, 1806–1838*. Chapel Hill: University of North Carolina Press, 1944.

Mitchell, Charles. "Law of Newspapers." In *Newspaper Press Directory*, 39–69. London: C. Mitchell, 1851.

———. *Newspaper Press Directory and Advertiser's Guide*. London: C. Mitchell, 1846.

Mitchell, Sally. "The Forgotten Woman of the Period: Penny Weekly Family Magazines of the 1840s and 1850s." In *A Widening Sphere: Changing Roles of Victorian Women*, edited by Martha Vicinus, 29–51. Bloomington: Indiana University Press, 1977.

———. *Frances Power Cobbe: Victorian Feminist, Journalist, Reformer*. Charlottesville: University of Virginia Press, 2004.

———. "*Good Words*." In *British Literary Magazines*, vol. 3, *The Victorian and Edwardian Age, 1837–1913*, edited by Alvin Sullivan, 145–9. Westport: Greenwood Press, 1984.

———. *The New Girl: Girls' Culture in England, 1880–1915*. New York: Columbia University Press, 1995.

"Modern Men." *Scots Observer* 1, nos. 20 and 22 (1889): 603–4.

Mogridge, G. "The Canker of Discontent." *British Workman* 1, no. 2 (February 1855): 1–2.

"Money Matters—The 'Linotype.' An Indictment of the Linotype Company, Limited, and Its Impossible Machine." *Saturday Review*, November 23, 1895, 686–7.

"The Monotype." *New Review* 17 (November 1897): 564–70.

Montgomery, Maureen E. *Gilded Prostitution: Status, Money, and Transatlantic Marriages, 1870–1914*. London: Routledge, 1989.

Morgan, Kenneth O. *The History of Wales*. Vol. 6, *Rebirth of a Nation: Wales 1880–1980*. Oxford: Clarendon/University of Wales Press, 1981.

Morris, Albert. *Scotland's Paper: The Scotsman, 1817–1992*. Edinburgh: Scotsman, 1992.

Morris, Frankie. *Artist of Wonderland: The Life, Political Cartoons, and Illustrations of Tenniel*. Charlottesville: University of Virginia Press, 2005.

Morrison, John. "The Oxford Movement and the British Periodicals." *Catholic Historical Review* 45, no. 2 (1959): 137–60.

Morrison, Robert. "William Blackwood and the Dynamics of Success." In *Print Culture and the Blackwood Tradition, 1805–1930*, edited by David Finkelstein, 21–48. Toronto: University of Toronto Press, 2006.

Moruzi, Kristine. *Constructing Girlhood through the Periodical Press, 1850–1915*. Aldershot: Ashgate, 2012.

———. "'The freedom suits me': Encouraging Girls to Settle in the Colonies." In *Relocating Victorian Settler Narratives: Transatlantic and Transpacific Views in the Long Nineteenth Century*, edited by Tamara Wagner, 177–92. London: Pickering & Chatto, 2011.

Mott, Frank Luther. *A History of American Magazines, 1741–1930*. 5 vols. Cambridge: Harvard University Press, 1958–68.

Mountjoy, Peter Roger. "Thomas Bywater Smithies, Editor of the *British Workman*." *Victorian Periodicals Review* 18, no. 2 (1985): 46–56.

"Mr. Disraeli's Speech at the Mansion House, August 4, 1875." *Examiner*, August 14, 1875, 913.

"Mozart's Sonatas and How to Play Them." *Magazine of Music* 11, no. 2 (1894): 35.

Mulford, Carla. "Benjamin Franklin and Transatlantic Literary Journalism." In *Transatlantic Literary Studies, 1660–1830*, edited by Eve Tavor Bannet and Susan Manning, 75–90. Cambridge: Cambridge University Press, 2012.

Mulvey, Christopher. *Anglo-American Landscapes: A Study of Nineteenth-Century Anglo-American Travel Literature*. Cambridge: Cambridge University Press, 1983.

———. *Transatlantic Manners: Social Patterns in Nineteenth-Century Anglo-American Travel Literature*. Cambridge: Cambridge University Press, 1990.

Murphy, Andrew. *Shakespeare for the People: Working-Class Readers, 1800–1900*. Cambridge: Cambridge University Press, 2008.

Murphy, G. Martin. "Northcote, James Spencer (1821–1907)." In *The Oxford Dictionary of National Biography*, edited by H.C.G. Matthew and Brian Harrison. Oxford: Oxford University Press, 2004. http://www.oxforddnb.com.

Murphy, James, ed. *The Oxford History of the Irish Book*. Vol. 4, *The Irish Book in English, 1800–1891*. Oxford: Oxford University Press, 2011.

Murphy, Paul Thomas. *Toward a Working-Class Canon: Literary Criticism in British Working-Class Periodicals, 1816–1858*. Columbus: Ohio State University Press, 1994.

Murray, Frank. "Band of Hope Review (1851–1937)." In *The Dictionary of Nineteenth-Century Journalism in Great Britain and Ireland*, edited by Laurel Brake and Marysa Demoor, 37. Ghent and London: Academia Press and the British Library, 2009.

———. "*British Workman* (1855–1921)." In *The Dictionary of Nineteenth-Century Journalism in Great Britain and Ireland*, edited by Laurel Brake and Marysa Demoor, 80. Ghent and London: Academia Press and the British Library, 2009.

———. "Often Taken Where a Tract Is Refused: T.B. Smithies, the *British Workman*, and the Popularisation of the Religious and Temperance Message." In *The Lure of Illustration in the Nineteenth Century: Picture and Press*, edited by Laurel Brake and Marysa Demoor, 149–67. London: Palgrave Macmillan, 2009.

Murray, Padmini Ray. "Newspapers." In *The Edinburgh History of the Book in Scotland*, vol. 3, *Ambition and Industry 1800–1880*, edited by Bill Bell, 370–81. Edinburgh: Edinburgh University Press, 2007.

Musgrave, Michael. *The Musical Life of the Crystal Palace*. Cambridge: Cambridge University Press, 1995.

"The Musical Standard." *Musical Standard* 1, no. 1 (1862): 1–2.

Mussell, James. *The Nineteenth-Century Press in the Digital Age*. Basingstoke: Palgrave Macmillan, 2012.

Mussell, James, and Suzanne Paylor. "Editions and Archives: Textual Editing and the *Nineteenth-Century Serials Edition*." In *Text Editing, Print and the Digital World*, edited by Marilyn Deegan and Kathryn Sutherland, 137–57. Farnham: Ashgate, 2009.

Musson, A.E. "Newspaper Printing in the Industrial Revolution." *Economic History Review* 10, no. 3 (1958): 411–26.

Nash, Sarah. "What's in a Name?: Signature, Criticism, and Authority in the *Fortnightly Review*." *Victorian Periodicals Review* 43, no. 1 (2010): 57–82.

"National Music and Musicians." *Citizen* 1, no. 3 (1840): 192–6.

Nattrass, Leonora. *William Cobbett: The Politics of Style*. Cambridge: Cambridge University Press, 1995.

"The Navy; Its Want of Men." *National Review* 9, no. 18 (1859): 394–423.

Nead, Lynda. *Victorian Babylon: People, Streets and Images in Nineteenth-Century London*. New Haven: Yale University Press, 2000.

"'Near' and 'Off' Side." *Sporting Magazine* 17 (February 1826): 243–4.

Nestor, Pauline. "A New Departure in Women's Publishing: *The English Woman's Journal* and *The Victoria Magazine*." *Victorian Periodicals Review* 15, no. 3 (1982): 93–106.

Newey, Katherine. "Shakespeare and the Wars of the Playbills." In *The Victorians and Shakespeare*, edited by Gail Marshall and Adrian Poole, 13–28. Basingstoke: Palgrave Macmillan, 2003.

Newman, John Henry. "Review of *The Theatre of the Greeks*." *London Review* 1 (January 1829): 153–71.

"New Series." *Missionary Magazine and Chronicle*, January 2, 1860, 1.

"News Notes." *Bookman* 11 (March 1897): 164.

"News Notes." *Bookman* 29 (March 1901): 171–3.

"Newspaper Editors and their Work." *Chambers's Journal* 19 (September 16, 1882): 585–7.

"Newspaper Literature." *Saturday Magazine* 9 (October 1, 1836): 132.

Nicholls, James. *The Politics of Alcohol: A History of the Drink Question in England*. Manchester: Manchester University Press, 2009.

Nicholson, Bob. "Counting Culture; or, How to Read Victorian Newspapers from a Distance." *Journal of Victorian Culture* 17, no. 2 (2012): 238–46.

———. "The Digital Turn." *Media History* 19, no. 1 (2013): 59–73.

———. "Jonathan's Jokes: American Humour in the Late-Victorian Press." *Media History* 18, no. 1 (2012): 33–49.

———. "Looming Large: America and the Late-Victorian Press, 1865–1902." PhD diss., University of Manchester, 2012.

———. "'You Kick the Bucket; We Do The Rest!': Jokes and the Culture of Reprinting in the Transatlantic Press." *Journal of Victorian Culture* 17, no. 3 (2012): 273–86.

Nicholson, John. "Popular Imperialism and the Provincial Press: Manchester Evening and Weekly Papers, 1895–1902." *Victorian Periodicals Review* 13, no. 3 (1980): 85–96.

Nicholson, Tony. "The Provincial Stead." In *W.T. Stead: Newspaper Revolutionary*, edited by Roger Luckhurst, Laurel Brake, James Mussell, and Ed King, 7–21. London: British Library, 2012.

Nicholson, Watson. *The Struggle for a Free Stage in London*. New York: Benjamin Blom, 1966.

Niessen, Olwen. "Temperance." In *Victorian Periodicals and Victorian Society*, edited by J. Don Vann and Rosemary Van Arsdel, 251–77. Toronto: University of Toronto Press, 1994.

Nimrod. "The Life of a Sportsman." *New Sporting Magazine* 2, no. 12 (1841): 333–9.

Nisbet, Ada. *British Comment on the United States: A Chronological Bibliography, 1832–1899*. London: University of California Press, 2001.

Noakes, Richard. "The *Boy's Own Paper* and Late-Victorian Juvenile Magazines." In *Science in the Nineteenth-Century Periodical: Reading the Magazine of Nature*, edited by Geoffrey Cantor, Gowan Dawson, Graeme Gooday, Richard Noakes, Sally Shuttleworth, and Jonathan R. Topham, 151–71. Cambridge: Cambridge University Press, 2004.

Nord, David Paul. *Communities of Journalism: A History of American Newspapers and Their Readers*. Urbana: University of Illinois Press, 2001.

"Norman MacColl." *Athenaeum* 4026 (December 24, 1904): 874.

Norris, Pippa. *Digital Divide: Civic Engagement, Information Poverty and the Internet Worldwide.* Cambridge: Cambridge University Press, 2001.

North, John. Introduction to *The Waterloo Directory of English Newspapers and Periodicals, 1800–1900.* Waterloo: North Waterloo Academic Press, 1994–2003. http://www.victorianperiodicals.com/series2/touroverview.asp.

———, ed. *The Waterloo Directory of English Newspapers and Periodicals, 1800–1900.* Series 1, 10 vols.; series 2, 20 vols. Waterloo: North Waterloo Academic Press, 1997, 2003.

———, ed. *The Waterloo Directory of Irish Newspapers and Periodicals, 1800–1900.* 2 vols. Waterloo: North Waterloo Academic Press, 1986.

"Notes of Latest News." *Lloyd's Weekly Newspaper,* July 3, 1881, 7.

Nowell-Smith, Simon. *The House of Cassell, 1848–1958.* London: Cassell, 1958.

Nugent, Walter. *Crossings: The Great Transatlantic Migrations, 1870–1914.* Bloomington: Indiana University Press, 1992.

Ó Ciosáin, Niall. "Oral Culture, Literacy, and Reading, 1800–1850." In *The Oxford History of the Irish Book,* vol. 4, edited by James H. Murphy, 173–91. Oxford: Oxford University Press, 2011.

[Oakley, C.S.]. "On Commencing Author." *Quarterly Review* 186 (1897): 90.

"The Obligations of the General Medical Council, Medical Schools, and Corporations in Relation to the Rights of Medical Men." *Lancet* 2, no. 3802 (1896): 136–8.

O'Connor, E. Foley. "*Chambers's Edinburgh Journal* (1832–1956)." In *The Dictionary of Nineteenth-Century Journalism in Great Britain and Ireland,* edited by Laurel Brake and Marysa Demoor, 106. Ghent and London: Academia Press and the British Library, 2009.

Odello, Denise. "British Brass Band Periodicals and the Construction of a Movement." *Victorian Periodicals Review* 47, no. 3 (2014): 432–53.

Official Descriptive and Illustrated Catalogue. 3 vols. London: Spicer Brothers, 1851.

Ogborn, Miles, and Charles W. J. Withers. "Introduction: Book Geography, Book History." In *Geographies of the Book,* edited by Miles Ogborn and Charles W. J. Withers, 1–25. Farnham: Ashgate, 2010.

O'Hara, Patricia. "'The Woman of To-day': The *Fin de Siècle* Woman of *The Music Hall and Theatre Review.*" *Victorian Periodicals Review* 30, no. 2 (1997): 141–56.

Oliphant, Margaret. *Annals of a Publishing House.* 3 vols. Edinburgh: William Blackwood and Sons, 1897.

———. *The Autobiography and Letters of Mrs. M.O.W. Oliphant (1899).* Edited by Linda H. Peterson. London: Pickering and Chatto, 2012.

———. "The Byways of Literature: Reading for the Million." *Blackwood's Edinburgh Magazine* 84 (August 1858): 200–16.

[———]. "Sensation Novels." *Blackwood's Magazine* 91 (1862): 564–84.

Olsen, Stephanie. *Juvenile Nation: Youth, Emotions and the Making of the Modern British Citizen, 1880–1914.* London: Bloomsbury, 2014.

"On Humility." *Christian Spectator* 1, no. 2 (1819): 61–2.

"On Materialism in Men of Science." *Lancet* 2, no. 2574 (1872): 934–5.

Onslow, Barbara. *Women of the Press in Nineteenth-Century Britain.* Basingstoke: Macmillan, 2000.

Ormond, Leonée. *Linley Sambourne: Illustrator and Punch Cartoonist.* London: Paul Holberton, 2010.

Otis, Laura. *Networking: Communicating with Bodies and Machines in the Nineteenth Century.* Ann Arbor: University of Michigan Press, 2001.

Oulton, Carolyn W. *Let the Flowers Go: A Life of Mary Cholmondeley.* London: Pickering and Chatto, 2009.

"Our Address." *Illustrated London News,* May 12, 1842, 1.

"Our Library Table." *Athenaeum* 2987 (January 24, 1885): 119.

"Our Prize Competition." *Boy's Own Paper* 1 (January 18, 1879): 16.

Owen, Bob. "Welsh American Newspapers and Periodicals." *National Library of Wales Journal* 6 (1950): 373–84.

Owen, Frank. *Tempestuous Journey: Lloyd George His Life and Times*. London: Hutchinson, 1954.

Owers, James, Rodney Carveth, and Alison Alexander. "An Introduction to Media Economics Theory and Practice." In *Media Economics: Theory and Practice*, 3rd ed., edited by Alison Alexander, James Owers, Rodney A. Carveth, C. Ann Hollifield, and Albert N. Greco, 3–47. New York: Routledge, 2003.

P.C.M. "The Evolution of Sex." *Nature* 41 (April 10, 1890): 531–2.

Palmegiano, Eugenia M. "The First Common Market: The British Press on Nineteenth-Century European Journalism." *Media History Monographs* 11, no. 1 (2008–9). http://facstaff.elon.edu/dcopeland/mhm/mhmjour11-1.pdf.

———. "The Indian Mutiny in the Mid-Victorian Press." *Journal of Newspaper and Periodical History* 7 (1991): 3–11.

———. *Perceptions of the Press in Nineteenth-Century British Periodicals: A Bibliography*. London: Anthem, 2012.

Palmer, Beth. "Dangerous and Foolish Work: Evangelicalism and Sensationalism in Ellen Wood's *Argosy Magazine*." *Women's Writing* 15, no. 2 (2008): 187–98.

———. *Women's Authorship and Editorship in Victorian Culture: Sensational Strategies*. Oxford: Oxford University Press, 2011.

Palmer, Fiona M. *Vincent Novello (1781–1861): Music for the Masses*. Aldershot: Ashgate, 2006.

Palmer, Samuel, ed. *Index to the Times Newspaper*. London: Samuel Palmer, 1868–1941.

Palmeri, Frank. "Cruikshank, Thackeray, and the Victorian Eclipse of Satire." *Studies in English Literature* 44, no. 4 (2004): 753–77.

Parikka, Jussi. *What Is Media Archaeology?* Cambridge: Polity Press, 2012.

"Paris Edition The New York Times." *New York Times*, April 15, 1900, 22.

Park, Robert. "Reflections on Communications and Culture." *American Journal of Sociology* 44 (1939): 191–205.

Parker, Mark. *Literary Magazines and British Romanticism*. Cambridge: Cambridge University Press, 2000.

Parkes, Bessie Rayner. "The Use of a Special Periodical." *Alexandra Magazine & Woman's Social and Industrial Advocate* 1 (September 1864): 257–63.

Parratt, Catriona M. "Athletic 'Womanhood': Exploring Sources for Female Sport in Victorian and Edwardian England." *Journal of Sport History* 16, no. 2 (1989): 140–57.

Parry, Ann. "The Grove Years, 1868–1883: A 'New Look' for Macmillan's Magazine?" *Victorian Periodicals Review* 19, no. 4 (1986): 149–57.

Parsons, Gerald, and James More, eds. *Religion in Victorian Britain*. 4 vols. Manchester: Manchester University Press, 1988.

Paterson's Roads. 15th ed. London: Thomas Carnan, 1811.

Paterson's Roads. 18th ed. London: Thomas Carnan, 1826.

Patessio, Mara. *Women and Public Life in Early Meiji Japan: The Development of the Feminist Movement*. Ann Arbor: University of Michigan, 2011.

Patessio, Mara, and Mariko Ogawa. "To Become a Woman Doctor in Early Meiji Japan (1868–1890): Women's Struggles and Ambitions." *Historia Scientiarum* 15, no. 2 (2005): 159–76.

Patten, Robert L. *Charles Dickens and His Publishers*. Oxford: Clarendon Press, 1978.

———. *George Cruikshank's Life, Times, and Art*. 2 vols. New Brunswick: Rutgers University Press, 1991–96.

Patten, Robert L., and David Finkelstein. "Editing *Blackwood's*; or, What Do Editors Do?" In *Print Culture and the Blackwood Tradition, 1805–1930*, edited by David Finkelstein, 146–83. Toronto: University of Toronto Press, 2006.

Pattijn, Joke. "Editing the Correspondence of a Victorian Editor: William Hepworth Dixon." Master's thesis, Ghent University, 2014. http://lib.ugent.be/fulltxt/RUG01/002/162/769/RUG01-002162769_2014_0001_AC.pdf.

Pattison, Mark. "Books and Critics." *Fortnightly Review* 22 (November 1877): 659–79.

Patton, Cynthia Ellen. "'Not a limitless possession': Health Advice and Readers' Agency in the *Girl's Own Paper*, 1880–1890." *Victorian Periodicals Review* 45, no. 3 (2012): 111–33.

Paz, Dennis, *Nineteenth-Century English Religious Traditions: Retrospect and Prospect*. Westport: Greenwood Press, 1995.

Pedlar, Neil. *The Imported Pioneers: Westerners Who Helped Build Modern Japan*. Folkstone: Japan Library, 1990.

Pelkey, Stanley C. "Music, Memory and the People in Selected British Periodicals of the Late Eighteenth and Early Nineteenth Centuries." *Music and History: Bridging the Disciplines*, edited by Jeffery H. Jackson and Stanley C. Pelkey, 61–83. Jackson: University Press of Mississippi, 2005.

"Penny Novels." *Macmillan's Magazine* 14 (June 1866): 96–105.

"Periodical Literature." *Athenaeum: Spirit of the English Magazines*, 3rd ser., 3 no. 9 (January 1830): 352–4.

"Periodicals." *Randolf County Journal* 1, no. 13 (March 25, 1858): 4.

Perry, Gail. *Spectacular Flirtations: Viewing the Actress in British Art and Theatre, 1768–1820*. New Haven: Yale University Press, 2008.

Peters, Lisa. *Politics, Publishing, and Personalities: Wrexham Newspapers 1848–1914*. Chester: University of Chester Press, 2011.

———. "A Troubled History of a Welsh Newspaper Publishing Company: The North Wales Constitutional Newspaper Company Limited, 1869–1878." In *The Moving Market: Continuity and Change in the Book Trade*, edited by Peter Isaac and Barry McKay, 117–25. New Castle: Oak Knoll Press, 2001.

Peterson, Linda H. *Becoming a Woman of Letters: Myths of Authorship and Facts of the Victorian Market*. Princeton: Princeton University Press, 2009.

Phegley, Jennifer. *Courtship and Marriage in Victorian England*. Santa Barbara: Praeger, 2011.

———. *Educating the Proper Woman Reader: Victorian Family Literary Magazines and the Cultural Health of the Nation*. Columbus: Ohio State University Press, 2004.

Pigeon, Stephan. "Anglo-American Cultures of Re-Printing in the *Ladies' Treasury* (1857–1895): Eliza Warren Francis's 'Scissors-and-Paste.'" Master's thesis, University of Windsor, 2013.

Pittard, Christopher. "'Cheap, healthful literature': *The Strand Magazine*, Fictions of Crime, and Purified Reading Communities." *Victorian Periodicals Review* 40, no. 1 (2007): 1–23.

Place, Jean-Michel, and André Vasseur. *Bibliographie des revues et journaux littéraires des XIXe et XXe Siècles*. 3 vols. Paris: J.M. Place, 1973–7.

Platt, Jane. "A Sweet, Saintly, Christian Business?: The *Anglican Parish Magazine*, 1859–1918." PhD diss., Lancaster University, 2011.

"Police." *Times*, August 23, 1889, 11.

Poole, William Frederick, and William Fletcher. *Poole's Index to Periodical Literature*. 7 vols. London: Kegan Paul, Tench, Trübner, 1882–1908.

Poovey, Mary. "Economics and Finance." In *The Cambridge History of Victorian Literature*, edited by Kate Flint, 388–404. Cambridge, Cambridge University Press, 2012.

———. *Uneven Developments: The Ideological Work of Gender in Mid-Victorian England*. Chicago: University of Chicago Press, 1988.

———. "Writing about Finance in Victorian England: Disclosure and Secrecy in the Culture of Investment." *Victorian Studies* 45, no. 1 (Autumn 2002): 17–41.

Porter, Bernard. *The Absent-Minded Imperialists*. Oxford: Oxford University Press, 2004.

Porter, G.R. *The Progress of the Nation*. Edited by F.W. Hirst. London: Methuen, 1912.

Porter, Michael. *Competitive Advantage: Creating and Sustaining Superior Performance*. New York: Simon and Schuster, 1985.

Portsmouth, Eveline. "The Position of Woman." *Woman's World* 1 (1888): 7–10.

"The Post-Office." *Times*, July 19, 1849, 7.

Potter, Sarah. "Declaration of 150 Female Volunteers in Birmingham and Its Vicinity." In *Political Women, 1800–1850*, edited by Ruth Frow and Edmund Frow, 50–3. London: Pluto Press, 1989.

Potter, Simon. *News and the British World: The Emergence of an Imperial Press System*. Oxford: Oxford University Press, 2003.

———, ed. *Newspapers and Empire in Ireland and Britain: Reporting the British Empire, c. 1857–1921*. Dublin: Four Courts Press, 2004.

Pound, Reginald. *Mirror of the Century: The Strand Magazine, 1891–1950*. London: A.S. Barnes, 1967.

Pound, Richard. "'The Gallery of Comicalities': An Introduction to the Caricatures of C.J. Grant (fl. c. 1830–1846)." *G.J. Saville Caricatures*. http://www.gjsaville-caricatures.co.uk/articles/GJGrant.

———. "Serial Journalism and the Transformation of English Graphic Satire, 1830–36." 2 vols. PhD diss., University of London, 2002.

Powell, Michael, and Terry Wyke. "Manchester Men and Manchester Magazines: Publishing Periodicals in the Provinces in the Nineteenth Century." In *Periodicals and Publishers: The Newspaper and Journal Trade, 1750–1914*, edited by John Hinks, Catherine Armstrong, and Matthew Day, 161–84. New Castle: Oak Knoll, 2009.

Powers, Ron. *Mark Twain: A Life*. London: Pocket Books, 2007.

[Praed, Winthrop Mackworth]. "My Partner." *New Monthly Magazine* 22 (January 1828): 353–4.

Prager, Arthur. *The Mahogany Tree: An Informal History of Punch*. New York: Hawthorn, 1979.

"Preface." *Christian Observer* 60 (1861): n.p.

"Preface." *Fine Arts Quarterly Review* 1 (May 1863): v–vi.

"Preparations for War." *Lloyd's Weekly*, November 24, 1850, 1.

Prévost, Stéphanie. "W.T. Stead and the Eastern Question." *19: Interdisciplinary Studies in the Long Nineteenth Century* 16 (2013). http://www.19.bbk.ac.uk/index.php/19/article/view/654/899.

Price, Leah. *How to Do Things with Books in Victorian Britain*. Princeton: Princeton University Press, 2012.

Price, R.G.G. *A History of Punch*. London: R. & R. Clarke, 1957.

Prince, Kathryn. *Shakespeare in the Victorian Periodicals*. New York: Routledge, 2008.

"Privilege of Counsel." *Law Times*, July 13, 1844, 294.

Prochaska, Frank. *Eminent Victorians on American Democracy: The View from Albion*. Oxford: Oxford University Press, 2012.

"Professional Manliness and Generosity." *North Wales Chronicle*, October 28, 1893, 5.

"Progress of the War." *Examiner*, July 22, 1854, 461–2.

"Prospectus." *Blackwood's Edinburgh Magazine* 1 (April 1817): n.p.

Pryce, W.T.R. "Language Areas in North-East Wales, c. 1800–1911." In *Language and Community in the Nineteenth Century*, edited by Geraint H. Jenkins, 21–61. Cardiff: University of Wales Press, 1998.

R.M.M. [Richard Monckton Milnes]. "Projected Railways in Westmoreland, in Answer to Mr. Wordsworth's Late Sonnet." *Examiner*, November 23, 1844, 745.

Radford, Joseph. "The War-Cry." *Northern Star*, November 21, 1840, 3.

Ramamurthy, Anandi. *Imperial Persuaders: Images of Africa and Asia in British Advertising*. Manchester: Manchester University Press, 2003.

The Ranger. "Life in the Woods." *Sporting Magazine* 298 (October 1865): 297–300.

Rantanen, Terhi. "The Globalization of Electronic News in the 19th Century." *Media, Culture, & Society* 19, no. 4 (1997): 605–20.

Ray, Gordon N. *Thackeray: The Age of Wisdom, 1847–1863*. New York: McGraw-Hill, 1958.

———. *Thackeray: The Uses of Adversity, 1811–1863*. New York: McGraw-Hill, 1955.

Raykoff, Ivan. "Piano, Telegraph, Typewriter: Listening to the Language of Touch." In *Media, Technology, and Literature in the Nineteenth Century: Image, Sound, Touch*, edited by Colette Colligan and Margaret Linley, 159–88. Farnham: Ashgate, 2011.

Read, Donald. *The Power of the News: The History of Reuters*. 2nd ed. Oxford: Oxford University Press, 1998.

———. *Press and People, 1790–1850: Opinion in Three English Cities*. London: Edward Arnold, 1961.

Recchio, Thomas. *Elizabeth Gaskell's* Cranford: *A Publishing History*. Farnham: Ashgate, 2009.

"Recollections of Derbyshire." *Citizen* 1, no. 1 (1839): 32–7.

Rees, R.D. "South Wales and Monmouthshire Newspapers under the Stamp Acts." *Welsh History Review* 1 (1960): 301–24.

Reid, Forrest. *Illustrators of the Eighteen Sixties: An Illustrated Survey of the Work of 58 British Artists*. 1928. Reprint, New York: Dover, 1975.

Reid, John Cowie. *Thomas Hood*. London: Routledge & Kegan Paul, 1963.

"Religious and Moral." *Friend* 1, no. 3 (1815): 61–2.

"Remarks upon Various Subjects by W. Hutton." *Gentleman's Magazine* 73 (January 1803): iv.

Rendall, Jane. "'A Moral Engine'?: Feminism, Liberalism and the *English Woman's Journal*." In *Equal or Different: Women's Politics 1800–1914*, edited by Jane Rendall, 112–38. Oxford: Basil Blackwell, 1987.

"Report from the Select Committee on Newspaper Stamps, 1851." *British Quarterly Review* 15 (February 1852): 135–62.

"A Reporter." *Wrexham Telegraph*, March 25, 1858, 4.

"Repose." *Saturday Review*, July 23, 1864, 110–11.

"Return of Mr. Cobbett." *Black Dwarf*, December 8, 1819, 801.

"Review of *The Siege of Rochelle*." *Musical Library: Monthly Supplement* 22 (January 1836): 32–4.

"A Revolution in Printing: The Story of the Linotype." *Chambers's Journal of Popular Literature, Science, and Arts* 14 (January 30, 1897): 69–71.

[Reynolds, G.W.M.]. "Lord Brougham's Vagaries." *Reynolds's Weekly Newspaper*, July 21, 1850, 2.

Richards, Jeffrey, ed. *Imperialism and Juvenile Literature*. Manchester: Manchester University Press, 1989.

———. *Imperialism and Music: Britain 1876–1953*. Manchester: Manchester University Press, 2001.

Richards, Leah, and Maurice Milne. "*Bell's Life in London*." In *The Dictionary of Nineteenth-Century Journalism in Great Britain and Ireland*, edited by Laurel Brake and Marysa Demoor, 46–7. Ghent and London: Academia Press and the British Library, 2009.

Richardson, Ruth, and Robert Thorne, eds. *The Builder: Illustrations Index*. London: Builder Group, 1994.

Richmond, Lesley, and Bridget Stockford. *Company Archives: The Survey of the Records of 1,000 of the First Registered Companies in England and Wales*. Aldershot: Gower Press, 1986.

Roberts, Brinley F. "Welsh Periodicals: A Survey." In *Investigating Victorian Journalism*, edited by Laurel Brake, Aled Jones, and Lionel Madden, 71–84. Basingstoke: Macmillan, 1990.

Roberts, F. David. "Still More Early Victorian Newspaper Editors." *Victorian Periodicals Newsletter* 18 (1972): 12–26.

Roberts, Helene E. "British Art Periodicals of the Eighteenth and Nineteenth Centuries." *Victorian Periodicals Newsletter* 9 (1970): 2–183.

Roberts, Steven. *Distant Writing: A History of the Telegraph Companies in Britain between 1838 and 1858*. 2006. http://distantwriting.co.uk.

Robinson, Howard. *Britain's Post Office: A History of Development from the Beginnings to the Present Day*. Oxford: Oxford University Press, 1953.

Robinson, Solveig C. "'Amazed at our success': The Langham Place Editors and the Emergence of a Feminist Critical Tradition." *Victorian Periodicals Review* 29, no. 2 (1996): 159–72.

Rochelson, Meri-Jane. "*Church of England Quarterly Review* (1837–1858)." In *The Dictionary of Nineteenth-Century Journalism in Great Britain and Ireland*, edited by Laurel Brake and Marysa Demoor, 118. Ghent and London: Academia Press and the British Library, 2009.

Rodensky, Lisa. "Middles." In *The Dictionary of Nineteenth-Century Journalism*, edited by Laurel Brake and Marysa Demoor, 411–12. Ghent and London: Academia Press and the British Library, 2009.

Rodgers, Beth. "Competing Girlhoods: Competition, Community, and Reader Contribution in the *Girl's Own Paper* and the *Girl's Realm*." *Victorian Periodicals Review* 45, no. 3 (2012): 277–300.

Rogala, Jozef. *The Genius of Mr. Punch*. Tokyo: Yurindo, 2006.

Rollin, Charles. *Histoire ancienne des Égyptiens, des Carthaginois, des Assyriens, des Babyloniens, des Mèdes et des Perses, des Macédoniens, des Grecs*. Paris: la Veuve Estiennes/les Frères Estienne, 1730–38.

Rollington, Ralph [John W. Allingham]. *A Brief History of Boys' Journals*. Leicester: H. Simpson, 1913.

Roper, Derek. *Reviewing before the Edinburgh, 1788–1802*. London: Methuen, 1978.

Rose, Jonathan, and Patricia Anderson, eds. *British Literary Publishing Houses, 1881–1965*. Vol. 112 of *The Dictionary of Literary Biography*. London: Gale, 1991.

Rosenberg, Tracy. "Breaking out of the Cage: Mona Caird and Her Reception in the Victorian Press." *Folio* 8 (2004): 9–12.

Rossetti, William Michael. *Fine Arts, Chiefly Contemporary*. London: Macmillan, 1867.

"The Roughs' Guide." *All the Year Round*, December 16, 1865, 492–6.

Rowlands, Walter. "Art Sales in America." *Art Journal*, September 1887, 293–5.

Rowntree, Joseph, and Arthur Sherwell. *The Temperance Problem and Social Reform*. 8th ed. London: Hodder and Stoughton, 1900.

Rubery, Matthew. *The Novelty of Newspapers*. Oxford: Oxford University Press, 2009.

———. "Victorian Print Culture, Journalism and the Novel." *Literature Compass* 7, no. 4 (2010): 290–300.

Rueschemayer, Dietrich. "Can One or a Few Cases Yield Theoretical Gains?" In *Comparative Historical Analysis in the Social Sciences*, edited by J. Mahoney and D. Rueschemeyer, 305–36. Cambridge: Cambridge University Press, 2003.

Rumbaugh, Liela. "*The Magazine of Art*." PhD diss., Northwestern University, 1969.

Ryan, James R. *Picturing Empire: Photography and the Visualization of the British Empire*. London: Reaktion, 1997.

Sabin, Roger. "Ally Sloper, Victorian Comic Hero: Interpreting a Comedy Type." In *Visual Communication*, edited by David Machin, 429–44. Berlin: De Gruyter Mouton, 2014.

Said, Edward. *Orientalism*. New York: Vintage, 1979.

Saintsbury, George. *A Last Scrapbook*. London: Macmillan, 1924.

Sala, George Augustus. "The Cant of Modern Criticism." *Belgravia* 4 (November 1867): 45–55.

———. *The Life and Adventures of George Augustus Sala Written by Himself*. London: Cassell, 1896.

———. *Things I Have Seen and People I Have Known*. 2 vols. London: Cassell, 1896.

Salesa, Damon. *Racial Crossings: Race, Intermarriage, and the Victorian British Empire*. Oxford: Oxford University Press, 2011.

Salmon, Edward. *Juvenile Literature as It Is*. London: Henry J. Drane, 1888.

"Salutatory." *Lorgnette*, December 8, 1883, 2.

Sanders, Mike. *The Poetry of Chartism: Aesthetics, Politics, History*. Cambridge: Cambridge University Press, 2009.

Sato, Tomoko, and Toshio Watanabe, eds. *Japan and Britain: An Aesthetic Dialogue, 1850–1930*. London: Lund Humphries in association with Barbican Art Gallery and the Setagaya Art Museum, 1991.

Saunders, J.W. *The Profession of English Letters*. London: Routledge and Kegan Paul, 1964.

Savory, Jerold J. "An Uncommon Comic Collection: Humorous Victorian Periodicals in the Newberry Library." *Victorian Periodicals Newsletter* 17 (1984): 94–102.

Schiau-Botea, Diana. "Performing Writing: *Le Chat Noir* (1881–95); *Le Courrier français* (1884–1913); and *Les Quat'z'arts* (1897–98)." In *The Oxford Critical and Cultural History of Modernist Magazines*, vol. 3, edited by Peter Brooker, Sascha Bru, Andrew Thacker, and Christian Weikop, 38–59. Oxford: Oxford University Press, 2013.

Schivelbusch, Wolfgang. *The Railway Journey: The Industrialization of Time and Space in the Nineteenth Century*. Berkeley: University of California Press, 1986.

Schmidt, Barbara Quinn. "Novelists, Publishers, and Fiction in Middle-Class Magazines: 1860–1880." *Victorian Periodicals Review* 17, no. 4 (1984): 142–53.

Scholes, Percy A. *The Mirror of Music 1844–1944: A Century of Musical Life in Britain as Reflected in the Pages of the Musical Times*. 2 vols. 1947. Reprint, Freeport: Books for Libraries Press, 1970.

Schroeder, Janice. "'Better Arguments': The *English Woman's Journal* and the Game of Public Opinion." *Victorian Periodicals Review* 35, no. 3 (2002): 243–71.

Schwarz, Alan. *The Numbers Game: Baseball's Lifelong Fascination with Statistics*. New York: St. Martin's, 2004.

"Scissors and Paste." *Chambers's Journal* 207 (December 14, 1867): 1–4.

Scodel, Joshua. *The English Poetic Epitaph: Commemoration and Conflict from Jonson to Wordsworth*. Ithaca: Cornell University Press, 1991.

Score, Melissa. "Pioneers of Social Progress?: Gender and Technology in British Printing Trade Union Journals, 1840–65." *Victorian Periodicals Review* 47, no. 2 (2014): 274–95.

Scotti, Pascal. *Out of Due Time: Wilfred Ward and the* Dublin Review. Washington, DC: Catholic University Press of America, 2006.

Scriven, Tom. "The Jim Crow Craze in London's Press and Streets, 1836–39." *Journal of Victorian Culture* 19, no. 1 (2014): 93–109.

Scrivener, Michael, ed. *Poetry and Reform: Periodical Verse from the English Democratic Press, 1792–1824*. Detroit: Wayne State University Press, 1992.

Secord, William. *Victorian Sensation: The Extraordinary Publication, Reception, and Secret Authorship of* Vestiges of the Natural History of Creation. Chicago: University of Chicago Press, 2000.

Seed, David. *American Travellers in Liverpool*. Liverpool: Liverpool University Press, 2008.

Sell's Dictionary of the World's Press. London: Sell, 1883–1921.

Shamgar, Beth. "Perceptions of Stylistic Change: A Study of the Reviews of New Music in the *Harmonicon* (1823–1833)." *Current Musicology* 42 (1986): 20–31.

[Shand, Alexander Innes]. "The Literary Life of Anthony Trollope." *Edinburgh Review* 159 (1884): 186–212.

Shattock, Joanne, ed. *The Cambridge Bibliography of English Literature*. Vol. 4, 1800–1900. Cambridge: Cambridge University Press, 1999.

———. "The Culture of Criticism." In *The Cambridge Companion to English Literature, 1830–1914*, edited by Joanne Shattock, 71–90. Cambridge: Cambridge University Press, 2010.

———. "*North British Review* (1844–1871)." In *The Dictionary of Nineteenth-Century Journalism in Great Britain and Ireland*, edited by Laurel Brake and Marysa Demoor, 457. Ghent and London: Academia Press and the British Library, 2009.

———. *Politics and Reviewers: The* Edinburgh *and the* Quarterly *in the Early Victorian Age*. Leicester: Leicester University Press, 1989.

———. "Reviews and Monthlies." In *The Edinburgh History of the Book in Scotland*, vol. 3, edited by Bill Bell, 343–57. Edinburgh: Edinburgh University Press, 2007.

———. "Tait's Edinburgh Magazine (1832–1861)." In *The Dictionary of Nineteenth-Century Journalism in Great Britain and Ireland*, edited by Laurel Brake and Marysa Demoor, 613–14. Ghent and London: Academia Press and the British Library, 2009.

Shattock, Joanne, and Michael Wolff, eds. *The Victorian Periodical Press: Samplings and Soundings*. Leicester: Leicester University Press, 1982.

Sheehy, Ian. "'The View from Fleet Street': Irish Nationalist Journalists in London and Their Attitudes towards Empire, 1892–1898." In *Newspapers and Empire in Ireland and Britain: Reporting the British Empire, c. 1857–1921*, edited by Simon Potter, 143–58. Dublin: Four Courts Press, 2004.

Sheets-Pyenson, Susan. "Popular Science Periodicals in Paris and London: The Emergence of a Low Scientific Culture, 1820–1875." *Annals of Science* 42 (1985): 549–72.

Shepard, Leslie. *The Broadside Ballad*. London: Herbert Jenkins, 1962.

———. *The History of Street Literature*. Newton Abbott, UK: David and Charles, 1973.

Shepherd, Jennifer. "The British Press and Turn-of-the-Century Developments in the Motoring Movement." *Victorian Periodicals Review* 38, no. 4 (2005): 379–91.

Sherratt, Tim. "4 Million Articles Later . . ." *Discontents: Working for the Triumph of Content over Form, Ideas over Control, People over Systems* (blog). June 29, 2012. http://discontents.com.au/shed/experiments/4-million-articles-later.

———. *The front page*. 2012. http://dhistory.org/frontpages.

Shiach, Morag. *Discourse on Popular Culture*. Cambridge: Polity Press, 1989.

Shillingsburg, Peter L. *Pegasus in Harness: Victorian Publishing and W.M. Thackeray*. Charlottesville: University Press of Virginia, 1992.

———. "Thackeray, William Makepeace (1811–1863)." In *The Oxford Dictionary of National Biography*, edited by H.C.G. Matthew and Brian Harrison. Oxford: Oxford University Press, 2004. http://www.oxforddnb.com.

Shiman, Lilian Lewis. *The Crusade against Drink in Victorian England*. London: Macmillan, 1988.

"Shot-Proof Men-of-War." *Lloyd's Weekly*, September 1, 1861, 8.

Showalter, Elaine. *Sexual Anarchy: Gender and Culture at the Fin de Siècle*. New York: Viking, 1990.

Silberstein-Loeb, Jonathan. "The Structure of the News Market in Britain, 1870–1914." *Business History Review* 83 (2009): 759–88.

Simmonds, P.L. "Art-Aids to Commerce." *Art Journal*, December 1872, 295–6.

Simmons, Jack. *The Victorian Railway*. New York: Thames & Hudson, 1991.

Sinfield, Alan. *The Wilde Century: Effeminacy, Oscar Wilde and the Queer Moment*. New York: Columbia University Press, 1994.

Sinnema, Peter. *Dynamics of the Pictured Page: Representing the Nation in the* Illustrated London News. Aldershot: Ashgate, 1998.

Slater, Michael. "Dickens, Charles John Huffam (1812–1870)." In *The Oxford Dictionary of National Biography*, edited by H.C.G. Matthew and Brian Harrison. Oxford: Oxford University Press, 2004. http://www.oxforddnb.com.

———. *Douglas Jerrold, 1803–1857*. London: Duckworth, 2002.

Smith, Adam. *An Inquiry into the Nature and Causes of the Wealth of Nations*. 2 vols. London: Strahan and Cadell, 1776.

Smith, George. "Our Birth and Parentage." *Cornhill Magazine* 10 (January 1901): 4–17.

Smith, Harold F. *American Travellers Abroad: A Bibliography of Accounts Published before 1900*. 2nd ed. London: Scarecrow Press, 1999.

Smith, Malvern Van Wyk. *Drummer Hodge: The Poetry of the Anglo-Boer War, 1899–1902*. Oxford: Clarendon Press, 1978.

Smith, Michelle J. *Empire in British Girls' Literature and Culture: Imperial Girls, 1880–1915*. Basingstoke: Palgrave Macmillan, 2011.

Smith, Olivia. *The Politics of Language, 1791–1819*. Oxford: Oxford University Press, 1984.

Smith, Peter. "The *Cornhill Magazine*, Number 1." *Review of English Literature* 4 (1963): 23–4.

Smithies, Thomas Bywater. "To The Boys and Girls of All Nations." *Band of Hope Review* 1, no. 1 (1851): 1.

Snigurowicz, Diana. "The Harmonicon." In *The Harmonicon, 1823–1833*, edited by Diana Snigurowicz, ix–xi. Ann Arbor: UMI, 1989. http://www.ripm.org/pdf/Introductions/HARintroEnglish.pdf.

———. "The Musical Standard." In *The Musical Standard, 1862–1871* [first series], edited by Diana Snigurowicz, ix–xiii. Ann Arbor: UMI, 1991. http://www.ripm.org/pdf/Introductions/MSTintroEnglish.pdf.

Solie, Ruth. "Music in a Victorian Mirror: *Macmillan's Magazine* in the Grove Years." In *Music in Other Words: Victorian Conversations*, 44–84. Berkeley: University of California Press, 2004.

"Soliloquy on the Periodical Press." *Polar Star of Entertainment* 2 (1830): 336–8.

Soussloff, Catherine M. *The Absolute Artist: The Historiography of a Concept*. Minneapolis: University of Minnesota Press, 1997.

Southward, John. *Progress in Printing and the Graphic Arts during the Victorian Era*. London: Simpkin, Marshall, Hamilton, Kent, 1897.

Spielmann, Marion Harry. "An Art Causerie." *Graphic* 70, no. 1819 (October 8, 1904): 472–4.

———. "An Art Causerie." *Graphic* 72, no. 1877 (November 18, 1905): 656.

———. "George F. Watts, R.A." *Graphic* 70, no. 1806 (July 9, 1904): 42–3.

———. *The History of "Punch."* London: Cassell, 1895.

———. "'The Magazine of Art'—Its Majority: A Retrospect." *Magazine of Art* 23 (May 1899): 316–20.

———. "The Rivals of 'Punch.' A Glance at the Illustrated Comic Press of Half a Century." *National Review* 25 (March–August 1895): 654–66.

———. "Simeon Solomon." *Jewish World*, December 7, 1906, 626.

———. "Valedictory." *Magazine of Art*, n.s., 2 (1904): 461.

"Spirit of the Public Journals: Periodical Literature." *Mirror of Literature*, December 26, 1829, 440–2.

Spivak, Gayatri Chakravorti. "Can the Subaltern Speak?" In *Global Literary Theory*, edited by Richard Lane, 521–9. New York: Routledge, 2013.

"Sporting Writers." *Saturday Review*, December 21, 1878, 778–9.

Springhall, John. "Disreputable Adolescent Reading: Low-Life, Women-in-Peril, and School Sport 'Penny Dreadfuls' from the 1860s to the 1890s." In *Disreputable Pleasures: Less Virtuous Victorians at Play*, edited by Mike Huggins and J.A. Mangan, 103–23. London: Frank Cass, 2004.

Srebrnik, Patricia. *Alexander Strahan: Victorian Publisher*. Ann Arbor: University of Michigan Press, 1986.

St. Clair, William. *The Reading Nation in the Romantic Period*. Cambridge: Cambridge University Press, 2004.

St. Helier, Lady. "The Ideal Husband." *Leisure Hour* 54 (June 1905): 626–8. *The Statutes at Large*. Vol. 12. Cambridge: Danby Pickering, 1762–66.

Stead, W.T. "The Future of Journalism." *Contemporary Review* 50 (November 1886): 663–79. Reprinted in *Victorian Print Media: A Reader*, edited by Andrew King and John Plunkett, 323–9. Oxford: Oxford University Press, 2005.

———. "Programme." *Review of Reviews* 1 (January 1890): 14.

Stead, W.T., and Eliza Hetherington, eds. *Index to the Periodical Literature of the World*. 11 vols. London: Review of Reviews, 1891–1900.

Stedman, Jane W. "Theatre." In *Victorian Periodicals and Victorian Society*, edited by J. Don Vann and Rosemary T. VanArsdel, 162–76. Toronto: University of Toronto Press, 1994.

Stedman Jones, Gareth. *Languages of Class: Studies in English Working Class History, 1832–1982*. Cambridge: Cambridge University Press, 1983.

Steedman, Ian. "Wicksteed, Philip Henry (1844–1927)." In *The Oxford Dictionary of National Biography*, edited by Lawrence Goldman. Oxford: Oxford University Press. http://www.oxforddnb.com.

Stephens, Meic. *New Companion to the Literature of Wales*. Cardiff: University of Wales Press, 1998.

———. "Y Traethodydd." In *The Oxford Companion to the Literature of Wales*, edited by Meic Stephens, 594. Oxford: Oxford University Press, 1986.

Stokes, John, and Mark W. Turner. *The Collected Works of Oscar Wilde*. 2 vols. Oxford: Oxford University Press, 2013.

Stone, James S. *Emily Faithfull: Victorian Champion of Women's Rights*. Toronto: Meany, 1994.

Storey, Graham. *Reuters' Century: 1851–1951*. London: Max Parrish, 1951.

Stowe, William. *Going Abroad: European Travel in Nineteenth-Century American Culture*. Princeton: Princeton University Press, 1994.

Stratman, Carl J. *A Bibliography of British Dramatic Periodicals, 1720–1960*. New York: New York Public Library, 1962.

Straus, Ralph. *Sala: The Portrait of an Eminent Victorian*. London: Constable, 1942.

Stubenrauch, Joseph. "Silent Preachers in the Age of Ingenuity: Faith, Commerce, and Religious Tracts in Early Nineteenth-Century Britain." *Church History* 80, no. 3 (2011): 547–74. http://www.thefreelibrary.com/Silent+preachers+in+the+age+of+ingenuity%3a+faith%2c+commerce%2c+and . . . -a0270730922.

"A Sub-Editor's Duties and Difficulties." *Blackburn Standard and Weekly Express* 55 (July 4, 1891): 5.

"Suggestions for the Licensed Victuallers." *Leader* 5 (September 2, 1854): 825.

Sullivan, Alvin, ed. *British Literary Magazines*. 4 vols. London: Greenwood Press, 1984.

Suriano, Gregory R. *The Pre-Raphaelite Illustrators*. London: British Library, 2000.

Surtees, Robert. *Jorrocks's Jaunts and Jollities: The Hunting, Shooting, Racing, Driving, Sailing, Eccentric and Extravagant Exploits of that Renowned Sporting Citizen, Mr. John Jorrocks*. 4th ed. London: George Routledge, 1874.

Sutherland, John. *Victorian Novelists and Publishers*. London: Bloomsbury, 2013.

Swale, Alistair. *The Meiji Restoration*. Basingstoke: Palgrave Macmillan, 2009.

Swinburne, Algernon C. "A New Year's Eve." *Nineteenth Century* 37 (February 1895): 367–8.

———. *The Poems of Algernon Charles Swinburne*. Vol. 2. New York and London: Harper, 1904.

Symons, Arthur. "Editorial Note." *Savoy* 1 (January 1896): 1.

T.H.S. "The Temptations of St. Anthony." Illustrated by George Cruickshank. *Bentley's Miscellany* 3 (January 1838): 100–104.

Tanner, Simon, Trevor Muñoz, and Pich Hemy Ros. "Measuring Mass Text Digitization Quality and Usefulness: Lessons Learned from Assessing the OCR Accuracy of the British Library's *19th Century Online Newspaper Archive*." *D-Lib Magazine* 15, no. 7/8 (2009). http://www.dlib.org/dlib/july09/munoz/07munoz.html.

Tate, Steve. "Binsead, Arthur Morris (1861–1914)." In *The Dictionary of Nineteenth-Century Journalism in Great Britain and Ireland*, edited by Laurel Brake and Marysa Demoor, 55. Ghent and London: Academia Press and the British Library, 2009.

Taunton, Matthew. "*Penny Magazine* (1832–1845); *Knight's Penny Magazine* (1846)." In *The Dictionary of Nineteenth-Century Journalism in Great Britain and Ireland*, edited by Laurel Brake and Marysa Demoor, 486–7. Ghent and London: Academia Press and the British Library, 2009.

Tave, Stuart M. *The Amiable Humourist: A Study in the Comic Theory and Criticism of the Eighteenth and Early Nineteenth Centuries*. Chicago: University of Chicago Press, 1960.

Taylor, Tom. "English Painting in 1862." *Fine Arts Quarterly Review* 1 (May 1863): 1–26.

Temperley, Nicholas. "MT and Musical Journalism, 1844." *Musical Times* 110, no. 1516 (1969): 583–6.

"Terriers: Replies to an Inquiry." *Sporting Magazine* 17 (February 1826): 244–5.

Test, George A. *Satire: Spirit and Art*. Tampa: University of South Florida Press, 1991.

Thackeray, William Makepeace. "Half-a-Crown's Worth of Cheap Knowledge." *Fraser's Magazine* 17 (March 1838): 279–90. Reprinted in *Victorian Print Media: A Reader*, edited by Andrew King and John Plunkett, 469–80. London: Routledge, 2004.

———. "On a Lazy, Idle Boy." *Cornhill Magazine* 1 (January 1860): 124–8.

———. "Thorns in the Cushion." *Cornhill Magazine* 2 (July 1860): 122–8.

Thieme, Hugo. *Bibliographie de la littérature française de 1800–1930*. Paris: E. Droz, 1933.

Thirlwell, Angela. *William and Lucy: The Other Rossettis*. New Haven: Yale University Press, 2003.

"This Is the Last page." *Kind Words for Boys and Girls* 1 (January 4, 1866): 8.

Thomas, David, ed. *Restoration and Georgian England, 1660–1788. Theatre in Europe: A Documentary History*. Cambridge: Cambridge University Press, 1989.

Thomas, Julia. *Pictorial Victorians: The Inscription of Values in Word and Image*. Athens: Ohio University Press, 2004.

Thomas, R. Maldwyn. "Hen Gefndir yr *Herald Cymraeg*." *Y Casglwr* 23 (1984): 10–11.

Thomas, Sue. *Chambers's Journal, 1854–1910: Indexes to Fiction*. Victorian Fiction Research Guide 17. Victorian Secrets. http://www.victoriansecrets.co.uk/victorian-fiction-research-guides/chambers-journal.

———. *Tinsley's Magazine (The Novel Review)*. Victorian Fiction Research Guide 7. Victorian Secrets. http://www.victoriansecrets.co.uk/victorian-fiction-research-guides/tinsleys-magazine.

Thompson, E.P. *William Morris: Romantic to Revolutionary*. Oakland and Pontypool: PM Press and Merlin Press, 2011.

Thompson, Nicola Diane. *Reviewing Sex: Gender and the Reception of Victorian Novels*. Basingstoke: Macmillan, 1996.

Tilley, Elizabeth. "Periodicals." In *The Oxford History of the Irish Book*, vol. 4, edited by James H. Murphy, 144–70. Oxford: Oxford University Press, 2011.

———. "Science, Industry, and Nationalism in the *Dublin Penny Journal*." In *Culture and Science in the Nineteenth-Century Media*, edited by Louise Henson, Geoffrey Cantor, Gowan Dawson, Richard Noakes, Sally Shuttleworth, and Jonathan R. Topham, 139–50. Aldershot: Ashgate, 2004.

"Tip Topics of the Turf." *Judy*, January 7, 1903, 12.

"To Our Readers." *Irish Penny Journal*, June 26, 1841, 416.

"To Our Readers." *Kind Words for Boys and Girls* 5 (1866): n.p.

"To the Men Who Work for a Greater Benefit to Others than to Themselves." *Northern Star*, December 15, 1838, 3.

"To the Noblemen, Gentlemen, and Middlemen of England, Scotland, and Wales." *Charter*, May 19, 1839, 272.

"To the Readers of 'Figaro in London' All over the World." *Figaro in London*, May 31, 1834, 87.

"To the Unrepresented Seven Millions of Working Men of England, Ireland and Scotland." *Poor Man's Guardian*, February 9, 1833, 45–6.

"To the Young Men of England." *Cobbett's Weekly Political Register*, March 10, 1832, 642.

"To Young Men, Who Have the Laudable Wish to be Married." *Cobbett's Weekly Political Register*, February 7, 1829, 183–4.

"Toco, took." In *The Routledge Dictionary of Historical Slang*, edited by Eric Partridge, abridged by Jacqueline Simpson, 5530. London: Routledge, 1973.

Topham, Jonathan. "Science, Natural Theology, and Practice of Christian Piety in Early-Nineteenth-Century Religious Magazines." In *Science Serialized: Representations of the Sciences in Nineteenth-Century Periodicals*, edited by Geoffrey Cantor and Sally Shuttleworth, 37–66. Cambridge: MIT Press, 2004.

———. "The Wesleyan Methodist Magazine and Religious Monthlies in Early Nineteenth-Century Britain." In *Science in the Nineteenth-Century Periodical: Reading the Magazine of Nature*, edited by Geoffrey Cantor, Gowan Dawson, Graeme Gooday, Richard Noakes, Sally Shuttleworth, and Jonathan R. Topham, 67–90. Cambridge: Cambridge University Press, 2004.

Toplis, Alison. "Ready-Made Clothing Advertisements in Two Provincial Newspapers, 1800–1850." *International Journal of Regional and Local Studies* 5 (2009): 85–103.

Tosh, John. "What Should Historians Do with Masculinity?: Reflections on Nineteenth-Century Britain." *History Workshop Journal* 38 (1994): 179–202.

Travis, Madelyn. "'Both English and Jewish': Negotiating Cultural Boundaries in *Young Israel*, 1897–1901." *Victorian Periodicals Review* 46, no. 1 (2013): 116–41.

Tredrey, F.D. *The House of Blackwood, 1804–1954*. Edinburgh: William Blackwood, 1954.

Tressell, Robert. *The Ragged-Trousered Philanthropists*. Oxford: Oxford University Press, 2005.

Trevor, John. "The Labour Church." *Labour Prophet* 1, no. 2 (1892): 16.

Trollope, Anthony. *Autobiography*. London: Blackwood, 1883.

———. "Introduction." *Saint Paul's Magazine* 1 (October 1867): 1–7.

———. "Mr. Freeman on the Morality of Hunting." *Fortnightly Review*, n.s., 6 (1869): 616–25.

"True Manliness." *Belfast News-Letter*, February 22, 1892, 6.

Tucker, Albert. "Military." In *Victorian Periodicals and Victorian Society*, edited by J. Don Vann and Rosemary T. VanArsdel, 62–80. Toronto: University of Toronto Press, 1994.

Tuckwell, Gertrude M., and Stephen Gwynn. *The Life of the Rt. Hon. Sir Charles W. Dilke*. London: John Murray, 1917.

Turner, E.S. *Boys Will Be Boys: The Story of Sweeney Todd, Deadwood Dick, Sexton Blake, Billy Bunter, Dick Barton, et al.* 1948. Reprint, Harmondsworth: Penguin, 1976.

Turner, Mark W. "Periodical Time in the Nineteenth Century." *Media History* 8, no. 2 (2002): 183–96.

———. *Trollope and the Magazines: Gendered Issues in Mid-Victorian Britain*. Basingstoke: Macmillan, 2000.

Tusan, Michelle. "Gleaners in the Holy Land: Women and the Missionary Press in Victorian Britain." *Nineteenth-Century Gender Studies* 6, no. 2 (2010). http://www.ncgsjournal.com/issue62/tusan.htm.

———. "Humanitarian Journalism: The Career of Lady Henry Somerset." In *Women in Journalism at the Fin de Siècle: Making a Name for Herself*, edited by Elizabeth Gray, 91–109. Houndmills: Palgrave, 2012.

———. *Smyrna's Ashes: Humanitarianism, Genocide, and the Birth of the Middle East*. Berkeley: University of California Press, 2012.

———. *Women Making News: Gender and Journalism in Modern Britain*. Chicago: University of Illinois Press, 2005.

———. "Writing *Stri Dharma*: International Feminism, Nationalist Politics, and Women's Press Advocacy in Colonial India." *Women's History Review* 12, no. 4 (2003): 623–49.

Twyman, Michael. *The British Library's Guide to Printing: History and Techniques*. Toronto: University of Toronto Press, 1998.

———. "The Illustration Revolution." In *The Cambridge History of the Book in Britain 1830–1914*, vol. 6, edited by David McKitterick, 117–43. Cambridge: Cambridge University Press, 2009.

———. *Printing 1770–1970: An Illustrated History of Its Development and Uses in England*. 1970. Reprint, London: The British Library, 1998.

United Kingdom Band of Hope Annual Report. London: UK Band of Hope Union, 1895.

"United States (by Telegraph)." *Standard*, June 9, 1881, 5.

"United States (by Telegraph)." *Standard*, June 10, 1881, 5.

Untitled. *Black Dwarf*, December 8, 1819, 801.

Untitled. *Bolton Literary Journal*, April 29, 1831, 1:26.

Untitled. *The Times*, January 9, 1829, 2.

Untitled. *Y Dywysogaeth*, Hydref [October] 21, 1881, 1.

Vallely, Fintan. *The Companion to Irish Traditional Music*. Cork: Cork University Press, 2011.

"The Value of Protectionist Relief." *Economist* 9 (June 7, 1851): 1.

Vamplew, Wray. "Cheny, John (fl. 1727–50)." In *The Oxford Dictionary of National Biography*. Oxford: Oxford University Press, 2004. http://www.oxforddnb.com.

Van Remoortel, Marianne. "New Contexts, New Meanings: Reprints of Dante Rossetti's and Christina Rossetti's Poetry in the American Press." *Journal of Pre-Raphaelite Studies* 22, no. 1 (2013): 75–86.

———. *Women, Work, and the Victorian Periodical: Living by the Press*. Houndmills: Palgrave Macmillan, 2015.

Van Vugt, William E. *Britain to America: Mid-Nineteenth-Century Immigrants to the United States*. Urbana: University of Illinois Press, 1999.

VanArsdel, Rosemary T. "Grove as Editor of *Macmillan's Magazine*, 1863–83." In *George Grove, Music and Victorian Culture*, edited by Michael Musgrave, 145–67. Basingstoke: Palgrave Macmillan, 2003.

Vann, J. Don. "Comic Periodicals." In *Victorian Periodicals and Victorian Society*, edited by J. Van Dann and Rosemary T. VanArsdel, 278–90. Toronto: University of Toronto Press, 1994.

———. *Victorian Novels in Serial*. New York: Modern Language Association, 1985.

Vann, J. Don, and Rosemary T. VanArsdel, eds. *Periodicals of Queen Victoria's Empire: An Exploration*. London: Mansell, 1996.

———, eds. *Victorian Periodicals and Victorian Society*. Toronto: University of Toronto Press, 1994.

Venn, J. "On the Diagrammatic and Mechanical Representation of Propositions and Reasonings." London, Dublin and Edinburgh *Philosophical Magazine and Journal of Science*, 5th ser., 10, no. 59 (July 1880): 1–18.

Villette, Solange, and Irene Hardhill. "Paris and Fashion: Reflections on the Role of the Parisian Fashion Industry in the Cultural Economy." *International Journal of Sociology and Social Policy* 30, no. 9/10 (2010): 461–71.

Vincent, David. *Literacy and Popular Culture*. Cambridge: Cambridge University Press, 1989.

"Visual Material." *Nineteenth-Century Serials Edition*. 2008. http://www.ncse.ac.uk/commentary/visual.html.

Vizetelly, Henry. *Glances Back Through Seventy Years: Autobiographical and Other Reminiscences*. 2 vols. London: Kegan Paul, Trench, Trubner, 1893.

Vogenauer, Stefan. "Law Journals in Nineteenth-Century England." *Edinburgh Law Review* 12 (2008): 26–50.

von Ungern-Sternberg, Jürgen. "Scientists." In *Brill's Encyclopedia of the First World War*, edited by Gerhard Hirschfeld, Gerd Krumeich, and Irina Renz. Leiden: Brill, 2012.

Vorachek, Laura. "Whitewashing Blackface Minstrelsy in Nineteenth-Century England: Female Banjo Players in *Punch*." *Victorians: A Journal of Culture and Literature* 123 (Spring 2013): 31–51.

W.G.C. "On Some Pictures in the Royal Academy Exhibition of 1855." *Fraser's Magazine* 51 (June 1855): 707–15.

Wagstaff, Rev. Frederick. "Temperance Work in the Pulpit. The Cry of the Craftsmen." *Temperance Worker and Band of Hope Conductor* 4, no. 40 (1876): 57.

Wakeman, Geoffrey. *Victorian Book Illustration: The Technical Revolution*. Newton Abbot, UK: David & Charles, 1973.

Walker, Andrew, ed. "The Development of the Provincial Press in England, c. 1780–1914." Special issue, *Journalism Studies* 7, no. 3 (August 2006).

Wall, Joseph Frazier. *Andrew Carnegie*. New York: Oxford University Press, 1970.

Wallis, George. "Art, Science, and Manufacture." *Art Journal*, October 1851, 245–52.

Walters, Huw. *Llyfryddiaeth Cylchgronau Cymreig, 1735–1850 / A Bibliography of Welsh Periodicals, 1735–1850*. Aberystwyth: National Library of Wales, 1993.

———. *Llyfryddiaeth Cylchgronau Cymreig, 1851–1900 / A Bibliography of Welsh Periodicals, 1851–1900*. Aberystwyth: National Library of Wales, 2003.

———. "The Periodical Press to 1914." In *A Nation and its Books: A History of the Book in Wales*, edited by Philip Henry Jones and Eiluned Rees, 197–208. Aberystwyth: National Library of Wales, 1998.

———. "The Welsh Language and the Periodical Press." In *The Welsh Language and Its Social Domains*, edited by Geraint H. Jenkins, 349–78. Cardiff: University of Wales Press, 2000.

———. *Y Wasg Gyfnodol Gymreig, 1935–1900 / The Welsh Periodical Press, 1935–1900*. Aberystwyth: National Library of Wales, 1987.

Walthall, Anne. *The Weak Body of a Useless Woman: Matsuo Taseko and the Meiji Restoration*. Chicago: University of Chicago Press, 1998.

[Walton, Isaak, and Charles Cotton]. *The Compleat Angler, or, the Contemplative Man's Recreation*, edited by Marjorie Swann. Oxford: Oxford University Press, 2014.

"War and Its Trophies." *Lloyd's Weekly*, June 11, 1843, 1.

"War—Army Estimates." *Champion*, March 22, 1840, 4.

Ward, William S. *British Periodicals and Newspapers, 1798–1832: A Bibliography of Secondary Sources*. Lexington: University of Kentucky Press, 1972.

Warner, William. *Protocols of Liberty: Communication Innovation and the American Revolution*. Chicago: University of Chicago Press, 2013. http://emc.english.ucsb.edu/imprint/warner/protocols/protocols_of_liberty_intro.html.

Warren, Lynne. "Women in Conference: Reading the Correspondence Columns in *Woman*, 1890–1910." In *Nineteenth-Century Media and the Construction of Identities*, edited by Laurel Brake, Bill Bell, and David Finkelstein, 122–34. London: Palgrave, 2000.

Waters, Cathy. "'Much of Sala, and but Little of Russia': 'A Journey Due North,' *Household Words*, and the Birth of a Special Correspondent." *Victorian Periodicals Review* 42, no. 2 (2009): 305–23.

Waters, Chris. *British Socialists and the Politics of Popular Culture, 1884–1914*. Manchester: Manchester University Press, 1990.

Watkins, John. "Address to the Women of England." *Chartist Circular* 1, no. 13 (1841): 49.

Watt, W. "Careless Sportsmen." *Sporting Magazine* 287 (November 1864): 365–71.

Waugh, Evelyn. *Waugh in Abyssinia*. With an introduction by John Maxwell Hamilton. Baton Rouge: Louisiana State University Press, 2007.

Weatherby, Charles, and James Weatherby. *The Racing Calendar for the Year 1847: Races to Come*. London: Reynell and Weight, 1847.

Webb, Maurice Everett, and Herbert Wigglesworth, eds. *Raffles Davison: A Record of His Life and Work from 1870 to 1926*. London: Batsford, 1927.

Webb, R.K. *The British Working Class Reader, 1790–1848: Literacy and Tension*. London: Allen and Unwin, 1957.

Webb, Sidney, and Beatrice Webb. *The History of Liquor Licensing, Principally from 1700 to 1830*. London: Longman, Green, 1903.

Weber, William. *Music and the Middle Class: The Social Structure of Concert Life in London, Paris, and Vienna*. London: Croom Helm, 1975.

Webster, Augusta. "My Loss," *Cornhill Magazine* 30 (October 1874): 474.

———. "The Swallows." *Cornhill Magazine* 29 (January 1874): 80.

Weedon, Alexis, *Victorian Publishing: The Economics of Book Production for a Mass Market, 1836–1916*. Farnham: Ashgate, 2003.

Weedon, Alexis, and Michael Bott. *British Book Trade Archives, 1830–1939: A Location Register*. History of the Book-on-demand, Series 5. Bristol: Simon Eliot and Michael Turner, 1996. http://british bookarchives.beds.ac.uk.

"Weekly Romance." *Saturday Review* 1 (March 8, 1856): 364–5.

Weeks, Jeffrey. *Sex, Politics and Society: The Regulation of Sexuality since 1800*. 3rd ed. Harlow: Pearson, 2012.

———. *Sexuality and Its Discontents*. London: Routledge and Kegan Paul, 1985.

Welland, Dennis. *Mark Twain in England*. London: Chatto & Windus, 1978.

West, Shearer. "Tom Taylor, William Powell Firth, and the British School of Art." *Victorian Studies* 33, no. 2 (1990): 307–26.

Wheeler, Thomas M. "Address from the London Delegate Council, to the Male and Female Chartists of Great Britain and Ireland." *English Chartist Circular* 1, no. 34 (n.d.): 133.

[Whibley, Charles]. "The Sins of Education." *Blackwood's Edinburgh Magazine* 165 (March 1899): 503–13.

White, Cynthia. *Women's Magazines, 1693–1968*. London: Michael Joseph, 1970.

White, Gleeson. *English Illustration: The Sixties, 1855–70*. London: Archibald Constable, 1897.

"Why Are Men Stronger than Women?" *Penny Illustrated Paper*, November 2, 1895, 290.

"Why I Don't Write Plays. I–XIX." *Pall Mall Gazette* 55 (August 31, 1892): 1–2; (September 1, 1892): 1–2; (September 2, 1892): 2; (September 5, 1892): 3; (September 7, 1892): 3; (September 8, 1892): 3; (September 9, 1892): 3; (September 10, 1892): 3; (September 12, 1892): 3; (September 13, 1892): 3; (September 20, 1892): 3.

"Why I Don't Write Plays." *Judy; or, the London Serio-Comic Journal*, September 28, 1892, 152.

Wicksteed, Philip. "Is the Labour Church a Class Church?" *Labour Prophet* 1, no. 1 (1892): 1.

Wickwar, William Hardy. *The Struggle for the Freedom of the Press: 1819–1832*. New York: Johnson Reprint, 1972.

Widén, Anne. "'Le roi est mort, vive le roi'; Languages and Leadership in Niecks's Liszt Obituary." In *Europe, Empire, and Spectacle in Nineteenth-Century British Music*, edited by Rachel Cowgill and Julian Rushton, 45–53. Aldershot: Ashgate, 2006.

Wiener, Joel H. "The Americanization of the British Press, 1830–1914." *Studies in Newspaper and Periodical History* 2, no. 1 (1994): 61–74.

———. *The Americanization of the British Press, 1830s–1914: Speed in the Age of Transatlantic Journalism*. Basingstoke: Palgrave Macmillan, 2011.

———. "Circulation and the Stamp Tax." In *Victorian Periodicals: A Guide to Research*, vol. 1, edited by J. Don Vann and Rosemary T. VanArsdel, 149–73. New York: Modern Language Association of America, 1978.

———, ed. *Innovators and Preachers: The Role of the Editor in Victorian England*. Westport: Greenwood Press, 1985.

———. *The War of the Unstamped: The Movement to Repeal the British Newspaper Tax, 1830–1836*. Ithaca: Cornell University Press, 1969.

Wiener, Joel H., and Mark Hampton, eds. *Anglo-American Media Interactions, 1850–1900*. Basingstoke: Palgrave, 2007.

Wilde, Oscar. *The Letters of Oscar Wilde*. Edited by Rupert Hart-Davis. New York: Harcourt, Brace & World, 1962.

Wiles, R.M. *Freshest Advices: Early Provincial Newspapers in England*. Columbus: Ohio State University Press, 1965.

Williams, Brid Gwenllian. "'Swyno merched ein gwlad allan o'u hogofau': delweddau o'r ferch yn *Y Frythones*, 1879–1891." MSc diss., University of Wales, Aberystwyth, 1998.

Williams, G.J. "Cyhoeddi llyfrau Cymraeg yn y bedwaredd ganrif ar bymtheg." *Journal of the Welsh Bibliographical Society* 9, no. 4 (April 1965): 152–61.

———. *Y wasg Gymraeg ddoe a heddiw*. Y Bala: Llyfrau'r Faner, 1970.

Williams, Glanmor. *Religion, Language, and Nationality in Wales: Historical Essays*. Cardiff: University of Wales Press, 1979.

Williams, J.E. Caerwyn. "Hanes cychwyn Y Traethodydd." *Llen Cymru* 14 (1981–82): 111–42.

———. "Hanes Y Traethodydd." *Y Traethodydd* 136 (1981): 34–49.

Williams, John. *Digest of Welsh Historical Statistics*. 2 vols. Cardiff: Welsh Office, 1985.

Williams, Kevin. *Read All About It!: A History of the British Newspaper*. Abingdon: Routledge, 2010.

Williams, Raymond. *Communications*. 3rd ed. Harmondsworth: Penguin, 1976.

Williams, Sian Rhiannon. "*Y Frythones*: Portread cyfriodolion merched y bedwaredd ganrif o bymtheg o Gymraes yr oes." *Llafur* 4 (1984): 43–56.

Williams, W. Alister. *The Encyclopeadia of Wrexham*. Rev. ed. Wrexham: Bridge Books, 2010.

Wilson, Charles. *First with the News: The History of W.H. Smith, 1792–1972*. London: W.H. Smith, 1985.

Wilson, David A. *Paine and Cobbett: The Transatlantic Connection*. Montreal: McGill-Queen's University Press, 1988.

Wilson, John. "Monologue, or Soliloquy on the Annuals." *Blackwood's Edinburgh Magazine* 26 (December 1829): 948–76.

Wilson Kimber, Marian. "Mr. Riddle's Readings: Music and Elocution in Nineteenth-Century Concert Life." *Nineteenth Century Studies* 21 (2007): 163–81.

Winskill, Peter T. *The Temperance Movement and Its Workers*. 4 vols. London: Blackie, 1891–92.

Winstanley, Michael. "News from Oldham: Edwin Butterworth and the Manchester Press, 1829–1848." *Manchester Region History Review* 4 (1990): 3–10.

Winston, Brian. *Media, Technology, and Society, A History: From the Telegraph to the Internet*. London: Routledge, 1998.

Wirgman, Charles, ed. *Japan Punch*. 10 vols. 1882–87. Reprint, Tokyo: Yoshudo Publishing, 1976.

"Woman's Mission." *Christian Mother's Magazine* 10, no. 2 (July 1845): 438–44.

Wood, Marcus. *Radical Satire and Print Culture, 1790–1827*. Oxford: Clarendon, 1994.

Wood, Naomi. "Angelic, Atavistic, Human: The Child of the Victorian Period." In *The Child in British Literature: Literary Constructions of Childhood, Medieval to Contemporary*, edited by Adrienne E. Gavin, 116–30. Houndmills: Palgrave Macmillan, 2012.

Wood, T. Martin. *George du Maurier: The Satirist of the Victorians*. New York: McBride, Nast, 1913.

Wolff, Michael. "Charting the Golden Stream: Thoughts on a Directory of Victorian Periodicals." *Victorian Periodicals Newsletter* 4 (1971): 23–38.

Woolf, Paul Jonathan. "Special Relationships: Anglo-American Love Affairs, Courtships, and Marriages in Fiction, 1821–1914." PhD diss., University of Birmingham, 2007.

Wordsworth, William. "The Ettrick Shepherd [Extempore Effusion, on reading, in the *Newcastle Journal*, the news of the death of the poet, James Hogg]." *Athenaeum* 424 (December 12, 1835): 930–1.

———. "On the Projected Kendal and Windermere Railway." *Morning Post*, October 16, 1844. Reprint, *Critic* 1 (November 1, 1844): 162. Reprinted as "On the Projected Windermere Railway." *Examiner*, October 19, 1844, 660.

"A Working Man." "Some Last Words about Mr. Kingsley's Sermon." *Christian Socialist*, August 16, 1861, 109.

"Working Men, Support your Order!" *Northern Star*, May 30, 1846, 6.

"The World Revolution Begun." *New York Herald*, August 6, 1858, 4.

Wright, Tom F. "Britain on the American Popular Lecture Circuit, 1844–1865." PhD diss., University of Cambridge, 2010.

Wyland, Russell M. "John Taylor Coleridge, Forgotten Editor of the *Quarterly Review*." *Victorian Periodicals Review* 44, no. 3 (2011): 215–35.

Wyman, Mark. *Round-Trip to America: The Immigrants Return to Europe, 1880–1930*. London: Cornell University Press, 1993.

Wynne, Deborah. *The Sensation Novel and the Victorian Family Magazine*. Basingstoke: Palgrave, 2001.

Yalden, Peter. "Association, Community, and the Origins of Secularisation; English and Welsh Nonconformity, c. 1850–1930." *Journal of Ecclesiastical History* 55, no. 2 (2004): 293–324.

Yates, Edmund. *Edmund Yates: His Recollections and Experiences*. 2 vols. London: Richard Bentley, 1884.

Yeomans, Henry. *Alcohol and Moral Regulations: Public Attitudes, Spirited Measures, and Victorian Hangovers*. London: Policy Press, 2014.

Yokoyama, Toshio. *Japan in the Victorian Mind: Studies of Stereotyped Images of a Nation, 1850–1880*. London: Macmillan, 1987.

Yonge, Charlotte M. "The Cumberland Street Children's Hospital." *Monthly Packet*, n.s., 11 (1871): 92–5.

Zeller, Suzanne. *Inventing Canada: Early Victorian Science and the Idea of a Transcontinental Nation*. Toronto: University of Toronto Press, 1987.

Zemitz, Thomas Milton. "Matt Morgan of 'Tomahawk' and English Cartooning, 1867–1870." *Victorian Studies* 19 (1975): 5–34.

Ziff, Larzer. *Return Passages: Great American Travel Writing, 1780–1910*. New Haven: Yale University Press, 2000.

Zon, Bennett. *Representing Non-Western Music in Nineteenth-Century Britain*. Rochester: University of Rochester Press, 2007.

Zwerdling, Alex. *Improvised Europeans: American Literary Expatriates and the Siege of London*. New York: Basic Books, 1998.

INDEX

Note: Page numbers with *f* indicate figures; those with *t* indicate tables.

A.1. 300
À Beckett, Arthur William 321
À Beckett, Gilbert 321, 369
À Becketts of Punch The (À Beckett) 321
Aberdare Times 197
Academy 9, 178, 378
Acke, Hanna 357
Ackermann, Rudolph 124, 125, 264, 377
Ackermann's Repository 262, 263*f*
Act for the Advancement of True Religion (1543) 329
Acting Manager 368
Act of Union (1801) 208–9
Actors by Gaslight 374
Adams Matthew 154
Addison, Joseph 378
Adrian, Arthur 322–3
Adventures of Philip, The (Thackeray) 288
advertisements; *see also* press directories: British identities and 156; in children's periodicals 294–5, 306; economics and 62, 71–2, 72*t*; *Englishwoman's Review* and 62; masculinity and 258; penny dreadfuls and 139; race and 61, 176; in religious periodicals 355, 359; duties on 43–6, 329
advertising agencies 53–5; *see also* newspaper press directories, Gordon & Gotch
Ady, Julia Cartwright 387
"A Father of Women" (Meynell) 88
Age (Westmacott) 240, 321
Aglaia 183
Ainsworth, Harrison 142
Ainsworth's Magazine 378
Albany Literary Journal 13
Alcohol and Drugs History Society 345
Alexandra Magazine 269
Allen, Grant 143, 144
Alleyn, Ellen 86; *see also* Rossetti, Christina

Alliance (*see* United Kingdom Alliance)
Alliance House Foundation 344
Alliance (Weekly) News 333, 345, 349, 350
Allingham, William 134
All the Year Round 21, 82, 94, 140, 242, 243, 246, 253, 291, 292
Ally Sloper's Half-Holiday 118, 318, 325–6
Altholz, Joseph 345, 357–8
Altick, Richard 63, 247, 278, 304, 322, 324, 325
Amalgamated Press 253
American Civil War, transatlantic relations and 166–7
American Masonick Record 13
American Notes (Dickens) 171
Amiable Humorist, The (Tave) 319
"Amos Barton" (Eliot) 83, 84
Amserau, Yr (The Times) 5, 196,
Analysis of Beauty, The (Hogarth) 378
Andersen, Hans Christian 301
Anderson, Benedict 2, 125, 154, 155, 368
Anderson, Patricia 115
Andrews, Alexander 66
Anglo-American Times 173
animal rights 254, 308
Annals of the Fine Arts 124, 377
Annals of the Four Masters 210
annuals 62, 67, 68*t*, 69, 69*f*, 264
anonymity *see also* authorship; 80, 90–1, 275
Answers to Correspondents 149
Anti-Corn Law League 344
Anti-Jacobin (Canning and Gifford) 319
Apperley, Charles James ("Nimrod") 310, 311, 312, 317
Applegarth, Augustus 34–7 (*see also* Vertical Roray Press)
Appleton, Charles Edward 178
Archaeologia Cambrensis 205

Archaeological Magazine of Bristol, Bath, and South Wales 205
Archer, William 369–70
archives 65–6; Bentley Papers 65; "British Publishers' Archives" microfilm series 65; digital 167, 173–4, 246; French 180–1; Gale Cengage newspaper 25; Irish 208; Japanese 181; Longman 65; Macmillan 65; political periodical 340–1; provincial newspapers and periodicals 221–2; publishers 232, 275; Welsh 194–6
Argosy 116, 140, 143, 285–7, 286*f*, 356, 378
Argument in Behalf of the Science of a Connoisseur, An (Richardson) 378
Arminian Magazine 335
Arnold, Matthew 135, 137, 171
Artist 377
Artist and Journal of Home Culture 258, 387
Artist's Repository and Drawing Magazine 377
Art Journal 377, 378, 379, 385–6
art periodicals 377–89; business of 380–1; commerce and 385–6; criticism and promotion of 381–5; future research for 388–9; overview of 377–80; specialist 386–8
Art-Union 62, 379
Arweinydd Annibynol, Yr (The Independent Leader) 201
Association for the Repeal of the Taxes on Knowledge 45–6; *see also* Taxes on Knowledge
Association of Irish Learned Journals 219–20
Atalanta 300, 303, 305, 339
Athelings, The (Oliphant) 83
Athenaeum 13, 47, 127, 243, 245; art and 378; editing of 97–8; "Our Weekly Gossip" column 148

INDEX

Athraw, Yr (The Teacher) 203
Athraw i Blentyn, Yr (The Teacher for Children) 204
Atlantic Monthly 141
Attardo, Salvatore 134
Au Bonheur des dames (Zola) 183
Auerbach, Jeffrey 264, 266
Augener and Co. 393
Aunt Judy's Magazine 144, 301, 304
"Aunt Judy's Magazine Cot" 305
Aurora Floyd (Braddon) 140
Ausytalydd, Yr (the Australian) 205
Authorship, *see* anonymity; celebrity; *Fate of Fenella*; foreign correspondents; journalism; journalists; penny-a-liners; pseudonymity; remuneration
Autobiography (Martineau) 79; (Trollope) 96
Autobiography of Mansie Wauch, The (Moir) 189
"Ave Maria in Rome" (Blinde) 135
Ayerton, William 392
Ayrshire Legatees, The (Galt) 139, 189

Bacon, Alice Mabel 183
Bacon, Richard Mackenzie 392
Badminton Magazine of Sports and Pastimes 313
Bagehot, Walter 81, 92, 187
Baird, Bridget 26
balaam-box 149
Balfe, Michael 212
Balfour, Clara Lucas 354
Balfour, Fairfax 280
Ballantyne, R.M. 296, 302
Ballin, Ada 313, 317
Band of Hope 344, 347, 351–2
Band of Hope Chronicle 345, 352
Band of Hope Review 333, 345, 347, 350, 351, 352, 356
Baner ac Amserau Cymru (Banner and Times of Wales) 196, 197, 198f, 203
Baner Cymru (Banner of Wales) 196
Banham, Christopher 296
Banim, John 214
Banjo World 394
Baron, Beth 160
Barrack Room Ballads (Kipling) 137
Barrett Browning, Elizabeth 124, 129
Barrow, George 83
Bashford, Christina 397–8
Batts, John S. 173
Baudelaire, Charles 7
Baudin, Dominique 179
Bax, Ernest Belfort 340
Baxter, W.G. 118
"Bayadere, The" (L.E.L.) 134
Beardsley, Aubrey 112, 118
Bebbington, David 357
Beckford, Peter 307
Bedyddiwr, Y (The Baptist) 201

Beegan, Gerry 106, 121
Beer, Gillian 178
Beer, Rachel 99–100
Beer Act (1830) 342–3
Beetham, Margaret 229, 250, 267, 277–8, 352
Beeton, Isabella 267
Beeton, Samuel 253, 267, 273, 282, 295, 298
Beeton's Christmas Annual 142–3
Begbie, Harold 29–31, 41
Beginnings of a Commercial Sporting Culture in Britain (Harvey) 308
Behrendt, Stephen 127
Beirniad, Y (The Critic) 203
Belfast News-Letter 250
Belgravia 82, 140, 287, 288
Bell, Acton 86; *see also* Brontë, Anne
Bell, Bill 186
Bell, John 261
Bell's Life in London 310–11, 319, 369
Bell's Sporting Weekly 374
Belton Castle (Trollope) 81
Ben Brierly's Journal 130
Bender, Jill 158
Bengry, Justin 257
Bennett, Arnold 94
Bennett, John 301
Bennett, Joseph 397
Bennett, Mary 301
Bennett, Scott 18–19
Benn's Media Directory 54
Bentley, George 84, 85
Bentley, James 172
Bentley, Richard 189
Bentley and Son 84
Bentley's Miscellany 82, 94, 136, 172
Besant, Walter 81, 141, 143
Bibliotheksdienst 179
Bibliothèque Nationale de France 179, 180
Bibliothèque numérique de Roubaix 181
Bickham, Troy 166
Billington, Louis 357
Bing, Siegfried 183–4
"Biographical Sketches of Illustrious Ladies" 148
biographies, as genre 90, 322–3; art criticism and 381–2; Carlyle and 77–8
"Birthday, A" (Rossetti) 87
Black Arrow, The (Stevenson) 301
Blackburn Standard and Weekly Express 93
Black Dwarf 319, 331, 333, 339
Blackmore, R.D. 189
Blackwood, John 83, 189
Blackwood, William, I 96–7, 185, 188
Blackwood, William, III 61, 189
Blackwoodians 188, 189
Blackwood's (Edinburgh) Magazine 1, 9, 13, 81, 82, 83, 87, 89, 90, 96–7,

124, 129, 132, 135, 139, 185, 186, 188, 191, 239, 241, 293, 318, 378
Blackwood's Lady's Magazine 262
Blatchford, Robert 251, 337
Blaythwayt, Raymond 148
Bledsoe, Robert Terrell 397
Blessington, Lady 264
Blevins, Cameron 26
Blinde, Mathilde 135
B.M.G.: A Journal Devoted to Banjo, Mandoline, and Guitar 394
Boddice, Rob 254
Bodichon, Barbara Leigh Smoth 269, 290
Bolton Literary Journal 231
Bookman 99
Book of Beauty 264
Bookseller 62–3, 67
Boos, Florence S. 130
Boswell, James 185
Boucher, William 118
Boucherett, Jessie 62, 269
Bourdieu, Pierre 381
Bow Bells 12, 180, 278, 282, 284–5, 285f
Boxer War 177
Boyce, Charlotte 129
Boyd, H.S. 135
Boyd, Kelly 306
"Boy's Exchange" 304
Boy's Friend 253, 298
Boys' Herald 253
Boy's Journal 295–6
Boys' Miscellany 296
Boys of England 296, 297f
Boy's Own Magazine 253, 295, 304
Boy's Own Paper 144–5, 253, 294, 295, 296, 299–300, 304, 355
Boys' Realm 253
Bradbury and Evans 95, 292
Braddon, Mary Elizabeth 89, 140, 141, 173, 264, 287, 288
Brake, Laurel 4, 7, 9, 186, 228, 329
Brantlinger, Patrick 323
Brett, Edwin J. 296
Brewing Trade Review 64, 71–4, 72t, 73f
Brewster, David 192
Brief History of Boys' Journals, A (Rollington) 305
Briggs, Julia 293
Bristol Temperance Herald 348
British and American Journal of Commerce 173
British and Foreign Review 78
British Critic 360
British Critic and Quarterly Theological Review 335
British Friend 360
British Journal of Inebriety 350
British Library 313, 231, 232
British Magazine 132

462

INDEX

British Medical Temperance Association 350
British Mother's Magazine, The 268, 337
British Newspaper Archive 23, 24, 66
British Newspapers, 1600-1900 25
British Protestant 335
"British Publishers' Archives" (microfilm series) 65
British Temperance Advocate 345, 349, 350
British Weekly 356
British Women's Temperance Association 344, 348
British Women's Temperance Journal/Wings 341, 348
British Workman 106, 116, 117f, 329–31, 330f, 333, 347, 351
British Workwoman 337, 338f
Brontë, Anne 86; *see also* Bell, Acton
Brontë, Branwell 231
Brooks, Shirley 324
Brothers, Ann 388
Brough, Robert 325
Brougham, Henry 77, 187
Brown, Ford Madox 116
Brown, Lucy 145
Brown, Stephen 211
Browne, H.K. 213, 215
Browne, Janet 178
Browning, Elizabeth Barrett 87
Browning, Robert 86
Bruce, Charles 135
Brut, Y (The Chronicle) 205
Bryce, James 171
Buchan, John 189
Builder 242, 378
Bulletin des Bibliothèques de France 180
Bulletin Quotidien de l'Exposition 40
Bulwer-Lytton, Edward 86, 370
Burke, Edmund 319, 378
Burlington Magazine 387
Burnand, F.C. 322
Burne-Jones, Edward 112, 116, 118
Burton, Antoinette 160
Busybody, or Men and Manners 319
Butler, Elizabeth 382
Butts, Dennis 293
Buzzetti, Dino 21–2

Cadbury, John 343
Cadets of Temperance 351
Cadogan, Mary 305
Caird, Mona 10
Cambrian 196
Cambrian Archaeological Association 205
Cambrian Daily Leader 197
Cambridge Bibliography of English Literature (Shattock) 66, 228
Campbell, Thomas 126
Canning, George 319
Carleton, William 210, 215, 217
Carlile, Richard 319, 331, 339

Carlyle, Thomas 7, 77–8, 92, 145, 190
Carnarvon Herald 197
Carnegie, Andrew 226–7
Carr, Henry Lascelles 200
Carver, Terrell 10
Casement, Roger 157
Cashel Byron's Profession (Shaw) 341
Cassell, John 343, 351, 356, 379–80
Cassell and Co. 253, 356
Cassell's (Illustrated) Family Magazine/Paper 84, 115, 141, 242, 253, 278, 300, 356
Catholic Herald 227
Catholic Penny Magazine 209
Cecire, Natalie 20
Celebrated Trials (Barrow) 83
celebrity (authors) 91, 125, 128, 148–9, 312
celebrity editors 90–1, 98, 310–11; Dickens as 94; examples of 91
Celt, Y (The Celt) 197
Cenadydd, Y (The Messenger) 201
Centre for Literary and Linguistic Computing 21
Century Guild Hobby Horse 387–8
Cesarini, David 357
Chadwick, Owen 357
Chalaby, Jean 165
Chalmers, Thomas 359
Chambers, Robert 185, 190
Chambers, William 185, 190
Chambers's Edinburgh Journal 52, 80, 90–1, 104, 143, 149, 185, 186, 190–1, 242, 243, 246, 277–8, 279
Chameleon 129
Champion, Henry Hyde 332
Chapman, Alison 129–30
Chapman, Jane 8
Chapman, John 80, 147
Chapman & Hall 94
"Characteristics" (Carlyle) 79
"Charge of the Light Brigade, The" (Tennyson) 87–8, 126
Charivari, Le 181
Charles O'Malley (Lever) 213, 215–19, 216f
Charter 251
Chartism 166, 190, 230, 332336, 340; poetry's role in 127–9
Chartist periodicals and newspapers 228, 332, 334; *Chartist* 332; *Chartist Circular* 340; *Cleave's Gazette* 166; *Northern Liberator* 166; *Northern Star* 146; *Red Republican* 62
Chase, Malcolm 332
Chase Act (1891) 52, 173
Chat noir, Le 181
Chatterbox 301
Children's Friend 294
children's periodicals 293–306; for boys 295–8; for boys and girls 300–1; definitions of childhood and 293;

editors and 303–5; future research for 305–6; gendered reading and 301–2; for girls 298–300; history of 293; market growth of 293–5
Child's Companion 294
Ching Ching's Own 326
Cholmondeley, Mary 84–5
Chorley, Henry Fothergill 264, 397
Christian Lady's Magazine, The 132, 268, 337
Christian Mothers' Magazine 268
Christian Observer 359, 363
Christian periodicals: Church of England 335–6, 347–8, 360–1
Christian Remembrancer 355
Christian Socialist: A Journal of Association 336
ChristianWorld 355
Christie, G.H. 189
"Chronicles of Carlingford" (Oliphant) 83
Chronicling America 27
Chums 253, 296, 302
Church Missionary Society 159
Church of England Quarterly Review 335
Church of England Temperance Chronicle 350
Church of England Temperance Magazine 334, 348, 350
Church of England Temperance Society 343
Chwarelwr Cymreig, Y (The Welsh Quarryman) 197
Circular to Bankers 242
circulating libraries 139
circulation 42, 47–8, 56–9t, 68t, 89, 181, 191–2, 195, 196, 213, 225, 231, 239, 279, 282, 287, 294, 303, 311, 331, 332, 333, 344, 345, 347, 348, 351, 355, 358, 368, 379, 380; colonial, 51, 242; economics and 63, 69–70; technology and 49–50; transatlantic 271; *see also* distribution
Citizen 211–13, 402t
Civilization in the United States (Arnold) 171
Clarion 242, 251, 337, 340, 341
Clarke, Erskine 301
Clarke, Mary Cowden 393
Clarke, Meaghan 389
class papers 46, 237
Cleave, John 334
Cleave's Gazette 166
Cleghorn, James 188
Clockmaker, The (Halliburton) 172
Clubbe, John 321
Cobbe, Frances Power 247
Cobbett, William 44, 146, 251, 319, 331
Cobbett's Political Register 146
Cobden, Richard 333
Codell, Julie 12, 157

463

INDEX

Coffee Tavern Gazette 350
Colburn, Henry 189, 242, 370
Cole, Henry 46
Coleridge, Samuel Taylor 87, 189
Collections Historical and Archeological Relating to Montgomeryshire 205
Collet, Collet Dobson 46
Collins, Wilkie 2, 140, 141, 173, 279, 280, 281–2
Coloured Comic 326
Combe, William 124
Comic Annual 321
Comic Cuts 326
Comic Magazine 321
Comic Offering 121, 321
comic/satiric periodicals 318–27; critical examples of 319–20; defining 318; early examples of 318–19; future research for 326–7; *Punch* 322–6; recent examples of 320–1; studies of 319; wood engraving and 114, 118–23; see also French periodicals, humor, *Simplicissimus*
Committee on Newspaper Stamps see House of Commons Select Committee on Newspaper Stamps
"Common Heroes" (series) 29
Commonsense 332
Communist Manifesto (Marx and Engels) 62
Companion for Youth 301
Company Archives 66
Conan Doyle, Arthur 157, 189
Conboy, Martin 169
Connected Histories 25, 26
Connors, Linda E. 357
Conrad, Joseph 157, 189
Conservative politics, press and 195, 197–200
Constable, Archibald 185, 186
Contagious Diseases Acts 270–1
Contemporary Review 147, 378
Conway, M.D. 81
Cook, Eliza 2, 89, 91, 134, 264
Cook, Thomas 343
Cooke, Simon 107, 116
Cooper, Victoria 396
Coover, James 395, 396
Copyright Act (1842) 48–9, 57t; (1911) 49, 59t; see also Chace Act
Copyright Commission 49, 58t
Corkran, Alice 300
Cornhill Magazine 18, 23, 82, 83, 85, 87, 96, 106, 116, 134, 140, 141, 285, 287–90, 289f
Corn Laws 44, 47, 56t, 57t
correspondence columns 53, 281, 291, 297f
Corresponding Societies 44
Cosmopolis 144
Cottam, John Charles 39
Cowan, Yuri 11

Courrier français, Le 181
Cowper, Edward 34
Cox, Edward 273
Cox, Horace 273
Craig, Edward Gordon 62
Craig, Patricia 305
Craik, Dinah 192, 301
Crane, Walter 129
Crawford, F. Marion 189
Crimean War 87–8, 158–9
Crime of the Congo, The (Conan Doyle) 157
Critic 125
Crone, J.S. 219
Cronicl Cymru (Chronicle of Wales) 197
Cross, Nigel 83–4
Cruikshank, George 121, 136, 321, 323, 379–80
"Cry of the Children, The" (Barrett Browning) 87, 124, 129
Curry, William 213
Curtis, L. Perry, Jr. 326
Curwen, John 393
Cwmni'r Wasg Genedlaethol Gymraeg (Welsh National Press Company) 200
Cyfaill Eglwysig, Y (The Ecclesiastical Friend) 204
Cyfaill o'r Hen Wlad yn America, Y (The Friend from the Old Country in America) 205
Cylch-grawn Cynmraeg (Welsh Magazine) 195
Cymmrodor, Y (The Welshman) 205
Cymmrodorion, Honourable Society of 205
Cymro, Y (The Welshman) 197
Cymru'r Plant (The Children's Wales) 204

Daily Mail 226
Daily News 5, 35, 38, 39, 94, 99
Daily Post 198
Daily Telegraph 10, 35, 222, 225
Daly, Kieran 396
Dalziel Brothers 106
Dalziel's Bible Gallery 106
Dance, Charles 271
"Danny Deever" (Kipling) 124
Danvers Jewels, The (Cholmondeley) 84, 85
Danvers Power, J. 72, 74
Dark Blue 137
Davenant, William 367
Davidson, John 137
Davies, Emily 290
Davis, Thomas 210
Davison, J.W. 392, 397
Dawson, Julia 340
Daybreak 159
Deacon's Newspaper Handbook 355
"Death of Orpheus and Eurydice, The" (Boyd) 135

"Death of the Lion, The" (James) 144
de Courcy, Beatrice 266
de Courcy, Margaret 266
Democracy in America (de Tocqueville) 171
Demoor, Marysa 7, 228
Dempster, Charlotte 189
de Nie, Michael 156
De Quincey, Thomas 189, 191, 192
de Sablé, Madame 147
de Tocqueville, Alexis 171
Detroit Free Press 173
Deutsche Nationalbibliothek 179
Deutsch-Ostafrikanische Zeitung 179
Dial 387
Diana Tempest (Cholmondeley) 84
Dickens, Charles 82, 92, 94–6, 140, 171, 246, 373; hybrid family magazines and 291–2
Dickens Journals Online 21, 140
Dicks, John 282
Diderot, Denis 378
Diggle, John 253
digitization 17–28; see also databases (in Bibliography); benefits of 17; features of 18–24; impact of, on nineteenth-century periodicals 17; metadata and 22–4; Optical Character Recognition and 20–2; overview of 17–18; printed periodicals and 24–8
Dilke, Charles Wentworth, I 97–8
Dilke, Charles Wentworth, III 98
Dinwiddy, J.R. 319
Dircks, Rudolf 144
Dirwestydd, Y (The Abstainer) 203
Dirwestydd Deheuol, Y (The Southern Abstainer) 203
Discourses on Art (Joshua Reynolds) 378
distribution 42–55; defined 42–3; fiscal/legal reform and 43–9; technology 49–55; timeline 56–9t
Diwygiwr, Y (The Reformer) 201
Dixon, Diana 293, 305
Dixon, Ella Hepworth 89
Dixon, Henry Hall ("The Druid") 312
Dixon, William Hepworth 97, 98
Dobson, Austin 96, 134
"Doctor's Family, The" (Oliphant) 83
Dombey and Son (Dickens) 82
Dome 116, 118
Domestic Manners of the Americans (Trollope) 171
Doran, John 98
Doughan, David 274
Doughty, Terri 305
Douglas, Alfred 129, 258
Douglas, Mary 382
Dovastan, John F.M. 126
Dowden, Edward 147
Doyle, Arthur Conan 142, 143, 144
Doyle, John 120, 321

464

INDEX

Doyle, Richard 105, 118
Dravod, Y (the Discussion) 205
"Dream of Gerontius, The" (Newman) 137
Drew, John 94
Drotner, Kirsten 305, 345
dual-publication system 83, 84, 87
Dublin Core 22
Dublin Penny Journal 177, 209, 210
Dublin Review 360
Dublin Satirist 319
Dublin University Magazine 86, 140, 213–19, 214f, 216f, 242
Dubois, Martin 360
Dudley and Midland Counties Express & Mining Gazette 223–4, 223f
Dudley Weekly Times 224
Duffy, Charles Gavan 210, 213, 217–18
Dumas, Alexandre 139
du Maurier, George 118, 288
Dunae, Patrick 295, 296, 302
Duncan, William 93
Dundee Advertiser 192
Dunton, John 261
Duval, Marie 118
Dyer, George 128
Dysgedydd, Y (The Instructor)
Dywysogaeth, Y (The Principality) 200, 202

Easley, Alexis 80
Eastern Question 158
Eaton, Daniel Isaac 319
Echo du Japon 184
economics, periodical 60–74; *see also* advertisements; authorship; capitalism and 60; defining 61; economic unit and 63–4; mark-up and 62; production costs 64–74; profit and 62; sample costs 67–74, 68t, 69f, 70f; theoretical issues 60–4
Economist 243, 255
Economist Historical Archive 25
Edgeworth, Maria 214, 267, 293
Edinburgh Monthly Magazine 188
Edinburgh Review 77, 78, 79, 81, 88, 92, 104, 146, 185, 191, 241, 256; and the rise of the literary journal 186–9
editors 89–101; *Athenaeum* 97–8; celebrity 91; children's periodicals and 303–5; Dickens as editor 92, 94–6; duties 91; process 90–4; Trollope as editor 96–7; types of 90
"Editor's Tales, An" (Trollope) 96, 99
Edwards, Lewis 203
Edwards, Owen M. 205
Edwards, P.D. 325
Egan, Pierce (the Elder) 312
Egg, Augustus 375
Eglwysydd, Yr (The Churchman) 201
Egoff, Sheila 305
Ehnes, Caley 131
Electric Telegraph Company 53

Elementary Education Act (1870) 294
Elias, John Roose 205
Eliot, George 80, 81, 83, 85, 141, 147, 189, 231, 291; *see also* Evans, Marian
Eliot, Simon 82
Empire, British, press and 153–62; British identities and 155–7; career writers of 157–9; colony and 159–62; studies of 153–5; war correspondents and 158–9
"End of the Month, The" (Swinburne) 137
Engels, Friedrich 331
"English Boy, The" (Hemans) 132–3
English Caricaturists and Graphic Humourists of the Nineteenth Century (Everitt) 324
English Chartist Circular 336
English Chartist Circular and Temperance Record 334, 343
English Constitution, The 81
English Girls' Journal, and Ladies' Magazine 298
English Illustrated Magazine 12
English Spy 319
"Englishwoman's Conversazione, The" 267, 270f, 273
Englishwoman's Domestic Magazine 141, 242, 267, 270f, 273, 282, 298
English Woman's Journal 10, 269, 270, 290
English Woman's Journal Company 269
English woman's Review of Social and Industrial Questions 62, 269, 290
Enkvist, Nils Erik 173
Entertaining Companion for the Fair Sex 261
Epstein, James A. 320
Era 373–6
Erickson, Lee 77
Escott, T.H.S. 288
Essay on Comedy and the Uses of the Comic Spirit, An (Meredith) 319
Essay on the Whole Art of Criticism as It Relates to Painting, An (Richardson) 378
Ettrick Shepherd 134; *see also* Hogg, James
Eurgrawn Wesleyaidd, Yr (The Wesleyan Magazine) 201
European Society for Periodical Research (ESPRit) 176, 248
Evangelical Alliance 355
Evangelical Christendom 355
Evangelical Magazine 359
Evans, Marian 80–1, 90; *see also* Eliot, George
Evening Chronicle 82
Evening Express 198
Everett-Green, Evelyn 302
Everitt, Graham 324
Every Boy's Magazine 116

Every Girl's Magazine 300
Ewing, Juliana 301
Examiner 87–8, 125, 242, 257, 319, 369, 378
"Extempore Effusion" (Wordsworth) 126–7

Faithfull, Emily 270, 285, 290
Family Friend 276–7, 277f
Family Herald 172, 242, 278, 279, 280, 281, 282, 361–2
family magazines 276–92; Dickens and hybrid 291–2; overview of 276–8; penny weekly 278–85; shilling monthly 285–91
Far from the Madding Crowd (Hardy) 134
Fate of Fenella, The (consecutive serial authorship) 142
Fawcett, Millicent 182
Fawcett, Trevor 388
Feldman, Paula R. 87
Fellinger, Imogen 394
"Female Education" (Martineau) 79
Female Missionary Intelligencer 159
Female Reformers of Blackburn 339–40
Female Spectator 261
Female Tatler 261
"Female Writers on Practical Divinity" (Martineau) 79
femininity, *see* gender, periodicals and; women; women's periodicals
feminist publications 10; *see also* women's periodicals; *English Woman's Journal* 269; *Englishwoman's Review* 62; Lady Somerset illustrates 159; Langham Place Circle and 290–1; socialist press and 340; *Woman's Signal* 157; *Young Woman* 300
Ferguson, Samuel 189
Fern, Fanny 172
Ferrier, Susan 189
fiction 81–5, 138–45; *see also* prose; sensation 145, 287–91
Fiddler 394
Field 310, 313, 314
Fielding, Sarah 293
Figaro in London (Gray) 104, 105f, 318, 321, 368–9
Financial Times 255
Fine Arts Quarterly Review 386
Finkelstein, David 8–9, 90, 157
Fletcher, Pamela 389
Fliegende Blätter 181
Follet, Le: le Journal du Grande Monde, Fashion and Polite Literature 262
foreign correspondents 70f, 157
Foreign Quarterly Review 78, 81, 177, 178
Forest Sanctuary, The (Hemans) 87
Forget-Me-Not 264
Fortnightly Review 81, 87, 88, 137, 148, 252, 254, 378
Foucault, Michel 358

INDEX

Fourth Estate, The (Hunt) 67
Fox, Celina 106, 114–15, 321
Fox, W.J. 356
"Fragment" (Landon) 86
Franklin, Benjamin 165
Fraser, Alexander Campbell 192
Fraser, Hilary 274
Fraser's Magazine 77, 78, 82, 86, 134, 135, 240, 318, 371
Free Church of Scotland 192
Freeman, Edward Augustus 254–5
Freeman's Journal 156, 219
French periodicals, transnational fashion/caricature and 179–81; *see also* Bulletin Quotidien de l'Exposition 1900, Charivari, Courrier français, Echo du Japon, Japon artistique, Mode illustrée, Moniteur dela mode, Tam-tam
frequency (of publication) 244
Friend 360
Friendship's Offering 264
front page, The (Sherratt) 27
Frost, John 129
Froude, J.A. 192
Frythones, Y (The British Woman) 204
Fulleylove, John 135
Fun 118, 127
Funny Bits 325
Funny Cuts 326
Fyfe, Aileen 357

Gale Cengage 23, 25, 26, 154, 306, 341
Gallica 179, 181
Galt, John 139, 189, 191
Garrett, Fitzroy 94
Gaskell, Elizabeth 92, 140, 141, 291
Gatty, Margaret 301
Gazette des Beaux-Arts 184
Geczy, Adam 183
Gee, Thomas 196, 197, 203
Geirgrawn, Y (The Magazine) 195
Gem 264
gender, periodicals and 249–59; future research for 259–9; *see also* femininity, masculinity overview of 249–51
gendered reading, children's periodicals and 301–2
Genedl Gymreig, Y (The Welsh Nation) 200
Gentleman's Magazine 126, 135, 250, 314, 369
Gentlewoman 142
George, David Lloyd 200
Georgiana, Duchess of Devonshire 135
Germ 86, 136, 378
German periodicals: *see* Deutsch-Ostafricanische Zeitung, Fliegende Blätter, Internazionale Wochenschrift, Literarisches Centralblatt, Missions-Blat, Simplicissimus

Germany, transnational science and 177–9
Gerrard, Teresa 281
Ghosts (Ibsen) 370
Gibson, Thomas Milner 45
Gifford, William 319
Gilbert, W.S. 192, 325
Gil Blas 181
Gilpin, William 378
Gilroy, Paul 161
Girl's Best Friend 300
Girl's Empire 300
Girl's Own Paper 145, 294, 298–300, 299f, 302, 304, 339, 355
Girl's Realm 300
Gissing, George 144
Gitelman, Lisa 31
Gladstone, William 192
Glasgow Courier 126
Glasgow Penny Post 130
Glasier, Katherine Bruce 340
Gleaner 159
Goblin Market and Other Poems (Christina Rossetti) 87
Goethe, Wolfgang von 78
Goldman, Paul 107, 116
Goleuad, Y (The Illuminator) 202
Good Templar Advocate and General Intelligencer 203
Good Templar's Watchword 350
Good Words 106, 116, 131, 186, 191, 335, 361
Good Words for the Young 191, 192, 301, 356
Google Books 17, 186
Gordon-Cumming, Constance 189
Gordon & Gotch 54
Gore, Catherine 191
Gozzoli, Benozzo 387
Grant, C.J. 120, 321
Grant, James 66
Graphic 40, 41, 83, 141, 142, 374
Gray, Donald J. 318, 321, 323, 326
Gray, Elizabeth F. 129, 132, 268
Gray, Maria 252
Greal, Y (the Miscellany) 201
Great Expectations (Dickens) 82, 140
Great Western Railway 53
Greeley, Horace 47
Green, Stephanie 274
Green Room 372
Greenwell, Dora 131
Greg, W.R. 192
Gregory, Barnard 321
Griffin, Dustin 319
Griffith Gaunt (Howells) 141
Gross, John 90
Grove, George 397
Grove Music Online 394
Guardian 242
Guide to the Turf 311
Guys, Constantin 7

Gwalia (Cambria) 197
Gweithiwr, Y (the Worker) 197
Gwerinwr, Y (the Common Man) 204
Gwir Fedyddiwr, Y (the True Baptist) 201
Gwladgarwr, Y (the Patriot) 197
Gwron Cymraeg, Y (The Welsh Hero) 196, 197
Gwyliedydd, Y (The Sentinel) 202
Gymraes, Y (the Welshwoman) 204, 205

Habermas, Jürgen 55
Haggard, H. Rider 142, 173, 303
Halévy, Elie 335
Halfpenny Owl 326
half-tone engraving 121–2, 122f
Hall, Samuel Carter 62, 67, 210, 379
Halliburton, Thomas Chandler 172
Hamerton, Philip Gilbert 387
Hampshire Telegraph 170
Hannam, June 340
Hannay, James 323
Hard Times (Dickens) 82
Hardy, Philip Dixon 210
Hardy, Thomas 85, 134, 141–2, 189, 192
Harmonicon 392, 395
Harmsworth, Alfred 63, 169, 296, 298
Harney, George Julian 146
Harper's Monthly Magazine 173
Harper's Weekly 141
Harris, Janice H. 290
Harrison, Brian 345, 350
Harrison, Debbie 256
Harte, Bret 143
Harvey, Adrian 308, 311
Harwood, Philip 99
Haskins, Katherine 389
HathiTrust Digital Library 17, 219
Hatton, Joseph 322
Haul, Yr (The Sun) 201
Hawthorne, Nathaniel 141
Hay, Mary Cecil 362
Hayley, Barbara 219–20
Hays, Matilda Mary 269
Hazlitt, William 146, 189, 378
Healey, Chadwyck 65
Healthy and Artistic Dress Union 183
Hearth and Home 148
Heart of Darkness (Conrad) 9, 157
Helmreich, Anne 389
Hemans, Felicia 87, 127, 132–3
Henderson, James 301
Henley, William Ernest 137, 380
Henty, G.A. 296
Herald 129
Herald Cymraeg, Yr (The Welsh Herald) 196
Herschel, John 81
Hervey, T.K. 97
Hetherington, Henry 44, 331, 334
Heuffer, Francis 397
Heywood, Abel 48, 228–9

466

INDEX

Hill, Frank 99
Hine, H.G. 102, 103f
Hitchman, Francis 280
Hive 335
Hobbs, Andrew 4–5, 124–5, 170
Hobsbawm, Eric 335
Hobson, J.A. 157, 158
Hogarth, George 397
Hogarth, William 378
Hogg, James 126–7, 134, 188
Hog's Wash (Eaton) 319
Hollis, Patricia 320
Holme, Charles 388
"Home" (1829, anonymous poem) 130
Home Chat 274
Home Rule movement 156
Hone, Ann 319
Hone, William 319
Hood, Thomas 129, 133, 143, 321, 325
Hook, Theodore 319, 321
Hopkins, Gerard Manley 360
Horne, Herbert 387
Horne, Richard Hengist 87
Horner, Francis 187
Houghton, Arthur Boyd 116
Household Narrative 46
Household Words 21, 52, 80, 82, 92, 94–5, 140, 141, 242, 243, 246, 291–2
House of Commons: Select Committee on Dramatic Literature 370; Select Committee on Newspaper Stamps 5, 6, 7, 42, 45, 49, 53, 55, 58t, 66, 231; *see also* law and the press
Housman, Laurence 118
Houston, Natalie 125, 133
Howells, William Dean 141
Howes, Craig 11
Howitt, Mary 80, 86, 264
Howitt, William 80
Howitt's Journal 80
Hudson, Henry 211
Hudson, William Elliot 211
Huett, Lorna 291
Huffman, James 182
Hughes, Linda K. 6, 8, 85–6, 116
Hughes, Meirion 396, 397, 398
Hughes, Tom 241, 310
Huish, Marcus 388
Hull Advertiser 192
Hull Band of Hope Advocate 348
humor, illustration and 118–23; *see also* comic/satiric periodicals
Humpherys, Anne 145, 321
Hunt, Frederick Knight 67
Hunt, John 257
Hunt, Karen 336–7, 340
Hunt, Leigh 89, 191, 257, 319, 369
Hutchison, George Andrew 296
Hyndman, Henry Mayers 340

ILEJ (Internet Library of Early Journals) 186
Illuminated Magazine 102, 103f
Illustrated Catholic Missions 360
Illustrated Exhibitor 379
Illustrated London News 5, 7, 10, 32, 35, 36, 52, 71, 104, 106, 108, 110f, 112, 114, 115, 129, 141, 145, 222, 242, 321
Illustrated London News Historical Archive 23, 25
Illustrated Magazine of Art 379–80
Illustrated Police News 145
Illustrated Sporting and Dramatic News 374
Illustrated Times 108
illustration 7–8, 12, 23, 33t, 48, 102–23, 136, 144, 209, 215, 276, 280, 284, 288, 295, 308, 314, 331, 337–8, 377, 379, 387, 401t; *see also* wood engraving; "black and white" surveys of 106, 116; fashion and, 106, 179, 183, 261–4, 266, 267, 273–4, 298; history of 106–7; humor and 118–23; magazine titles and 106; overview of 102–7; photomechanical reprographic processes of 106; pictorial 112, 114f; process reprographic techniques and 121–2, 122f; uses/absence of 104; wood engraved 107–18
Illustrations of Political Economy (Martineau) 60–1
ImageGrid (Baird and Blevin) 26
imagined community (Anderson) 2, 125, 132, 154, 368
Independent Order of Good Templars 344
Independent Order of Rechabites 344
Index to Current Literature (Low) 18
Index to Periodical Literature (Poole) 18
Index to the Periodical Literature of the World (Stead) 1
Index to the Times Newspaper (Palmer) 18
India 4, 154, 156–7, 160–2
industrialization 42, 307–8
"Influence of Rationalism, The" (Eliot) 81
Inheritance (Ferrier) 189
Innovators and Preachers (Weiner) 89
Institute of Journalists 99
International Association of Academies 177
Internationale Wochenschrift für Wissenschaft, Kunst und Technik (International Weekly for Science, Art, and Technology) 178
International Union for the Protection of Literary and Artistic Works 52
Internet Archive 17, 186, 232
Irish Book Lover, The 219
Irish Builder 219

Irish Independent 156
Irish Penny Journal 9, 210
Irish periodicals 155–6, 158–9, 208–20; overview of 208–10; source material for study of 219–20; *see also Citizen, Dublin* [periodical titles], *Kottabos, Lyra Ecclesiastica*
IrishWorld (Ní Bhroiméil) 158–9
Ireland, representations of 120, 324, 326; *see also* Irish periodicals
Isis 339
Isle of Man Guardian and Rechabite Journal 350

Jack Sheppard (Ainsworth) 142
Jackson, Kate 94
Jackson, Mason 106
James, Henry 144, 171
James, Louis 175, 284, 321, 323
Jameson, Anna 12, 269
"Janet's Repentance" (Eliot) 83
Janowitz, Anne 127–8
Japan Gazette Hong List and Directory 184
Japan Herald 184
Japan Punch 184
Japan Society 183, 388
Japan Weekly Mail 184
Japon Artistique 184, 404t
Jeffrey, Francis 77, 92, 187
Jensz, Felicity 177, 357
Jerdan, William 86
Jerome, Jerome K. 173
Jerrold, Douglas 91, 322, 324, 336
Jerrold, Walter 322
Jewish Chronicle 355
Jo: A Chronicle of Banjo, Guitar, and Mandoline News 394
Jockey Club 307, 314
Joe Miller the Younger 118
"Johannes Agricola in Meditation" (Browning) 86
John Bull 240, 319, 321, 369
John Curwen and Sons 393
John Johnson Collection of Printed Ephemera 25
John Marchmont's Legacy (Braddon) 140
"Johnny Ludlow" (series, Ellen Wood) 143
Johnson, Samuel 84, 185
Johnson-Hill, Erin 395
Johnston, Anna 159
Johnston, Ellen 130
Johnston, Judith 274
Johnstone, Christian Isobel 89, 189, 191
Joker 326
Jones, Evan 204
Jones, Hannah Maria 84
Jones, Owen 202
Jones, Thomas 196, 197
Jordell, Daniel 180

INDEX

Jorum of "Punch," A (Mayhew) 321
Journal des Débats 139
Journal pour rire (Philipon) 181
journalism: definition 7, 79–80, 90, 96, 238–9, 366–8, 371, 374–5; fiction and, 157; illustrated, *see* Illustration; poetry and 125; "scissors-and-paste" 149, 371; transatlantic communication and 164, 165–7; *see also* New Journalism.
journalists: definition 7; foreign correspondents, 68*t*, 70*t*, 71, 157, 169; penny-a-liners 149; remuneration; war correspondents 158; women, 250–1; working conditions of 29–31
"Journey to the Centre of the Earth" (Verne) 296
Judy 118, 133, 325, 369
Junior Church of England Temperance Society 351
Jurist 256
Justice 332, 340
Justice of the Peace 256
Juvenile Rechabite 351, 352
Juvenile Templar 352

Kaleidoscope 80, 250
Kant, Immanuel 378
Kassler, Jamie 394
Katie Stewart (Oliphant) 83, 189
Kaul, Chandrika 155, 156–7, 161
Kavanagh, Robin 209
Keats, John 124, 189
Keble, John 146
Keene, Charles 118
Keepsake 87, 264
Kendall, May 133–4
Kent, Christopher 325, 398
Kenyon, George 200
Kidnapped (Stevenson) 301
Killigrew, Thomas 367
Kim (Kipling) 141
Kindred Societies 74
Kind Words 303
King, Andrew 172, 252, 279, 282
Kingsley, Charles 142, 192, 301, 336
Kingston, W.H.G. 295, 296, 302
Kipling, Rudyard 124, 141, 144, 157
Kittler, Friedrich 32
Kitton, Frederick G. 323
Klancher, Jon P. 319
Klein, Thoralf 177
Knight, Charles 191
Knight, Mark 11
Knight, Richard Payne 378
Koenig cylinder press 34
Kooistra, Lorraine Janzen 136
Kottabos 86
Krummel, D.W. 395
Kunzle, David 121, 320
Kyprianides, Christine 397

La Belle Assemblée 148, 180, 261
Labour Leader 251, 334, 337, 340
Labour Prophet 251, 336
Lacy, Thomas Hailes 374
Ladies' Cabinet of Fashion, Music, and Romance 144, 264, 266
Ladies' Companion 266
Ladies' Diary 261
Ladies' Fashionable Repository 261–2
Ladies' Gazette of Fashion 262
Ladies' Mercury 261
Ladies' Pocket Magazine 262
Ladies' Treasury 84, 172
Lady's Curiosity 261
Lady's Magazine 261
Lady's Monthly Museum 135
Lady's Museum 261
Lady's Newspaper 271–3, 272f
Lady's Realm 84, 274
Lady's Weekly Magazine 261
Lamb, Charles 146
Lambert, Ernest Orger 39
Lancet 10, 108, 256
Landon, Laetitia Elizabeth (L.E.L.) 86–7, 264
Landow, George 388
Landseer, Edwin 134
Langham Place Circle 290
Langley, Leanne 391, 395
Language of the Walls, The 375
Larsen, Timothy 357
"Last Sark. Written in 1859, The" (Johnston) 130
Last Scrap Book, A (Saintsbury) 99
Latané, David E. 322
Lauterbach, Edward S. 325
law and the press, the *see* Copyright Act; House of Commons; libel; Taxes on Knowledge
Law, Graham 5, 140, 141, 142
Law Magazine 256
Lawrence, D.H. 144
Law Times 10, 256
Layard, George Somes 323, 324
"Lay of the Trilobite" (Kendall) 133–4
Leader 5, 78, 240
Leary, Patrick 23, 61, 322, 324
Ledbetter, Kathryn 132
Leech, John 118
Leeds Mercury 38
legal periodicals 186–9, 192, 256, 352–3
Leighton, Frederick 288
Leith, Alicia 300
L.E.L. *see* Landon
Lemon, Mark 95, 323
Leng, John 192
Lessons for the Swinish Multitude (Spence) 319

Lever, Charles 210, 213–19
Lewes, Agnes 83
Lewes, George Henry 78–9, 80, 96
Lewis, Harriet 172
libel 44, 127, 320
Liberal 319
Liberal/Whig politics, press and 70–1, 146–7; *see also* Edinburgh Review
Liberator 164
"Liberty: An Ode" (J.H.) 133
library editions 246
Library of the Fine Arts 377
Licensed Victuallers' Association 373
Liddle, Dallas 91
"Life of an Editor, The" (anon.) 91–2
Life of a Sportsman (Nimrod) 317
Life of Schiller, The (Carlyle) 78
Liggins, Emma 300
Linley Sambourne: Illustrator and Punch Cartoonist (Ormond) 323
Linotype 6, 29–30, 32*t*, 38–41, 41*f*, 59*t*
Linotype Company 31, 32, 39–40
Linton, Eliza Lynn 96
Lippincott's Magazine 143
literacy rates 1, 57–9*t*, 115, 227–8
Literarisches Centralblatt für Deutschland 178
Literary and Scientific Mirror 250
Literary Chronicle and Weekly Review 135, 240
Literary Examiner 240
Literary Gazette 86, 134, 240
Literary Guardian and Spectator of Books, Sciences and Fine Arts, the Drama 369
Literary Souvenir 264
lithography 102, 106–7, 121
Littell's Living Age 52
Liverpool Albion 316
Liverpool Dramatic Censor 372
Liverpool Dramatic Journal 370–1
Liverpool Mercury 250, 253
Livesey, Joseph 345, 348
Llais y Wlad (Voice of the Country) 197
Llan, Y (the Church) 202
Llan a'r Dywysogaeth, Y (The Church and the Principality) 203
Llandaff Diocesan Magazine 201
Llenor, Y (The Litterateur) 203
Lloyd, Edward 64
Lloyd's Weekly News 173, 244
Locke, John 293
Locker, Frederick 134
Lockhart, John Gibson 188–9
Lodge, Sara 321
log-rolling 97–8; *see also* puffing, reviews and reviewing
London American Register 173
London and Provincial Music Trades Review 395
London Charivari 318

INDEX

London Journal 5, 84, 115, 136, 172, 180, 242, 243, 244, 252, 278, 279, 280, 281f, 282, 283f
London Labour and the London Poor 321
London Magazine 146–7, 188
London Press Directory and Advertiser's Handbook 352–3
London Reader 278
London Review 89
London Society 140
London Working Men's Associations 336
Looking Glass 120
Lootens, Tricia 132
Lorgnette 372
Lorrequer, Harry 213
Lost Visions 23, 123
Loti, Pierre 183
"Love On" (Cook) 134
Lover, Samuel 210
Low, Sampson 18, 173
Lowe, Helen 273
Lowell, James Russell 173
Ludgate Magazine 143
Lunn, Henry Charles 393

Macbeth, Robert Walker 12
MacColl, Norman 98
MacDonald, George 96, 143, 301, 303, 361
MacDonald, Mary Lu 357
MacFarlane, Helen 62
Mackay, R.W. 80
MacKenzie, John 156
Mackmurdo, Arthur 387
Macleod, Donald 191
Macleod, Norman 191
Macmillan, Alexander 87
Macmillan's Magazine 61, 82, 87, 140, 241, 280, 282, 285
Madame Chrysanthème (Loti) 183
Madden, Richard Robert 219
"Madhouse Cells" (Browning) 86
"Maga" 83, 188 (see *Blackwood's Edinburgh Magazine*)
Magasin des demoiselles, Le 179
Magazine (student art) 388
magazine, defined 82; see also *Ainsworth's, Alexandra, Archaeological, Arminian, Artist's Repository, Aunt Judy's, Badminton, Blackwood's, Blackwood's Lady's, Boy's Own, British, British Literary, British Mother's, Burlington, Cassell's, Catholic Penny, Christian Lady's, Christian Mothers', Church of England Temperance, Comic, Cornhill, Cylch-grawn Cymraeg, Dublin University, Edinburgh Monthly, English Girls', English Illustrated, Englishwoman's Domestic, Eurgrawn Wesleyaidd, Evangelical, Every Boy's, Every Girl's, Fraser's, Geirgrawn,*

Gentleman's, Harper's, Illuminated, Illustrated Magazine of Art, Ladies' Pocket, Lady's, Lady's Weekly, Law, Lippincott's, Llandaff Diocesan, London, Ludgate, Macmillan's, Mechanic's, Methodist Temperance, Metropolitan, Minim, Missionary, Monthly, Monthly Magazine of Music, Mothers', Musical, New British Lady's, New Monthly, New Sporting, New Universal, Oriental Sporting, Oxford and Cambridge, Pall Mall, Parish, Pearson's, Penny, Poetical, Protestant Penny, Quarterly Musical, Rechabite and Temperance, Saint Paul's, St James's, Saturday, Scots, Servant's, Sporting, Strand, Studio, Tait's Edinburgh, Temperance, University, Victoria, Violin Monthly, Wesleyan Methodist, Windsor, Young Englishwoman, Young Ladies'
Magazine of Art 377, 378, 379–80, 386
Magazine of Music 391
Magazine of the Fine Arts 377
Maginn, William 189, 239–40, 247
Maguire, Tom 129
Maidment, Brian 80, 320–1, 368
Mainzer's Musical Times and Singing Class Circular 393
Maitland, J.A. Fuller 397
Malik, Rachel 142
Manchester and Salford Advertiser 227
Manchester Guardian 48, 225
Manchester Weekly Times 226
Man in the Moon 118, 325
Manual of Book-keeping for Booksellers, Publishers and Stationers 64–5, 69
Mapping Texts 26
"Marathon" (J.S.B.) 135
Marchant, Bessie 302
mark-up 21–2, 62
Marriage (Ferrier) 189
"Marriage" (Caird) 10
Married Women's Property Act (1882) 270–1, 290
Marryat, Florence 89
Marryat, Frederick 139, 302
Marston Lynch (Brough) 325
Martin, Robert Bernard 319
Martin Chuzzlewit (Dickens) 82
Martineau, Harriet 5, 60–1, 79–80, 191
Martyn, Caroline 340
Marvel 298
Marx, Eleanor 340
Marxists Internet Archive, The 341
Marylebone Cricket Club 307
masculinity 10, 89–90, 252–5; class-based definitions of 251–2; professional masculinities 255–7; at fin de siècle 257–8
Mass Image, The (author) 106

mass-market periodical 190–1; see also *Answers to Correspondents, Bow Bells, Cassell's, London Journal, Reynolds's Miscellany, Strand, Tit-Bits*; see also New Journalism, popular press, religion, temperance periodicals
Masson, David 87, 192
Master Humphrey's Clock 94
Maturin, Charles Robert 214
Maurice, F.D. 336
Maxwell, John 141
Maxwell, William Hamilton 312
Mayhew, Athol 321
Mayhew, Henry 321, 324
Mayne, John 126
May's Press Guide 195
McAllister, Annemarie 11
McCalman, Iain 320
McClure's 141
McGann, Jerome 21–2
McGlashan, James 213, 217
McKay, Enda 219–20
McKelvy, William 358
McLean, Thomas 120
McNeely, Sarah 397
McNicholas, Anthony 357
Meade, L.T. 300, 303
Mechanic's Magazine 108
Media and the British Empire (Kaul) 155, 161
Media History 239
Medical Pioneer 350
Medical Temperance Journal 350
Medical Temperance Review 350
Meiji Shinbun Zasshi Bunko 182
Meliora 350
Melrose, Andrew 300
Menzies, John 53
Menzies, Stephen 300
Mercury 80
Meredith, George 319
Mergenthaler, Ottmar 38
Merle, Gibbons 91, 92
Merry England 356
"Mervaunee" (Allingham) 134
Methodist Temperance Magazine 350
Methodist Times 242
Metropolitan Magazine 67
Meynell, Alice 88
Middles, definition 240
Mill, J.S. 191
Millais, John Everett 96, 112, 116, 288
Miller, Bonny H. 398–9
Miller, Elizabeth C. 128, 129
Miller, Henry J. 323
Milnes, Richard Monckton 126
Minim: A Musical Magazine for Everybody 391, 394
Minor Spy, The 368
Mirror of Literature 13, 108
Mirror of Music, The 396
Miscellaneous Repository 195

469

INDEX

Missionary Chronicle 355
Missionary Magazine and Chronicle 362–3
missionary press 159–60
Missions-Blat 177
Miss Kilmansegg and Her Precious Leg (Hood) 133
Mitchell, Charles 53, 54–5
Mitchell, Sally 276, 278, 279, 302, 305
Mitchell's Newspaper Press Directory 4, 5, 178, 231, 237–8, 355–6
Mitford, Mary Russell 264
Mode illustrée, La 179
Modernist Journals Project, The 181
modernist periodicals 118, 181
Moir, Douglas M. 189
Molesworth, Mary 303
Moniteur de la mode, Le 179
Monotype 38
Monte Cristo (Dumas) 139
Montefiore, Dora 340
Month 137, 360
Monthly Magazine 82, 87, 135
Monthly Magazine of Music 391
Monthly Mirror of Literature and Fashion 253
Monthly Musical Record 393–4
Monthly Packet of Evening Readings for Younger Members of the Church of England 294, 298, 303, 339
Monthly Repository 79, 80, 86, 242, 356
Monthly Review 84
Moral Reformer 348
Morel, E.D. 157
Morgan, Matt 118, 325
Moritz, E.R. 72
Morley, Samuel 329
Morning Advertiser 71
Morning Chronicle 82, 321
Morning Post 125
Mornings in Bow Street 121
Morris, Frankie 323
Morris, Mowbray 47
Morris, William 129, 137
Morton, John 1–13
Moruzi, Kristine 10, 339
Mother's Friend, The 337
Mothers' Magazine 337
Mozley, Thomas 360
"Mr. Disraeli's Speech at the Mansion House, August 4, 1875" (anonymous) 127
"Mr. Gilfil's Love Story" (Eliot) 83
Mulford, Carla 165
Munro, Neil 189
Murphy, Paul Thomas 331–2, 339
Murray, John 85, 188
Murray, Padmini 186
Musical Herald and Tonic Sol-fa Reporter 393
Musical Library: Monthly Supplement 212
Musical Magazine 391

Musical Opinion and Trade Review 393, 394, 395
Musical Standard 393
Musical Times 390, 391, 392, 393, 396
Musical Times and Singing Class Circular 393
Musical World 392–3
Music and Romance 264
music periodicals 390–9; current research on 395–7; future research for 397–9; overview of 390–5
Mussell, James 2–3, 6, , 329, 340, 375,
Mutch, Deborah 11
"My Cottage Home" ("C.P.") 131
"My Loss" (Webster) 134
"My Partner" (Praed) 133
Myriade 180–1
Mystères de Paris, Les (Sue) 139
Mysteries of London, The (Reynolds) 139

Nagasaki Shipping List and Advertiser 184
Nation 214
National British Women's Temperance Association 344
National British Women's Total Abstinence Union 344
National Football Museum 313
national, concept of the 2–4, 8–9, 78–9, 125, 132–3, 153–233, 238–9, 247–8, 301–3, 366–8, 377, 383; *see also* imagined community; Ireland; Irish periodicals; provincial press; Scotland; Scottish periodicals; Wales; Welsh periodicals
nationalism 155–6
National Library of Wales 206
National Register of Archives 65
National Sporting Library 313
National Temperance Advocate and Herald 345, 347
National Temperance Chronicle 349
National Temperance League 349, 350, 351
National Temperance Society 351
"Natural History of German Life, The" (Eliot) 80
Nature 255
Nesbit, Edith 129
Nestor, Pauline 269–70
Nevinson, Henry 158, 247
Newbolt, Henry 84
New Bon Ton 319
New British Lady's Magazine 253
Newcastle Chronicle 38, 93
Newcastle Journal 126
Newcastle Weekly Courant 170
Newey, Katherine 12
New Journalism 228, 233, 382; art-press endorsements and 380–1; as competition for Scottish periodicals 192; newspaper jokes as characteristic of 166; wholesale newspaper trade study of 229
Newman, John Henry 137, 360
New Monthly Belle Assemblée 264, 265f, 266
New Monthly Magazine 5, 133, 134, 135, 241, 242, 369, 370
Newnes, George 55, 94, 169, 192
Newport Presbyterian 201
news agencies 29, 170
Newsagents' Publishing Company 296
News of the World 242
Newspaper, definitions: 4–6, 43–4, 108, 201, 237–40, 311, 364; cost model compared to periodicals, 67–72; editors, 90–1, 202; form 145, 150; and gender 204, 252, 271–4; and poetry 85, 125–7, 210; and serial fiction 139, 141; subeditors 92–4; *see also Aberdare Times, Amserau, Anglo-American Times, Baner ac Amserau Cymru, Baner Cymru, Blackburn Standard, Brut, Bulletin Quotidian de l'Exposition 1900, Cambrian Daily Leader, Caernarvon Herald, Cymro, Cronicl Cymru, Chwarylwr Cymreig, Daily Mail, Daily News, Daily Post, Daily Telegraph, Deutsch-Ostafrikanische Zeitung, Dudley and Midland, Dudley Weekly, Dundee Advertiser, Evening Chronicle, Evening Express, Financial Times, Genedle Cymeig, Glasgow Courier, Glasgow Penny Post, Gwalia, Gladgarwr, Gwron Cymraeg, Gwythiwr, Hampshire Telegraph, Herald Cymraeg, Hull Advertiser, Illustrated London News, Illustrated Police News, Illustrated Times, Irish Independent, Isle of Man Guardian, Japan Herald, Japan Weekly Mail, Jewish Chronicle, Journal des Débats, Leader, Leeds Mercury, Liverpool Albion, Liverpool Mercury, Lloyd's Weekly News, Manchester and Salford Advertiser, Manchester Guardian, Mercury (Staffordshire), Morning Advertiser, Morning Chronicle, Morning Post, Nagasaki Shipping List, Newcastle Chronicle, Newcastle Journal, Newcastle Weekly Courant, News of the World, New York Courier, New York Herald, New York Times, New York Tribune, New York World, North Eastern Daily Gazette, Northern Star, North Wales Chronicle, North Wales Gazette, North Wales Observer, Norwich and Norfolk Independent, Pall Mall Gazette, Papyr Newydd, Police Reporter, Political Register, Poor Man's Guardian, Queen, Red Republican, Reynolds's Weekly News, Scotsman, Scots Observer, Times, Times of India, Sunday Times, Standard, South Wales Daily Post, South Wales News, South Wales Echo, Udgorn Rhyddid,*

470

INDEX

Tarian y Gwythiwr, Weekly Dispatch, Weekly Telegraph, Western Mail, Western Weekly News, Wrexham and Denbigh Advertiser, Wrexham Guardian
Newspaper Press 66
NEWSPLAN Wales/Cymru 206
New Sporting Magazine 254, 308, 310
New Statesman 243
NewsVault 25
New Universal Magazine 135
New Woman 144, 257, 339, 404t, 405t
"New Year's Eve, A" (Swinburne) 127
NewYork Courier 52
NewYorker 243
NewYork Herald 163, 164, 167
NewYork Times 40
NewYork Tribune 38, 47
NewYorkWorld 168
Ní Bhroiméil, Úna 158–9
Nice Bits 325
Nicholas Nickleby (Dickens) 82
Nicholls, James 342–3
Nicholson, Bob 8, 371
Nicholson, Renton 322, 323
Niessen, Olwen C. 345, 353
NINES: Nineteenth-Century Scholarship Online 25–6
Nineteenth Century 127, 378
Nineteenth-Century British Pamphlets 25
Nineteenth-Century British Library Newspapers 25, 239
Nineteenth-Century Collections Online 25
Nineteenth-Century Serials Edition 4, 23–4, 226, 341
Nineteenth-Century UK Periodicals 25, 26, 186, 306
Nonconformist 335
North, Christopher 97
North, John I 246
North America (Trollope) 171
North and South (Gaskell) 92, 141
North British Review 192
North-Eastern Daily Gazette 225
Northern Liberator 166
Northern Star 128, 146, 222, 228, 239, 242, 244, 251, 332, 336, 343
North Wales Chronicle 197, 250
North Wales Gazette 196, 197
North Wales Observer and Express 200
Norton, Caroline 264
Norwich and Norfolk Independent 46
Notes 395
Novello, J. Alfred 392, 393, 396
Novelty 325
Novoscotian 172
Nuggets 326

obituaries 126, 150
Observations on the RiverWye (Gilpin) 378
Observer 5, 99
O'Connell, Daniel 209
O'Connor, Feargus 146, 332, 334, 336

O'Connor, T.P. 156, 169
"Ode, Translated from the Persian of the Poet Hafez" (anon.) 135
"Ode on a Grecian Urn" (Keats) 124
"Ode to Liberty" (Dyer) 128
O'Donovan, John 210
Official Descriptive and Illustrated Catalogue 36
O'Hara, Patricia 396–7
Old Curiosity Shop, The (Dickens) 82
"Old Home, The" ("F.J.C.") 130–1
"Old Saloon" (Blackwood's meeting place) 188
Oliphant, Margaret 82–3, 84, 85, 96, 141, 189, 279, 291
Oliver Twist (Dickens) 82
Olsen, Stephanie 10, 345,
"On Atoms" (Herschel) 81
Once a Week 12, 86, 106, 113f, 116
On Political Economy (Chalmers) 359
Onslow, Barbara 89, 305–6
On the Line 347
Onward 333, 346f, 347, 351–2
Onward Reciter 351
Optical Character Recognition (OCR) 20–1, 22; see also digitization
oral cultures 1, 208
Oriental Sporting Magazine 316
Ormond, Leonée 323
Our Celebrities: A Portrait Gallery 148
Our First Tiff (Macbeth) 12
Our Own Fireside 335
Our Young Folks' Weekly Budget 301
Overland Route 316
Owen, David 201
Oxford and Cambridge Magazine 137
Oxford Critical and Cultural History of Modernist Magazines 181
Oxford Movement 132

Page 62
Pall Mall Gazette 18, 240, 369, 370
Pall Mall Magazine 29, 30f
Palmegiano, Eugenia 175, 232
Palmer, Beth 8
Palmer, Samuel 18
Palmeri, Frank 323, 324
paper duty 43–9; see also Taxes on Knowledge
"Paper War" 160
Papyr Newydd Cymraeg, Y (The Welsh Newspaper) 196
Pardoe, Julia 84
Parikka, Jussi 32, 38
Parish Magazine 227
Parkes, Bessie Rayner 269, 290
Parnell, Charles Stewart 209
Parratt, Catriona 313
Parry, John 375
Partridge, Samuel 351
"Passage of the Mountain of Saint Gothard" (Georgiana) 135

Past and Present (Egg) 375
Pater, Walter 7, 388
Patten, Robert L. 321, 324
Pattison, Mark 193
Paz, Denis 357
Pearce, Isabella Bream 340
Pearson, Arthur 63
Pearson's Magazine 308, 309f
Pen and the Book, The (Besant) 81
"Pencil Marks in a Book of Devotion" (Greenwell) 131
penny-a-liners 68t, 91, 149
penny bloods 48, 139, 278
penny dreadfuls 139, 278, 295–6, 301
Penny Magazine 12, 104, 108, 115, 191, 243, 277–8, 279, 355
Penny Novelist 139
Penny Story-Teller 139
penny weekly family magazines 278–85; see also mass-market periodical, popular press
People's Friend 52, 192
People's Journal 130, 192
Periodical Accounts 177
periodicals, definition of: 4–6, 9, 25, 237–40; chronology of nineteenth-century 400–5; cost model compared to newspapers 67–72; fiction contributions 81–5; poetry 85–8; religious mode of reading 200–3; writing for 77–88; French 179–81; German 177–9; Irish 208–20; Japanese 181–4; Scottish 185–93; Welsh 194–207
Perpetual Curate, The (Oliphant) 83
"Personal Recollections of Abraham Lincoln" (Conway) 81
Peters, Charles 298–9
Peters, Lisa 5, 8, 9, 192
Peter Simple (Marryat) 139
Peterson, Linda H. 7
Petrie, George 209
Phegley, Jennifer 10
Philharmonic Society 392
Phillpot, Clive 388
Philosophical Enquiry into the Origin of Our Ideas of the Sublime and Beautiful, A (Burke) 378
photography 112–14; half-tone engraving and 121–2, 122f; process methods and 121
Pianotyp 38, 39
Pickwick Papers, The (Dickens) 82, 84, 140
Pictorial Comic Life 326
Pigeon, Stephan 172
Pig's Meat (Spence) 319
Pinwell, G.J. 116
Pirkis, Catherine Louisa 143
"Pitfall, The" (Cholmondeley) 84
Pittard, Christopher 143
Pluck 298
Poe, Edgar Allan 143

471

Poetess Archive 25
Poetical Magazine 124, 125, 133
poetry 124–37; entertainment 133–5; home, nation, faith sanctities of 130–3; love 134–5; news cycle and 125–7; overview of 124–5; periodicals and writing 85–8; politics and periodical 127–30; seasonal/month lyrics and 136; special features and 135–7; suffrage and 129–30; translation and 135–6
Poet's Corner 125
Polar Star of Entertainment and Popular Science 13
Police Reporter 46
Political Drama 120, 120f
Political Register 10, 44, 251, 319, 331
Poole, William Frederick 18
Poor Man's Guardian 44, 48, 229, 251, 323–4, 331
Poovey, Mary 60
popular press 38–9, 169
"Porphyria's Lover" (Browning) 86
Portfolio 387
Portsmouth, Evelyn 274–5
Post Office, distribution and 46–7, 49–52, 53
Potter, Simon 155, 156
Pound, Richard J. 321
Powell, Michael 229
Praed, Winthrop Mackworth 133, 325
Prager, Arthur 322
Pre-Raphaelites 86, 116, 136, 382, 383
Press Association 53
press directories: geography and 8; *Deacon's Newspaper Handbook* 355; *Mitchell's Advertising Press Directory* 4, 5, 54, 178, 231, 237–8, 355–6; newspaper 175, 238; *Sell's Dictionary of the World's Press* 3–4, 178, 238
press models: categories of 237; frequency, price, geography and 240–5; remediation and 245–8; *see also* magazine, newspaper, periodical
Preston Temperance Advocate 348
Price, R.G.G. 322
Price, Uvedale 378
Pringle, Thomas 188
Prisoners (Cholmondeley) 84
Private Eye 243
Proceedings of the Old Bailey Online 25
Proceedings of the Royal Musical Association 391
process reprographic techniques 121–2, 122f
"Procris" (Tomson) 134
Procter, Adelaide 136
Procter, John 118
professional journals 255–6
profit, defined 62
Progressionist 348
Progress of the Intellect, The (Mackay) 80

Prophetic Bell 313
ProQuest 26, 154, 341
prose 138–50; fiction 138–45; non-fiction 145–50; overview of 138
Protestant Journal 335
Protestant Penny Magazine 209
provincial press 170, 221–33; cannibalised by London press, 92–3; characteristics of 223–7, 224f, 225f; definitions 222–3, 238; effect of Stamp Duty on, 48; French, 180; overview of 221–2; poetry in, 124–5; primary sources/methodology 231–3; readerships 227; sales procedures, 62; secondary sources 228–9; technology, 38; theoretical models for 230–1; *see also* Press Association
Puck 325
puffing 89, 97, 366, 375
Punch 5, 12, 47, 54, 61, 85, 95, 104f, 105, 114, 118, 120–1, 127, 129, 133, 240, 242, 243, 300, 318, 321, 322–6, 369
Punch Historical Archive 25, 322
Puppet Show 118, 119f, 325
"Pyramids, The" (anon.) 135

Quarterly Musical Magazine and Review 390, 392, 395
Quarterly Review 77, 81, 88, 146, 148, 188, 191, 241, 256
Quarterly Review of Jurisprudence 256
Queen: The Lady's Newspaper and Court Chronicle 242, 267, 273–4, 273f
Quelch, Harry 340
Quest 388
Quintessence of Ibsenism, The (Shaw) 370
Quiver 116, 335, 356
Quiz: The Satirist 326
Quizziology of the British Drama, The (À Beckett) 369
Quorum 258

race: advertisements and 61, 176; Victorian imperialist understandings of 160–1; orientalism and 181, 183
Racing Calendar 314–15
Radford, Joseph 128–9
radical politics, press and 127, 320
Railway Signal, or Lights along the Line 353
railways: 54, 125–6, 325, distribution and 30–1, 33t, 51, 53, 56–9t145, 331; sporting literature and 308, 310; see also *On the Line*
Ramamurthy, Anandi 156, 160
Rambler 91, 360
Randolph County Journal 13
Ray, Gordon N. 322
Reade, Charles 138, 141
reading aloud 227
Rechabite and Temperance Magazine 350

Rechabites 350
"Recollections of a Police-Officer" 143
Record, The 335, 361
"Rector, The" (Oliphant) 83
recycling (reprinting) 7, 11–13, 27, 52, 112, 125–6, 135, 137, 172–3, 208, 212, 221–3, 233, 265–6, 271, 316, 379, 392
Red Dragon 204
Red Pottage (Cholmondeley) 84, 85
Red Republican 62
Reed, Talbot Baines 296
Rees, David 201
Rees, Sarah Jane 204–5
Reeves, William 387
Reform Act (1832) 190
Reformists' Register 319
Reid, Forrest 116, 288
Reid, John Cowie 321
Reid, Mayne 295, 296
religion: children's magazines and 294; overview of 355–7; periodical press and 200–3; *versus* quantitative 362–4; reading 358–62; scholarship on 357–8
Religious Tract Society 253, 294, 295, 298, 355, 360
remuneration: authors 61, 68t, 77–9, 82–5, 87, 96, 140, 185, 186, 290; compositors, 39; editors, 68t, 94–6; journalists, 68t, 149
Répertoire Bibliographique des Principales Revues Françaises 180
Reports of the Commissioners of Enquiry into the State of Education in Wales 194–5
Repository of Arts 377
Representative 240
reprinting, *see* recycling
Republican 331
republication 106; *see also* recycling, serialization
Research Society for Victorian Periodicals 229
Reuters 29, 71, 168
Revue Blanche, La 179
reviews (as periodical genre) 77–9, 81, 241–2, 252; *see also* Band of Hope, Brewing Trade, British and Foreign, Contemporary, Dublin University, Edinburgh, Englishwoman's, Foreign Quarterly, Fortnightly, Literary Chronicle, London, New Monthly, North British, Quarterly Review, Review of Reviews, Saturday, Sporting, Universal, Westminster
reviews and reviewing 5, 12, 18, 61, 78–9, 80, 97–8, 146–8, 186–8, 212, 215, 221–2, 252, 268, 279–80, 290–1, 300, 337, 369–70, 375, 380–1, 383–5, 391–4, 395–6;

INDEX

anonymous 81; signed 148; *see also* log-rolling, puffing
Review of Reviews 18, 99, 100f, 149, 173
Revolutionary War, transatlantic relations and 166
Reynolds, G.W.M. 5, 91, 139, 146, 247, 351
Reynolds, Joshua 378
Reynolds's Miscellany 5, 115, 225, 278, 279
Reynolds's Weekly Newspaper 146, 244
Rich, Henry 45
Richards, Jeffrey 302
Richards, Richard 202
Richardson, Jonathan 378
Rintoul, Robert 369
Roberts, Helene 388
Rollington, Ralph 305
Romance of the Harem (Pardoe) 84
"Rome" (Landon) 86
Romola (Eliot) 81, 83, 141
Rosenberg, Adolphus 326
Rosenberg's Little Journal 326
Ross, Charles Henry 118
Rossetti, Christina 86, 87; *see also* Alleyn, Ellen
Rossetti, Dante Gabriel 116, 118, 137
Rossetti, William Michael 381
Rossetti Archive 25–6
Routledge 300
Rowlandson, Thomas 124
Royal Academy of Music 391
Rubery, Matthew 157
Ruff, William 311
Russell, W.H. 247

Sacred Harmonic Society 392
Said, Edward 153
Saint Paul's Magazine 96, 138–9, 140, 285, 287
Saintsbury, George 99
St. Clair, William 63
St. James's Magazine 140, 285
St. Paul's 285, 287
Sala, George Augustus 138, 169, 287, 288, 325
sales: bookshops and 185–6; of daily papers 42; mark-up and 62; penny stamp and 48; profit and 62–3; subscription 42, 55, 71–2; *see also* circulation, distribution
Salesa, Damon 160
Salmon, Edward 300
Sanders, Mike 128
Sartor Resartus (Carlyle) 78
satire *see* comic/satiric periodicals
Satirist (Gregory) 319, 321
Saturday Magazine 104, 108, 109f, 355
Saturday Night 310
Saturday Review 1–2, 39, 99, 139, 240, 242, 245, 312
Savoy 144, 387

Scarlet Letter, The (Hawthorne) 141
Scenes and Hymns (Hemans) 87
Scenes from Rejected Comedies (author) 369
Scenes of Clerical Life (Evans) 81, 83
Schmidt, Barbara Quinn 285
Scholarly and Academic Information Navigator 182
Scholes, Percy 396
Schoolmaster's Tour, The (Combe) 124, 133, 136
Schwarz, Alan 314
science periodicals 175, 176, 177–9
SciPer: Science in the Nineteenth-Century Periodical 25, 178
"scissors-and-paste" journalism 149
Score, Melissa 39
Scotland 4, 8–9, 155
Scottish periodicals 185–93; distribution in 53; *Edinburgh Review* 186–9; late-century developments in 192–3; mass-market periodical and 190–1; monthly 191–2; overview of 185–6; religious periodicals in 200–1; possible connections with Welsh 203, 207
Scots Magazine 135, 188
Scotsman 47
Scots (later *National*) *Observer* 124, 137, 250
Scott, John 188–9
Scott, Walter 146, 185, 187–8
Scourge 319
Scriven, Thomas 166
Scudder, Samuel 177
Seditious Publications Act (1816) 329, 331
self-improvement 190, 242, 278, 284
Sell's Dictionary of the World's Press 3–4, 178, 238
sensation fiction 145, 287–91
Sepoy Rebellion 126
Seren Cymru (Star of Wales) 202
Seren Gomer (Star of Gomer) 196, 201
serialization 83, 85, 94, 140–2, 212, 215
Servant's Magazine 337
Seymour, Robert 104, 105f, 321
Shamgar, Beth 395–6
Sharples, Eliza 339
Shattock, Joanne 186, 228
Shaw, George Bernard 341, 370, 397
She (Haggard) 142
Sheets-Pyenson, Susan 178
Sheridan, Louisa 321
Sherratt, Tim 27
shilling monthlies 140, 276, 285–91
Shillingsburg, Peter L. 85
short story genre 143–5
Showalter, Elaine 257
"Sign of Four, The" (Doyle) 143
"Silly Novels by Lady Novelists" (Eliot) 80

Simplicissimus 181
Sinnema, Peter 106, 115–16, 366
Sir Charles Danvers (Cholmondeley) 84
Sketch 149, 374
Sketches 120
"Sketches of London" (Dickens) 82
Slater, Michael 322
Smith, Adam 48
Smith, Albert 324
Smith, Egerton 250
Smith, Eliza 126
Smith, George 83, 85, 141
Smith, James 361–2
Smith, Michelle 302
Smith, Olivia 319
Smith, Peter 287
Smith, Sydney 77, 187
Smith Bodichon, Barbara Leigh 269
Smithies, Thomas Bywater 329, 350–1
Smythies, Harriette Maria 84
Social Democratic Federation 332
socialism *see* social purpose periodicals
social purpose periodicals 328–41; class politics and 328–32; gender issues and 337–40; in Internet age 340–1; overview of 328; religion and class issues 335–7; temperance and 333–4
Society for the Diffusion of Useful Knowledge 191
Society for the Promotion of Christian Knowledge 355
Society of Authors 81
Society of British Musicians 391, 392
Society of Women Journalists 99
Solicitors' Journal 256
Solomon, Simeon 137
Somerset, Henry 157
"Song, Translated from the French" (Alpheus) 135
"Song of the Shirt" (Hood) 129
Songs of Affections (Hemans) 87
"Sonnet, Translated from Petrarcha" (A.S.) 135
Sons of Temperance 344, 350
Soussloff, Catherine 382
Southcott, Joanna 361
Southey, Robert 77
South Wales Daily News 198
South Wales Daily Post 197
South Wales Echo 198
Southworth, E.D.E.N. 172
Spectator 86, 240, 242, 243, 245, 316, 369, 378
Spence, Thomas 319
Spencer, Herbert 192
Spielmann, Marion Harry 322, 380, 382–3
Spirit Lamp 258
Spivak, G. 159
Sporting Chronicle 310, 313, 319
Sporting Gazette 313
Sporting Life 310

INDEX

Sporting Magazine 254, 307, 308, 311, 314
sporting periodicals 254–5, 307–17; distinctions between 311; format variety in 310; future research for 315–17; gender and 313; illustration and 310–11; origins of 307–8; readerships 313–14; statistics and 314–15; technology and 308–10; writers for 312–13
Sporting Review 254
Sporting Times 312
Sports Illustrated 243
Sportsman 254
Stables, Gordon 296
Stamp Act (1712) 141
stamp duty 43–9; *see also* House of Commons; Taxes on Knowledge
Standard 35, 168, 222, 240
Stanley, Henry Morton 149
"Stanzas from the Grande Chartreuse" (Arnold) 135
Star of Temperance 333
Staunch Teetotaller 348
Stead, W.T. 18, 99, 149, 169, 173, 192, 229, 231
Steam-Boat, The (Galt) 139
Stedman, Jane W. 366
Steele, Richard 378
Stephen, Fitzjames 240
Stephen, Leslie 96, 134
Stevenson, Robert Louis 301, 303, 387
Stock Exchange Year Book 66
Storey, Samuel 226–7
"Story of Nala and Damayanti, The" (Bruce) 135
Stowe, Harriet Beecher 172, 267
Strad 390, 392, 394
Strahan, Alexander 96, 191, 301, 361
Strand Magazine 3, 122f, 142, 143, 144, 148, 193
Stratman, Carl J. 368
Straus, Ralph 325
"Street Sketches" (Dickens) 82
Stri Dharma 160
Strings 394
Stroud Free Press 46
Studies in Newspaper and Periodical History 239
Studio: An Illustrated Magazine of Fine and Applied Arts 258, 388
sub-editors 92–4
Sue, Eugène 139
"Suffering Christian, The" (Henwood) 131–2
Sullivan, Frank J. 118
Sunday at Home 253, 355
Sunday in London 121
Sunday Scholar's Reward 294
Sunday Times 99
Sunday Times Digital Archive 25, 99
Surtees, Robert Smith 254, 310, 317

Sutherland, John 140
Swan, Annie 89, 264, 274
Swinburne, Algernon Charles 86, 127, 135, 137
S.W. Partridge & Co. 351
Sylvia's Home Journal 298
syndication 140–2

Tablet 355
Tait, William 191
Tait's Edinburgh Magazine 89, 186, 189, 191
Talfourd, Thomas Noon 370
Tam-tam, Le 181
Tarian y Gweithiwr (the Worker's Shield) 197
Tave, Stuart M. 319
Taxes on Knowledge 44–8, 71; *see also* advertisements, duties on; House of Commons, law and the press, paper duty, stamp duty, unstamped newspapers, "War of the Unstamped"
Taylor, Charles 377
technical journals 108
technology: distribution 49–55; overview of 29–32; photomechanical 121–2; production 29–41; timeline of 33–4t; *see also* Koenig cylinder press, Linotype, lithography, Pianotyp rotary press, telegraph, transatlantic cable, Walter press
Teetotaler 351
Teetotal Essayist 351
Teetotal Times 351
Teetotal Times and Essayist 351
telegraph 29, 52–3, 71, 163–5, 230
Telescope 240
Temperance Bells 348
Temperance Caterer 350
Temperance Chronicle 348, 350
Temperance Lancet 350
Temperance Magazine and Review 333
Temperance Mirror 349, 349f
Temperance Monthly Visitor 348
temperance movement 342–4
temperance periodicals 342–54; for adults 348–51; characteristics of 345–8; for children 351–2; future research for 352–4; overview of 342; scholarship on 345; as social purpose periodicals 333–4; temperance movement and 342–4
Temperance Record 349
Temperance Union of the Women of South Wales 204
Temperance Worker and Band of Hope Conductor 333, 334
Temperley, Nicholas 396
Templar (and Templar Journal) / Templar Journal and Treasury 350

Temple Bar 82, 84, 85, 140, 285, 287
"Temptations of St. Anthony, The" (T.H.S.) 136
Tenniel, John 118
Tennyson, Alfred 87, 192
Tess of the d'Urbervilles (Hardy) 142
Thackeray, Anne 291
Thackeray, William Makepeace 2, 85, 231, 287, 322
theater, periodical press and 365–76; discursive function of 366–73; the *Era* 373–6; overview of 365–6
Theatrical Journal 5
Theatrical Licensing Act (1737) 367
Theatrical Programme and Entr'acte 375
Thelwall, John 128
Thieme, Hugo 180
"Thirty Bob a Week" (Davidson) 137
Thomas, W.F. 118
Thompson, E.P. 321, 324, 335
1,000 Answers to 1,000 Questions 149
Tilley, Elizabeth 8, 9, 177
Tillotson, W.F. 142
Tillotson's Fiction Syndicate 71
Times, The 3, 5, 32, 35, 36, 44, 45, 47, 52, 53, 55, 61, 91, 145, 158, 163–4, 222, 225, 228, 239
Times Digital Archive, The 25
Times of India 154
Tindall, William 369
Tinsley's 61, 285
Tit-Bits 94, 149, 192, 242
Tittle Tattle 326
Tlysau yr Hen Oesoedd (Gems of Past Ages) 195
"To a Michaelmas Daisy" (Landon) 86
Toby 325
To-Day: A Monthly Magazine of Scientific Socialism 129, 341
Tomahawk 118, 325
Tom Brown at Oxford (Hughes) 241
Tom Brown's Schooldays (Hughes) 310
"To Minna, Translated from the German of Schiller" (O.) 135
Tomson, Graham R. 134
Tonic Sol-fa Reporter 391, 393
Tonna, Charlotte Elizabeth 132
Topham, John 357
Tory politics, press and 44, 77, 188–9; Welsh periodicals/newspapers and 196–200
"To the Memory of the Princess Charlotte" (anonymous) 126
Toulmin, Camilla 264
Town (Nicholson) 322
Town Talk 326
trade periodicals 2, 72, 104, 175, 179
Traethodydd, Y (The Essayist) 203
Transactions of the Honourable Society of Cymmrodorion 205
transatlantic cable 29, 53

474

INDEX

transatlantic relations 163–74; American Civil War and 166–7; as Anglo-American invention 165–7; digital transatlantic and 173–4; history of 163–5; interest in America and 167–70, 168*f*; Revolutionary War and 166

translation 78, 139, 176, 182–3, 210, 392; poetry and 135–6

transnational connections, comparative approach to 175–84; advantages/hindrances of 175–7; French 179–81; German 177–9; Japanese 181–4; overview of 175

travelogues 170–1

Treasure Island (Stevenson) 301

Tressell, Robert 317

Trevor, John 336

Tribune 128

Trollope, Anthony 81, 85, 96–7, 138–9, 141, 171, 189, 192, 254–5, 287, 361

Trollope, Frances 171

Troubadour 394

Truth 242

Trysorfa Gwybodaeth (Treasury of Knowledge) 195

Trysorfa y Plant (the Children's Treasury) 204

Trysorfa Ysprydol, Y (the Spiritual Treasury) 195

Turner, Ernest S. 305

Tusan, Michelle 8

Twain, Mark 157, 171, 172

Tweedie, William 351

"Two Loves" (Douglas) 129

Tynan, Katherine 303

Tyst Cymreig, Y (the Welsh Witness) 202

Tywysydd yr Ieuainc (Guide for Young People) 204

Udgorn Rhyddid (The Trumpet of Freedom) 200

Uncle Tom's Cabin (Stowe) 172

United Kingdom Alliance for the Suppression of the Traffic in all Intoxicating Liquors (the Alliance) 62, 333, 344, 345, 347

United Kingdom Railway Union 347

Universal Review 134

University Magazine 12

Unknown Mayhew, The (Yeo and Thompson) 321

unstamped newspapers 43–6, 237, 320

"Uphill" (Rossetti) 87

urbanization 230, 368

VanArsdel, Rosemary T. 3, 154, 161

Vanity Fair 135, 318

Vann, J. Don 3, 154, 161, 318

Van Remoortel, Marianne 90

Verne, Jules 296

Vertical Rotary Press, Applegarth's 32, 34–7, 35*f*, 37*f*

Victoria Magazine 270, 285, 290–1

Victorian Periodicals Review 3, 66, 229

Victoria Press 10, 290

Victoria Regia 270

Vincent, Henry 334

Violin 394

Violin Monthly Magazine 394

Violin Times 392, 394

Viral Texts 27

Virtue, James 96

"Vitaï Lampada" (Newbolt) 310

Vizetelly, Henry 325

Vogue 243, 274

Vorachek, Laura 12

Vote 160

Waghorn, Thomas 316

Wagstaff, Frederic 334

Wakley, Thomas 256

Wales 4, 8–9; and rugby union 313; *see also* Welsh periodicals

Walker, Frederick 288

Walter, John, II 34

Walter, John, III 35

Walter press 35

Walters, Huw 206

Walton, Isaak 307

War Cry 242, 359

"War-Cry, The" (Radford) 128–9

Ward, Artemus 171, 173

Ward, William S. 66

"War of the Unstamped" 44; *see also* Taxes on Knowledge, unstamped newspapers

Warren, Lynne 94

Warren, Samuel 189

Waterloo Directory The 1, 3, 66, 208, 223, 228, 231, 246

Waugh, Evelyn 144, 157, 158

Waugh in Abyssinia (Waugh) 158

Webster, Augusta 134

Weekly Apollo 261

Weekly Dispatch 5

Weekly Record of the Temperance Movement 349

Weekly Telegraph 225

Weekly Visitor 111*f*

Weeks, Jeffrey 257

Wehr-Wolf, The (Reynolds) 139

Welland, Dennis 173

Wellesley Index to Victorian Periodicals, The 3, 6, 19, 66, 85–6

Welsh, Charles 296

Welsh Church Press, The 202

Welsh Journals Online 203, 206

Welsh periodicals 194–207; *Baner ac Amserau Cymru* 43, 198*f*; history of 195–6; overview of 194–5; politics and 196–200; primary/secondary sources of 206–7; religion and 200–3; targeted audience of 203–5; *Wrexham and Denbigh Advertiser* 2, 199*f*

Werin, Y (The People) 200

Wesleyan-Methodist Magazine 131, 355

Western European Studies Section (WessWeb) 178

Western Mail 198, 200, 250

Western Temperance Herald 348

Western Weekly News 226

"West Indian Anecdote, A" (Landon) 86

Westmacott, Charles Molloy 321

Westminster Review 5, 10, 77, 78, 80, 81, 89, 91, 104, 147, 241, 246

White, Cynthia 267

White, Gleeson 116

White Ribbon 348

White Ribbon Society 344

W.H. Smith 47, 53–4

Whymper, Josiah 116

Whyte-Melville, George John 312

Wickwar, William Hardy 319

Widén, Anne 396

Wiener, Joel H. 89, 169–70, 320

Wilde, Oscar 86, 189, 258, 274

William Blake Archive 26

William Morris Internet Archive 341

William Reeves publishing house 399

Williams, George Washington 157

Williams, Raymond 55

Williams, William 202

William-Wynn, Watkin 200

Wills, W.H. 92, 291

Wilson, John 13, 188

Wilson, Margaret Harries 264

Wilson, William Carus 294

Windsor Magazine 148

Wings 348

Winllan, Y (the Vineyard) 204

Wirgman, Charles 184

Woman 94

Woman at Home 274

Womanhood 274, 313, 317

Woman in White, The (Collins) 140, 141

Woman's Herald 271

Woman Question 269, 340

Woman's Signal 157, 271

Woman's World 274

Woman Worker 340

women: editors 10, 89–90, 99, 264–5; Japanese, periodicals 181–4; poems supporting suffrage and 129–30; readers, illustration and 106; religious/domestic periodical poetry and 132–3; writers 10, 79–88, 159, 172, 189, 291

women's and expatriate periodicals 181–4; *see also Echo du Japon, Studio*

Women's Freedom League 160

Women's India Association 160

women's interests, periodicals and 260–7

women's news 271–4

women's opportunities, periodicals and 274–5
Women's Penny Paper 129, 271
women's periodicals 260–75; future research for 275; overview of 260; women's interests and, value of 260–7; women's news and 271–4; women's opportunities and, developing 274–5; women's roles and, expanding 268–71; religious, 268
Women's Total Abstinence Union 344, 348
Wood, Ellen Price 89, 140, 143, 264, 285, 287, 356, 361
Wood, Marcus 319
Wood, T. Martin 323
wood engraving 107–18; categories of 108; comic 114, 118–23; history of 107; pictorial 110, 112, 114, 116; as representation 108, 110
Woodward, B.B. 386
Wooler, Thomas J. 319, 331, 333
Wordsworth, Dorothy 378

Wordsworth, William 87, 125–6, 189
Workers Onward 352
working-class periodicals 11; *see also* social purpose periodicals; children, 294, 296, 300, 306; men, 251–2, 329; women, 130, 337–8, 340; and art 379–90
Workman's Times 242
World of Fashion and Continental Feuilletons 262
World's Comic 326
World War I 88, 295, 344
Worth, Charles 179
Wrexham and Denbigh Advertiser 197, 199f, 202
Wrexham Guardian 197, 200
Wrexham Temperance Messenger 203
Wyke, Terry 229

Yates, Edmund 325
Year's Art (Huish) 388
Yeast (Kingsley) 142
Yeats, W.B. 118, 137

yellowback 54
Yellow Book 116, 118, 137, 144, 387
Yellow Nineties Online 25
Yeo, Leslie 321
Ymwelydd, Yr (The Visitor) 205
Yonge, Charlotte M. 89, 142, 264, 298, 303, 339
Young Briton 301
Young England 303
Young Englishman 298, 301
Young Englishwoman 298
Young Gentleman's Journal 296
Young Ireland movement 210, 214, 217–18
Young Ladies' Magazine of Theology, History, Philosophy, and General Knowledge 298
Young Ladies of Great Britain 298
Young Woman 300, 339
Youthful Teetotaler 351

Zefys 179
Zeller, Suzanne 177
Zon, Bennett 397